story by
GEORGE R.R. MARTIN

sequential adaptation
DANIEL ABRAHAM

color
DIGIKORE STUDIOS

pencils
RAFA LOPEZ

covers & chapter

inks
RUBEN

editor in chief WILLIAM CHRISTENSEN • creative director MARK SEIFERT • managing editor JIM KUHORIC
director of sales & marketing KEITH DAVIDSEN • director of events DAVID MARKS • production assistant ARIANA OSBORNE

www.avatarpress.com   www.twitter.com/avatarpress   www.facebook.com/avatarpresscomics

GEORGE R.R. MARTIN'S FEVRE DREAM COLLECTED. June 2011. Published by Avatar Press, Inc., 515 N. Century Blvd. Rantoul, IL 61866. ©2011
Avatar Press, Inc. Fevre Dream and all related properties TM & ©2011 George R.R. Martin. All characters as depicted in this story are over the age of 18.
The stories, characters, and institutions mentioned in this magazine are entirely fictional. Printed in Canada.

CHAPTER 1

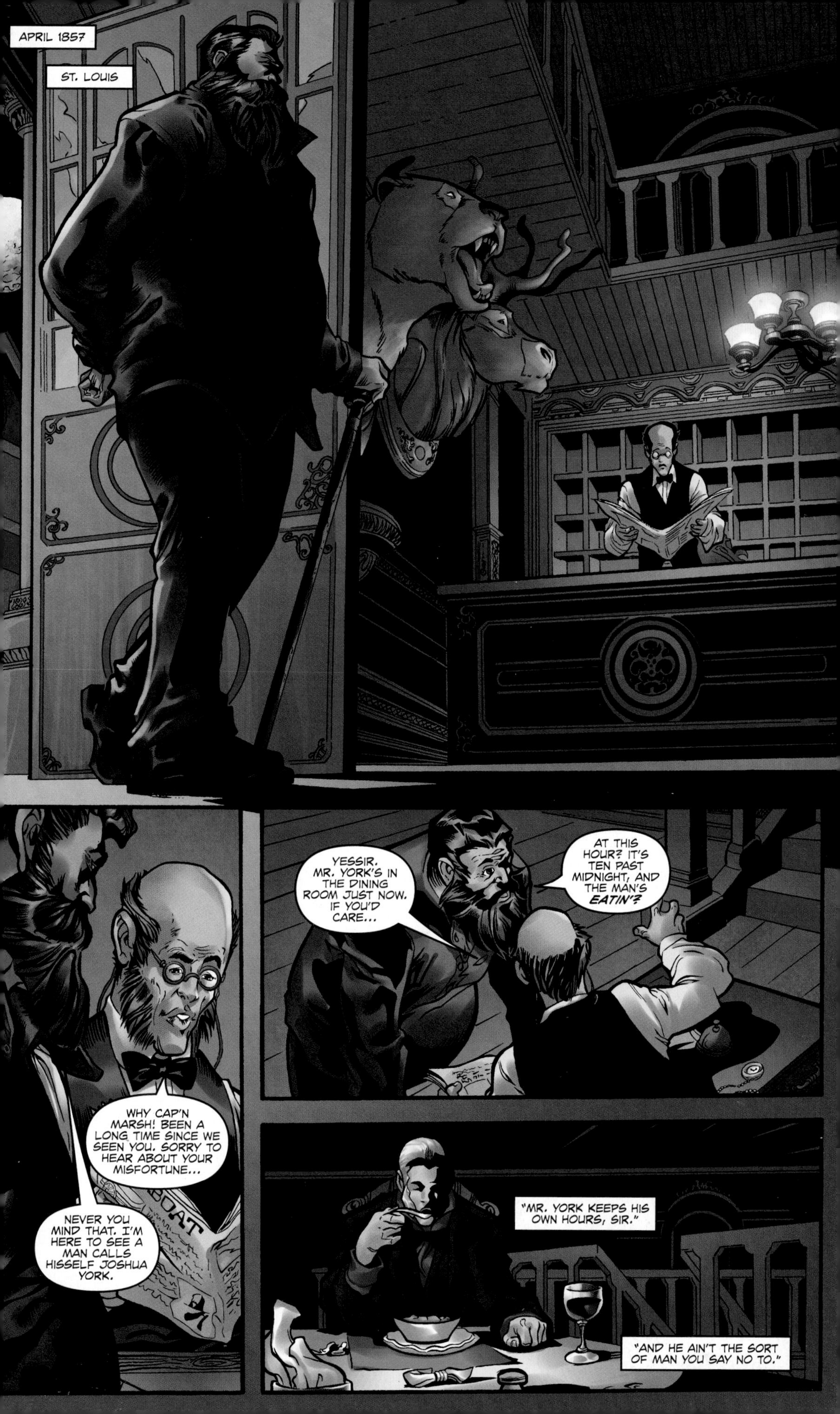
APRIL 1857
ST. LOUIS
WHY CAP'N MARSH! BEEN A LONG TIME SINCE WE SEEN YOU. SORRY TO HEAR ABOUT YOUR MISFORTUNE...
NEVER YOU MIND THAT. I'M HERE TO SEE A MAN CALLS HISSELF JOSHUA YORK.
YESSIR. MR. YORK'S IN THE DINING ROOM JUST NOW. IF YOU'D CARE...
AT THIS HOUR? IT'S TEN PAST MIDNIGHT, AND THE MAN'S *EATIN'?*
"MR. YORK KEEPS HIS OWN HOURS, SIR."
"AND HE AIN'T THE SORT OF MAN YOU SAY NO TO."

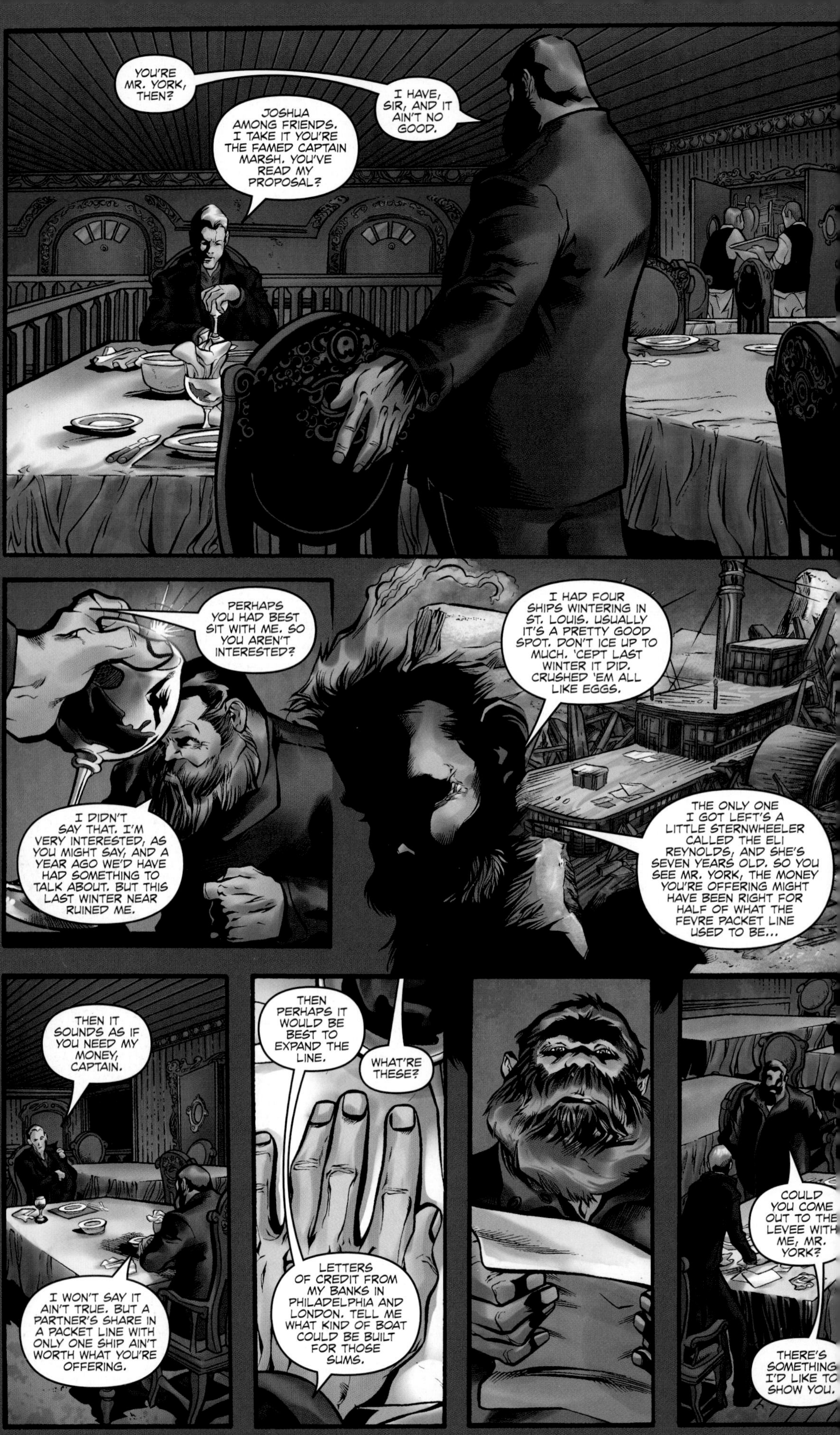
YOU'RE MR. YORK, THEN?
I HAVE, SIR, AND IT AIN'T NO GOOD.
JOSHUA AMONG FRIENDS. I TAKE IT YOU'RE THE FAMED CAPTAIN MARSH. YOU'VE READ MY PROPOSAL?
PERHAPS YOU HAD BEST SIT WITH ME. SO YOU AREN'T INTERESTED?
I DIDN'T SAY THAT. I'M VERY INTERESTED, AS YOU MIGHT SAY, AND A YEAR AGO WE'D HAVE HAD SOMETHING TO TALK ABOUT. BUT THIS LAST WINTER NEAR RUINED ME.
I HAD FOUR SHIPS WINTERING IN ST. LOUIS. USUALLY IT'S A PRETTY GOOD SPOT. DON'T ICE UP TO MUCH. 'CEPT LAST WINTER IT DID. CRUSHED 'EM ALL LIKE EGGS.
THE ONLY ONE I GOT LEFT'S A LITTLE STERNWHEELER CALLED THE ELI REYNOLDS, AND SHE'S SEVEN YEARS OLD. SO YOU SEE MR. YORK, THE MONEY YOU'RE OFFERING MIGHT HAVE BEEN RIGHT FOR HALF OF WHAT THE FEVRE PACKET LINE USED TO BE...
THEN IT SOUNDS AS IF YOU NEED MY MONEY, CAPTAIN.
I WON'T SAY IT AIN'T TRUE. BUT A PARTNER'S SHARE IN A PACKET LINE WITH ONLY ONE SHIP AIN'T WORTH WHAT YOU'RE OFFERING.
THEN PERHAPS IT WOULD BE BEST TO EXPAND THE LINE.
WHAT'RE THESE?
LETTERS OF CREDIT FROM MY BANKS IN PHILADELPHIA AND LONDON. TELL ME WHAT KIND OF BOAT COULD BE BUILT FOR THOSE SUMS.
COULD YOU COME OUT TO THE LEVEE WITH ME, MR. YORK?
THERE'S SOMETHING I'D LIKE TO SHOW YOU.

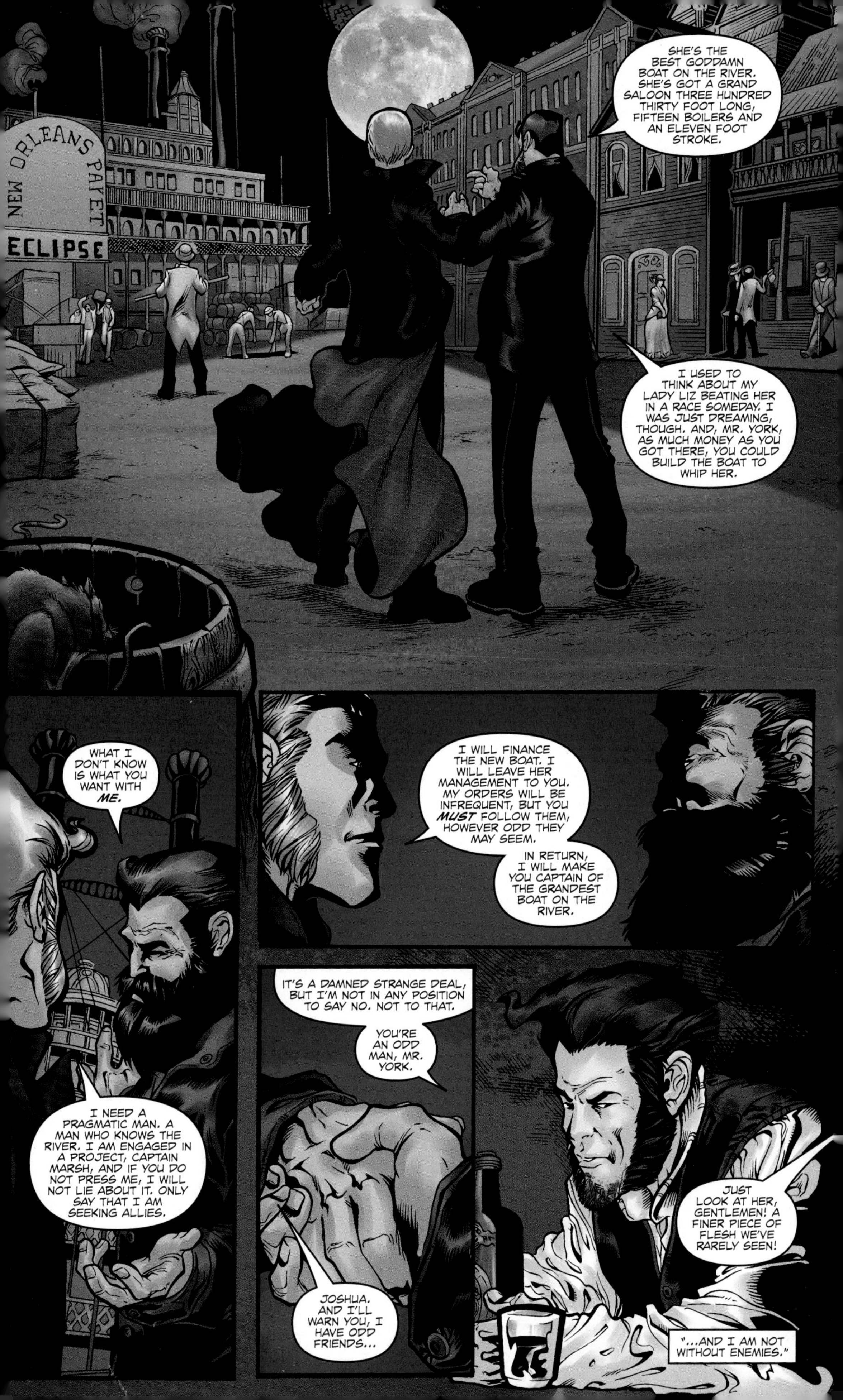

NEW ORLEANS PAYET
ECLIPSE
SHE'S THE BEST GODDAMN BOAT ON THE RIVER. SHE'S GOT A GRAND SALOON THREE HUNDRED THIRTY FOOT LONG, FIFTEEN BOILERS AND AN ELEVEN FOOT STROKE.
I USED TO THINK ABOUT MY LADY LIZ BEATING HER IN A RACE SOMEDAY. I WAS JUST DREAMING, THOUGH. AND, MR. YORK, AS MUCH MONEY AS YOU GOT THERE, YOU COULD BUILD THE BOAT TO WHIP HER.
WHAT I DON'T KNOW IS WHAT YOU WANT WITH ME.
I NEED A PRAGMATIC MAN. A MAN WHO KNOWS THE RIVER. I AM ENGAGED IN A PROJECT, CAPTAIN MARSH, AND IF YOU DO NOT PRESS ME, I WILL NOT LIE ABOUT IT. ONLY SAY THAT I AM SEEKING ALLIES.
I WILL FINANCE THE NEW BOAT. I WILL LEAVE HER MANAGEMENT TO YOU. MY ORDERS WILL BE INFREQUENT, BUT YOU MUST FOLLOW THEM, HOWEVER ODD THEY MAY SEEM.
IN RETURN, I WILL MAKE YOU CAPTAIN OF THE GRANDEST BOAT ON THE RIVER.
IT'S A DAMNED STRANGE DEAL, BUT I'M NOT IN ANY POSITION TO SAY NO. NOT TO THAT.
YOU'RE AN ODD MAN, MR. YORK.
JOSHUA. AND I'LL WARN YOU, I HAVE ODD FRIENDS...
JUST LOOK AT HER, GENTLEMEN! A FINER PIECE OF FLESH WE'VE RARELY SEEN!
"...AND I AM NOT WITHOUT ENEMIES."

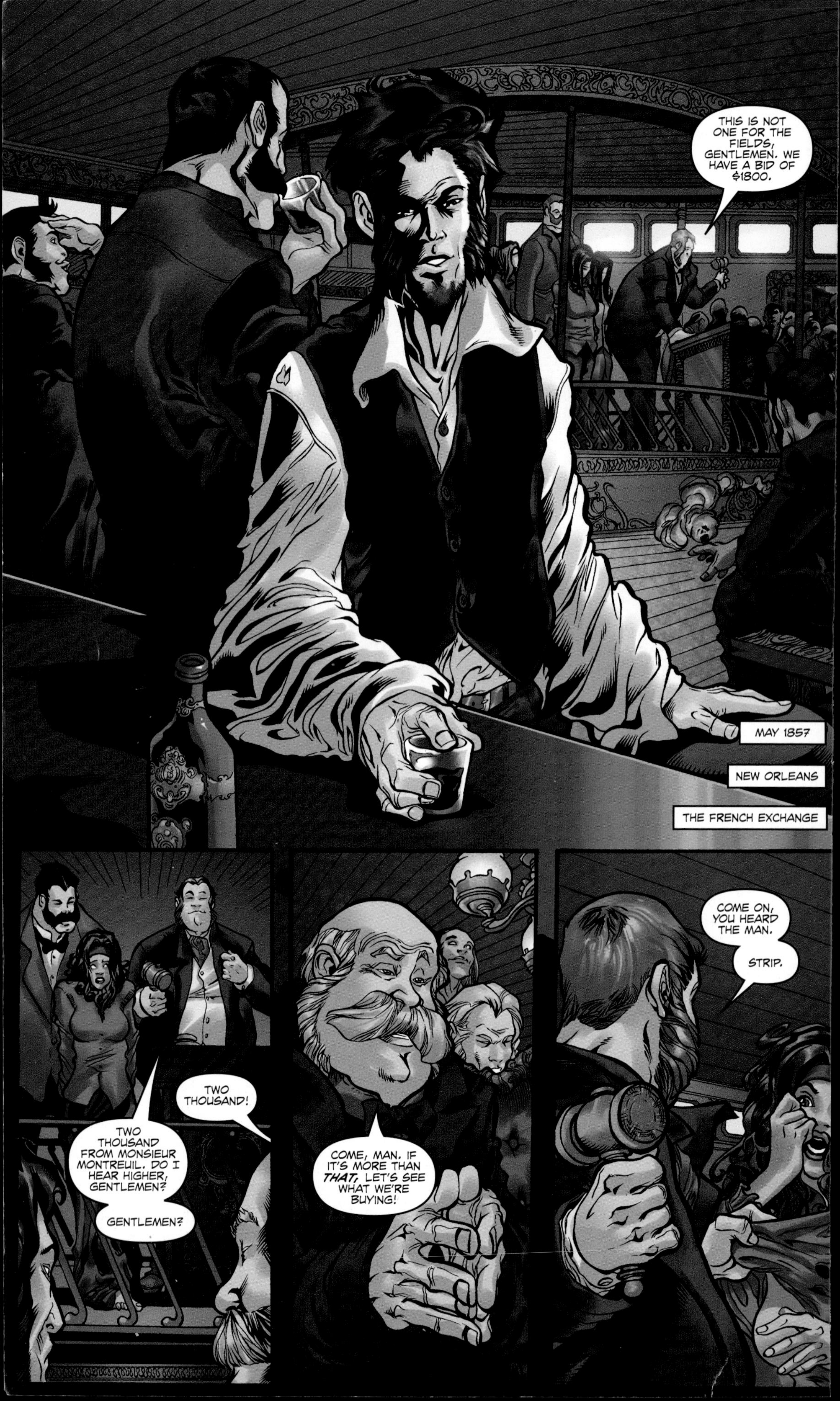
THIS IS NOT ONE FOR THE FIELDS, GENTLEMEN. WE HAVE A BID OF $1800.
MAY 1857
NEW ORLEANS
THE FRENCH EXCHANGE
TWO THOUSAND!
TWO THOUSAND FROM MONSIEUR MONTREUIL. DO I HEAR HIGHER, GENTLEMEN?
GENTLEMEN?
COME, MAN. IF IT'S MORE THAN *THAT,* LET'S SEE WHAT WE'RE BUYING!
COME ON, YOU HEARD THE MAN.
STRIP.

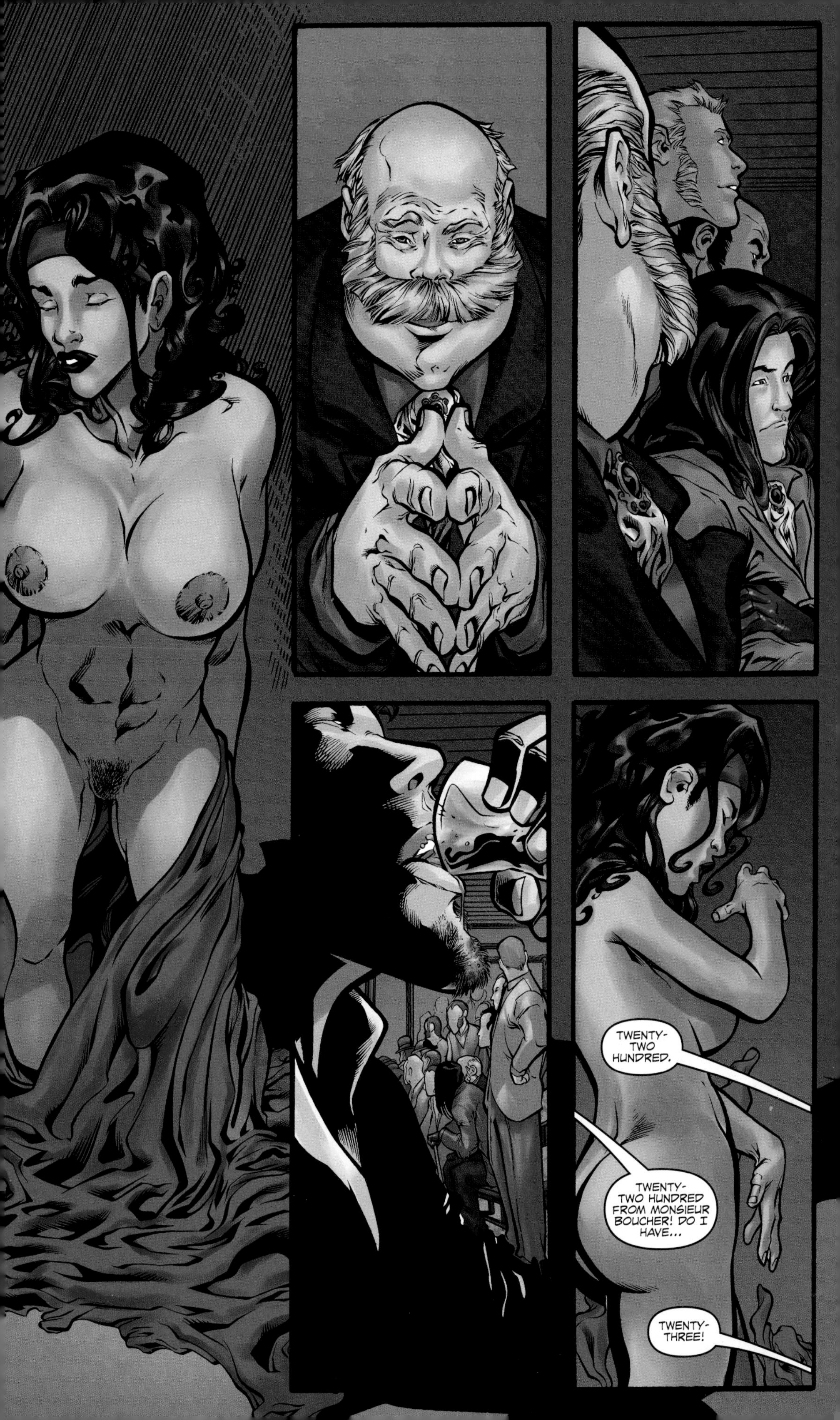
TWENTY-TWO HUNDRED.
TWENTY-TWO HUNDRED FROM MONSIEUR BOUCHER! DO I HAVE...
TWENTY-THREE!

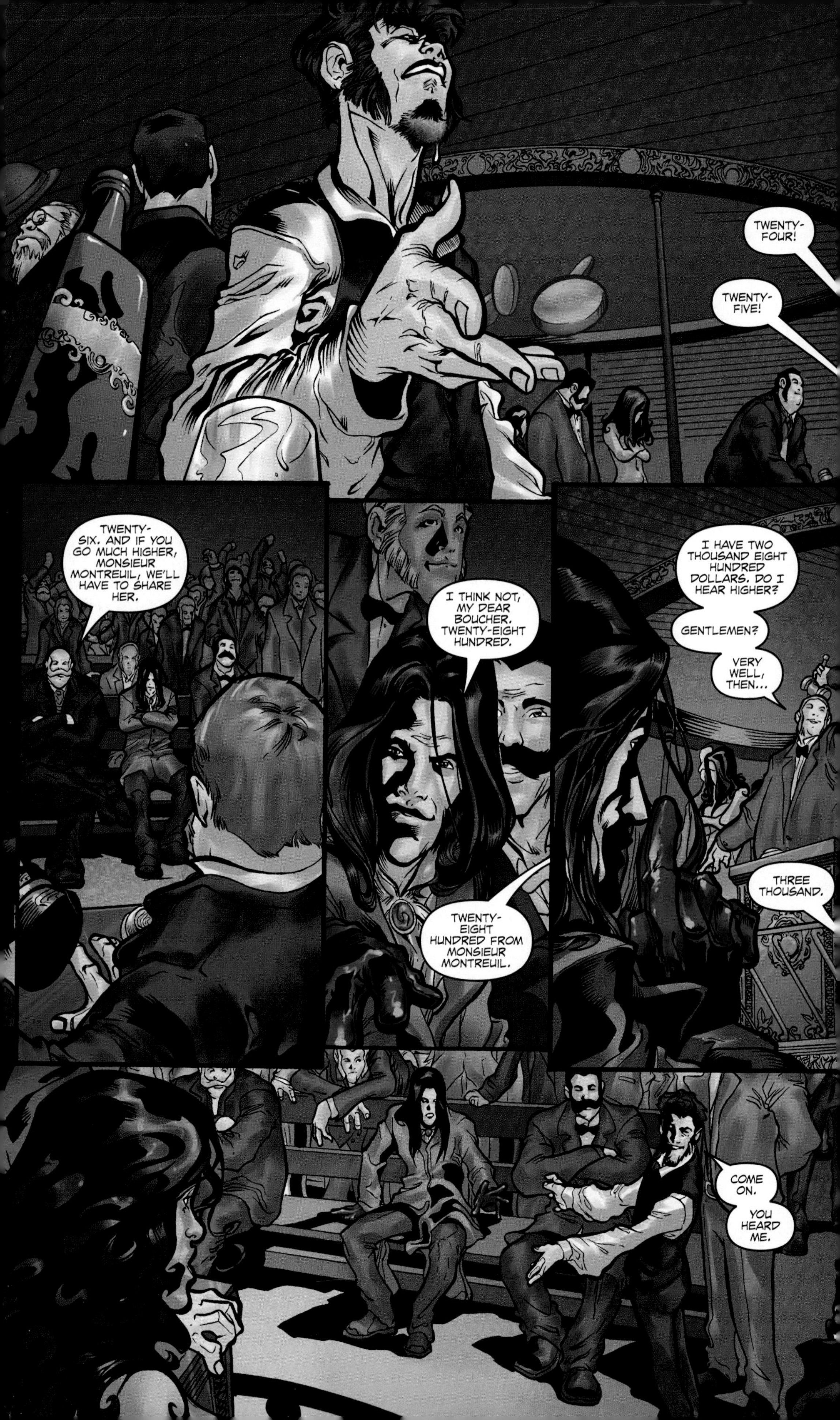
TWENTY-FOUR!
TWENTY-FIVE!
TWENTY-SIX. AND IF YOU GO MUCH HIGHER, MONSIEUR MONTREUIL, WE'LL HAVE TO SHARE HER.
I THINK NOT, MY DEAR BOUCHER. TWENTY-EIGHT HUNDRED.
TWENTY-EIGHT HUNDRED FROM MONSIEUR MONTREUIL.
I HAVE TWO THOUSAND EIGHT HUNDRED DOLLARS. DO I HEAR HIGHER?
GENTLEMEN?
VERY WELL, THEN...
THREE THOUSAND.
COME ON.
YOU HEARD ME.

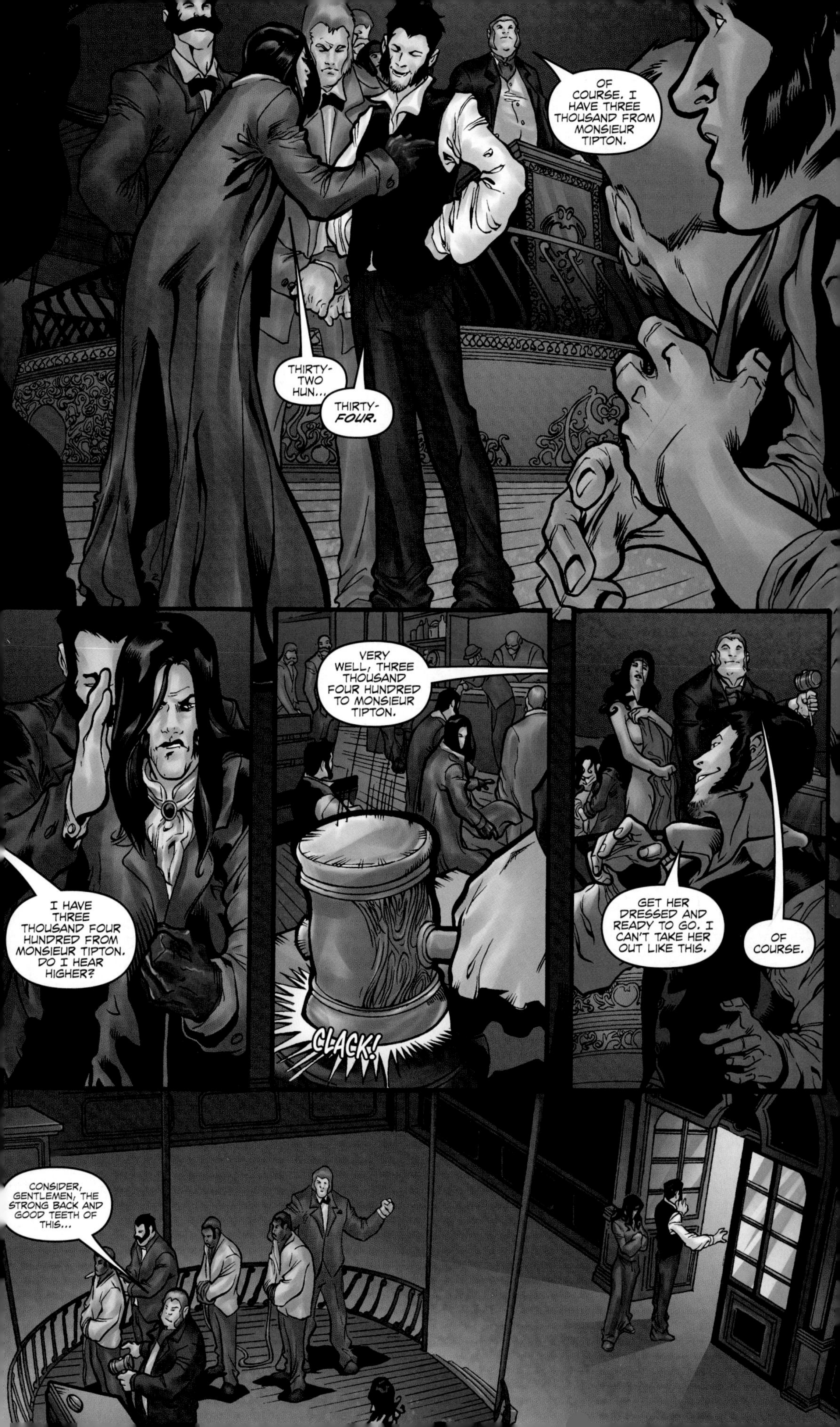
OF COURSE. I HAVE THREE THOUSAND FROM MONSIEUR TIPTON.
THIRTY-TWO HUN...
THIRTY-FOUR.
I HAVE THREE THOUSAND FOUR HUNDRED FROM MONSIEUR TIPTON. DO I HEAR HIGHER?
VERY WELL, THREE THOUSAND FOUR HUNDRED TO MONSIEUR TIPTON.
CLACK!
GET HER DRESSED AND READY TO GO. I CAN'T TAKE HER OUT LIKE THIS.
OF COURSE.
CONSIDER, GENTLEMEN, THE STRONG BACK AND GOOD TEETH OF THIS...

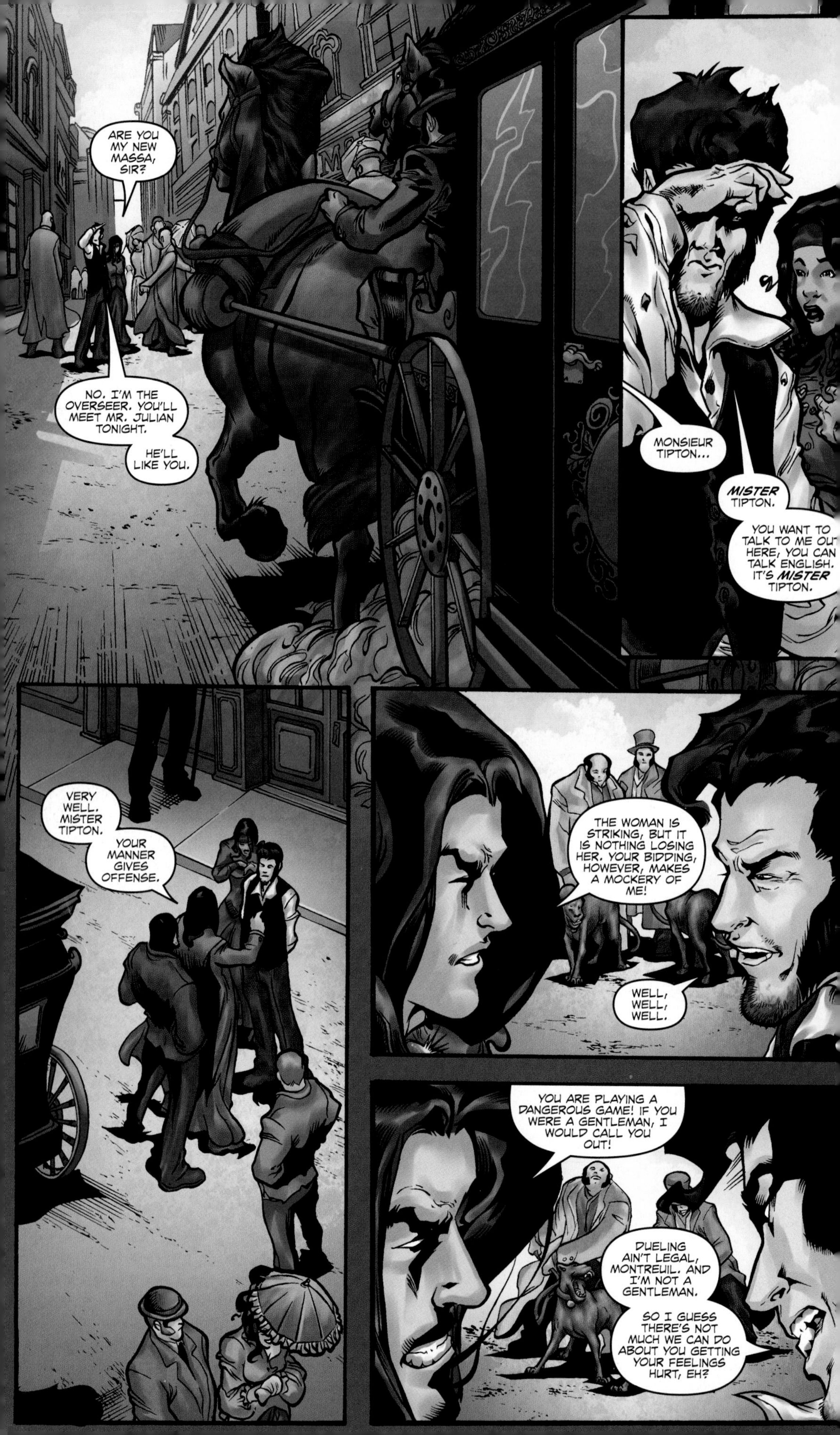
ARE YOU MY NEW MASSA, SIR?
NO. I'M THE OVERSEER. YOU'LL MEET MR. JULIAN TONIGHT.
HE'LL LIKE YOU.
MONSIEUR TIPTON...
MISTER TIPTON.
YOU WANT TO TALK TO ME OUT HERE, YOU CAN TALK ENGLISH. IT'S *MISTER* TIPTON.
VERY WELL. MISTER TIPTON.
YOUR MANNER GIVES OFFENSE.
THE WOMAN IS STRIKING, BUT IT IS NOTHING LOSING HER. YOUR BIDDING, HOWEVER, MAKES A MOCKERY OF ME!
WELL, WELL, WELL.
YOU ARE PLAYING A DANGEROUS GAME! IF YOU WERE A GENTLEMAN, I WOULD CALL YOU OUT!
DUELING AIN'T LEGAL, MONTREUIL. AND I'M NOT A GENTLEMAN.
SO I GUESS THERE'S NOT MUCH WE CAN DO ABOUT YOU GETTING YOUR FEELINGS HURT, EH?

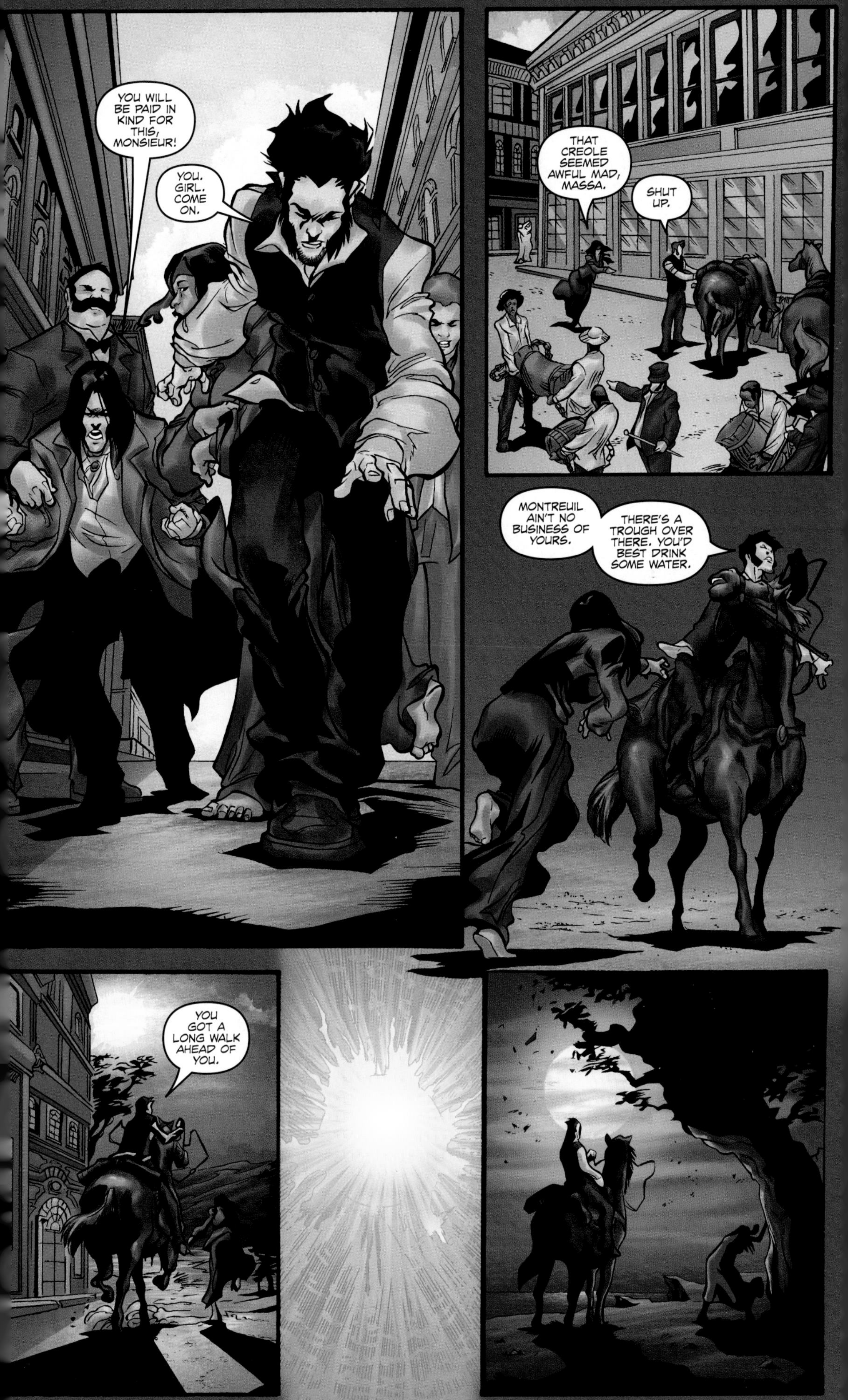
YOU WILL BE PAID IN KIND FOR THIS, MONSIEUR!
YOU. GIRL. COME ON.
THAT CREOLE SEEMED AWFUL MAD, MASSA.
SHUT UP.
MONTREUIL AIN'T NO BUSINESS OF YOURS.
THERE'S A TROUGH OVER THERE. YOU'D BEST DRINK SOME WATER.
YOU GOT A LONG WALK AHEAD OF YOU.

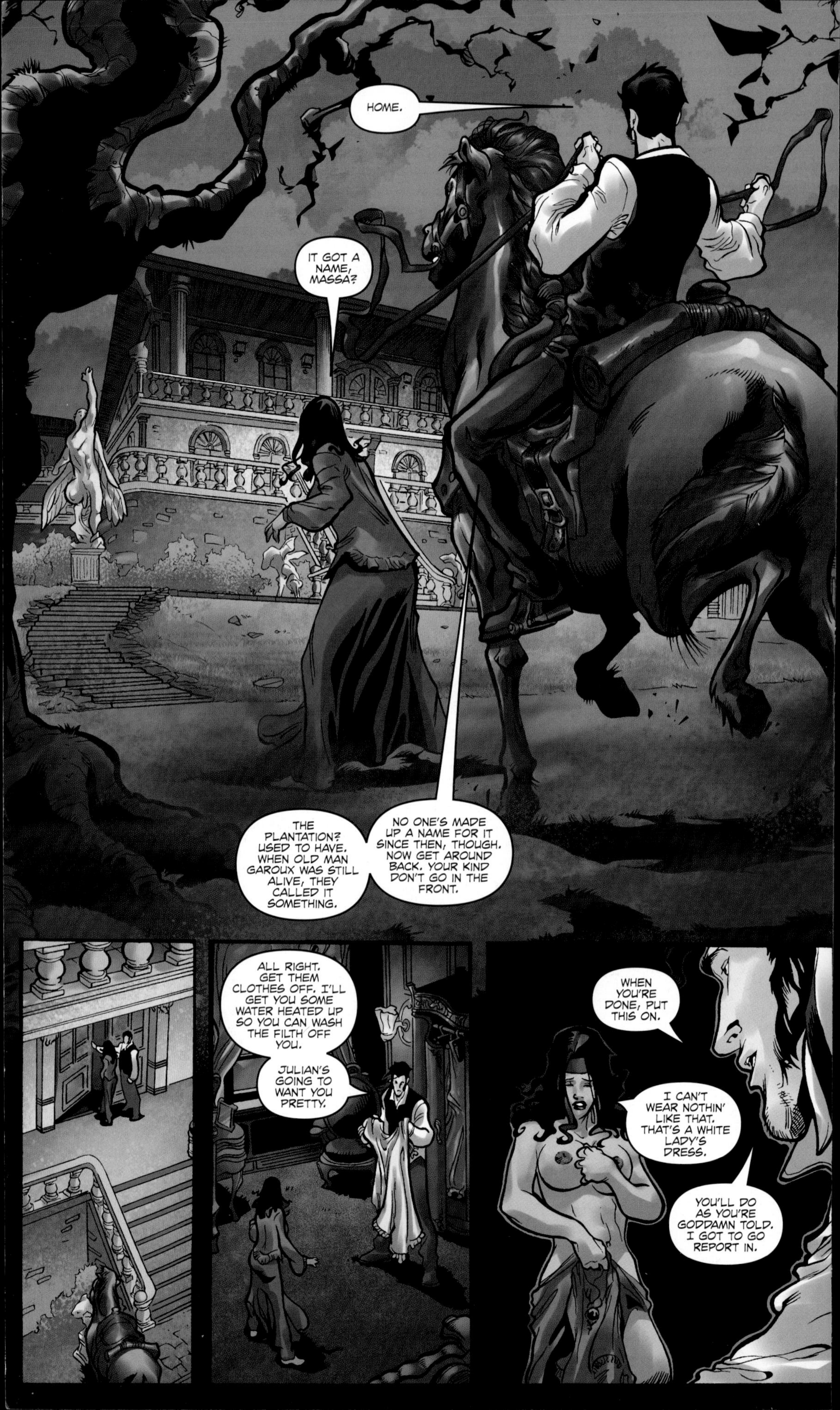
HOME.
IT GOT A NAME, MASSA?
THE PLANTATION? USED TO HAVE. WHEN OLD MAN GAROUX WAS STILL ALIVE, THEY CALLED IT SOMETHING.
NO ONE'S MADE UP A NAME FOR IT SINCE THEN, THOUGH. NOW GET AROUND BACK. YOUR KIND DON'T GO IN THE FRONT.
ALL RIGHT. GET THEM CLOTHES OFF. I'LL GET YOU SOME WATER HEATED UP SO YOU CAN WASH THE FILTH OFF YOU.
JULIAN'S GOING TO WANT YOU PRETTY.
WHEN YOU'RE DONE, PUT THIS ON.
I CAN'T WEAR NOTHIN' LIKE THAT. THAT'S A WHITE LADY'S DRESS.
YOU'LL DO AS YOU'RE GODDAMN TOLD. I GOT TO GO REPORT IN.

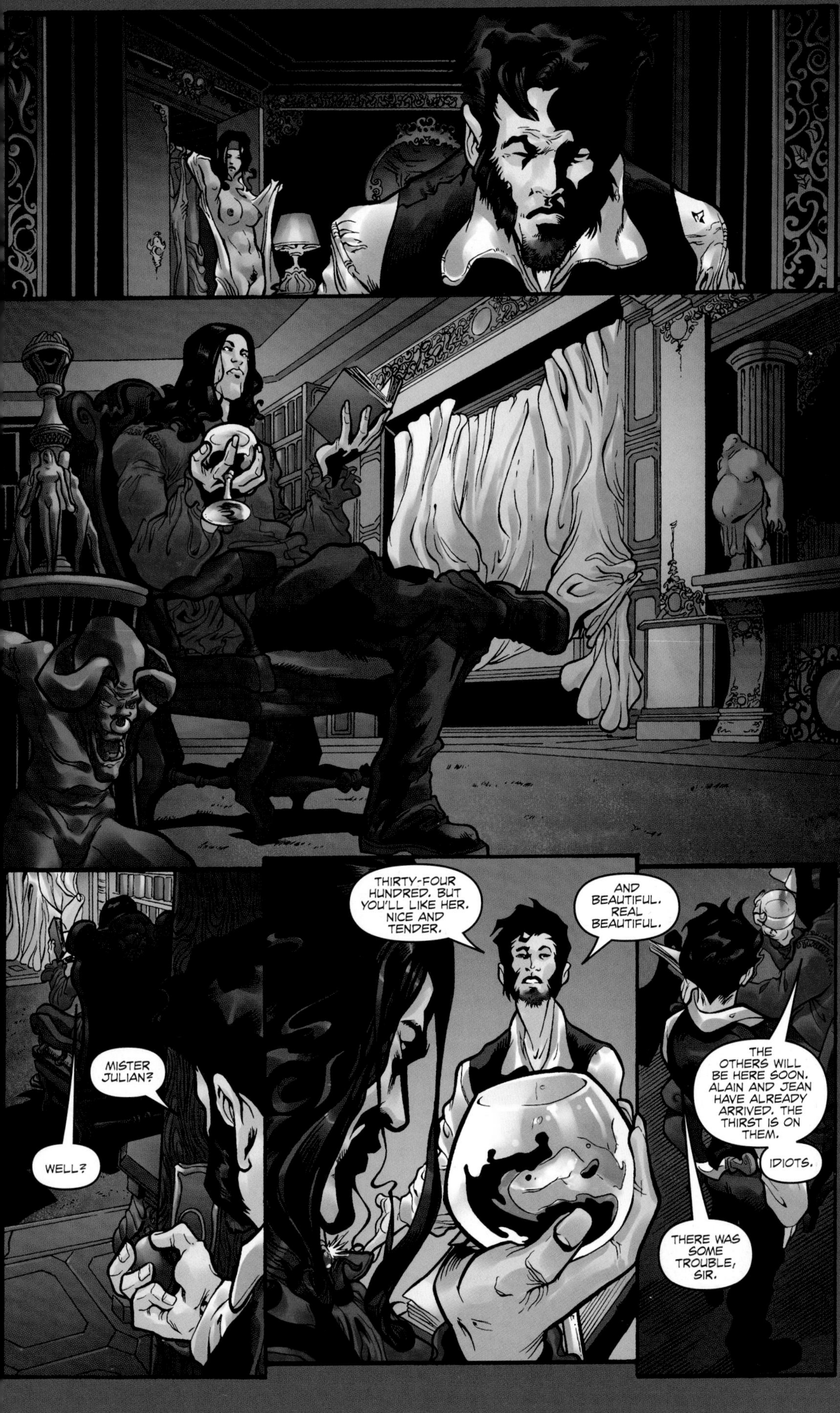

MISTER JULIAN?
WELL?
THIRTY-FOUR HUNDRED. BUT YOU'LL LIKE HER. NICE AND TENDER.
AND BEAUTIFUL. REAL BEAUTIFUL.
THE OTHERS WILL BE HERE SOON. ALAIN AND JEAN HAVE ALREADY ARRIVED. THE THIRST IS ON THEM.
IDIOTS.
THERE WAS SOME TROUBLE, SIR.

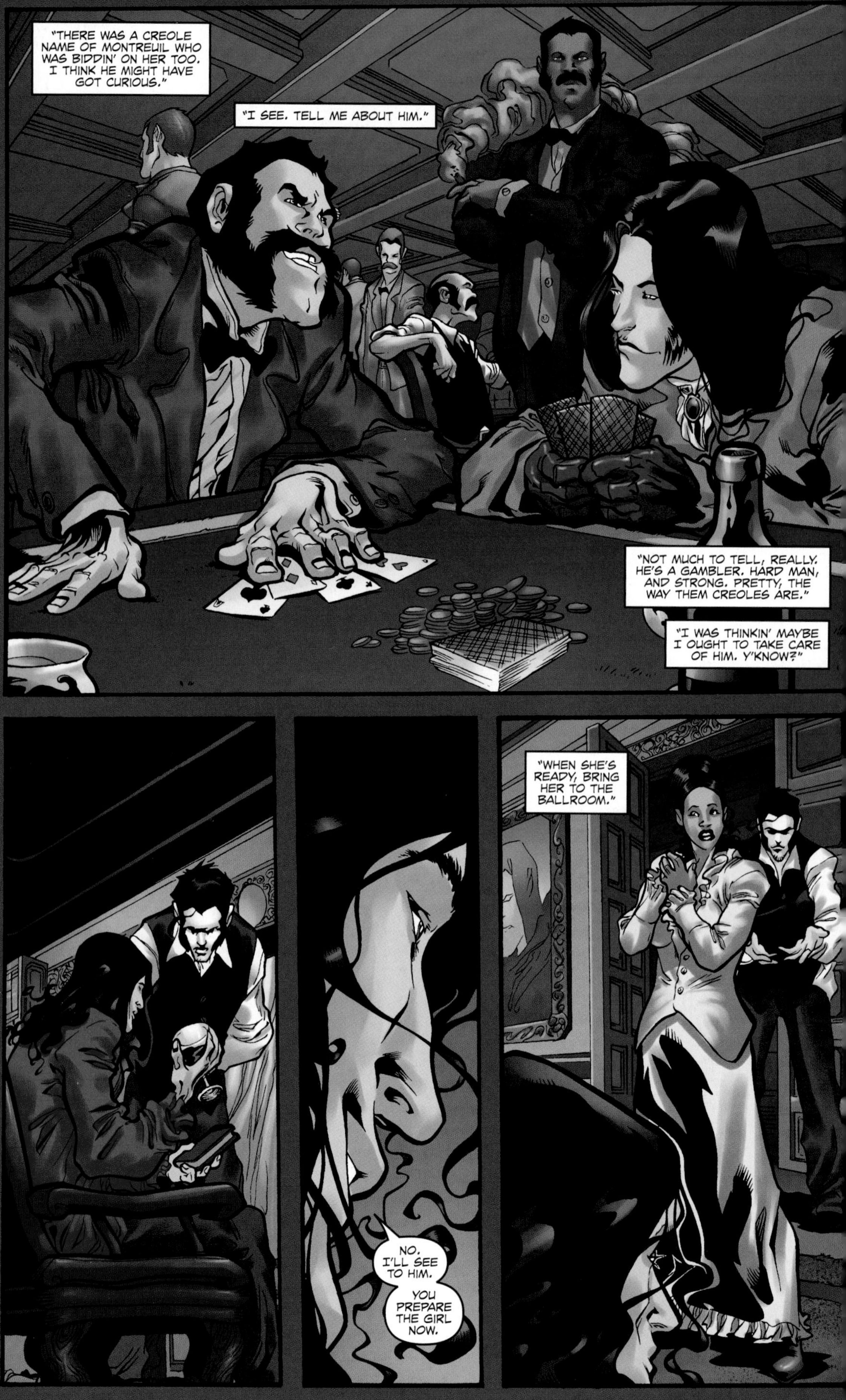
"THERE WAS A CREOLE NAME OF MONTREUIL WHO WAS BIDDIN' ON HER TOO. I THINK HE MIGHT HAVE GOT CURIOUS."
"I SEE. TELL ME ABOUT HIM."
"NOT MUCH TO TELL, REALLY. HE'S A GAMBLER. HARD MAN, AND STRONG. PRETTY, THE WAY THEM CREOLES ARE."
"I WAS THINKIN' MAYBE I OUGHT TO TAKE CARE OF HIM. Y'KNOW?"
NO. I'LL SEE TO HIM.
YOU PREPARE THE GIRL NOW.
"WHEN SHE'S READY, BRING HER TO THE BALLROOM."

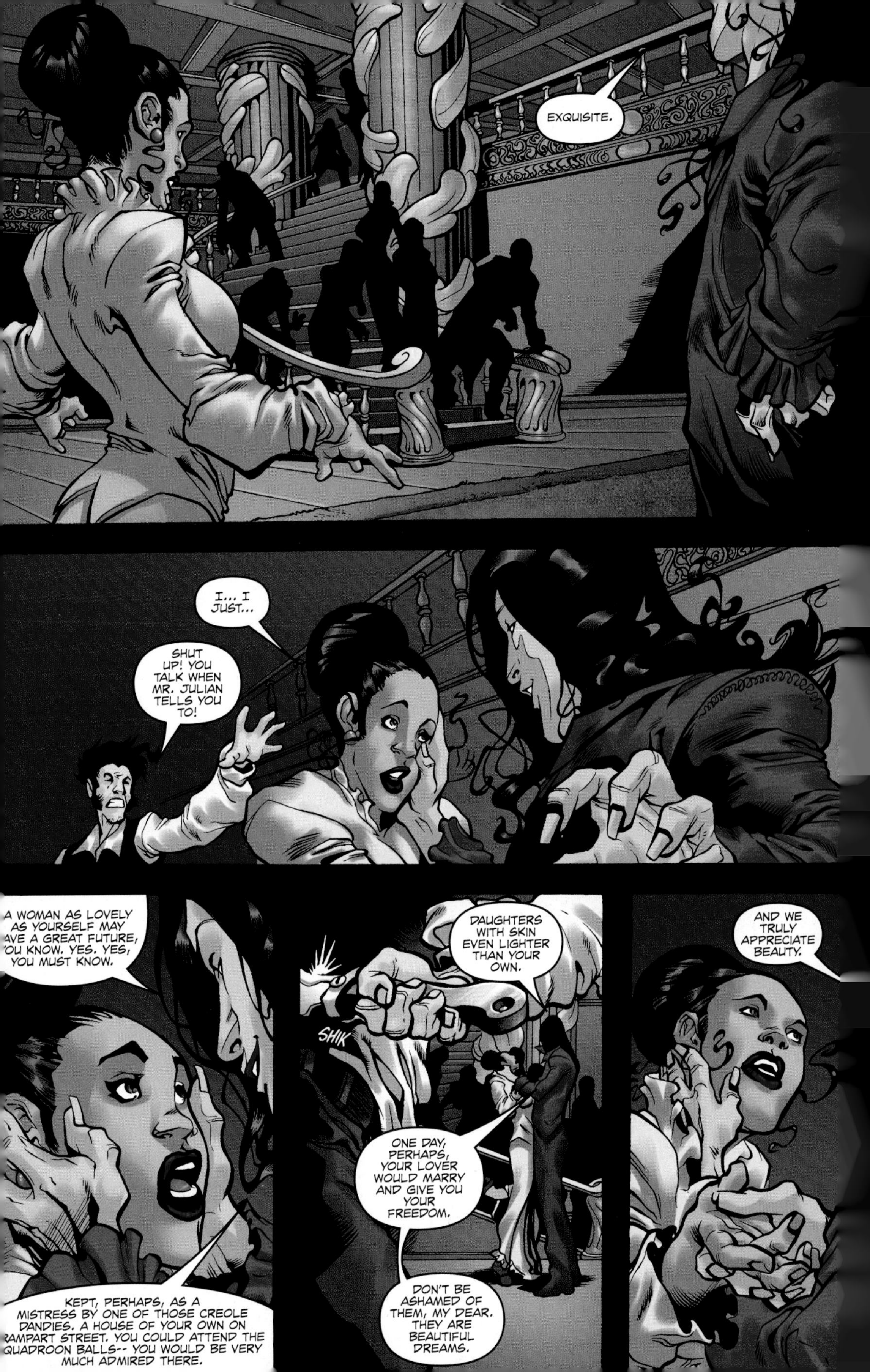
EXQUISITE.
I... I JUST...
SHUT UP! YOU TALK WHEN MR. JULIAN TELLS YOU TO!
A WOMAN AS LOVELY AS YOURSELF MAY AVE A GREAT FUTURE, OU KNOW. YES. YES, YOU MUST KNOW.
KEPT, PERHAPS, AS A MISTRESS BY ONE OF THOSE CREOLE DANDIES. A HOUSE OF YOUR OWN ON RAMPART STREET. YOU COULD ATTEND THE QUADROON BALLS-- YOU WOULD BE VERY MUCH ADMIRED THERE.
SHIK
DAUGHTERS WITH SKIN EVEN LIGHTER THAN YOUR OWN.
ONE DAY, PERHAPS, YOUR LOVER WOULD MARRY AND GIVE YOU YOUR FREEDOM.
DON'T BE ASHAMED OF THEM, MY DEAR. THEY ARE BEAUTIFUL DREAMS.
AND WE TRULY APPRECIATE BEAUTY.

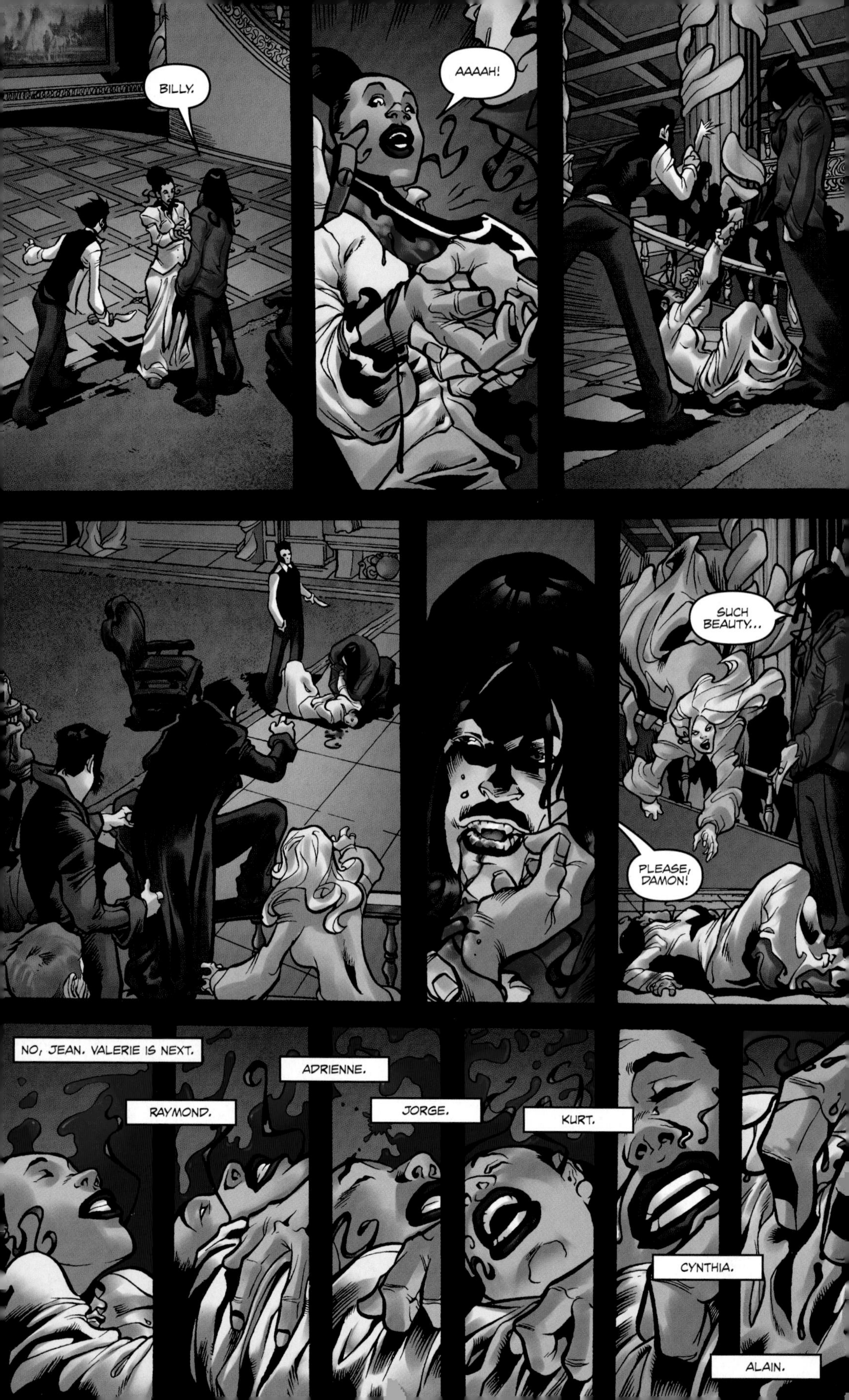
BILLY.
AAAAH!
SUCH BEAUTY...
PLEASE, DAMON!
NO, JEAN. VALERIE IS NEXT.
RAYMOND.
ADRIENNE.
JORGE.
KURT.
CYNTHIA.
ALAIN.

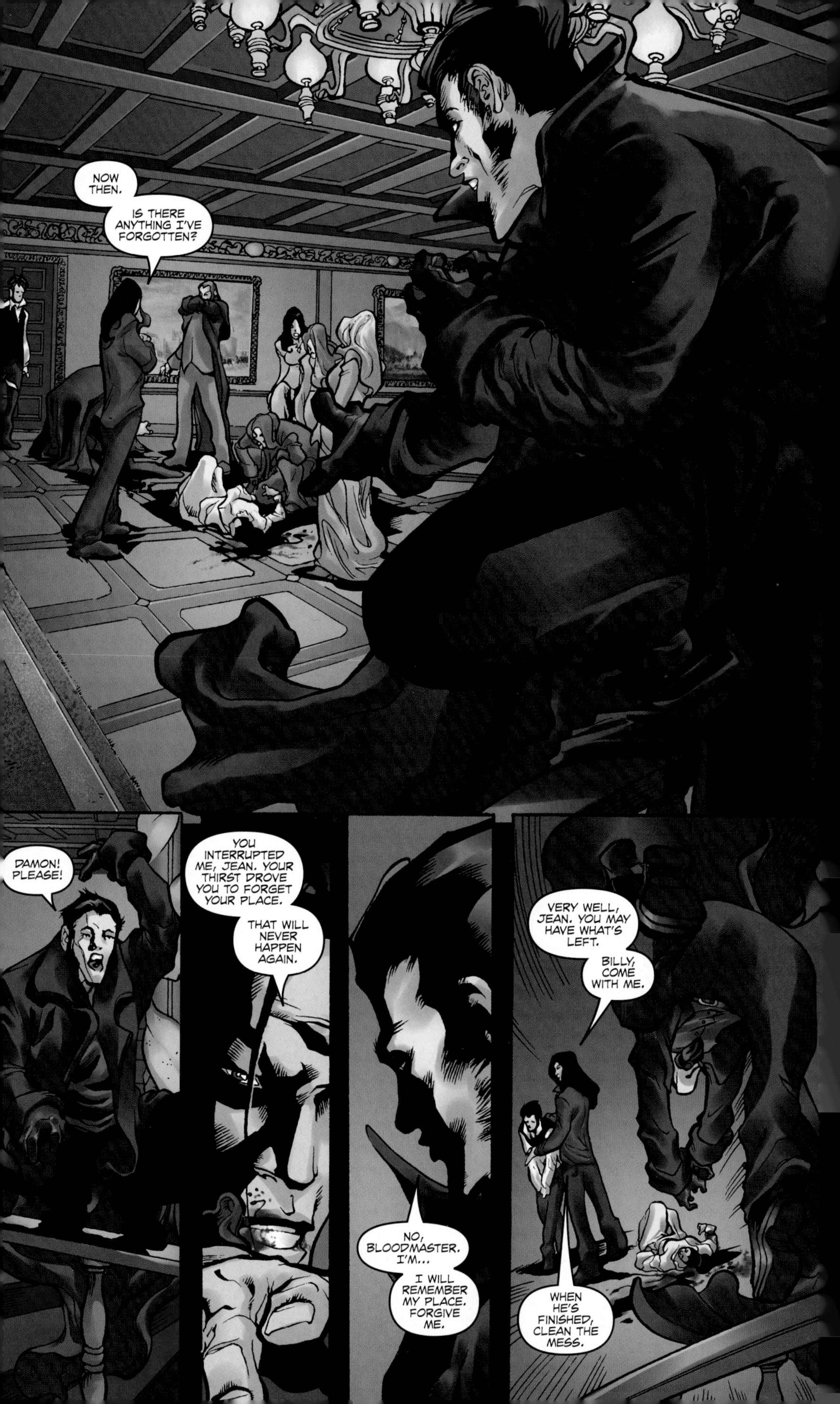

NOW THEN.
IS THERE ANYTHING I'VE FORGOTTEN?
DAMON! PLEASE!
YOU INTERRUPTED ME, JEAN. YOUR THIRST DROVE YOU TO FORGET YOUR PLACE.
THAT WILL NEVER HAPPEN AGAIN.
NO, BLOODMASTER. I'M...
I WILL REMEMBER MY PLACE. FORGIVE ME.
VERY WELL, JEAN. YOU MAY HAVE WHAT'S LEFT.
BILLY, COME WITH ME.
WHEN HE'S FINISHED, CLEAN THE MESS.

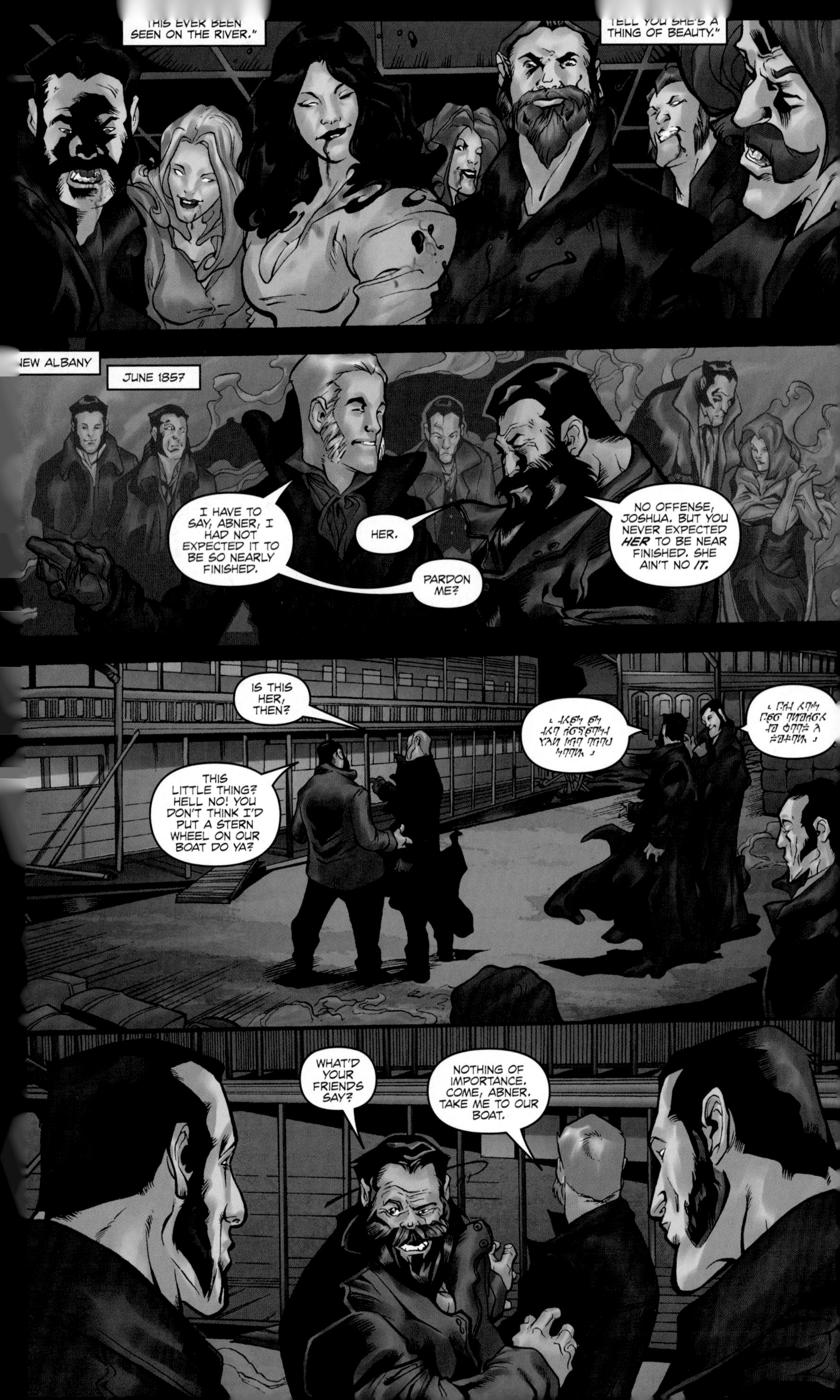
THIS EVER BEEN SEEN ON THE RIVER."
TELL YOU SHE'S A THING OF BEAUTY."
NEW ALBANY
JUNE 1857
I HAVE TO SAY, ABNER, I HAD NOT EXPECTED IT TO BE SO NEARLY FINISHED.
HER.
PARDON ME?
NO OFFENSE, JOSHUA. BUT YOU NEVER EXPECTED HER TO BE NEAR FINISHED. SHE AIN'T NO IT.
IS THIS HER, THEN?
THIS LITTLE THING? HELL NO! YOU DON'T THINK I'D PUT A STERN WHEEL ON OUR BOAT DO YA?
WHAT'D YOUR FRIENDS SAY?
NOTHING OF IMPORTANCE. COME, ABNER. TAKE ME TO OUR BOAT.

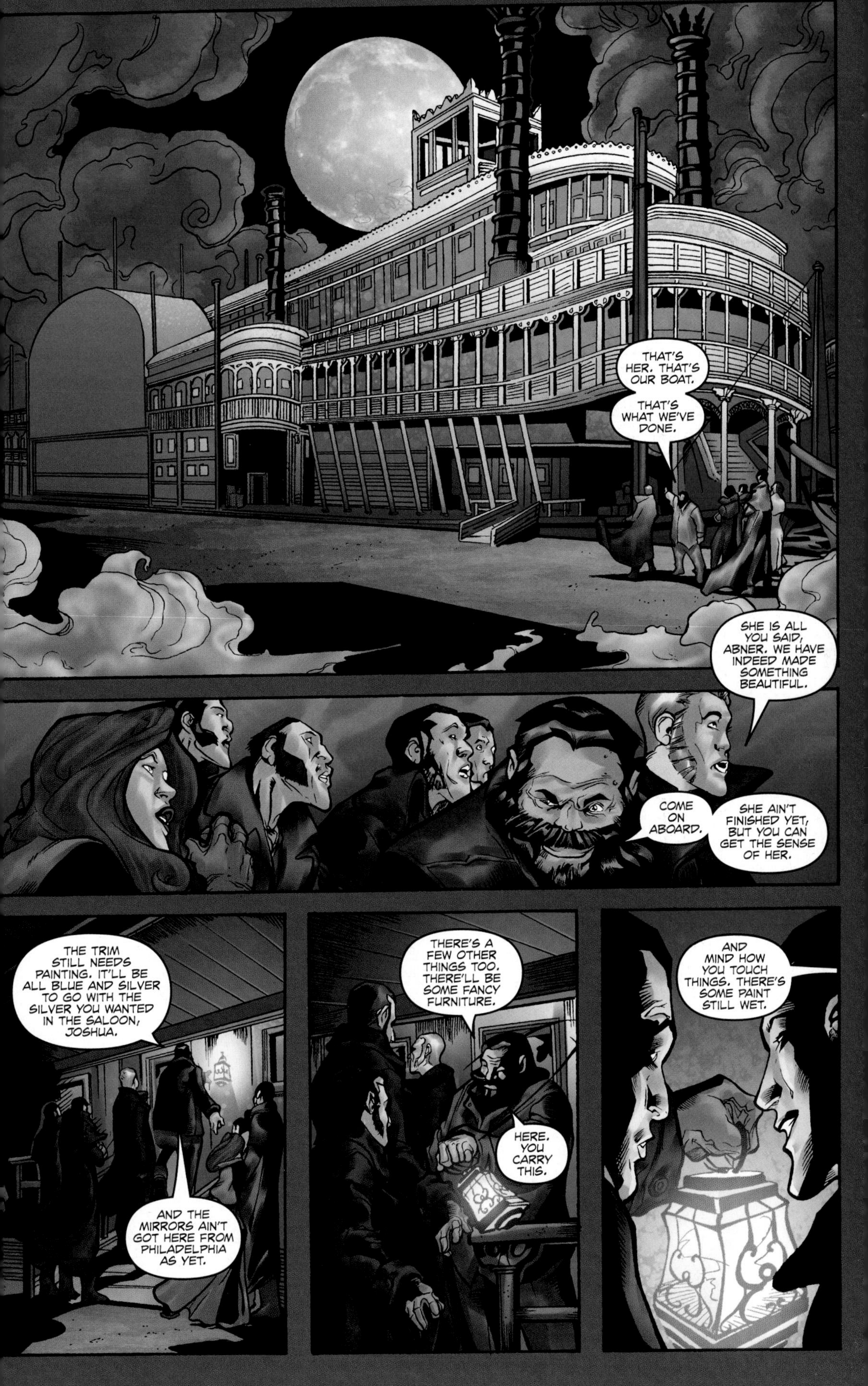
THAT'S HER. THAT'S OUR BOAT.
THAT'S WHAT WE'VE DONE.
SHE IS ALL YOU SAID, ABNER. WE HAVE INDEED MADE SOMETHING BEAUTIFUL.
COME ON ABOARD.
SHE AIN'T FINISHED YET, BUT YOU CAN GET THE SENSE OF HER.
THE TRIM STILL NEEDS PAINTING. IT'LL BE ALL BLUE AND SILVER TO GO WITH THE SILVER YOU WANTED IN THE SALOON, JOSHUA.
AND THE MIRRORS AIN'T GOT HERE FROM PHILADELPHIA AS YET.
THERE'S A FEW OTHER THINGS TOO. THERE'LL BE SOME FANCY FURNITURE.
HERE. YOU CARRY THIS.
AND MIND HOW YOU TOUCH THINGS. THERE'S SOME PAINT STILL WET.

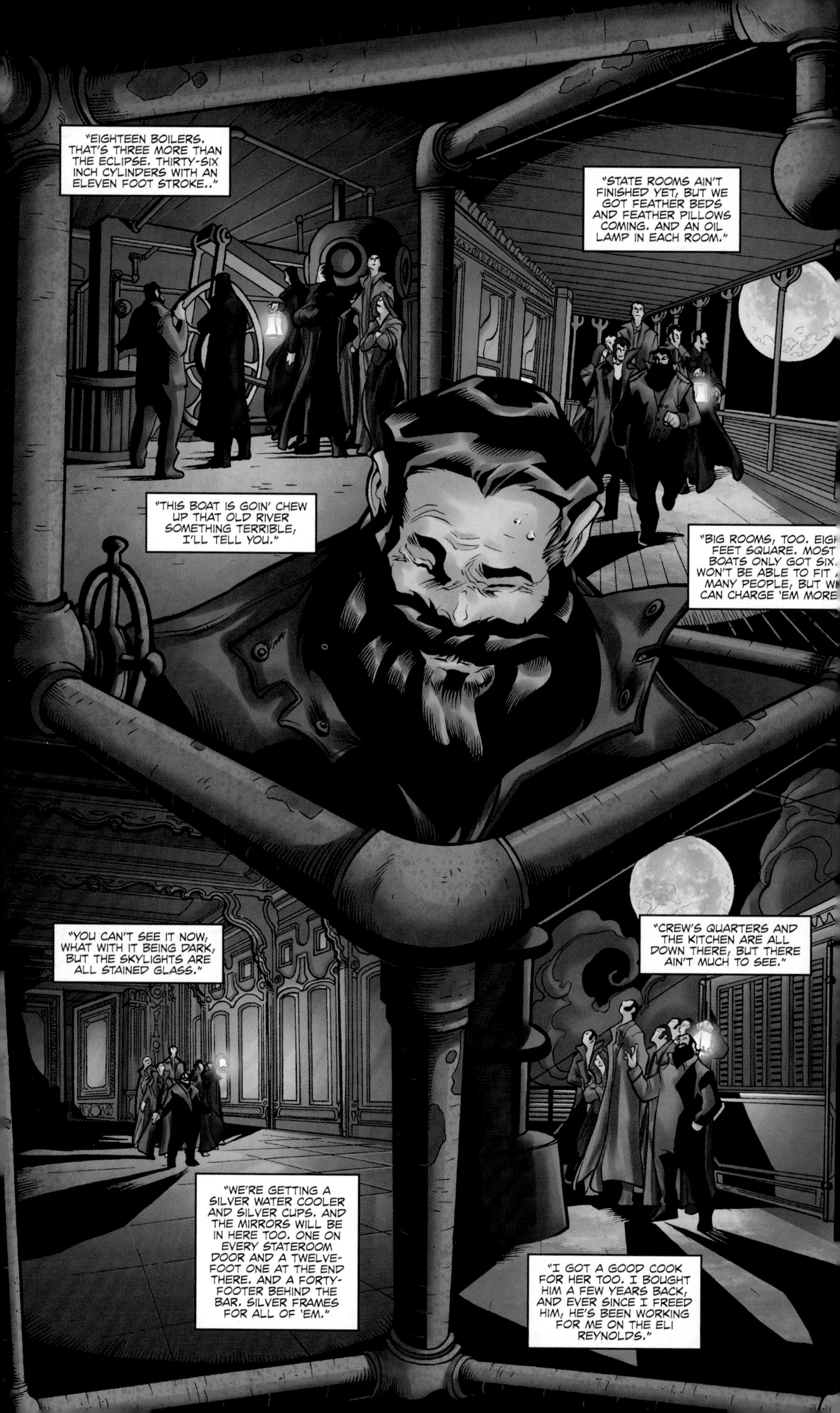
"EIGHTEEN BOILERS. THAT'S THREE MORE THAN THE ECLIPSE. THIRTY-SIX INCH CYLINDERS WITH AN ELEVEN FOOT STROKE.."
"STATE ROOMS AIN'T FINISHED YET, BUT WE GOT FEATHER BEDS AND FEATHER PILLOWS COMING. AND AN OIL LAMP IN EACH ROOM."
"THIS BOAT IS GOIN' CHEW UP THAT OLD RIVER SOMETHING TERRIBLE, I'LL TELL YOU."
"BIG ROOMS, TOO. EIG FEET SQUARE. MOST BOATS ONLY GOT SIX WON'T BE ABLE TO FIT MANY PEOPLE, BUT W CAN CHARGE 'EM MORE
"YOU CAN'T SEE IT NOW, WHAT WITH IT BEING DARK, BUT THE SKYLIGHTS ARE ALL STAINED GLASS."
"CREW'S QUARTERS AND THE KITCHEN ARE ALL DOWN THERE, BUT THERE AIN'T MUCH TO SEE."
"WE'RE GETTING A SILVER WATER COOLER AND SILVER CUPS. AND THE MIRRORS WILL BE IN HERE TOO. ONE ON EVERY STATEROOM DOOR AND A TWELVE-FOOT ONE AT THE END THERE. AND A FORTY-FOOTER BEHIND THE BAR. SILVER FRAMES FOR ALL OF 'EM."
"I GOT A GOOD COOK FOR HER TOO. I BOUGHT HIM A FEW YEARS BACK, AND EVER SINCE I FREED HIM, HE'S BEEN WORKING FOR ME ON THE ELI REYNOLDS."

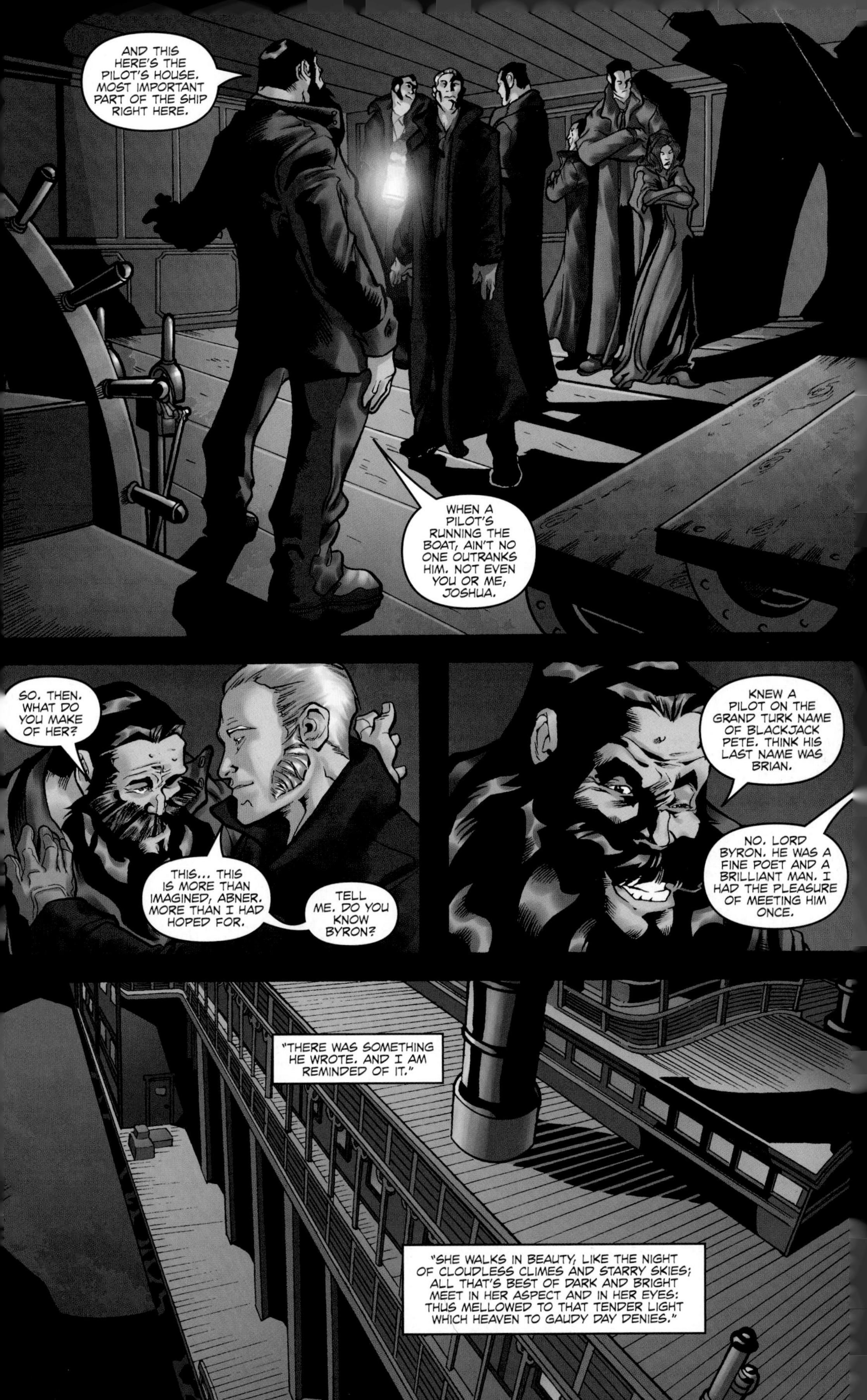
AND THIS HERE'S THE PILOT'S HOUSE. MOST IMPORTANT PART OF THE SHIP RIGHT HERE.
WHEN A PILOT'S RUNNING THE BOAT, AIN'T NO ONE OUTRANKS HIM. NOT EVEN YOU OR ME, JOSHUA.
SO. THEN. WHAT DO YOU MAKE OF HER?
THIS... THIS IS MORE THAN IMAGINED, ABNER. MORE THAN I HAD HOPED FOR.
TELL ME. DO YOU KNOW BYRON?
KNEW A PILOT ON THE GRAND TURK NAME OF BLACKJACK PETE. THINK HIS LAST NAME WAS BRIAN.
NO. LORD BYRON. HE WAS A FINE POET AND A BRILLIANT MAN. I HAD THE PLEASURE OF MEETING HIM ONCE.
"THERE WAS SOMETHING HE WROTE. AND I AM REMINDED OF IT."
"SHE WALKS IN BEAUTY, LIKE THE NIGHT OF CLOUDLESS CLIMES AND STARRY SKIES; ALL THAT'S BEST OF DARK AND BRIGHT MEET IN HER ASPECT AND IN HER EYES: THUS MELLOWED TO THAT TENDER LIGHT WHICH HEAVEN TO GAUDY DAY DENIES."

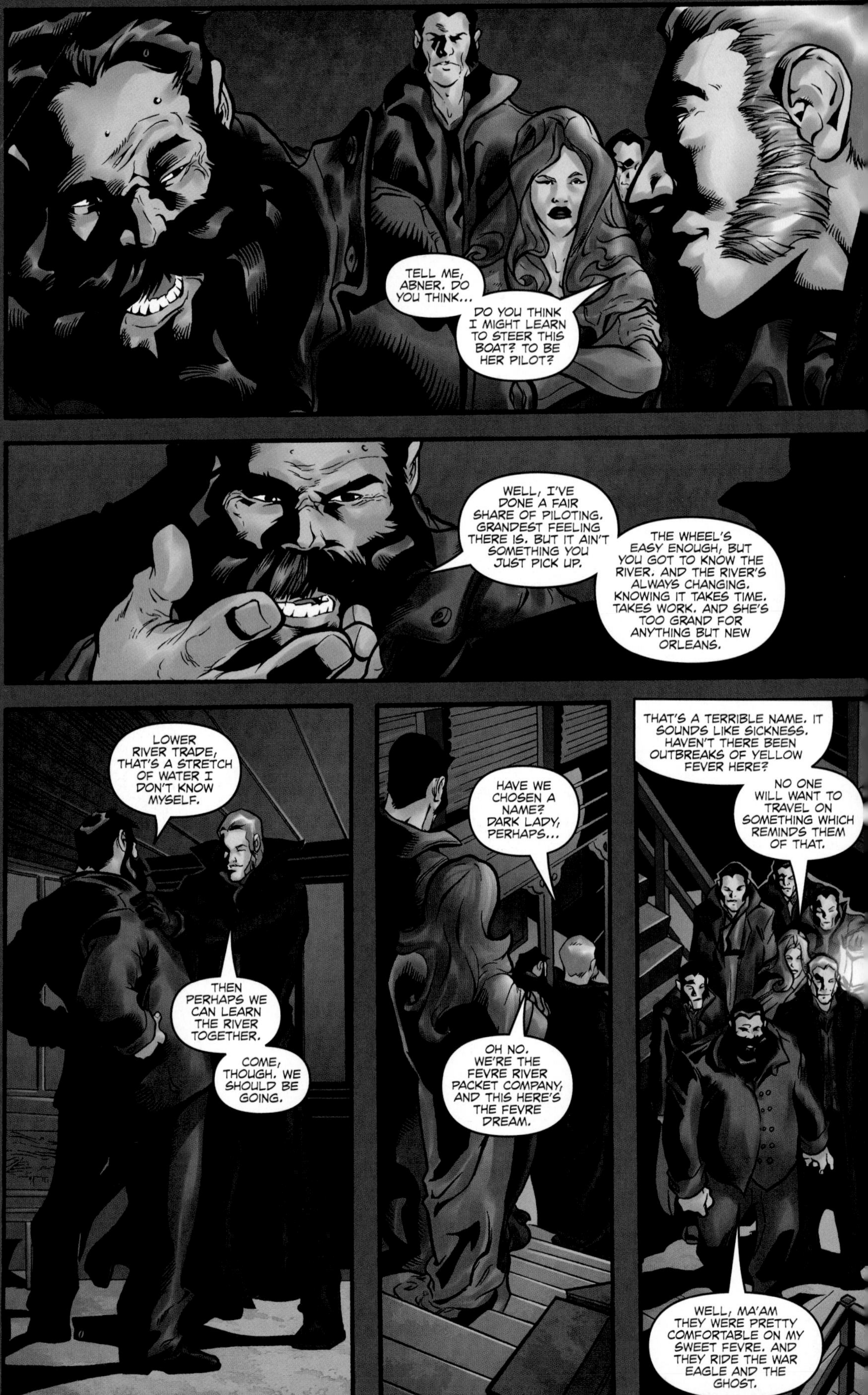
TELL ME, ABNER. DO YOU THINK...
DO YOU THINK I MIGHT LEARN TO STEER THIS BOAT? TO BE HER PILOT?
WELL, I'VE DONE A FAIR SHARE OF PILOTING. GRANDEST FEELING THERE IS. BUT IT AIN'T SOMETHING YOU JUST PICK UP.
THE WHEEL'S EASY ENOUGH, BUT YOU GOT TO KNOW THE RIVER. AND THE RIVER'S ALWAYS CHANGING. KNOWING IT TAKES TIME. TAKES WORK. AND SHE'S TOO GRAND FOR ANYTHING BUT NEW ORLEANS.
LOWER RIVER TRADE, THAT'S A STRETCH OF WATER I DON'T KNOW MYSELF.
THEN PERHAPS WE CAN LEARN THE RIVER TOGETHER.
COME, THOUGH. WE SHOULD BE GOING.
HAVE WE CHOSEN A NAME? DARK LADY, PERHAPS...
OH NO. WE'RE THE FEVRE RIVER PACKET COMPANY, AND THIS HERE'S THE FEVRE DREAM.
THAT'S A TERRIBLE NAME. IT SOUNDS LIKE SICKNESS. HAVEN'T THERE BEEN OUTBREAKS OF YELLOW FEVER HERE?
NO ONE WILL WANT TO TRAVEL ON SOMETHING WHICH REMINDS THEM OF THAT.
WELL, MA'AM THEY WERE PRETTY COMFORTABLE ON MY SWEET FEVRE. AND THEY RIDE THE WAR EAGLE AND THE GHOST.

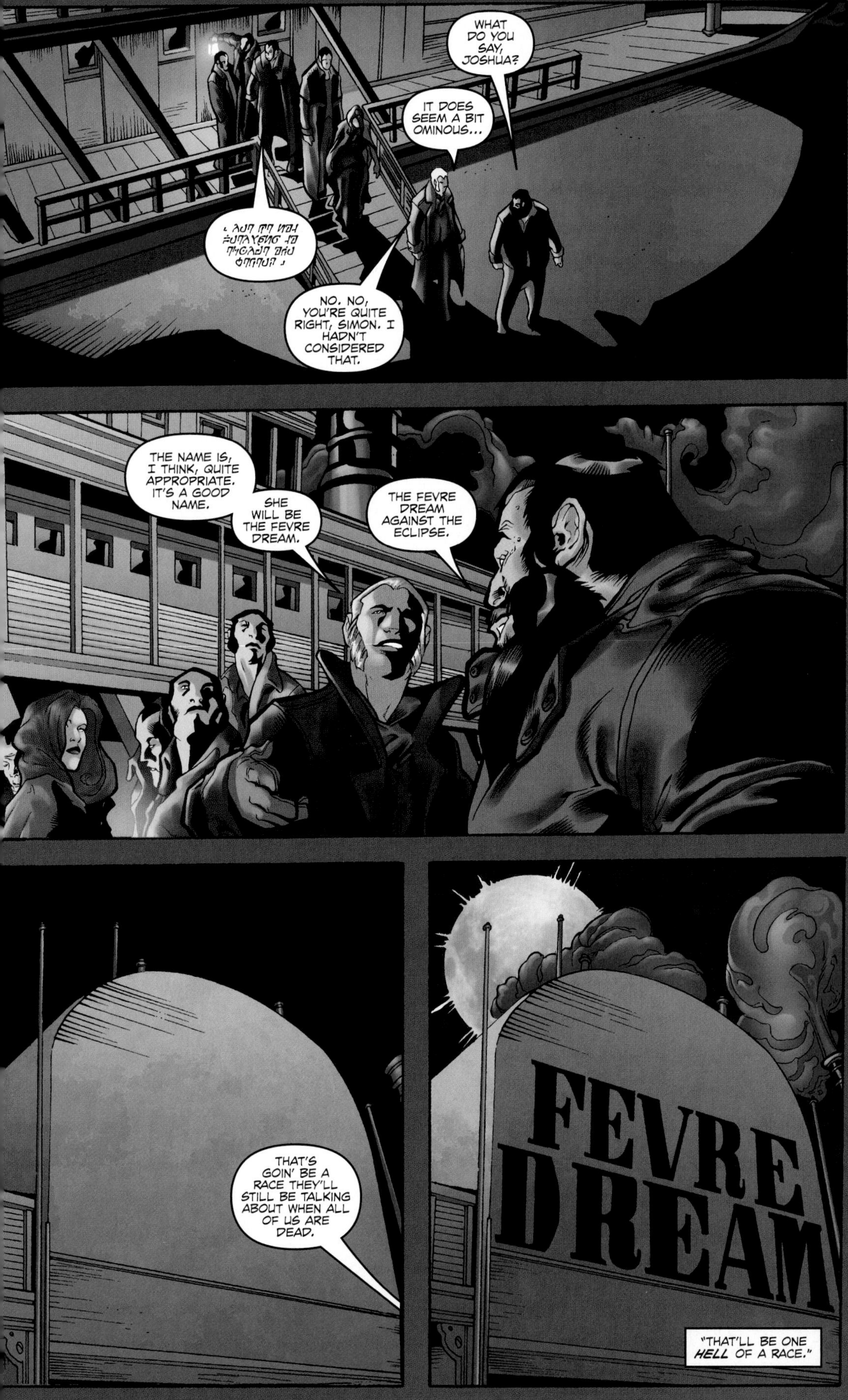
WHAT DO YOU SAY, JOSHUA?
IT DOES SEEM A BIT OMINOUS...
NO. NO, YOU'RE QUITE RIGHT, SIMON. I HADN'T CONSIDERED THAT.
THE NAME IS, I THINK, QUITE APPROPRIATE. IT'S A GOOD NAME.
SHE WILL BE THE FEVRE DREAM.
THE FEVRE DREAM AGAINST THE ECLIPSE.
THAT'S GOIN' BE A RACE THEY'LL STILL BE TALKING ABOUT WHEN ALL OF US ARE DEAD.
FEVRE DREAM
"THAT'LL BE ONE *HELL* OF A RACE."

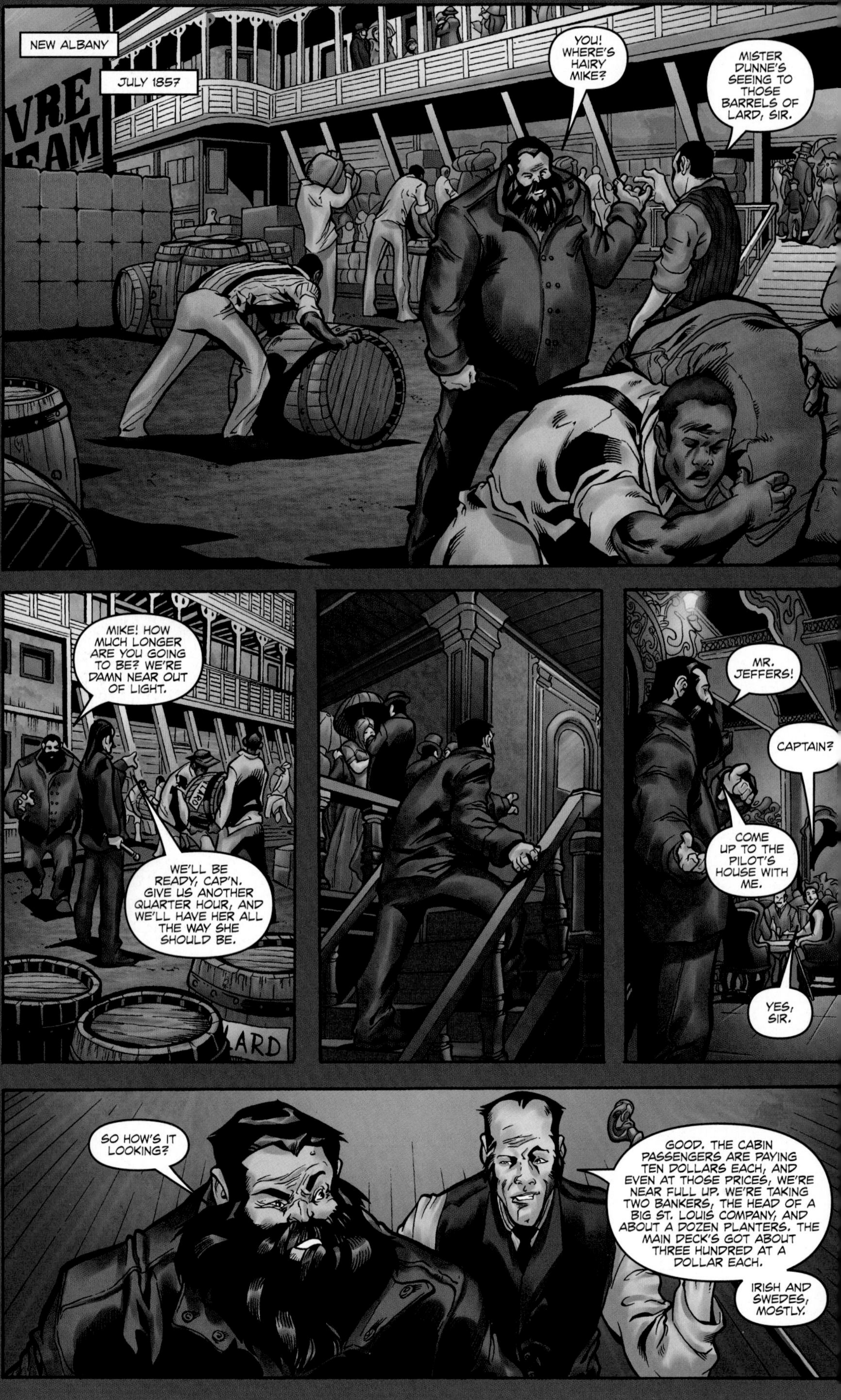
NEW ALBANY
JULY 1857
YOU! WHERE'S HAIRY MIKE?
MISTER DUNNE'S SEEING TO THOSE BARRELS OF LARD, SIR.
MIKE! HOW MUCH LONGER ARE YOU GOING TO BE? WE'RE DAMN NEAR OUT OF LIGHT.
WE'LL BE READY, CAP'N. GIVE US ANOTHER QUARTER HOUR, AND WE'LL HAVE HER ALL THE WAY SHE SHOULD BE.
MR. JEFFERS!
CAPTAIN?
COME UP TO THE PILOT'S HOUSE WITH ME.
YES, SIR.
SO HOW'S IT LOOKING?
GOOD. THE CABIN PASSENGERS ARE PAYING TEN DOLLARS EACH, AND EVEN AT THOSE PRICES, WE'RE NEAR FULL UP. WE'RE TAKING TWO BANKERS, THE HEAD OF A BIG ST. LOUIS COMPANY, AND ABOUT A DOZEN PLANTERS. THE MAIN DECK'S GOT ABOUT THREE HUNDRED AT A DOLLAR EACH.
IRISH AND SWEDES, MOSTLY.

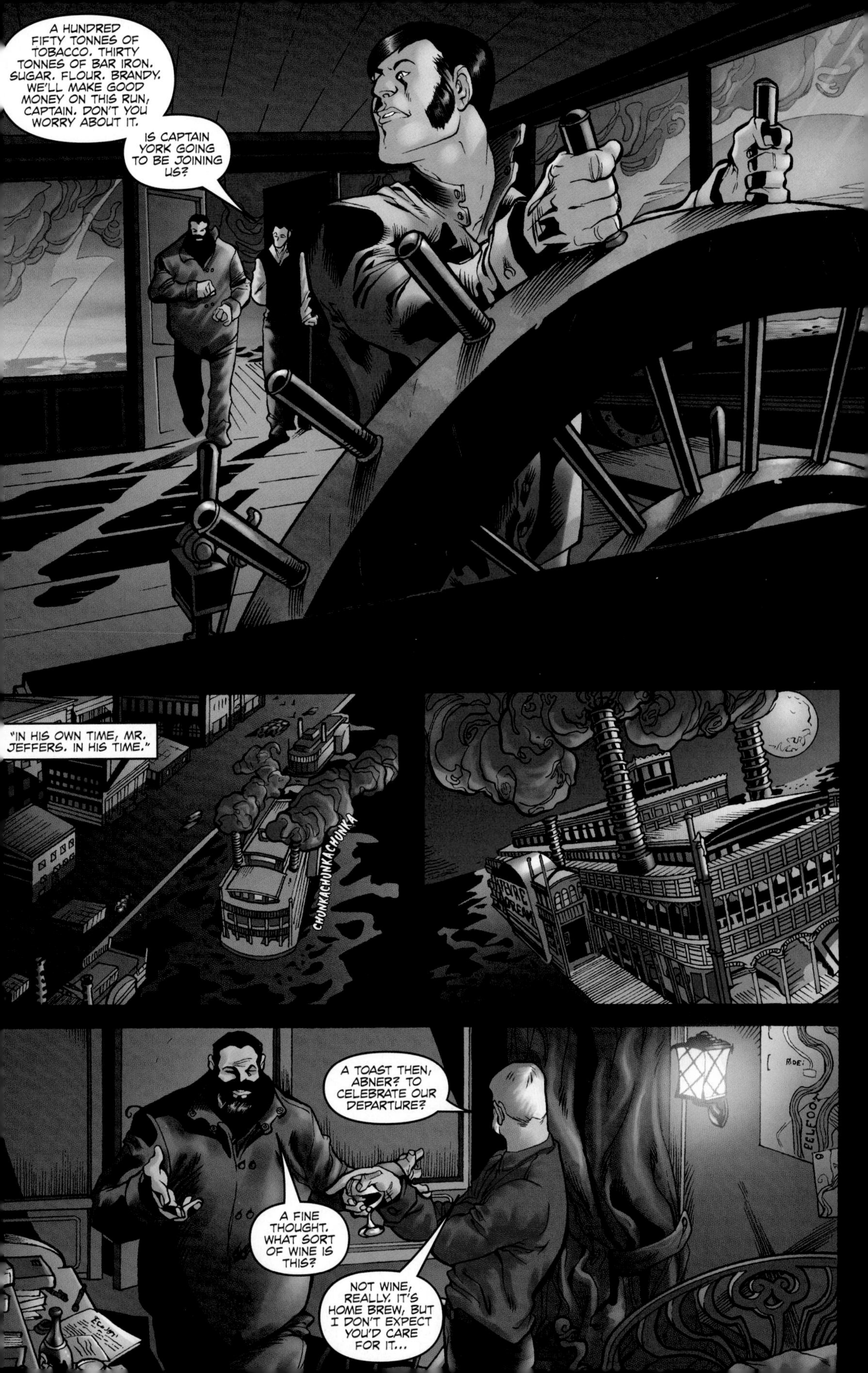

A HUNDRED FIFTY TONNES OF TOBACCO. THIRTY TONNES OF BAR IRON. SUGAR. FLOUR. BRANDY. WE'LL MAKE GOOD MONEY ON THIS RUN, CAPTAIN. DON'T YOU WORRY ABOUT IT.
IS CAPTAIN YORK GOING TO BE JOINING US?
"IN HIS OWN TIME, MR. JEFFERS. IN HIS TIME."
CHUNKACHUNKACHUNKA
A TOAST THEN, ABNER? TO CELEBRATE OUR DEPARTURE?
A FINE THOUGHT. WHAT SORT OF WINE IS THIS?
NOT WINE, REALLY. IT'S HOME BREW, BUT I DON'T EXPECT YOU'D CARE FOR IT...

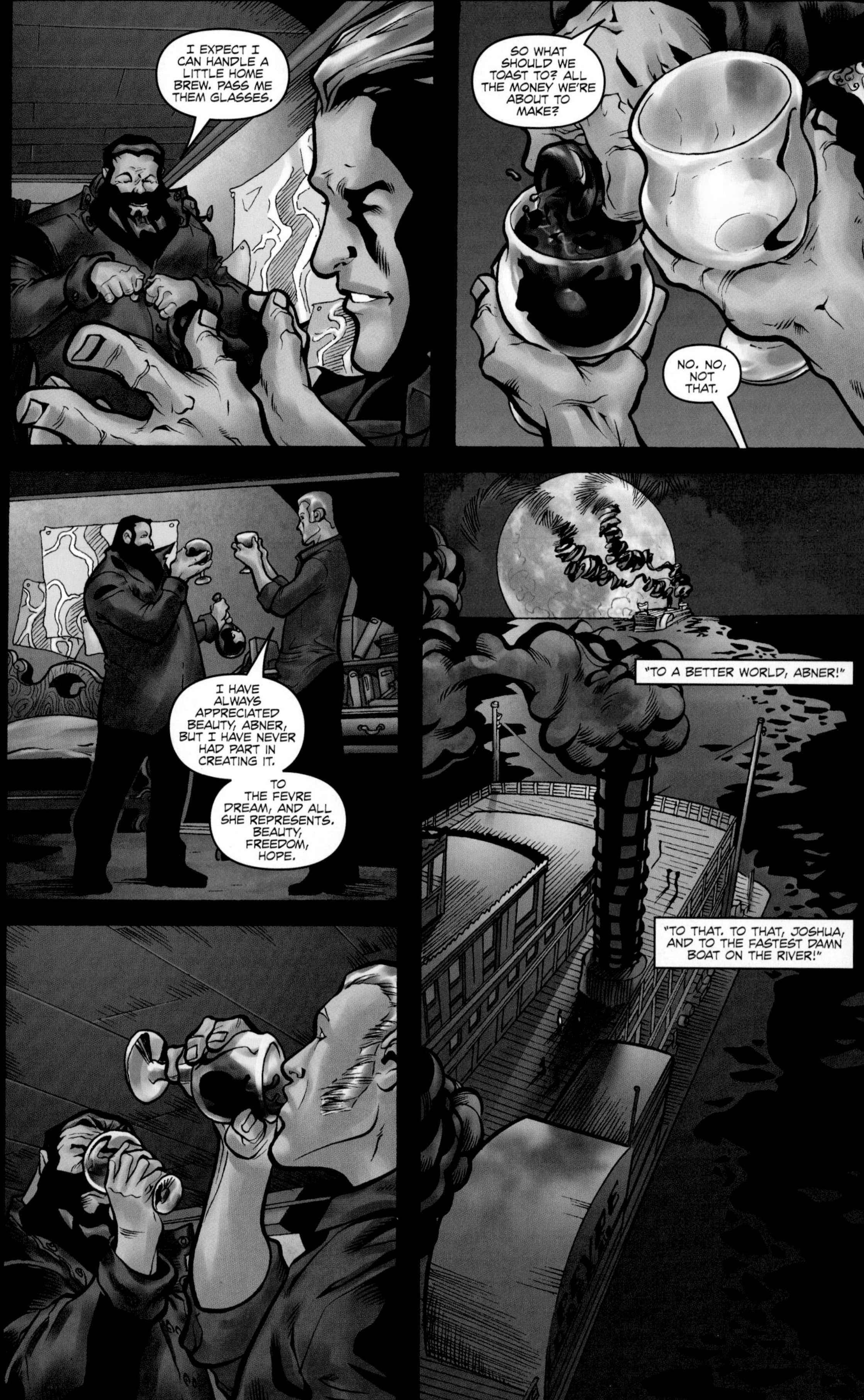
I EXPECT I CAN HANDLE A LITTLE HOME BREW. PASS ME THEM GLASSES.
SO WHAT SHOULD WE TOAST TO? ALL THE MONEY WE'RE ABOUT TO MAKE?
NO. NO, NOT THAT.
I HAVE ALWAYS APPRECIATED BEAUTY, ABNER, BUT I HAVE NEVER HAD PART IN CREATING IT.
TO THE FEVRE DREAM, AND ALL SHE REPRESENTS. BEAUTY, FREEDOM, HOPE.
"TO A BETTER WORLD, ABNER!"
"TO THAT. TO THAT, JOSHUA, AND TO THE FASTEST DAMN BOAT ON THE RIVER!"

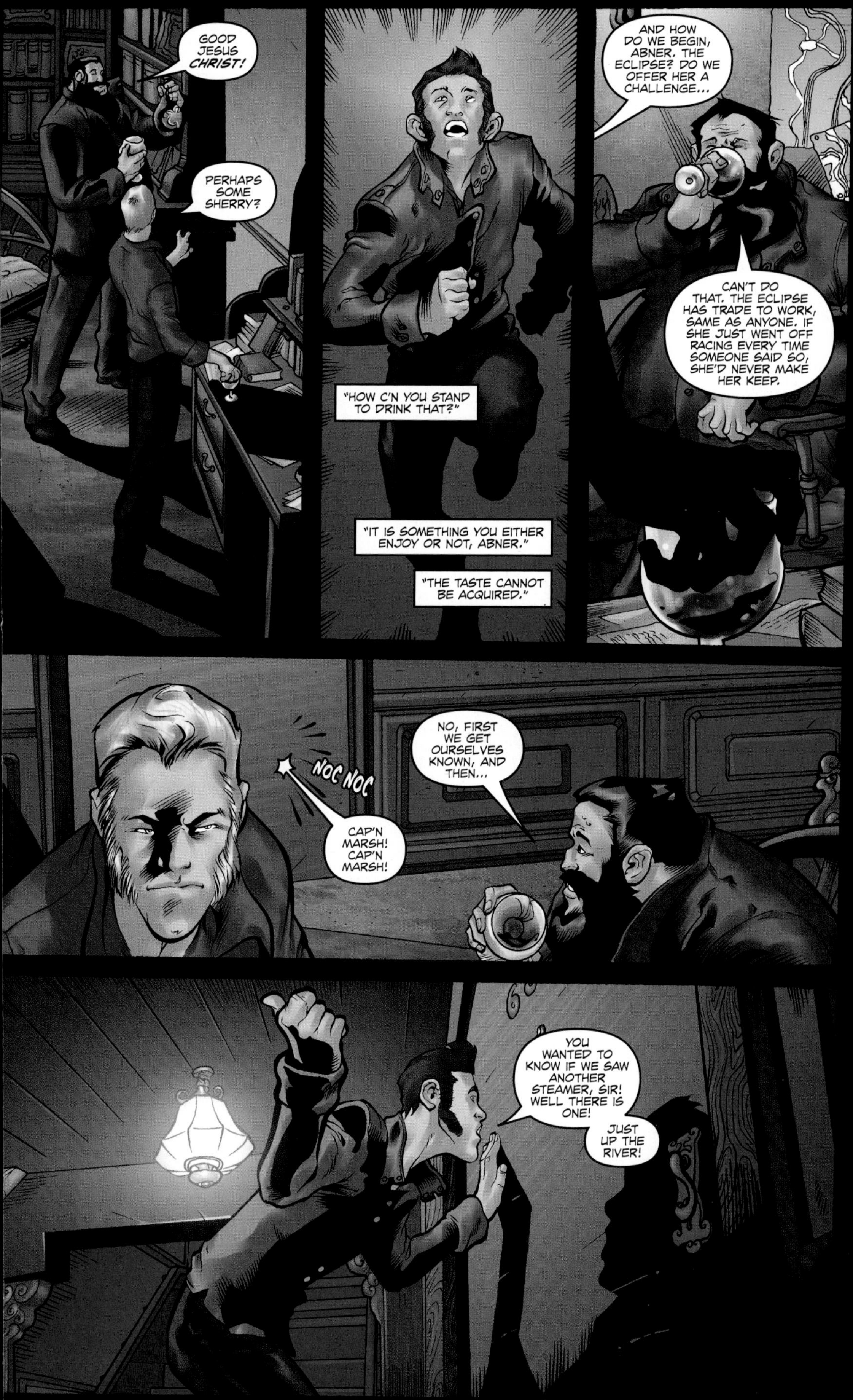
GOOD JESUS CHRIST!
PERHAPS SOME SHERRY?
"HOW C'N YOU STAND TO DRINK THAT?"
"IT IS SOMETHING YOU EITHER ENJOY OR NOT, ABNER."
"THE TASTE CANNOT BE ACQUIRED."
AND HOW DO WE BEGIN, ABNER. THE ECLIPSE? DO WE OFFER HER A CHALLENGE...
CAN'T DO THAT. THE ECLIPSE HAS TRADE TO WORK, SAME AS ANYONE. IF SHE JUST WENT OFF RACING EVERY TIME SOMEONE SAID SO, SHE'D NEVER MAKE HER KEEP.
NO, FIRST WE GET OURSELVES KNOWN, AND THEN...
NOC NOC
CAP'N MARSH! CAP'N MARSH!
YOU WANTED TO KNOW IF WE SAW ANOTHER STEAMER, SIR! WELL THERE IS ONE!
JUST UP THE RIVER!

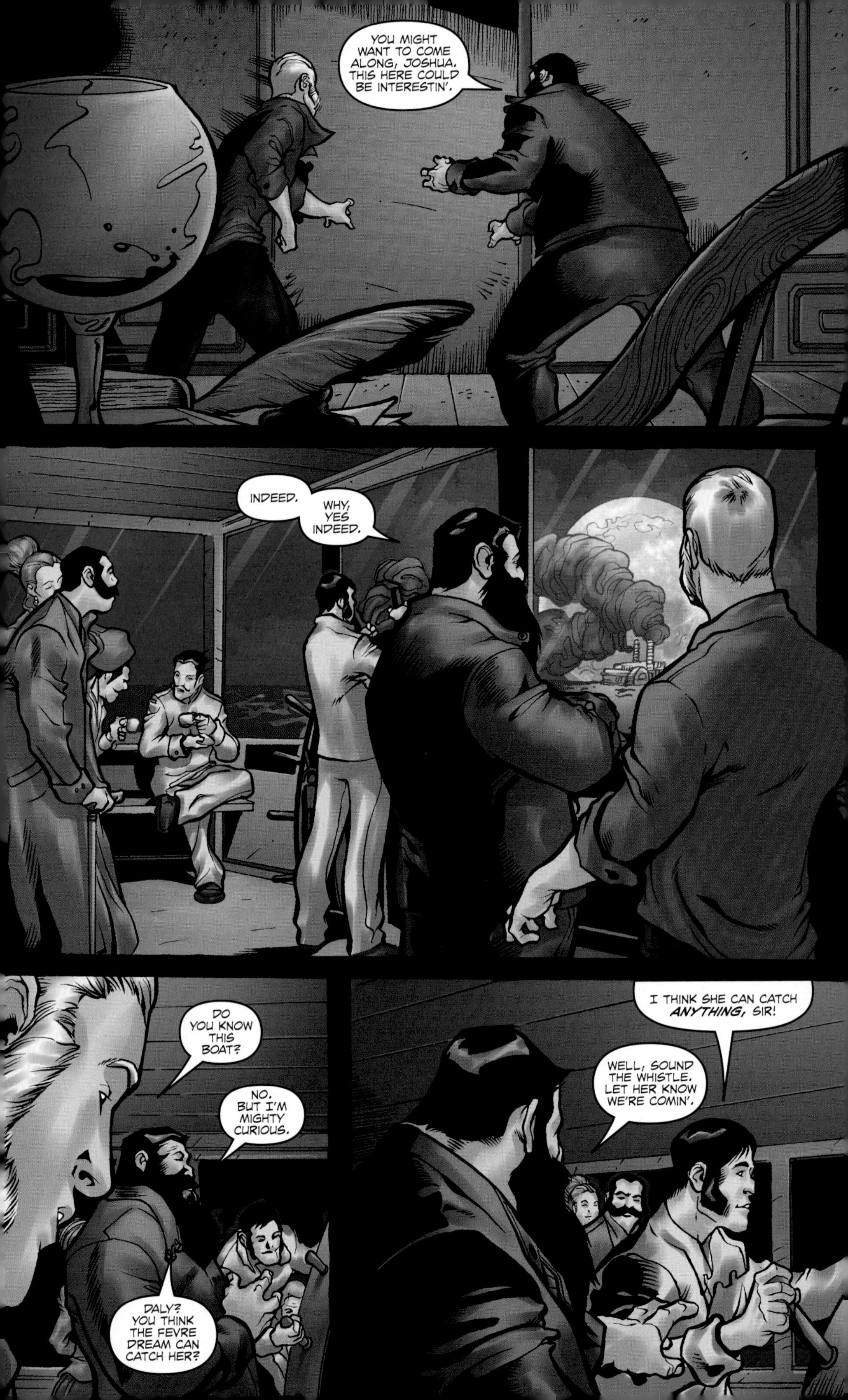
YOU MIGHT WANT TO COME ALONG, JOSHUA. THIS HERE COULD BE INTERESTIN'.
INDEED.
WHY, YES INDEED.
DO YOU KNOW THIS BOAT?
NO, BUT I'M MIGHTY CURIOUS.
DALY? YOU THINK THE FEVRE DREAM CAN CATCH HER?
I THINK SHE CAN CATCH *ANYTHING,* SIR!
WELL, SOUND THE WHISTLE. LET HER KNOW WE'RE COMIN'.

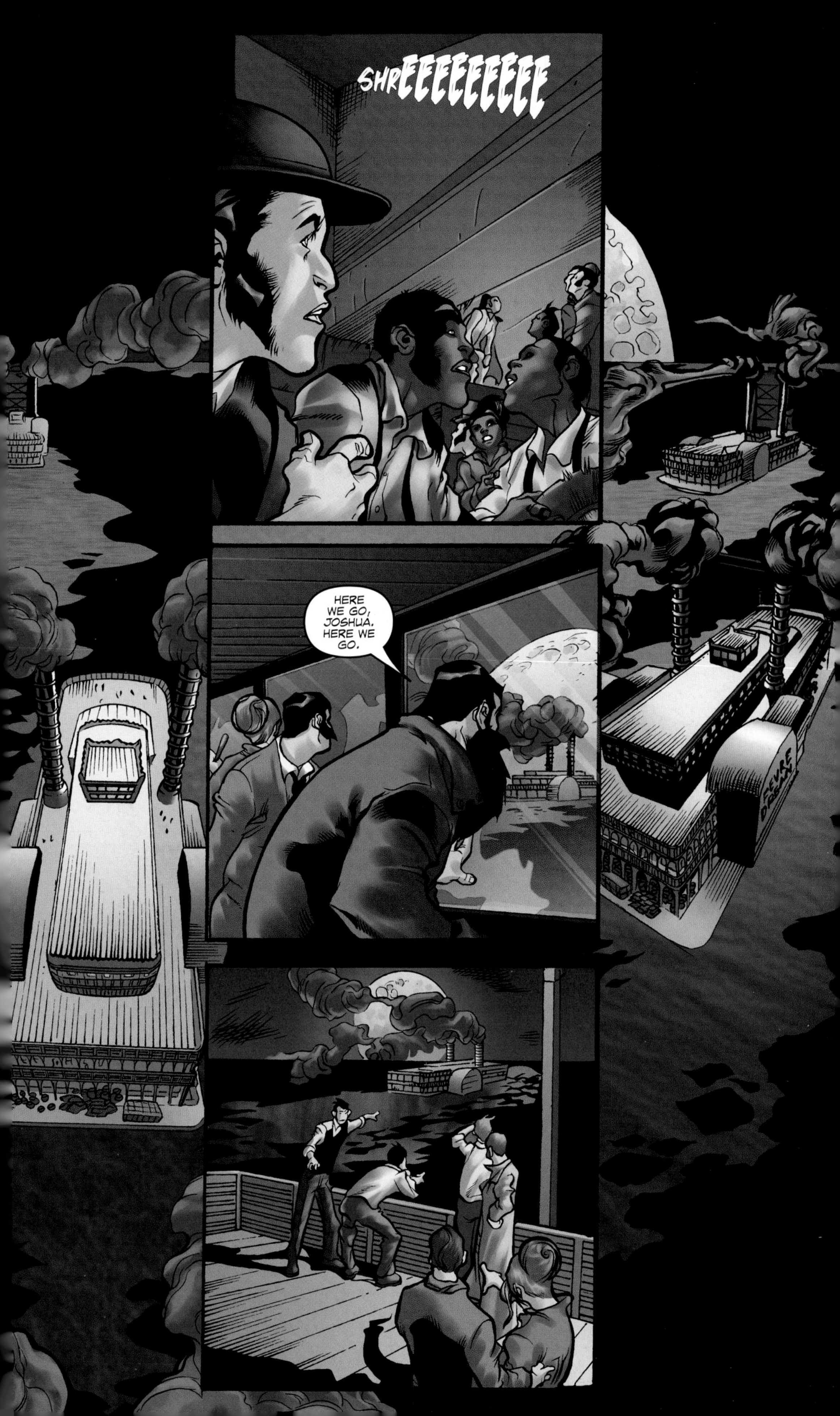
SHREEEEEEEEE
HERE WE GO, JOSHUA. HERE WE GO.
FEVRE DREAM

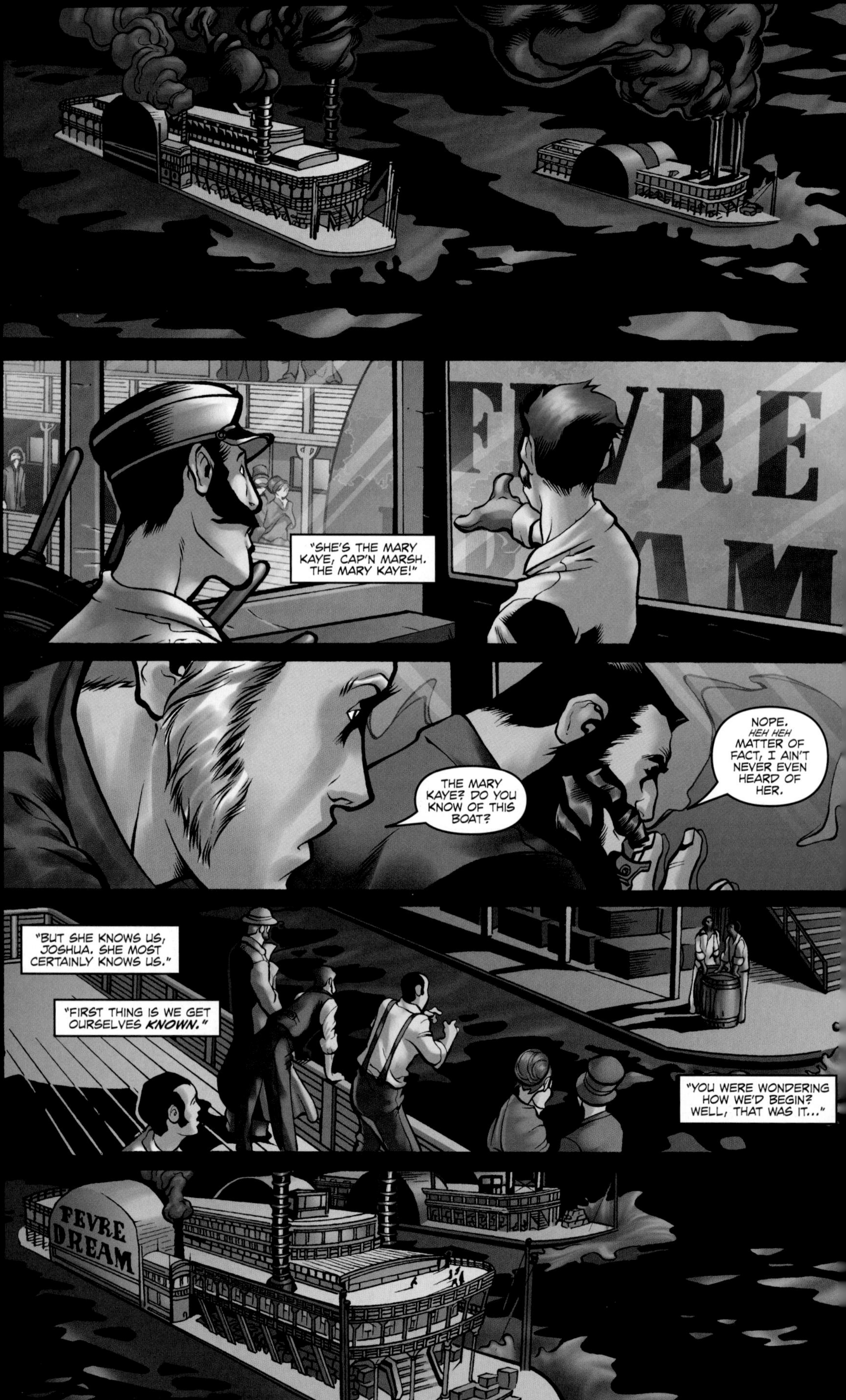

"SHE'S THE MARY KAYE, CAP'N MARSH. THE MARY KAYE!"
THE MARY KAYE? DO YOU KNOW OF THIS BOAT?
NOPE. HEH HEH MATTER OF FACT, I AIN'T NEVER EVEN HEARD OF HER.
"BUT SHE KNOWS US, JOSHUA. SHE MOST CERTAINLY KNOWS US."
"FIRST THING IS WE GET OURSELVES KNOWN."
"YOU WERE WONDERING HOW WE'D BEGIN? WELL, THAT WAS IT..."
FEVRE DREAM

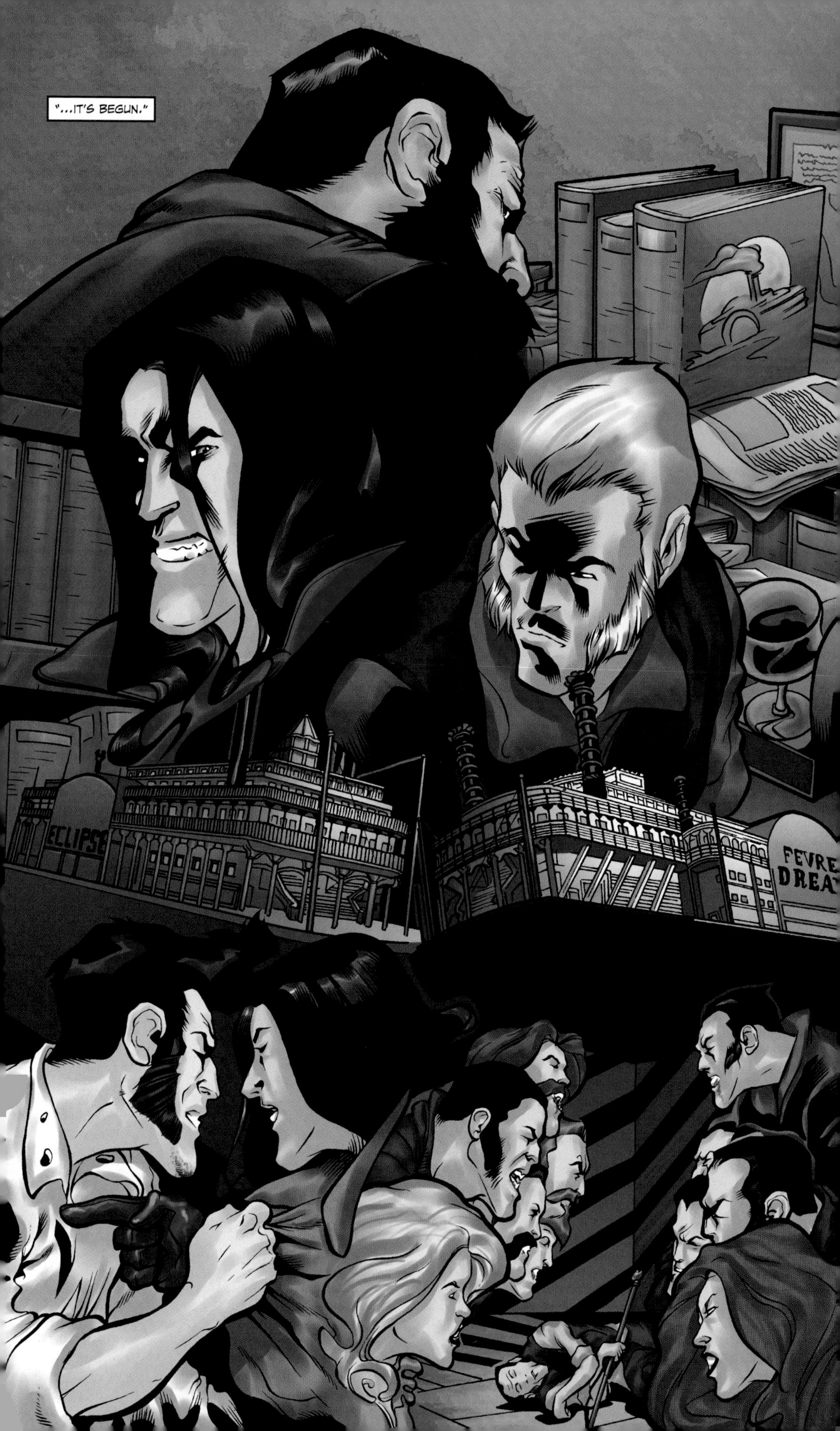
"...IT'S BEGUN."
ECLIPSE
FEVRE
DREA

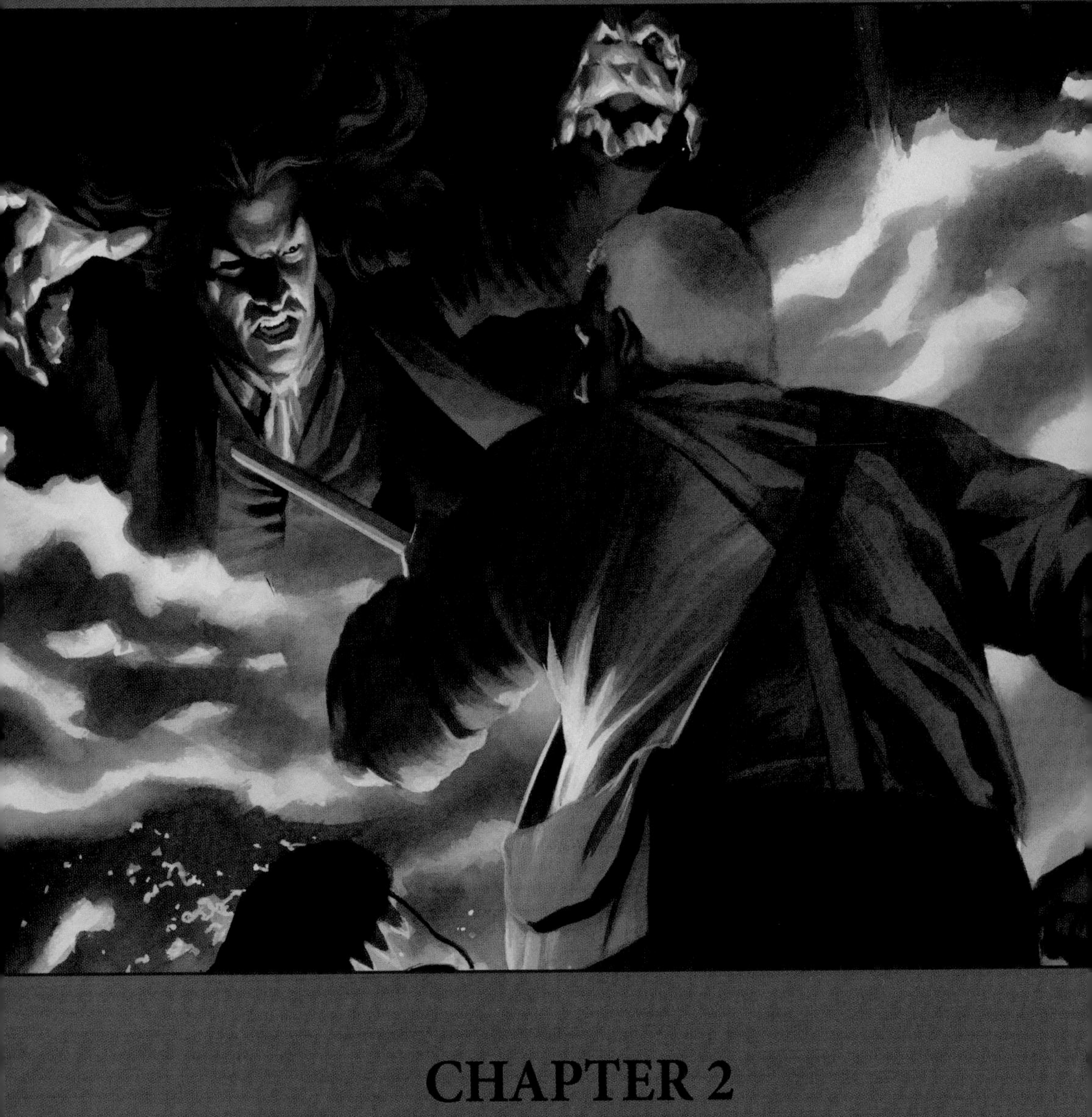

CHAPTER 2

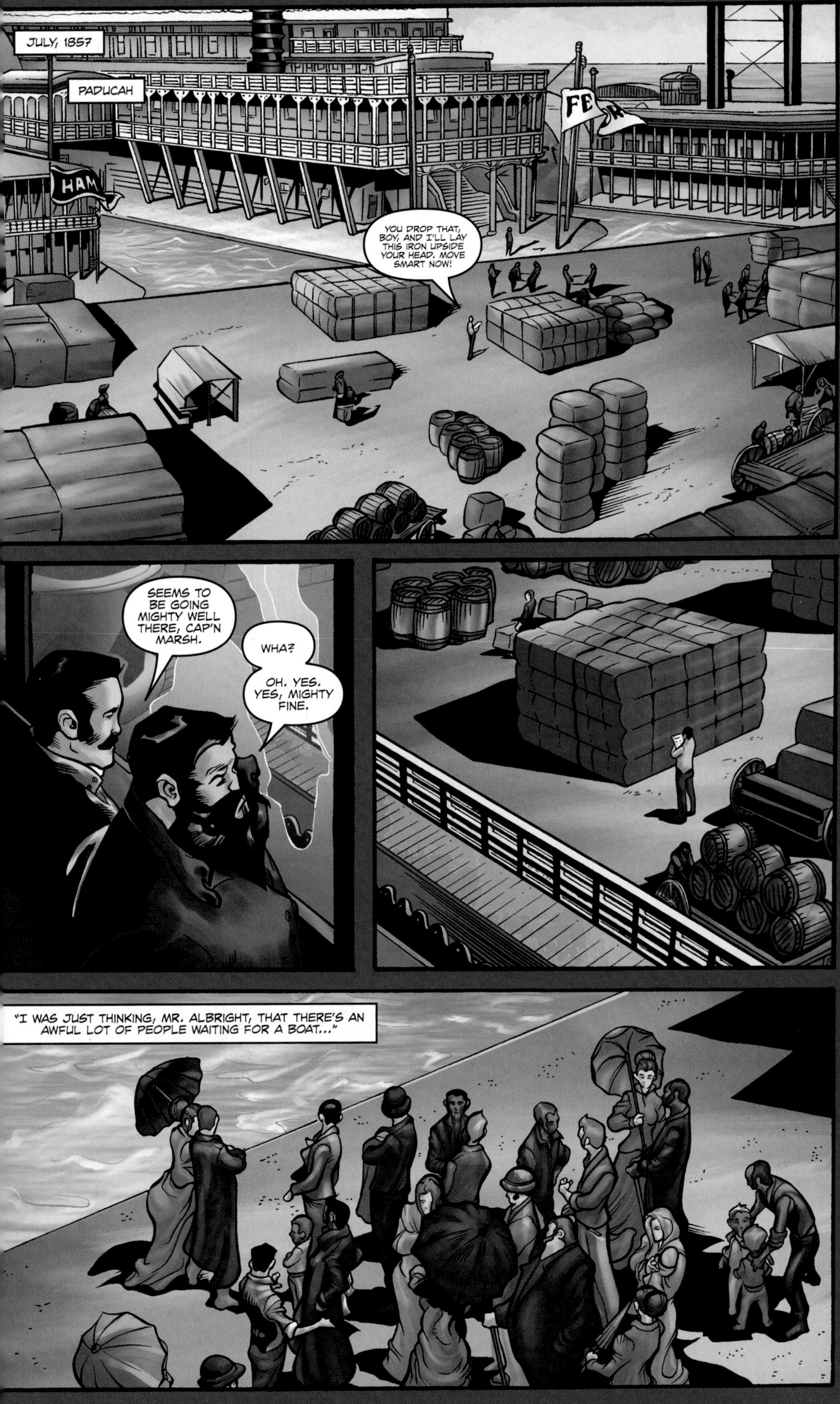
JULY, 1857
PADUCAH
HAM
FE
YOU DROP THAT, BOY, AND I'LL LAY THIS IRON UPSIDE YOUR HEAD. MOVE SMART NOW!
SEEMS TO BE GOING MIGHTY WELL THERE, CAP'N MARSH.
WHA?
OH. YES. YES, MIGHTY FINE.
"I WAS JUST THINKING, MR. ALBRIGHT, THAT THERE'S AN AWFUL LOT OF PEOPLE WAITING FOR A BOAT..."

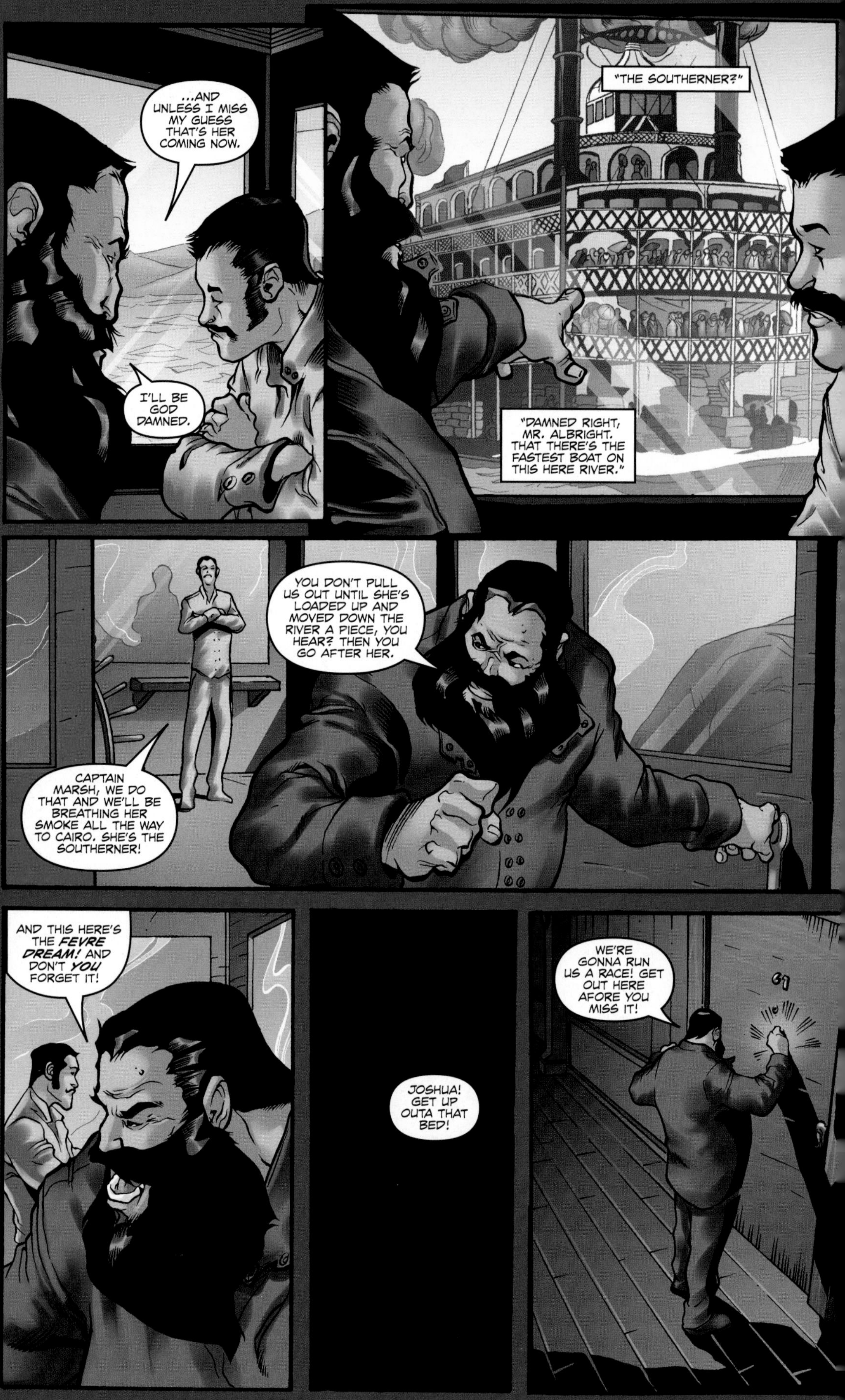
...AND UNLESS I MISS MY GUESS THAT'S HER COMING NOW.
I'LL BE GOD DAMNED.
"THE SOUTHERNER?"
"DAMNED RIGHT, MR. ALBRIGHT. THAT THERE'S THE FASTEST BOAT ON THIS HERE RIVER."
YOU DON'T PULL US OUT UNTIL SHE'S LOADED UP AND MOVED DOWN THE RIVER A PIECE, YOU HEAR? THEN YOU GO AFTER HER.
CAPTAIN MARSH, WE DO THAT AND WE'LL BE BREATHING HER SMOKE ALL THE WAY TO CAIRO. SHE'S THE SOUTHERNER!
AND THIS HERE'S THE *FEVRE DREAM!* AND DON'T *YOU* FORGET IT!
JOSHUA! GET UP OUTA THAT BED!
WE'RE GONNA RUN US A RACE! GET OUT HERE AFORE YOU MISS IT!

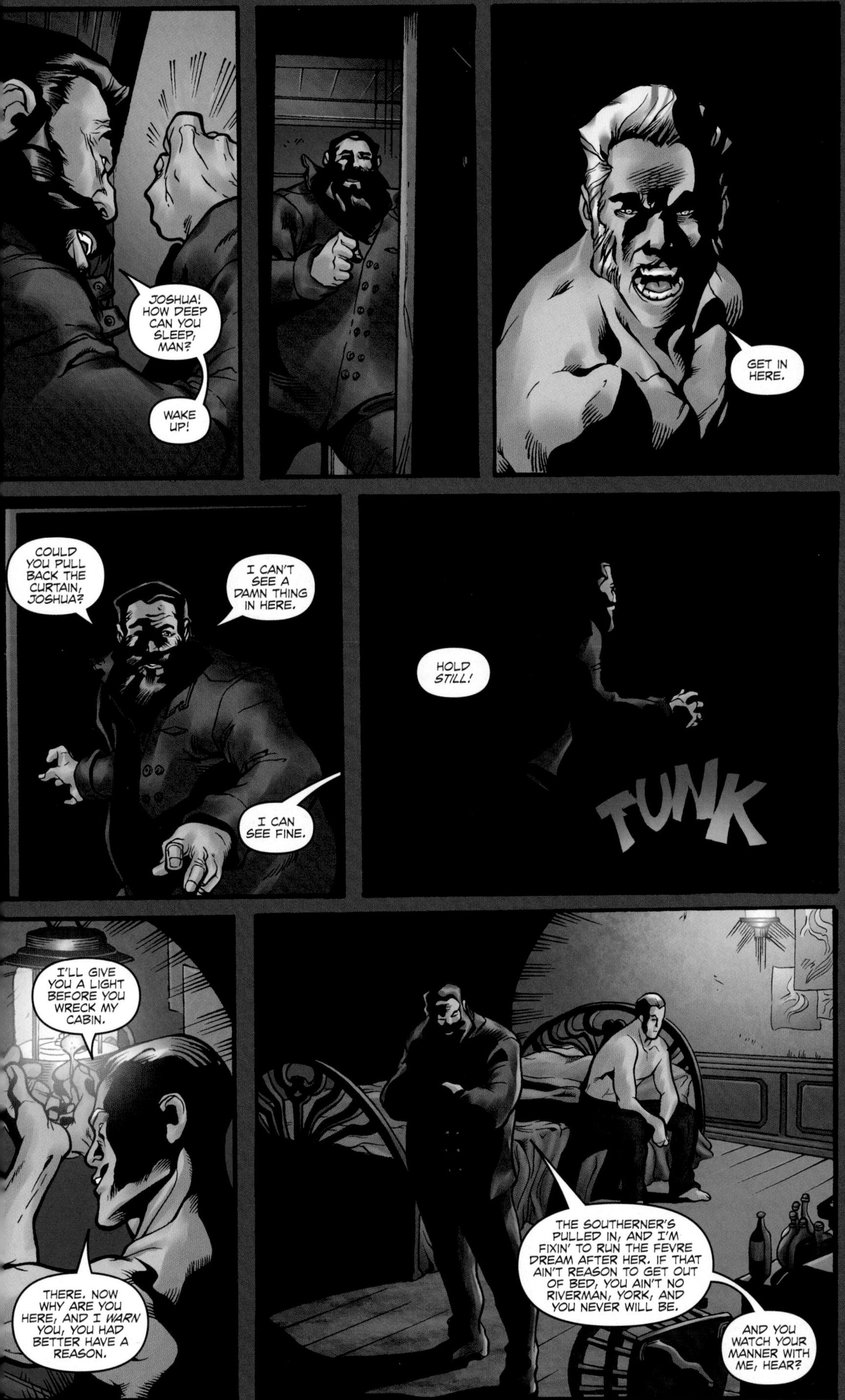
JOSHUA! HOW DEEP CAN YOU SLEEP, MAN?
WAKE UP!
GET IN HERE.
COULD YOU PULL BACK THE CURTAIN, JOSHUA?
I CAN'T SEE A DAMN THING IN HERE.
I CAN SEE FINE.
HOLD STILL!
TUNK
I'LL GIVE YOU A LIGHT BEFORE YOU WRECK MY CABIN.
THERE. NOW WHY ARE YOU HERE, AND I *WARN* YOU, YOU HAD BETTER HAVE A REASON.
THE SOUTHERNER'S PULLED IN, AND I'M FIXIN' TO RUN THE FEVRE DREAM AFTER HER. IF THAT AIN'T REASON TO GET OUT OF BED, YOU AIN'T NO RIVERMAN, YORK, AND YOU NEVER WILL BE.
AND YOU WATCH YOUR MANNER WITH ME, HEAR?

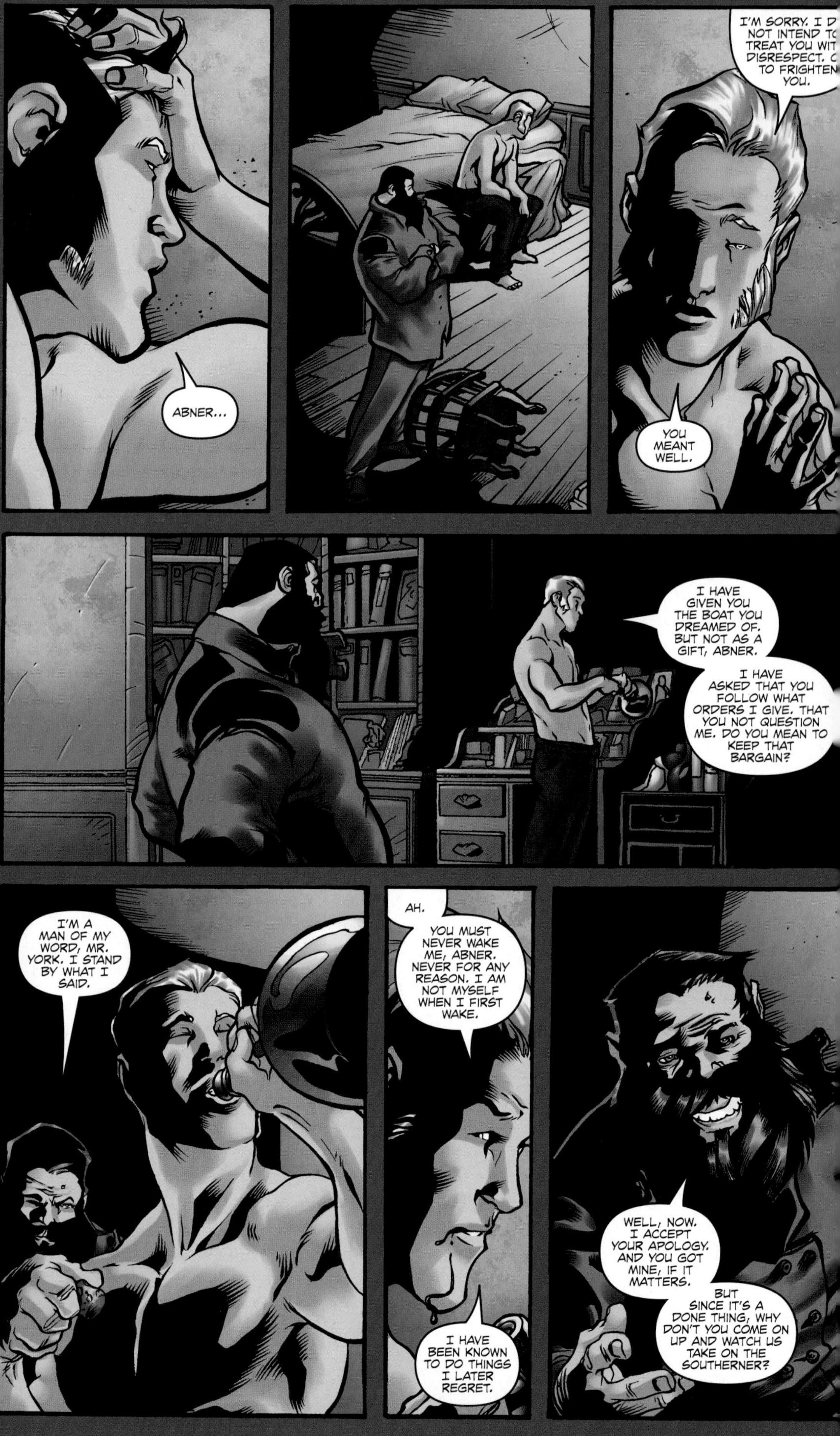
ABNER...
I'M SORRY. I D
NOT INTEND TO
TREAT YOU WIT
DISRESPECT. O
TO FRIGHTEN
YOU.
YOU MEANT WELL.
I HAVE GIVEN YOU THE BOAT YOU DREAMED OF. BUT NOT AS A GIFT, ABNER.
I HAVE ASKED THAT YOU FOLLOW WHAT ORDERS I GIVE. THAT YOU NOT QUESTION ME. DO YOU MEAN TO KEEP THAT BARGAIN?
I'M A MAN OF MY WORD, MR. YORK. I STAND BY WHAT I SAID.
AH.
YOU MUST NEVER WAKE ME, ABNER. NEVER FOR ANY REASON. I AM NOT MYSELF WHEN I FIRST WAKE.
I HAVE BEEN KNOWN TO DO THINGS I LATER REGRET.
WELL, NOW. I ACCEPT YOUR APOLOGY. AND YOU GOT MINE, IF IT MATTERS.
BUT SINCE IT'S A DONE THING, WHY DON'T YOU COME ON UP AND WATCH US TAKE ON THE SOUTHERNER?

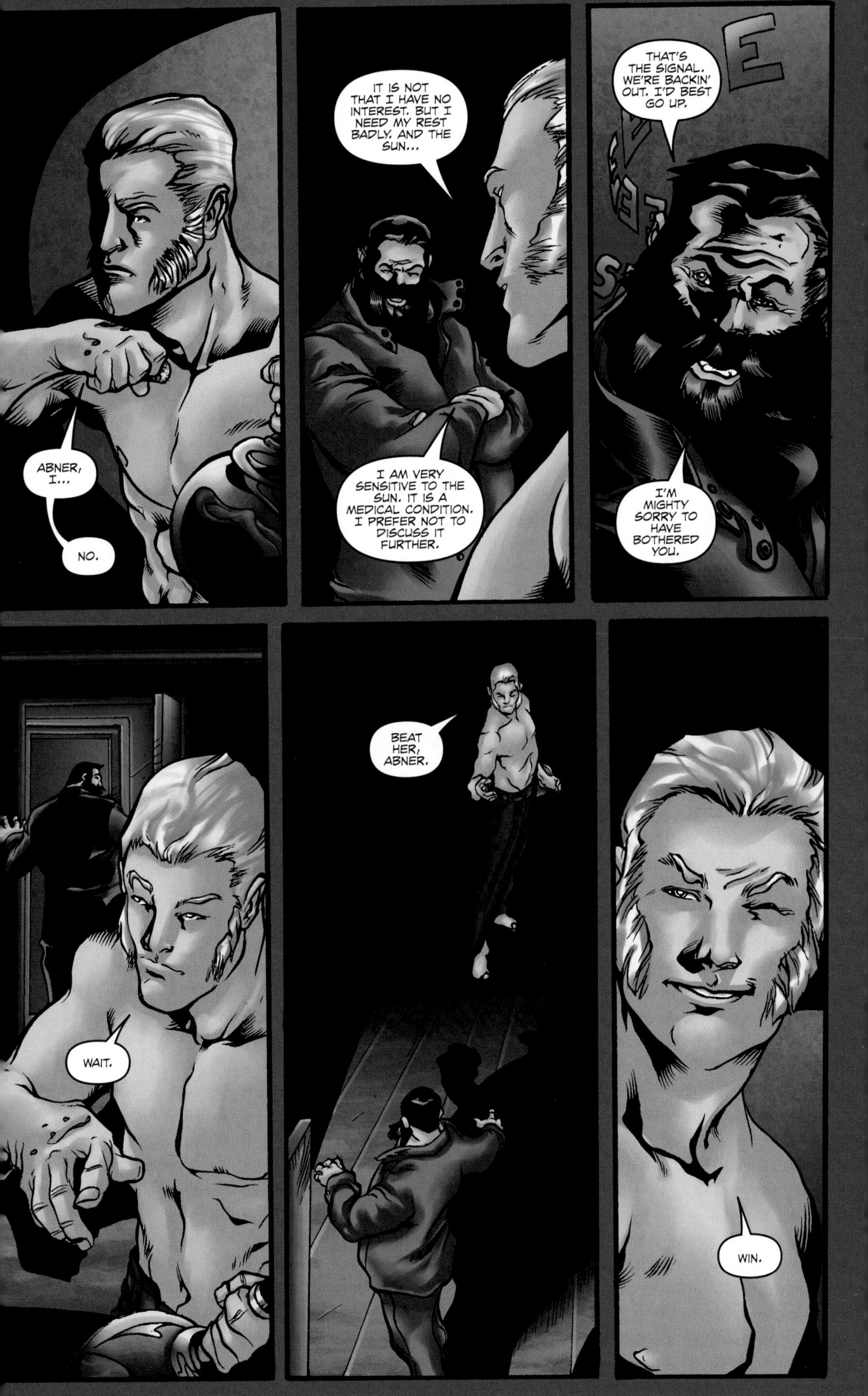
ABNER, I...
NO.
IT IS NOT THAT I HAVE NO INTEREST. BUT I NEED MY REST BADLY. AND THE SUN...
I AM VERY SENSITIVE TO THE SUN. IT IS A MEDICAL CONDITION. I PREFER NOT TO DISCUSS IT FURTHER.
THAT'S THE SIGNAL. WE'RE BACKIN' OUT. I'D BEST GO UP.
I'M MIGHTY SORRY TO HAVE BOTHERED YOU.
WAIT.
BEAT HER, ABNER.
WIN.

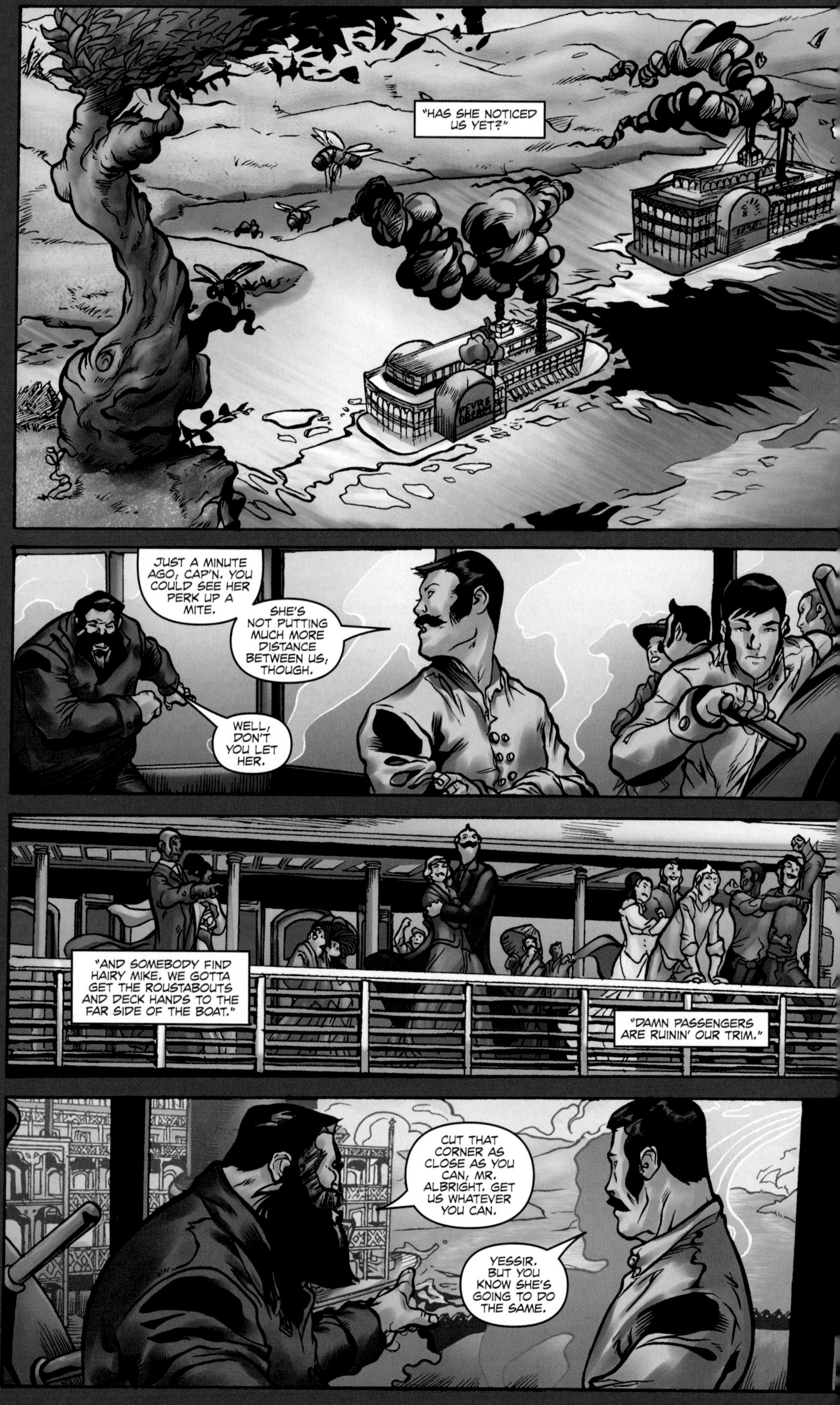

"HAS SHE NOTICED US YET?"
JUST A MINUTE AGO, CAP'N. YOU COULD SEE HER PERK UP A MITE.
SHE'S NOT PUTTING MUCH MORE DISTANCE BETWEEN US, THOUGH.
WELL, DON'T YOU LET HER.
"AND SOMEBODY FIND HAIRY MIKE. WE GOTTA GET THE ROUSTABOUTS AND DECK HANDS TO THE FAR SIDE OF THE BOAT."
"DAMN PASSENGERS ARE RUININ' OUR TRIM."
CUT THAT CORNER AS CLOSE AS YOU CAN, MR. ALBRIGHT. GET US WHATEVER YOU CAN.
YESSIR. BUT YOU KNOW SHE'S GOING TO DO THE SAME.

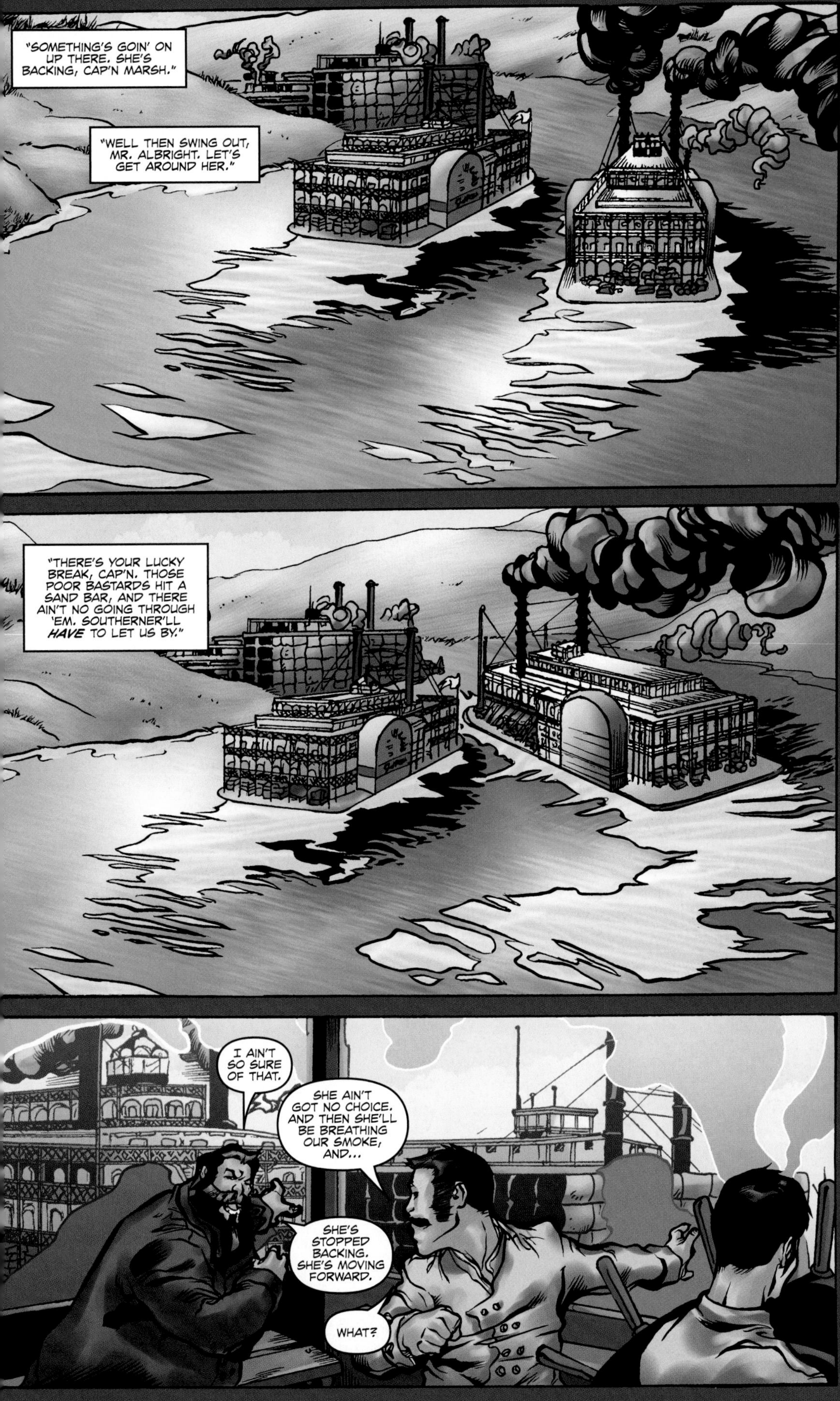
"SOMETHING'S GOIN' ON UP THERE. SHE'S BACKING, CAP'N MARSH."
"WELL THEN SWING OUT, MR. ALBRIGHT. LET'S GET AROUND HER."
"THERE'S YOUR LUCKY BREAK, CAP'N. THOSE POOR BASTARDS HIT A SAND BAR, AND THERE AIN'T NO GOING THROUGH 'EM. SOUTHERNER'LL *HAVE* TO LET US BY."
I AIN'T SO SURE OF THAT.
SHE AIN'T GOT NO CHOICE. AND THEN SHE'LL BE BREATHING OUR SMOKE, AND...
SHE'S STOPPED BACKING. SHE'S MOVING FORWARD.
WHAT?

"THAT IDJIT!"

NO PILOT IN HIS RIGHT *MIND*...

YOU'D BEST START BACKING YOURSELF, IF YOU'RE LOOKIN' TO LET HIM BY.

"I AIN'T BACKING. LET *HIM* BACK."

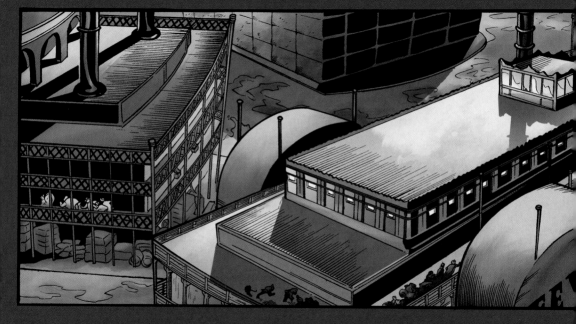

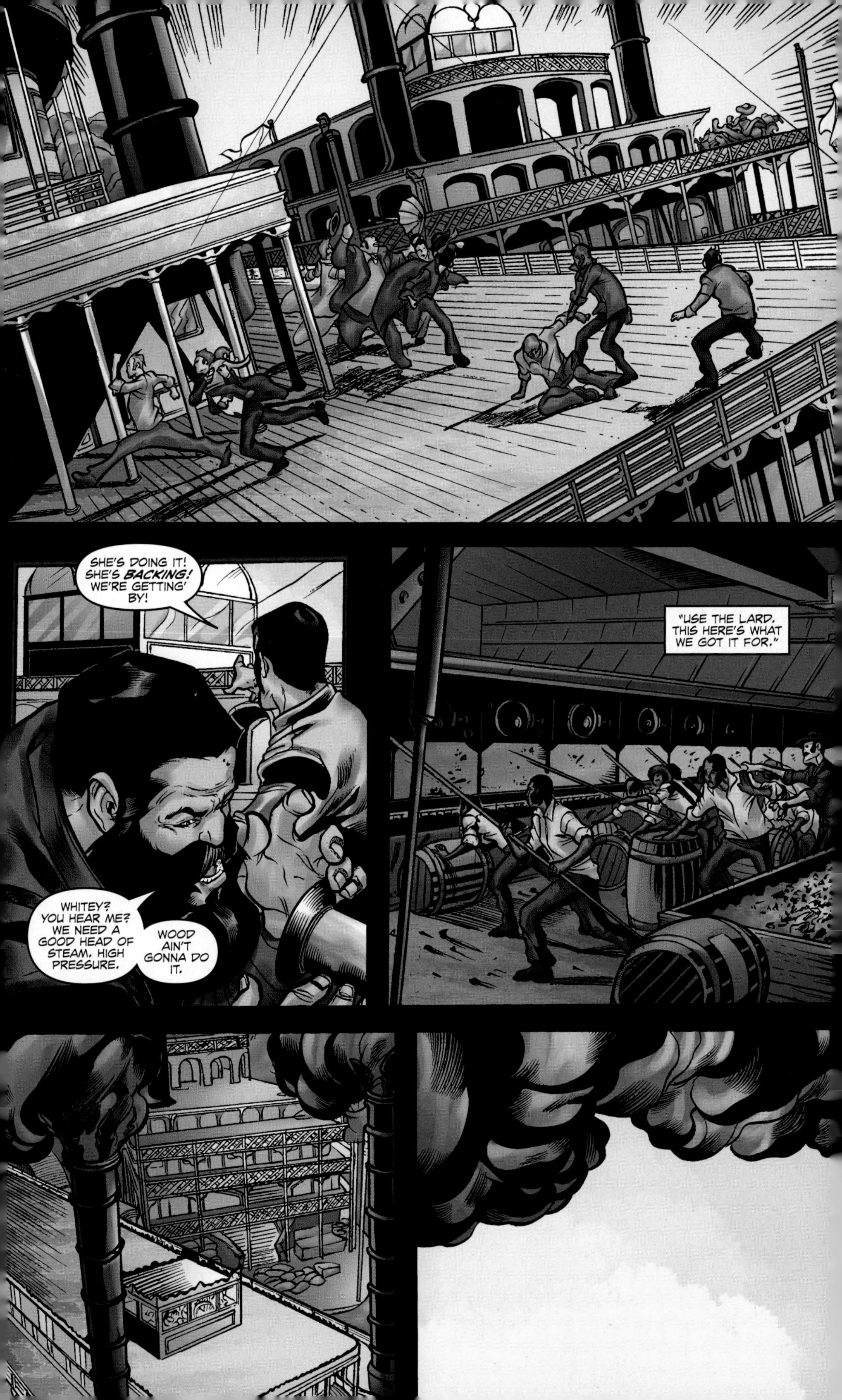

SHE'S DOING IT! SHE'S *BACKING!* WE'RE GETTING' BY!
WHITEY? YOU HEAR ME? WE NEED A GOOD HEAD OF STEAM. HIGH PRESSURE.
WOOD AIN'T GONNA DO IT.
"USE THE LARD. THIS HERE'S WHAT WE GOT IT FOR."

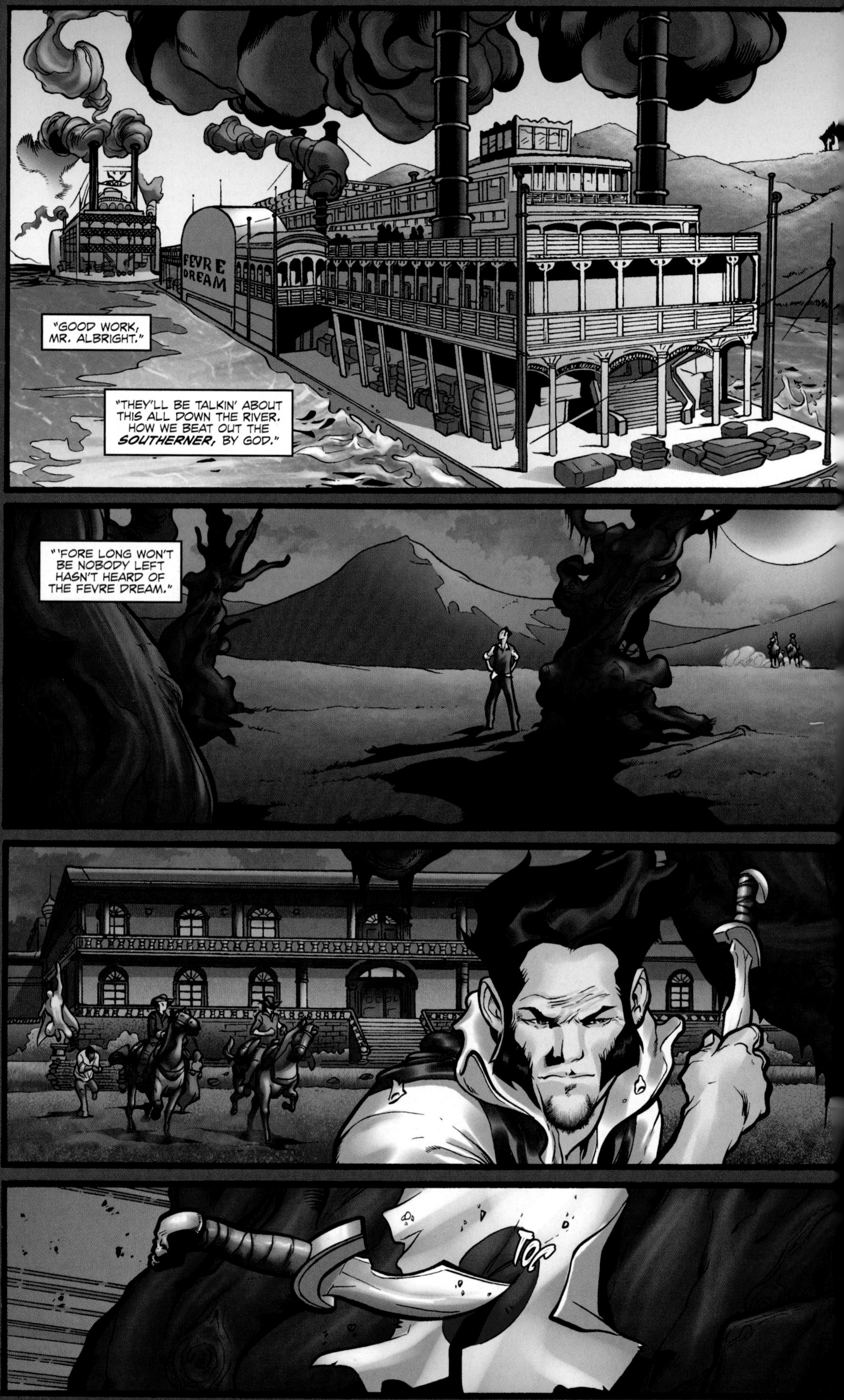
"GOOD WORK, MR. ALBRIGHT."
"THEY'LL BE TALKIN' ABOUT THIS ALL DOWN THE RIVER. HOW WE BEAT OUT THE SOUTHERNER, BY GOD."
FEVRE DREAM
"'FORE LONG WON'T BE NOBODY LEFT HASN'T HEARD OF THE FEVRE DREAM."
TOC

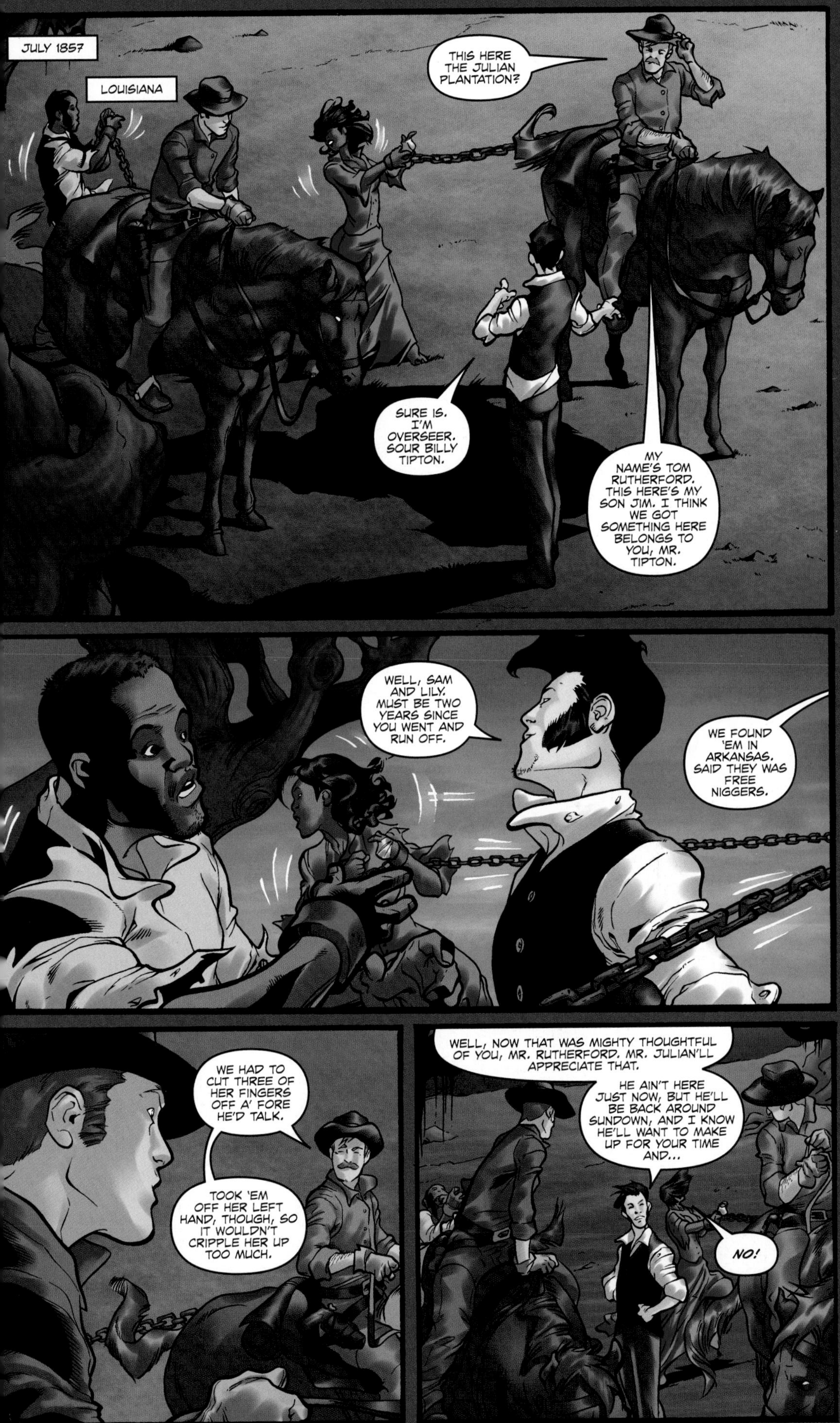
JULY 1857
LOUISIANA
THIS HERE THE JULIAN PLANTATION?
SURE IS. I'M OVERSEER. SOUR BILLY TIPTON.
MY NAME'S TOM RUTHERFORD. THIS HERE'S MY SON JIM. I THINK WE GOT SOMETHING HERE BELONGS TO YOU, MR. TIPTON.
WELL, SAM AND LILY. MUST BE TWO YEARS SINCE YOU WENT AND RUN OFF.
WE FOUND 'EM IN ARKANSAS. SAID THEY WAS FREE NIGGERS.
WE HAD TO CUT THREE OF HER FINGERS OFF A' FORE HE'D TALK.
TOOK 'EM OFF HER LEFT HAND, THOUGH, SO IT WOULDN'T CRIPPLE HER UP TOO MUCH.
WELL, NOW THAT WAS MIGHTY THOUGHTFUL OF YOU, MR. RUTHERFORD. MR. JULIAN'LL APPRECIATE THAT.
HE AIN'T HERE JUST NOW, BUT HE'LL BE BACK AROUND SUNDOWN, AND I KNOW HE'LL WANT TO MAKE UP FOR YOUR TIME AND...
NO!

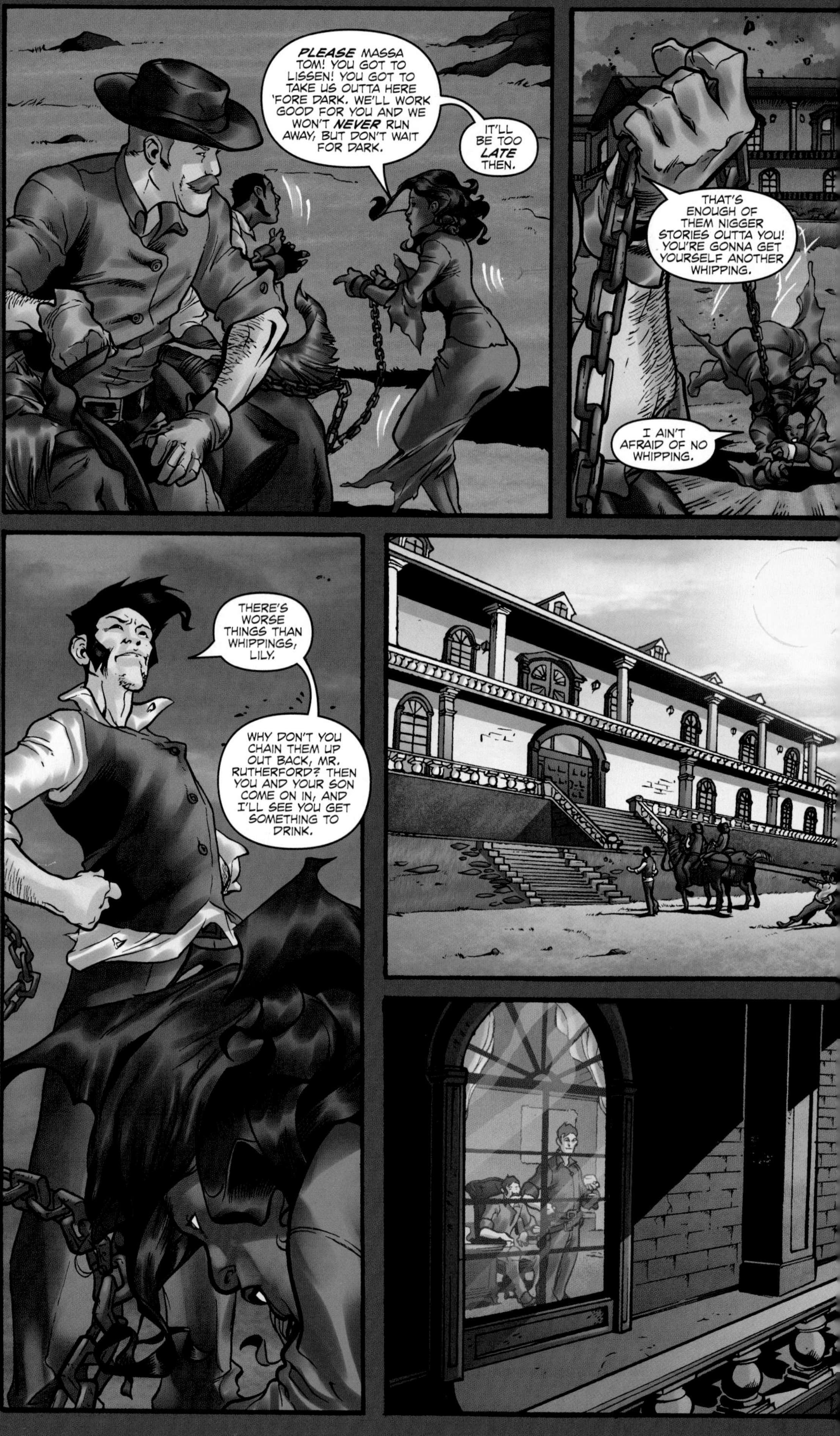
PLEASE MASSA TOM! YOU GOT TO LISSEN! YOU GOT TO TAKE US OUTTA HERE 'FORE DARK. WE'LL WORK GOOD FOR YOU AND WE WON'T NEVER RUN AWAY, BUT DON'T WAIT FOR DARK.
IT'LL BE TOO LATE THEN.
THAT'S ENOUGH OF THEM NIGGER STORIES OUTTA YOU! YOU'RE GONNA GET YOURSELF ANOTHER WHIPPING.
I AIN'T AFRAID OF NO WHIPPING.
THERE'S WORSE THINGS THAN WHIPPINGS, LILY.
WHY DON'T YOU CHAIN THEM UP OUT BACK, MR. RUTHERFORD? THEN YOU AND YOUR SON COME ON IN, AND I'LL SEE YOU GET SOMETHING TO DRINK.

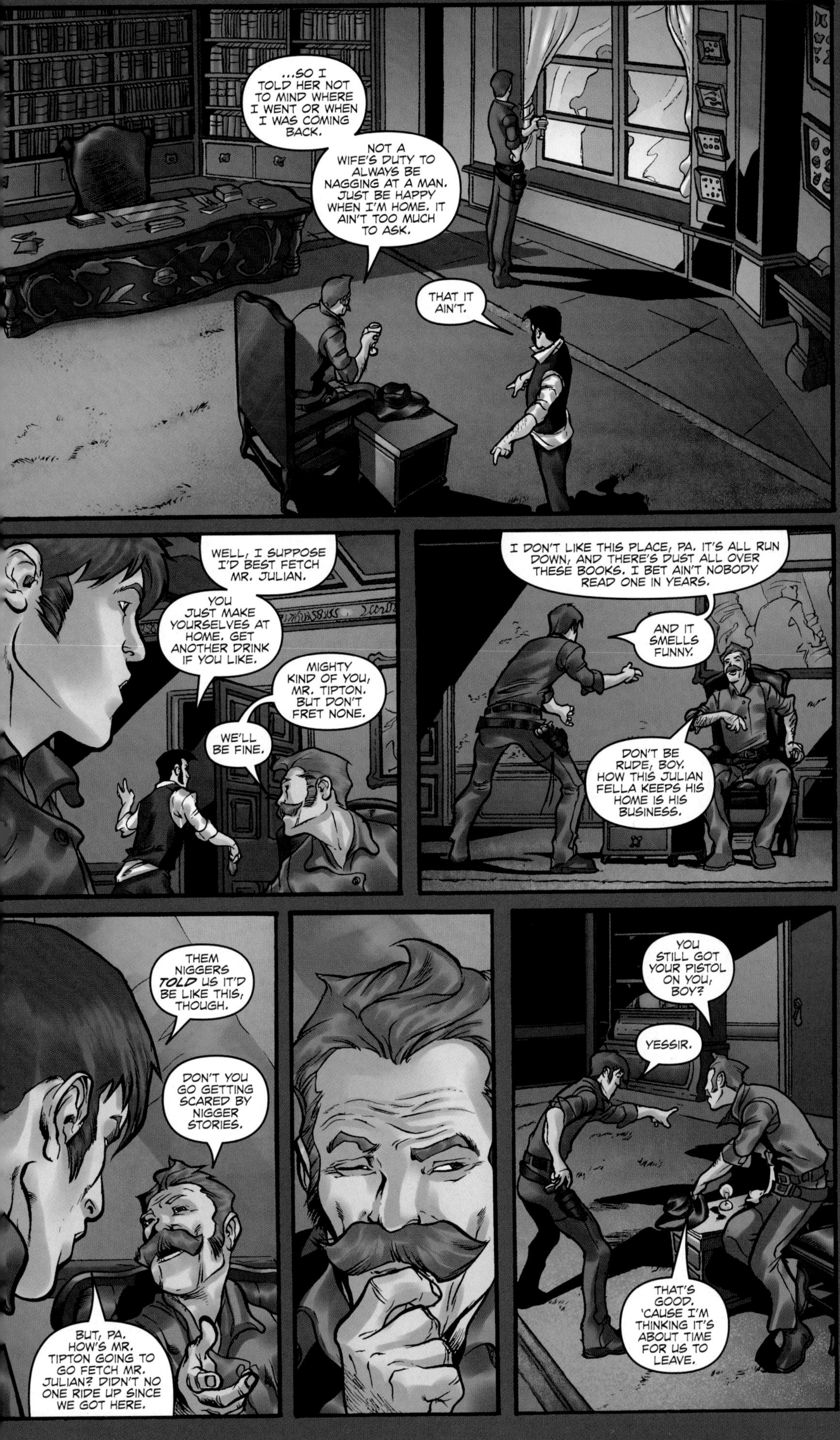
...SO I TOLD HER NOT TO MIND WHERE I WENT OR WHEN I WAS COMING BACK.
NOT A WIFE'S DUTY TO ALWAYS BE NAGGING AT A MAN. JUST BE HAPPY WHEN I'M HOME. IT AIN'T TOO MUCH TO ASK.
THAT IT AIN'T.
WELL, I SUPPOSE I'D BEST FETCH MR. JULIAN.
YOU JUST MAKE YOURSELVES AT HOME. GET ANOTHER DRINK IF YOU LIKE.
MIGHTY KIND OF YOU, MR. TIPTON. BUT DON'T FRET NONE.
WE'LL BE FINE.
I DON'T LIKE THIS PLACE, PA. IT'S ALL RUN DOWN, AND THERE'S DUST ALL OVER THESE BOOKS. I BET AIN'T NOBODY READ ONE IN YEARS.
AND IT SMELLS FUNNY.
DON'T BE RUDE, BOY. HOW THIS JULIAN FELLA KEEPS HIS HOME IS HIS BUSINESS.
THEM NIGGERS *TOLD* US IT'D BE LIKE THIS, THOUGH.
DON'T YOU GO GETTING SCARED BY NIGGER STORIES.
BUT, PA. HOW'S MR. TIPTON GOING TO GO FETCH MR. JULIAN? DIDN'T NO ONE RIDE UP SINCE WE GOT HERE.
YOU STILL GOT YOUR PISTOL ON YOU, BOY?
YESSIR.
THAT'S GOOD. 'CAUSE I'M THINKING IT'S ABOUT TIME FOR US TO LEAVE.

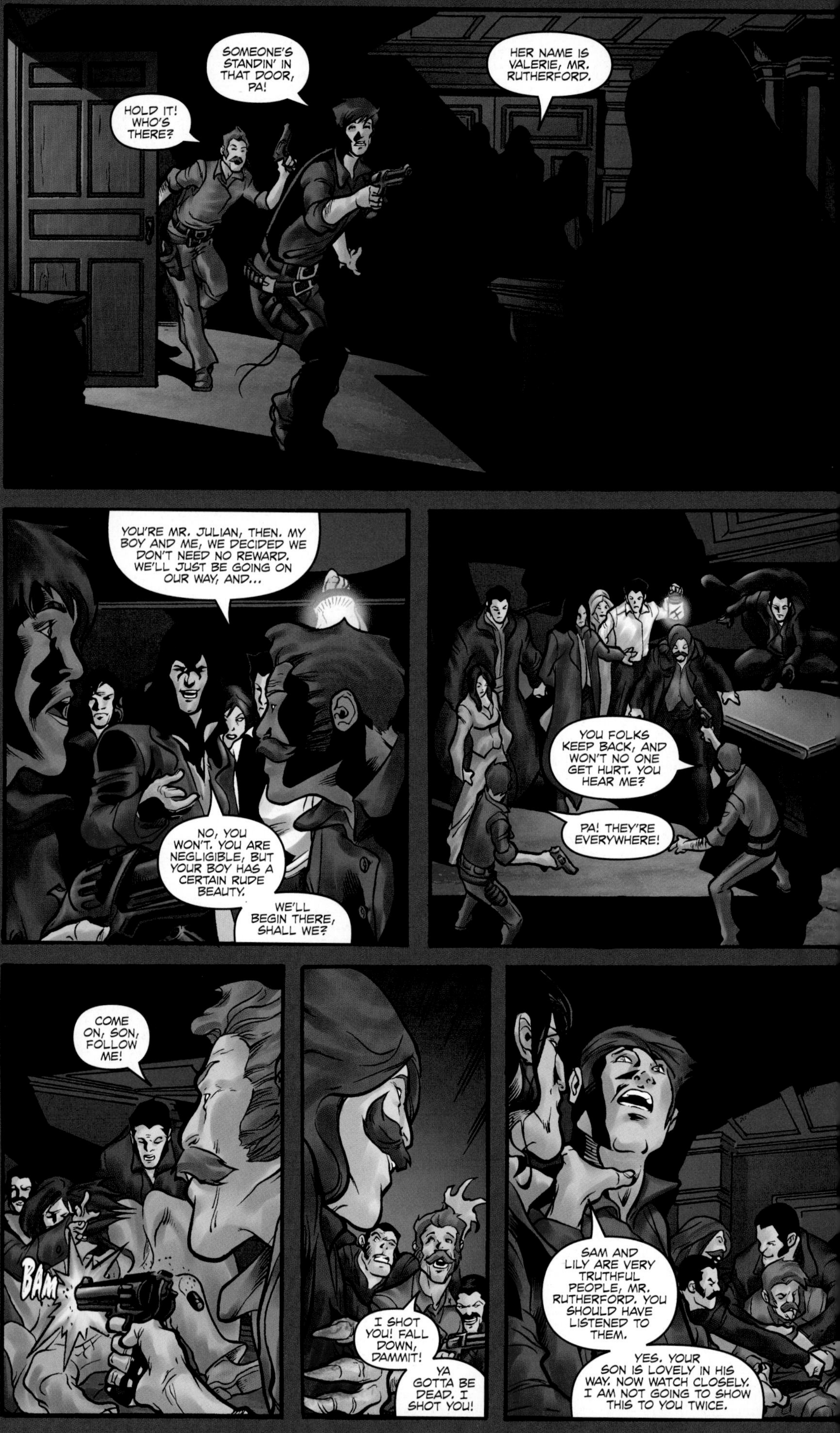
HOLD IT! WHO'S THERE?
SOMEONE'S STANDIN' IN THAT DOOR, PA!
HER NAME IS VALERIE, MR. RUTHERFORD.
YOU'RE MR. JULIAN, THEN. MY BOY AND ME, WE DECIDED WE DON'T NEED NO REWARD. WE'LL JUST BE GOING ON OUR WAY, AND...
NO, YOU WON'T. YOU ARE NEGLIGIBLE, BUT YOUR BOY HAS A CERTAIN RUDE BEAUTY.
WE'LL BEGIN THERE, SHALL WE?
YOU FOLKS KEEP BACK, AND WON'T NO ONE GET HURT. YOU HEAR ME?
PA! THEY'RE EVERYWHERE!
COME ON, SON, FOLLOW ME!
BAM
I SHOT YOU! FALL DOWN, DAMMIT!
YA GOTTA BE DEAD. I SHOT YOU!
SAM AND LILY ARE VERY TRUTHFUL PEOPLE, MR. RUTHERFORD. YOU SHOULD HAVE LISTENED TO THEM.
YES. YOUR SON IS LOVELY IN HIS WAY. NOW WATCH CLOSELY. I AM NOT GOING TO SHOW THIS TO YOU TWICE.

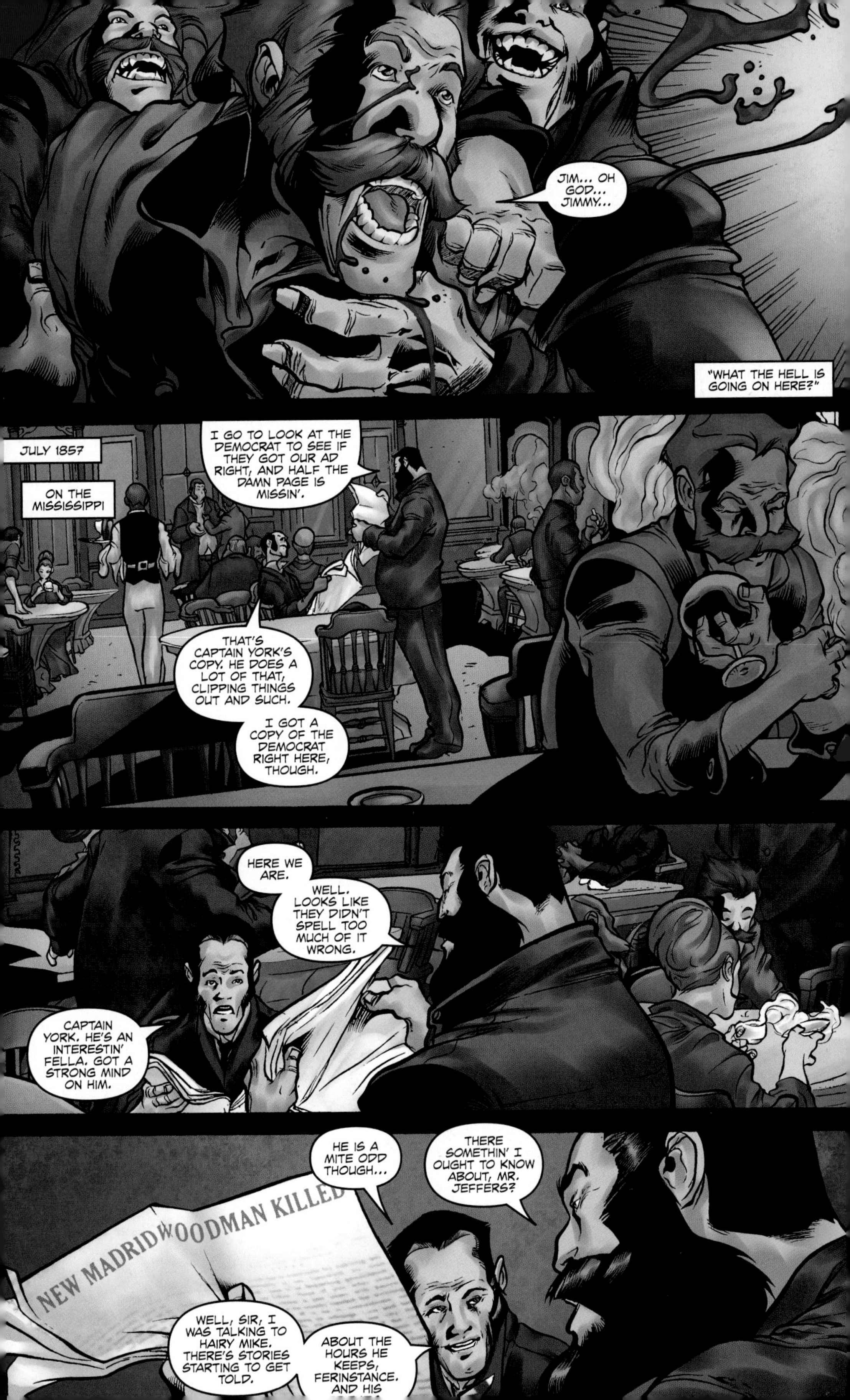
JIM... OH GOD... JIMMY...
"WHAT THE HELL IS GOING ON HERE?"
JULY 1857
ON THE MISSISSIPPI
I GO TO LOOK AT THE DEMOCRAT TO SEE IF THEY GOT OUR AD RIGHT, AND HALF THE DAMN PAGE IS MISSIN'.
THAT'S CAPTAIN YORK'S COPY. HE DOES A LOT OF THAT, CLIPPING THINGS OUT AND SUCH.
I GOT A COPY OF THE DEMOCRAT RIGHT HERE, THOUGH.
HERE WE ARE.
WELL. LOOKS LIKE THEY DIDN'T SPELL TOO MUCH OF IT WRONG.
CAPTAIN YORK. HE'S AN INTERESTIN' FELLA. GOT A STRONG MIND ON HIM.
NEW MADRID WOODMAN KILLED
HE IS A MITE ODD THOUGH...
THERE SOMETHIN' I OUGHT TO KNOW ABOUT, MR. JEFFERS?
WELL, SIR, I WAS TALKING TO HAIRY MIKE. THERE'S STORIES STARTING TO GET TOLD.
ABOUT THE HOURS HE KEEPS, FERINSTANCE. AND HIS

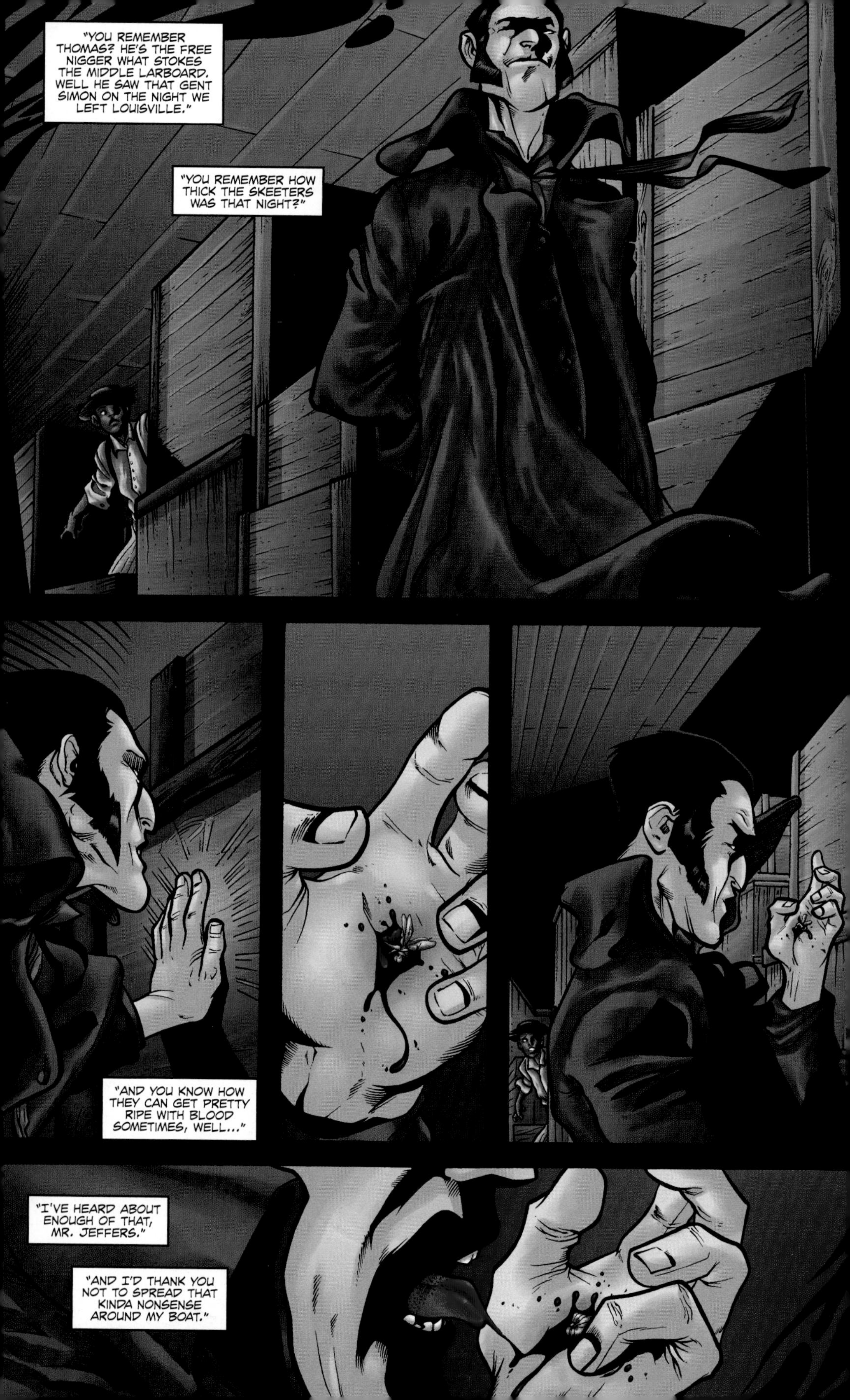
"YOU REMEMBER THOMAS? HE'S THE FREE NIGGER WHAT STOKES THE MIDDLE LARBOARD. WELL HE SAW THAT GENT SIMON ON THE NIGHT WE LEFT LOUISVILLE."
"YOU REMEMBER HOW THICK THE SKEETERS WAS THAT NIGHT?"
"AND YOU KNOW HOW THEY CAN GET PRETTY RIPE WITH BLOOD SOMETIMES, WELL..."
"I'VE HEARD ABOUT ENOUGH OF THAT, MR. JEFFERS."
"AND I'D THANK YOU NOT TO SPREAD THAT KINDA NONSENSE AROUND MY BOAT."

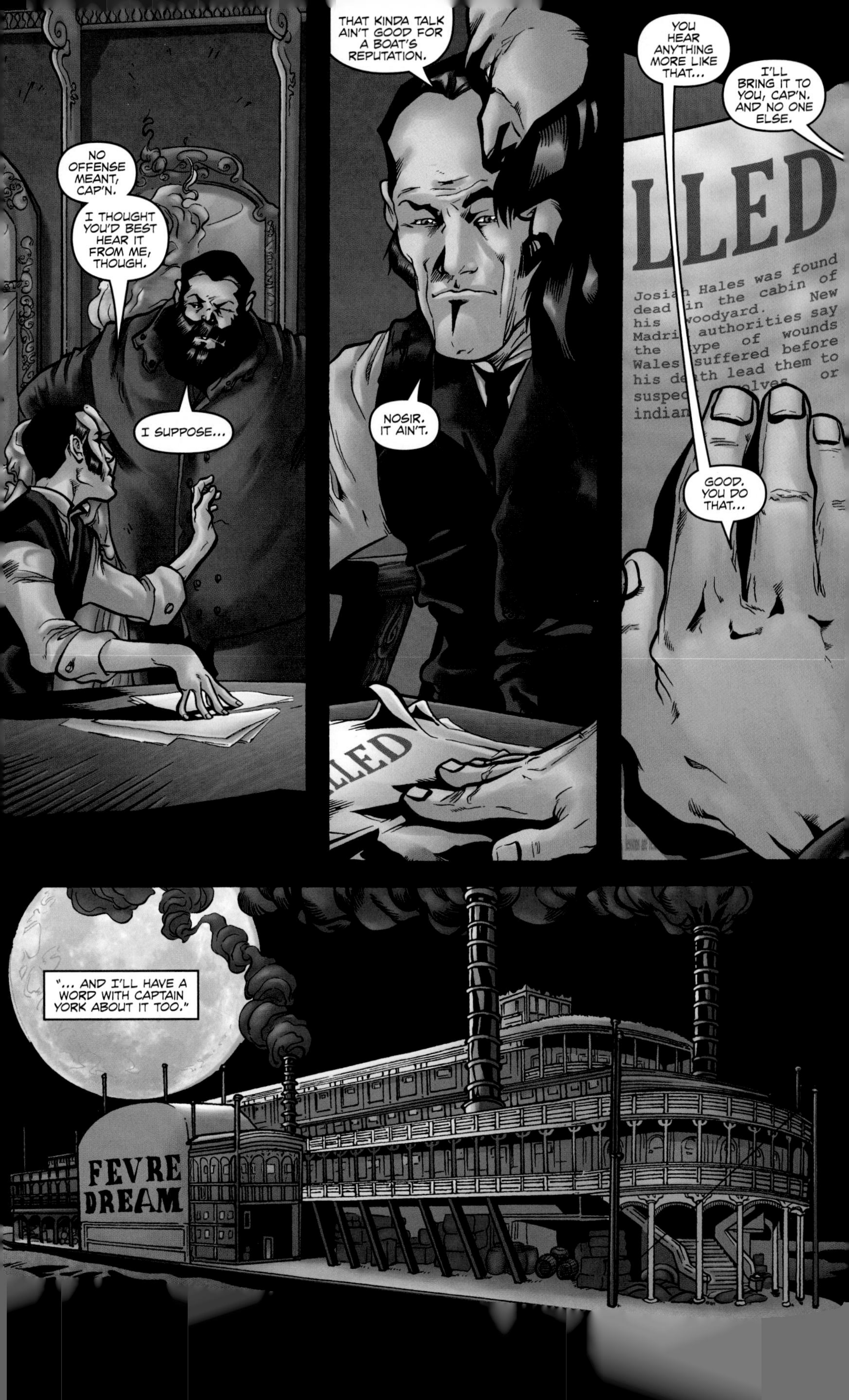
NO OFFENSE MEANT, CAP'N.
I THOUGHT YOU'D BEST HEAR IT FROM ME, THOUGH.
I SUPPOSE...
THAT KINDA TALK AIN'T GOOD FOR A BOAT'S REPUTATION.
NOSIR. IT AIN'T.
LLED
YOU HEAR ANYTHING MORE LIKE THAT...
I'LL BRING IT TO YOU, CAP'N. AND NO ONE ELSE.
GOOD. YOU DO THAT...
LLED
Josiah Hales was found dead in the cabin of his woodyard. New Madrid authorities say the type of wounds Wales suffered before his death lead them to suspec olves or indian
"... AND I'LL HAVE A WORD WITH CAPTAIN YORK ABOUT IT TOO."
FEVRE DREAM

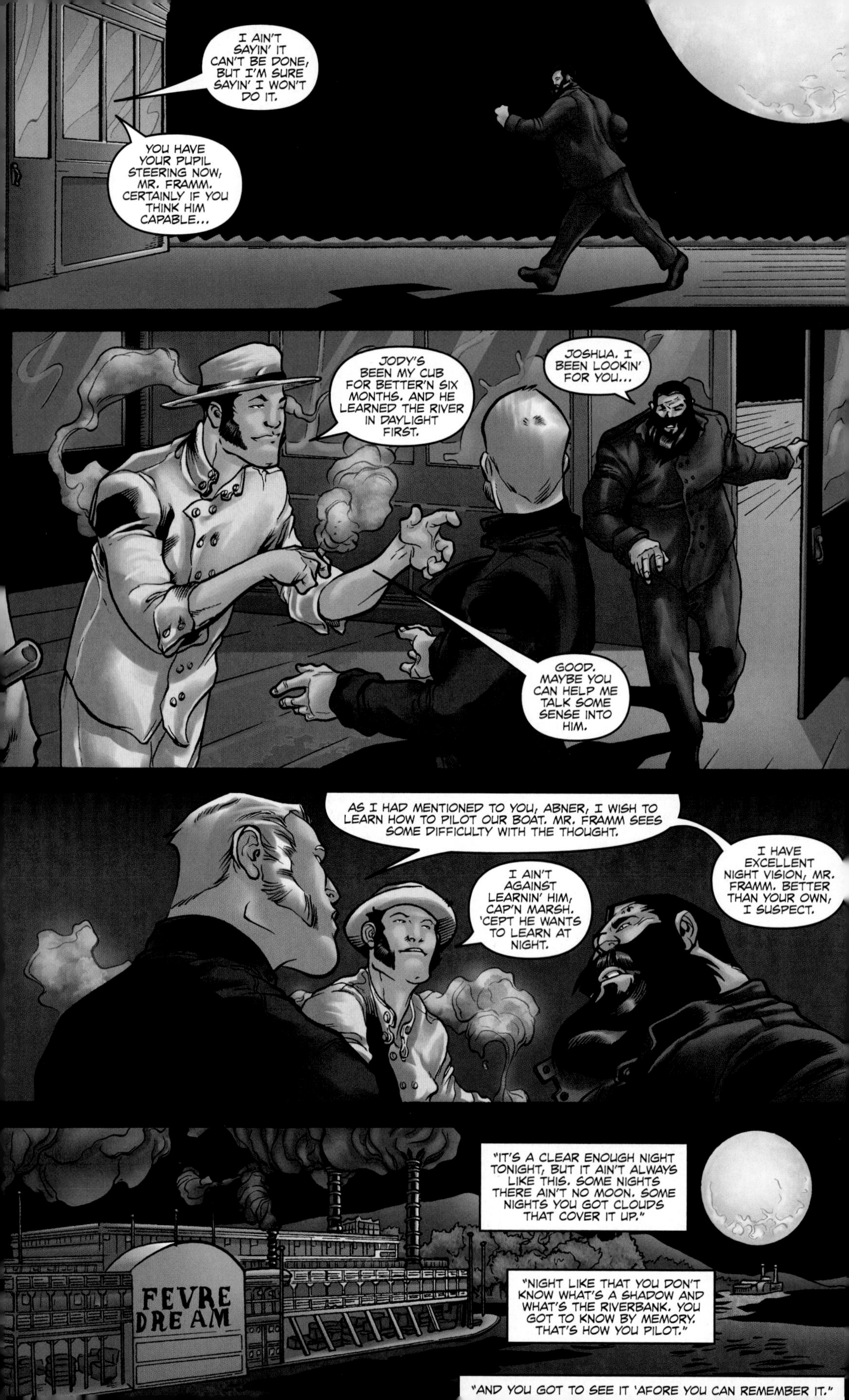
I AIN'T SAYIN' IT CAN'T BE DONE, BUT I'M SURE SAYIN' I WON'T DO IT.
YOU HAVE YOUR PUPIL STEERING NOW, MR. FRAMM. CERTAINLY IF YOU THINK HIM CAPABLE...
JODY'S BEEN MY CUB FOR BETTER'N SIX MONTHS. AND HE LEARNED THE RIVER IN DAYLIGHT FIRST.
JOSHUA. I BEEN LOOKIN' FOR YOU...
GOOD. MAYBE YOU CAN HELP ME TALK SOME SENSE INTO HIM.
AS I HAD MENTIONED TO YOU, ABNER, I WISH TO LEARN HOW TO PILOT OUR BOAT. MR. FRAMM SEES SOME DIFFICULTY WITH THE THOUGHT.
I AIN'T AGAINST LEARNIN' HIM, CAP'N MARSH. 'CEPT HE WANTS TO LEARN AT NIGHT.
I HAVE EXCELLENT NIGHT VISION, MR. FRAMM. BETTER THAN YOUR OWN, I SUSPECT.
FEVRE DREAM
"IT'S A CLEAR ENOUGH NIGHT TONIGHT, BUT IT AIN'T ALWAYS LIKE THIS. SOME NIGHTS THERE AIN'T NO MOON. SOME NIGHTS YOU GOT CLOUDS THAT COVER IT UP."
"NIGHT LIKE THAT YOU DON'T KNOW WHAT'S A SHADOW AND WHAT'S THE RIVERBANK. YOU GOT TO KNOW BY MEMORY. THAT'S HOW YOU PILOT."
"AND YOU GOT TO SEE IT 'AFORE YOU CAN REMEMBER IT."

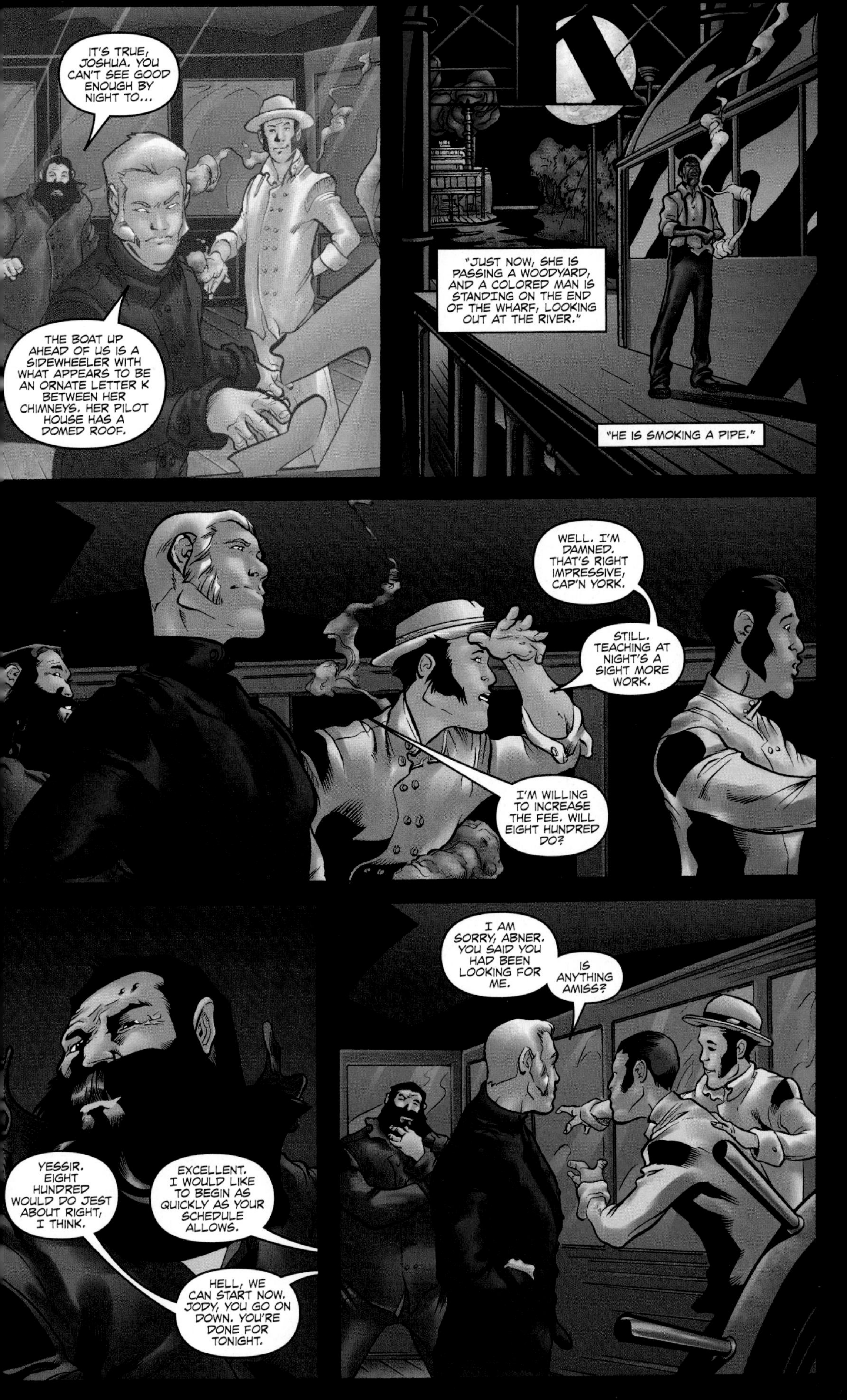
IT'S TRUE, JOSHUA. YOU CAN'T SEE GOOD ENOUGH BY NIGHT TO...
THE BOAT UP AHEAD OF US IS A SIDEWHEELER WITH WHAT APPEARS TO BE AN ORNATE LETTER K BETWEEN HER CHIMNEYS. HER PILOT HOUSE HAS A DOMED ROOF.
"JUST NOW, SHE IS PASSING A WOODYARD, AND A COLORED MAN IS STANDING ON THE END OF THE WHARF, LOOKING OUT AT THE RIVER."
"HE IS SMOKING A PIPE."
WELL. I'M DAMNED. THAT'S RIGHT IMPRESSIVE, CAP'N YORK.
STILL. TEACHING AT NIGHT'S A SIGHT MORE WORK.
I'M WILLING TO INCREASE THE FEE. WILL EIGHT HUNDRED DO?
YESSIR. EIGHT HUNDRED WOULD DO JEST ABOUT RIGHT, I THINK.
EXCELLENT. I WOULD LIKE TO BEGIN AS QUICKLY AS YOUR SCHEDULE ALLOWS.
HELL, WE CAN START NOW. JODY, YOU GO ON DOWN. YOU'RE DONE FOR TONIGHT.
I AM SORRY, ABNER. YOU SAID YOU HAD BEEN LOOKING FOR ME.
IS ANYTHING AMISS?

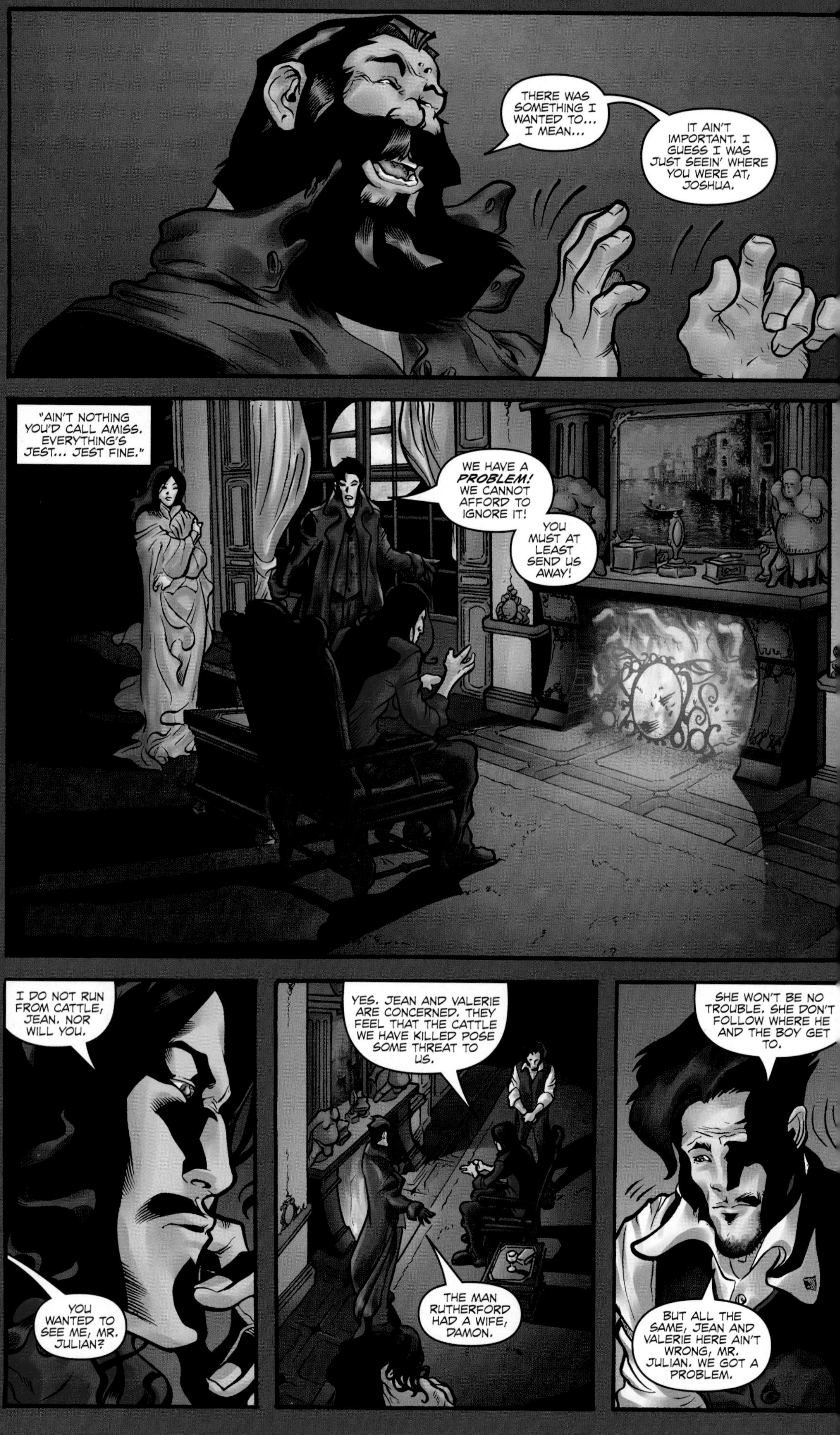
THERE WAS SOMETHING I WANTED TO... I MEAN...
IT AIN'T IMPORTANT. I GUESS I WAS JUST SEEIN' WHERE YOU WERE AT, JOSHUA.
"AIN'T NOTHING YOU'D CALL AMISS. EVERYTHING'S JEST... JEST FINE."
WE HAVE A PROBLEM! WE CANNOT AFFORD TO IGNORE IT!
YOU MUST AT LEAST SEND US AWAY!
I DO NOT RUN FROM CATTLE, JEAN. NOR WILL YOU.
YOU WANTED TO SEE ME, MR. JULIAN?
YES. JEAN AND VALERIE ARE CONCERNED. THEY FEEL THAT THE CATTLE WE HAVE KILLED POSE SOME THREAT TO US.
THE MAN RUTHERFORD HAD A WIFE, DAMON.
SHE WON'T BE NO TROUBLE. SHE DON'T FOLLOW WHERE HE AND THE BOY GET TO.
BUT ALL THE SAME, JEAN AND VALERIE HERE AIN'T WRONG, MR. JULIAN. WE GOT A PROBLEM.

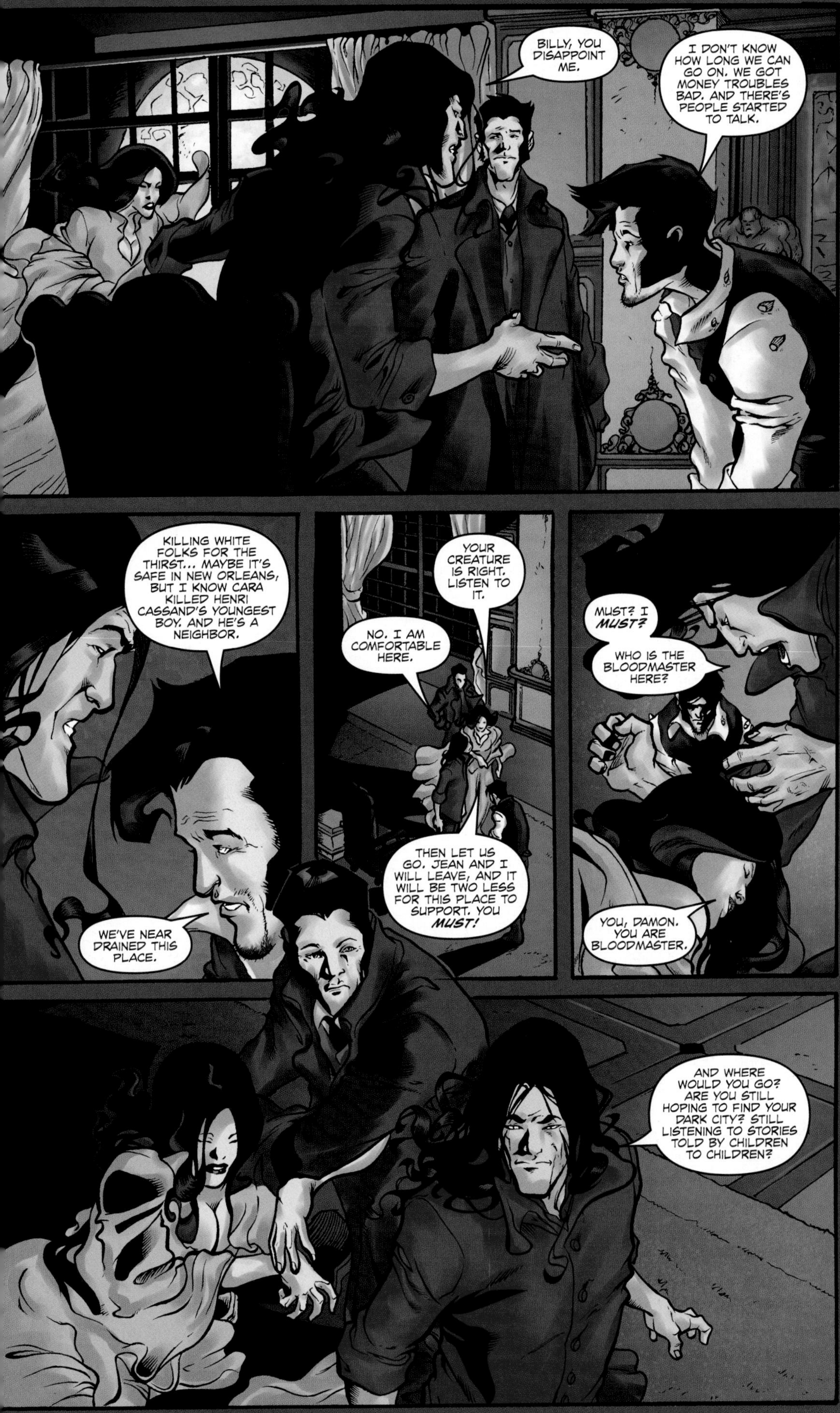
BILLY, YOU DISAPPOINT ME.
I DON'T KNOW HOW LONG WE CAN GO ON. WE GOT MONEY TROUBLES BAD. AND THERE'S PEOPLE STARTED TO TALK.
KILLING WHITE FOLKS FOR THE THIRST... MAYBE IT'S SAFE IN NEW ORLEANS, BUT I KNOW CARA KILLED HENRI CASSAND'S YOUNGEST BOY. AND HE'S A NEIGHBOR.
WE'VE NEAR DRAINED THIS PLACE.
YOUR CREATURE IS RIGHT. LISTEN TO IT.
NO. I AM COMFORTABLE HERE.
THEN LET US GO. JEAN AND I WILL LEAVE, AND IT WILL BE TWO LESS FOR THIS PLACE TO SUPPORT. YOU *MUST!*
MUST? I *MUST?*
WHO IS THE BLOODMASTER HERE?
YOU, DAMON. YOU ARE BLOODMASTER.
AND WHERE WOULD YOU GO? ARE YOU STILL HOPING TO FIND YOUR DARK CITY? STILL LISTENING TO STORIES TOLD BY CHILDREN TO CHILDREN?

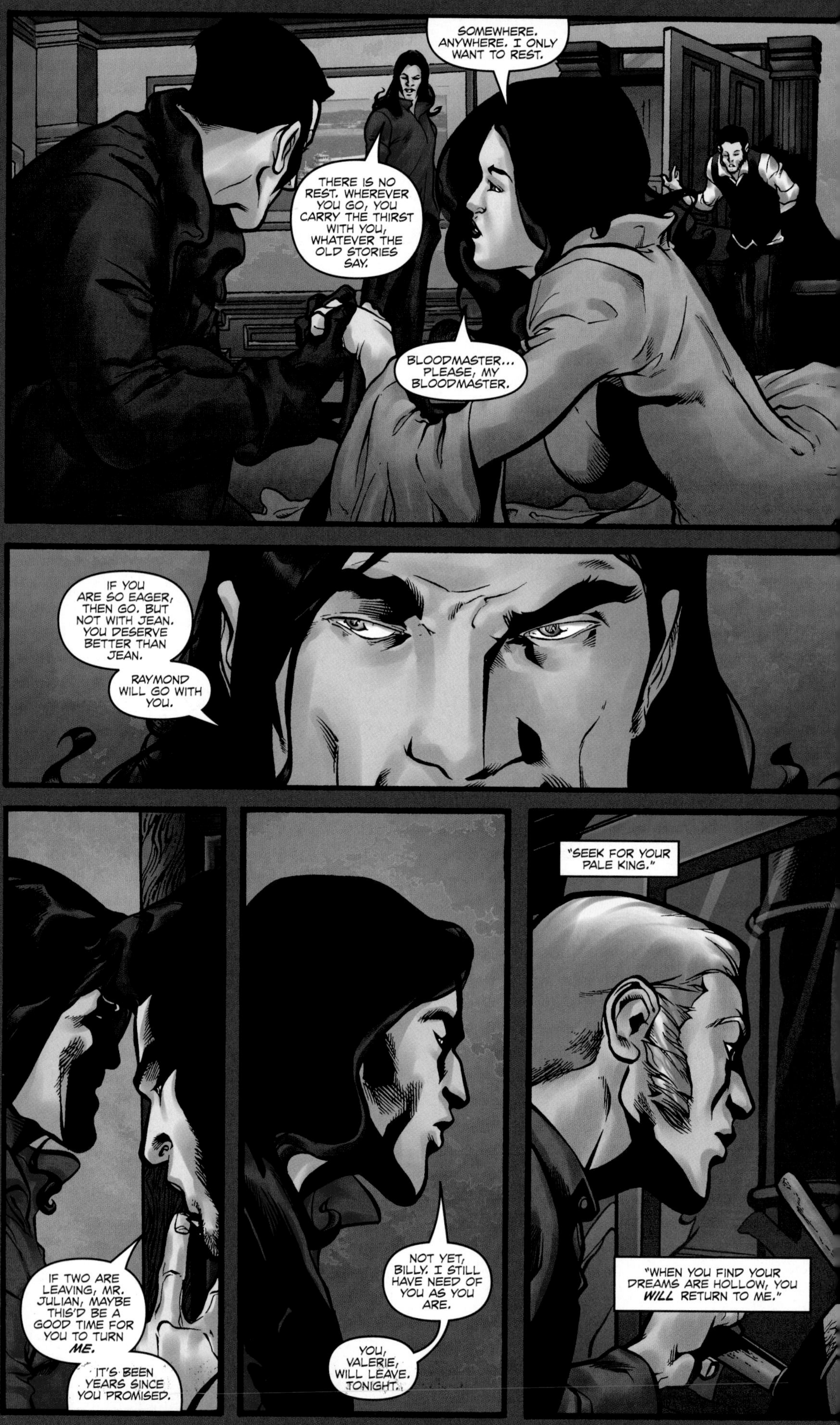
SOMEWHERE. ANYWHERE. I ONLY WANT TO REST.
THERE IS NO REST. WHEREVER YOU GO, YOU CARRY THE THIRST WITH YOU, WHATEVER THE OLD STORIES SAY.
BLOODMASTER... PLEASE, MY BLOODMASTER.
IF YOU ARE SO EAGER, THEN GO. BUT NOT WITH JEAN. YOU DESERVE BETTER THAN JEAN.
RAYMOND WILL GO WITH YOU.
IF TWO ARE LEAVING, MR. JULIAN, MAYBE THIS'D BE A GOOD TIME FOR YOU TO TURN ***ME.***
IT'S BEEN YEARS SINCE YOU PROMISED.
NOT YET, BILLY. I STILL HAVE NEED OF YOU AS YOU ARE.
YOU, VALERIE, WILL LEAVE. TONIGHT.
"SEEK FOR YOUR PALE KING."
"WHEN YOU FIND YOUR DREAMS ARE HOLLOW, YOU ***WILL*** RETURN TO ME."

CHAPTER 3

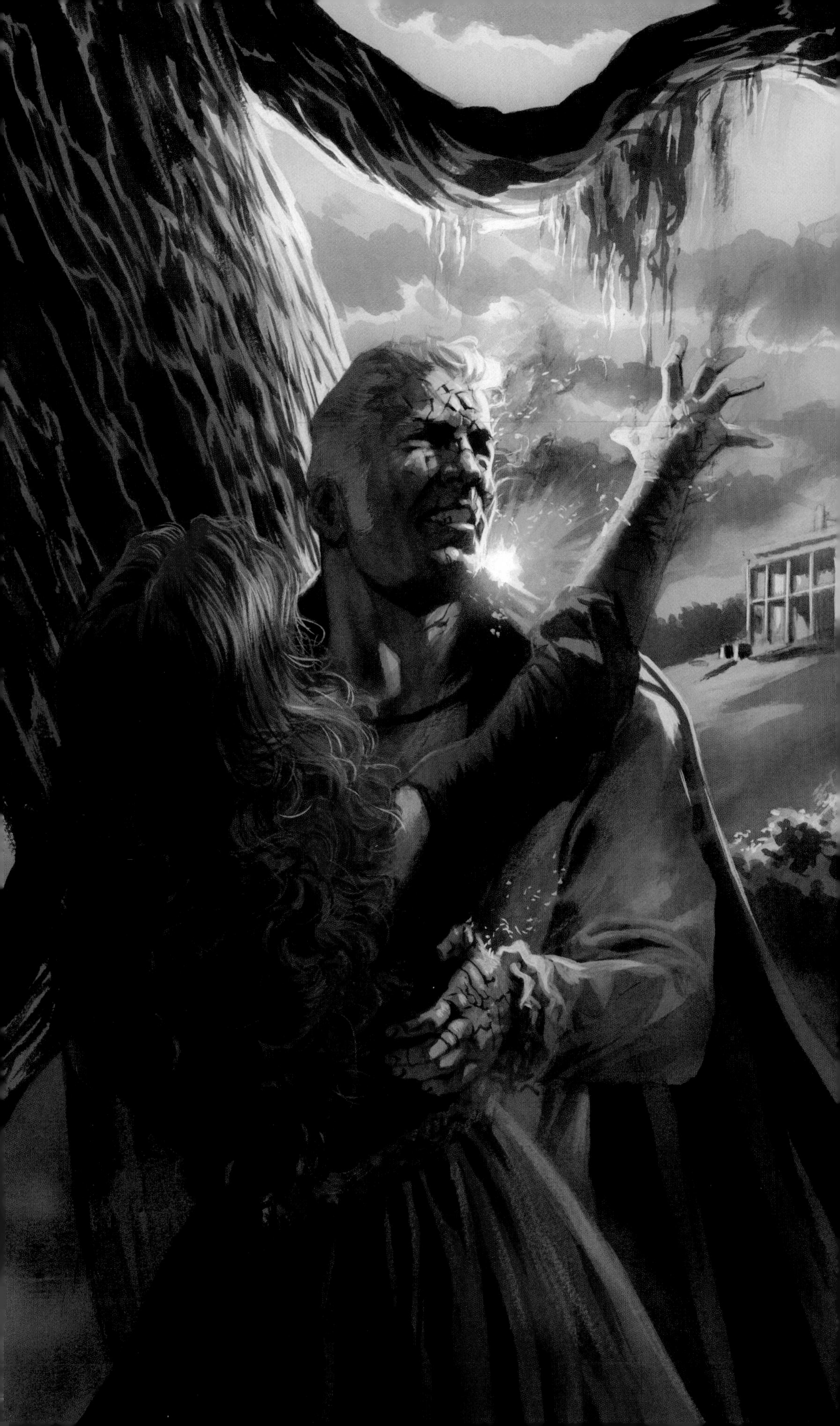

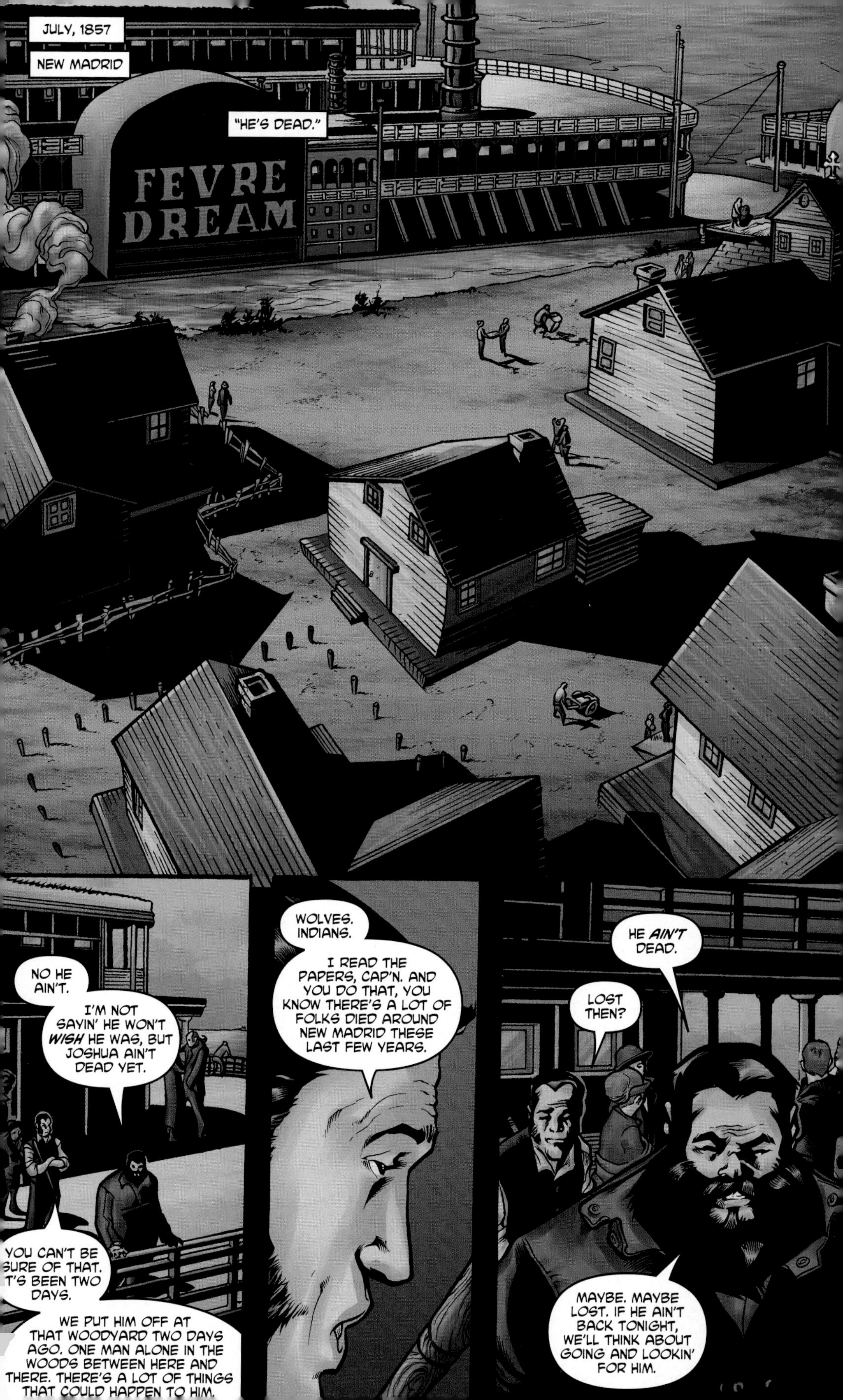
JULY, 1857
NEW MADRID
"HE'S DEAD."
FEVRE DREAM
NO HE AIN'T.
I'M NOT SAYIN' HE WON'T *WISH* HE WAS, BUT JOSHUA AIN'T DEAD YET.
YOU CAN'T BE SURE OF THAT. IT'S BEEN TWO DAYS.
WE PUT HIM OFF AT THAT WOODYARD TWO DAYS AGO. ONE MAN ALONE IN THE WOODS BETWEEN HERE AND THERE. THERE'S A LOT OF THINGS THAT COULD HAPPEN TO HIM.
WOLVES. INDIANS.
I READ THE PAPERS, CAP'N. AND YOU DO THAT, YOU KNOW THERE'S A LOT OF FOLKS DIED AROUND NEW MADRID THESE LAST FEW YEARS.
HE *AIN'T* DEAD.
LOST THEN?
MAYBE. MAYBE LOST. IF HE AIN'T BACK TONIGHT, WE'LL THINK ABOUT GOING AND LOOKIN' FOR HIM.

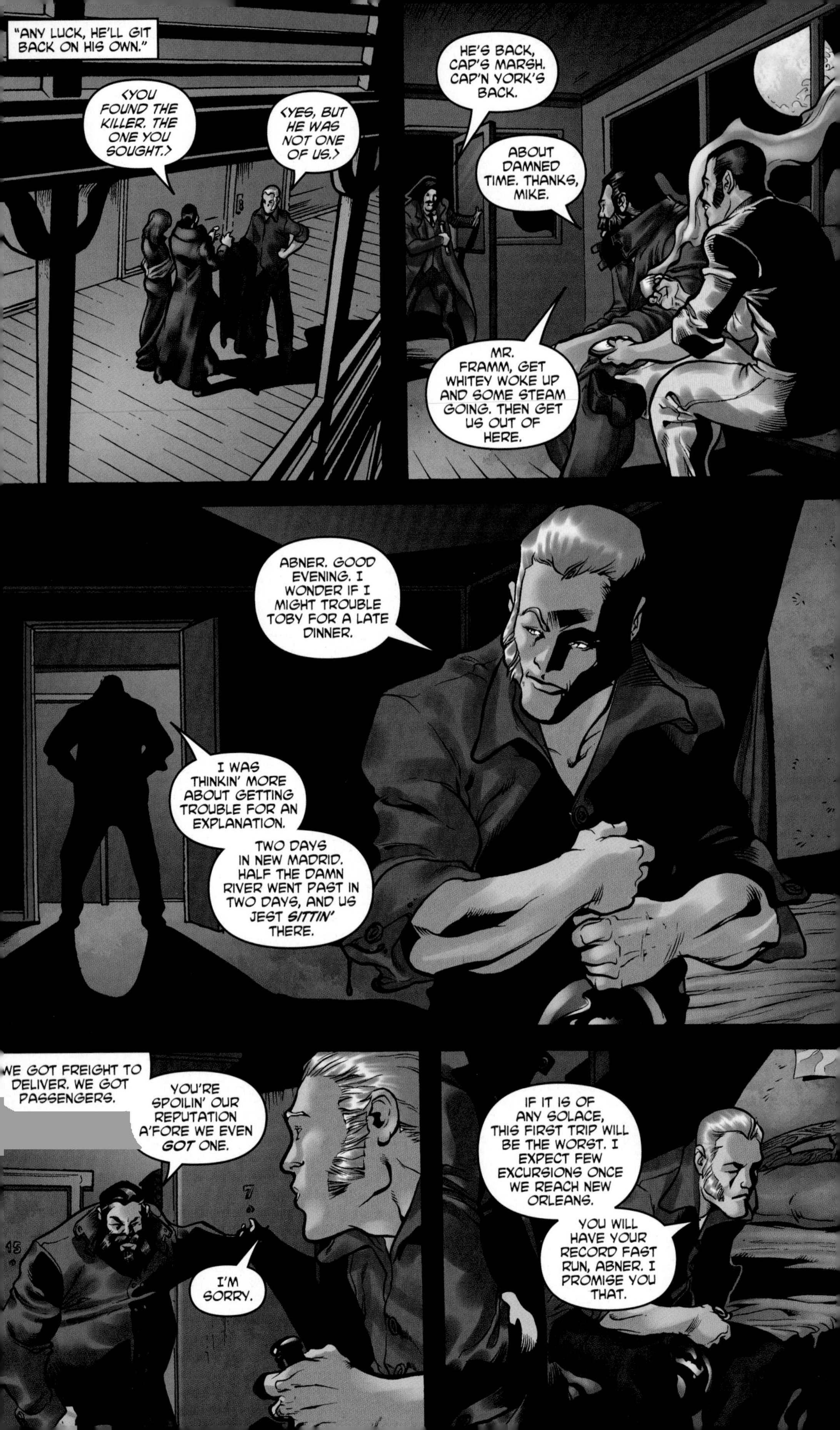
"ANY LUCK, HE'LL GIT BACK ON HIS OWN."
<YOU FOUND THE KILLER. THE ONE YOU SOUGHT.>
<YES, BUT HE WAS NOT ONE OF US.>
HE'S BACK, CAP'S MARSH. CAP'N YORK'S BACK.
ABOUT DAMNED TIME. THANKS, MIKE.
MR. FRAMM, GET WHITEY WOKE UP AND SOME STEAM GOING. THEN GET US OUT OF HERE.
ABNER. GOOD EVENING. I WONDER IF I MIGHT TROUBLE TOBY FOR A LATE DINNER.
I WAS THINKIN' MORE ABOUT GETTING TROUBLE FOR AN EXPLANATION.
TWO DAYS IN NEW MADRID. HALF THE DAMN RIVER WENT PAST IN TWO DAYS, AND US JEST *SITTIN'* THERE.
WE GOT FREIGHT TO DELIVER. WE GOT PASSENGERS.
YOU'RE SPOILIN' OUR REPUTATION A'FORE WE EVEN *GOT* ONE.
I'M SORRY.
IF IT IS OF ANY SOLACE, THIS FIRST TRIP WILL BE THE WORST. I EXPECT FEW EXCURSIONS ONCE WE REACH NEW ORLEANS.
YOU WILL HAVE YOUR RECORD FAST RUN, ABNER. I PROMISE YOU THAT.

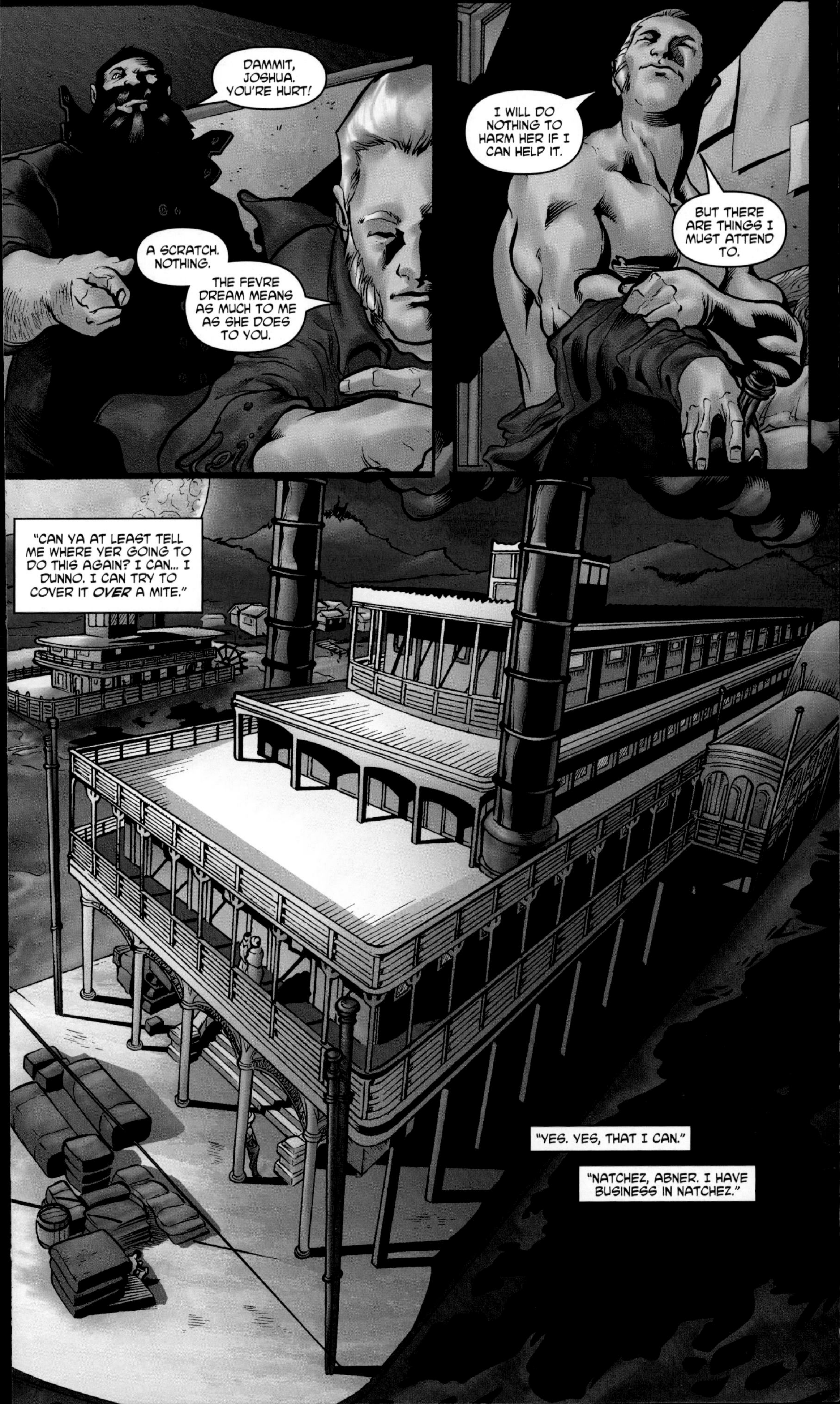
DAMMIT, JOSHUA. YOU'RE HURT!
A SCRATCH. NOTHING.
THE FEVRE DREAM MEANS AS MUCH TO ME AS SHE DOES TO YOU.
I WILL DO NOTHING TO HARM HER IF I CAN HELP IT.
BUT THERE ARE THINGS I MUST ATTEND TO.
"CAN YA AT LEAST TELL ME WHERE YER GOING TO DO THIS AGAIN? I CAN... I DUNNO. I CAN TRY TO COVER IT OVER A MITE."
"YES. YES, THAT I CAN."
"NATCHEZ, ABNER. I HAVE BUSINESS IN NATCHEZ."

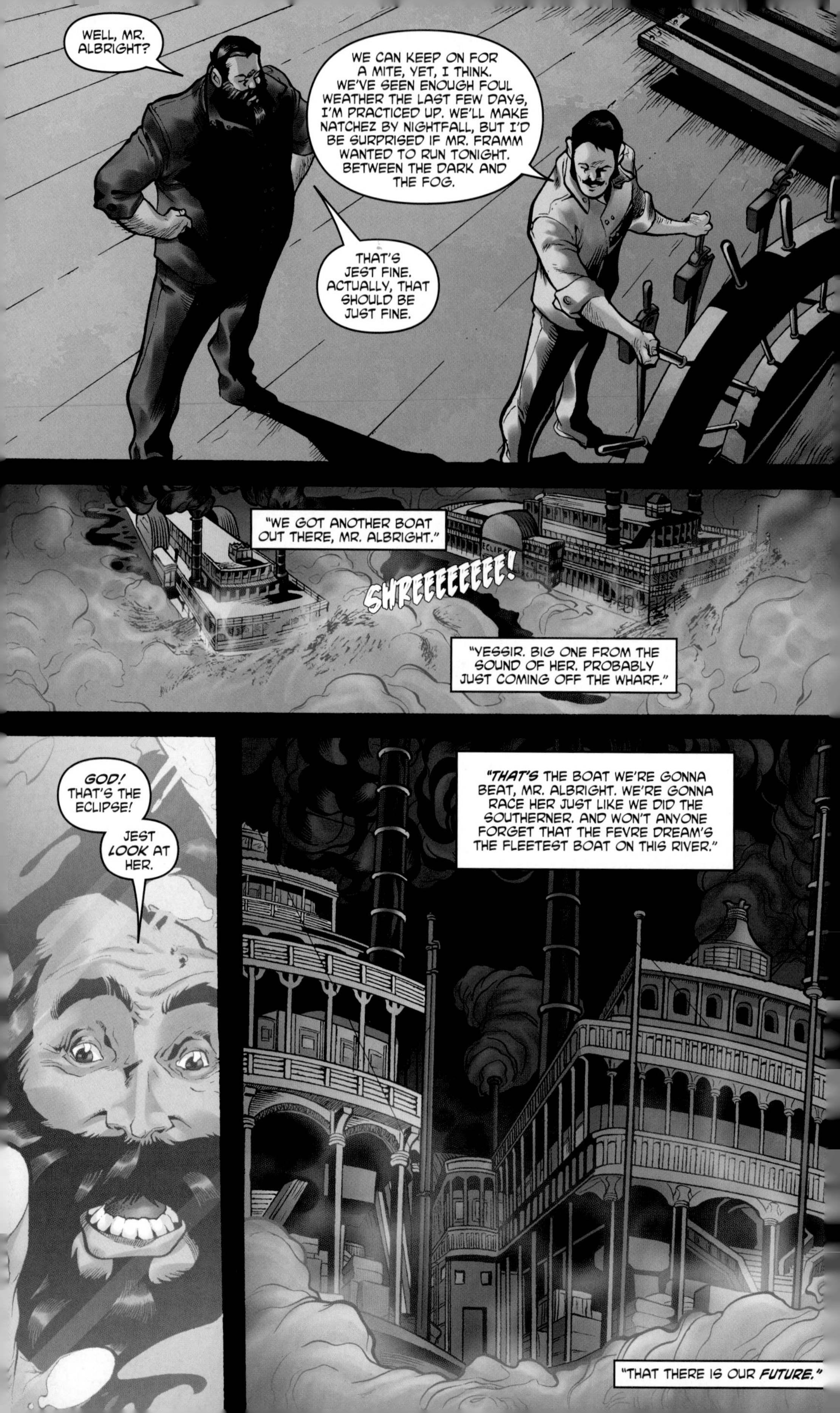
WELL, MR. ALBRIGHT?
WE CAN KEEP ON FOR A MITE, YET, I THINK. WE'VE SEEN ENOUGH FOUL WEATHER THE LAST FEW DAYS, I'M PRACTICED UP. WE'LL MAKE NATCHEZ BY NIGHTFALL, BUT I'D BE SURPRISED IF MR. FRAMM WANTED TO RUN TONIGHT. BETWEEN THE DARK AND THE FOG.
THAT'S JEST FINE. ACTUALLY, THAT SHOULD BE JUST FINE.
"WE GOT ANOTHER BOAT OUT THERE, MR. ALBRIGHT."
SHREEEEEEEE!
"YESSIR. BIG ONE FROM THE SOUND OF HER. PROBABLY JUST COMING OFF THE WHARF."
GOD! THAT'S THE ECLIPSE!
JEST LOOK AT HER.
"THAT'S THE BOAT WE'RE GONNA BEAT, MR. ALBRIGHT. WE'RE GONNA RACE HER JUST LIKE WE DID THE SOUTHERNER. AND WON'T ANYONE FORGET THAT THE FEVRE DREAM'S THE FLEETEST BOAT ON THIS RIVER."
"THAT THERE IS OUR FUTURE."

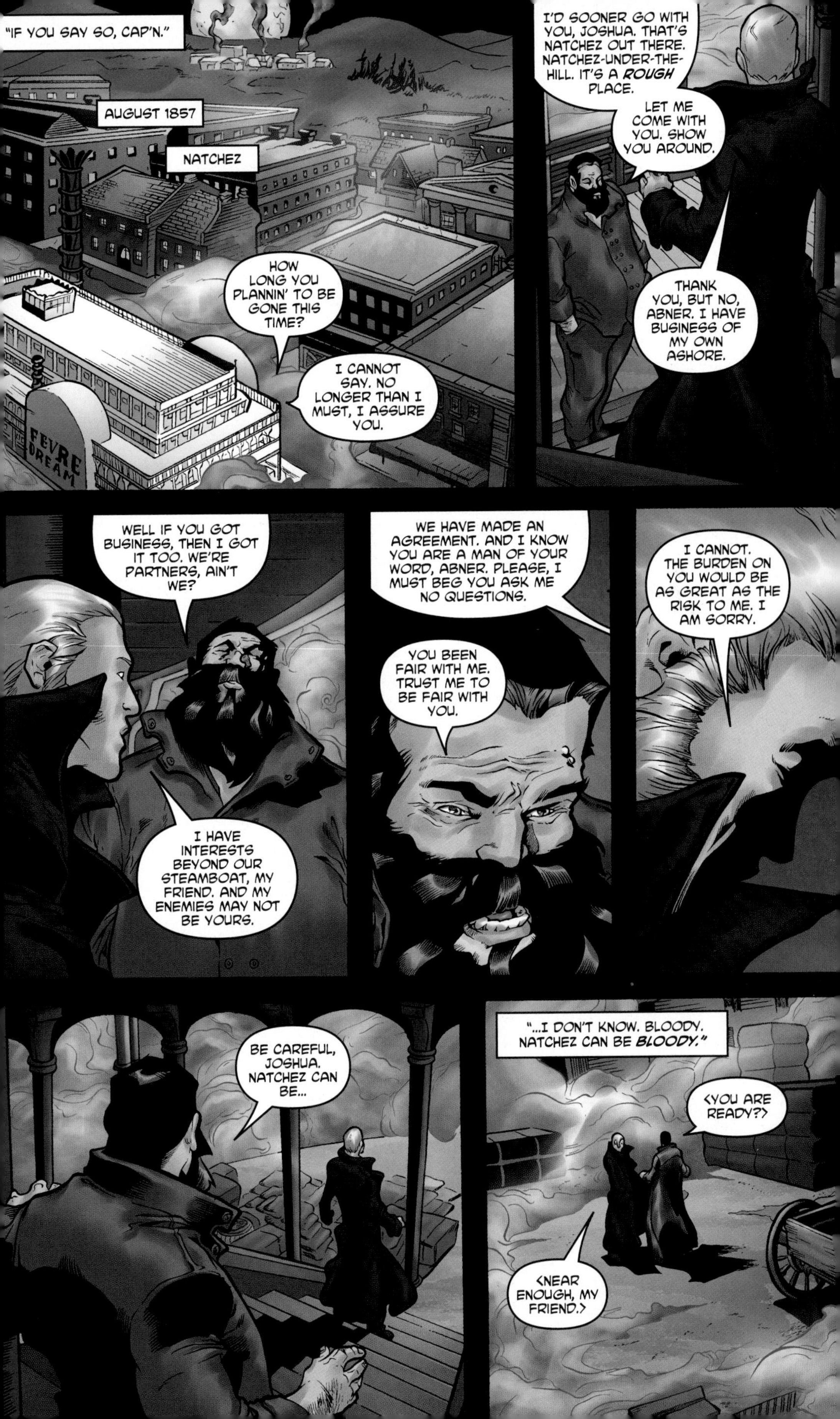
"IF YOU SAY SO, CAP'N."
AUGUST 1857
NATCHEZ
HOW LONG YOU PLANNIN' TO BE GONE THIS TIME?
I CANNOT SAY. NO LONGER THAN I MUST, I ASSURE YOU.
FEVRE DREAM
I'D SOONER GO WITH YOU, JOSHUA. THAT'S NATCHEZ OUT THERE. NATCHEZ-UNDER-THE-HILL. IT'S A *ROUGH* PLACE.
LET ME COME WITH YOU. SHOW YOU AROUND.
THANK YOU, BUT NO, ABNER. I HAVE BUSINESS OF MY OWN ASHORE.
WELL IF YOU GOT BUSINESS, THEN I GOT IT TOO. WE'RE PARTNERS, AIN'T WE?
I HAVE INTERESTS BEYOND OUR STEAMBOAT, MY FRIEND. AND MY ENEMIES MAY NOT BE YOURS.
WE HAVE MADE AN AGREEMENT. AND I KNOW YOU ARE A MAN OF YOUR WORD, ABNER. PLEASE, I MUST BEG YOU ASK ME NO QUESTIONS.
YOU BEEN FAIR WITH ME. TRUST ME TO BE FAIR WITH YOU.
I CANNOT. THE BURDEN ON YOU WOULD BE AS GREAT AS THE RISK TO ME. I AM SORRY.
BE CAREFUL, JOSHUA. NATCHEZ CAN BE...
"...I DON'T KNOW. BLOODY. NATCHEZ CAN BE *BLOODY.*"
<YOU ARE READY?>
<NEAR ENOUGH, MY FRIEND.>

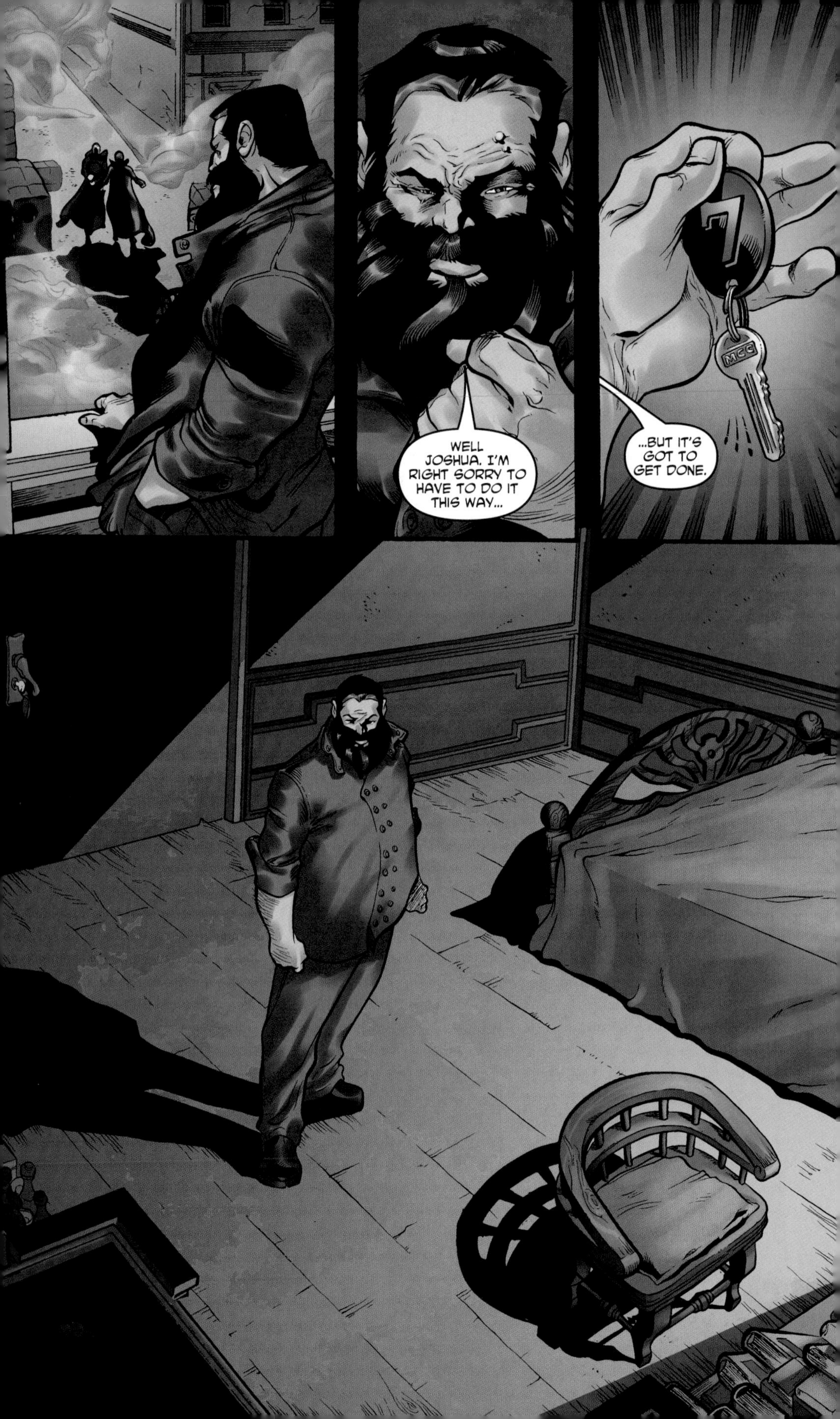
WELL JOSHUA. I'M RIGHT SORRY TO HAVE TO DO IT THIS WAY...
...BUT IT'S GOT TO GET DONE.
MCG

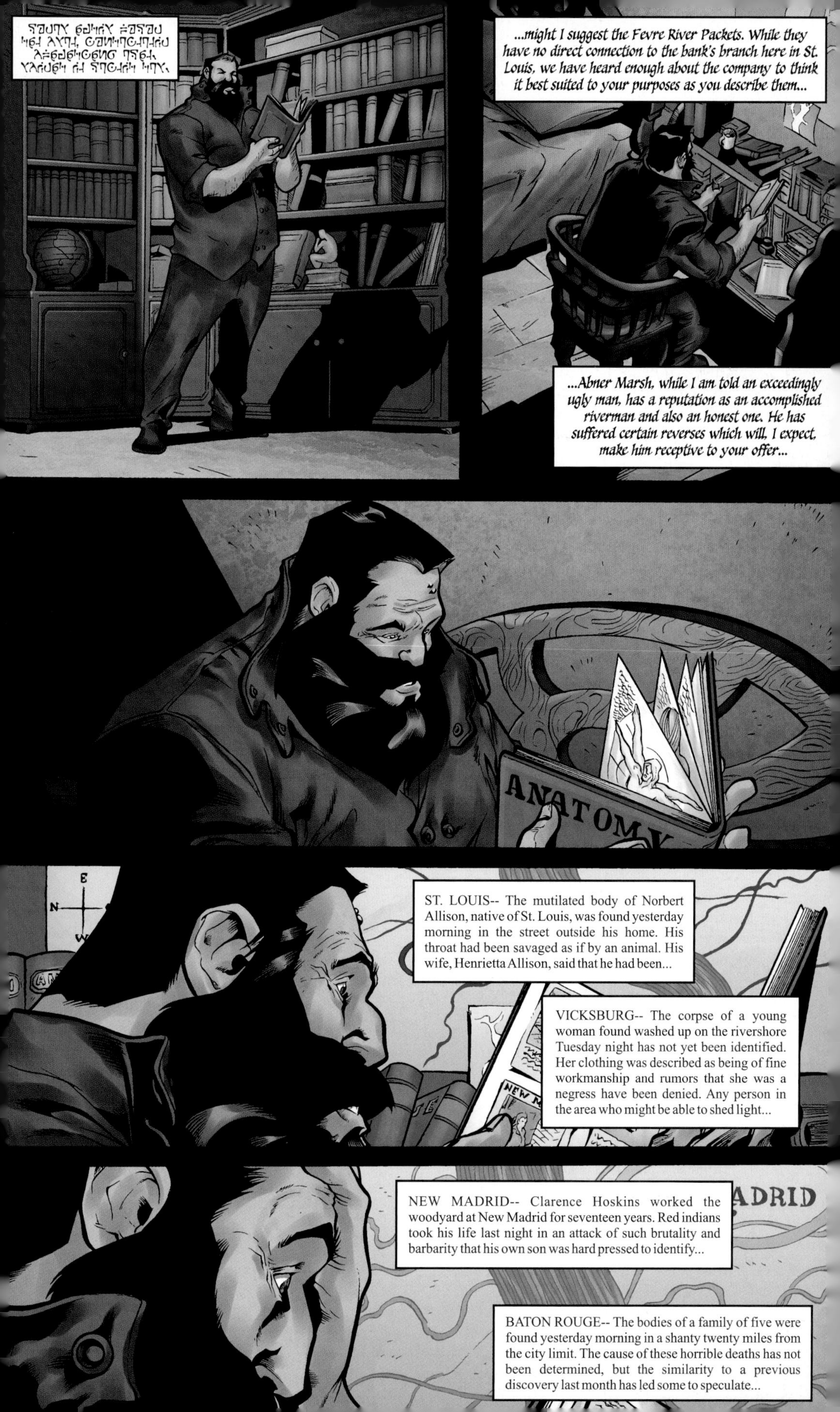
...might I suggest the Fevre River Packets. While they have no direct connection to the bank's branch here in St. Louis, we have heard enough about the company to think it best suited to your purposes as you describe them...
...Abner Marsh, while I am told an exceedingly ugly man, has a reputation as an accomplished riverman and also an honest one. He has suffered certain reverses which will, I expect, make him receptive to your offer...
ANATOMY
ST. LOUIS-- The mutilated body of Norbert Allison, native of St. Louis, was found yesterday morning in the street outside his home. His throat had been savaged as if by an animal. His wife, Henrietta Allison, said that he had been...
VICKSBURG-- The corpse of a young woman found washed up on the rivershore Tuesday night has not yet been identified. Her clothing was described as being of fine workmanship and rumors that she was a negress have been denied. Any person in the area who might be able to shed light...
NEW MADRID-- Clarence Hoskins worked the woodyard at New Madrid for seventeen years. Red indians took his life last night in an attack of such brutality and barbarity that his own son was hard pressed to identify...
BATON ROUGE-- The bodies of a family of five were found yesterday morning in a shanty twenty miles from the city limit. The cause of these horrible deaths has not been determined, but the similarity to a previous discovery last month has led some to speculate...

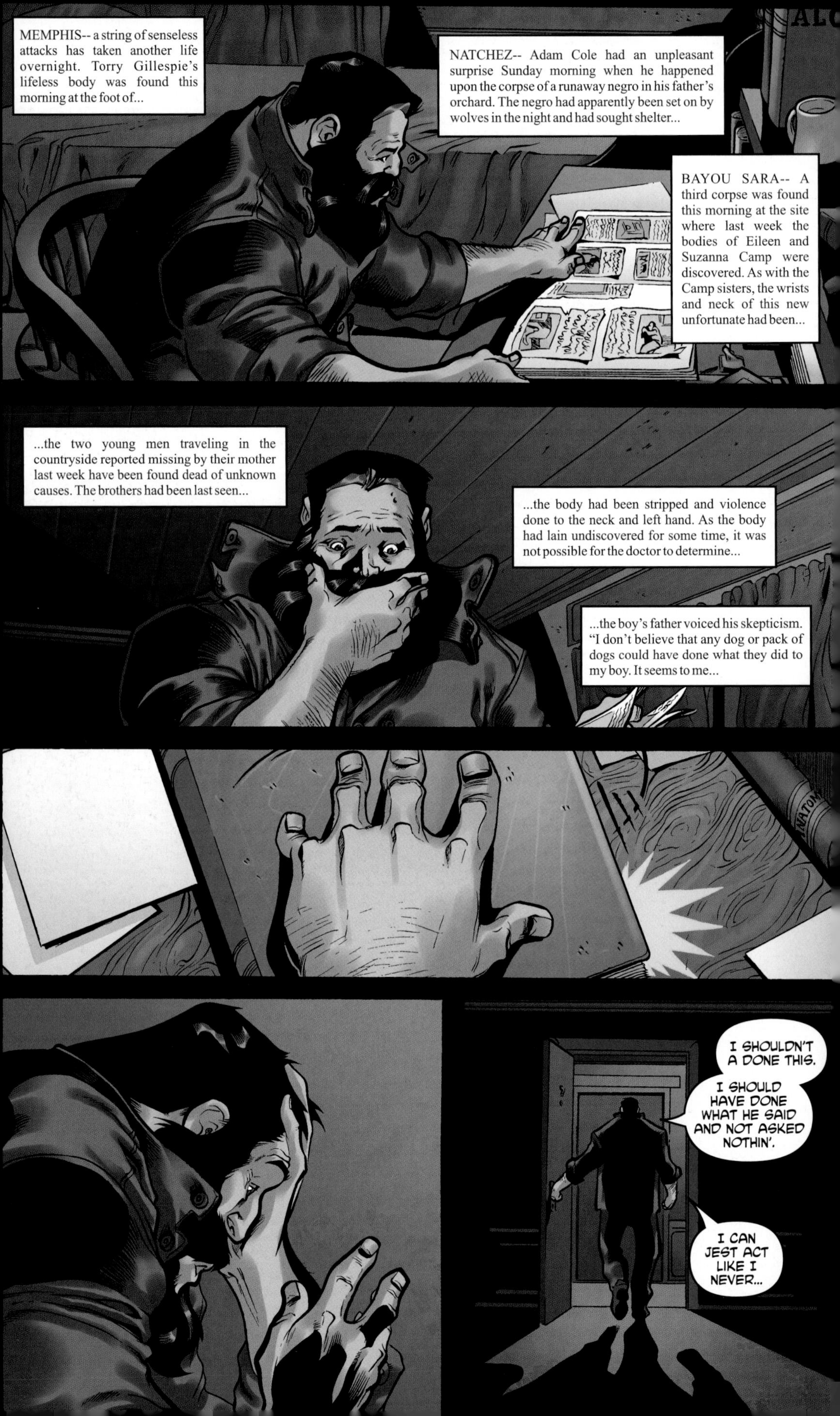

MEMPHIS-- a string of senseless attacks has taken another life overnight. Torry Gillespie's lifeless body was found this morning at the foot of...
NATCHEZ-- Adam Cole had an unpleasant surprise Sunday morning when he happened upon the corpse of a runaway negro in his father's orchard. The negro had apparently been set on by wolves in the night and had sought shelter...
BAYOU SARA-- A third corpse was found this morning at the site where last week the bodies of Eileen and Suzanna Camp were discovered. As with the Camp sisters, the wrists and neck of this new unfortunate had been...
...the two young men traveling in the countryside reported missing by their mother last week have been found dead of unknown causes. The brothers had been last seen...
...the body had been stripped and violence done to the neck and left hand. As the body had lain undiscovered for some time, it was not possible for the doctor to determine...
...the boy's father voiced his skepticism. "I don't believe that any dog or pack of dogs could have done what they did to my boy. It seems to me...
I SHOULDN'T A DONE THIS.
I SHOULD HAVE DONE WHAT HE SAID AND NOT ASKED NOTHIN'.
I CAN JEST ACT LIKE I NEVER...

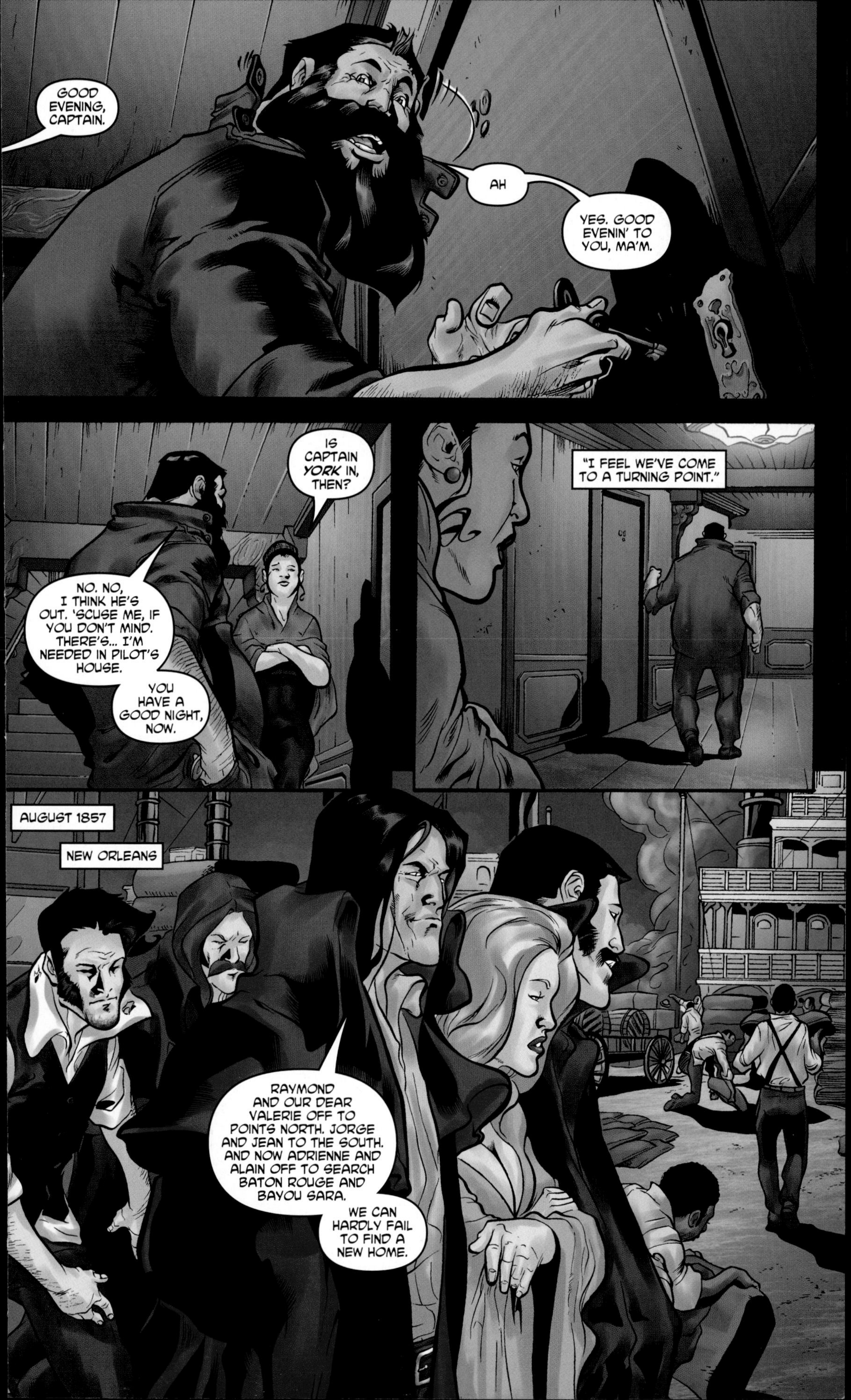

GOOD EVENING, CAPTAIN.
AH
YES. GOOD EVENIN' TO YOU, MA'M.
IS CAPTAIN YORK IN, THEN?
NO. NO, I THINK HE'S OUT. 'SCUSE ME, IF YOU DON'T MIND. THERE'S... I'M NEEDED IN PILOT'S HOUSE.
YOU HAVE A GOOD NIGHT, NOW.
"I FEEL WE'VE COME TO A TURNING POINT."
AUGUST 1857
NEW ORLEANS
RAYMOND AND OUR DEAR VALERIE OFF TO POINTS NORTH. JORGE AND JEAN TO THE SOUTH. AND NOW ADRIENNE AND ALAIN OFF TO SEARCH BATON ROUGE AND BAYOU SARA.
WE CAN HARDLY FAIL TO FIND A NEW HOME.

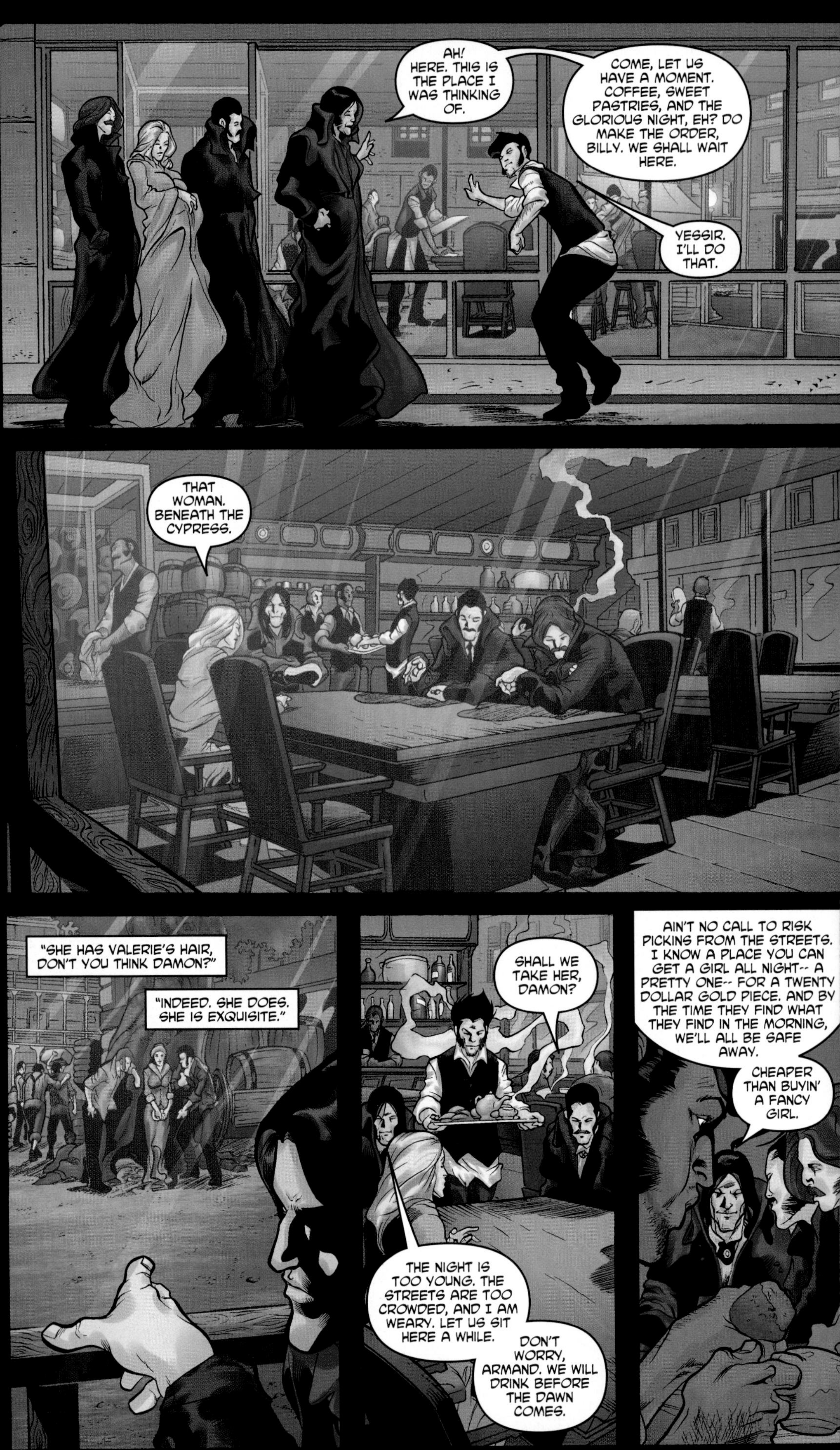
AH! HERE. THIS IS THE PLACE I WAS THINKING OF.
COME, LET US HAVE A MOMENT. COFFEE, SWEET PASTRIES, AND THE GLORIOUS NIGHT, EH? DO MAKE THE ORDER, BILLY. WE SHALL WAIT HERE.
YESSIR. I'LL DO THAT.
THAT WOMAN. BENEATH THE CYPRESS.
"SHE HAS VALERIE'S HAIR, DON'T YOU THINK DAMON?"
"INDEED. SHE DOES. SHE IS EXQUISITE."
SHALL WE TAKE HER, DAMON?
THE NIGHT IS TOO YOUNG. THE STREETS ARE TOO CROWDED, AND I AM WEARY. LET US SIT HERE A WHILE.
DON'T WORRY, ARMAND. WE WILL DRINK BEFORE THE DAWN COMES.
AIN'T NO CALL TO RISK PICKINS FROM THE STREETS. I KNOW A PLACE YOU CAN GET A GIRL ALL NIGHT-- A PRETTY ONE-- FOR A TWENTY DOLLAR GOLD PIECE. AND BY THE TIME THEY FIND WHAT THEY FIND IN THE MORNING, WE'LL ALL BE SAFE AWAY.
CHEAPER THAN BUYIN' A FANCY GIRL.

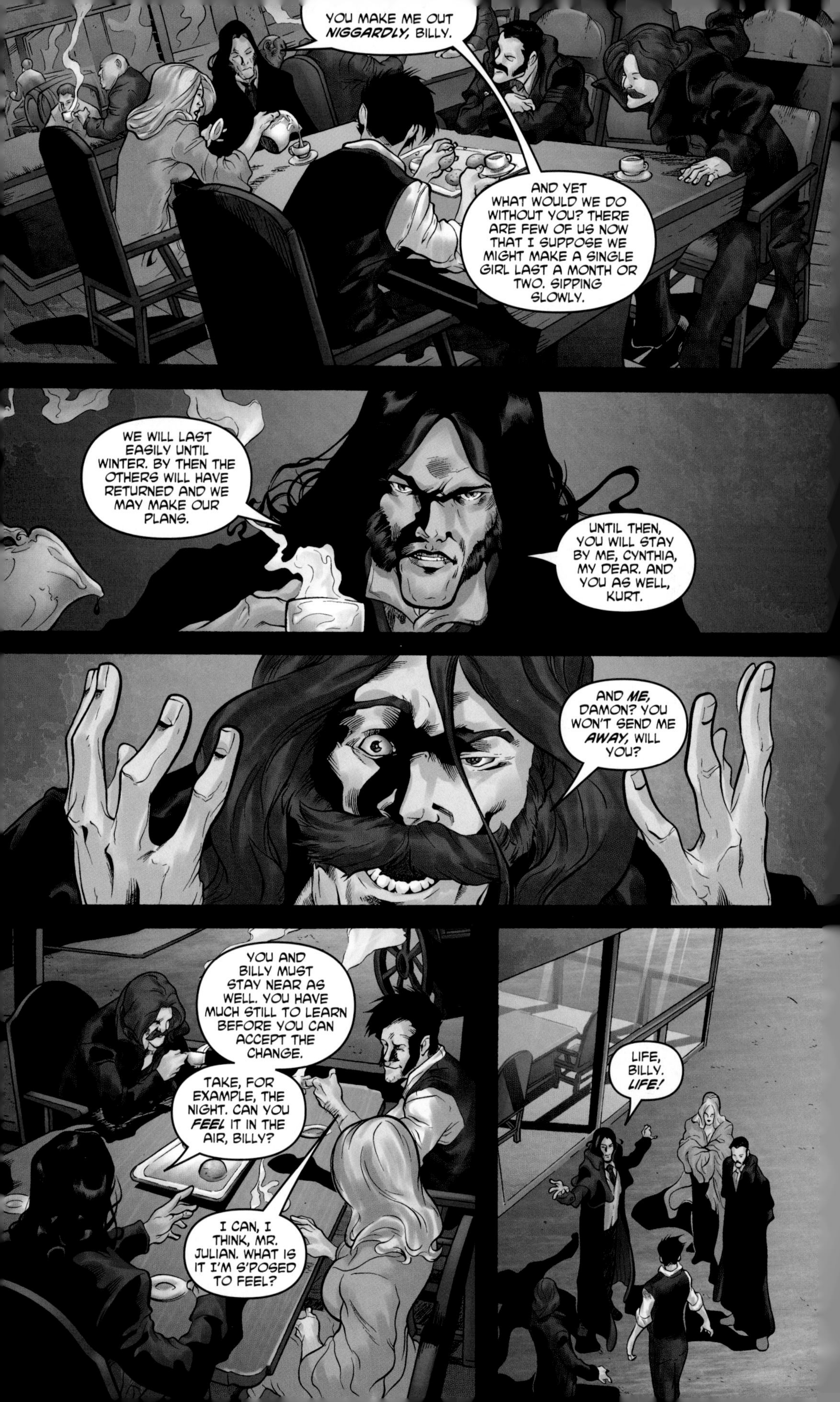
YOU MAKE ME OUT *NIGGARDLY,* BILLY.
AND YET WHAT WOULD WE DO WITHOUT YOU? THERE ARE FEW OF US NOW THAT I SUPPOSE WE MIGHT MAKE A SINGLE GIRL LAST A MONTH OR TWO. SIPPING SLOWLY.
WE WILL LAST EASILY UNTIL WINTER. BY THEN THE OTHERS WILL HAVE RETURNED AND WE MAY MAKE OUR PLANS.
UNTIL THEN, YOU WILL STAY BY ME, CYNTHIA, MY DEAR. AND YOU AS WELL, KURT.
AND *ME,* DAMON? YOU WON'T SEND ME *AWAY,* WILL YOU?
YOU AND BILLY MUST STAY NEAR AS WELL. YOU HAVE MUCH STILL TO LEARN BEFORE YOU CAN ACCEPT THE CHANGE.
TAKE, FOR EXAMPLE, THE NIGHT. CAN YOU *FEEL* IT IN THE AIR, BILLY?
I CAN, I THINK, MR. JULIAN. WHAT IS IT I'M S'POSED TO FEEL?
LIFE, BILLY. *LIFE!*

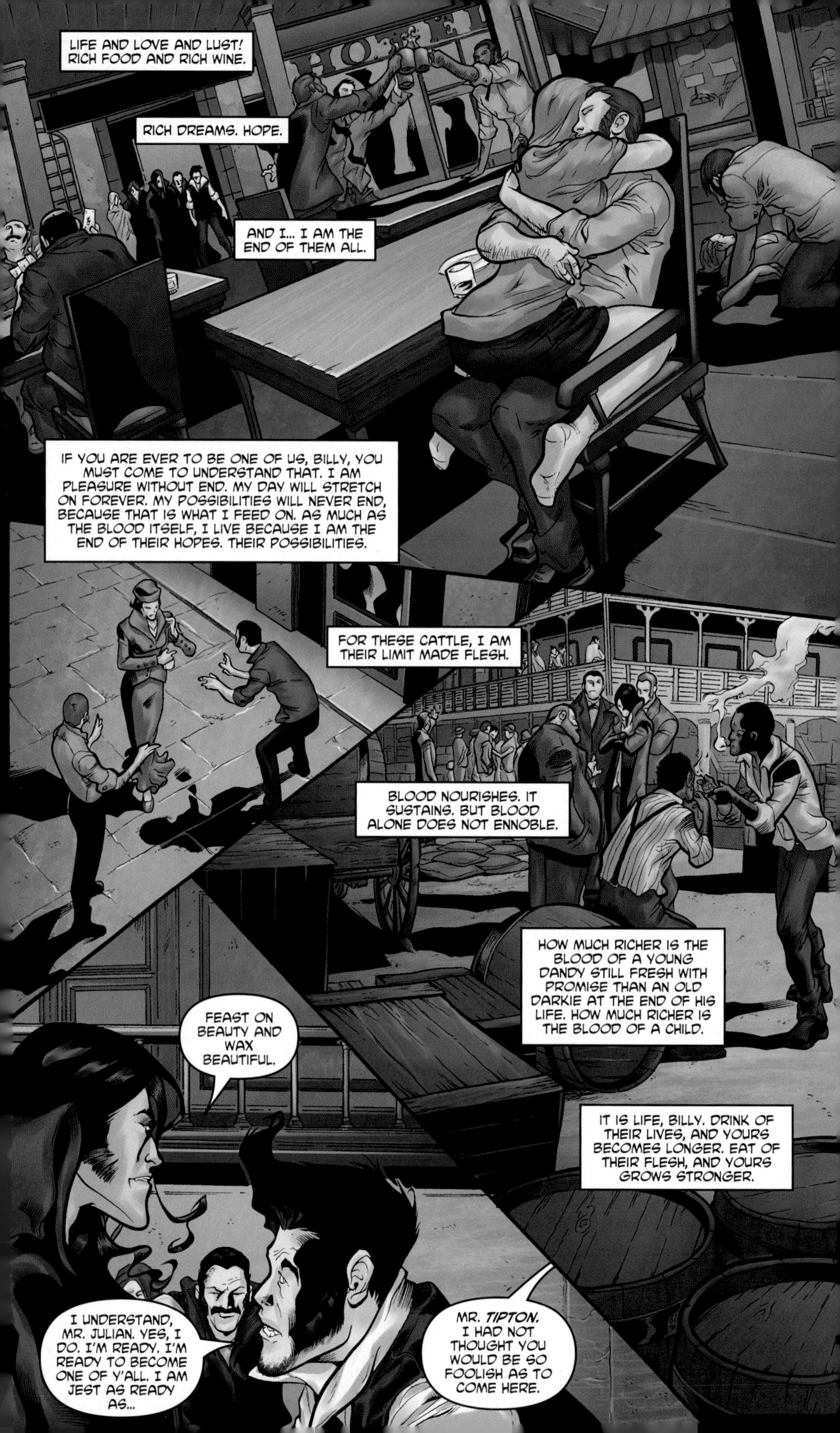
LIFE AND LOVE AND LUST! RICH FOOD AND RICH WINE.
RICH DREAMS. HOPE.
AND I... I AM THE END OF THEM ALL.
IF YOU ARE EVER TO BE ONE OF US, BILLY, YOU MUST COME TO UNDERSTAND THAT. I AM PLEASURE WITHOUT END. MY DAY WILL STRETCH ON FOREVER. MY POSSIBILITIES WILL NEVER END, BECAUSE THAT IS WHAT I FEED ON. AS MUCH AS THE BLOOD ITSELF, I LIVE BECAUSE I AM THE END OF THEIR HOPES. THEIR POSSIBILITIES.
FOR THESE CATTLE, I AM THEIR LIMIT MADE FLESH.
BLOOD NOURISHES. IT SUSTAINS. BUT BLOOD ALONE DOES NOT ENNOBLE.
HOW MUCH RICHER IS THE BLOOD OF A YOUNG DANDY STILL FRESH WITH PROMISE THAN AN OLD DARKIE AT THE END OF HIS LIFE. HOW MUCH RICHER IS THE BLOOD OF A CHILD.
FEAST ON BEAUTY AND WAX BEAUTIFUL.
IT IS LIFE, BILLY. DRINK OF THEIR LIVES, AND YOURS BECOMES LONGER. EAT OF THEIR FLESH, AND YOURS GROWS STRONGER.
I UNDERSTAND, MR. JULIAN. YES, I DO. I'M READY. I'M READY TO BECOME ONE OF Y'ALL. I AM JEST AS READY AS...
MR. *TIPTON.* I HAD NOT THOUGHT YOU WOULD BE SO FOOLISH AS TO COME HERE.

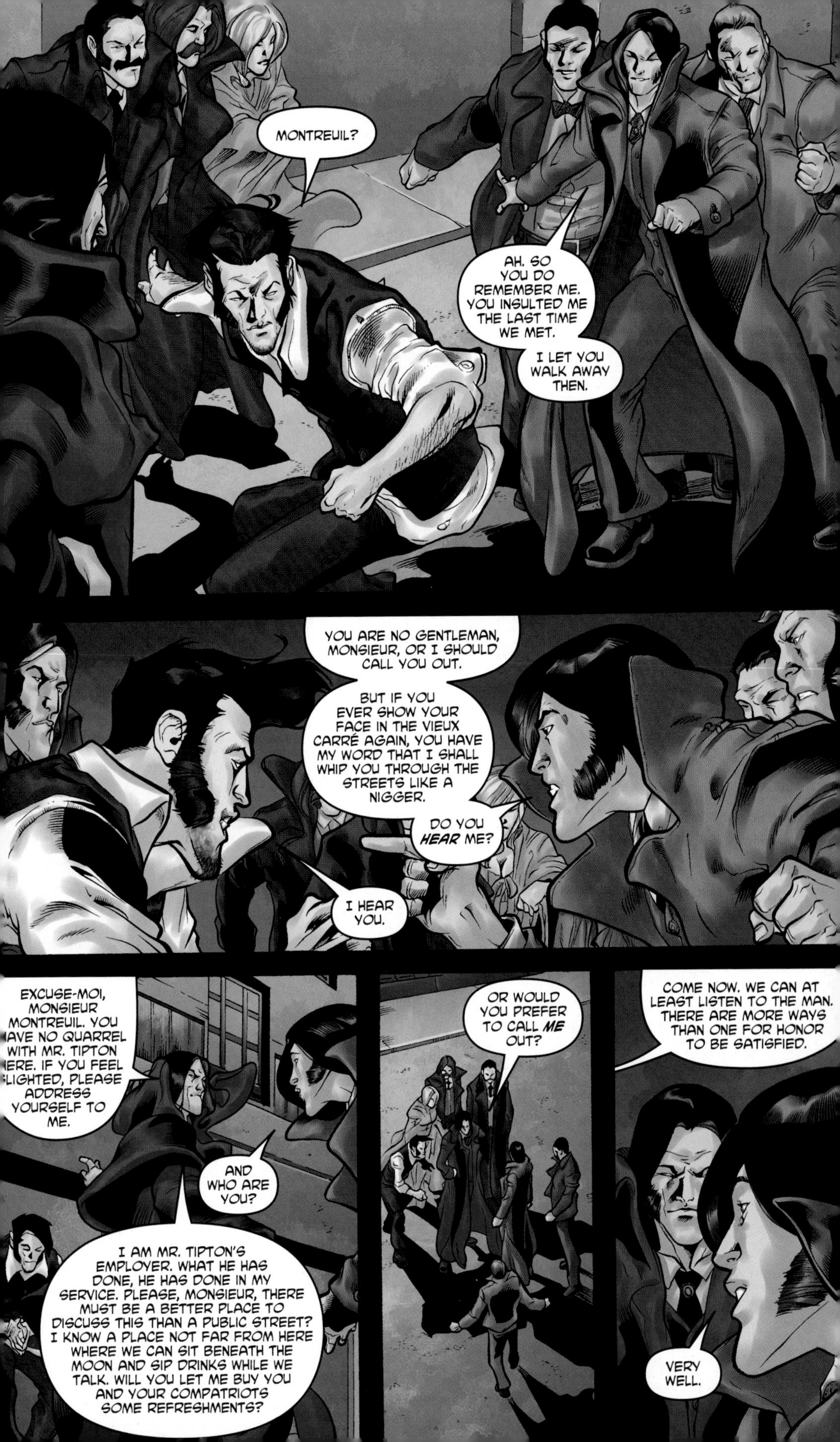
MONTREUIL?
AH. SO YOU DO REMEMBER ME. YOU INSULTED ME THE LAST TIME WE MET.
I LET YOU WALK AWAY THEN.
YOU ARE NO GENTLEMAN, MONSIEUR, OR I SHOULD CALL YOU OUT.
BUT IF YOU EVER SHOW YOUR FACE IN THE VIEUX CARRÉ AGAIN, YOU HAVE MY WORD THAT I SHALL WHIP YOU THROUGH THE STREETS LIKE A NIGGER.
DO YOU *HEAR* ME?
I HEAR YOU.
EXCUSE-MOI, MONSIEUR MONTREUIL. YOU AVE NO QUARREL WITH MR. TIPTON ERE. IF YOU FEEL LIGHTED, PLEASE ADDRESS YOURSELF TO ME.
AND WHO ARE YOU?
I AM MR. TIPTON'S EMPLOYER. WHAT HE HAS DONE, HE HAS DONE IN MY SERVICE. PLEASE, MONSIEUR, THERE MUST BE A BETTER PLACE TO DISCUSS THIS THAN A PUBLIC STREET? I KNOW A PLACE NOT FAR FROM HERE WHERE WE CAN SIT BENEATH THE MOON AND SIP DRINKS WHILE WE TALK. WILL YOU LET ME BUY YOU AND YOUR COMPATRIOTS SOME REFRESHMENTS?
OR WOULD YOU PREFER TO CALL *ME* OUT?
COME NOW. WE CAN AT LEAST LISTEN TO THE MAN. THERE ARE MORE WAYS THAN ONE FOR HONOR TO BE SATISFIED.
VERY WELL.

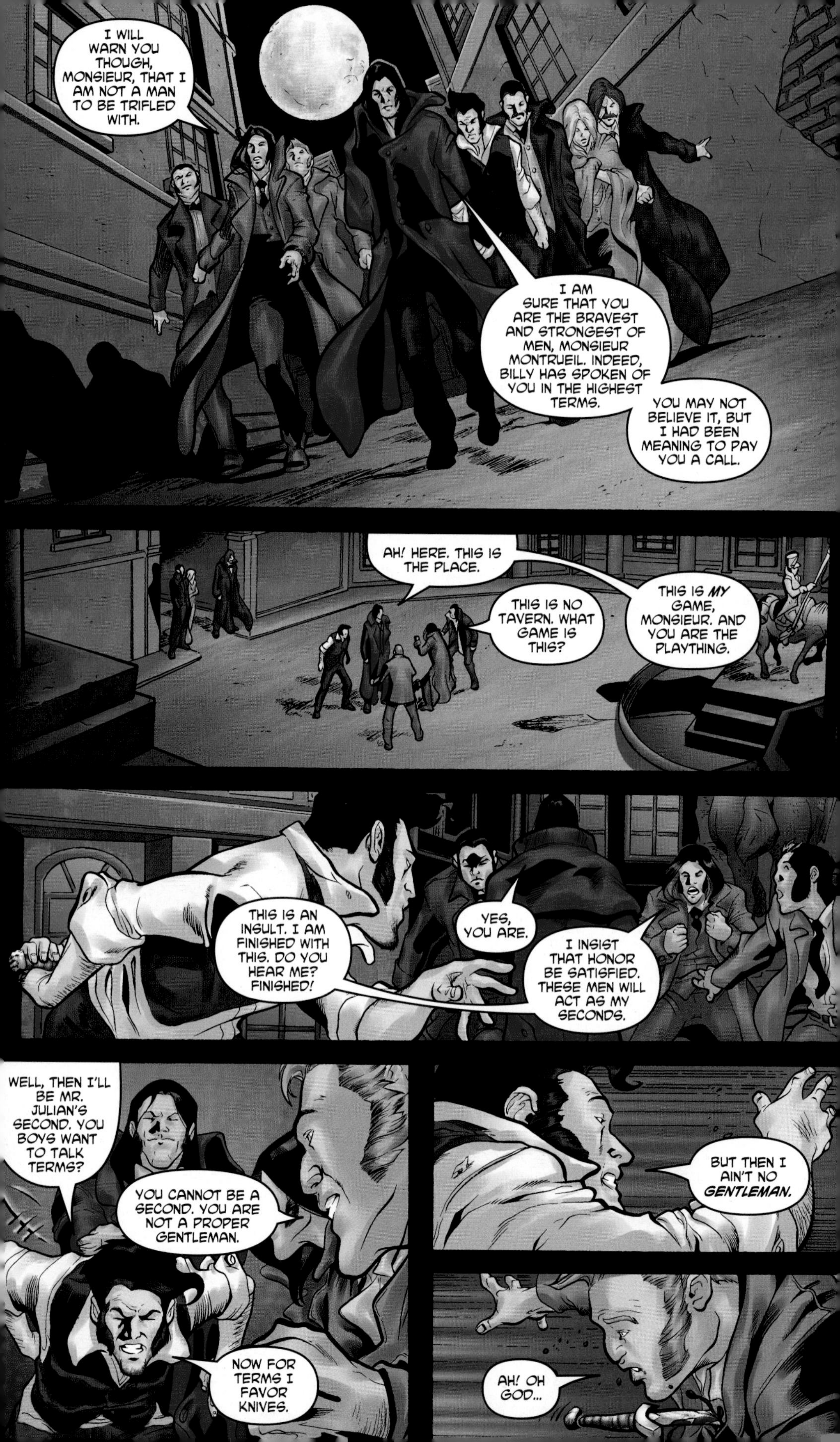
I WILL WARN YOU THOUGH, MONSIEUR, THAT I AM NOT A MAN TO BE TRIFLED WITH.
I AM SURE THAT YOU ARE THE BRAVEST AND STRONGEST OF MEN, MONSIEUR MONTRUEIL. INDEED, BILLY HAS SPOKEN OF YOU IN THE HIGHEST TERMS.
YOU MAY NOT BELIEVE IT, BUT I HAD BEEN MEANING TO PAY YOU A CALL.
AH! HERE. THIS IS THE PLACE.
THIS IS NO TAVERN. WHAT GAME IS THIS?
THIS IS *MY* GAME, MONSIEUR. AND YOU ARE THE PLAYTHING.
THIS IS AN INSULT. I AM FINISHED WITH THIS. DO YOU HEAR ME? FINISHED!
YES, YOU ARE.
I INSIST THAT HONOR BE SATISFIED. THESE MEN WILL ACT AS MY SECONDS.
WELL, THEN I'LL BE MR. JULIAN'S SECOND. YOU BOYS WANT TO TALK TERMS?
YOU CANNOT BE A SECOND. YOU ARE NOT A PROPER GENTLEMAN.
NOW FOR TERMS I FAVOR KNIVES.
BUT THEN I AIN'T NO ***GENTLEMAN.***
AH! OH GOD...

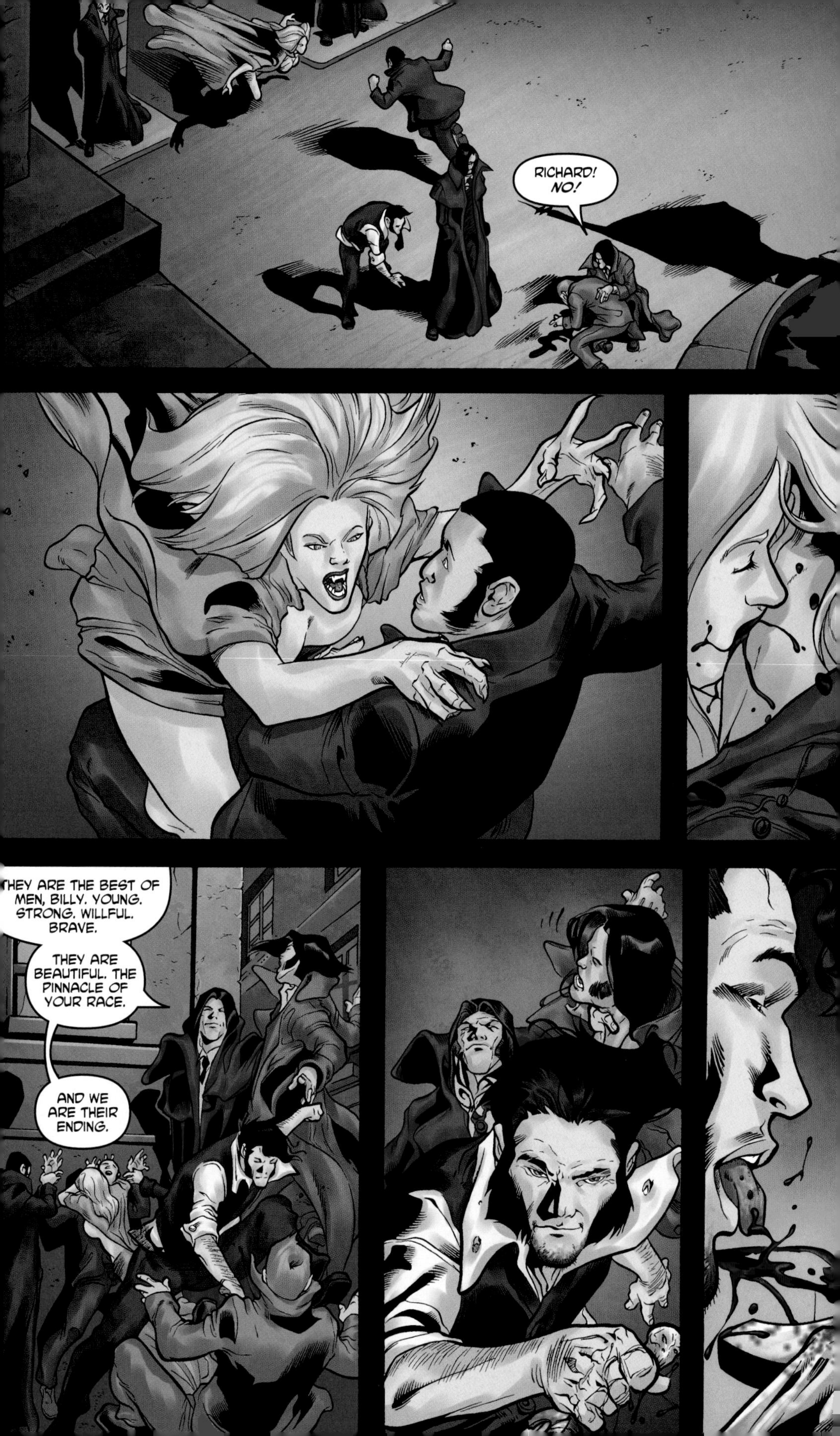
RICHARD! NO!
THEY ARE THE BEST OF MEN, BILLY. YOUNG. STRONG. WILLFUL. BRAVE.
THEY ARE BEAUTIFUL. THE PINNACLE OF YOUR RACE.
AND WE ARE THEIR ENDING.

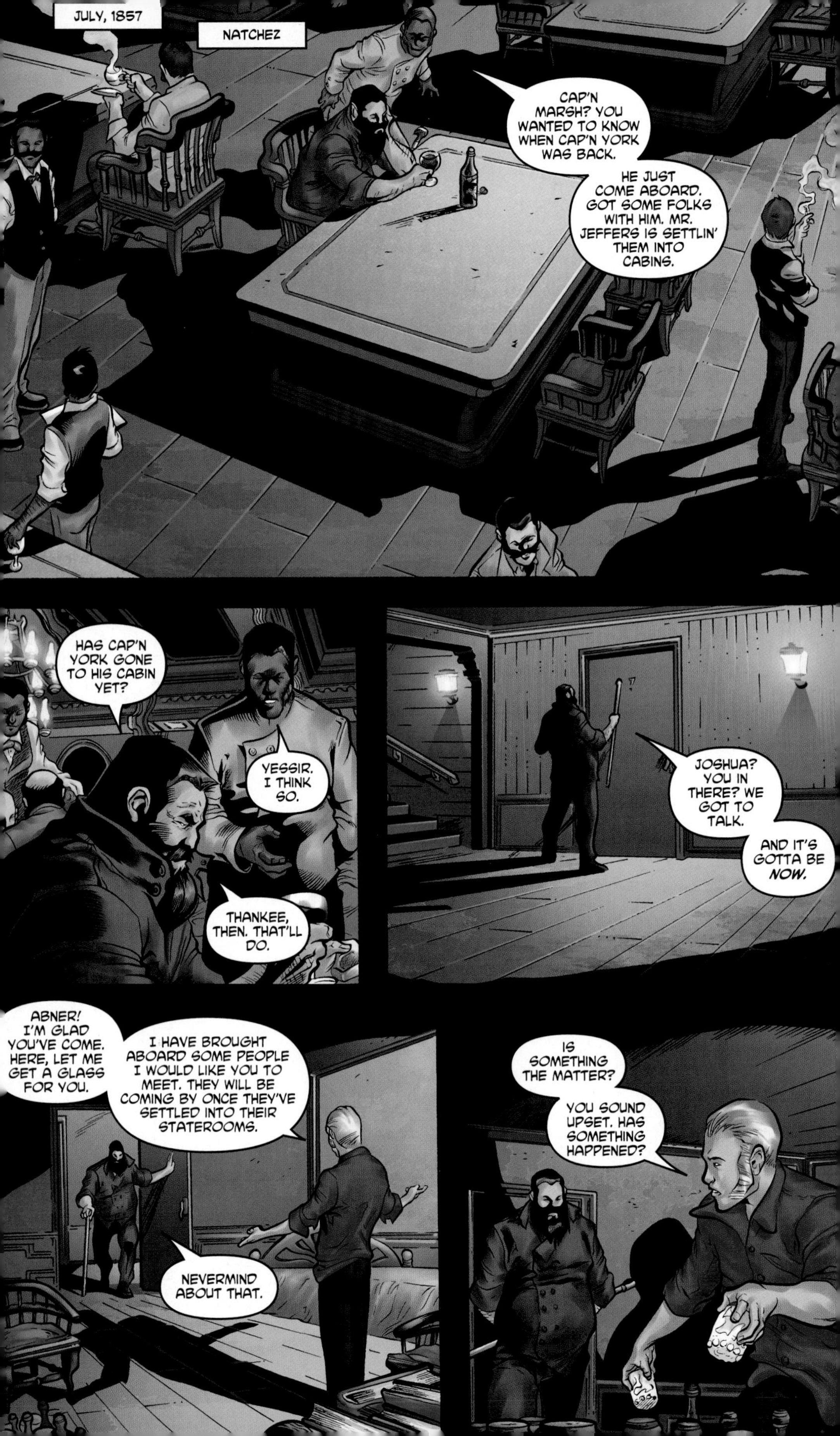

JULY, 1857
NATCHEZ
CAP'N MARSH? YOU WANTED TO KNOW WHEN CAP'N YORK WAS BACK.
HE JUST COME ABOARD. GOT SOME FOLKS WITH HIM. MR. JEFFERS IS SETTLIN' THEM INTO CABINS.
HAS CAP'N YORK GONE TO HIS CABIN YET?
YESSIR. I THINK SO.
THANKEE, THEN. THAT'LL DO.
7
JOSHUA? YOU IN THERE? WE GOT TO TALK.
AND IT'S GOTTA BE *NOW.*
ABNER! I'M GLAD YOU'VE COME. HERE, LET ME GET A GLASS FOR YOU.
I HAVE BROUGHT ABOARD SOME PEOPLE I WOULD LIKE YOU TO MEET. THEY WILL BE COMING BY ONCE THEY'VE SETTLED INTO THEIR STATEROOMS.
NEVERMIND ABOUT THAT.
IS SOMETHING THE MATTER?
YOU SOUND UPSET. HAS SOMETHING HAPPENED?

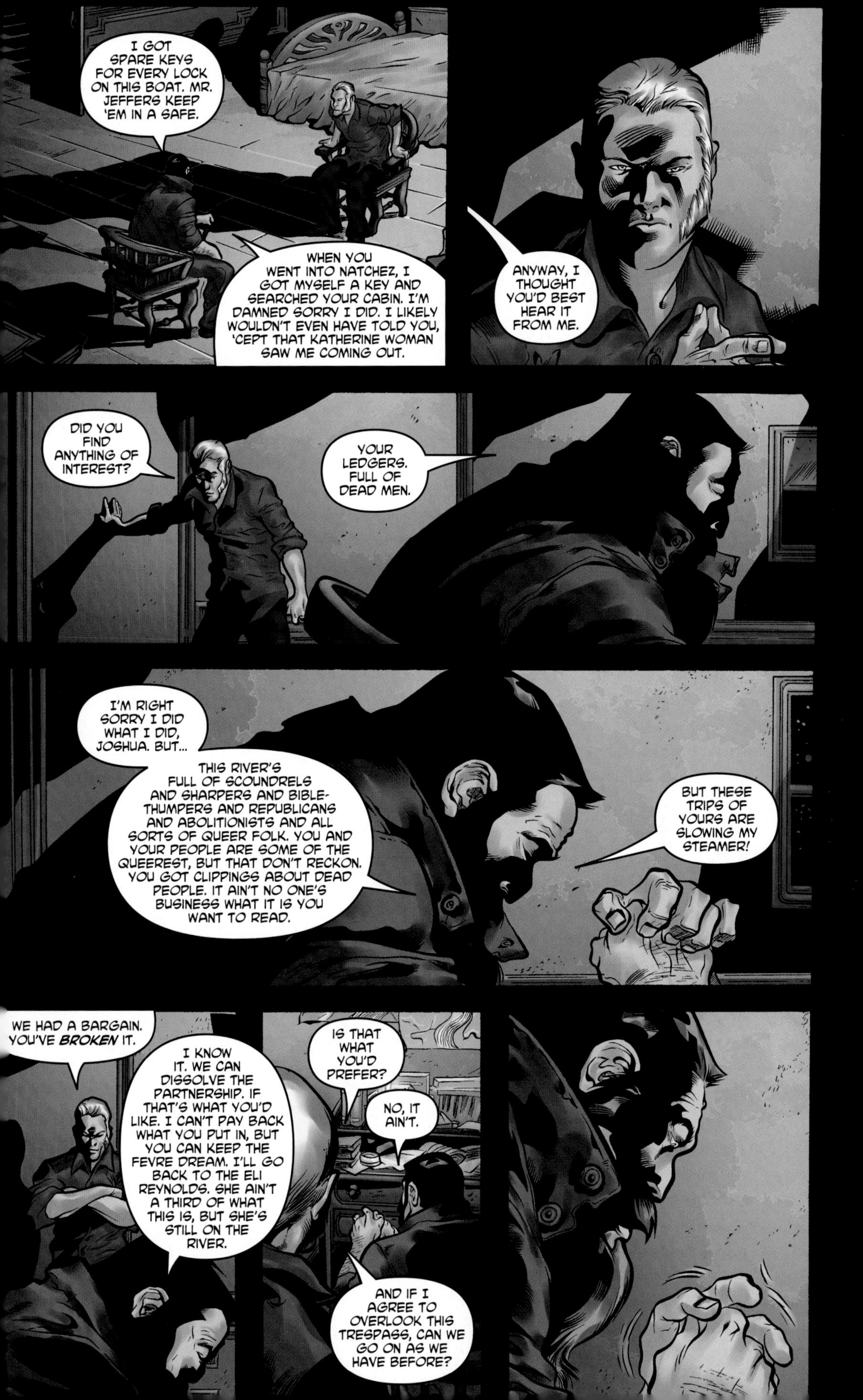

I GOT SPARE KEYS FOR EVERY LOCK ON THIS BOAT. MR. JEFFERS KEEP 'EM IN A SAFE.
WHEN YOU WENT INTO NATCHEZ, I GOT MYSELF A KEY AND SEARCHED YOUR CABIN. I'M DAMNED SORRY I DID. I LIKELY WOULDN'T EVEN HAVE TOLD YOU, 'CEPT THAT KATHERINE WOMAN SAW ME COMING OUT.
ANYWAY, I THOUGHT YOU'D BEST HEAR IT FROM ME.
DID YOU FIND ANYTHING OF INTEREST?
YOUR LEDGERS. FULL OF DEAD MEN.
I'M RIGHT SORRY I DID WHAT I DID, JOSHUA. BUT...
THIS RIVER'S FULL OF SCOUNDRELS AND SHARPERS AND BIBLE-THUMPERS AND REPUBLICANS AND ABOLITIONISTS AND ALL SORTS OF QUEER FOLK. YOU AND YOUR PEOPLE ARE SOME OF THE QUEEREST, BUT THAT DON'T RECKON. YOU GOT CLIPPINGS ABOUT DEAD PEOPLE. IT AIN'T NO ONE'S BUSINESS WHAT IT IS YOU WANT TO READ.
BUT THESE TRIPS OF YOURS ARE SLOWING MY STEAMER!
WE HAD A BARGAIN. YOU'VE *BROKEN* IT.
I KNOW IT. WE CAN DISSOLVE THE PARTNERSHIP. IF THAT'S WHAT YOU'D LIKE. I CAN'T PAY BACK WHAT YOU PUT IN, BUT YOU CAN KEEP THE FEVRE DREAM. I'LL GO BACK TO THE ELI REYNOLDS. SHE AIN'T A THIRD OF WHAT THIS IS, BUT SHE'S STILL ON THE RIVER.
IS THAT WHAT YOU'D PREFER?
NO, IT AIN'T.
AND IF I AGREE TO OVERLOOK THIS TRESPASS, CAN WE GO ON AS WE HAVE BEFORE?

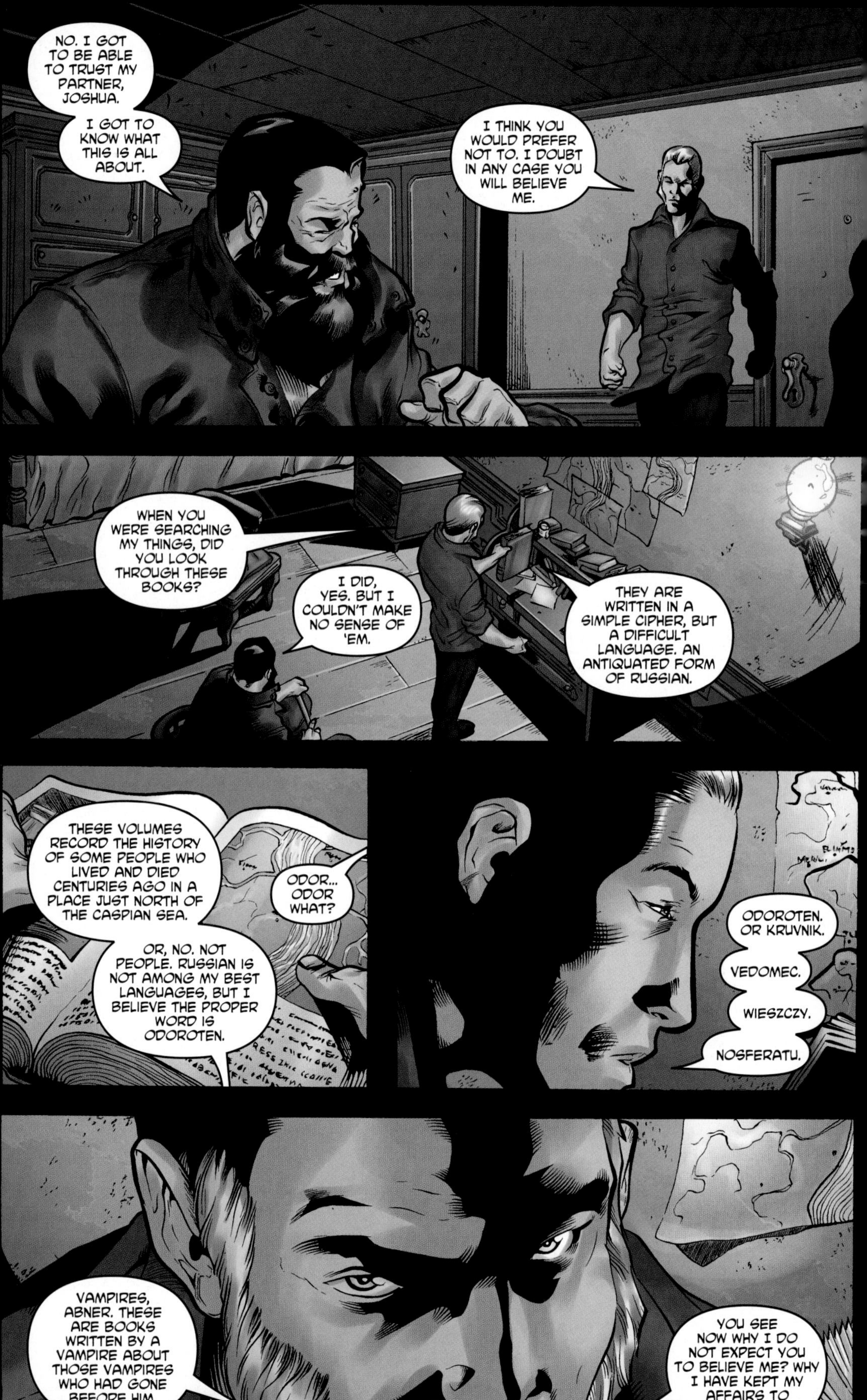
NO. I GOT TO BE ABLE TO TRUST MY PARTNER, JOSHUA.
I GOT TO KNOW WHAT THIS IS ALL ABOUT.
I THINK YOU WOULD PREFER NOT TO. I DOUBT IN ANY CASE YOU WILL BELIEVE ME.
WHEN YOU WERE SEARCHING MY THINGS, DID YOU LOOK THROUGH THESE BOOKS?
I DID, YES. BUT I COULDN'T MAKE NO SENSE OF 'EM.
THEY ARE WRITTEN IN A SIMPLE CIPHER, BUT A DIFFICULT LANGUAGE. AN ANTIQUATED FORM OF RUSSIAN.
THESE VOLUMES RECORD THE HISTORY OF SOME PEOPLE WHO LIVED AND DIED CENTURIES AGO IN A PLACE JUST NORTH OF THE CASPIAN SEA.
OR, NO. NOT PEOPLE. RUSSIAN IS NOT AMONG MY BEST LANGUAGES, BUT I BELIEVE THE PROPER WORD IS ODOROTEN.
ODOR... ODOR WHAT?
ODOROTEN. OR KRUVNIK.
VEDOMEC.
WIESZCZY.
NOSFERATU.
VAMPIRES, ABNER. THESE ARE BOOKS WRITTEN BY A VAMPIRE ABOUT THOSE VAMPIRES WHO HAD GONE BEFORE HIM.
YOU SEE NOW WHY I DO NOT EXPECT YOU TO BELIEVE ME? WHY I HAVE KEPT MY AFFAIRS TO MYSELF?

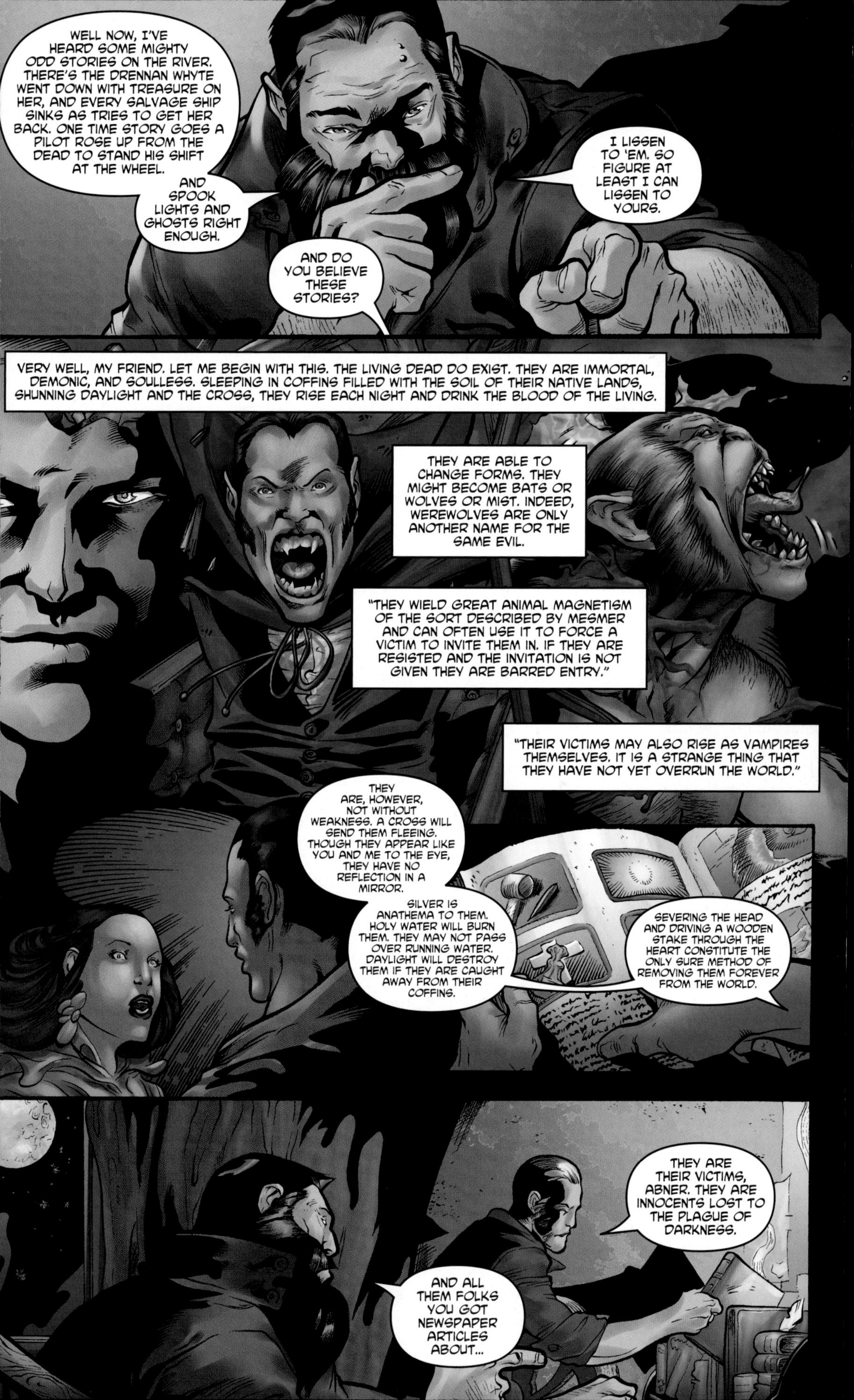
WELL NOW, I'VE HEARD SOME MIGHTY ODD STORIES ON THE RIVER. THERE'S THE DRENNAN WHYTE WENT DOWN WITH TREASURE ON HER, AND EVERY SALVAGE SHIP SINKS AS TRIES TO GET HER BACK. ONE TIME STORY GOES A PILOT ROSE UP FROM THE DEAD TO STAND HIS SHIFT AT THE WHEEL.
AND SPOOK LIGHTS AND GHOSTS RIGHT ENOUGH.
AND DO YOU BELIEVE THESE STORIES?
I LISSEN TO 'EM. SO FIGURE AT LEAST I CAN LISSEN TO YOURS.
VERY WELL, MY FRIEND. LET ME BEGIN WITH THIS. THE LIVING DEAD DO EXIST. THEY ARE IMMORTAL, DEMONIC, AND SOULLESS. SLEEPING IN COFFINS FILLED WITH THE SOIL OF THEIR NATIVE LANDS, SHUNNING DAYLIGHT AND THE CROSS, THEY RISE EACH NIGHT AND DRINK THE BLOOD OF THE LIVING.
THEY ARE ABLE TO CHANGE FORMS. THEY MIGHT BECOME BATS OR WOLVES OR MIST. INDEED, WEREWOLVES ARE ONLY ANOTHER NAME FOR THE SAME EVIL.
"THEY WIELD GREAT ANIMAL MAGNETISM OF THE SORT DESCRIBED BY MESMER AND CAN OFTEN USE IT TO FORCE A VICTIM TO INVITE THEM IN. IF THEY ARE RESISTED AND THE INVITATION IS NOT GIVEN THEY ARE BARRED ENTRY."
"THEIR VICTIMS MAY ALSO RISE AS VAMPIRES THEMSELVES. IT IS A STRANGE THING THAT THEY HAVE NOT YET OVERRUN THE WORLD."
THEY ARE, HOWEVER, NOT WITHOUT WEAKNESS. A CROSS WILL SEND THEM FLEEING. THOUGH THEY APPEAR LIKE YOU AND ME TO THE EYE, THEY HAVE NO REFLECTION IN A MIRROR.
SILVER IS ANATHEMA TO THEM. HOLY WATER WILL BURN THEM. THEY MAY NOT PASS OVER RUNNING WATER. DAYLIGHT WILL DESTROY THEM IF THEY ARE CAUGHT AWAY FROM THEIR COFFINS.
SEVERING THE HEAD AND DRIVING A WOODEN STAKE THROUGH THE HEART CONSTITUTE THE ONLY SURE METHOD OF REMOVING THEM FOREVER FROM THE WORLD.
AND ALL THEM FOLKS YOU GOT NEWSPAPER ARTICLES ABOUT...
THEY ARE THEIR VICTIMS, ABNER. THEY ARE INNOCENTS LOST TO THE PLAGUE OF DARKNESS.

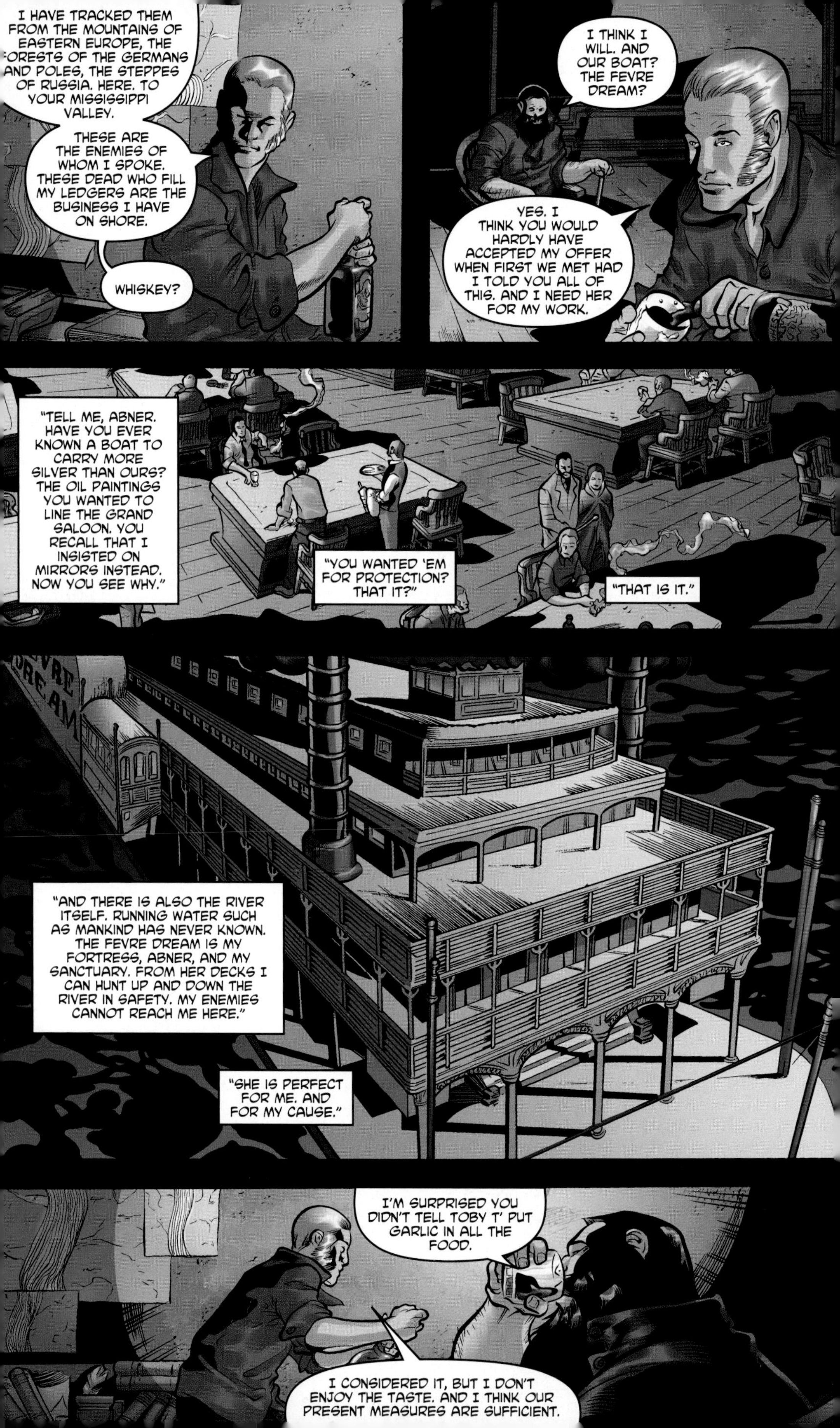

I HAVE TRACKED THEM FROM THE MOUNTAINS OF EASTERN EUROPE, THE FORESTS OF THE GERMANS AND POLES, THE STEPPES OF RUSSIA. HERE. TO YOUR MISSISSIPPI VALLEY.
THESE ARE THE ENEMIES OF WHOM I SPOKE. THESE DEAD WHO FILL MY LEDGERS ARE THE BUSINESS I HAVE ON SHORE.
WHISKEY?
I THINK I WILL. AND OUR BOAT? THE FEVRE DREAM?
YES. I THINK YOU WOULD HARDLY HAVE ACCEPTED MY OFFER WHEN FIRST WE MET HAD I TOLD YOU ALL OF THIS. AND I NEED HER FOR MY WORK.
"TELL ME, ABNER. HAVE YOU EVER KNOWN A BOAT TO CARRY MORE SILVER THAN OURS? THE OIL PAINTINGS YOU WANTED TO LINE THE GRAND SALOON. YOU RECALL THAT I INSISTED ON MIRRORS INSTEAD. NOW YOU SEE WHY."
"YOU WANTED 'EM FOR PROTECTION? THAT IT?"
"THAT IS IT."
FEVRE DREAM
"AND THERE IS ALSO THE RIVER ITSELF. RUNNING WATER SUCH AS MANKIND HAS NEVER KNOWN. THE FEVRE DREAM IS MY FORTRESS, ABNER, AND MY SANCTUARY. FROM HER DECKS I CAN HUNT UP AND DOWN THE RIVER IN SAFETY. MY ENEMIES CANNOT REACH ME HERE."
"SHE IS PERFECT FOR ME. AND FOR MY CAUSE."
I'M SURPRISED YOU DIDN'T TELL TOBY T' PUT GARLIC IN ALL THE FOOD.
I CONSIDERED IT, BUT I DON'T ENJOY THE TASTE. AND I THINK OUR PRESENT MEASURES ARE SUFFICIENT.

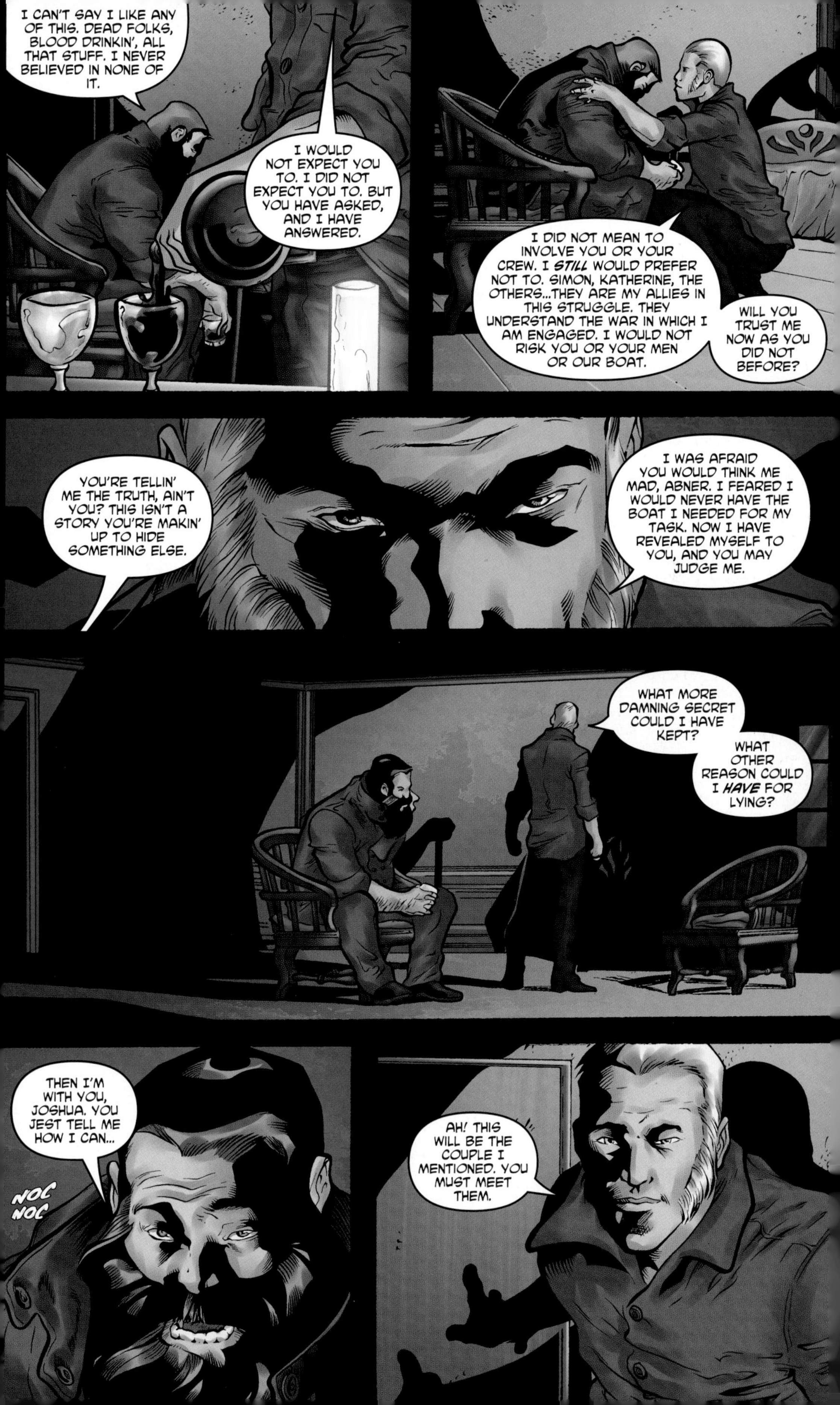
I CAN'T SAY I LIKE ANY OF THIS. DEAD FOLKS, BLOOD DRINKIN', ALL THAT STUFF. I NEVER BELIEVED IN NONE OF IT.
I WOULD NOT EXPECT YOU TO. I DID NOT EXPECT YOU TO. BUT YOU HAVE ASKED, AND I HAVE ANSWERED.
I DID NOT MEAN TO INVOLVE YOU OR YOUR CREW. I *STILL* WOULD PREFER NOT TO. SIMON, KATHERINE, THE OTHERS...THEY ARE MY ALLIES IN THIS STRUGGLE. THEY UNDERSTAND THE WAR IN WHICH I AM ENGAGED. I WOULD NOT RISK YOU OR YOUR MEN OR OUR BOAT.
WILL YOU TRUST ME NOW AS YOU DID NOT BEFORE?
YOU'RE TELLIN' ME THE TRUTH, AIN'T YOU? THIS ISN'T A STORY YOU'RE MAKIN' UP TO HIDE SOMETHING ELSE.
I WAS AFRAID YOU WOULD THINK ME MAD, ABNER. I FEARED I WOULD NEVER HAVE THE BOAT I NEEDED FOR MY TASK. NOW I HAVE REVEALED MYSELF TO YOU, AND YOU MAY JUDGE ME.
WHAT MORE DAMNING SECRET COULD I HAVE KEPT?
WHAT OTHER REASON COULD I *HAVE* FOR LYING?
THEN I'M WITH YOU, JOSHUA. YOU JEST TELL ME HOW I CAN...
NOC NOC
AH! THIS WILL BE THE COUPLE I MENTIONED. YOU MUST MEET THEM.

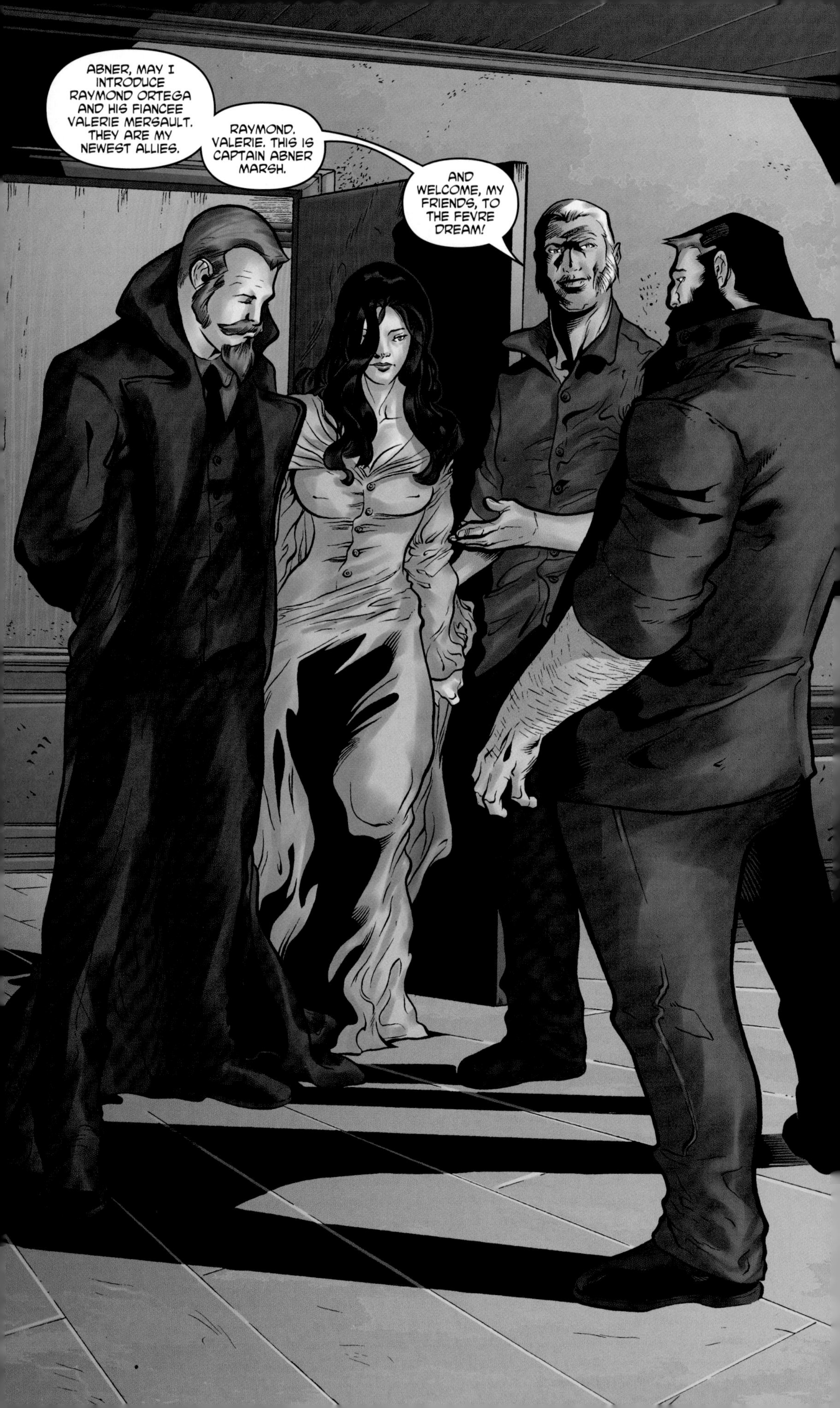
ABNER, MAY I INTRODUCE RAYMOND ORTEGA AND HIS FIANCEE VALERIE MERSAULT. THEY ARE MY NEWEST ALLIES.
RAYMOND. VALERIE. THIS IS CAPTAIN ABNER MARSH.
AND WELCOME, MY FRIENDS, TO THE FEVRE DREAM!

CHAPTER 4

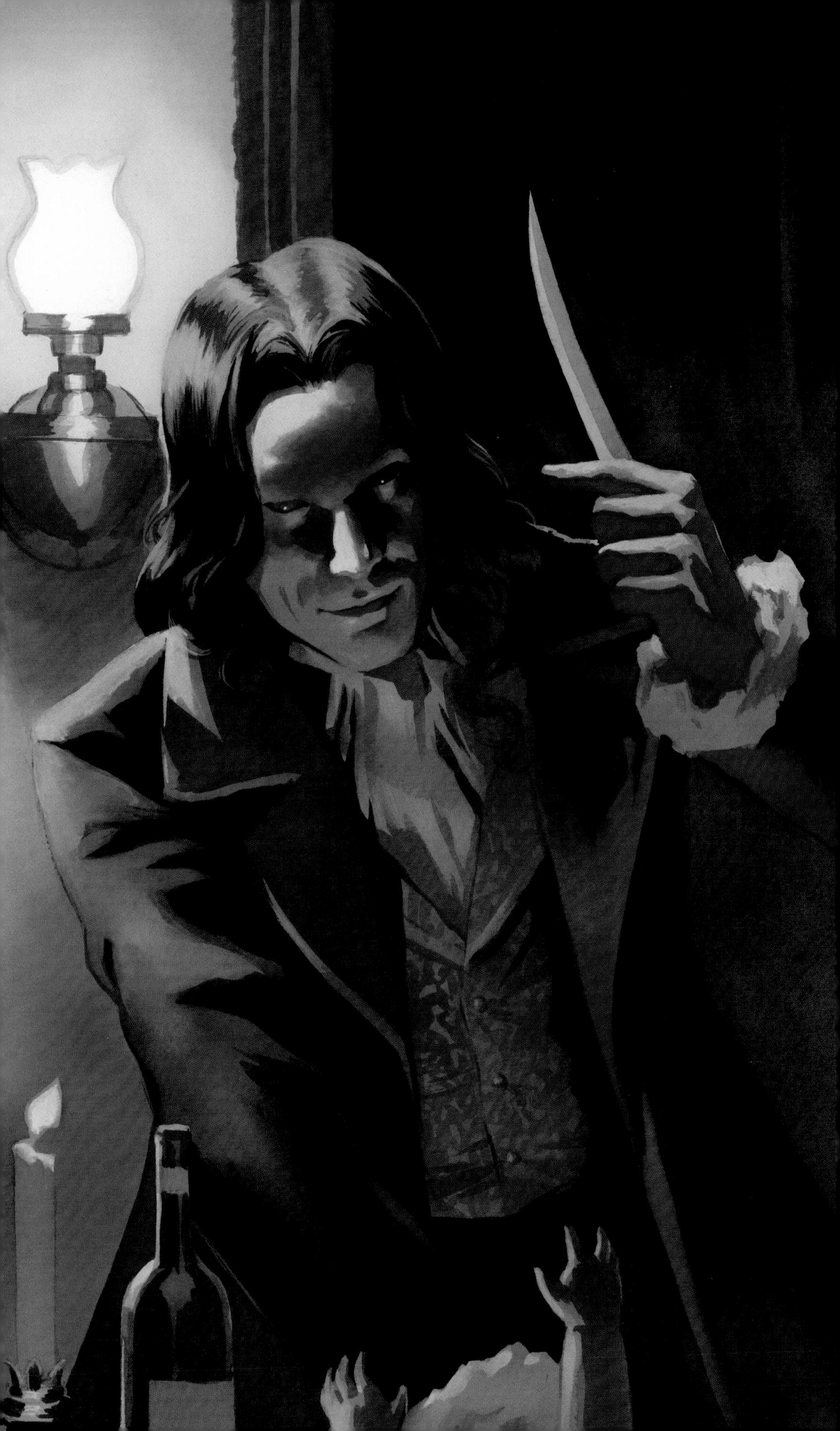

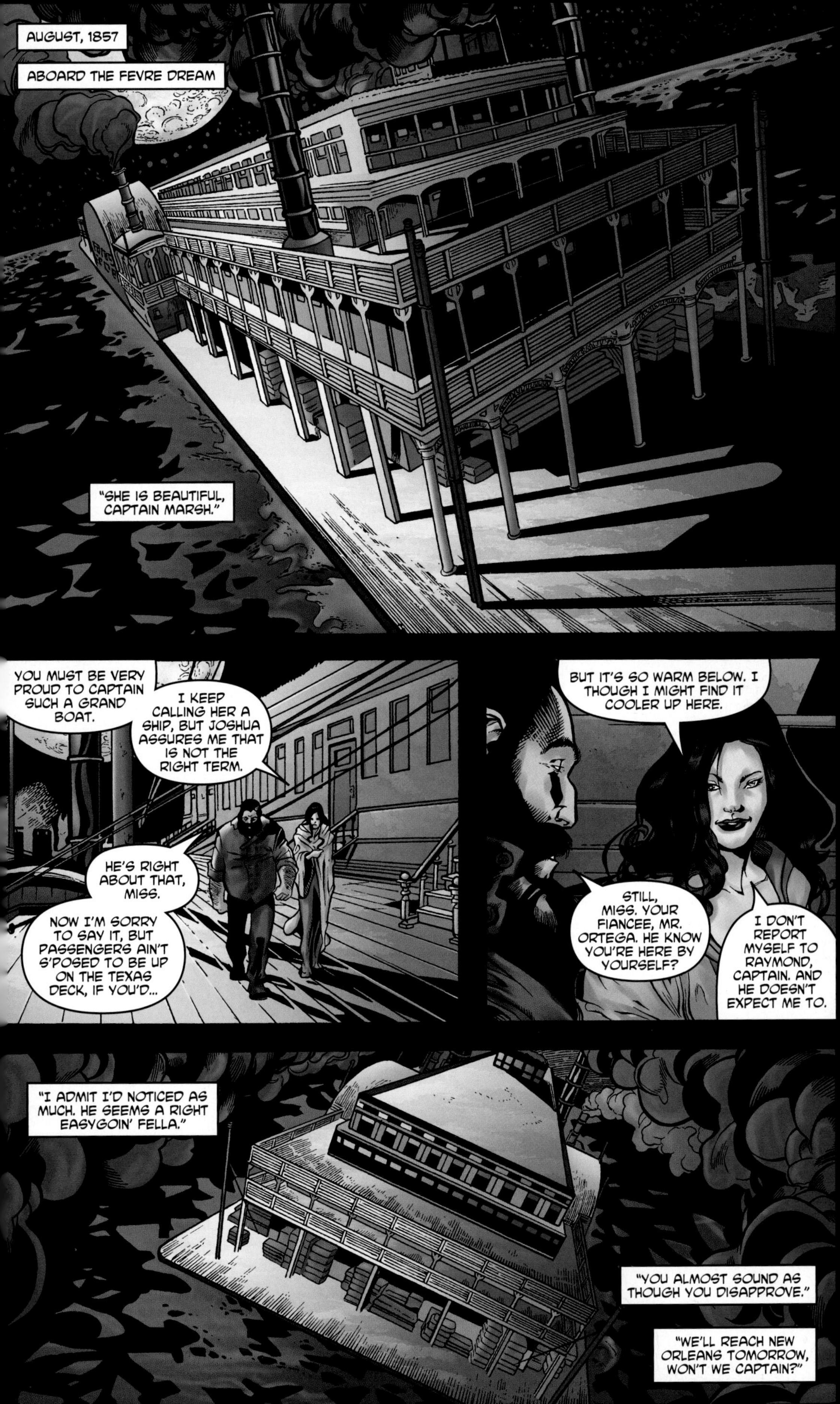
AUGUST, 1857
ABOARD THE FEVRE DREAM
"SHE IS BEAUTIFUL, CAPTAIN MARSH."
YOU MUST BE VERY PROUD TO CAPTAIN SUCH A GRAND BOAT.
I KEEP CALLING HER A SHIP, BUT JOSHUA ASSURES ME THAT IS NOT THE RIGHT TERM.
HE'S RIGHT ABOUT THAT, MISS.
NOW I'M SORRY TO SAY IT, BUT PASSENGERS AIN'T S'POSED TO BE UP ON THE TEXAS DECK, IF YOU'D...
BUT IT'S SO WARM BELOW. I THOUGH I MIGHT FIND IT COOLER UP HERE.
STILL, MISS. YOUR FIANCEE, MR. ORTEGA. HE KNOW YOU'RE HERE BY YOURSELF?
I DON'T REPORT MYSELF TO RAYMOND, CAPTAIN. AND HE DOESN'T EXPECT ME TO.
"I ADMIT I'D NOTICED AS MUCH. HE SEEMS A RIGHT EASYGOIN' FELLA."
"YOU ALMOST SOUND AS THOUGH YOU DISAPPROVE."
"WE'LL REACH NEW ORLEANS TOMORROW, WON'T WE CAPTAIN?"

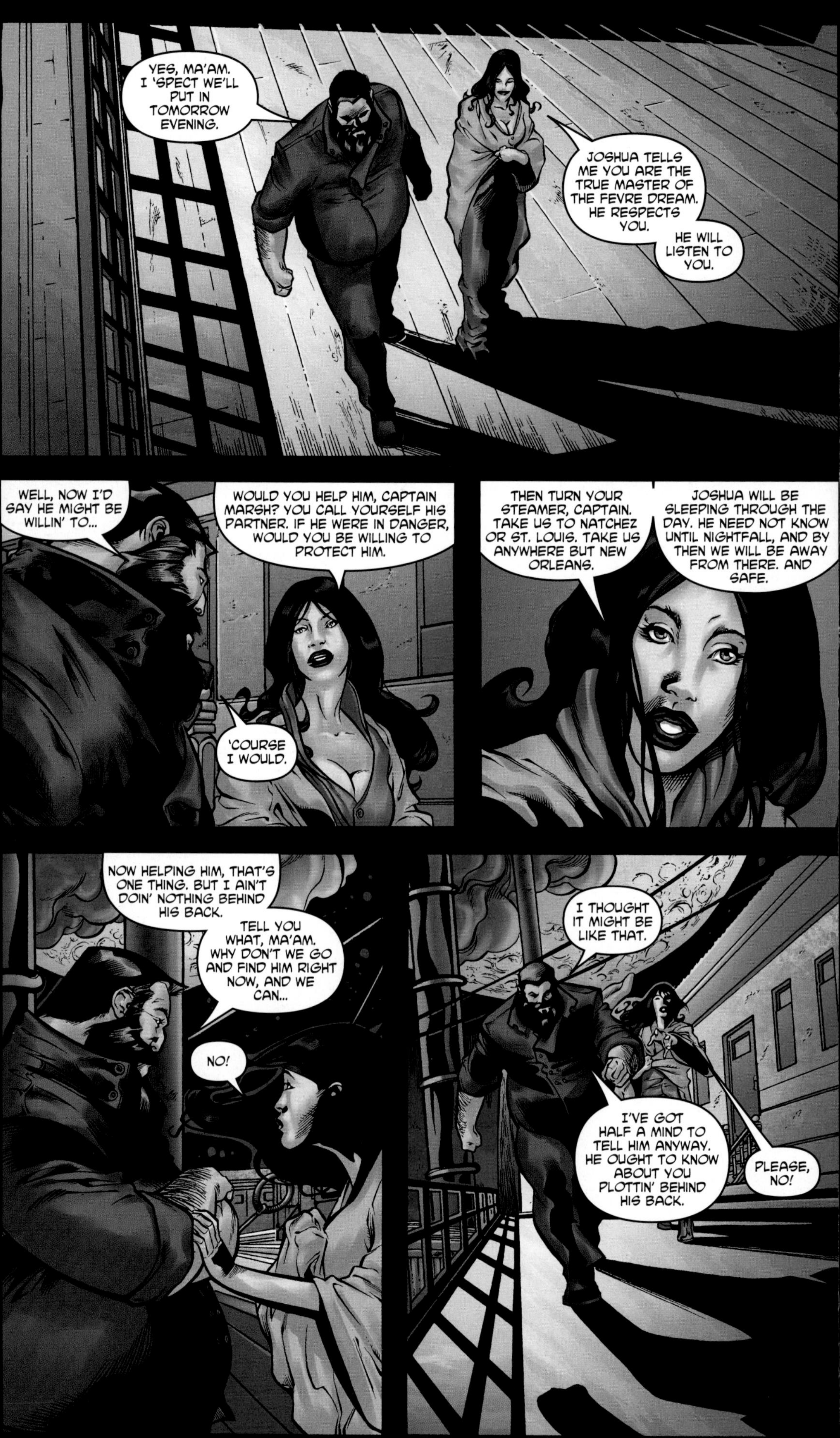
YES, MA'AM. I 'SPECT WE'LL PUT IN TOMORROW EVENING.
JOSHUA TELLS ME YOU ARE THE TRUE MASTER OF THE FEVRE DREAM. HE RESPECTS YOU.
HE WILL LISTEN TO YOU.
WELL, NOW I'D SAY HE MIGHT BE WILLIN' TO...
WOULD YOU HELP HIM, CAPTAIN MARSH? YOU CALL YOURSELF HIS PARTNER. IF HE WERE IN DANGER, WOULD YOU BE WILLING TO PROTECT HIM.
'COURSE I WOULD.
THEN TURN YOUR STEAMER, CAPTAIN. TAKE US TO NATCHEZ OR ST. LOUIS. TAKE US ANYWHERE BUT NEW ORLEANS.
JOSHUA WILL BE SLEEPING THROUGH THE DAY. HE NEED NOT KNOW UNTIL NIGHTFALL, AND BY THEN WE WILL BE AWAY FROM THERE. AND SAFE.
NOW HELPING HIM, THAT'S ONE THING. BUT I AIN'T DOIN' NOTHING BEHIND HIS BACK.
TELL YOU WHAT, MA'AM. WHY DON'T WE GO AND FIND HIM RIGHT NOW, AND WE CAN...
NO!
I THOUGHT IT MIGHT BE LIKE THAT.
I'VE GOT HALF A MIND TO TELL HIM ANYWAY. HE OUGHT TO KNOW ABOUT YOU PLOTTIN' BEHIND HIS BACK.
PLEASE, NO!

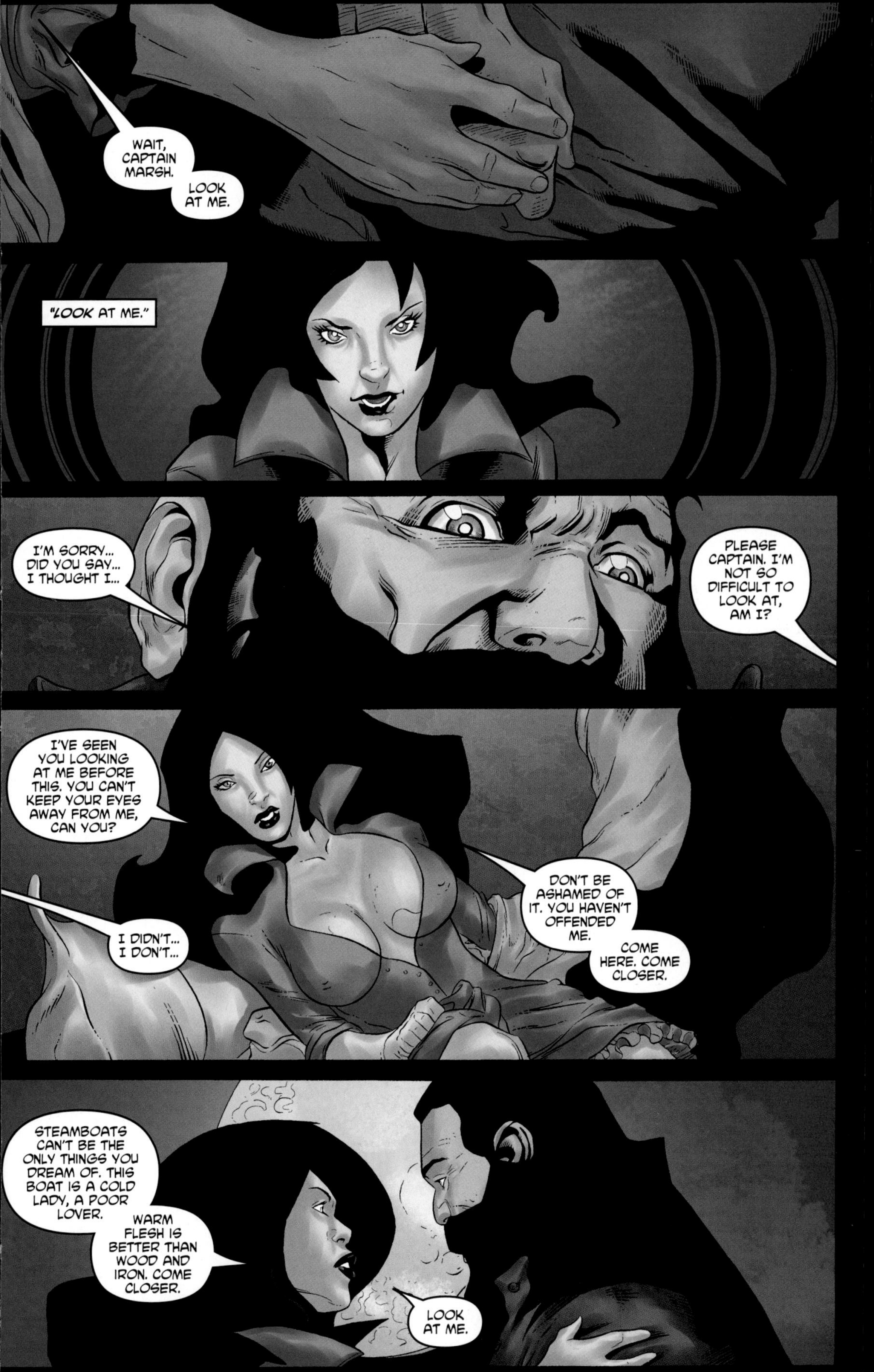
WAIT, CAPTAIN MARSH.
LOOK AT ME.
"LOOK AT ME."
I'M SORRY... DID YOU SAY... I THOUGHT I...
PLEASE CAPTAIN. I'M NOT SO DIFFICULT TO LOOK AT, AM I?
I'VE SEEN YOU LOOKING AT ME BEFORE THIS. YOU CAN'T KEEP YOUR EYES AWAY FROM ME, CAN YOU?
I DIDN'T... I DON'T...
DON'T BE ASHAMED OF IT. YOU HAVEN'T OFFENDED ME.
COME HERE. COME CLOSER.
STEAMBOATS CAN'T BE THE ONLY THINGS YOU DREAM OF. THIS BOAT IS A COLD LADY, A POOR LOVER.
WARM FLESH IS BETTER THAN WOOD AND IRON. COME CLOSER.
LOOK AT ME.

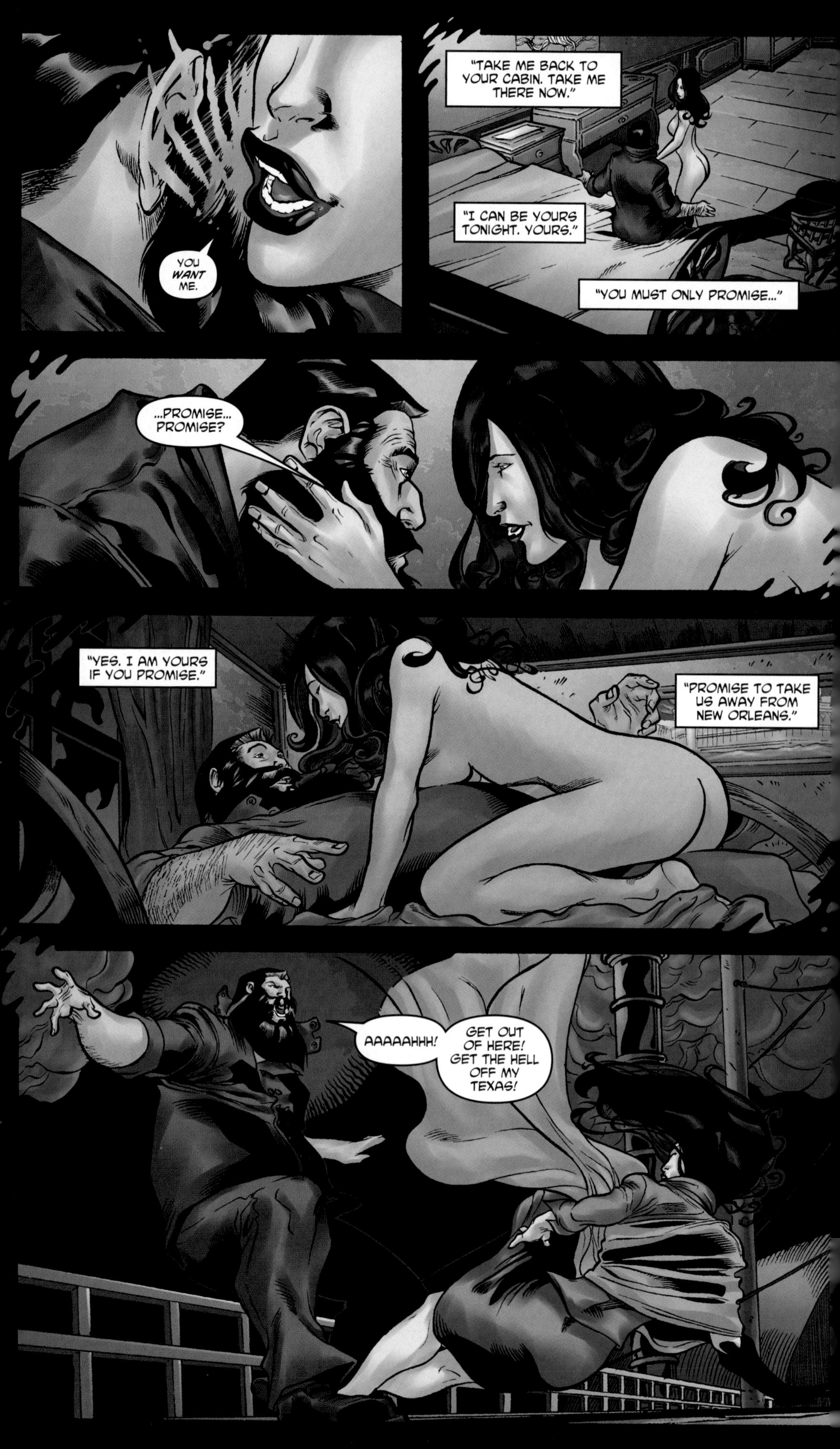
YOU *WANT* ME.
"TAKE ME BACK TO YOUR CABIN. TAKE ME THERE NOW."
"I CAN BE YOURS TONIGHT. YOURS."
"YOU MUST ONLY PROMISE..."
...PROMISE... PROMISE?
"YES. I AM YOURS IF YOU PROMISE."
"PROMISE TO TAKE US AWAY FROM NEW ORLEANS."
AAAAAHHH!
GET OUT OF HERE! GET THE HELL OFF MY TEXAS!

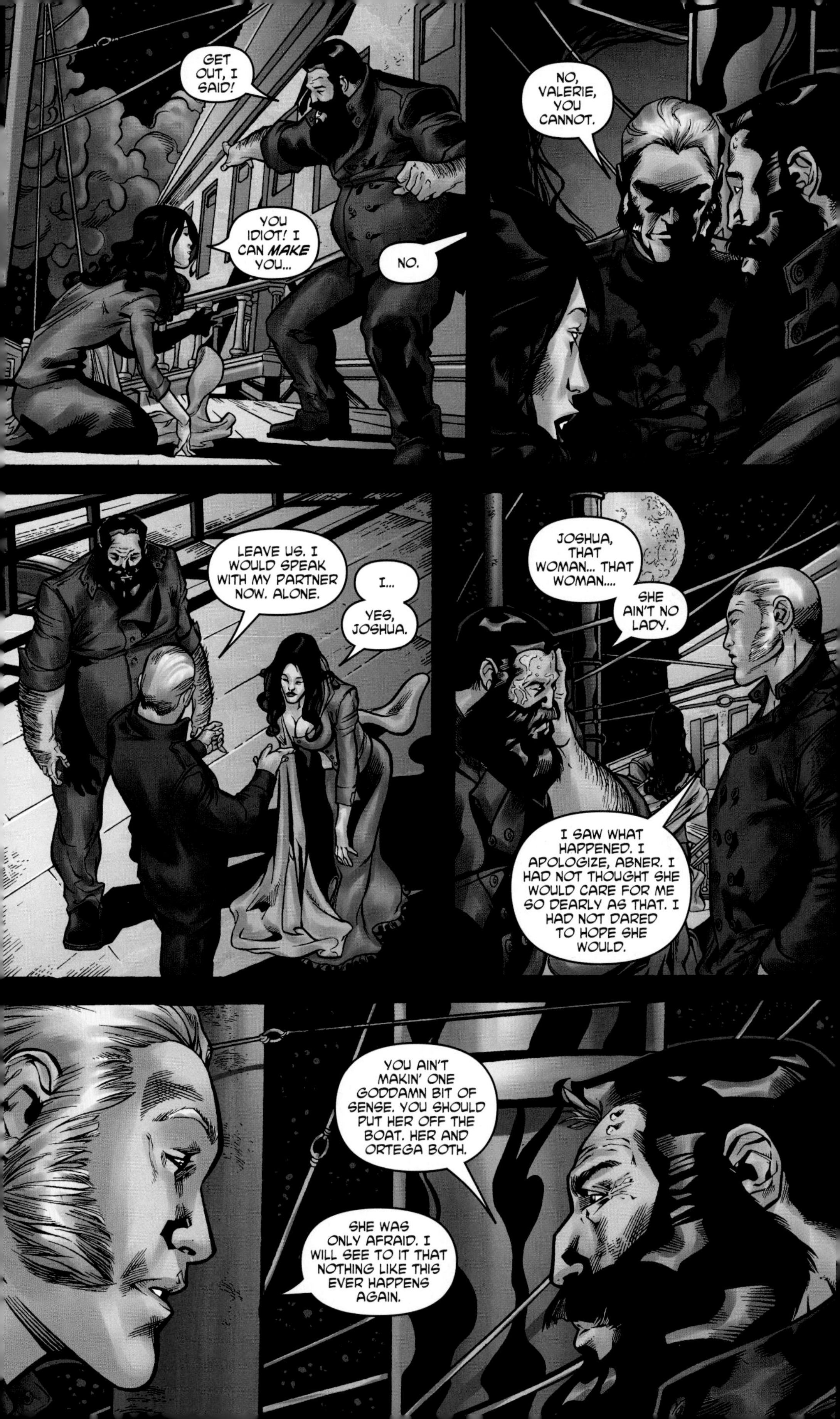
GET OUT, I SAID!
YOU IDIOT! I CAN *MAKE* YOU...
NO.
NO, VALERIE, YOU CANNOT.
LEAVE US. I WOULD SPEAK WITH MY PARTNER NOW. ALONE.
I...
YES, JOSHUA.
JOSHUA, THAT WOMAN... THAT WOMAN....
SHE AIN'T NO LADY.
I SAW WHAT HAPPENED. I APOLOGIZE, ABNER. I HAD NOT THOUGHT SHE WOULD CARE FOR ME SO DEARLY AS THAT. I HAD NOT DARED TO HOPE SHE WOULD.
YOU AIN'T MAKIN' ONE GODDAMN BIT OF SENSE. YOU SHOULD PUT HER OFF THE BOAT. HER AND ORTEGA BOTH.
SHE WAS ONLY AFRAID. I WILL SEE TO IT THAT NOTHING LIKE THIS EVER HAPPENS AGAIN.

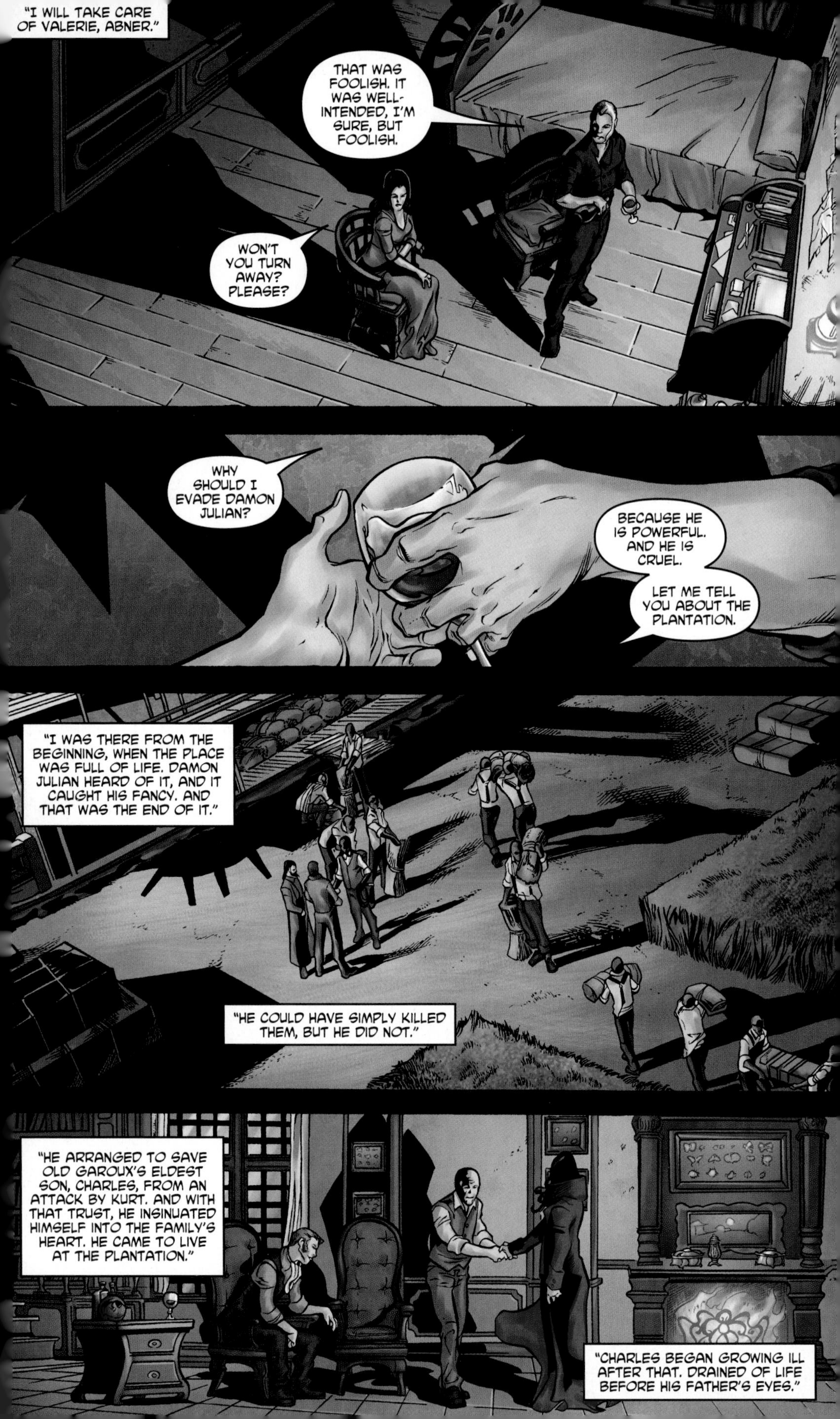
"I WILL TAKE CARE OF VALERIE, ABNER."
THAT WAS FOOLISH. IT WAS WELL-INTENDED, I'M SURE, BUT FOOLISH.
WON'T YOU TURN AWAY? PLEASE?
WHY SHOULD I EVADE DAMON JULIAN?
BECAUSE HE IS POWERFUL. AND HE IS CRUEL.
LET ME TELL YOU ABOUT THE PLANTATION.
"I WAS THERE FROM THE BEGINNING, WHEN THE PLACE WAS FULL OF LIFE. DAMON JULIAN HEARD OF IT, AND IT CAUGHT HIS FANCY. AND THAT WAS THE END OF IT."
"HE COULD HAVE SIMPLY KILLED THEM, BUT HE DID NOT."
"HE ARRANGED TO SAVE OLD GAROUX'S ELDEST SON, CHARLES, FROM AN ATTACK BY KURT. AND WITH THAT TRUST, HE INSINUATED HIMSELF INTO THE FAMILY'S HEART. HE CAME TO LIVE AT THE PLANTATION."
"CHARLES BEGAN GROWING ILL AFTER THAT. DRAINED OF LIFE BEFORE HIS FATHER'S EYES."

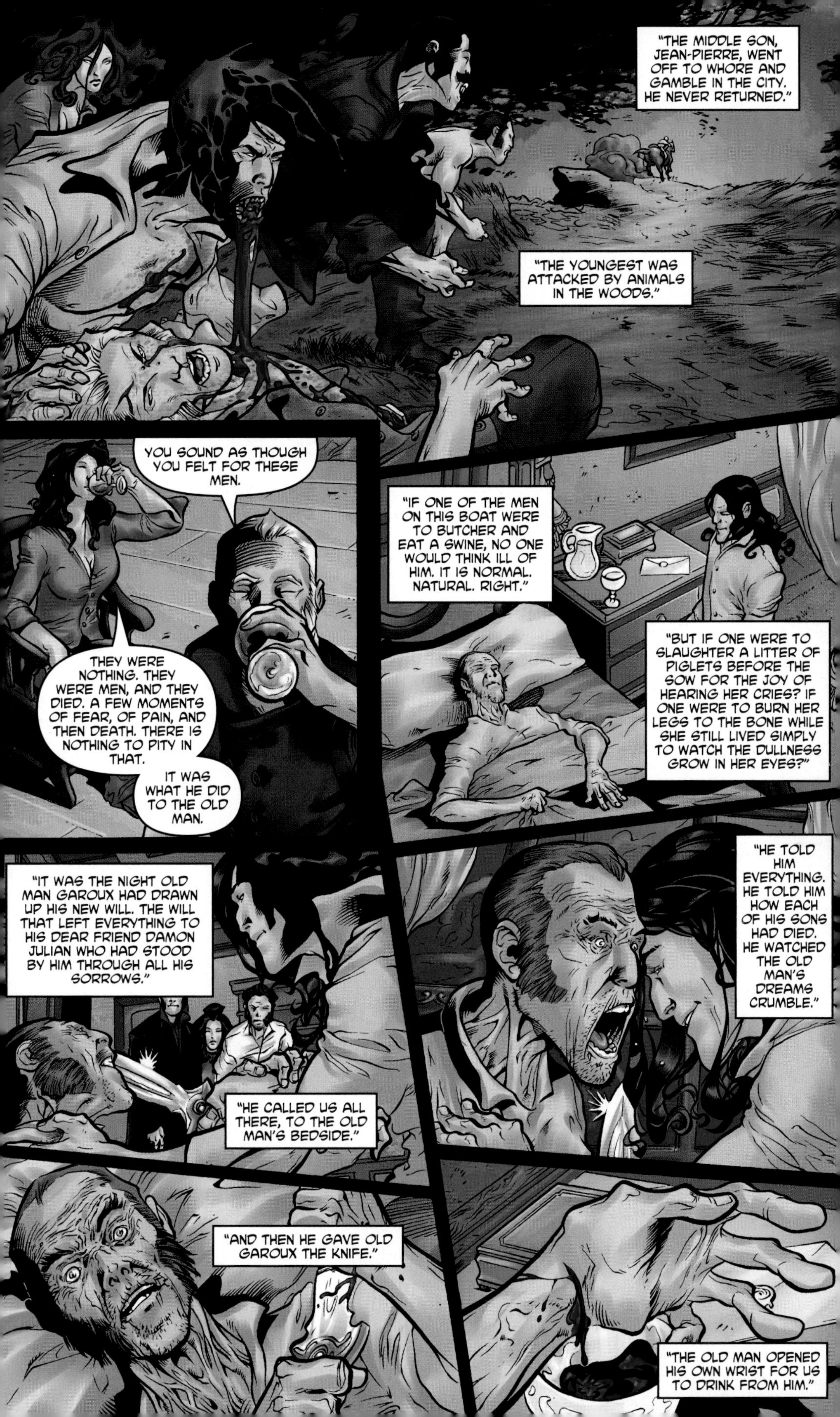
"THE MIDDLE SON, JEAN-PIERRE, WENT OFF TO WHORE AND GAMBLE IN THE CITY. HE NEVER RETURNED."
"THE YOUNGEST WAS ATTACKED BY ANIMALS IN THE WOODS."
YOU SOUND AS THOUGH YOU FELT FOR THESE MEN.
THEY WERE NOTHING. THEY WERE MEN, AND THEY DIED. A FEW MOMENTS OF FEAR, OF PAIN, AND THEN DEATH. THERE IS NOTHING TO PITY IN THAT.
IT WAS WHAT HE DID TO THE OLD MAN.
"IF ONE OF THE MEN ON THIS BOAT WERE TO BUTCHER AND EAT A SWINE, NO ONE WOULD THINK ILL OF HIM. IT IS NORMAL. NATURAL. RIGHT."
"BUT IF ONE WERE TO SLAUGHTER A LITTER OF PIGLETS BEFORE THE SOW FOR THE JOY OF HEARING HER CRIES? IF ONE WERE TO BURN HER LEGS TO THE BONE WHILE SHE STILL LIVED SIMPLY TO WATCH THE DULLNESS GROW IN HER EYES?"
"IT WAS THE NIGHT OLD MAN GAROUX HAD DRAWN UP HIS NEW WILL. THE WILL THAT LEFT EVERYTHING TO HIS DEAR FRIEND DAMON JULIAN WHO HAD STOOD BY HIM THROUGH ALL HIS SORROWS."
"HE CALLED US ALL THERE, TO THE OLD MAN'S BEDSIDE."
"HE TOLD HIM EVERYTHING. HE TOLD HIM HOW EACH OF HIS SONS HAD DIED. HE WATCHED THE OLD MAN'S DREAMS CRUMBLE."
"AND THEN HE GAVE OLD GAROUX THE KNIFE."
"THE OLD MAN OPENED HIS OWN WRIST FOR US TO DRINK FROM HIM."

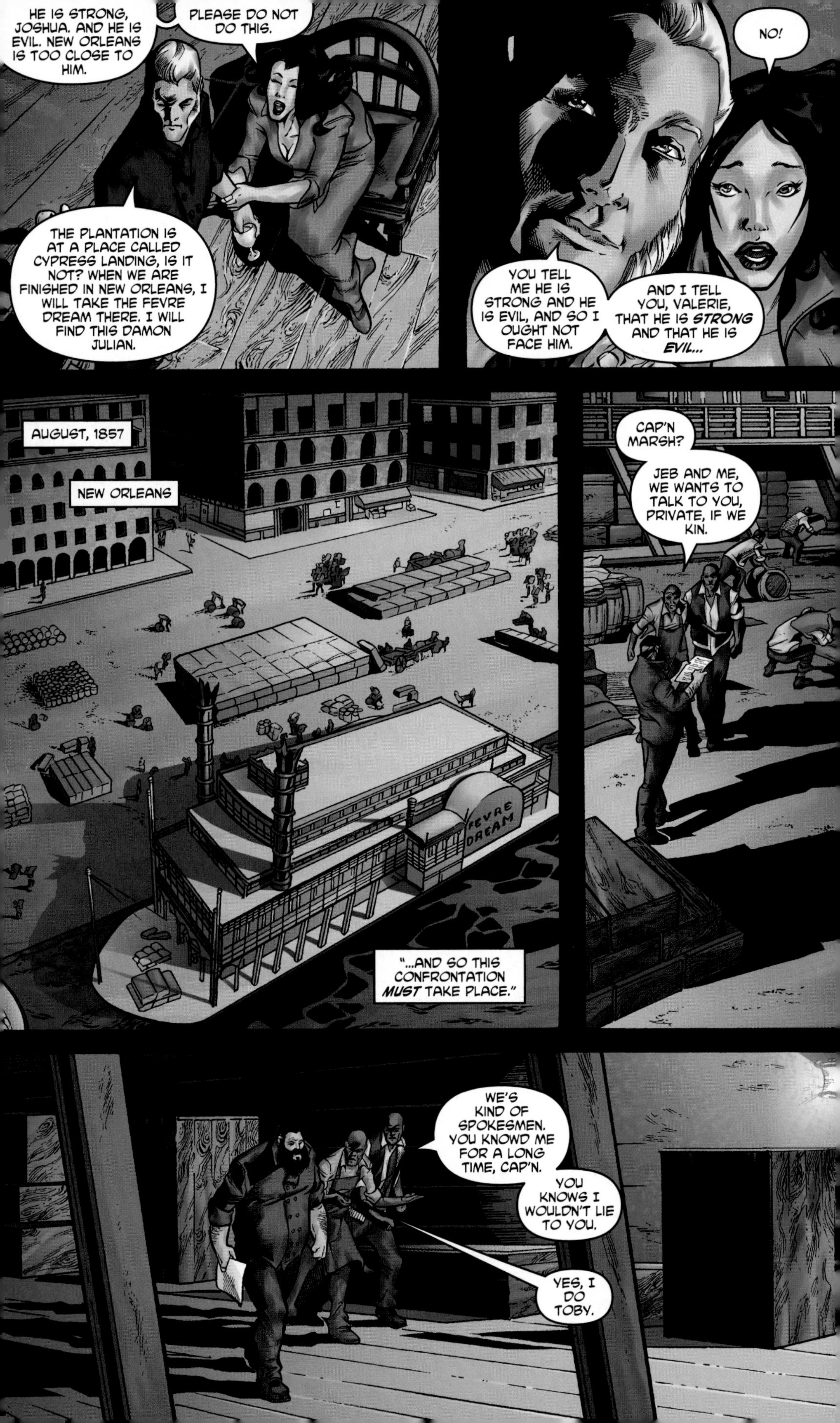
HE IS STRONG, JOSHUA. AND HE IS EVIL. NEW ORLEANS IS TOO CLOSE TO HIM.
PLEASE DO NOT DO THIS.
THE PLANTATION IS AT A PLACE CALLED CYPRESS LANDING, IS IT NOT? WHEN WE ARE FINISHED IN NEW ORLEANS, I WILL TAKE THE FEVRE DREAM THERE. I WILL FIND THIS DAMON JULIAN.
NO!
YOU TELL ME HE IS STRONG AND HE IS EVIL, AND SO I OUGHT NOT FACE HIM.
AND I TELL YOU, VALERIE, THAT HE IS STRONG AND THAT HE IS EVIL...
AUGUST, 1857
NEW ORLEANS
FEVRE DREAM
"...AND SO THIS CONFRONTATION MUST TAKE PLACE."
CAP'N MARSH?
JEB AND ME, WE WANTS TO TALK TO YOU, PRIVATE, IF WE KIN.
WE'S KIND OF SPOKESMEN. YOU KNOWD ME FOR A LONG TIME, CAP'N.
YOU KNOWS I WOULDN'T LIE TO YOU.
YES, I DO TOBY.

WHAT'S THIS ABOUT?

THERE'S TALK YOU'RE TAKIN' US DOWN TO CYPRESS LANDING. NOW I AIN'T BEEN THERE MYSELF, BUT THERE'S STORIES 'BOUT THAT PLACE.

ALL THE NIGGERS RUN OFF FROM THAT PLACE CAUSE OF THINGS WENT ON DOWN THERE.

BAD THINGS, CAP'N. *TERRIBLE* THINGS.

AIN'T NOTHING GOIN' TO HAPPEN DOWN THERE I NEED A COOK AND A BARBER FOR. YOU TWO WANT TO WAIT IN NEW ORLEANS, I WON'T OBJECT.

IT AIN'T JUST US. THE STOKERS...

DAMMIT. I *DO* NEED THEM.

THEY GON' RUN. YOU KIN SET HAIRY MIKE ON 'EM OR GIVE 'EM DOUBLE WAGES AND IT WON'T MAKE NO DIF'RENCE.

THEY SCARED, CAP'N.

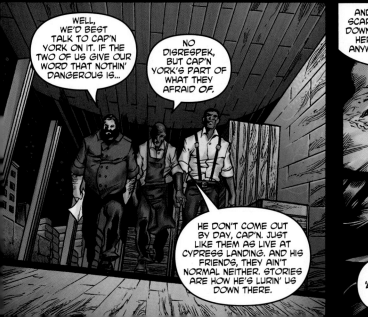

WELL, WE'D BEST TALK TO CAP'N YORK ON IT. IF THE TWO OF US GIVE OUR WORD THAT NOTHIN' DANGEROUS IS...

NO DISRESPEK, BUT CAP'N YORK'S PART OF WHAT THEY AFRAID *OF*.

HE DON'T COME OUT BY DAY, CAP'N. JUST LIKE THEM AS LIVE AT CYPRESS LANDING. AND HIS FRIENDS, THEY AIN'T NORMAL NEITHER. STORIES ARE HOW HE'S LURIN' US DOWN THERE.

AND WHAT IS IT THEY'RE SCARED'LL HAPPEN TO 'EM DOWN THERE CAN'T HAPPEN HERE OR NATCHEZ OR ANYWHERE ELSE ON THE RIVER?

THAT THEY'LL GET *'ET*, SUH. THAT'S WHAT THEY SCARED OF.

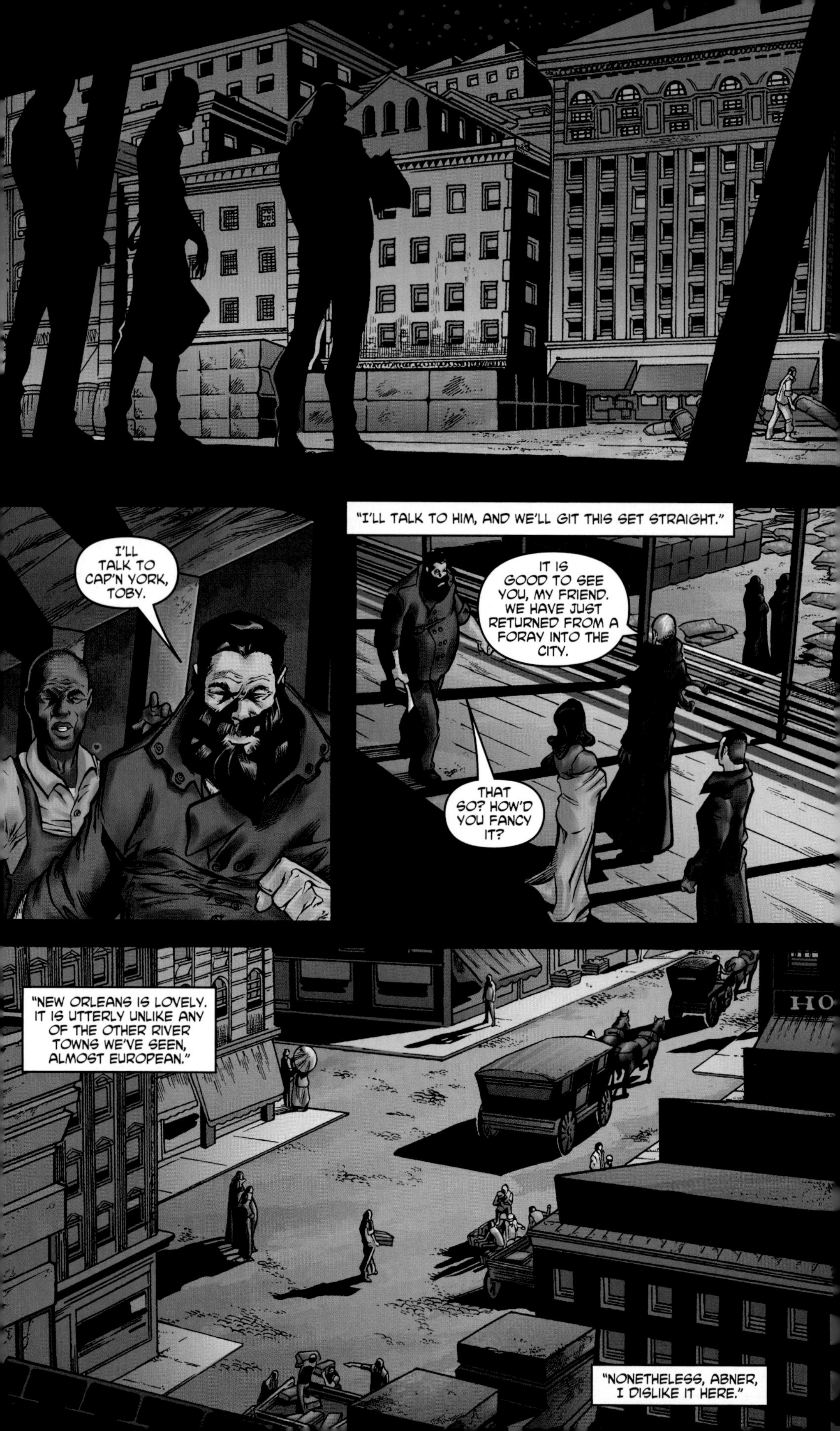

I'LL TALK TO CAP'N YORK, TOBY.
"I'LL TALK TO HIM, AND WE'LL GIT THIS SET STRAIGHT."
IT IS GOOD TO SEE YOU, MY FRIEND. WE HAVE JUST RETURNED FROM A FORAY INTO THE CITY.
THAT SO? HOW'D YOU FANCY IT?
"NEW ORLEANS IS LOVELY. IT IS UTTERLY UNLIKE ANY OF THE OTHER RIVER TOWNS WE'VE SEEN, ALMOST EUROPEAN."
HO
"NONETHELESS, ABNER, I DISLIKE IT HERE."

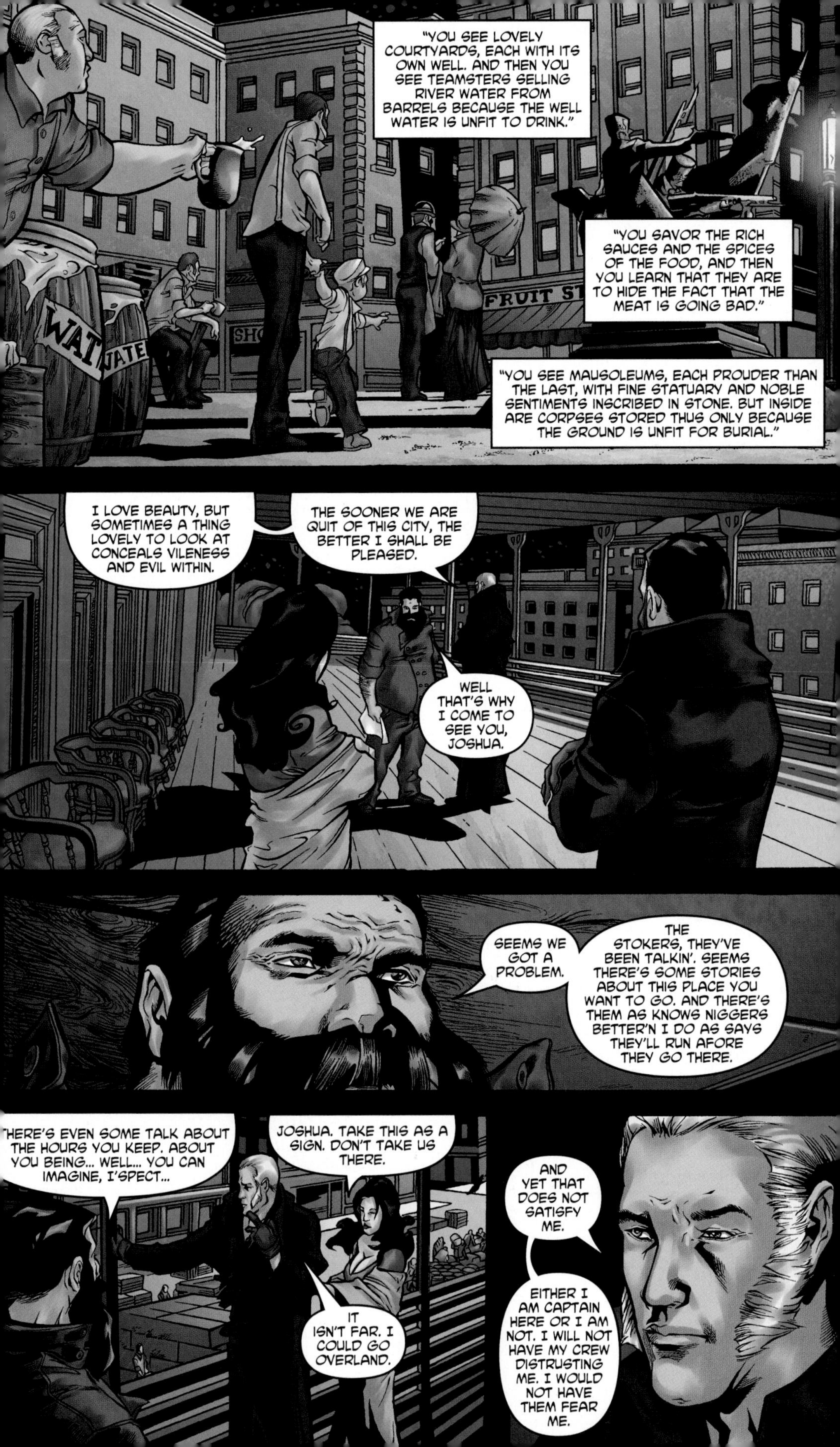

"YOU SEE LOVELY COURTYARDS, EACH WITH ITS OWN WELL. AND THEN YOU SEE TEAMSTERS SELLING RIVER WATER FROM BARRELS BECAUSE THE WELL WATER IS UNFIT TO DRINK."
WAT
WATE
SHO
FRUIT ST
"YOU SAVOR THE RICH SAUCES AND THE SPICES OF THE FOOD, AND THEN YOU LEARN THAT THEY ARE TO HIDE THE FACT THAT THE MEAT IS GOING BAD."
"YOU SEE MAUSOLEUMS, EACH PROUDER THAN THE LAST, WITH FINE STATUARY AND NOBLE SENTIMENTS INSCRIBED IN STONE. BUT INSIDE ARE CORPSES STORED THUS ONLY BECAUSE THE GROUND IS UNFIT FOR BURIAL."
I LOVE BEAUTY, BUT SOMETIMES A THING LOVELY TO LOOK AT CONCEALS VILENESS AND EVIL WITHIN.
THE SOONER WE ARE QUIT OF THIS CITY, THE BETTER I SHALL BE PLEASED.
WELL THAT'S WHY I COME TO SEE YOU, JOSHUA.
SEEMS WE GOT A PROBLEM.
THE STOKERS, THEY'VE BEEN TALKIN'. SEEMS THERE'S SOME STORIES ABOUT THIS PLACE YOU WANT TO GO. AND THERE'S THEM AS KNOWS NIGGERS BETTER'N I DO AS SAYS THEY'LL RUN AFORE THEY GO THERE.
THERE'S EVEN SOME TALK ABOUT THE HOURS YOU KEEP. ABOUT YOU BEING... WELL... YOU CAN IMAGINE, I'SPECT...
JOSHUA. TAKE THIS AS A SIGN. DON'T TAKE US THERE.
IT ISN'T FAR. I COULD GO OVERLAND.
AND YET THAT DOES NOT SATISFY ME.
EITHER I AM CAPTAIN HERE OR I AM NOT. I WILL NOT HAVE MY CREW DISTRUSTING ME. I WOULD NOT HAVE THEM FEAR ME.

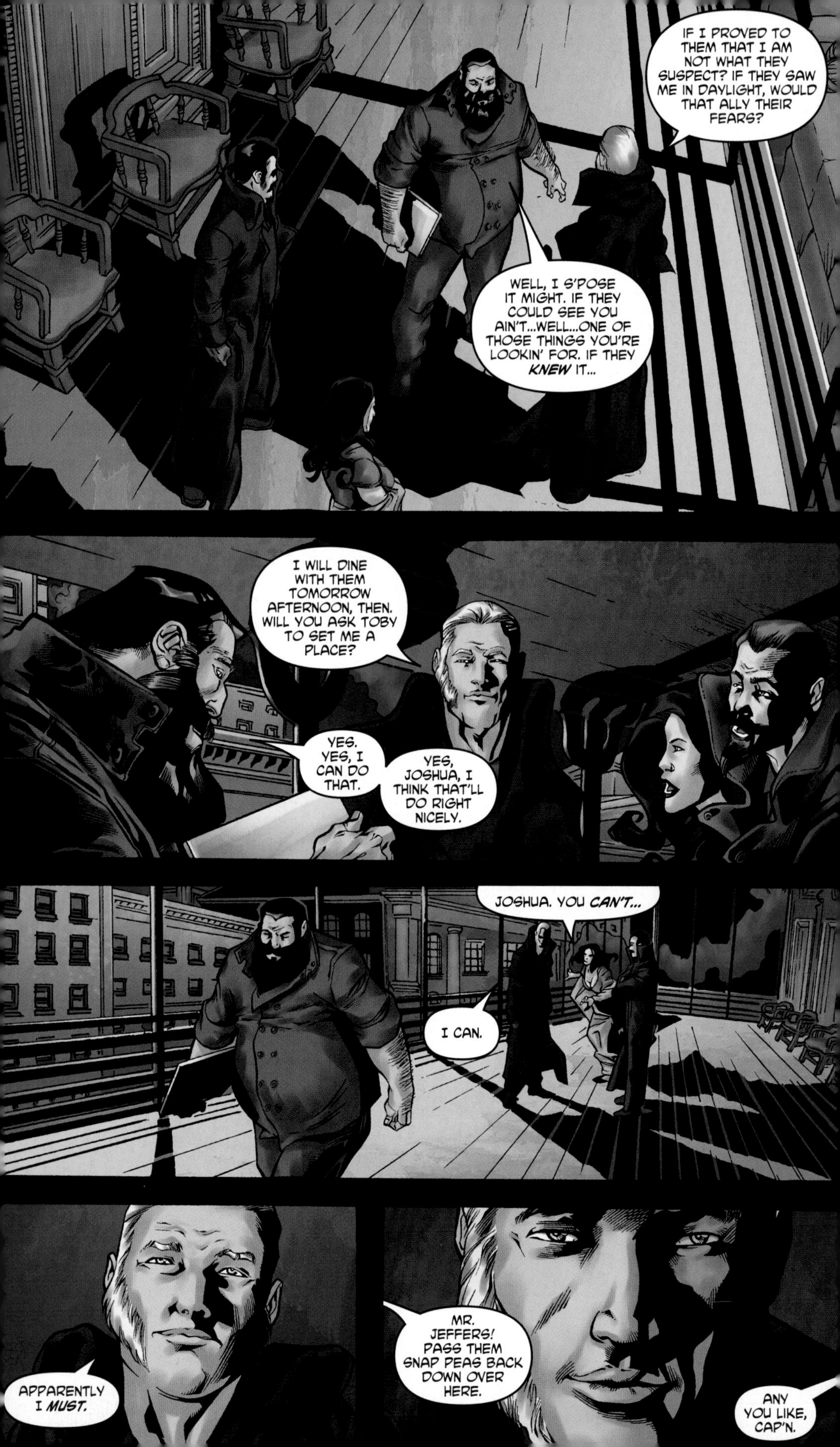
IF I PROVED TO THEM THAT I AM NOT WHAT THEY SUSPECT? IF THEY SAW ME IN DAYLIGHT, WOULD THAT ALLY THEIR FEARS?
WELL, I S'POSE IT MIGHT. IF THEY COULD SEE YOU AIN'T...WELL...ONE OF THOSE THINGS YOU'RE LOOKIN' FOR. IF THEY *KNEW* IT...
I WILL DINE WITH THEM TOMORROW AFTERNOON, THEN. WILL YOU ASK TOBY TO SET ME A PLACE?
YES. YES, I CAN DO THAT.
YES, JOSHUA, I THINK THAT'LL DO RIGHT NICELY.
JOSHUA. YOU *CAN'T*...
I CAN.
APPARENTLY I *MUST.*
MR. JEFFERS! PASS THEM SNAP PEAS BACK DOWN OVER HERE.
ANY YOU LIKE, CAP'N.

DAMN IT, JOSHUA. I WISH YOU'D COME T' DINNER WITH US MORE OFTEN. WE COULD EAT LIKE THIS EVERY DAY.

I THINK NOT. I STILL PREFER NIGHT.

I CAST MY LOT WITH LORD BYRON. DAY IS FAR TOO GAUDY.

EH?

YOU'VE FORGOTTEN THE POEM I RECITED ON THE DOCKS OF NEW ALBANY. IT WAS THE FIRST TIME I SAW THE FEVRE DREAM, AND IT FITS HER SO WELL.

SHE WALKS IN BEAUTY...

...LIKE THE NIGHT.

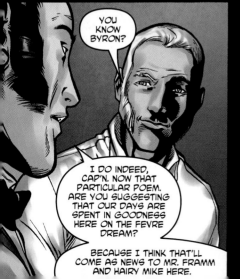

YOU KNOW BYRON?

I DO INDEED, CAP'N. NOW THAT PARTICULAR POEM. ARE YOU SUGGESTING THAT OUR DAYS ARE SPENT IN GOODNESS HERE ON THE FEVRE DREAM?

BECAUSE I THINK THAT'LL COME AS NEWS TO MR. FRAMM AND HAIRY MIKE HERE.

HEY, NOW. JUST 'CAUSE I GOT THREE WIVES DON'T MEAN I AIN'T GOOD. WHY MOST EVERY ONE OF 'EM 'UD VOUCH FOR ME.

WHAT THE HELL ARE YOU TWO TALKIN' ABOUT?

MR. JEFFERS IS REMINDING ME OF THE FINAL STANZA OF THAT POEM.

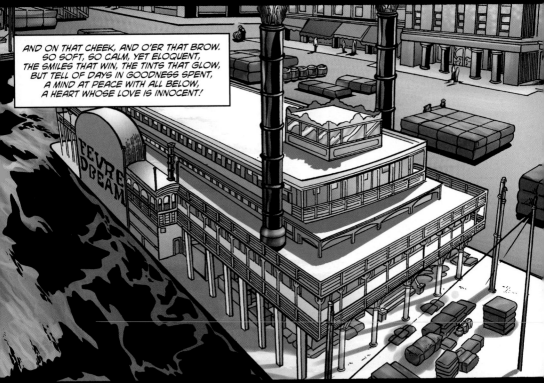

AND ON THAT CHEEK, AND O'ER THAT BROW.
SO SOFT, SO CALM, YET ELOQUENT,
THE SMILES THAT WIN, THE TINTS THAT GLOW,
BUT TELL OF DAYS IN GOODNESS SPENT,
A MIND AT PEACE WITH ALL BELOW,
A HEART WHOSE LOVE IS INNOCENT!

AND ARE WE INNOCENT, CAPTAIN YORK?

NO ONE IS ENTIRELY INNOCENT. BUT THE POEM SPEAKS TO ME NONETHELESS. THE NIGHT IS BEAUTIFUL, AND WE CAN HOPE TO FIND PEACE IN NOBILITY IN ITS DARK SPLENDOR.

TOBY! THERE YOU ARE! C'MON OVER HERE.

YESSUH.

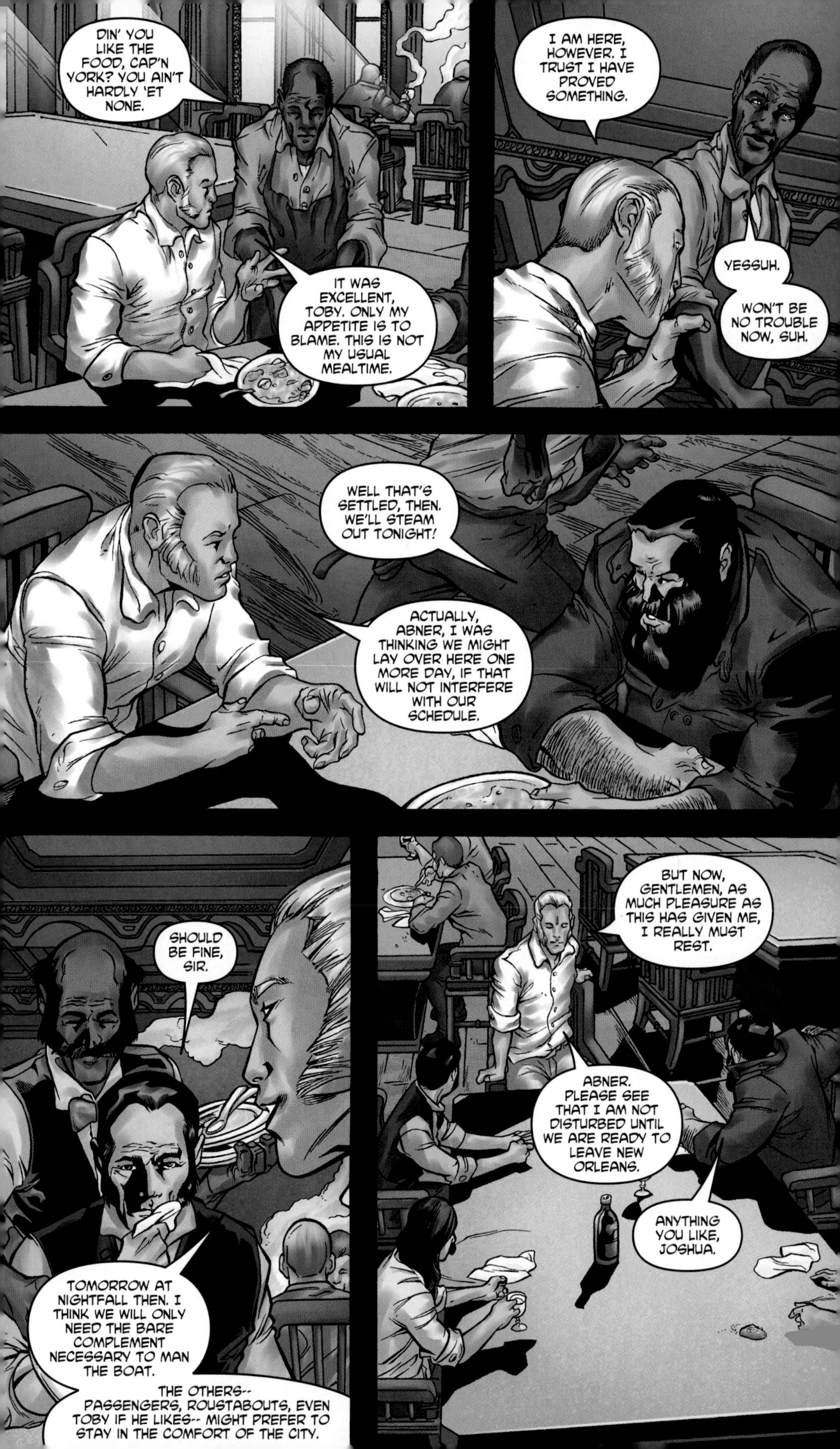
DIN' YOU LIKE THE FOOD, CAP'N YORK? YOU AIN'T HARDLY 'ET NONE.
IT WAS EXCELLENT, TOBY. ONLY MY APPETITE IS TO BLAME. THIS IS NOT MY USUAL MEALTIME.
I AM HERE, HOWEVER. I TRUST I HAVE PROVED SOMETHING.
YESSUH.
WON'T BE NO TROUBLE NOW, SUH.
WELL THAT'S SETTLED, THEN. WE'LL STEAM OUT TONIGHT!
ACTUALLY, ABNER, I WAS THINKING WE MIGHT LAY OVER HERE ONE MORE DAY, IF THAT WILL NOT INTERFERE WITH OUR SCHEDULE.
SHOULD BE FINE, SIR.
TOMORROW AT NIGHTFALL THEN. I THINK WE WILL ONLY NEED THE BARE COMPLEMENT NECESSARY TO MAN THE BOAT.
THE OTHERS-- PASSENGERS, ROUSTABOUTS, EVEN TOBY IF HE LIKES-- MIGHT PREFER TO STAY IN THE COMFORT OF THE CITY.
BUT NOW, GENTLEMEN, AS MUCH PLEASURE AS THIS HAS GIVEN ME, I REALLY MUST REST.
ABNER. PLEASE SEE THAT I AM NOT DISTURBED UNTIL WE ARE READY TO LEAVE NEW ORLEANS.
ANYTHING YOU LIKE, JOSHUA.

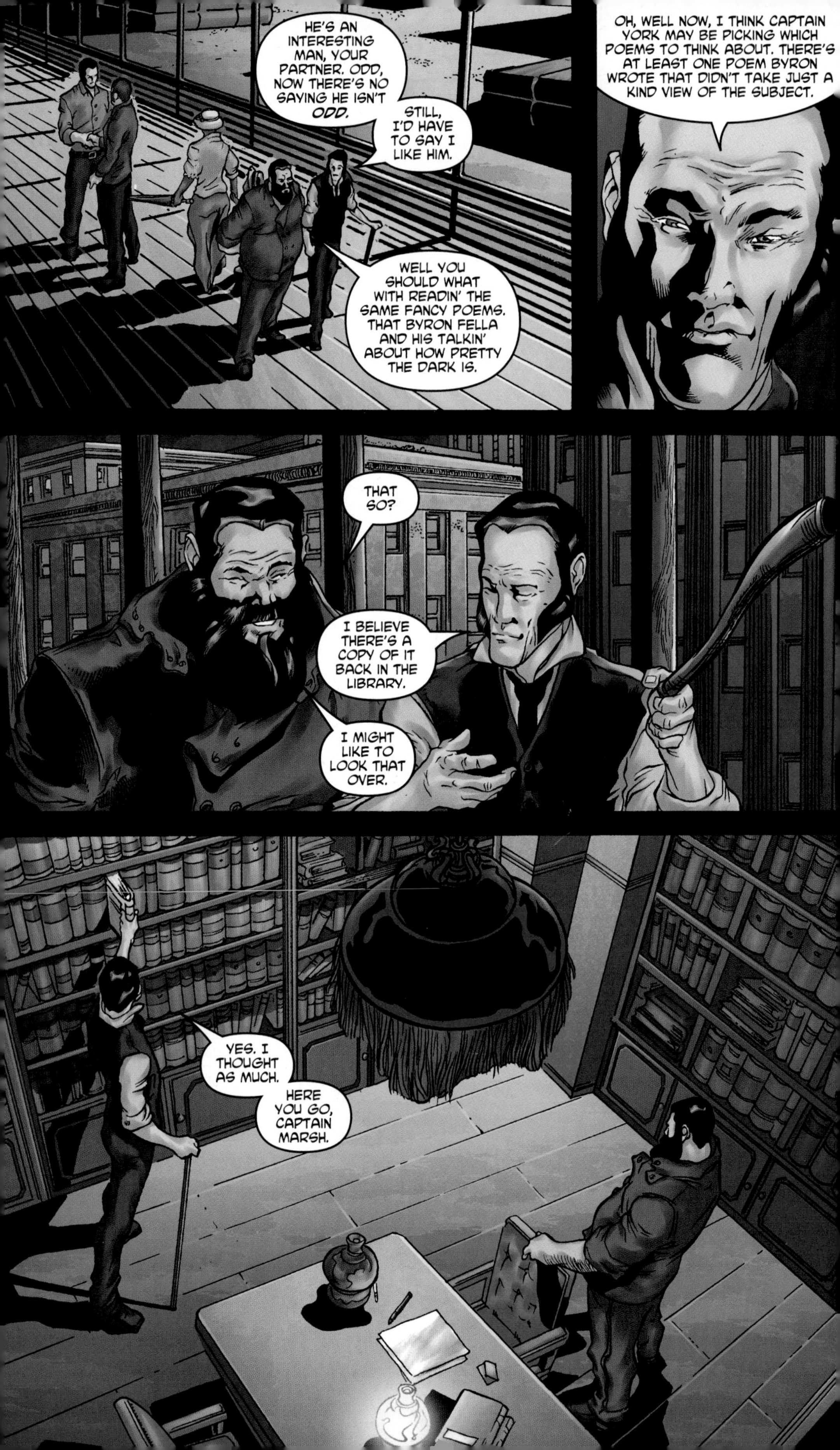

HE'S AN INTERESTING MAN, YOUR PARTNER. ODD, NOW THERE'S NO SAYING HE ISN'T *ODD*.
STILL, I'D HAVE TO SAY I LIKE HIM.
WELL YOU SHOULD WHAT WITH READIN' THE SAME FANCY POEMS. THAT BYRON FELLA AND HIS TALKIN' ABOUT HOW PRETTY THE DARK IS.
OH, WELL NOW, I THINK CAPTAIN YORK MAY BE PICKING WHICH POEMS TO THINK ABOUT. THERE'S AT LEAST ONE POEM BYRON WROTE THAT DIDN'T TAKE JUST A KIND VIEW OF THE SUBJECT.
THAT SO?
I BELIEVE THERE'S A COPY OF IT BACK IN THE LIBRARY.
I MIGHT LIKE TO LOOK THAT OVER.
YES. I THOUGHT AS MUCH.
HERE YOU GO, CAPTAIN MARSH.

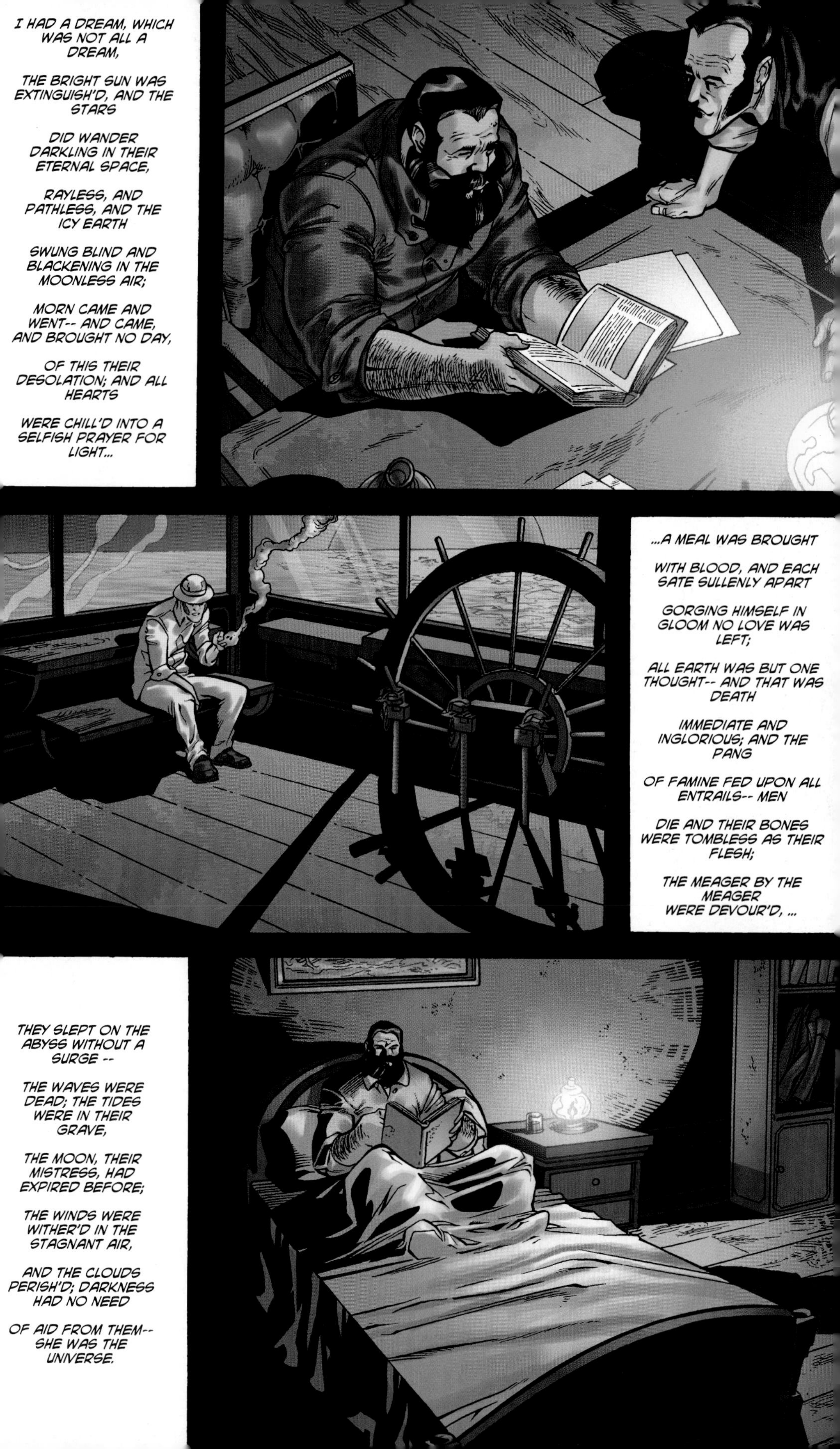
I HAD A DREAM, WHICH WAS NOT ALL A DREAM,
THE BRIGHT SUN WAS EXTINGUISH'D, AND THE STARS
DID WANDER DARKLING IN THEIR ETERNAL SPACE,
RAYLESS, AND PATHLESS, AND THE ICY EARTH
SWUNG BLIND AND BLACKENING IN THE MOONLESS AIR;
MORN CAME AND WENT-- AND CAME, AND BROUGHT NO DAY,
OF THIS THEIR DESOLATION; AND ALL HEARTS
WERE CHILL'D INTO A SELFISH PRAYER FOR LIGHT...
...A MEAL WAS BROUGHT
WITH BLOOD, AND EACH SATE SULLENLY APART
GORGING HIMSELF IN GLOOM NO LOVE WAS LEFT;
ALL EARTH WAS BUT ONE THOUGHT-- AND THAT WAS DEATH
IMMEDIATE AND INGLORIOUS; AND THE PANG
OF FAMINE FED UPON ALL ENTRAILS-- MEN
DIE AND THEIR BONES WERE TOMBLESS AS THEIR FLESH;
THE MEAGER BY THE MEAGER WERE DEVOUR'D, ...
THEY SLEPT ON THE ABYSS WITHOUT A SURGE --
THE WAVES WERE DEAD; THE TIDES WERE IN THEIR GRAVE,
THE MOON, THEIR MISTRESS, HAD EXPIRED BEFORE;
THE WINDS WERE WITHER'D IN THE STAGNANT AIR,
AND THE CLOUDS PERISH'D; DARKNESS HAD NO NEED
OF AID FROM THEM-- SHE WAS THE UNIVERSE.

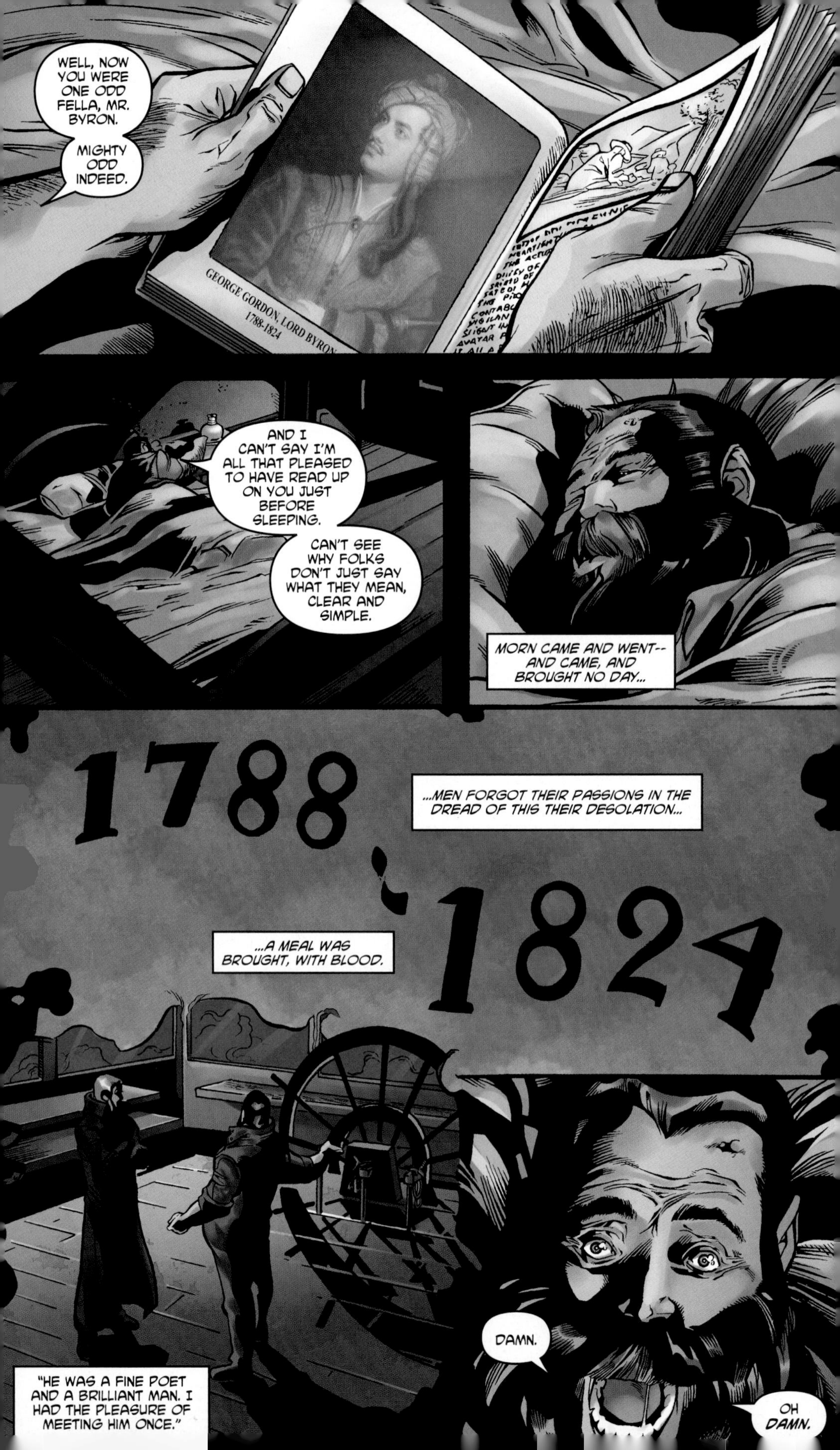
WELL, NOW YOU WERE ONE ODD FELLA, MR. BYRON.
MIGHTY ODD INDEED.
GEORGE GORDON, LORD BYRON 1788-1824
AND I CAN'T SAY I'M ALL THAT PLEASED TO HAVE READ UP ON YOU JUST BEFORE SLEEPING.
CAN'T SEE WHY FOLKS DON'T JUST SAY WHAT THEY MEAN, CLEAR AND SIMPLE.
MORN CAME AND WENT-- AND CAME, AND BROUGHT NO DAY...
1788
...MEN FORGOT THEIR PASSIONS IN THE DREAD OF THIS THEIR DESOLATION...
1824
...A MEAL WAS BROUGHT, WITH BLOOD.
DAMN.
"HE WAS A FINE POET AND A BRILLIANT MAN. I HAD THE PLEASURE OF MEETING HIM ONCE."
OH DAMN.

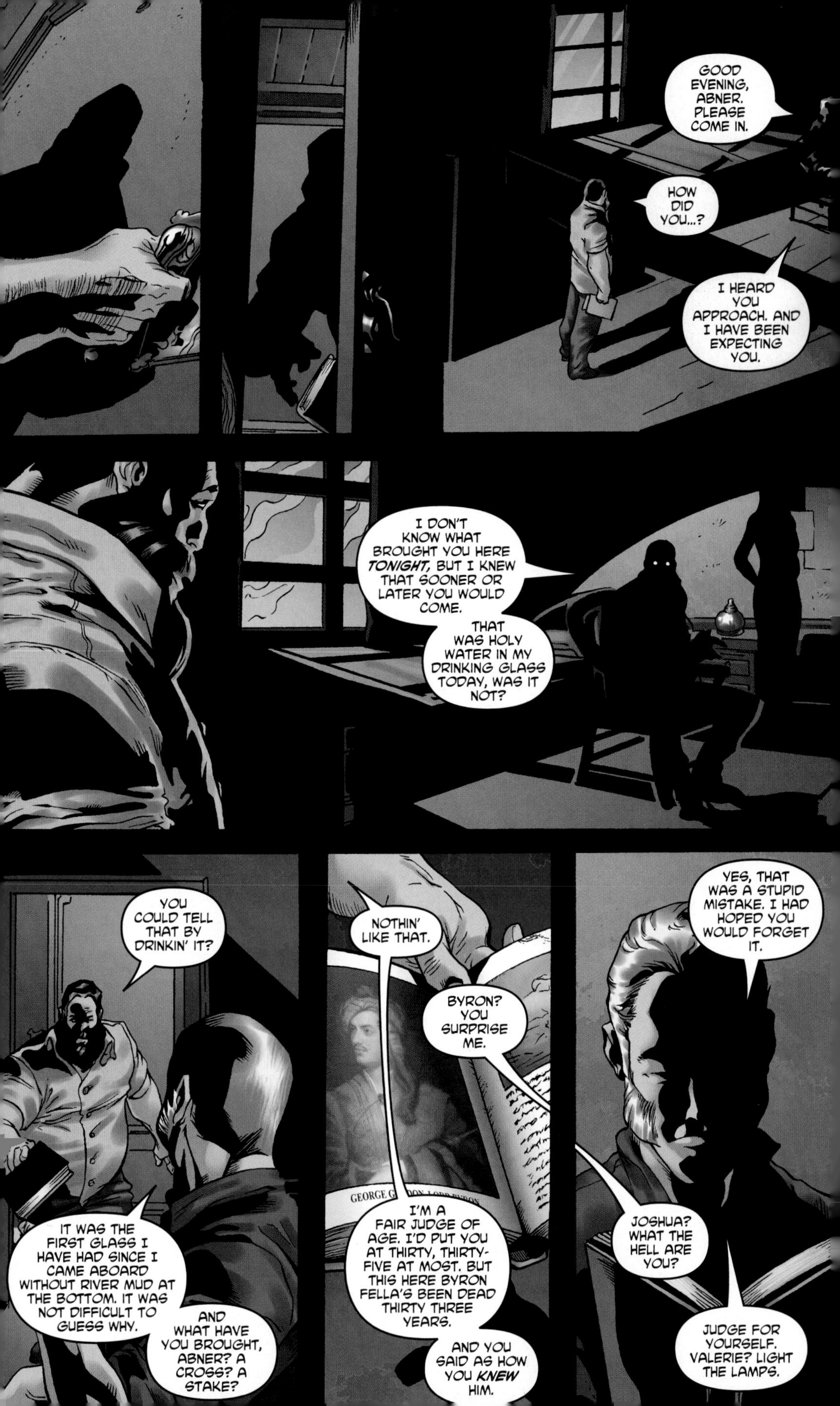
GOOD EVENING, ABNER. PLEASE COME IN.
HOW DID YOU...?
I HEARD YOU APPROACH. AND I HAVE BEEN EXPECTING YOU.
I DON'T KNOW WHAT BROUGHT YOU HERE *TONIGHT,* BUT I KNEW THAT SOONER OR LATER YOU WOULD COME.
THAT WAS HOLY WATER IN MY DRINKING GLASS TODAY, WAS IT NOT?
YOU COULD TELL THAT BY DRINKIN' IT?
IT WAS THE FIRST GLASS I HAVE HAD SINCE I CAME ABOARD WITHOUT RIVER MUD AT THE BOTTOM. IT WAS NOT DIFFICULT TO GUESS WHY.
AND WHAT HAVE YOU BROUGHT, ABNER? A CROSS? A STAKE?
NOTHIN' LIKE THAT.
BYRON? YOU SURPRISE ME.
I'M A FAIR JUDGE OF AGE. I'D PUT YOU AT THIRTY, THIRTY-FIVE AT MOST. BUT THIS HERE BYRON FELLA'S BEEN DEAD THIRTY THREE YEARS.
AND YOU SAID AS HOW YOU *KNEW* HIM.
YES, THAT WAS A STUPID MISTAKE. I HAD HOPED YOU WOULD FORGET IT.
JOSHUA? WHAT THE HELL ARE YOU?
JUDGE FOR YOURSELF. VALERIE? LIGHT THE LAMPS.

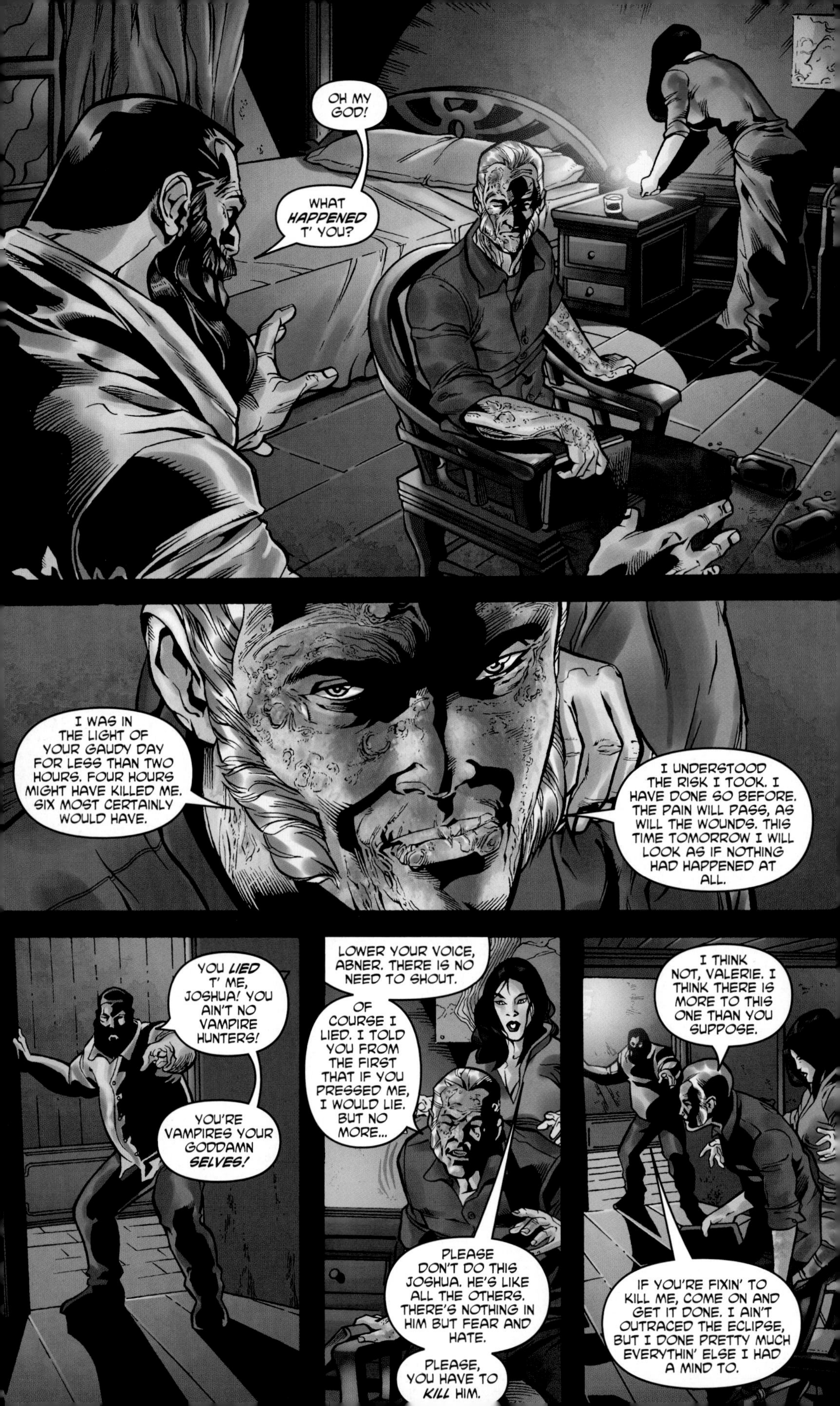
OH MY GOD!
WHAT HAPPENED T' YOU?
I WAS IN THE LIGHT OF YOUR GAUDY DAY FOR LESS THAN TWO HOURS. FOUR HOURS MIGHT HAVE KILLED ME. SIX MOST CERTAINLY WOULD HAVE.
I UNDERSTOOD THE RISK I TOOK. I HAVE DONE SO BEFORE. THE PAIN WILL PASS, AS WILL THE WOUNDS. THIS TIME TOMORROW I WILL LOOK AS IF NOTHING HAD HAPPENED AT ALL.
YOU LIED T' ME, JOSHUA! YOU AIN'T NO VAMPIRE HUNTERS!
YOU'RE VAMPIRES YOUR GODDAMN SELVES!
LOWER YOUR VOICE, ABNER. THERE IS NO NEED TO SHOUT.
OF COURSE I LIED. I TOLD YOU FROM THE FIRST THAT IF YOU PRESSED ME, I WOULD LIE. BUT NO MORE...
PLEASE DON'T DO THIS JOSHUA. HE'S LIKE ALL THE OTHERS. THERE'S NOTHING IN HIM BUT FEAR AND HATE.
PLEASE, YOU HAVE TO KILL HIM.
I THINK NOT, VALERIE. I THINK THERE IS MORE TO THIS ONE THAN YOU SUPPOSE.
IF YOU'RE FIXIN' TO KILL ME, COME ON AND GET IT DONE. I AIN'T OUTRACED THE ECLIPSE, BUT I DONE PRETTY MUCH EVERYTHIN' ELSE I HAD A MIND TO.

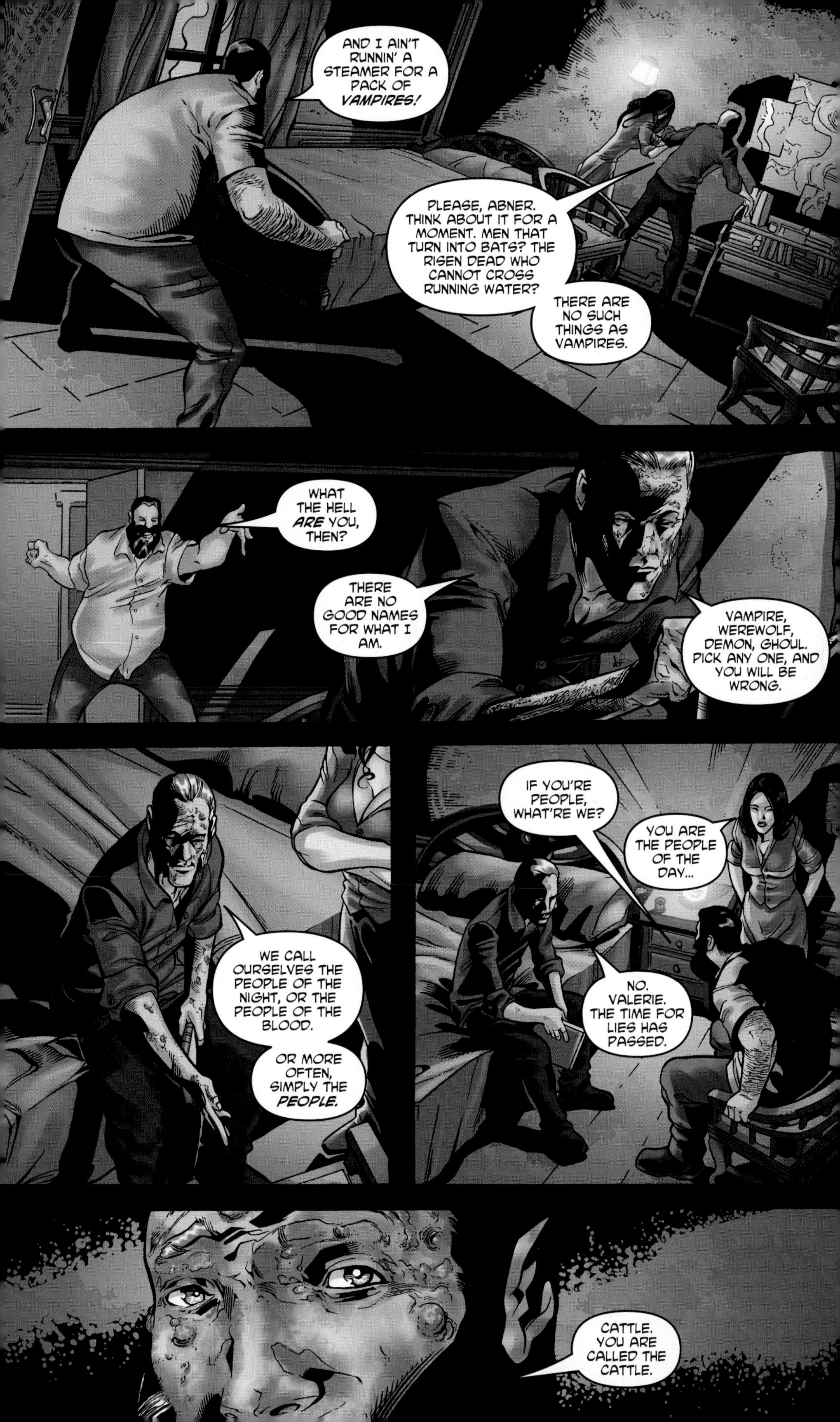
AND I AIN'T RUNNIN' A STEAMER FOR A PACK OF *VAMPIRES!*
PLEASE, ABNER. THINK ABOUT IT FOR A MOMENT. MEN THAT TURN INTO BATS? THE RISEN DEAD WHO CANNOT CROSS RUNNING WATER?
THERE ARE NO SUCH THINGS AS VAMPIRES.
WHAT THE HELL *ARE* YOU, THEN?
THERE ARE NO GOOD NAMES FOR WHAT I AM.
VAMPIRE, WEREWOLF, DEMON, GHOUL. PICK ANY ONE, AND YOU WILL BE WRONG.
WE CALL OURSELVES THE PEOPLE OF THE NIGHT, OR THE PEOPLE OF THE BLOOD.
OR MORE OFTEN, SIMPLY THE *PEOPLE.*
IF YOU'RE PEOPLE, WHAT'RE WE?
YOU ARE THE PEOPLE OF THE DAY...
NO. VALERIE. THE TIME FOR LIES HAS PASSED.
CATTLE. YOU ARE CALLED THE CATTLE.

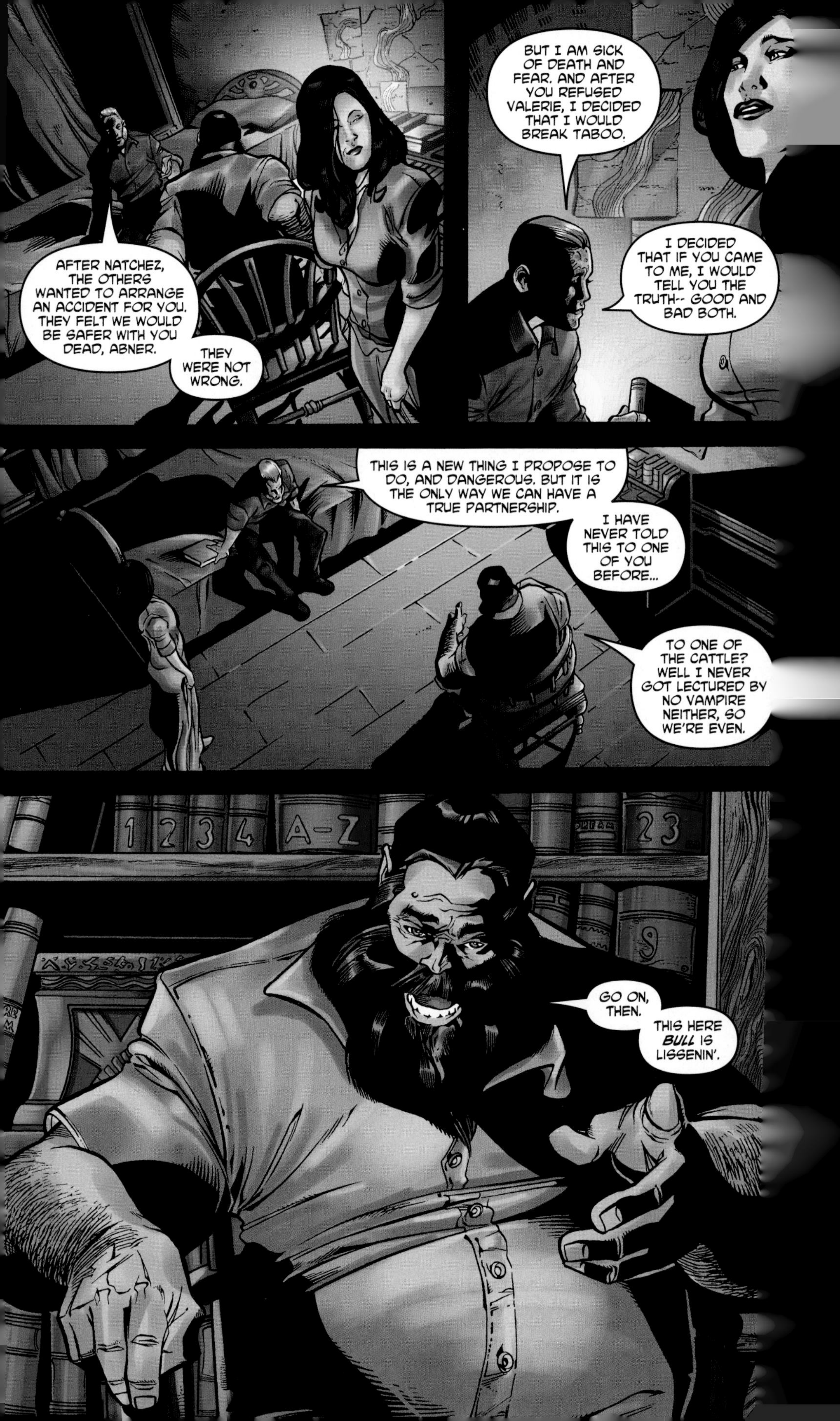
AFTER NATCHEZ, THE OTHERS WANTED TO ARRANGE AN ACCIDENT FOR YOU. THEY FELT WE WOULD BE SAFER WITH YOU DEAD, ABNER.
THEY WERE NOT WRONG.
BUT I AM SICK OF DEATH AND FEAR. AND AFTER YOU REFUSED VALERIE, I DECIDED THAT I WOULD BREAK TABOO.
I DECIDED THAT IF YOU CAME TO ME, I WOULD TELL YOU THE TRUTH-- GOOD AND BAD BOTH.
THIS IS A NEW THING I PROPOSE TO DO, AND DANGEROUS. BUT IT IS THE ONLY WAY WE CAN HAVE A TRUE PARTNERSHIP.
I HAVE NEVER TOLD THIS TO ONE OF YOU BEFORE...
TO ONE OF THE CATTLE? WELL I NEVER GOT LECTURED BY NO VAMPIRE NEITHER, SO WE'RE EVEN.
GO ON, THEN.
THIS HERE *BULL* IS LISSENIN'.

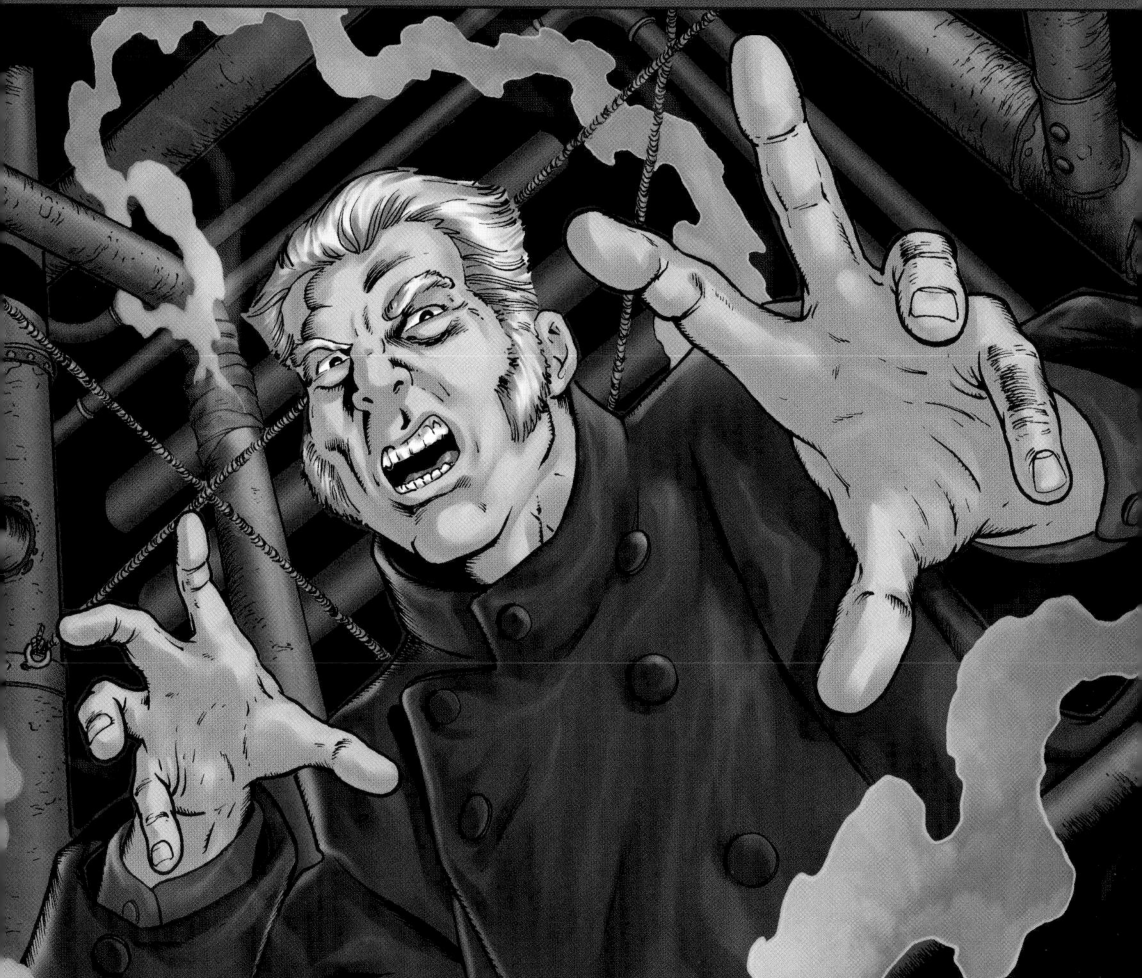

CHAPTER 5

Mississippi
River
Genevieve
Pilot Knob
Ohio
Paducah
Columbus
Union

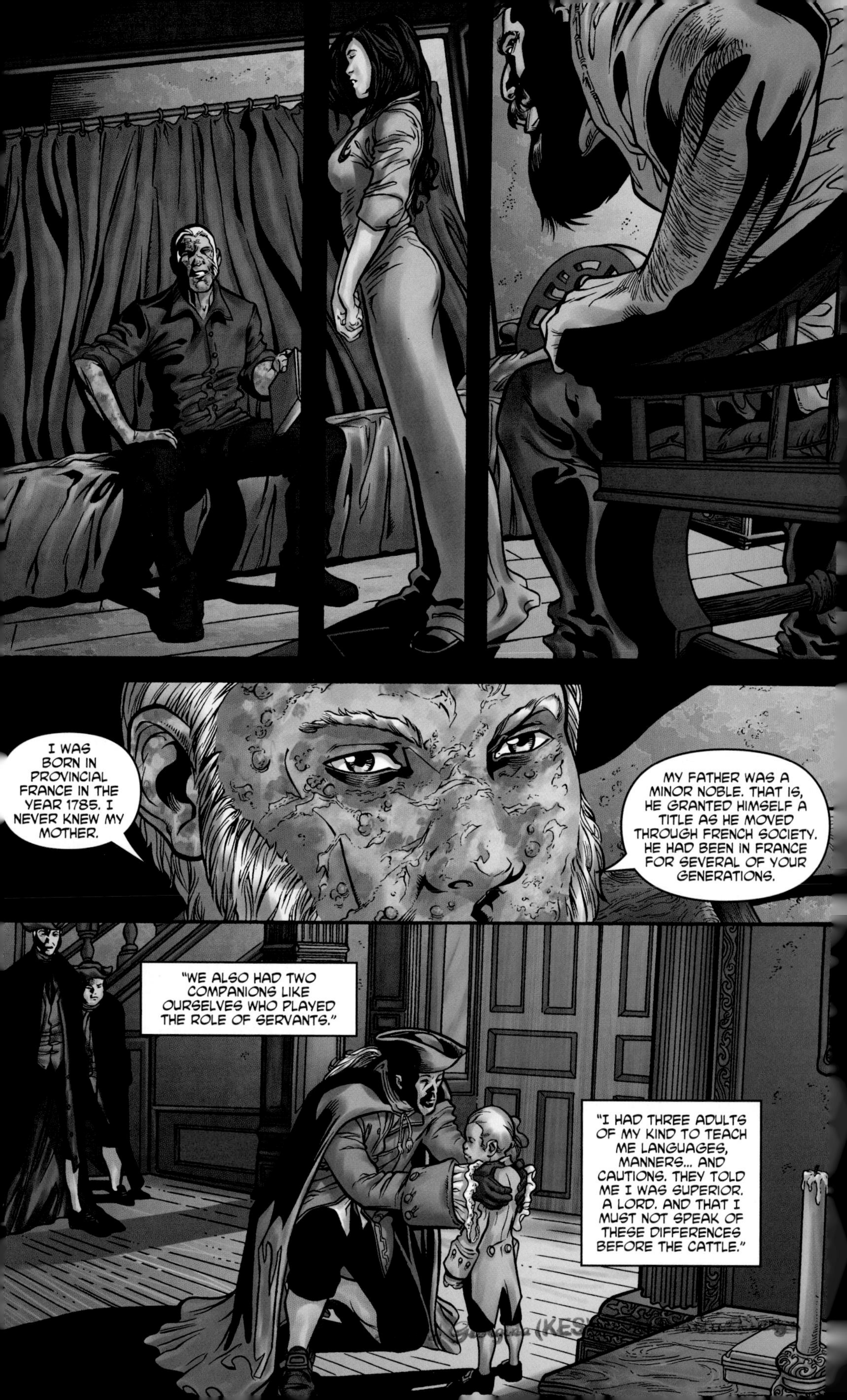
I WAS BORN IN PROVINCIAL FRANCE IN THE YEAR 1785. I NEVER KNEW MY MOTHER.
MY FATHER WAS A MINOR NOBLE. THAT IS, HE GRANTED HIMSELF A TITLE AS HE MOVED THROUGH FRENCH SOCIETY. HE HAD BEEN IN FRANCE FOR SEVERAL OF YOUR GENERATIONS.
"WE ALSO HAD TWO COMPANIONS LIKE OURSELVES WHO PLAYED THE ROLE OF SERVANTS."
"I HAD THREE ADULTS OF MY KIND TO TEACH ME LANGUAGES, MANNERS... AND CAUTIONS. THEY TOLD ME I WAS SUPERIOR. A LORD. AND THAT I MUST NOT SPEAK OF THESE DIFFERENCES BEFORE THE CATTLE."

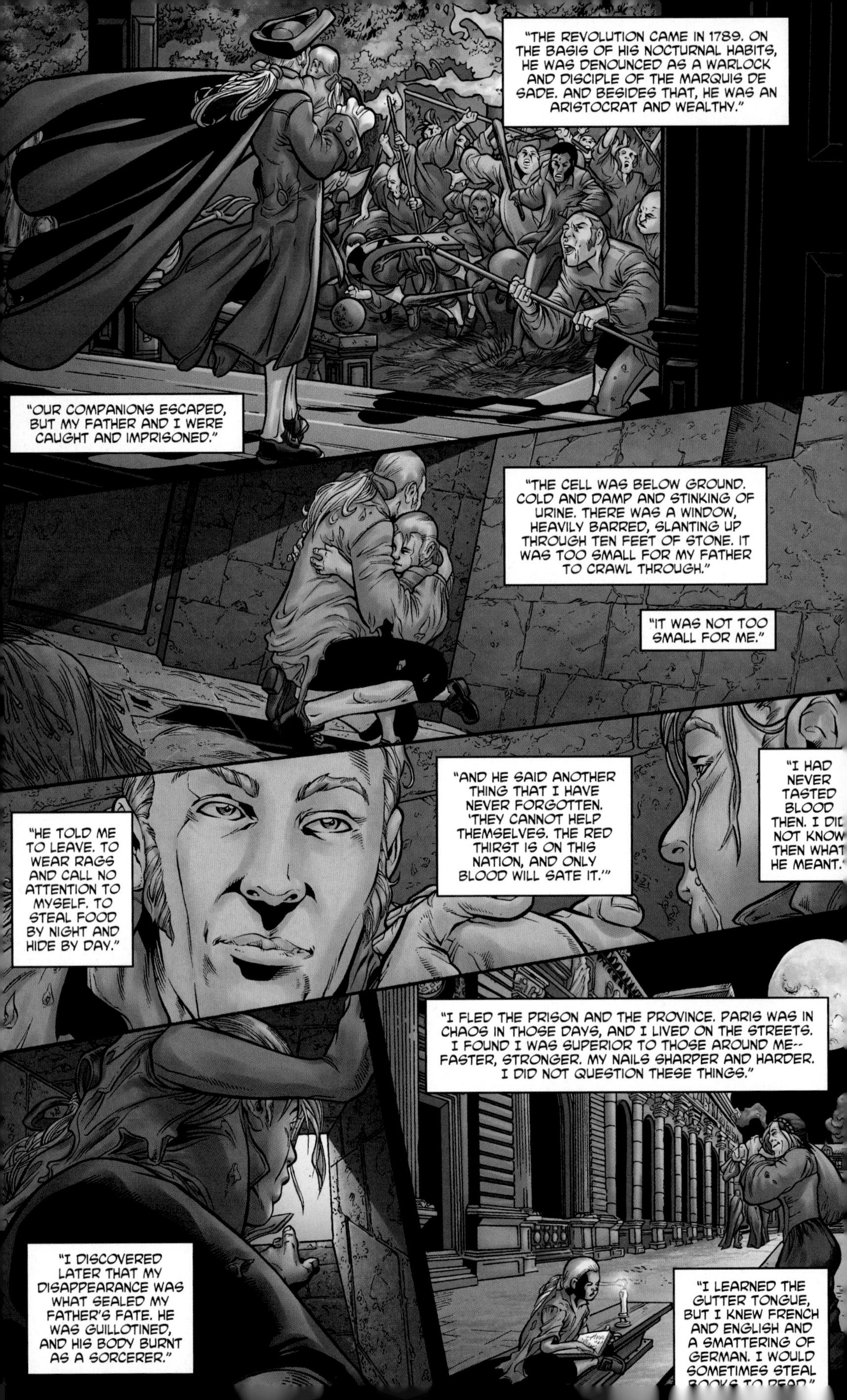
"THE REVOLUTION CAME IN 1789. ON THE BASIS OF HIS NOCTURNAL HABITS, HE WAS DENOUNCED AS A WARLOCK AND DISCIPLE OF THE MARQUIS DE SADE. AND BESIDES THAT, HE WAS AN ARISTOCRAT AND WEALTHY."
"OUR COMPANIONS ESCAPED, BUT MY FATHER AND I WERE CAUGHT AND IMPRISONED."
"THE CELL WAS BELOW GROUND. COLD AND DAMP AND STINKING OF URINE. THERE WAS A WINDOW, HEAVILY BARRED, SLANTING UP THROUGH TEN FEET OF STONE. IT WAS TOO SMALL FOR MY FATHER TO CRAWL THROUGH."
"IT WAS NOT TOO SMALL FOR ME."
"HE TOLD ME TO LEAVE. TO WEAR RAGS AND CALL NO ATTENTION TO MYSELF. TO STEAL FOOD BY NIGHT AND HIDE BY DAY."
"AND HE SAID ANOTHER THING THAT I HAVE NEVER FORGOTTEN. 'THEY CANNOT HELP THEMSELVES. THE RED THIRST IS ON THIS NATION, AND ONLY BLOOD WILL SATE IT.'"
"I HAD NEVER TASTED BLOOD THEN. I DID NOT KNOW THEN WHAT HE MEANT."
"I FLED THE PRISON AND THE PROVINCE. PARIS WAS IN CHAOS IN THOSE DAYS, AND I LIVED ON THE STREETS. I FOUND I WAS SUPERIOR TO THOSE AROUND ME-- FASTER, STRONGER. MY NAILS SHARPER AND HARDER. I DID NOT QUESTION THESE THINGS."
"I DISCOVERED LATER THAT MY DISAPPEARANCE WAS WHAT SEALED MY FATHER'S FATE. HE WAS GUILLOTINED, AND HIS BODY BURNT AS A SORCERER."
"I LEARNED THE GUTTER TONGUE, BUT I KNEW FRENCH AND ENGLISH AND A SMATTERING OF GERMAN. I WOULD SOMETIMES STEAL

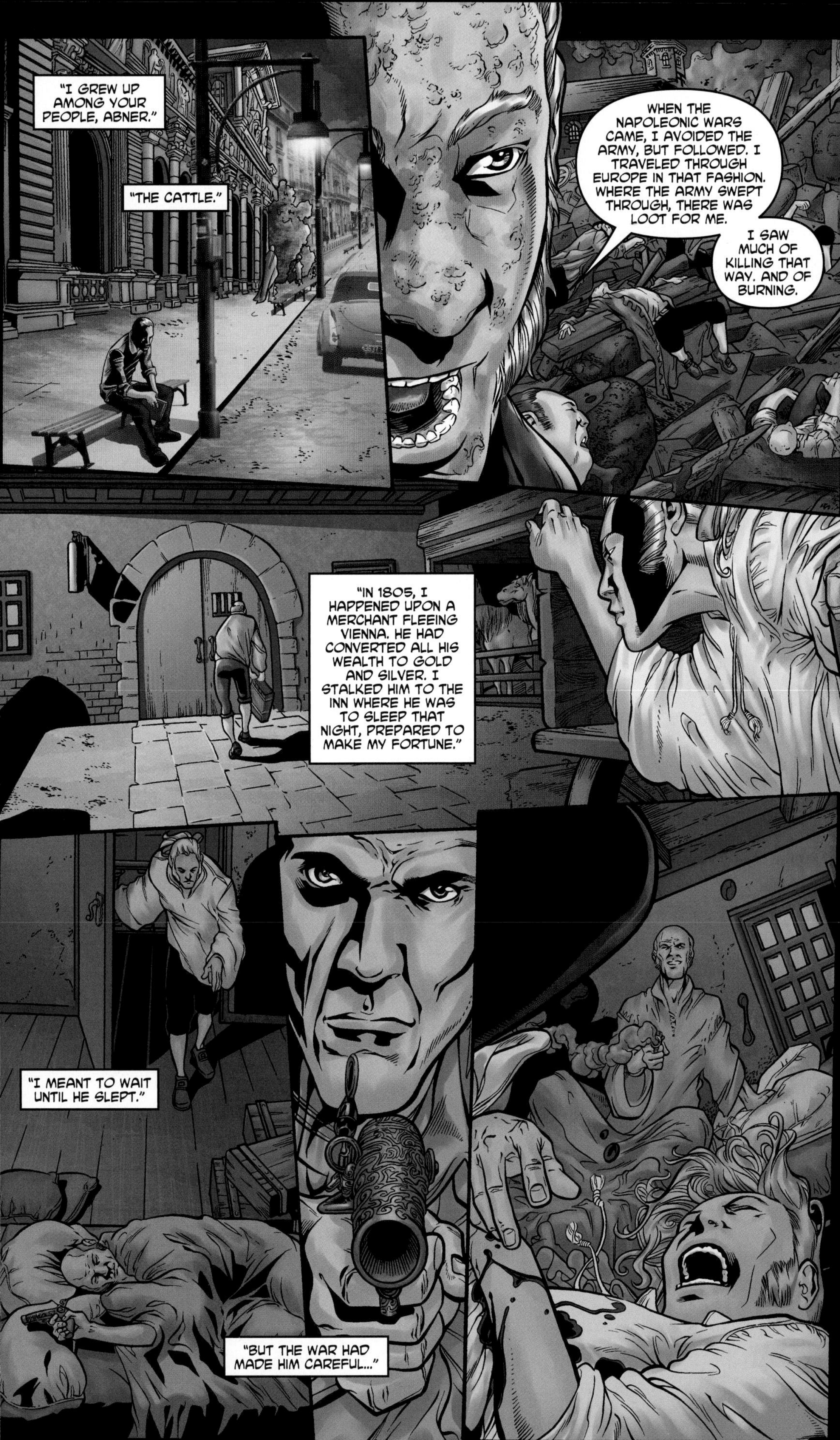
"I GREW UP AMONG YOUR PEOPLE, ABNER."
"THE CATTLE."
WHEN THE NAPOLEONIC WARS CAME, I AVOIDED THE ARMY, BUT FOLLOWED. I TRAVELED THROUGH EUROPE IN THAT FASHION. WHERE THE ARMY SWEPT THROUGH, THERE WAS LOOT FOR ME.
I SAW MUCH OF KILLING THAT WAY. AND OF BURNING.
"IN 1805, I HAPPENED UPON A MERCHANT FLEEING VIENNA. HE HAD CONVERTED ALL HIS WEALTH TO GOLD AND SILVER. I STALKED HIM TO THE INN WHERE HE WAS TO SLEEP THAT NIGHT, PREPARED TO MAKE MY FORTUNE."
"I MEANT TO WAIT UNTIL HE SLEPT."
"BUT THE WAR HAD MADE HIM CAREFUL..."

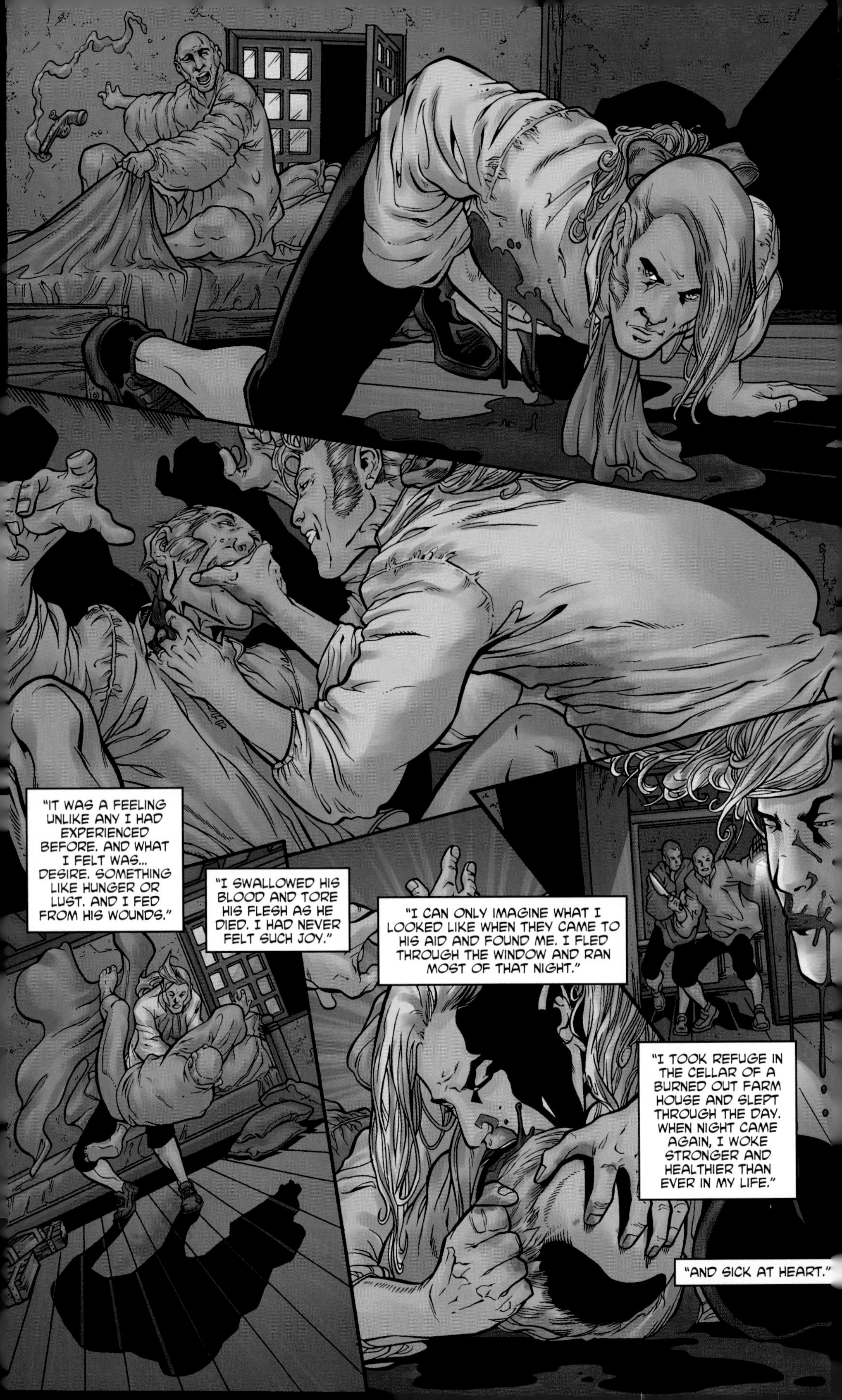
"IT WAS A FEELING UNLIKE ANY I HAD EXPERIENCED BEFORE. AND WHAT I FELT WAS... DESIRE. SOMETHING LIKE HUNGER OR LUST. AND I FED FROM HIS WOUNDS."
"I SWALLOWED HIS BLOOD AND TORE HIS FLESH AS HE DIED. I HAD NEVER FELT SUCH JOY."
"I CAN ONLY IMAGINE WHAT I LOOKED LIKE WHEN THEY CAME TO HIS AID AND FOUND ME. I FLED THROUGH THE WINDOW AND RAN MOST OF THAT NIGHT."
"I TOOK REFUGE IN THE CELLAR OF A BURNED OUT FARM HOUSE AND SLEPT THROUGH THE DAY. WHEN NIGHT CAME AGAIN, I WOKE STRONGER AND HEALTHIER THAN EVER IN MY LIFE."
"AND SICK AT HEART."

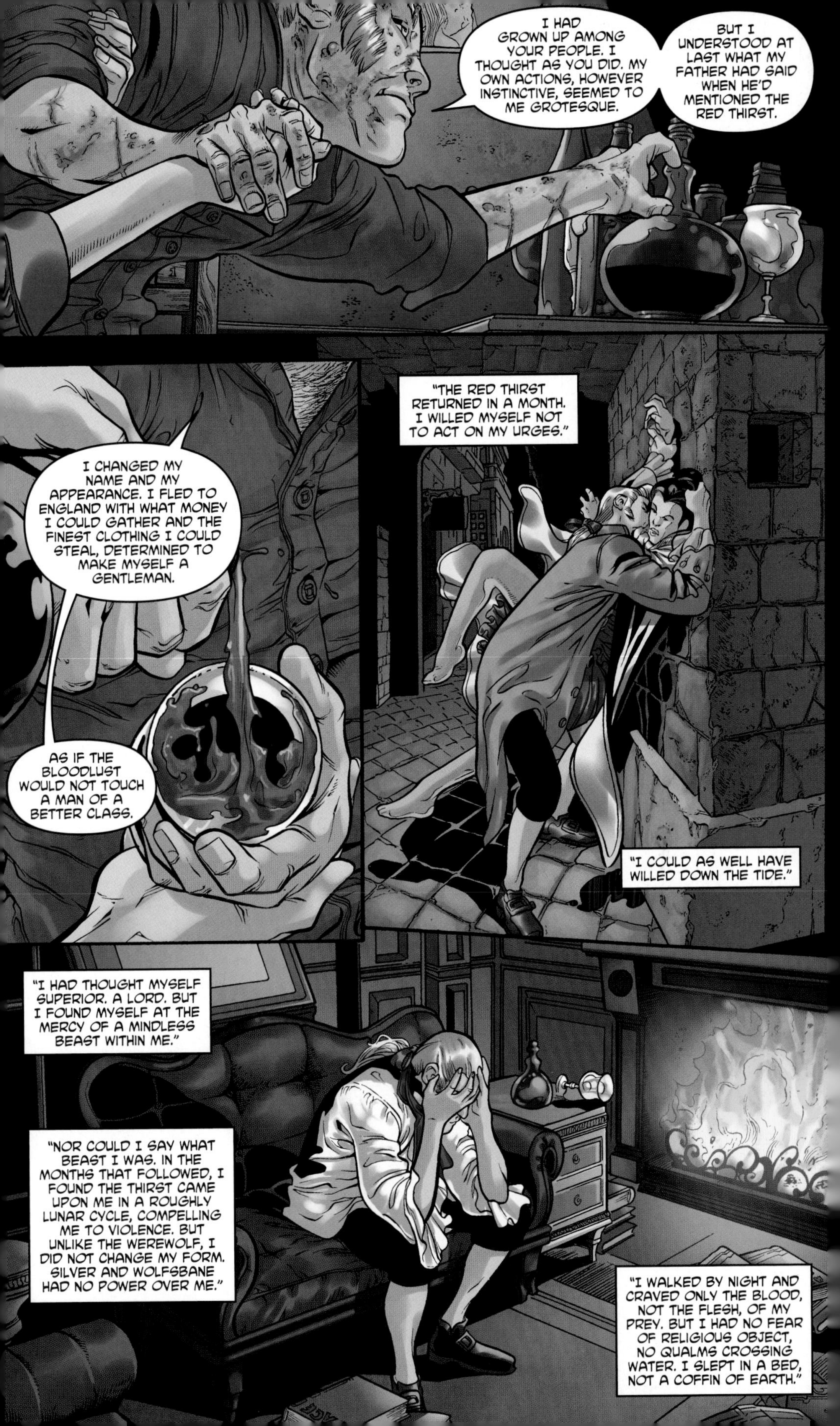
I HAD GROWN UP AMONG YOUR PEOPLE. I THOUGHT AS YOU DID. MY OWN ACTIONS, HOWEVER INSTINCTIVE, SEEMED TO ME GROTESQUE.
BUT I UNDERSTOOD AT LAST WHAT MY FATHER HAD SAID WHEN HE'D MENTIONED THE RED THIRST.
I CHANGED MY NAME AND MY APPEARANCE. I FLED TO ENGLAND WITH WHAT MONEY I COULD GATHER AND THE FINEST CLOTHING I COULD STEAL, DETERMINED TO MAKE MYSELF A GENTLEMAN.
AS IF THE BLOODLUST WOULD NOT TOUCH A MAN OF A BETTER CLASS.
"THE RED THIRST RETURNED IN A MONTH. I WILLED MYSELF NOT TO ACT ON MY URGES."
"I COULD AS WELL HAVE WILLED DOWN THE TIDE."
"I HAD THOUGHT MYSELF SUPERIOR. A LORD. BUT I FOUND MYSELF AT THE MERCY OF A MINDLESS BEAST WITHIN ME."
"NOR COULD I SAY WHAT BEAST I WAS. IN THE MONTHS THAT FOLLOWED, I FOUND THE THIRST CAME UPON ME IN A ROUGHLY LUNAR CYCLE, COMPELLING ME TO VIOLENCE. BUT UNLIKE THE WEREWOLF, I DID NOT CHANGE MY FORM. SILVER AND WOLFSBANE HAD NO POWER OVER ME."
"I WALKED BY NIGHT AND CRAVED ONLY THE BLOOD, NOT THE FLESH, OF MY PREY. BUT I HAD NO FEAR OF RELIGIOUS OBJECT, NO QUALMS CROSSING WATER. I SLEPT IN A BED, NOT A COFFIN OF EARTH."

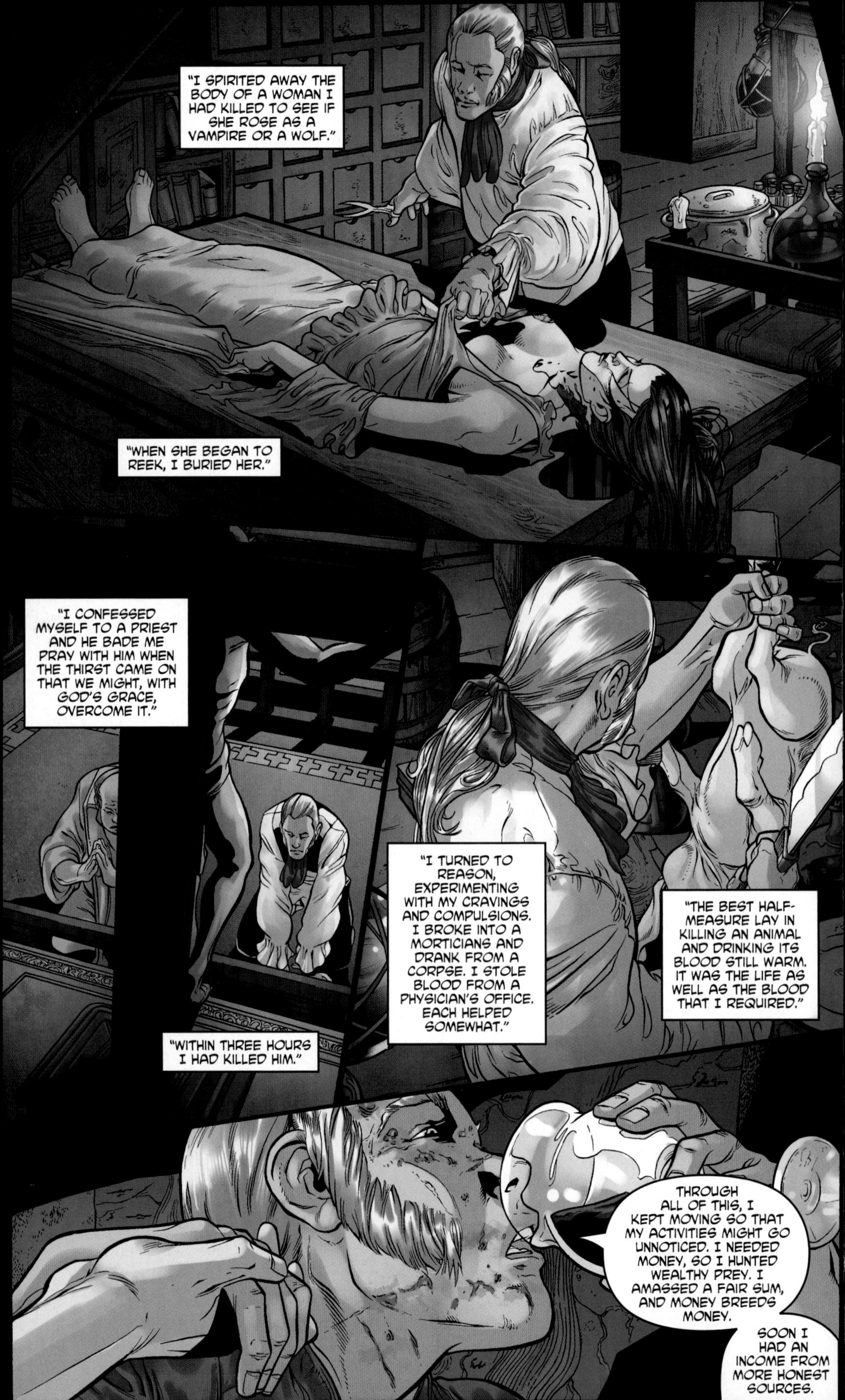
"I SPIRITED AWAY THE BODY OF A WOMAN I HAD KILLED TO SEE IF SHE ROSE AS A VAMPIRE OR A WOLF."
"WHEN SHE BEGAN TO REEK, I BURIED HER."
"I CONFESSED MYSELF TO A PRIEST AND HE BADE ME PRAY WITH HIM WHEN THE THIRST CAME ON THAT WE MIGHT, WITH GOD'S GRACE, OVERCOME IT."
"WITHIN THREE HOURS I HAD KILLED HIM."
"I TURNED TO REASON, EXPERIMENTING WITH MY CRAVINGS AND COMPULSIONS. I BROKE INTO A MORTICIANS AND DRANK FROM A CORPSE. I STOLE BLOOD FROM A PHYSICIAN'S OFFICE. EACH HELPED SOMEWHAT."
"THE BEST HALF-MEASURE LAY IN KILLING AN ANIMAL AND DRINKING ITS BLOOD STILL WARM. IT WAS THE LIFE AS WELL AS THE BLOOD THAT I REQUIRED."
THROUGH ALL OF THIS, I KEPT MOVING SO THAT MY ACTIVITIES MIGHT GO UNNOTICED. I NEEDED MONEY, SO I HUNTED WEALTHY PREY. I AMASSED A FAIR SUM, AND MONEY BREEDS MONEY.
SOON I HAD AN INCOME FROM MORE HONEST SOURCES.

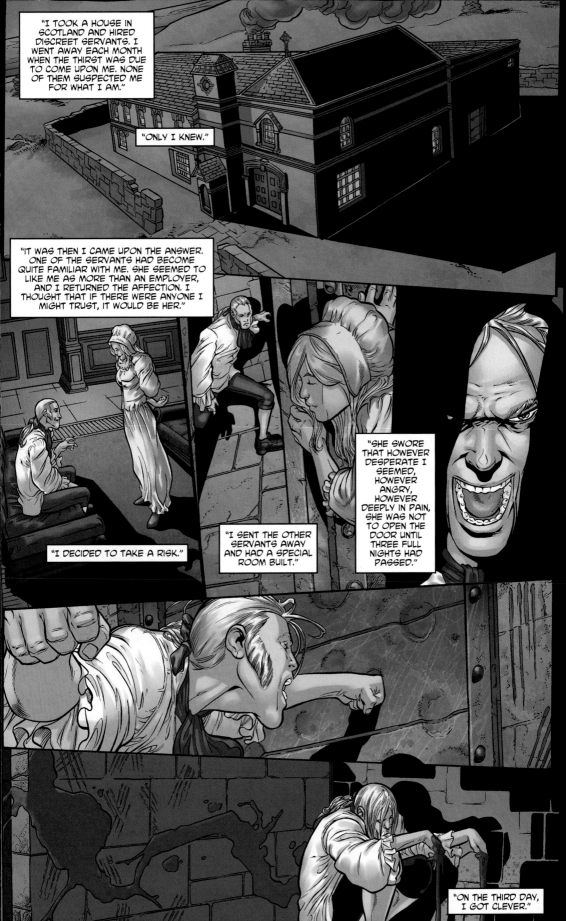

"I TOOK A HOUSE IN SCOTLAND AND HIRED DISCREET SERVANTS. I WENT AWAY EACH MONTH WHEN THE THIRST WAS DUE TO COME UPON ME. NONE OF THEM SUSPECTED ME FOR WHAT I AM."

"ONLY I KNEW."

"IT WAS THEN I CAME UPON THE ANSWER. ONE OF THE SERVANTS HAD BECOME QUITE FAMILIAR WITH ME. SHE SEEMED TO LIKE ME AS MORE THAN AN EMPLOYER, AND I RETURNED THE AFFECTION. I THOUGHT THAT IF THERE WERE ANYONE I MIGHT TRUST, IT WOULD BE HER."

"I DECIDED TO TAKE A RISK."

"I SENT THE OTHER SERVANTS AWAY AND HAD A SPECIAL ROOM BUILT."

"SHE SWORE THAT HOWEVER DESPERATE I SEEMED, HOWEVER ANGRY, HOWEVER DEEPLY IN PAIN, SHE WAS NOT TO OPEN THE DOOR UNTIL THREE FULL NIGHTS HAD PASSED."

"ON THE THIRD DAY, I GOT CLEVER."

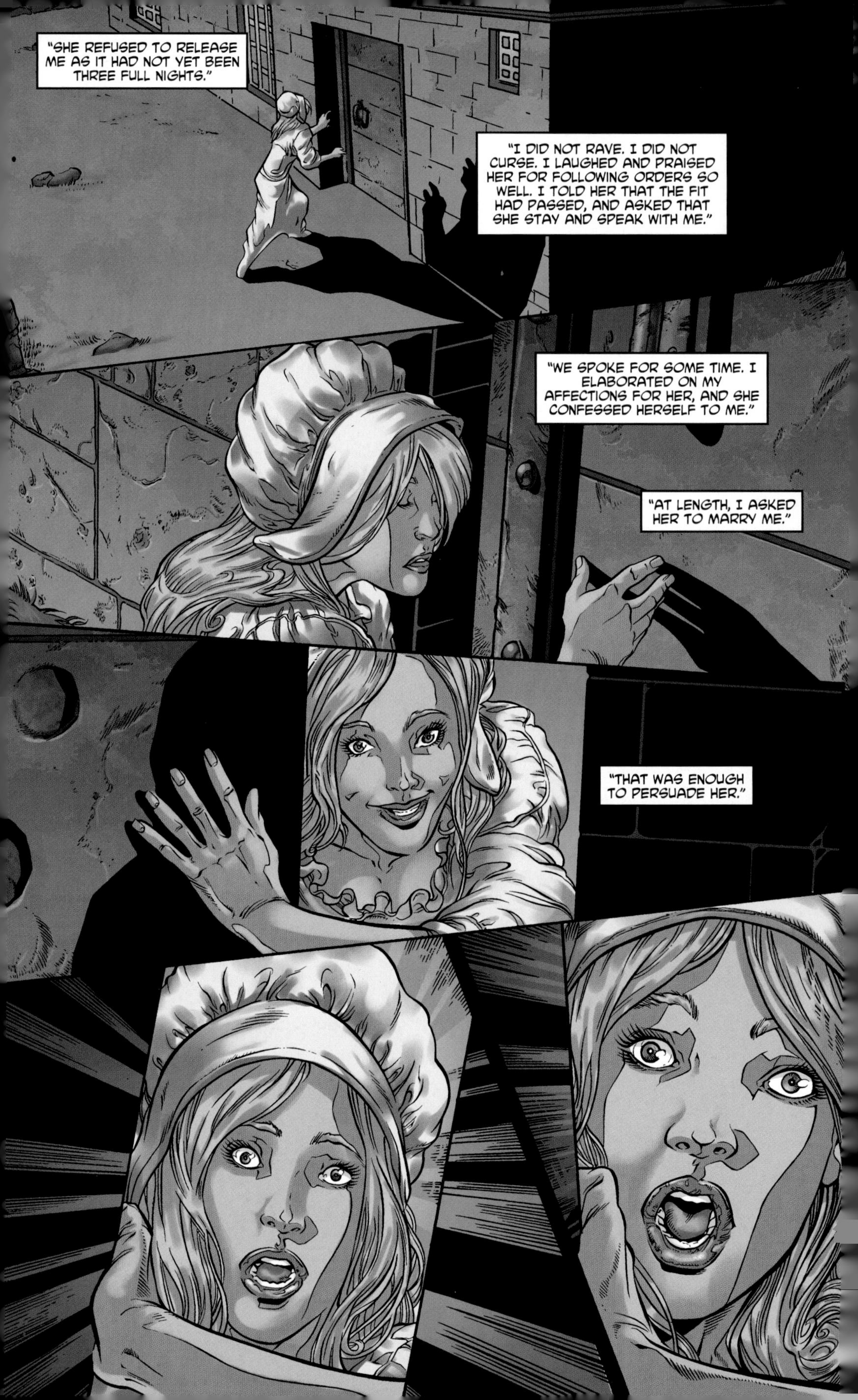
"SHE REFUSED TO RELEASE ME AS IT HAD NOT YET BEEN THREE FULL NIGHTS."
"I DID NOT RAVE. I DID NOT CURSE. I LAUGHED AND PRAISED HER FOR FOLLOWING ORDERS SO WELL. I TOLD HER THAT THE FIT HAD PASSED, AND ASKED THAT SHE STAY AND SPEAK WITH ME."
"WE SPOKE FOR SOME TIME. I ELABORATED ON MY AFFECTIONS FOR HER, AND SHE CONFESSED HERSELF TO ME."
"AT LENGTH, I ASKED HER TO MARRY ME."
"THAT WAS ENOUGH TO PERSUADE HER."

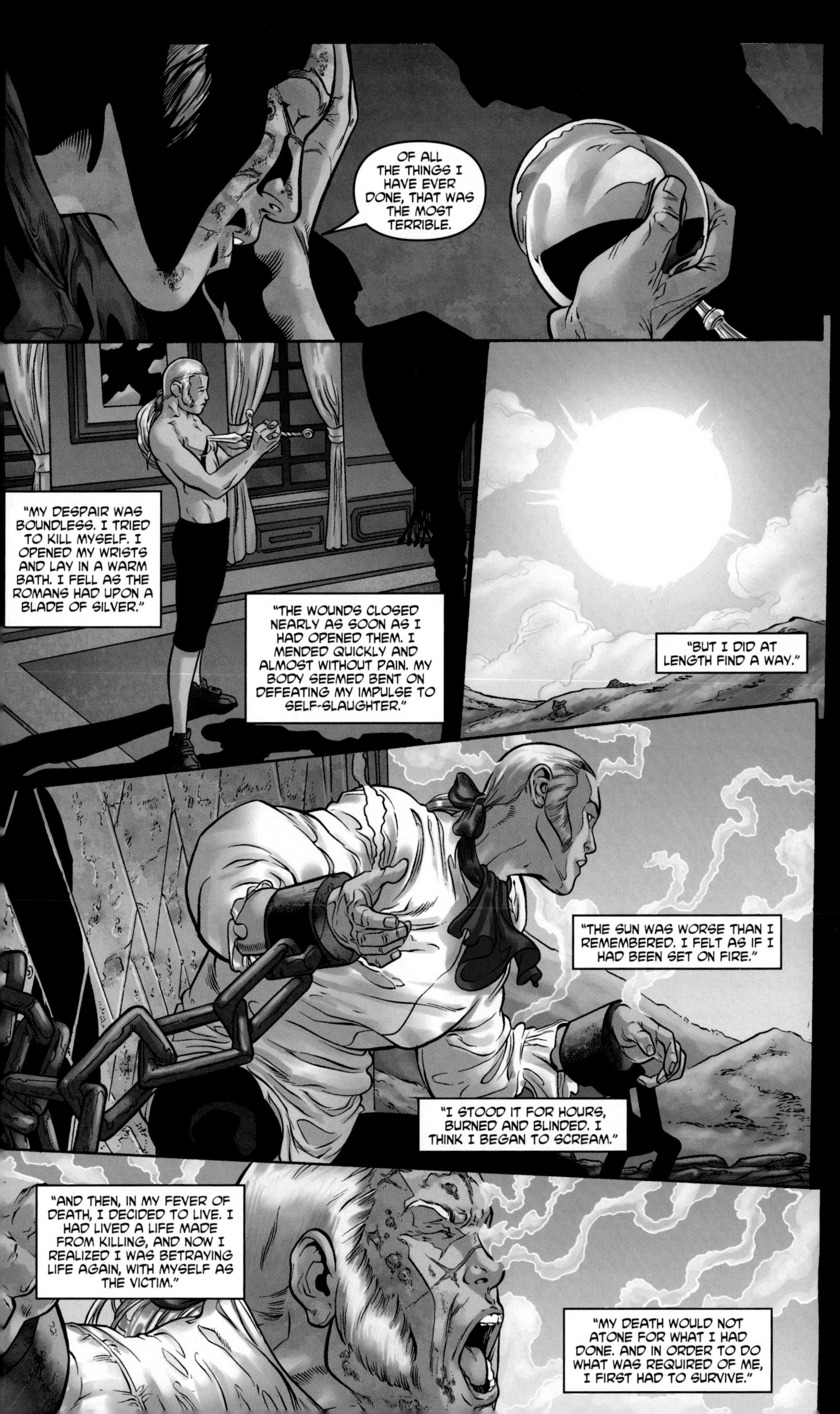
OF ALL THE THINGS I HAVE EVER DONE, THAT WAS THE MOST TERRIBLE.
"MY DESPAIR WAS BOUNDLESS. I TRIED TO KILL MYSELF. I OPENED MY WRISTS AND LAY IN A WARM BATH. I FELL AS THE ROMANS HAD UPON A BLADE OF SILVER."
"THE WOUNDS CLOSED NEARLY AS SOON AS I HAD OPENED THEM. I MENDED QUICKLY AND ALMOST WITHOUT PAIN. MY BODY SEEMED BENT ON DEFEATING MY IMPULSE TO SELF-SLAUGHTER."
"BUT I DID AT LENGTH FIND A WAY."
"THE SUN WAS WORSE THAN I REMEMBERED. I FELT AS IF I HAD BEEN SET ON FIRE."
"I STOOD IT FOR HOURS, BURNED AND BLINDED. I THINK I BEGAN TO SCREAM."
"AND THEN, IN MY FEVER OF DEATH, I DECIDED TO LIVE. I HAD LIVED A LIFE MADE FROM KILLING, AND NOW I REALIZED I WAS BETRAYING LIFE AGAIN, WITH MYSELF AS THE VICTIM."
"MY DEATH WOULD NOT ATONE FOR WHAT I HAD DONE. AND IN ORDER TO DO WHAT WAS REQUIRED OF ME, I FIRST HAD TO SURVIVE."

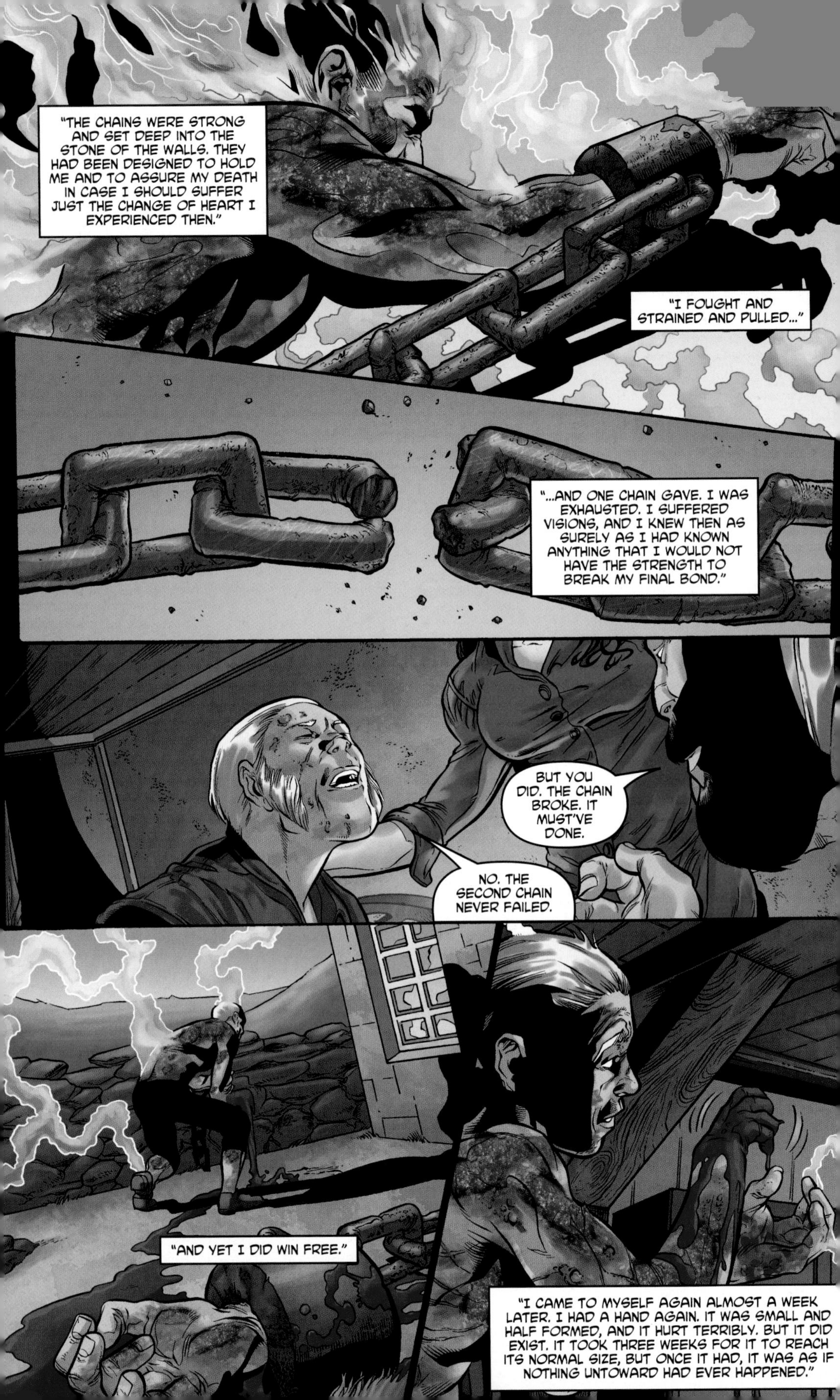
"THE CHAINS WERE STRONG AND SET DEEP INTO THE STONE OF THE WALLS. THEY HAD BEEN DESIGNED TO HOLD ME AND TO ASSURE MY DEATH IN CASE I SHOULD SUFFER JUST THE CHANGE OF HEART I EXPERIENCED THEN."
"I FOUGHT AND STRAINED AND PULLED..."
"...AND ONE CHAIN GAVE. I WAS EXHAUSTED. I SUFFERED VISIONS, AND I KNEW THEN AS SURELY AS I HAD KNOWN ANYTHING THAT I WOULD NOT HAVE THE STRENGTH TO BREAK MY FINAL BOND."
BUT YOU DID. THE CHAIN BROKE. IT MUST'VE DONE.
NO. THE SECOND CHAIN NEVER FAILED.
"AND YET I DID WIN FREE."
"I CAME TO MYSELF AGAIN ALMOST A WEEK LATER. I HAD A HAND AGAIN. IT WAS SMALL AND HALF FORMED, AND IT HURT TERRIBLY. BUT IT DID EXIST. IT TOOK THREE WEEKS FOR IT TO REACH ITS NORMAL SIZE, BUT ONCE IT HAD, IT WAS AS IF NOTHING UNTOWARD HAD EVER HAPPENED."

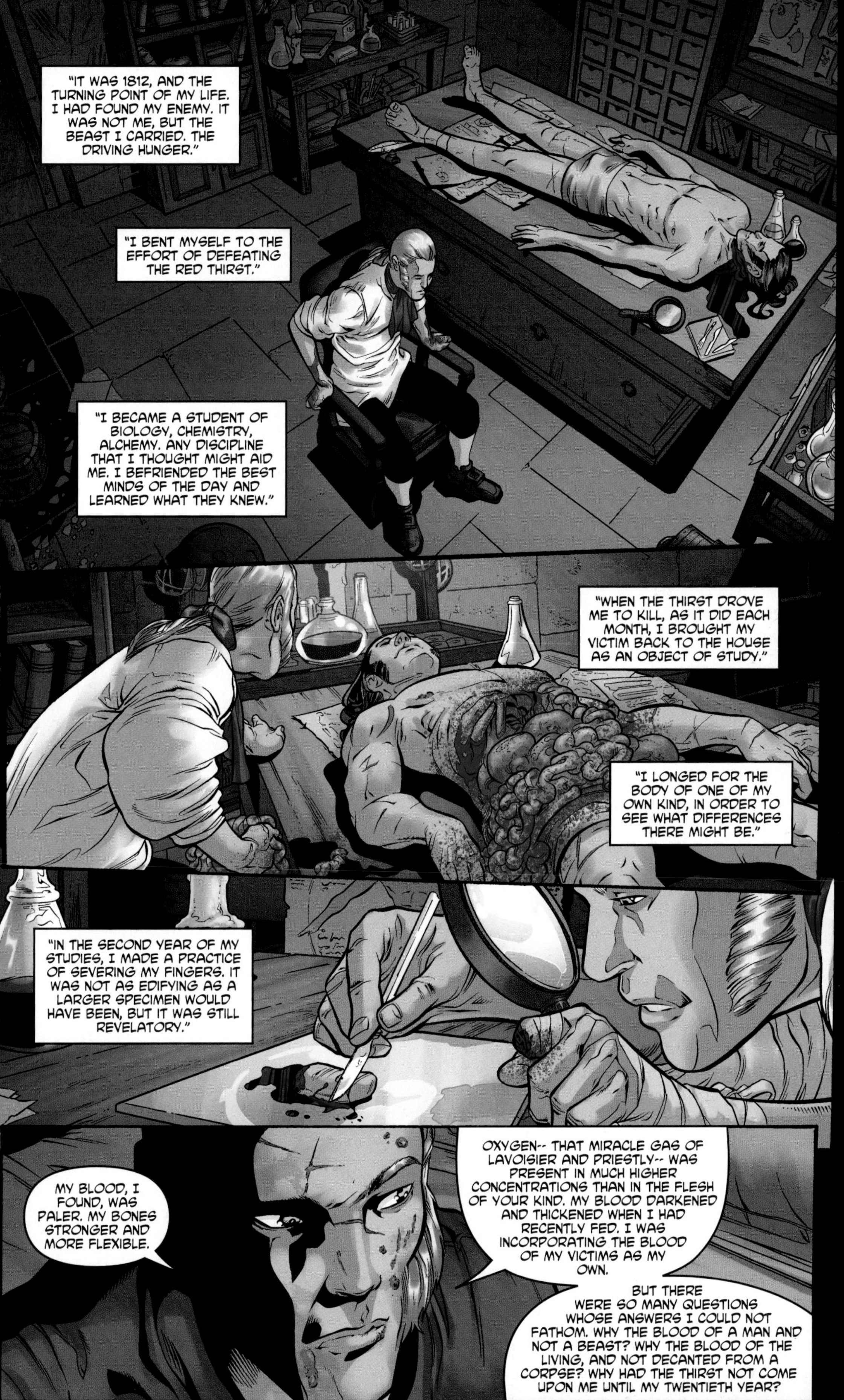
"IT WAS 1812, AND THE TURNING POINT OF MY LIFE. I HAD FOUND MY ENEMY. IT WAS NOT ME, BUT THE BEAST I CARRIED. THE DRIVING HUNGER."
"I BENT MYSELF TO THE EFFORT OF DEFEATING THE RED THIRST."
"I BECAME A STUDENT OF BIOLOGY, CHEMISTRY, ALCHEMY. ANY DISCIPLINE THAT I THOUGHT MIGHT AID ME. I BEFRIENDED THE BEST MINDS OF THE DAY AND LEARNED WHAT THEY KNEW."
"WHEN THE THIRST DROVE ME TO KILL, AS IT DID EACH MONTH, I BROUGHT MY VICTIM BACK TO THE HOUSE AS AN OBJECT OF STUDY."
"I LONGED FOR THE BODY OF ONE OF MY OWN KIND, IN ORDER TO SEE WHAT DIFFERENCES THERE MIGHT BE."
"IN THE SECOND YEAR OF MY STUDIES, I MADE A PRACTICE OF SEVERING MY FINGERS. IT WAS NOT AS EDIFYING AS A LARGER SPECIMEN WOULD HAVE BEEN, BUT IT WAS STILL REVELATORY."
MY BLOOD, I FOUND, WAS PALER. MY BONES STRONGER AND MORE FLEXIBLE.
OXYGEN-- THAT MIRACLE GAS OF LAVOISIER AND PRIESTLY-- WAS PRESENT IN MUCH HIGHER CONCENTRATIONS THAN IN THE FLESH OF YOUR KIND. MY BLOOD DARKENED AND THICKENED WHEN I HAD RECENTLY FED. I WAS INCORPORATING THE BLOOD OF MY VICTIMS AS MY OWN.
BUT THERE WERE SO MANY QUESTIONS WHOSE ANSWERS I COULD NOT FATHOM. WHY THE BLOOD OF A MAN AND NOT A BEAST? WHY THE BLOOD OF THE LIVING, AND NOT DECANTED FROM A CORPSE? WHY HAD THE THIRST NOT COME UPON ME UNTIL MY TWENTIETH YEAR?

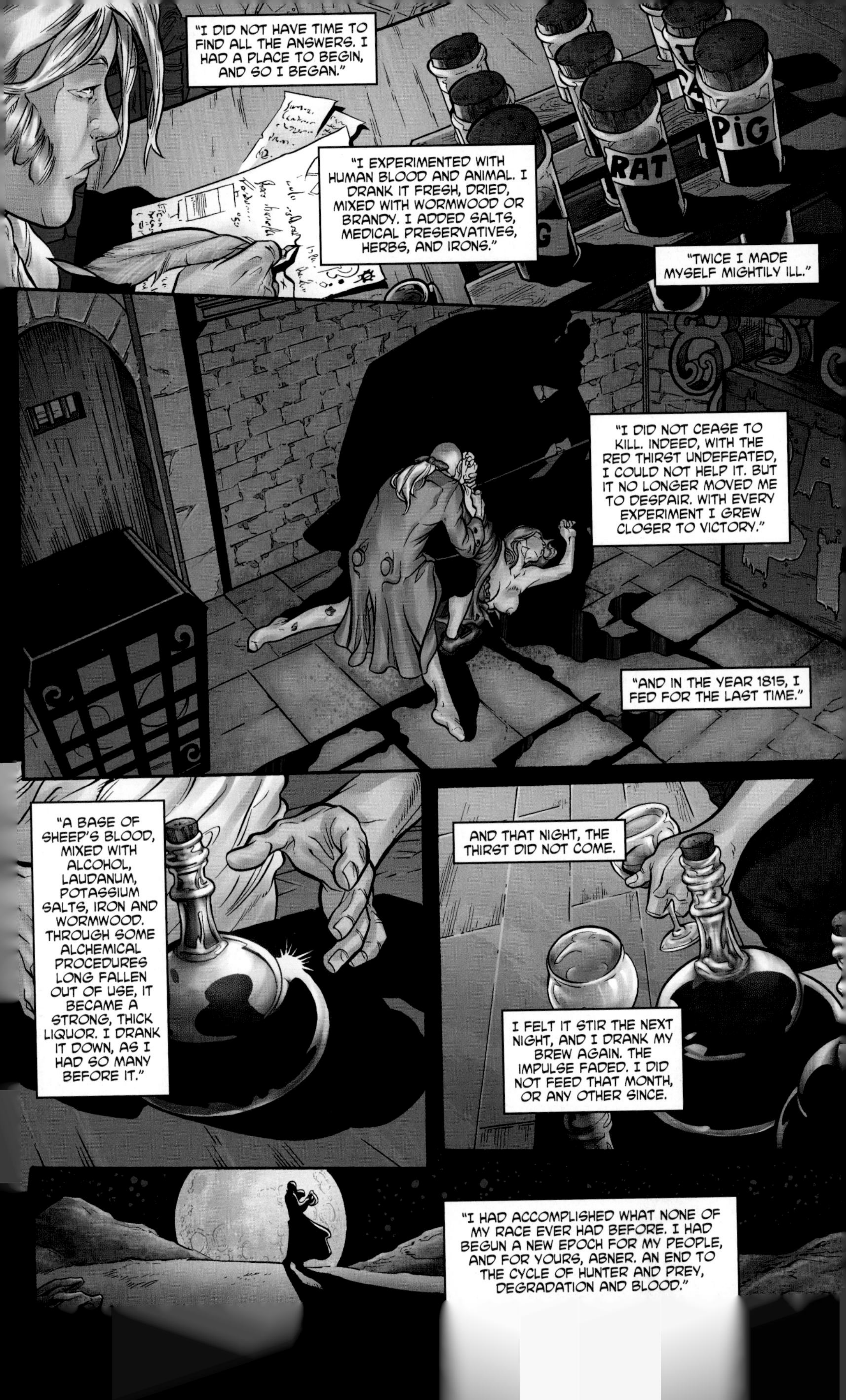
"I DID NOT HAVE TIME TO FIND ALL THE ANSWERS. I HAD A PLACE TO BEGIN, AND SO I BEGAN."
"I EXPERIMENTED WITH HUMAN BLOOD AND ANIMAL. I DRANK IT FRESH, DRIED, MIXED WITH WORMWOOD OR BRANDY. I ADDED SALTS, MEDICAL PRESERVATIVES, HERBS, AND IRONS."
RAT
PIG
"TWICE I MADE MYSELF MIGHTILY ILL."
"I DID NOT CEASE TO KILL. INDEED, WITH THE RED THIRST UNDEFEATED, I COULD NOT HELP IT. BUT IT NO LONGER MOVED ME TO DESPAIR. WITH EVERY EXPERIMENT I GREW CLOSER TO VICTORY."
"AND IN THE YEAR 1815, I FED FOR THE LAST TIME."
"A BASE OF SHEEP'S BLOOD, MIXED WITH ALCOHOL, LAUDANUM, POTASSIUM SALTS, IRON AND WORMWOOD. THROUGH SOME ALCHEMICAL PROCEDURES LONG FALLEN OUT OF USE, IT BECAME A STRONG, THICK LIQUOR. I DRANK IT DOWN, AS I HAD SO MANY BEFORE IT."
AND THAT NIGHT, THE THIRST DID NOT COME.
I FELT IT STIR THE NEXT NIGHT, AND I DRANK MY BREW AGAIN. THE IMPULSE FADED. I DID NOT FEED THAT MONTH, OR ANY OTHER SINCE.
"I HAD ACCOMPLISHED WHAT NONE OF MY RACE EVER HAD BEFORE. I HAD BEGUN A NEW EPOCH FOR MY PEOPLE, AND FOR YOURS, ABNER. AN END TO THE CYCLE OF HUNTER AND PREY, DEGRADATION AND BLOOD."

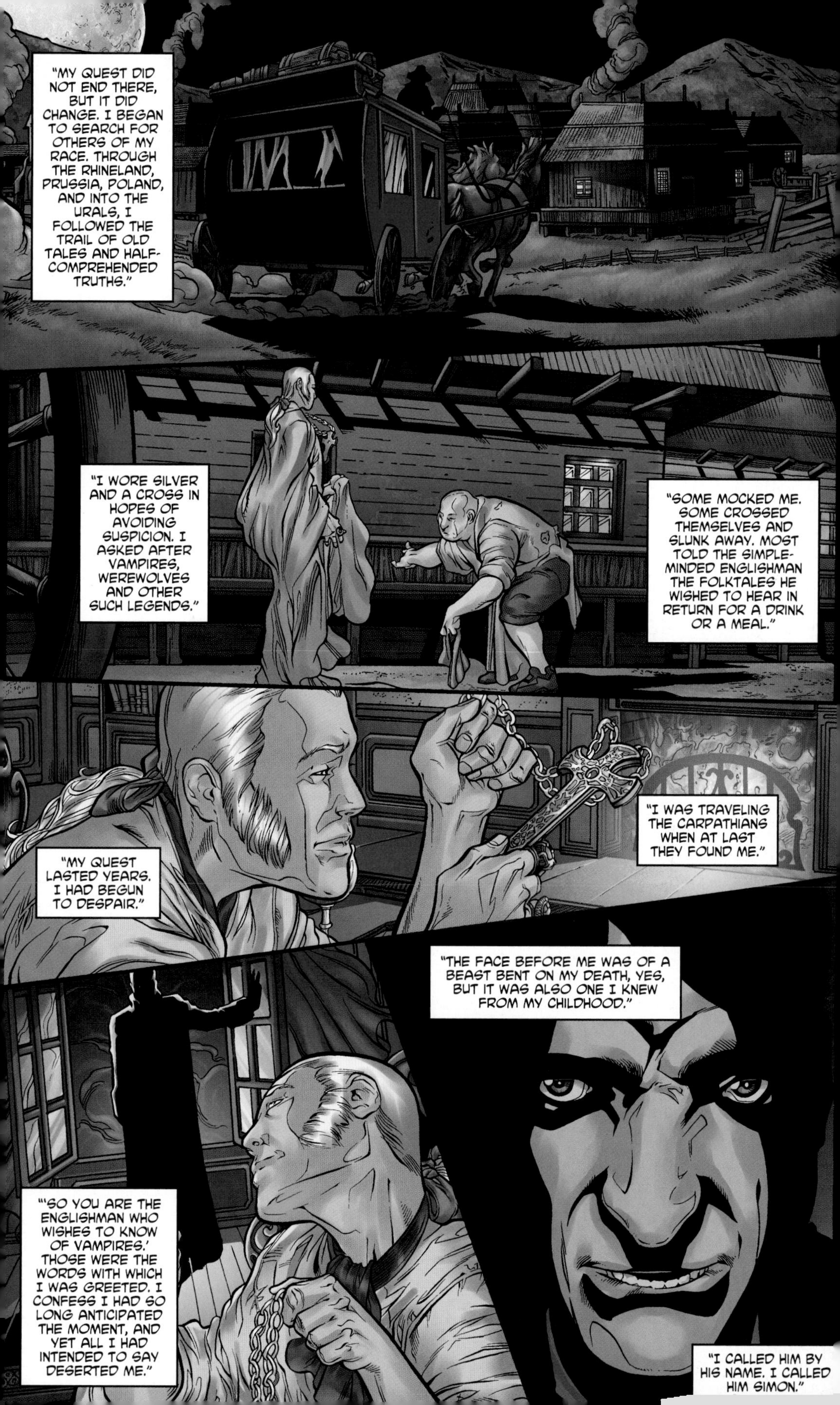
"MY QUEST DID NOT END THERE, BUT IT DID CHANGE. I BEGAN TO SEARCH FOR OTHERS OF MY RACE. THROUGH THE RHINELAND, PRUSSIA, POLAND, AND INTO THE URALS, I FOLLOWED THE TRAIL OF OLD TALES AND HALF-COMPREHENDED TRUTHS."
"I WORE SILVER AND A CROSS IN HOPES OF AVOIDING SUSPICION. I ASKED AFTER VAMPIRES, WEREWOLVES AND OTHER SUCH LEGENDS."
"SOME MOCKED ME. SOME CROSSED THEMSELVES AND SLUNK AWAY. MOST TOLD THE SIMPLE-MINDED ENGLISHMAN THE FOLKTALES HE WISHED TO HEAR IN RETURN FOR A DRINK OR A MEAL."
"MY QUEST LASTED YEARS. I HAD BEGUN TO DESPAIR."
"I WAS TRAVELING THE CARPATHIANS WHEN AT LAST THEY FOUND ME."
"THE FACE BEFORE ME WAS OF A BEAST BENT ON MY DEATH, YES, BUT IT WAS ALSO ONE I KNEW FROM MY CHILDHOOD."
"'SO YOU ARE THE ENGLISHMAN WHO WISHES TO KNOW OF VAMPIRES.' THOSE WERE THE WORDS WITH WHICH I WAS GREETED. I CONFESS I HAD SO LONG ANTICIPATED THE MOMENT, AND YET ALL I HAD INTENDED TO SAY DESERTED ME."
"I CALLED HIM BY HIS NAME. I CALLED HIM SIMON."

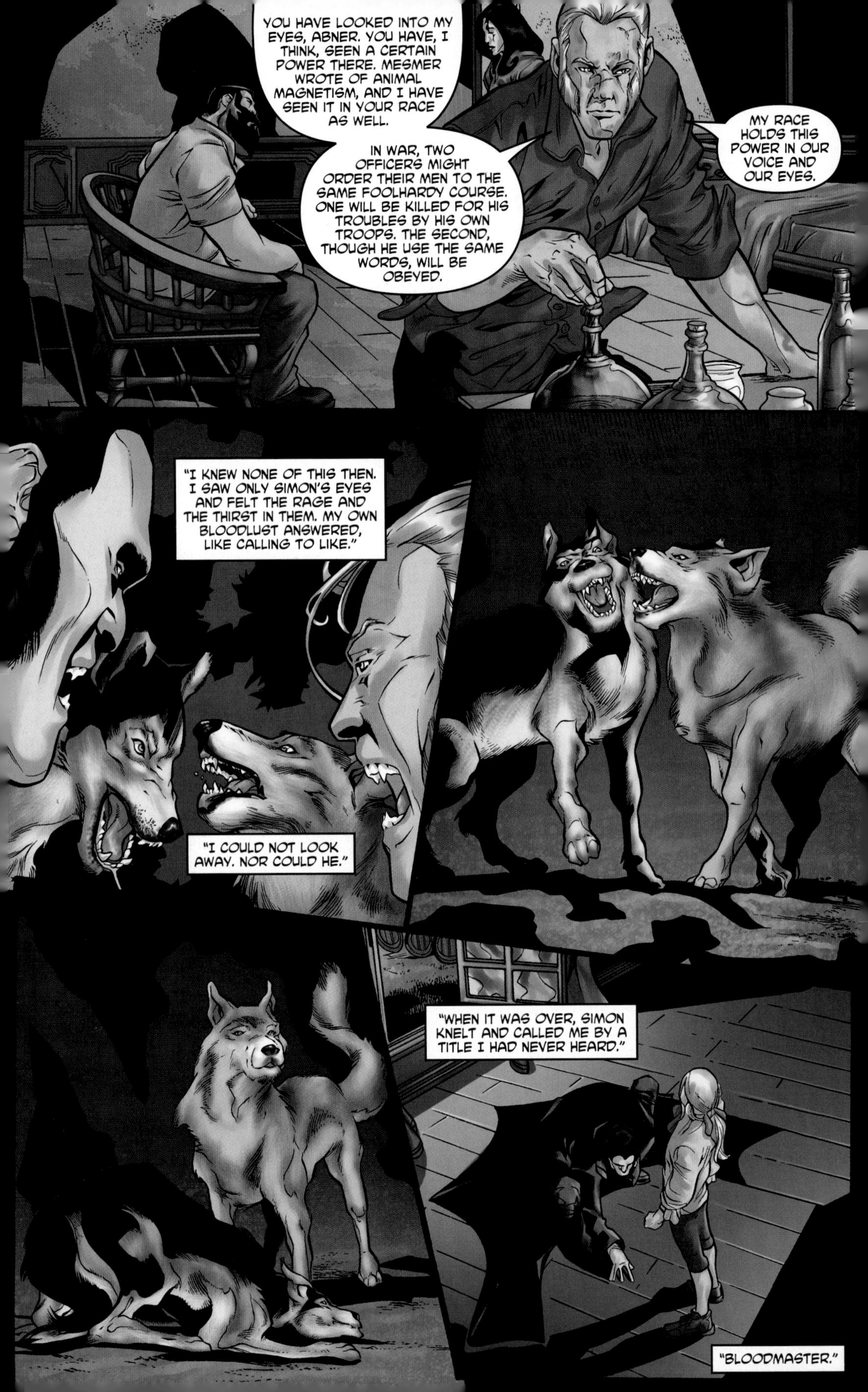
YOU HAVE LOOKED INTO MY EYES, ABNER. YOU HAVE, I THINK, SEEN A CERTAIN POWER THERE. MESMER WROTE OF ANIMAL MAGNETISM, AND I HAVE SEEN IT IN YOUR RACE AS WELL.
IN WAR, TWO OFFICERS MIGHT ORDER THEIR MEN TO THE SAME FOOLHARDY COURSE. ONE WILL BE KILLED FOR HIS TROUBLES BY HIS OWN TROOPS. THE SECOND, THOUGH HE USE THE SAME WORDS, WILL BE OBEYED.
MY RACE HOLDS THIS POWER IN OUR VOICE AND OUR EYES.
"I KNEW NONE OF THIS THEN. I SAW ONLY SIMON'S EYES AND FELT THE RAGE AND THE THIRST IN THEM. MY OWN BLOODLUST ANSWERED, LIKE CALLING TO LIKE."
"I COULD NOT LOOK AWAY. NOR COULD HE."
"WHEN IT WAS OVER, SIMON KNELT AND CALLED ME BY A TITLE I HAD NEVER HEARD."
"BLOODMASTER."

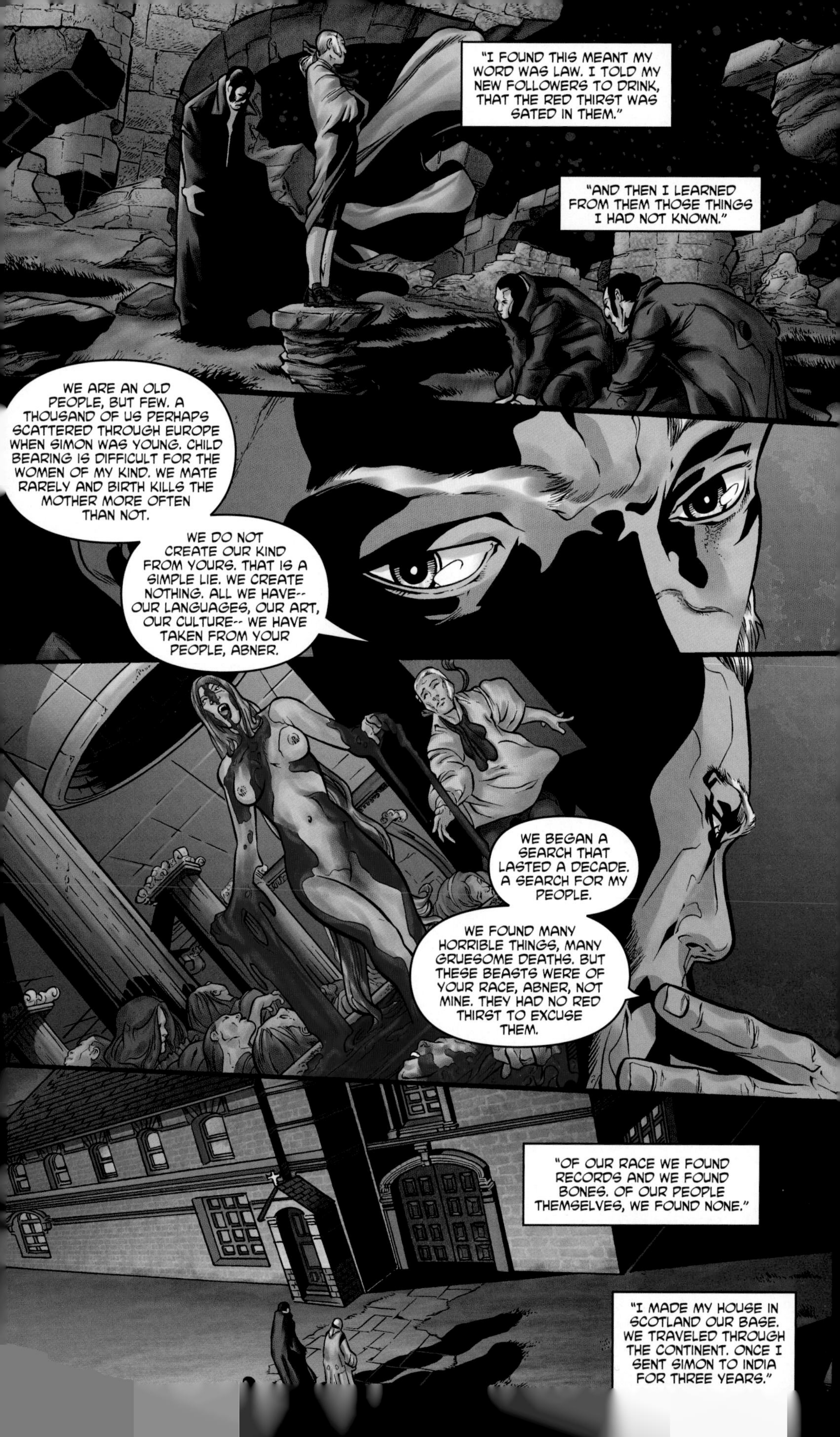
"I FOUND THIS MEANT MY WORD WAS LAW. I TOLD MY NEW FOLLOWERS TO DRINK, THAT THE RED THIRST WAS SATED IN THEM."
"AND THEN I LEARNED FROM THEM THOSE THINGS I HAD NOT KNOWN."
WE ARE AN OLD PEOPLE, BUT FEW. A THOUSAND OF US PERHAPS SCATTERED THROUGH EUROPE WHEN SIMON WAS YOUNG. CHILD BEARING IS DIFFICULT FOR THE WOMEN OF MY KIND. WE MATE RARELY AND BIRTH KILLS THE MOTHER MORE OFTEN THAN NOT.
WE DO NOT CREATE OUR KIND FROM YOURS. THAT IS A SIMPLE LIE. WE CREATE NOTHING. ALL WE HAVE-- OUR LANGUAGES, OUR ART, OUR CULTURE-- WE HAVE TAKEN FROM YOUR PEOPLE, ABNER.
WE BEGAN A SEARCH THAT LASTED A DECADE. A SEARCH FOR MY PEOPLE.
WE FOUND MANY HORRIBLE THINGS, MANY GRUESOME DEATHS. BUT THESE BEASTS WERE OF YOUR RACE, ABNER, NOT MINE. THEY HAD NO RED THIRST TO EXCUSE THEM.
"OF OUR RACE WE FOUND RECORDS AND WE FOUND BONES. OF OUR PEOPLE THEMSELVES, WE FOUND NONE."
"I MADE MY HOUSE IN SCOTLAND OUR BASE. WE TRAVELED THROUGH THE CONTINENT. ONCE I SENT SIMON TO INDIA FOR THREE YEARS."

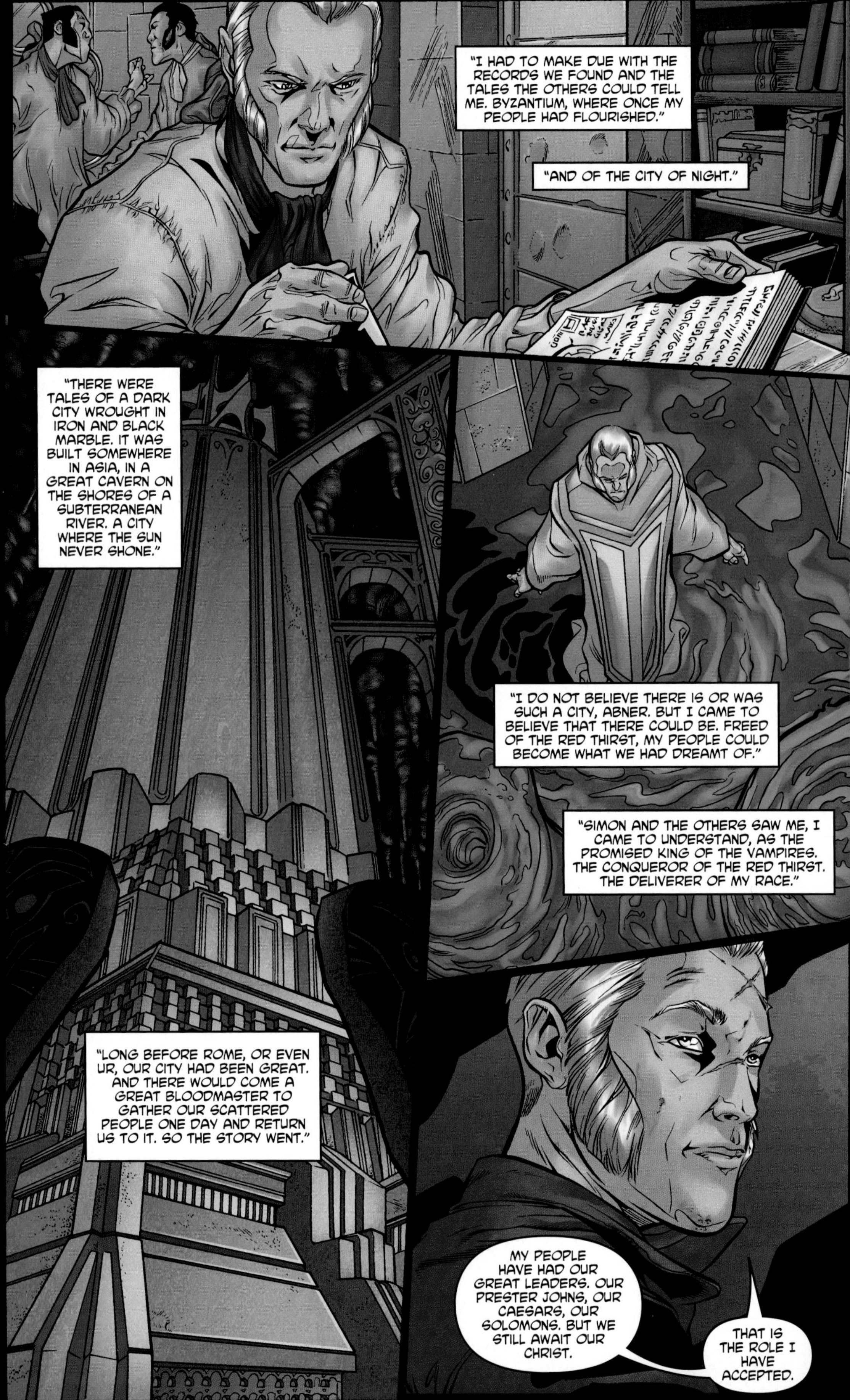
"I HAD TO MAKE DUE WITH THE RECORDS WE FOUND AND THE TALES THE OTHERS COULD TELL ME. BYZANTIUM, WHERE ONCE MY PEOPLE HAD FLOURISHED."
"AND OF THE CITY OF NIGHT."
"THERE WERE TALES OF A DARK CITY WROUGHT IN IRON AND BLACK MARBLE. IT WAS BUILT SOMEWHERE IN ASIA, IN A GREAT CAVERN ON THE SHORES OF A SUBTERRANEAN RIVER. A CITY WHERE THE SUN NEVER SHONE."
"I DO NOT BELIEVE THERE IS OR WAS SUCH A CITY, ABNER. BUT I CAME TO BELIEVE THAT THERE COULD BE. FREED OF THE RED THIRST, MY PEOPLE COULD BECOME WHAT WE HAD DREAMT OF."
"SIMON AND THE OTHERS SAW ME, I CAME TO UNDERSTAND, AS THE PROMISED KING OF THE VAMPIRES. THE CONQUEROR OF THE RED THIRST. THE DELIVERER OF MY RACE."
"LONG BEFORE ROME, OR EVEN UR, OUR CITY HAD BEEN GREAT. AND THERE WOULD COME A GREAT BLOODMASTER TO GATHER OUR SCATTERED PEOPLE ONE DAY AND RETURN US TO IT. SO THE STORY WENT."
MY PEOPLE HAVE HAD OUR GREAT LEADERS. OUR PRESTER JOHNS, OUR CAESARS, OUR SOLOMONS. BUT WE STILL AWAIT OUR CHRIST.
THAT IS THE ROLE I HAVE ACCEPTED.

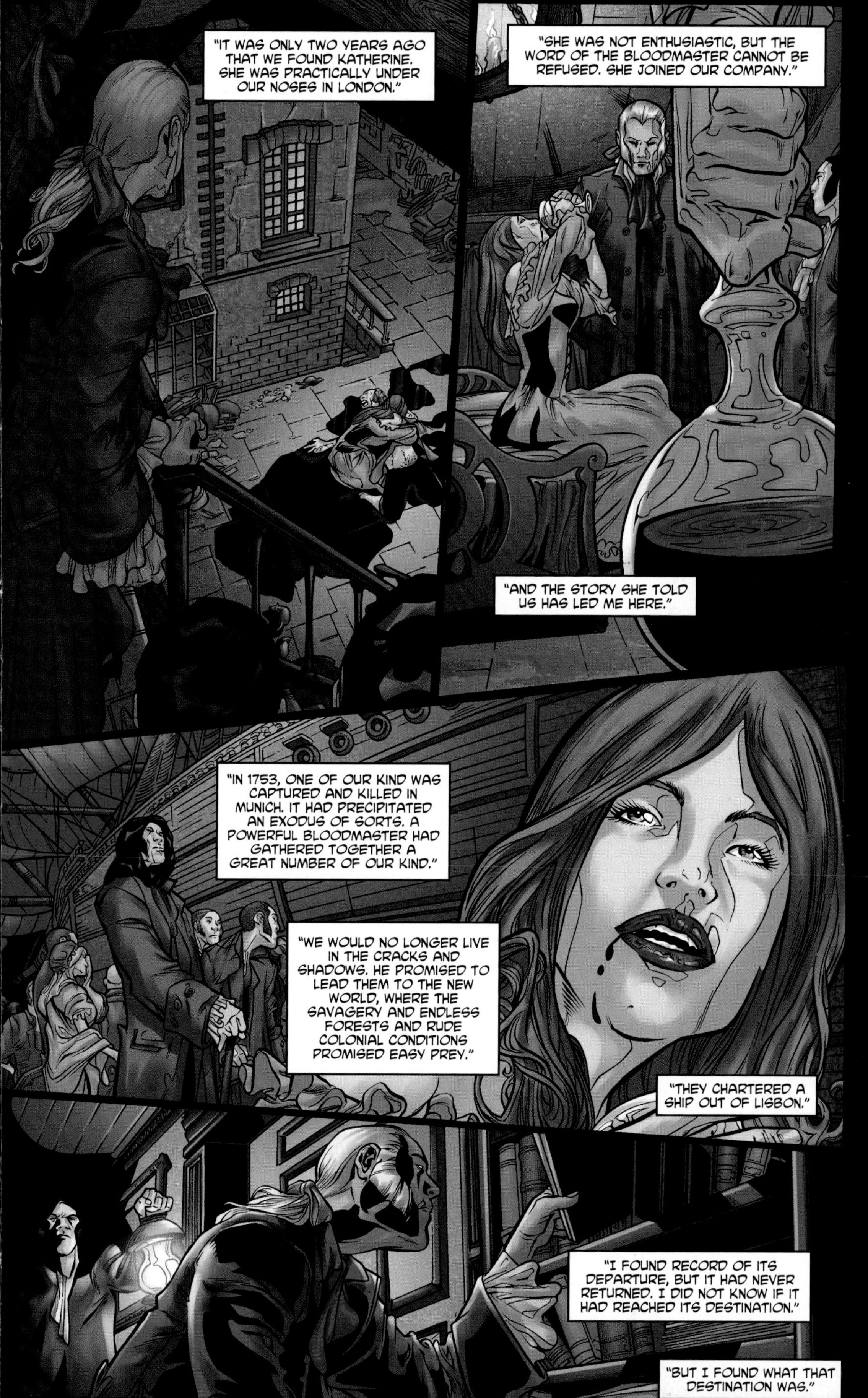
"IT WAS ONLY TWO YEARS AGO THAT WE FOUND KATHERINE. SHE WAS PRACTICALLY UNDER OUR NOSES IN LONDON."
"SHE WAS NOT ENTHUSIASTIC, BUT THE WORD OF THE BLOODMASTER CANNOT BE REFUSED. SHE JOINED OUR COMPANY."
"AND THE STORY SHE TOLD US HAS LED ME HERE."
"IN 1753, ONE OF OUR KIND WAS CAPTURED AND KILLED IN MUNICH. IT HAD PRECIPITATED AN EXODUS OF SORTS. A POWERFUL BLOODMASTER HAD GATHERED TOGETHER A GREAT NUMBER OF OUR KIND."
"WE WOULD NO LONGER LIVE IN THE CRACKS AND SHADOWS. HE PROMISED TO LEAD THEM TO THE NEW WORLD, WHERE THE SAVAGERY AND ENDLESS FORESTS AND RUDE COLONIAL CONDITIONS PROMISED EASY PREY."
"THEY CHARTERED A SHIP OUT OF LISBON."
"I FOUND RECORD OF ITS DEPARTURE, BUT IT HAD NEVER RETURNED. I DID NOT KNOW IF IT HAD REACHED ITS DESTINATION."
"BUT I FOUND WHAT THAT DESTINATION WAS."

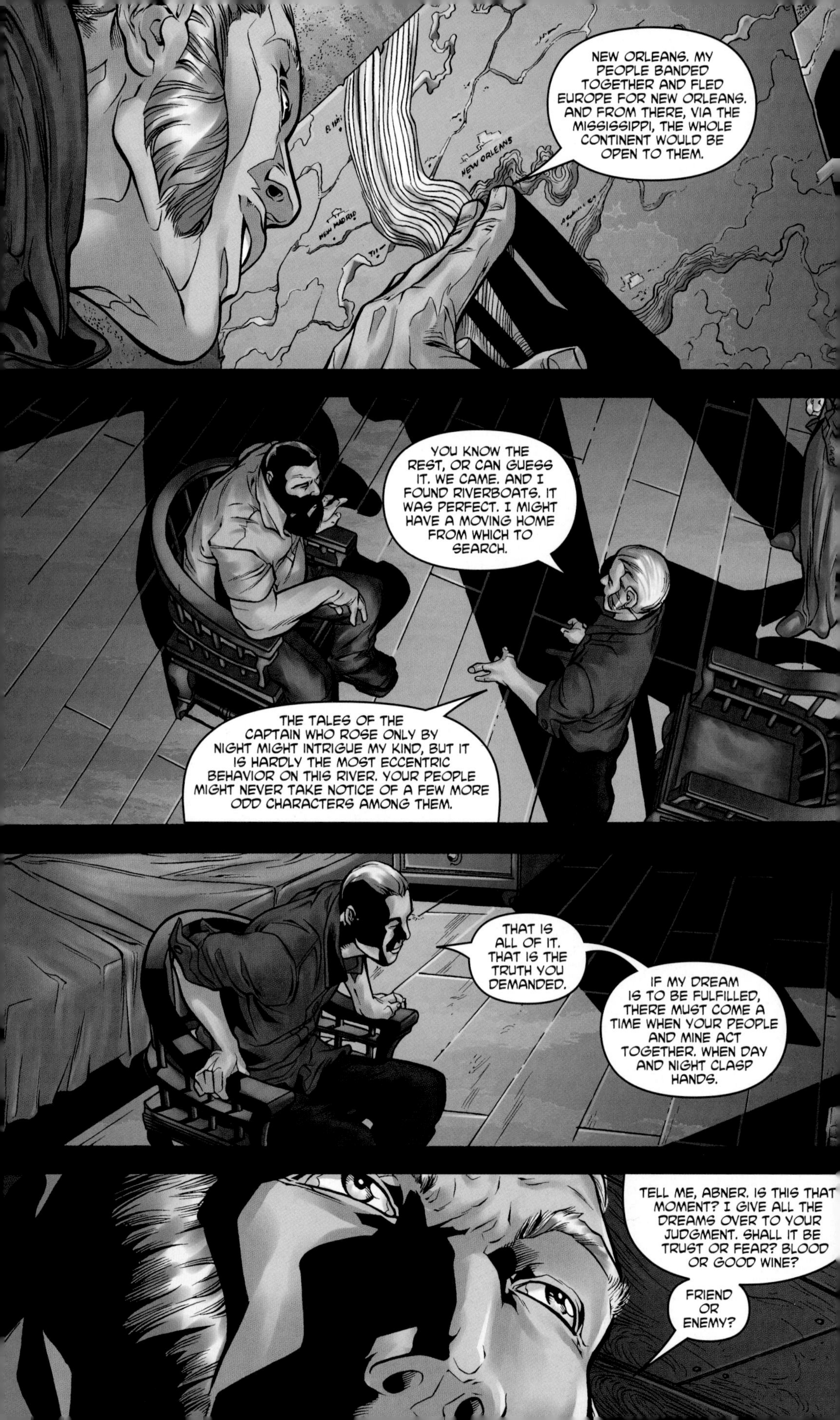
NEW ORLEANS
NEW MADRID
NEW ORLEANS. MY PEOPLE BANDED TOGETHER AND FLED EUROPE FOR NEW ORLEANS. AND FROM THERE, VIA THE MISSISSIPPI, THE WHOLE CONTINENT WOULD BE OPEN TO THEM.
YOU KNOW THE REST, OR CAN GUESS IT. WE CAME. AND I FOUND RIVERBOATS. IT WAS PERFECT. I MIGHT HAVE A MOVING HOME FROM WHICH TO SEARCH.
THE TALES OF THE CAPTAIN WHO ROSE ONLY BY NIGHT MIGHT INTRIGUE MY KIND, BUT IT IS HARDLY THE MOST ECCENTRIC BEHAVIOR ON THIS RIVER. YOUR PEOPLE MIGHT NEVER TAKE NOTICE OF A FEW MORE ODD CHARACTERS AMONG THEM.
THAT IS ALL OF IT. THAT IS THE TRUTH YOU DEMANDED.
IF MY DREAM IS TO BE FULFILLED, THERE MUST COME A TIME WHEN YOUR PEOPLE AND MINE ACT TOGETHER. WHEN DAY AND NIGHT CLASP HANDS.
TELL ME, ABNER. IS THIS THAT MOMENT? I GIVE ALL THE DREAMS OVER TO YOUR JUDGMENT. SHALL IT BE TRUST OR FEAR? BLOOD OR GOOD WINE?
FRIEND OR ENEMY?

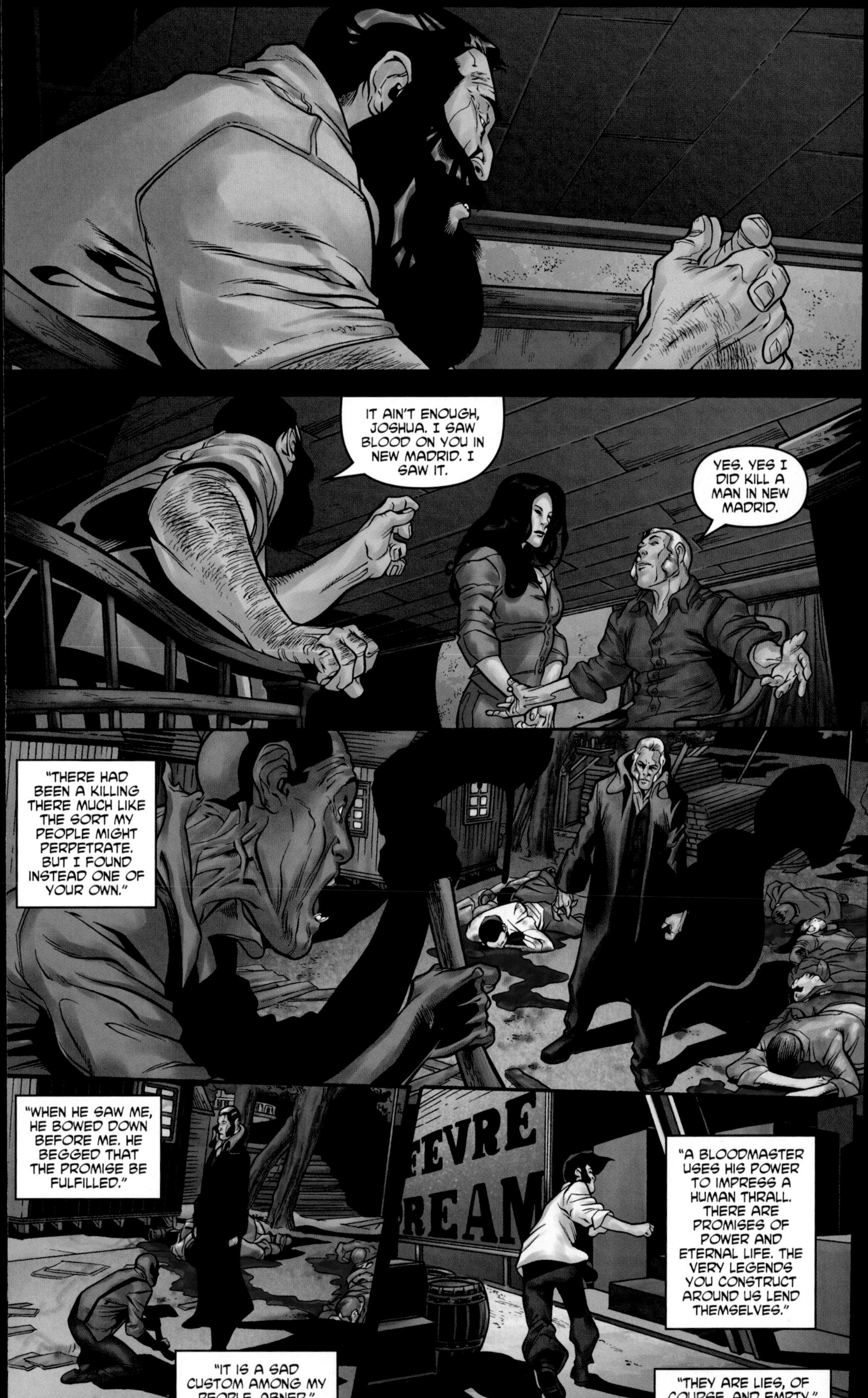
IT AIN'T ENOUGH, JOSHUA. I SAW BLOOD ON YOU IN NEW MADRID. I SAW IT.
YES. YES I DID KILL A MAN IN NEW MADRID.
"THERE HAD BEEN A KILLING THERE MUCH LIKE THE SORT MY PEOPLE MIGHT PERPETRATE. BUT I FOUND INSTEAD ONE OF YOUR OWN."
"WHEN HE SAW ME, HE BOWED DOWN BEFORE ME. HE BEGGED THAT THE PROMISE BE FULFILLED."
EEVRE
REAM
"IT IS A SAD CUSTOM AMONG MY PEOPLE, ABNER."
"A BLOODMASTER USES HIS POWER TO IMPRESS A HUMAN THRALL. THERE ARE PROMISES OF POWER AND ETERNAL LIFE. THE VERY LEGENDS YOU CONSTRUCT AROUND US LEND THEMSELVES."
"THEY ARE LIES, OF COURSE, AND EMPTY."

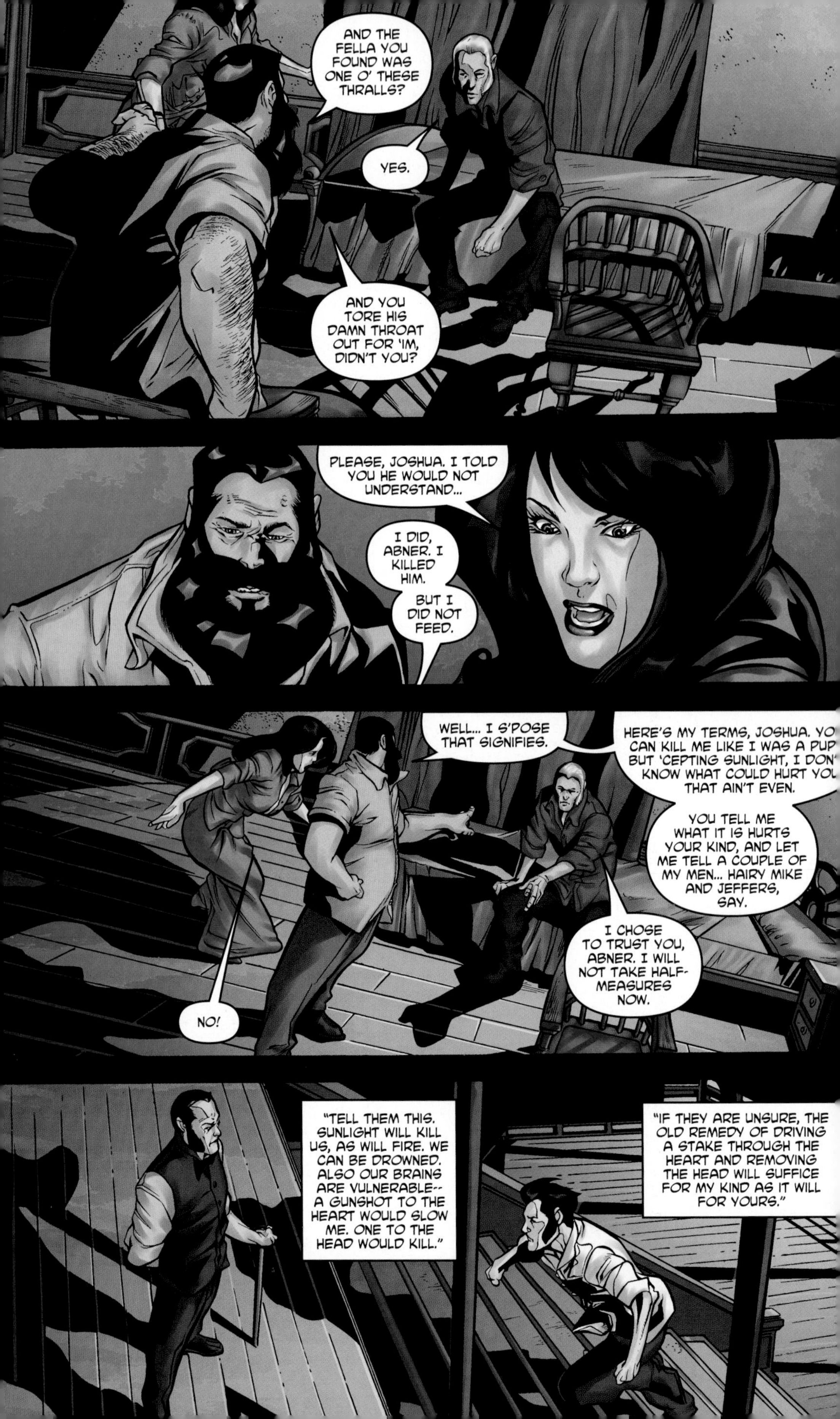
AND THE FELLA YOU FOUND WAS ONE O' THESE THRALLS?
YES.
AND YOU TORE HIS DAMN THROAT OUT FOR 'IM, DIDN'T YOU?
PLEASE, JOSHUA. I TOLD YOU HE WOULD NOT UNDERSTAND...
I DID, ABNER. I KILLED HIM.
BUT I DID NOT FEED.
WELL... I S'POSE THAT SIGNIFIES.
HERE'S MY TERMS, JOSHUA. YO CAN KILL ME LIKE I WAS A PUP BUT 'CEPTING SUNLIGHT, I DON' KNOW WHAT COULD HURT YOU THAT AIN'T EVEN.
YOU TELL ME WHAT IT IS HURTS YOUR KIND, AND LET ME TELL A COUPLE OF MY MEN... HAIRY MIKE AND JEFFERS, SAY.
NO!
I CHOSE TO TRUST YOU, ABNER. I WILL NOT TAKE HALF-MEASURES NOW.
"TELL THEM THIS. SUNLIGHT WILL KILL US, AS WILL FIRE. WE CAN BE DROWNED. ALSO OUR BRAINS ARE VULNERABLE-- A GUNSHOT TO THE HEART WOULD SLOW ME. ONE TO THE HEAD WOULD KILL."
"IF THEY ARE UNSURE, THE OLD REMEDY OF DRIVING A STAKE THROUGH THE HEART AND REMOVING THE HEAD WILL SUFFICE FOR MY KIND AS IT WILL FOR YOURS."

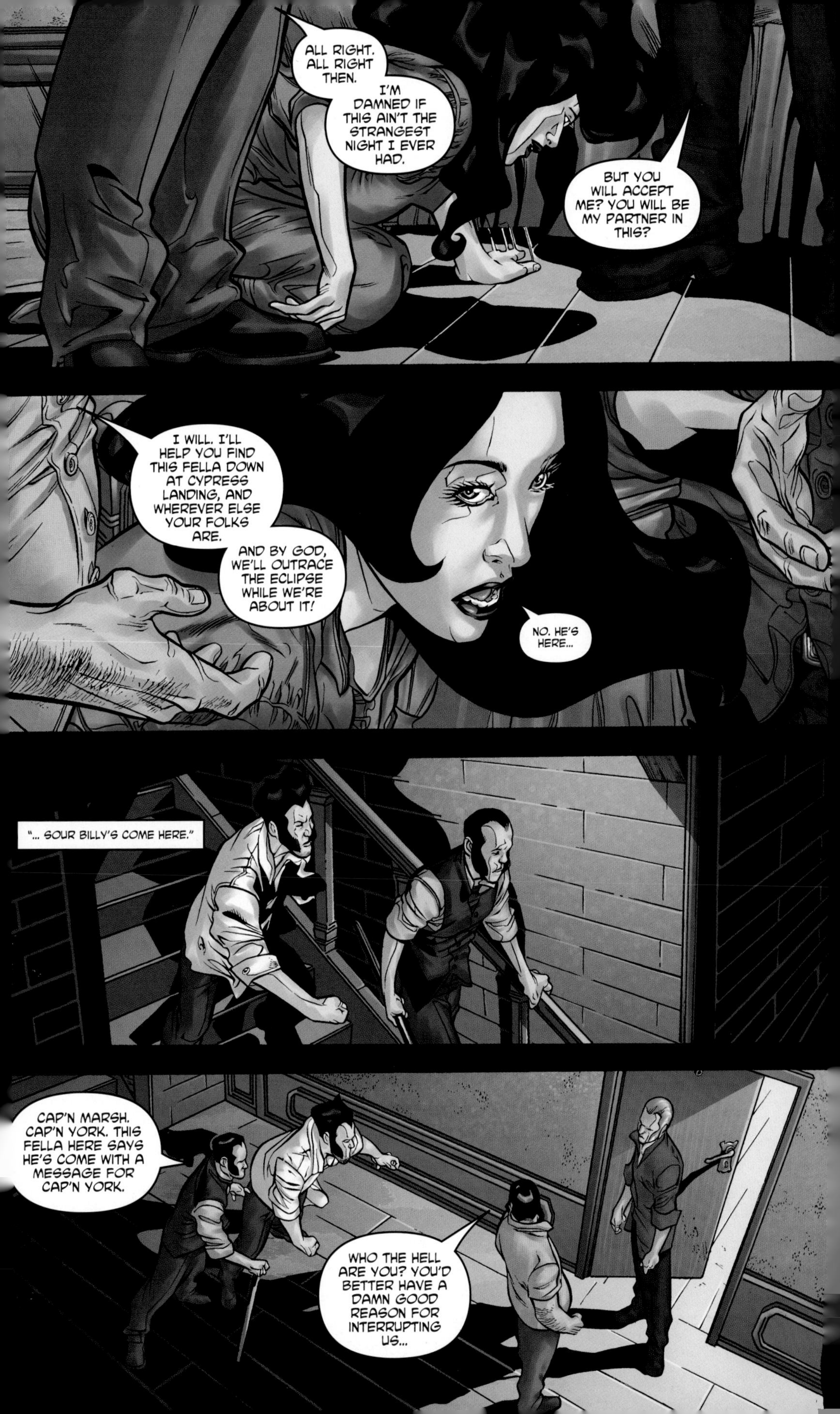
ALL RIGHT. ALL RIGHT THEN.
I'M DAMNED IF THIS AIN'T THE STRANGEST NIGHT I EVER HAD.
BUT YOU WILL ACCEPT ME? YOU WILL BE MY PARTNER IN THIS?
I WILL. I'LL HELP YOU FIND THIS FELLA DOWN AT CYPRESS LANDING, AND WHEREVER ELSE YOUR FOLKS ARE.
AND BY GOD, WE'LL OUTRACE THE ECLIPSE WHILE WE'RE ABOUT IT!
NO. HE'S HERE...
"... SOUR BILLY'S COME HERE."
CAP'N MARSH. CAP'N YORK. THIS FELLA HERE SAYS HE'S COME WITH A MESSAGE FOR CAP'N YORK.
WHO THE HELL ARE YOU? YOU'D BETTER HAVE A DAMN GOOD REASON FOR INTERRUPTING US...

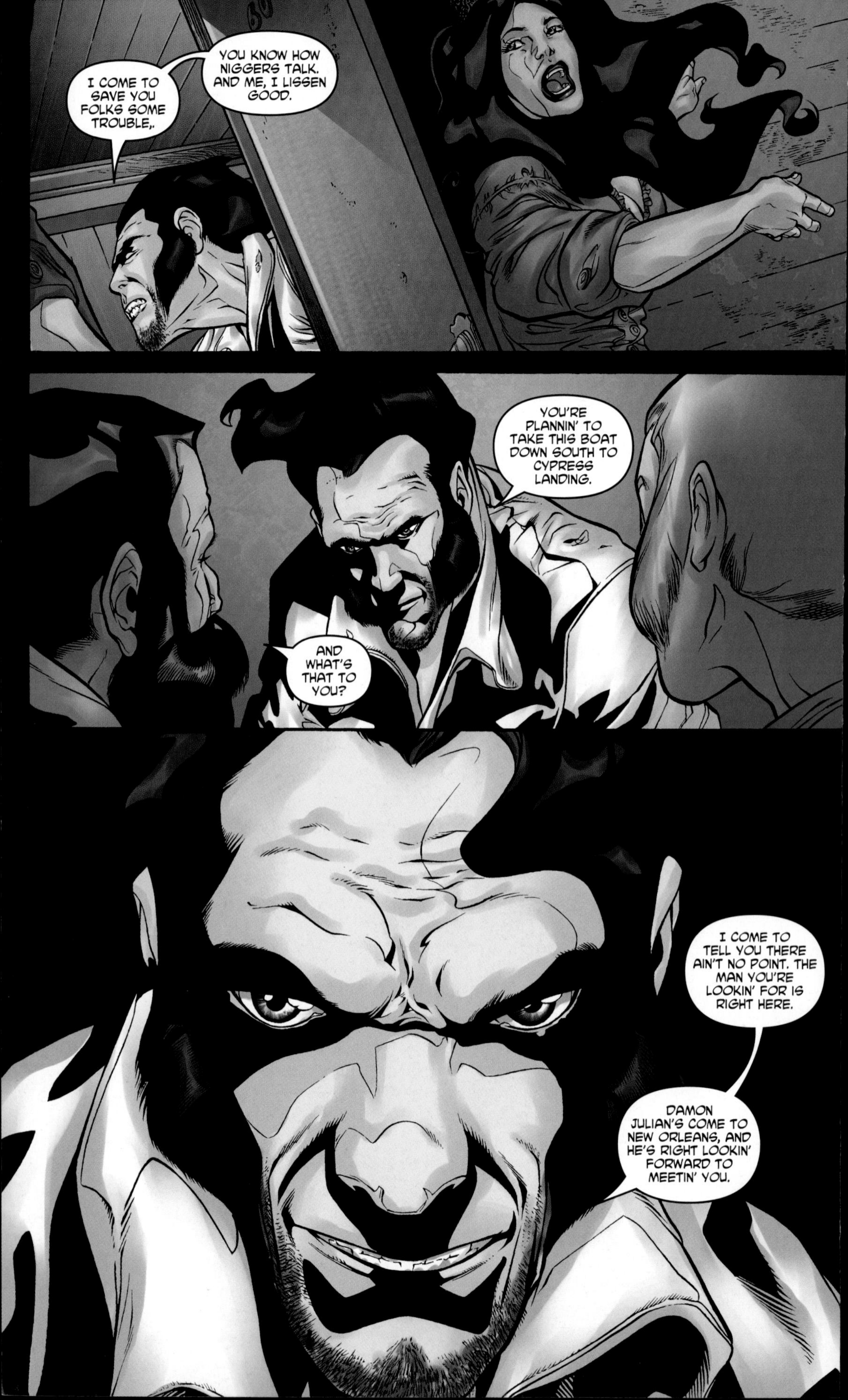
I COME TO SAVE YOU FOLKS SOME TROUBLE,.
YOU KNOW HOW NIGGERS TALK. AND ME, I LISSEN GOOD.
YOU'RE PLANNIN' TO TAKE THIS BOAT DOWN SOUTH TO CYPRESS LANDING.
AND WHAT'S THAT TO YOU?
I COME TO TELL YOU THERE AIN'T NO POINT. THE MAN YOU'RE LOOKIN' FOR IS RIGHT HERE.
DAMON JULIAN'S COME TO NEW ORLEANS, AND HE'S RIGHT LOOKIN' FORWARD TO MEETIN' YOU.

CHAPTER 6

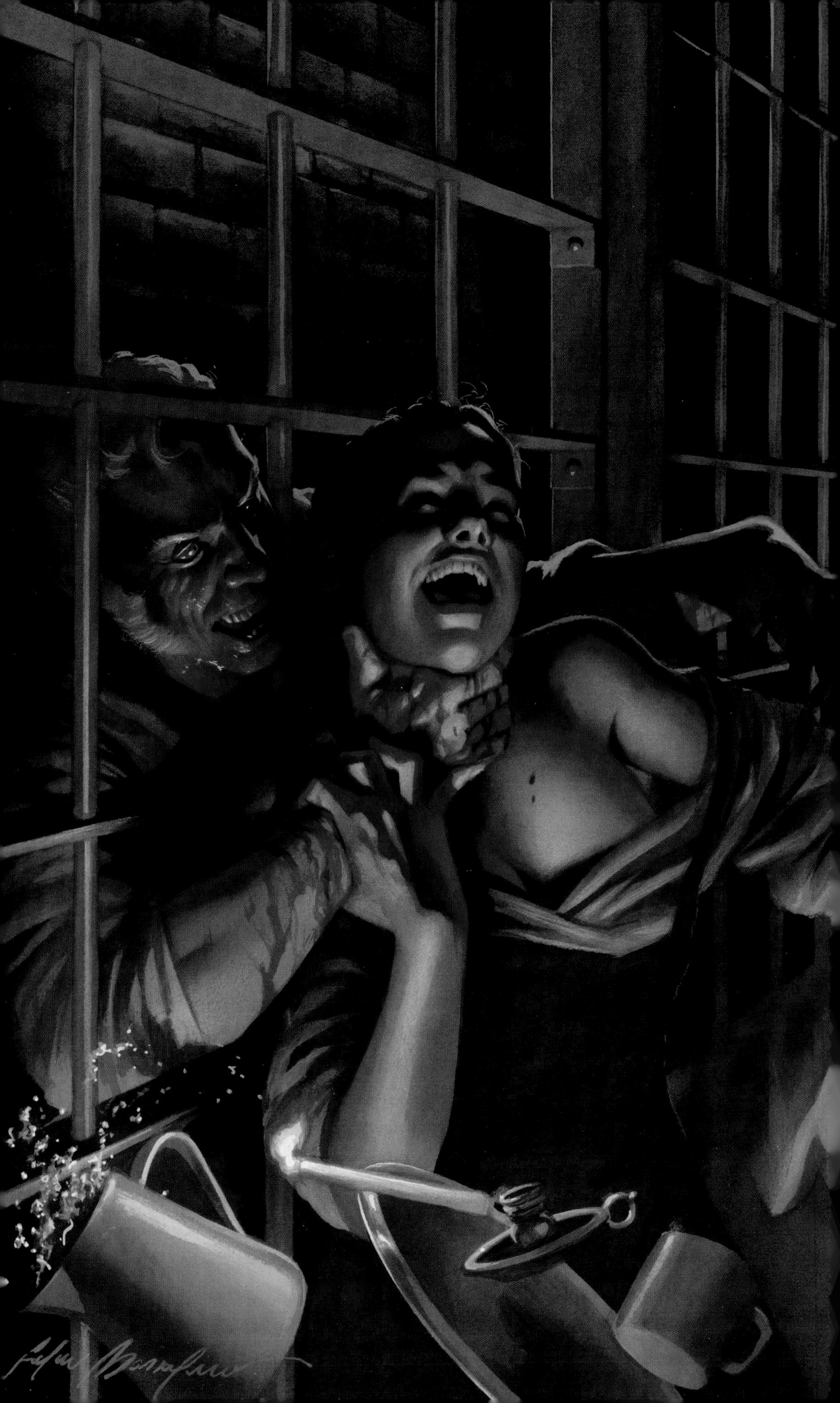

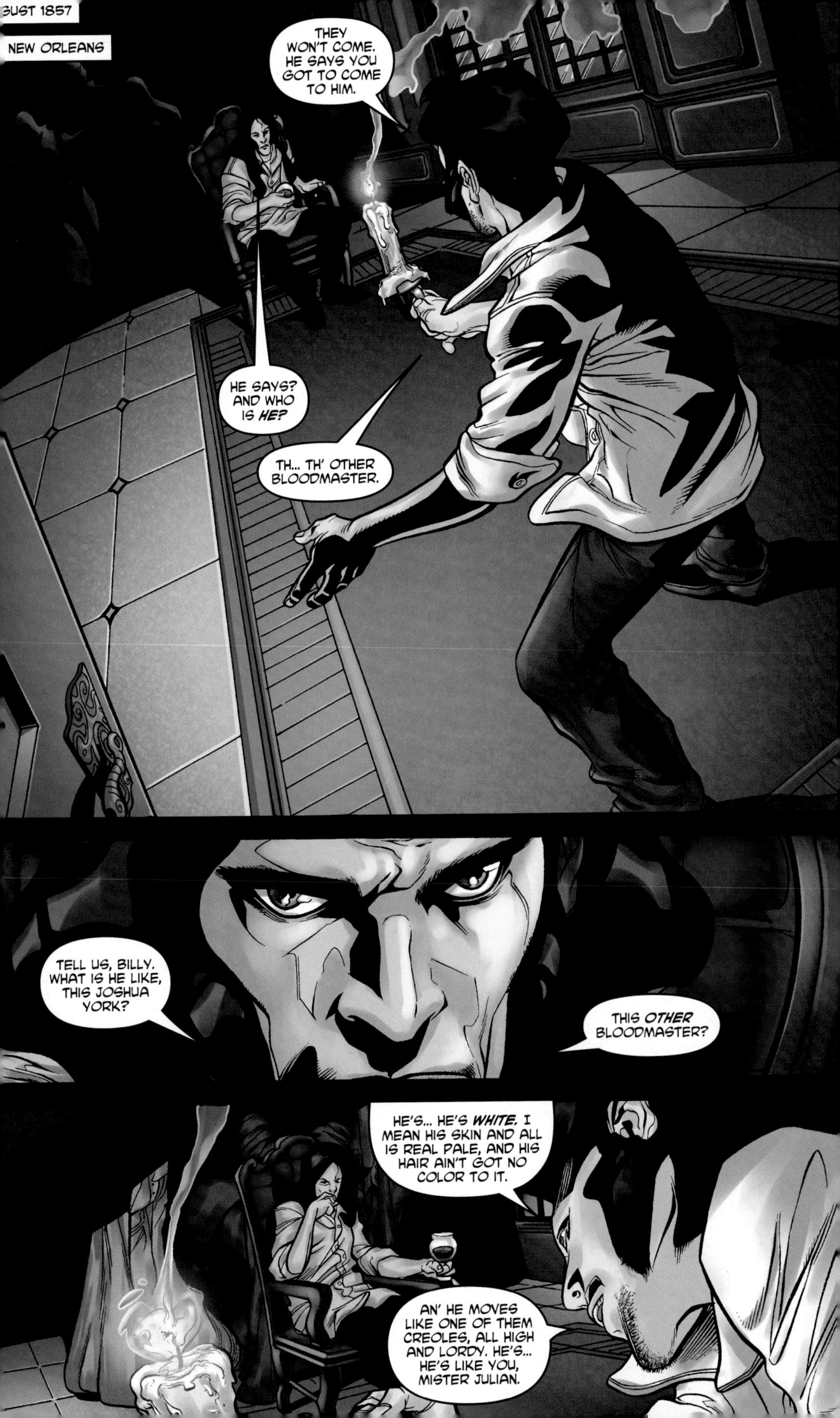
GUST 1857
NEW ORLEANS
THEY WON'T COME. HE SAYS YOU GOT TO COME TO HIM.
HE SAYS? AND WHO IS *HE?*
TH... TH' OTHER BLOODMASTER.
TELL US, BILLY. WHAT IS HE LIKE, THIS JOSHUA YORK?
THIS *OTHER* BLOODMASTER?
HE'S... HE'S *WHITE.* I MEAN HIS SKIN AND ALL IS REAL PALE, AND HIS HAIR AIN'T GOT NO COLOR TO IT.
AN' HE MOVES LIKE ONE OF THEM CREOLES, ALL HIGH AND LORDY. HE'S... HE'S LIKE YOU, MISTER JULIAN.

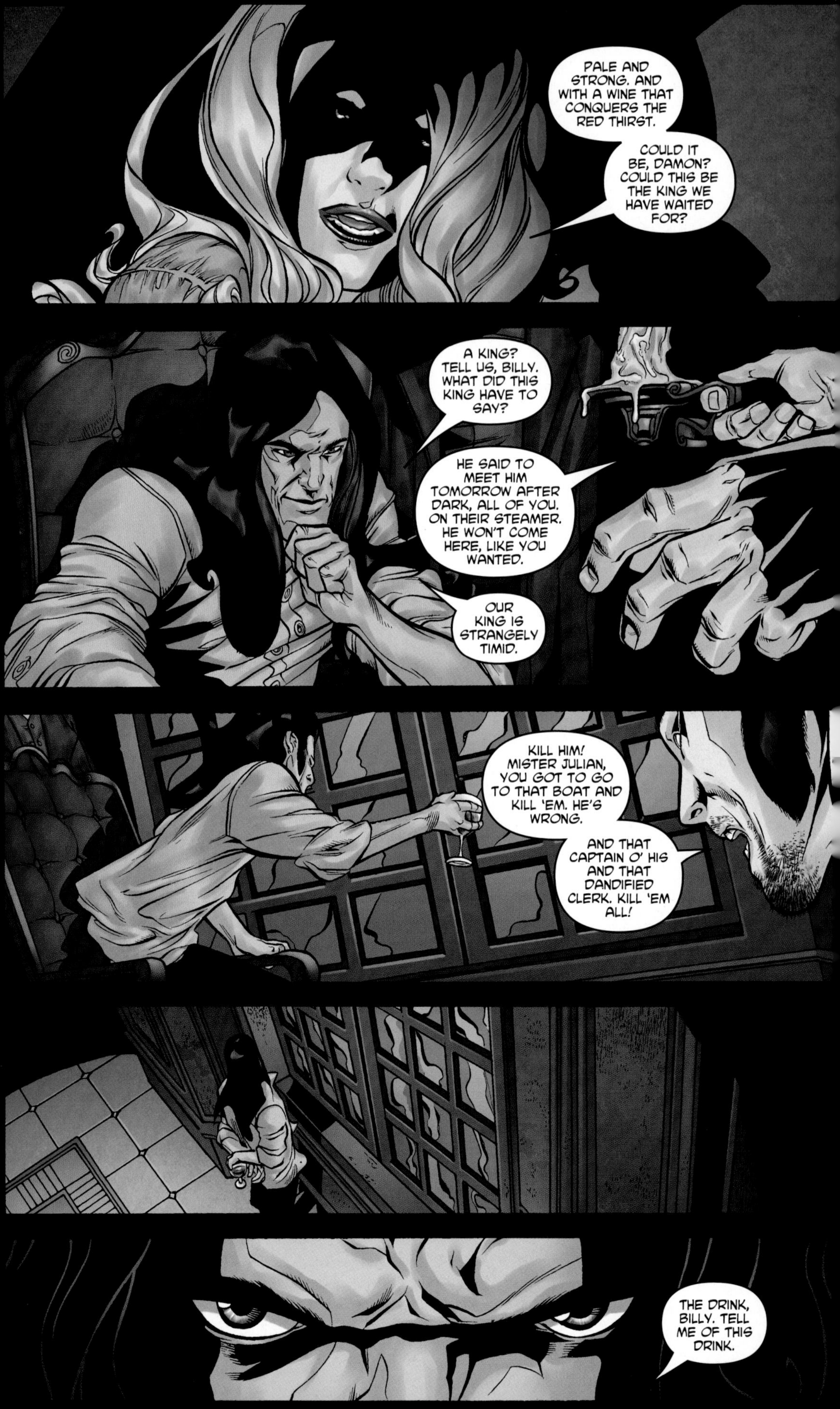
PALE AND STRONG. AND WITH A WINE THAT CONQUERS THE RED THIRST.
COULD IT BE, DAMON? COULD THIS BE THE KING WE HAVE WAITED FOR?
A KING? TELL US, BILLY. WHAT DID THIS KING HAVE TO SAY?
HE SAID TO MEET HIM TOMORROW AFTER DARK, ALL OF YOU. ON THEIR STEAMER. HE WON'T COME HERE, LIKE YOU WANTED.
OUR KING IS STRANGELY TIMID.
KILL HIM! MISTER JULIAN, YOU GOT TO GO TO THAT BOAT AND KILL 'EM. HE'S WRONG.
AND THAT CAPTAIN O' HIS AND THAT DANDIFIED CLERK. KILL 'EM ALL!
THE DRINK, BILLY. TELL ME OF THIS DRINK.

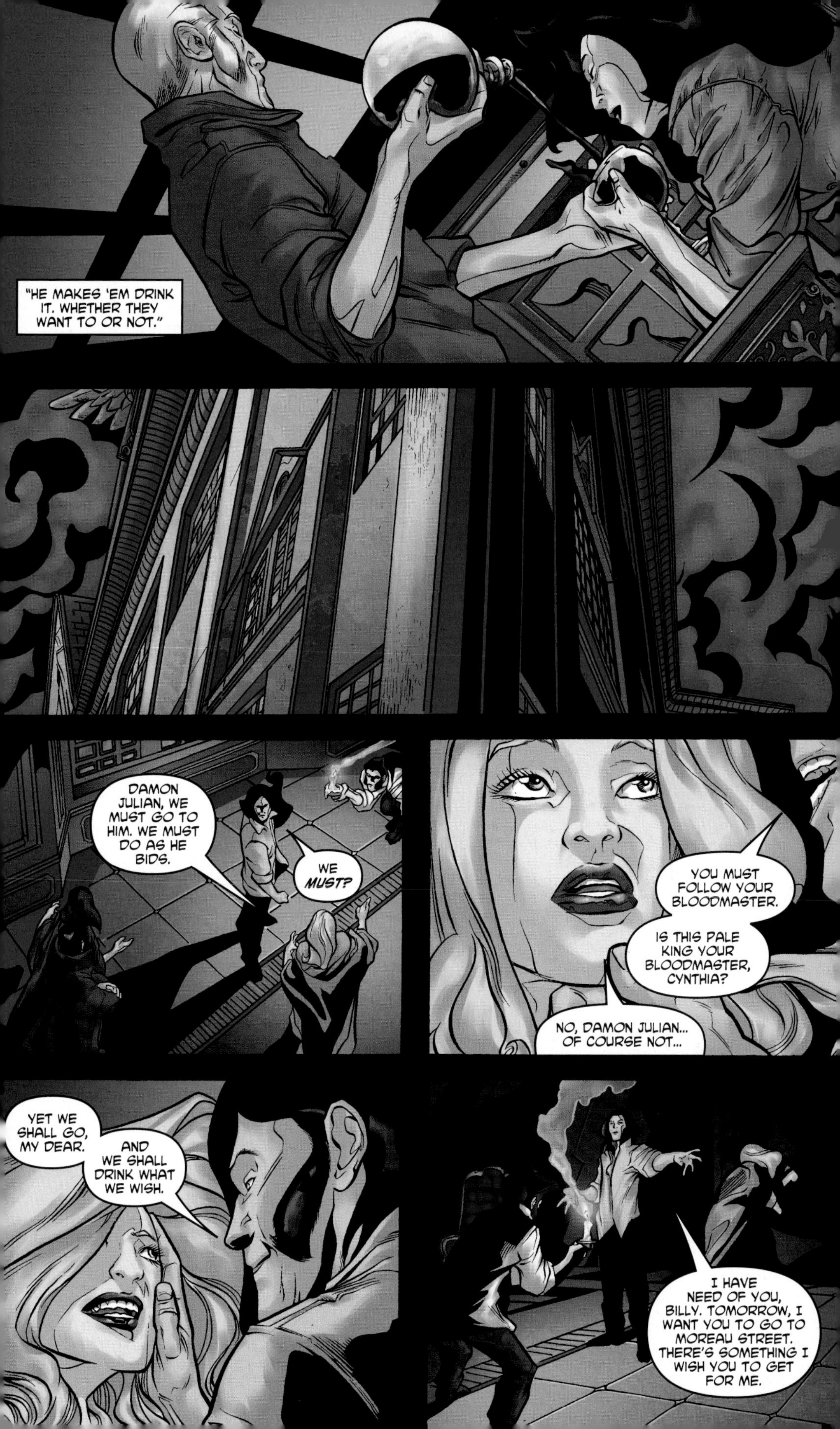
"HE MAKES 'EM DRINK IT. WHETHER THEY WANT TO OR NOT."
DAMON JULIAN, WE MUST GO TO HIM. WE MUST DO AS HE BIDS.
WE *MUST*?
YOU MUST FOLLOW YOUR BLOODMASTER.
IS THIS PALE KING YOUR BLOODMASTER, CYNTHIA?
NO, DAMON JULIAN... OF COURSE NOT...
YET WE SHALL GO, MY DEAR.
AND WE SHALL DRINK WHAT WE WISH.
I HAVE NEED OF YOU, BILLY. TOMORROW, I WANT YOU TO GO TO MOREAU STREET. THERE'S SOMETHING I WISH YOU TO GET FOR ME.

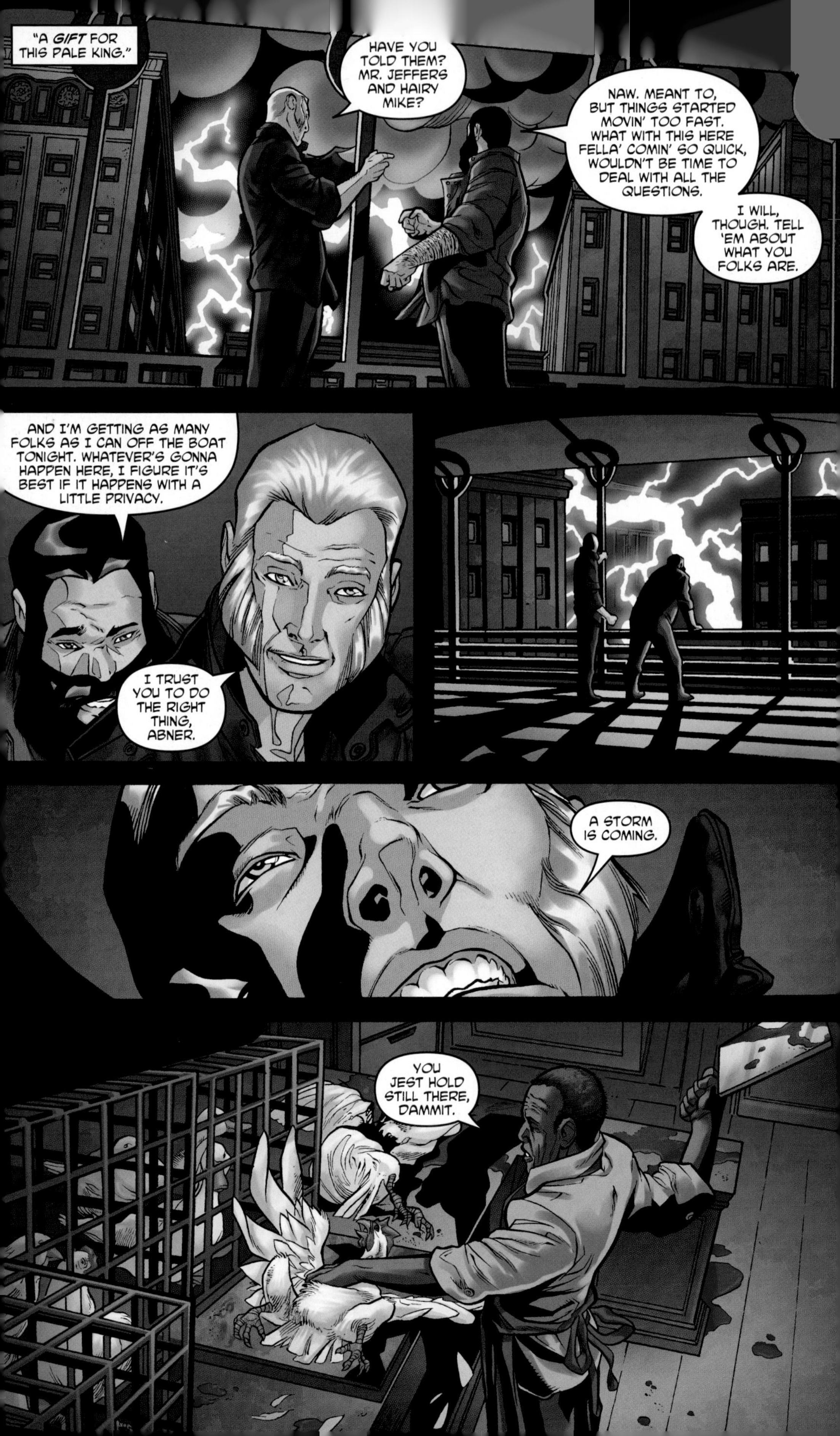
"A *GIFT* FOR THIS PALE KING."
HAVE YOU TOLD THEM? MR. JEFFERS AND HAIRY MIKE?
NAW. MEANT TO, BUT THINGS STARTED MOVIN' TOO FAST. WHAT WITH THIS HERE FELLA' COMIN' SO QUICK, WOULDN'T BE TIME TO DEAL WITH ALL THE QUESTIONS.
I WILL, THOUGH. TELL 'EM ABOUT WHAT YOU FOLKS ARE.
AND I'M GETTING AS MANY FOLKS AS I CAN OFF THE BOAT TONIGHT. WHATEVER'S GONNA HAPPEN HERE, I FIGURE IT'S BEST IF IT HAPPENS WITH A LITTLE PRIVACY.
I TRUST YOU TO DO THE RIGHT THING, ABNER.
A STORM IS COMING.
YOU JEST HOLD STILL THERE, DAMMIT.

TOBY.

WHY CAP'N MARSH. WHAT KIN I DO FER YOU?

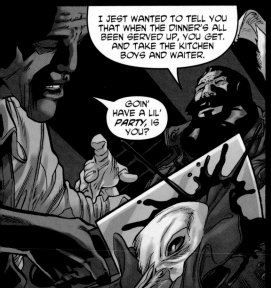

I JEST WANTED TO TELL YOU THAT WHEN THE DINNER'S ALL BEEN SERVED UP, YOU GET. AND TAKE THE KITCHEN BOYS AND WAITER.

GOIN' HAVE A LIL' *PARTY*, IS YOU?

YOU KNOW I NEVER HELD MUCH WITH SLAVERY, EVEN IF I NEVER DONE MUCH AGAINST IT. IF THEM ABOLITIONISTS JEST WEREN'T SUCH BIBLE THUMPERS...

I BEEN THINKIN' THAT IT AIN'T RIGHT, ONE KIND A PEOPLE JEST... USIN' ANOTHER LIKE THAT. IT'S GOTTA END. BETTER PEACEFUL, BUT EVEN BLOODY, IT'S BETTER ENDED.

CAP'N. THIS HERE'S *SLAVE* COUNTRY. TALK LIKE THAT GON' GET YOU KILT.

MAY BE AS IT COULD. BUT RIGHT'S RIGHT.

AND I JEST WANTED YOU TO KNOW AS I KNEW THAT. THERE'S TIMES FOLKS DON'T SAY THINGS THEY OUGHTTA.

ABOUT THIS DINNER TONIGHT...

YESSUH?

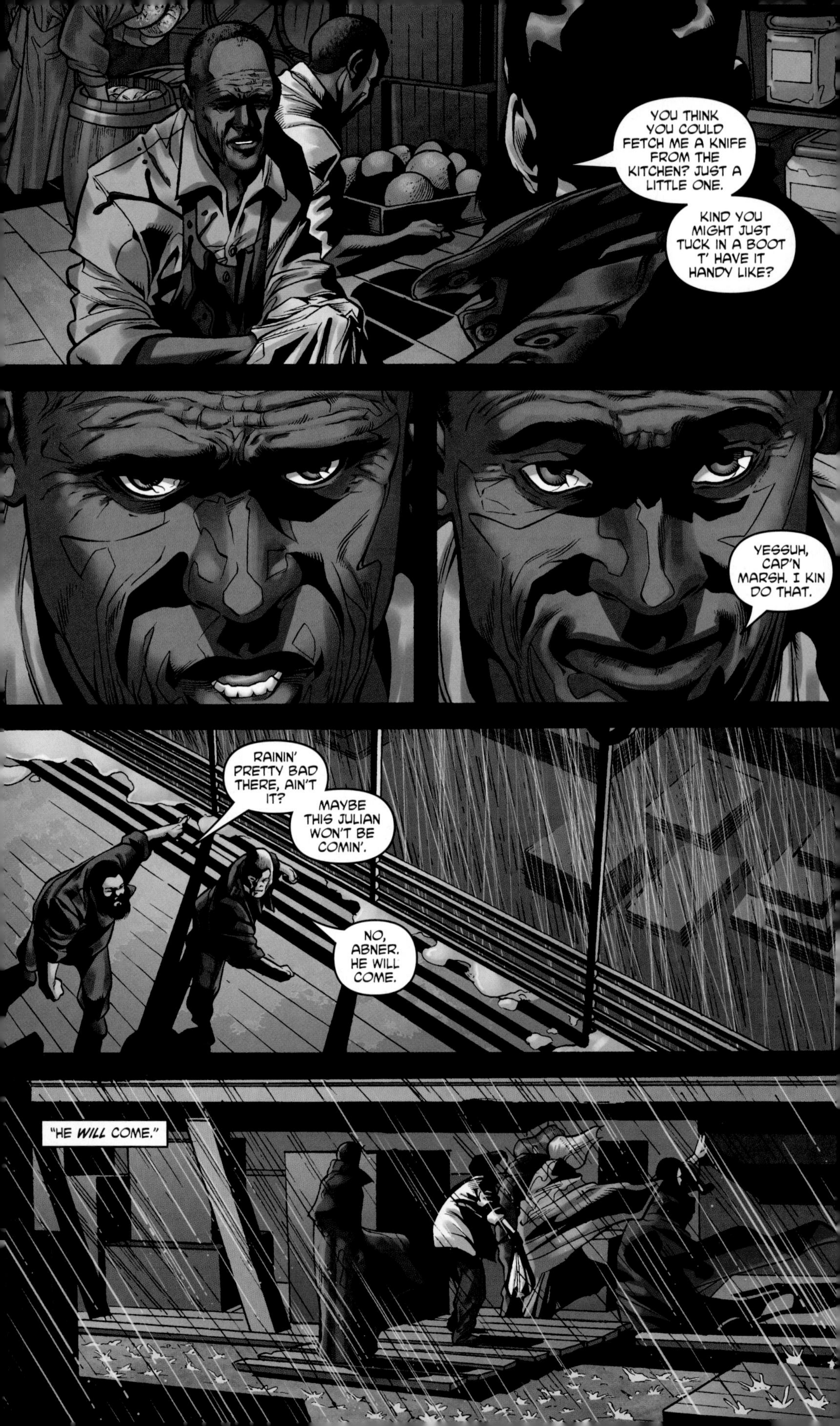
YOU THINK YOU COULD FETCH ME A KNIFE FROM THE KITCHEN? JUST A LITTLE ONE.
KIND YOU MIGHT JUST TUCK IN A BOOT T' HAVE IT HANDY LIKE?
YESSUH, CAP'N MARSH. I KIN DO THAT.
RAININ' PRETTY BAD THERE, AIN'T IT?
MAYBE THIS JULIAN WON'T BE COMIN'.
NO, ABNER. HE WILL COME.
"HE WILL COME."

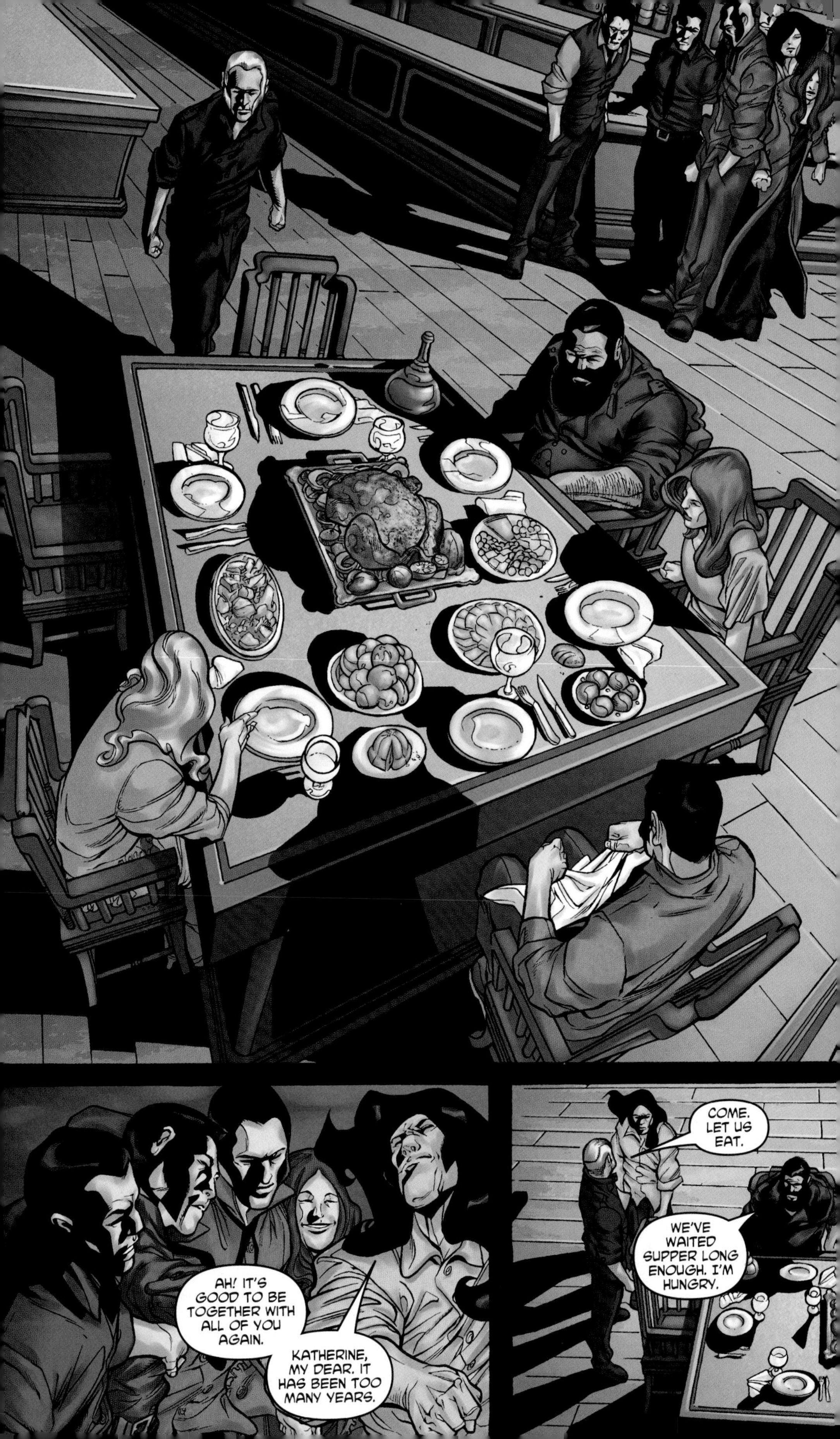
AH! IT'S GOOD TO BE TOGETHER WITH ALL OF YOU AGAIN.
KATHERINE, MY DEAR. IT HAS BEEN TOO MANY YEARS.
COME. LET US EAT.
WE'VE WAITED SUPPER LONG ENOUGH. I'M HUNGRY.

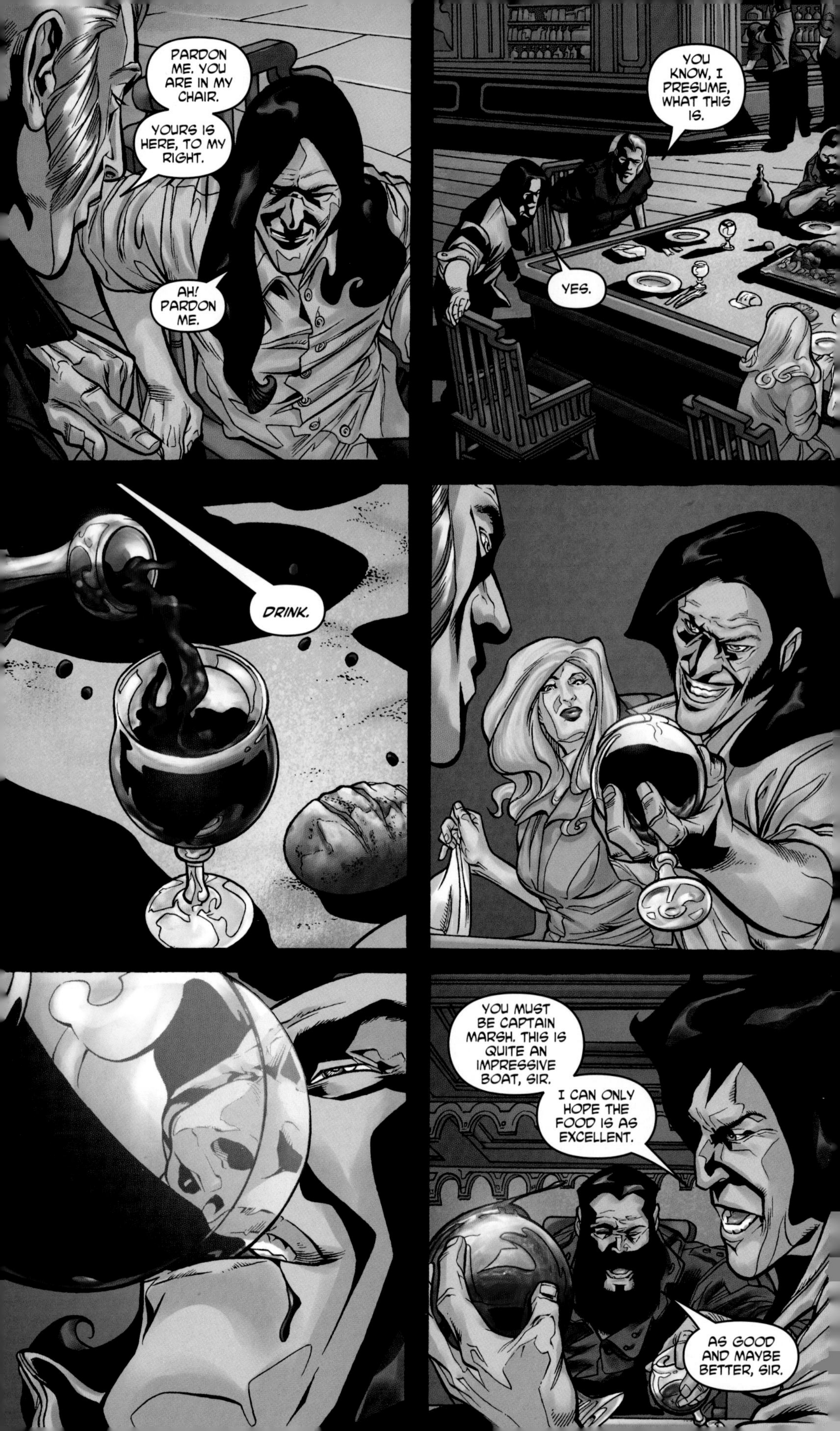
PARDON ME. YOU ARE IN MY CHAIR.
YOURS IS HERE, TO MY RIGHT.
AH! PARDON ME.
YOU KNOW, I PRESUME, WHAT THIS IS.
YES.
DRINK.
YOU MUST BE CAPTAIN MARSH. THIS IS QUITE AN IMPRESSIVE BOAT, SIR.
I CAN ONLY HOPE THE FOOD IS AS EXCELLENT.
AS GOOD AND MAYBE BETTER, SIR.

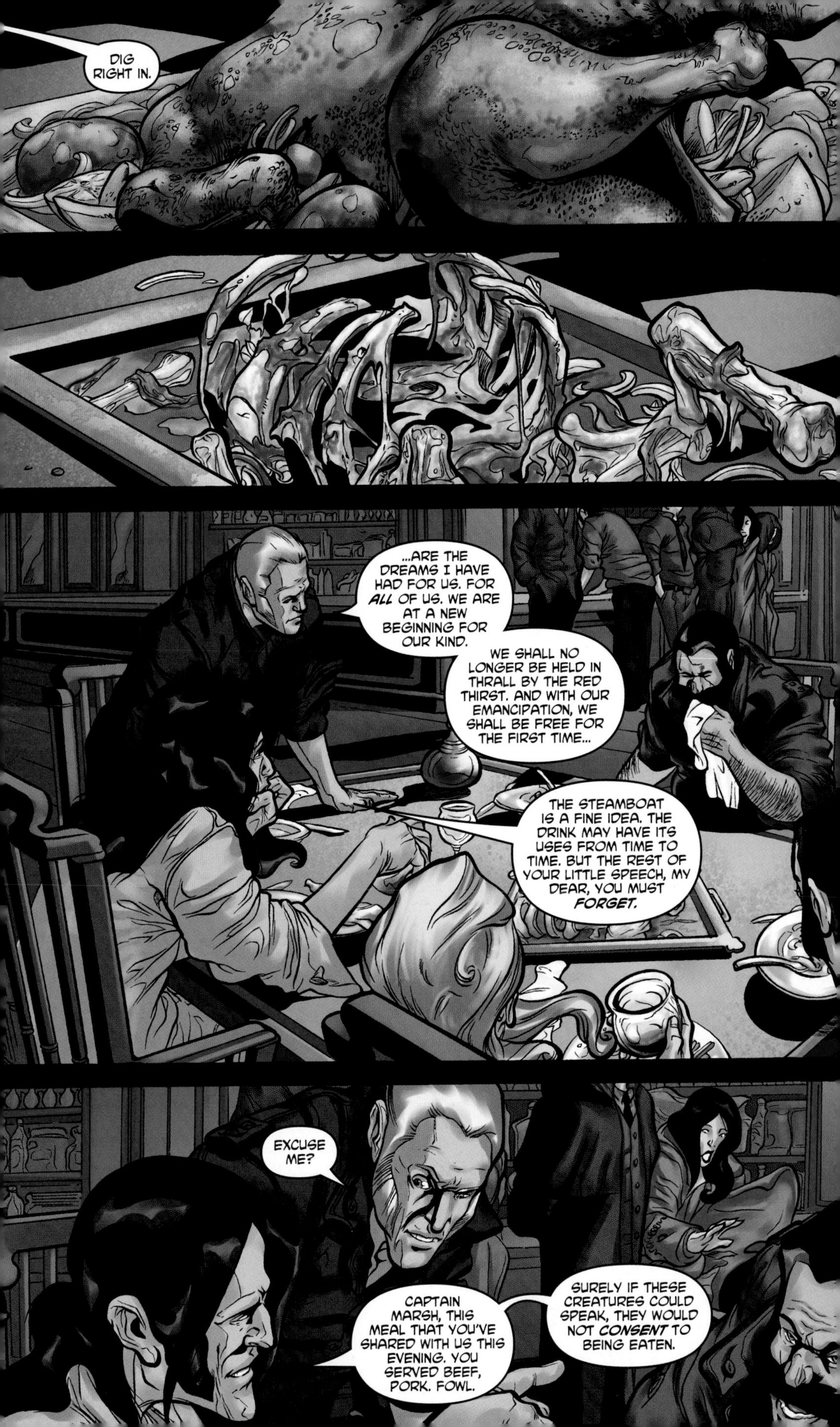
DIG RIGHT IN.
...ARE THE DREAMS I HAVE HAD FOR US. FOR ALL OF US. WE ARE AT A NEW BEGINNING FOR OUR KIND.
WE SHALL NO LONGER BE HELD IN THRALL BY THE RED THIRST. AND WITH OUR EMANCIPATION, WE SHALL BE FREE FOR THE FIRST TIME...
THE STEAMBOAT IS A FINE IDEA. THE DRINK MAY HAVE ITS USES FROM TIME TO TIME. BUT THE REST OF YOUR LITTLE SPEECH, MY DEAR, YOU MUST FORGET.
EXCUSE ME?
CAPTAIN MARSH, THIS MEAL THAT YOU'VE SHARED WITH US THIS EVENING. YOU SERVED BEEF, PORK. FOWL.
SURELY IF THESE CREATURES COULD SPEAK, THEY WOULD NOT CONSENT TO BEING EATEN.

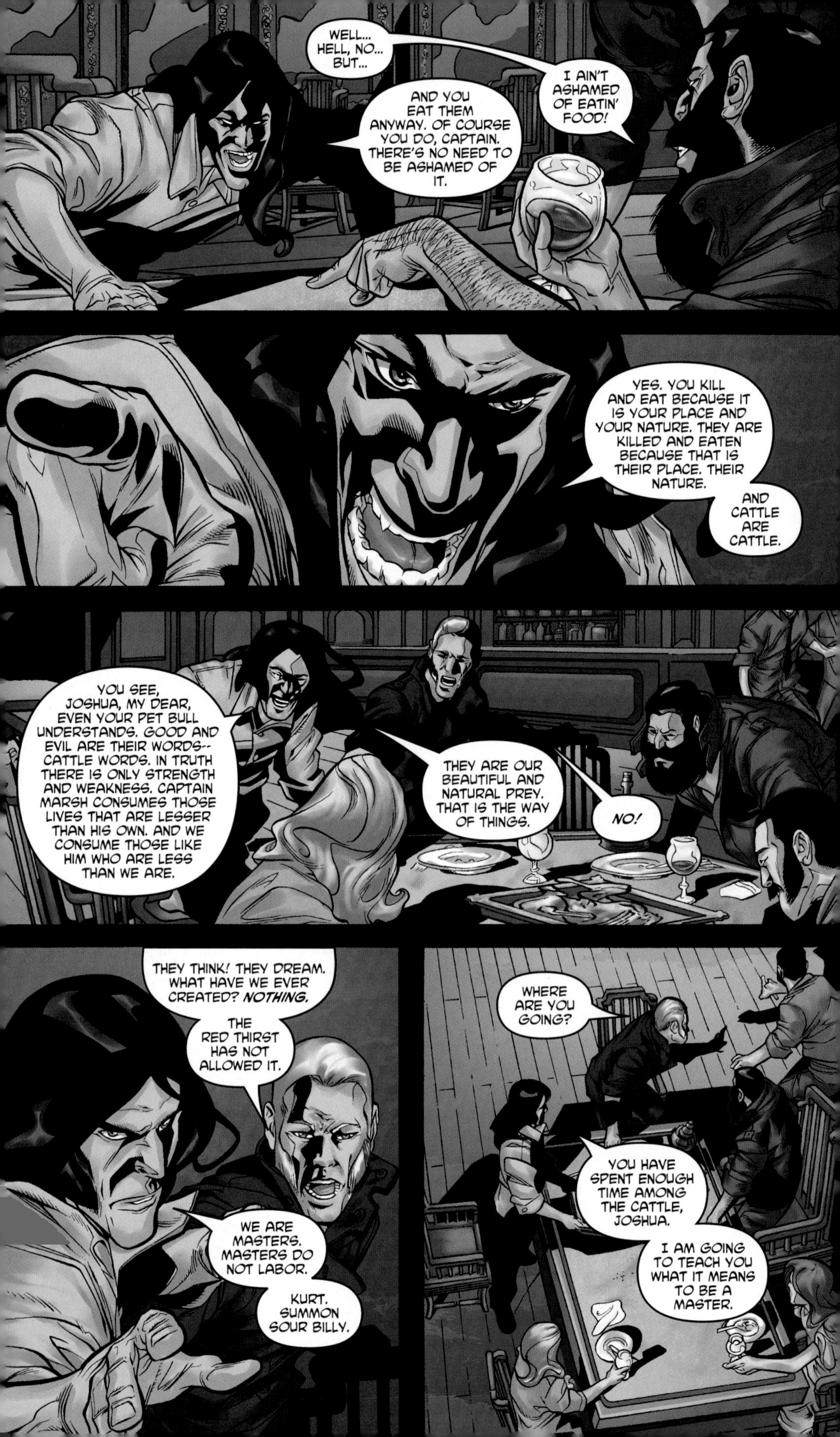
WELL... HELL, NO... BUT...
AND YOU EAT THEM ANYWAY. OF COURSE YOU DO, CAPTAIN. THERE'S NO NEED TO BE ASHAMED OF IT.
I AIN'T ASHAMED OF EATIN' FOOD!
YES. YOU KILL AND EAT BECAUSE IT IS YOUR PLACE AND YOUR NATURE. THEY ARE KILLED AND EATEN BECAUSE THAT IS THEIR PLACE. THEIR NATURE.
AND CATTLE ARE CATTLE.
YOU SEE, JOSHUA, MY DEAR, EVEN YOUR PET BULL UNDERSTANDS. GOOD AND EVIL ARE THEIR WORDS--CATTLE WORDS. IN TRUTH THERE IS ONLY STRENGTH AND WEAKNESS. CAPTAIN MARSH CONSUMES THOSE LIVES THAT ARE LESSER THAN HIS OWN. AND WE CONSUME THOSE LIKE HIM WHO ARE LESS THAN WE ARE.
THEY ARE OUR BEAUTIFUL AND NATURAL PREY. THAT IS THE WAY OF THINGS.
NO!
THEY THINK! THEY DREAM. WHAT HAVE WE EVER CREATED? NOTHING.
THE RED THIRST HAS NOT ALLOWED IT.
WE ARE MASTERS. MASTERS DO NOT LABOR.
KURT. SUMMON SOUR BILLY.
WHERE ARE YOU GOING?
YOU HAVE SPENT ENOUGH TIME AMONG THE CATTLE, JOSHUA.
I AM GOING TO TEACH YOU WHAT IT MEANS TO BE A MASTER.

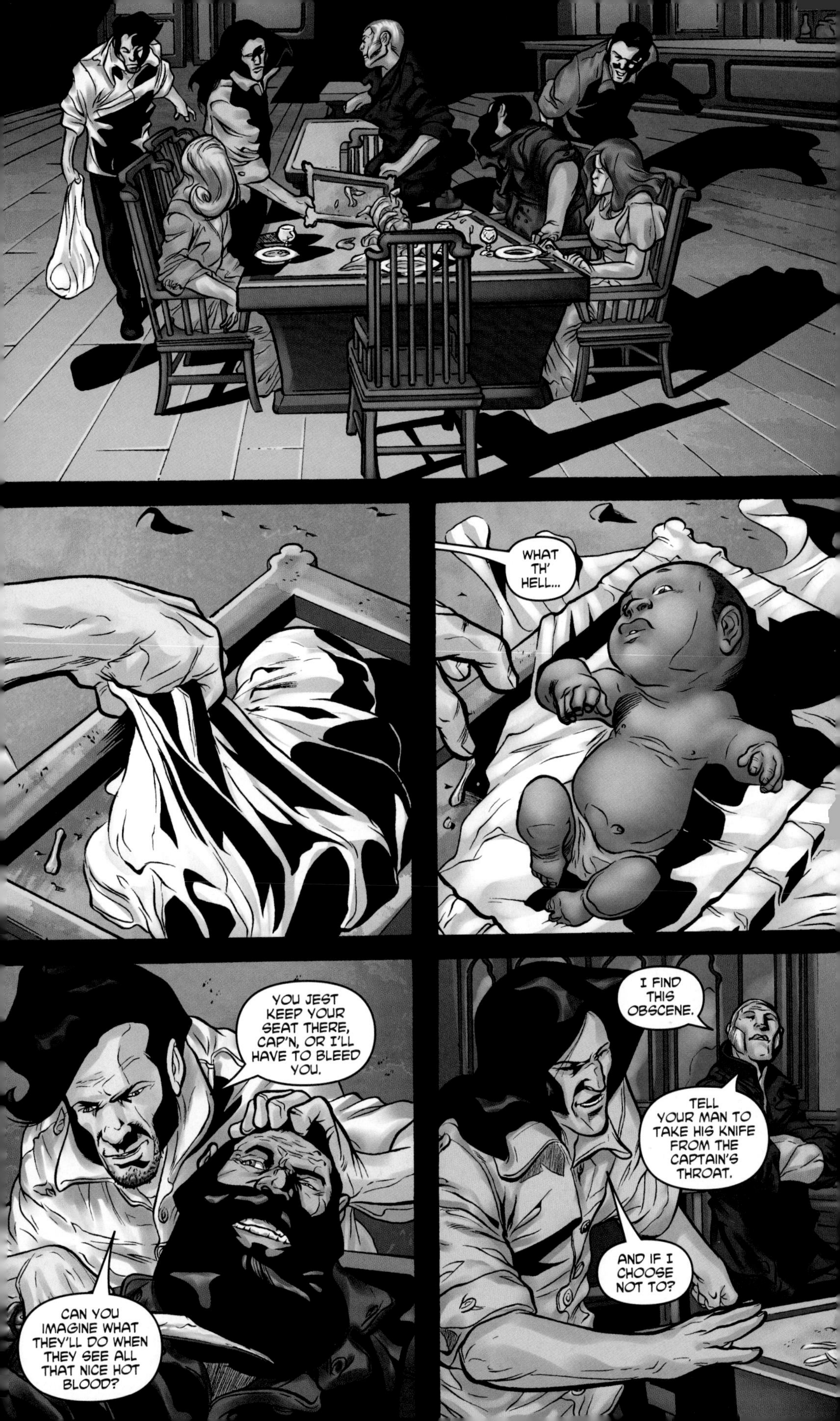
WHAT TH' HELL...
YOU JEST KEEP YOUR SEAT THERE, CAP'N, OR I'LL HAVE TO BLEED YOU.
CAN YOU IMAGINE WHAT THEY'LL DO WHEN THEY SEE ALL THAT NICE HOT BLOOD?
I FIND THIS OBSCENE.
TELL YOUR MAN TO TAKE HIS KNIFE FROM THE CAPTAIN'S THROAT.
AND IF I CHOOSE NOT TO?

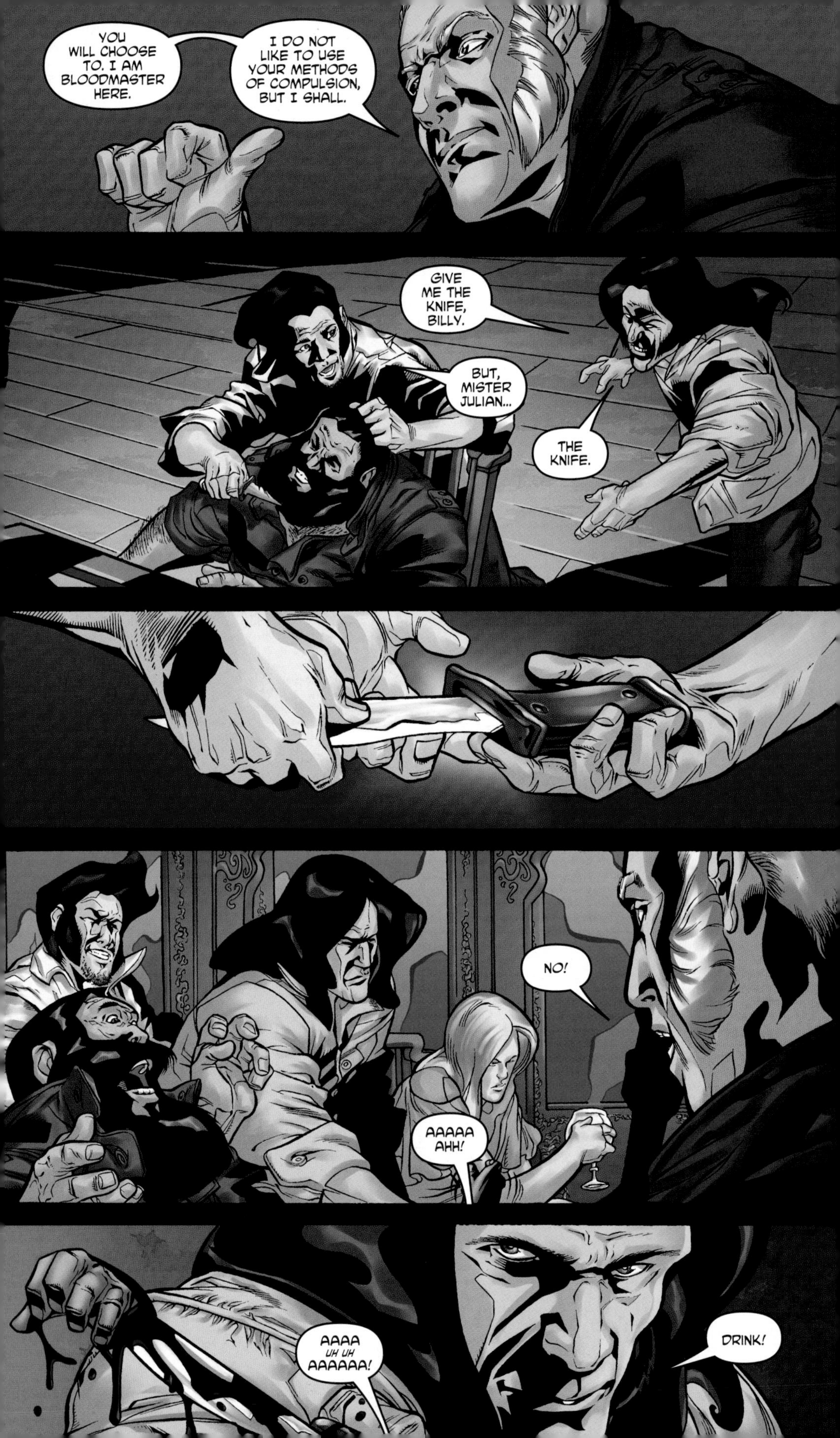
I DO NOT LIKE TO USE YOUR METHODS OF COMPULSION, BUT I SHALL.
YOU WILL CHOOSE TO. I AM BLOODMASTER HERE.
GIVE ME THE KNIFE, BILLY.
BUT, MISTER JULIAN...
THE KNIFE.
NO!
AAAAA AHH!
AAAA UH UH AAAAAA!
DRINK!

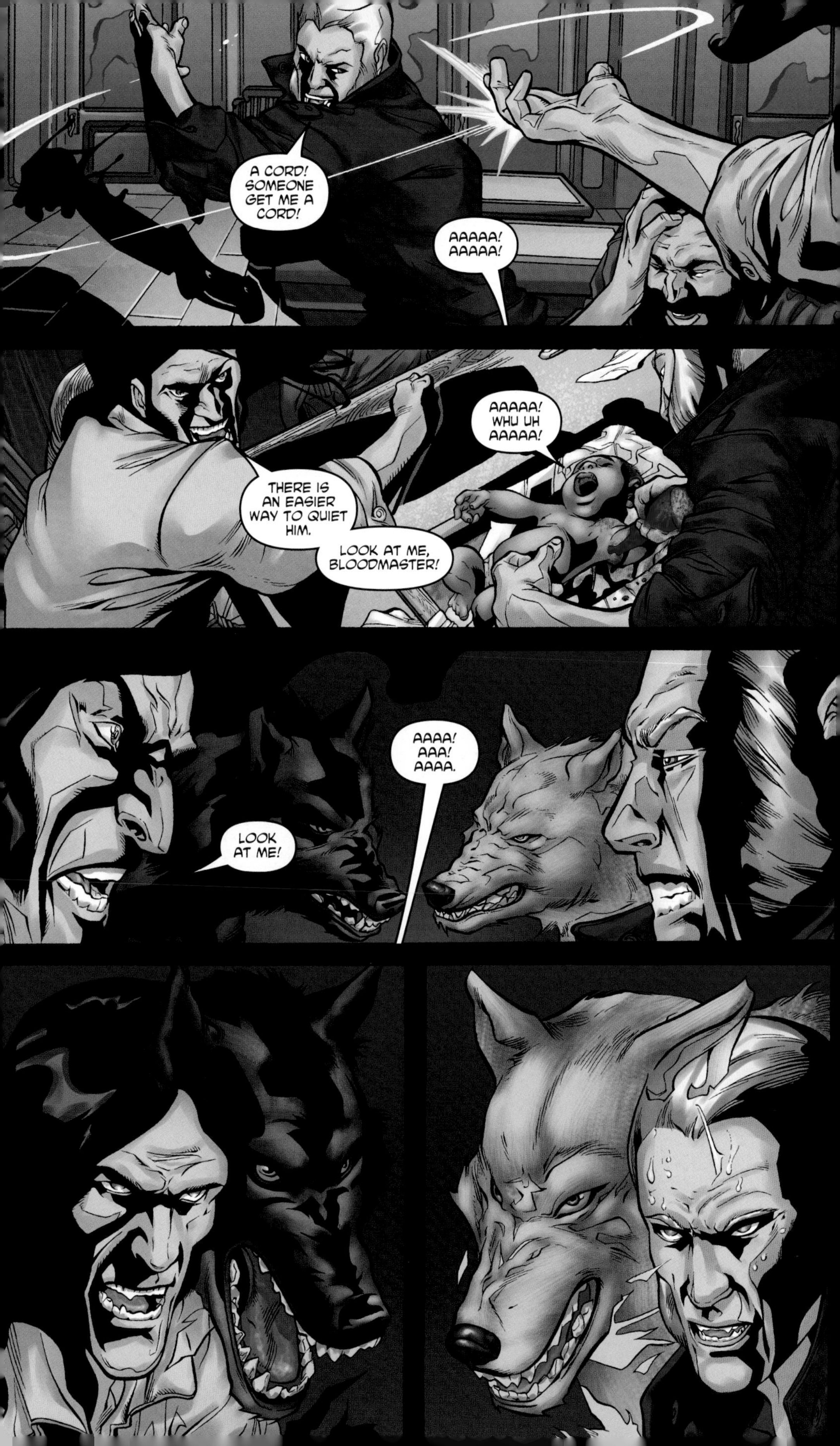
A CORD! SOMEONE GET ME A CORD!
AAAAA! AAAAA!
AAAAA! WHU UH AAAAA!
THERE IS AN EASIER WAY TO QUIET HIM.
LOOK AT ME, BLOODMASTER!
AAAA! AAA! AAAA.
LOOK AT ME!

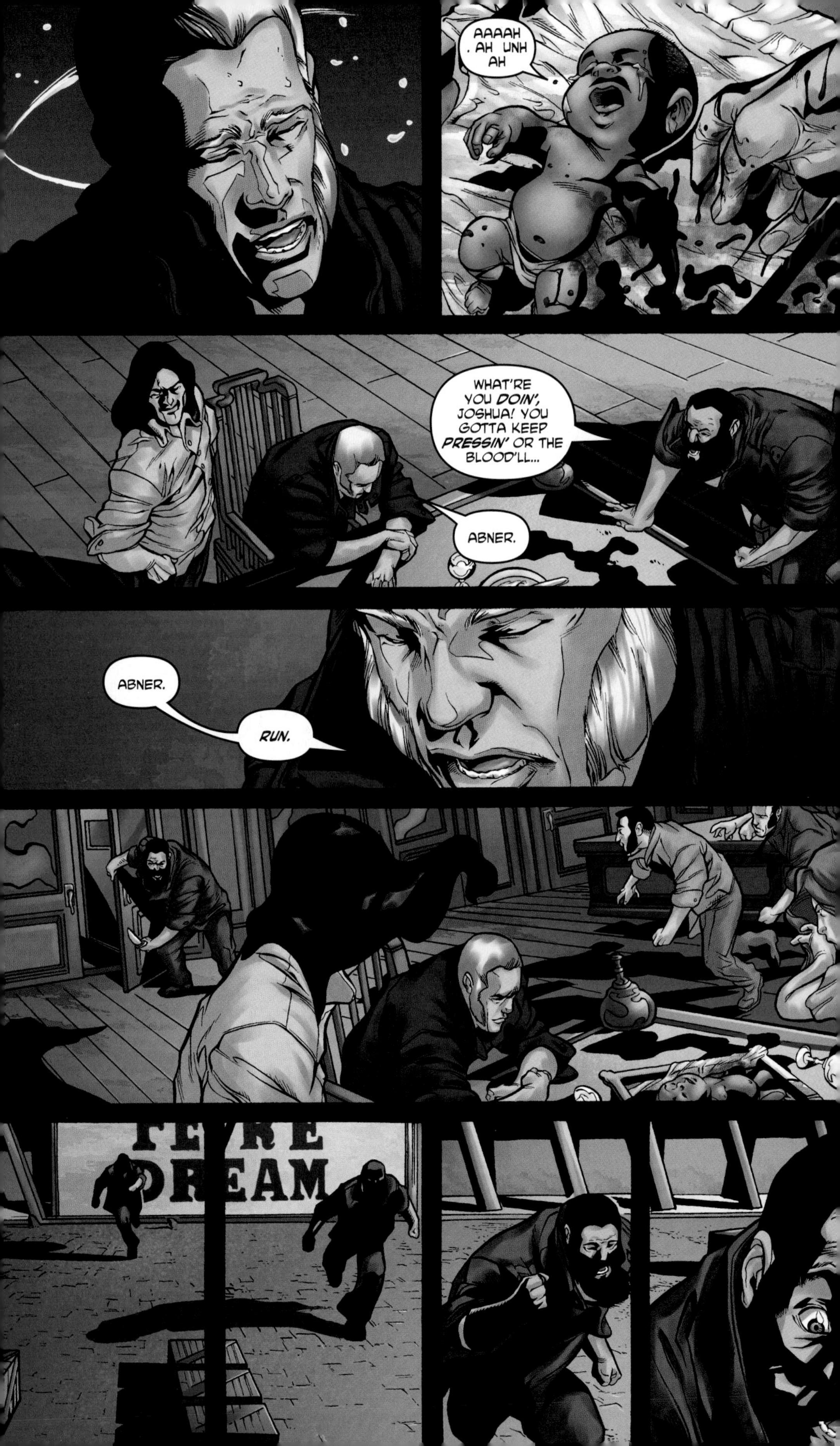
AAAAH . AH UNH AH
WHAT'RE YOU DOIN', JOSHUA! YOU GOTTA KEEP PRESSIN' OR THE BLOOD'LL...
ABNER.
ABNER.
RUN.
DREAM

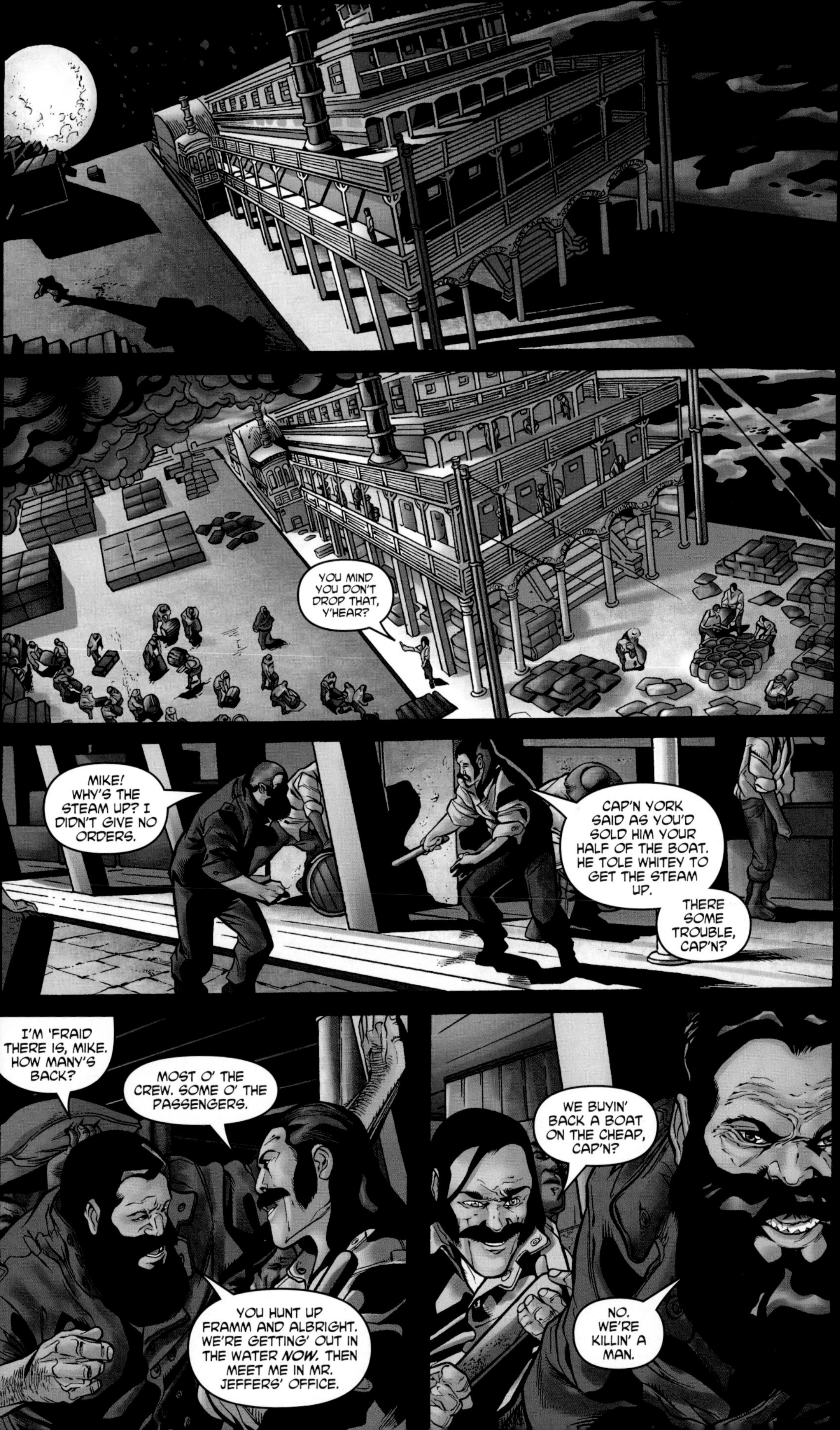
YOU MIND YOU DON'T DROP THAT, Y'HEAR?
MIKE! WHY'S THE STEAM UP? I DIDN'T GIVE NO ORDERS.
CAP'N YORK SAID AS YOU'D SOLD HIM YOUR HALF OF THE BOAT. HE TOLE WHITEY TO GET THE STEAM UP.
THERE SOME TROUBLE, CAP'N?
I'M 'FRAID THERE IS, MIKE. HOW MANY'S BACK?
MOST O' THE CREW. SOME O' THE PASSENGERS.
YOU HUNT UP FRAMM AND ALBRIGHT. WE'RE GETTING' OUT IN THE WATER NOW. THEN MEET ME IN MR. JEFFERS' OFFICE.
WE BUYIN' BACK A BOAT ON THE CHEAP, CAP'N?
NO. WE'RE KILLIN' A MAN.

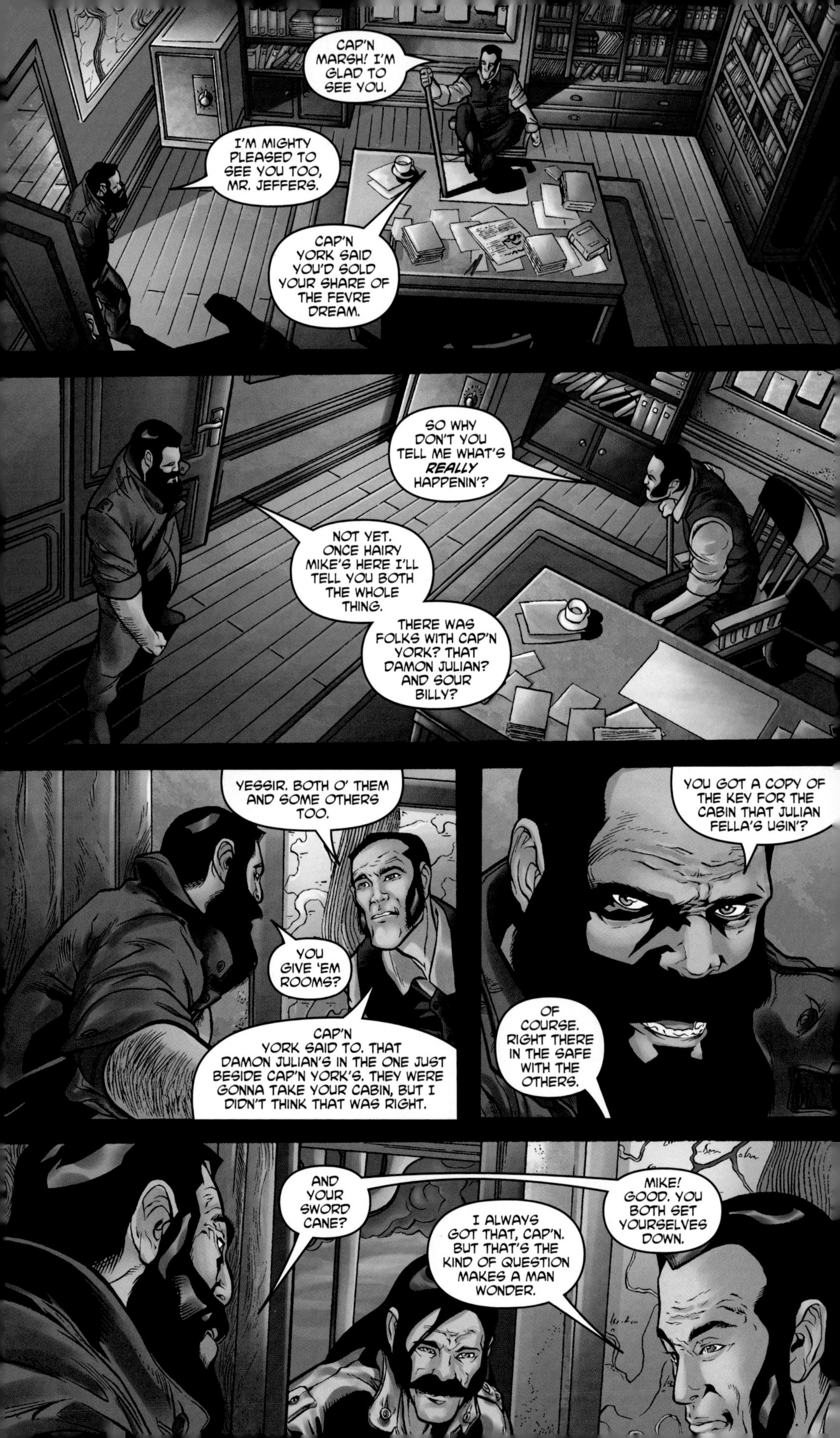
CAP'N MARSH! I'M GLAD TO SEE YOU.
I'M MIGHTY PLEASED TO SEE YOU TOO, MR. JEFFERS.
CAP'N YORK SAID YOU'D SOLD YOUR SHARE OF THE FEVRE DREAM.
SO WHY DON'T YOU TELL ME WHAT'S *REALLY* HAPPENIN'?
NOT YET. ONCE HAIRY MIKE'S HERE I'LL TELL YOU BOTH THE WHOLE THING.
THERE WAS FOLKS WITH CAP'N YORK? THAT DAMON JULIAN? AND SOUR BILLY?
YESSIR. BOTH O' THEM AND SOME OTHERS TOO.
YOU GIVE 'EM ROOMS?
CAP'N YORK SAID TO. THAT DAMON JULIAN'S IN THE ONE JUST BESIDE CAP'N YORK'S. THEY WERE GONNA TAKE YOUR CABIN, BUT I DIDN'T THINK THAT WAS RIGHT.
YOU GOT A COPY OF THE KEY FOR THE CABIN THAT JULIAN FELLA'S USIN'?
OF COURSE. RIGHT THERE IN THE SAFE WITH THE OTHERS.
AND YOUR SWORD CANE?
I ALWAYS GOT THAT, CAP'N. BUT THAT'S THE KIND OF QUESTION MAKES A MAN WONDER.
MIKE! GOOD. YOU BOTH SET YOURSELVES DOWN.

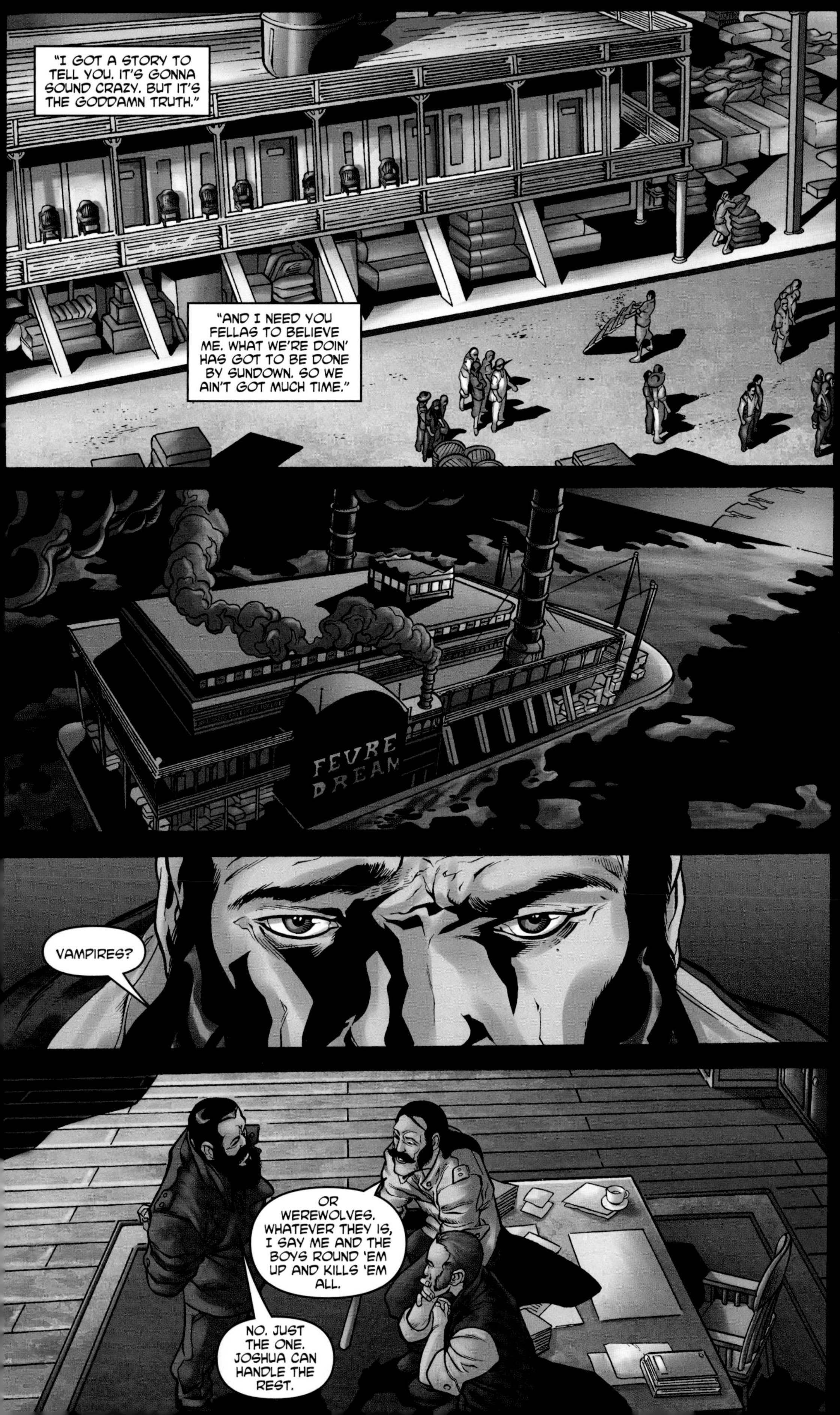
"I GOT A STORY TO TELL YOU. IT'S GONNA SOUND CRAZY. BUT IT'S THE GODDAMN TRUTH."
"AND I NEED YOU FELLAS TO BELIEVE ME. WHAT WE'RE DOIN' HAS GOT TO BE DONE BY SUNDOWN. SO WE AIN'T GOT MUCH TIME."
FEVRE DREAM
VAMPIRES?
OR WEREWOLVES. WHATEVER THEY IS, I SAY ME AND THE BOYS ROUND 'EM UP AND KILLS 'EM ALL.
NO. JUST THE ONE. JOSHUA CAN HANDLE THE REST.

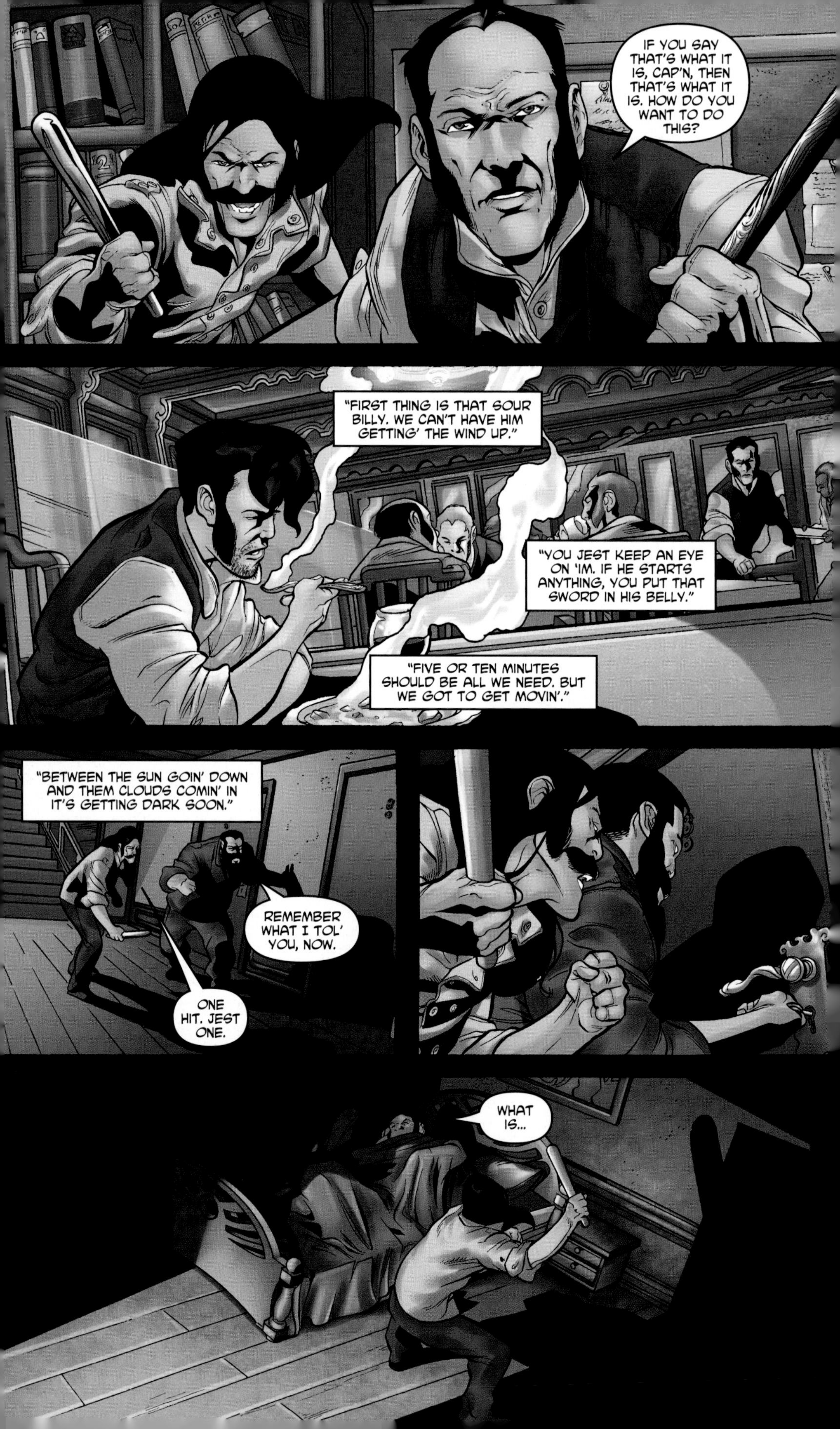
IF YOU SAY THAT'S WHAT IT IS, CAP'N, THEN THAT'S WHAT IT IS. HOW DO YOU WANT TO DO THIS?
"FIRST THING IS THAT SOUR BILLY. WE CAN'T HAVE HIM GETTING' THE WIND UP."
"YOU JEST KEEP AN EYE ON 'IM. IF HE STARTS ANYTHING, YOU PUT THAT SWORD IN HIS BELLY."
"FIVE OR TEN MINUTES SHOULD BE ALL WE NEED. BUT WE GOT TO GET MOVIN'."
"BETWEEN THE SUN GOIN' DOWN AND THEM CLOUDS COMIN' IN IT'S GETTING DARK SOON."
REMEMBER WHAT I TOL' YOU, NOW.
ONE HIT. JEST ONE.
WHAT IS...

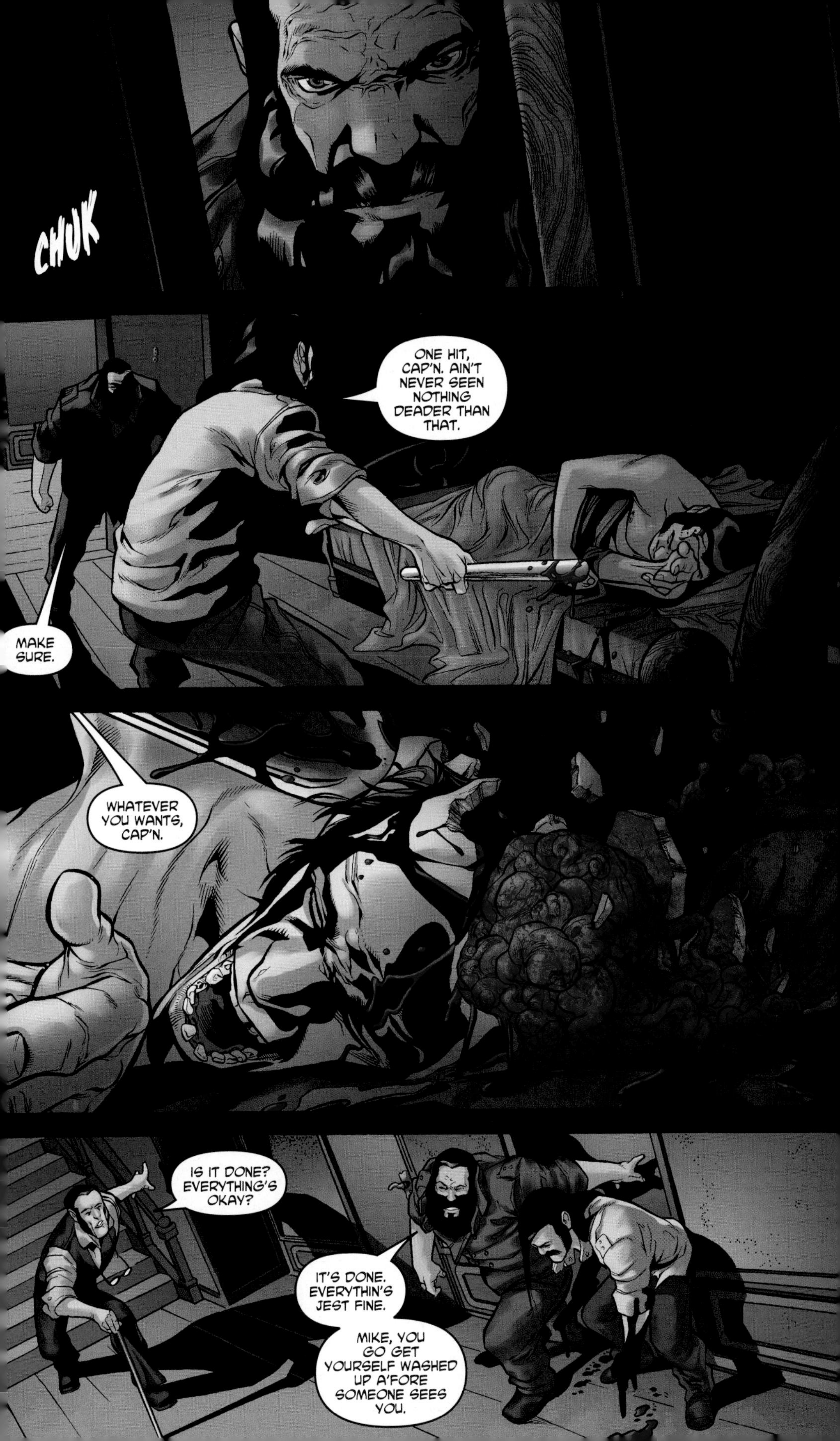
CHUK
ONE HIT, CAP'N. AIN'T NEVER SEEN NOTHING DEADER THAN THAT.
MAKE SURE.
WHATEVER YOU WANTS, CAP'N.
IS IT DONE? EVERYTHING'S OKAY?
IT'S DONE. EVERYTHIN'S JEST FINE.
MIKE, YOU GO GET YOURSELF WASHED UP A'FORE SOMEONE SEES YOU.

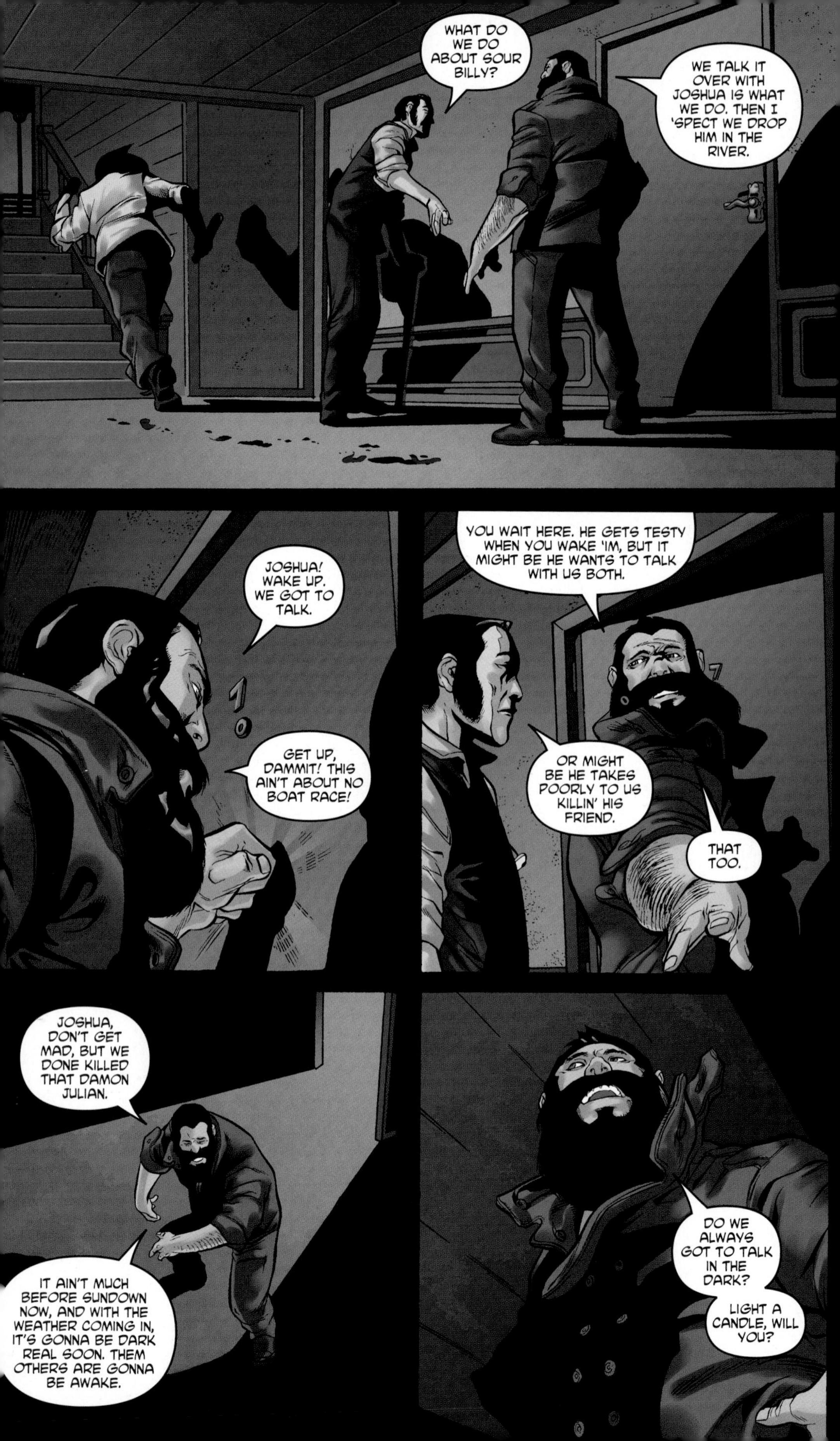
WHAT DO WE DO ABOUT SOUR BILLY?
WE TALK IT OVER WITH JOSHUA IS WHAT WE DO. THEN I 'SPECT WE DROP HIM IN THE RIVER.
JOSHUA! WAKE UP. WE GOT TO TALK.
GET UP, DAMMIT! THIS AIN'T ABOUT NO BOAT RACE!
YOU WAIT HERE. HE GETS TESTY WHEN YOU WAKE 'IM, BUT IT MIGHT BE HE WANTS TO TALK WITH US BOTH.
OR MIGHT BE HE TAKES POORLY TO US KILLIN' HIS FRIEND.
THAT TOO.
JOSHUA, DON'T GET MAD, BUT WE DONE KILLED THAT DAMON JULIAN.
IT AIN'T MUCH BEFORE SUNDOWN NOW, AND WITH THE WEATHER COMING IN, IT'S GONNA BE DARK REAL SOON. THEM OTHERS ARE GONNA BE AWAKE.
DO WE ALWAYS GOT TO TALK IN THE DARK?
LIGHT A CANDLE, WILL YOU?

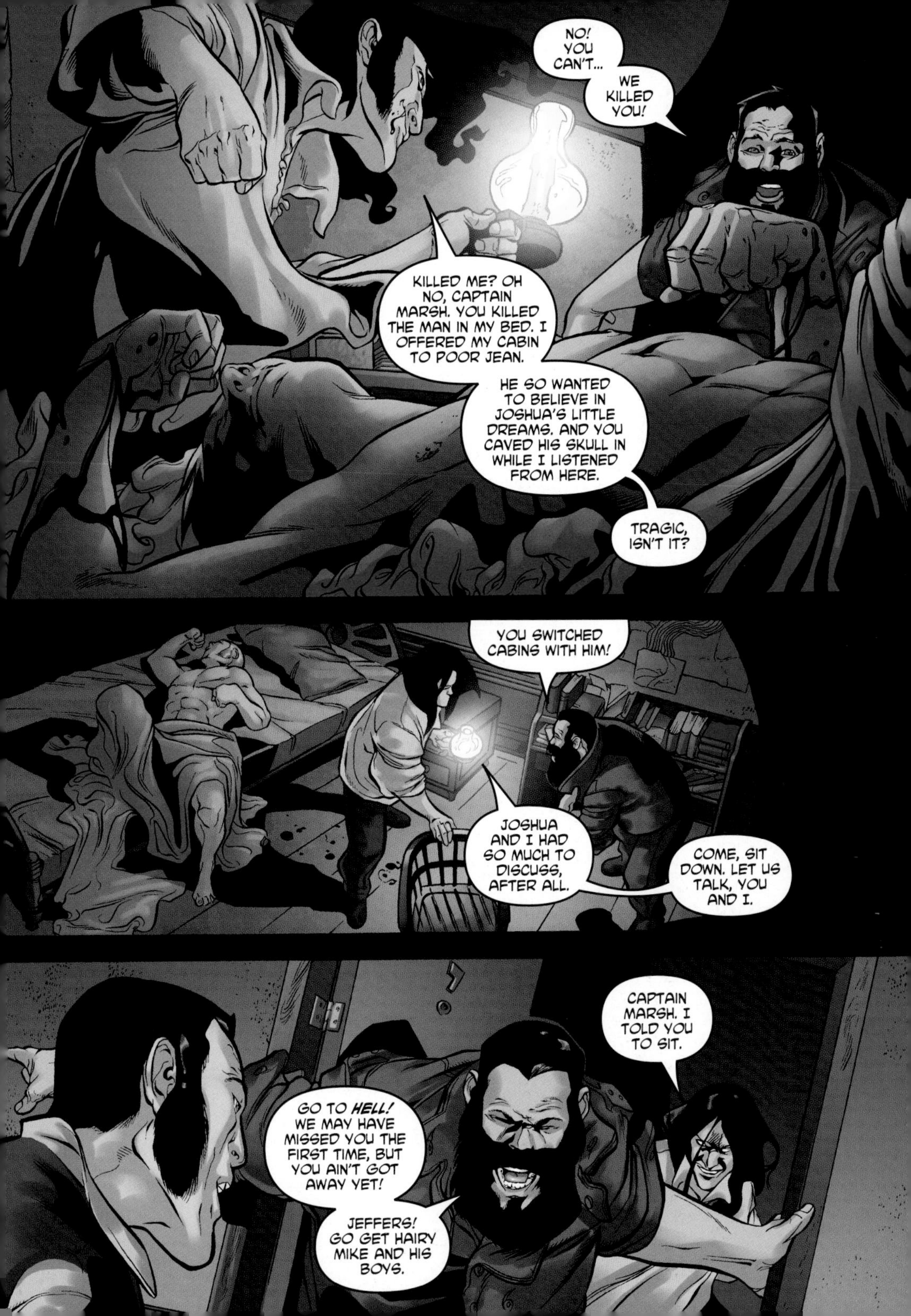
NO! YOU CAN'T...
WE KILLED YOU!
KILLED ME? OH NO, CAPTAIN MARSH. YOU KILLED THE MAN IN MY BED. I OFFERED MY CABIN TO POOR JEAN.
HE SO WANTED TO BELIEVE IN JOSHUA'S LITTLE DREAMS. AND YOU CAVED HIS SKULL IN WHILE I LISTENED FROM HERE.
TRAGIC, ISN'T IT?
YOU SWITCHED CABINS WITH HIM!
JOSHUA AND I HAD SO MUCH TO DISCUSS, AFTER ALL.
COME, SIT DOWN. LET US TALK, YOU AND I.
CAPTAIN MARSH. I TOLD YOU TO SIT.
GO TO HELL! WE MAY HAVE MISSED YOU THE FIRST TIME, BUT YOU AIN'T GOT AWAY YET!
JEFFERS! GO GET HAIRY MIKE AND HIS BOYS.

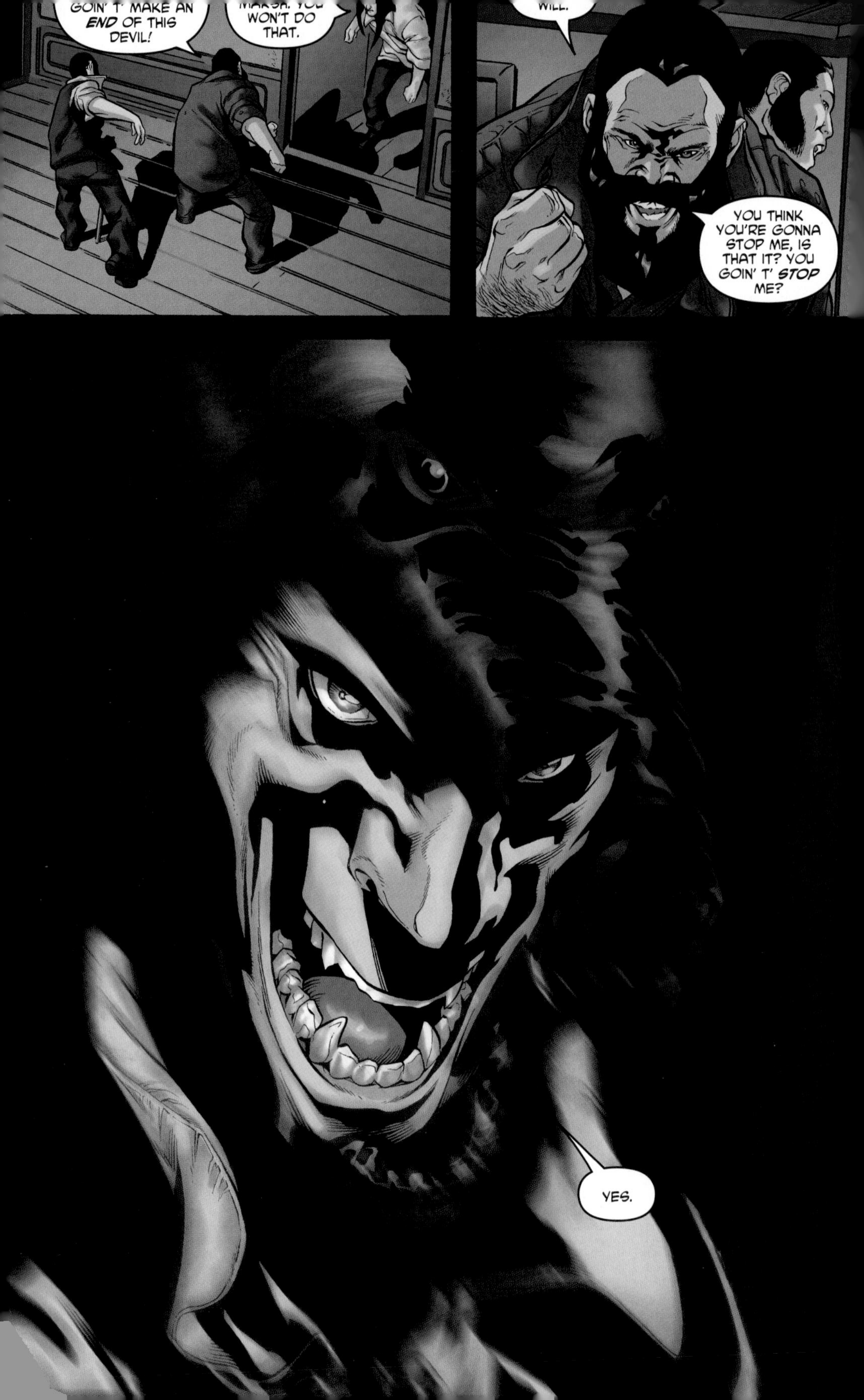
GOIN' T' MAKE AN END OF THIS DEVIL!
WON'T DO THAT.
WILL.
YOU THINK YOU'RE GONNA STOP ME, IS THAT IT? YOU GOIN' T' STOP ME?
YES.

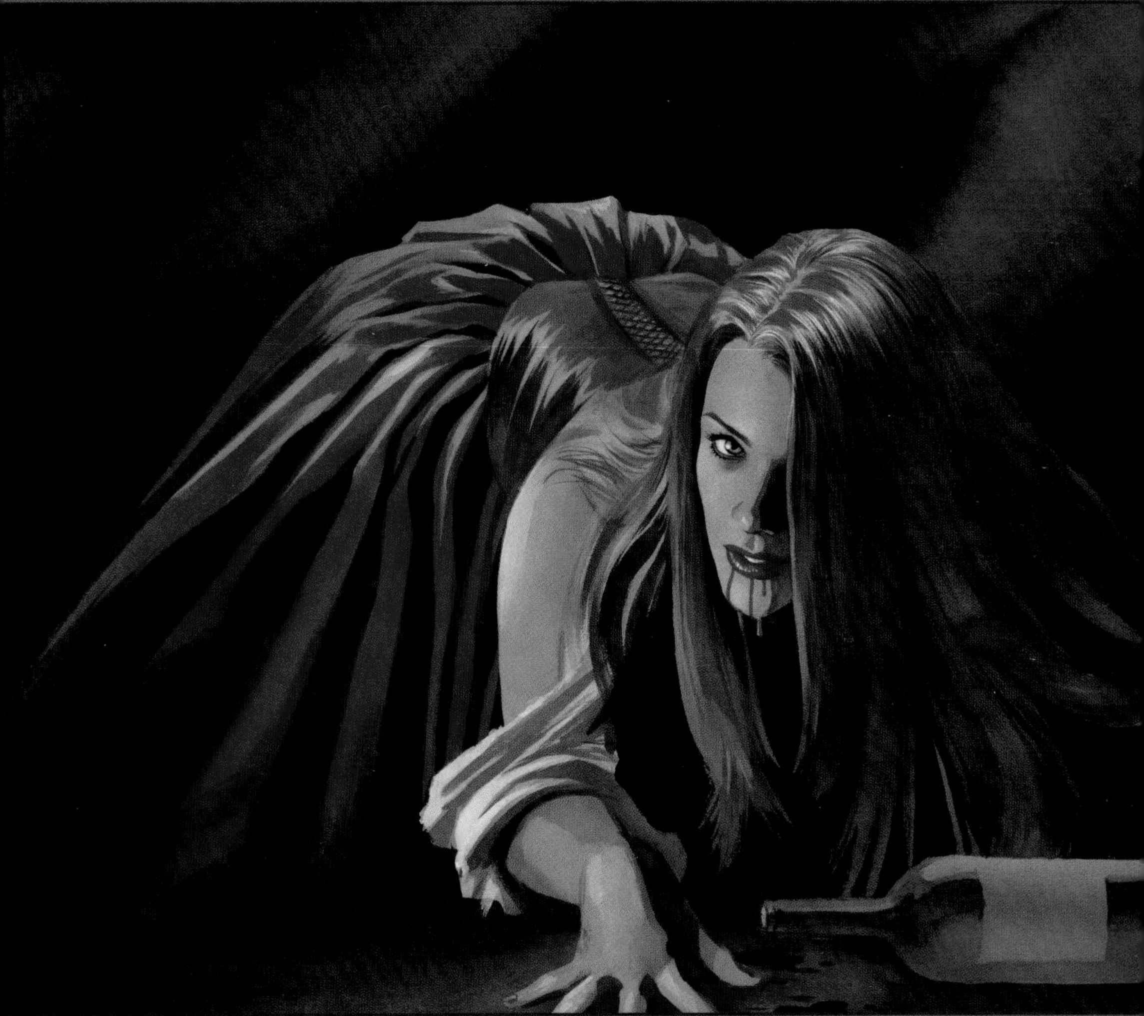

CHAPTER 7

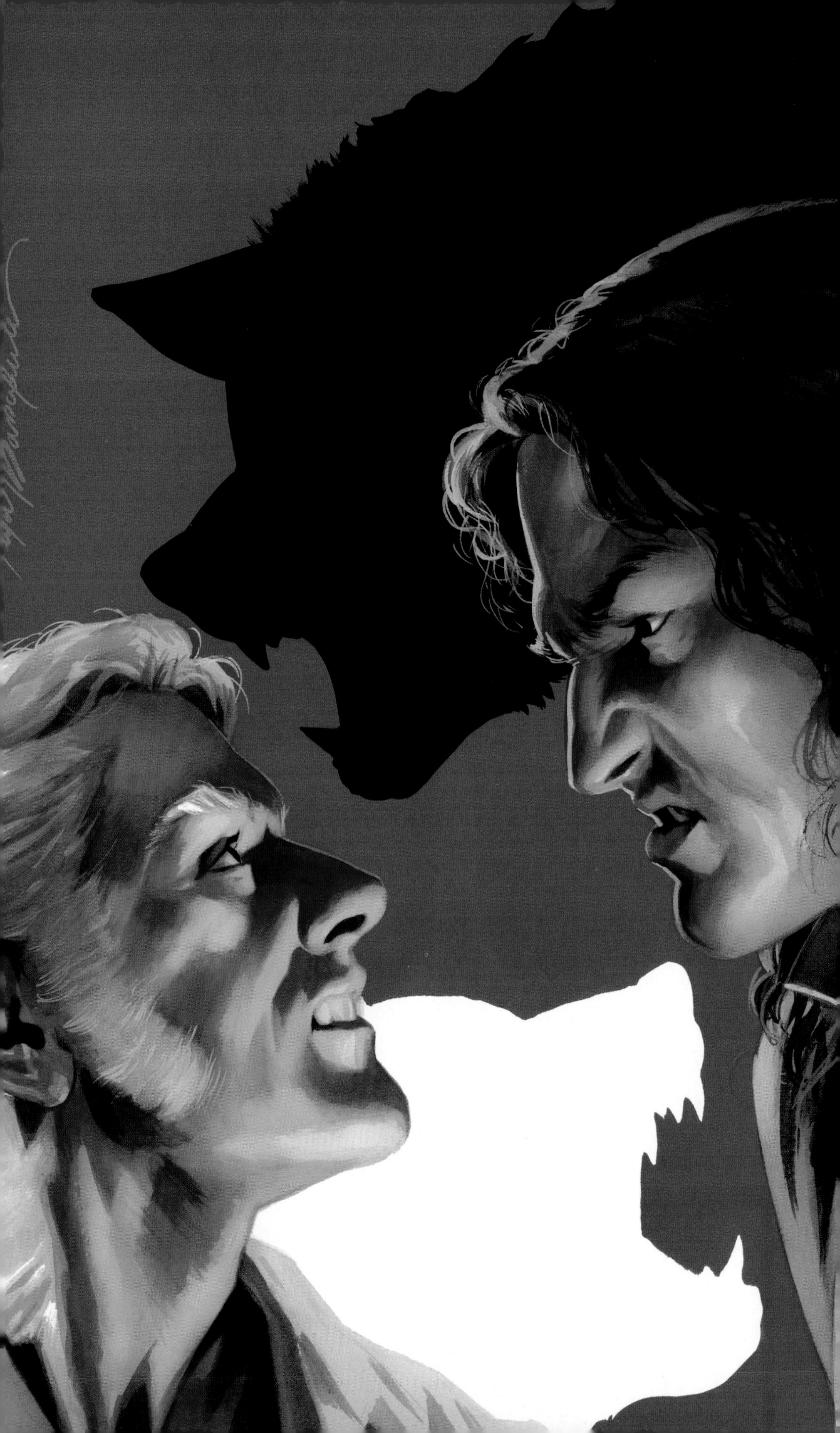

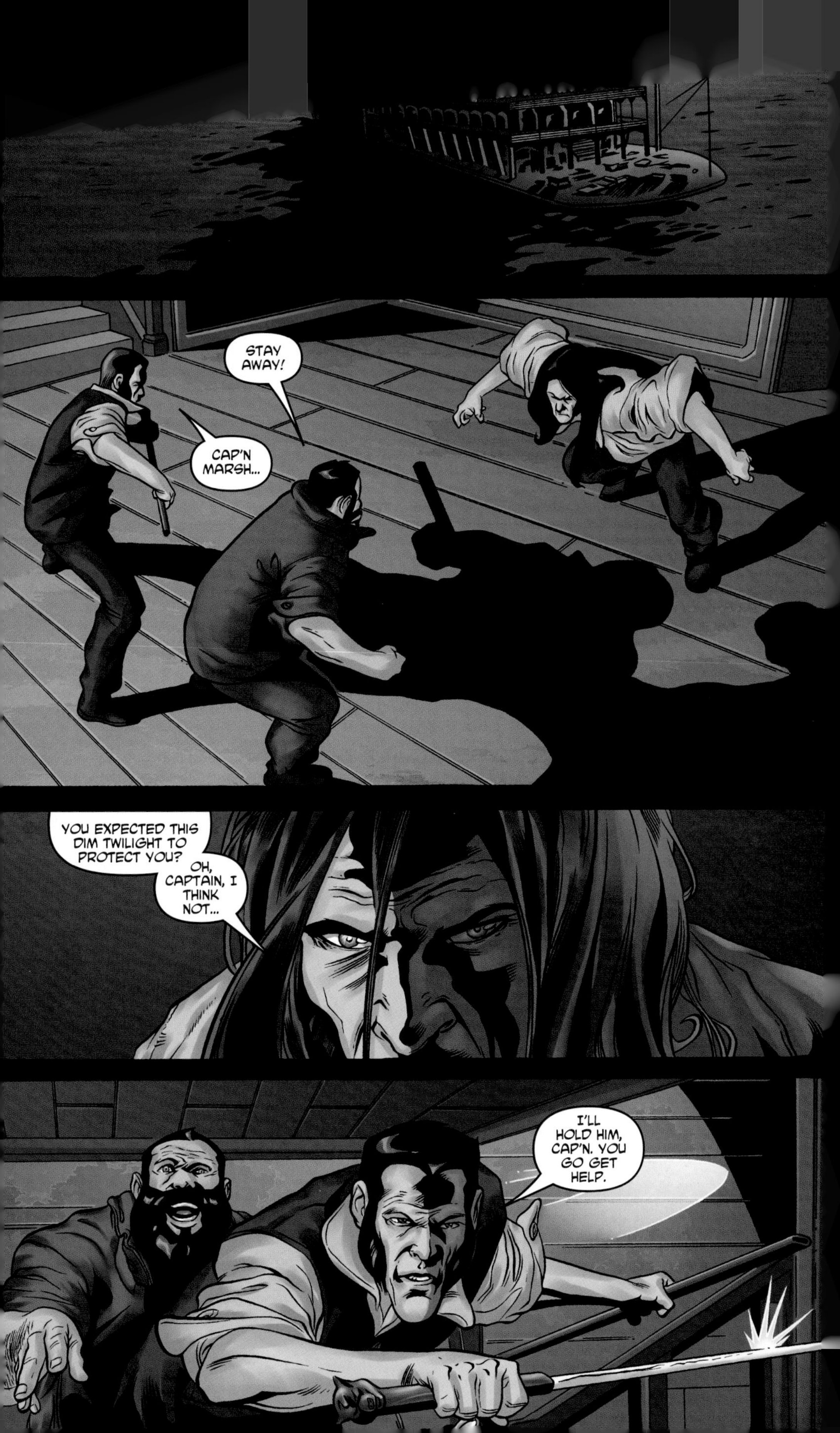
STAY AWAY!
CAP'N MARSH...
YOU EXPECTED THIS DIM TWILIGHT TO PROTECT YOU?
OH, CAPTAIN, I THINK NOT...
I'LL HOLD HIM, CAP'N. YOU GO GET HELP.

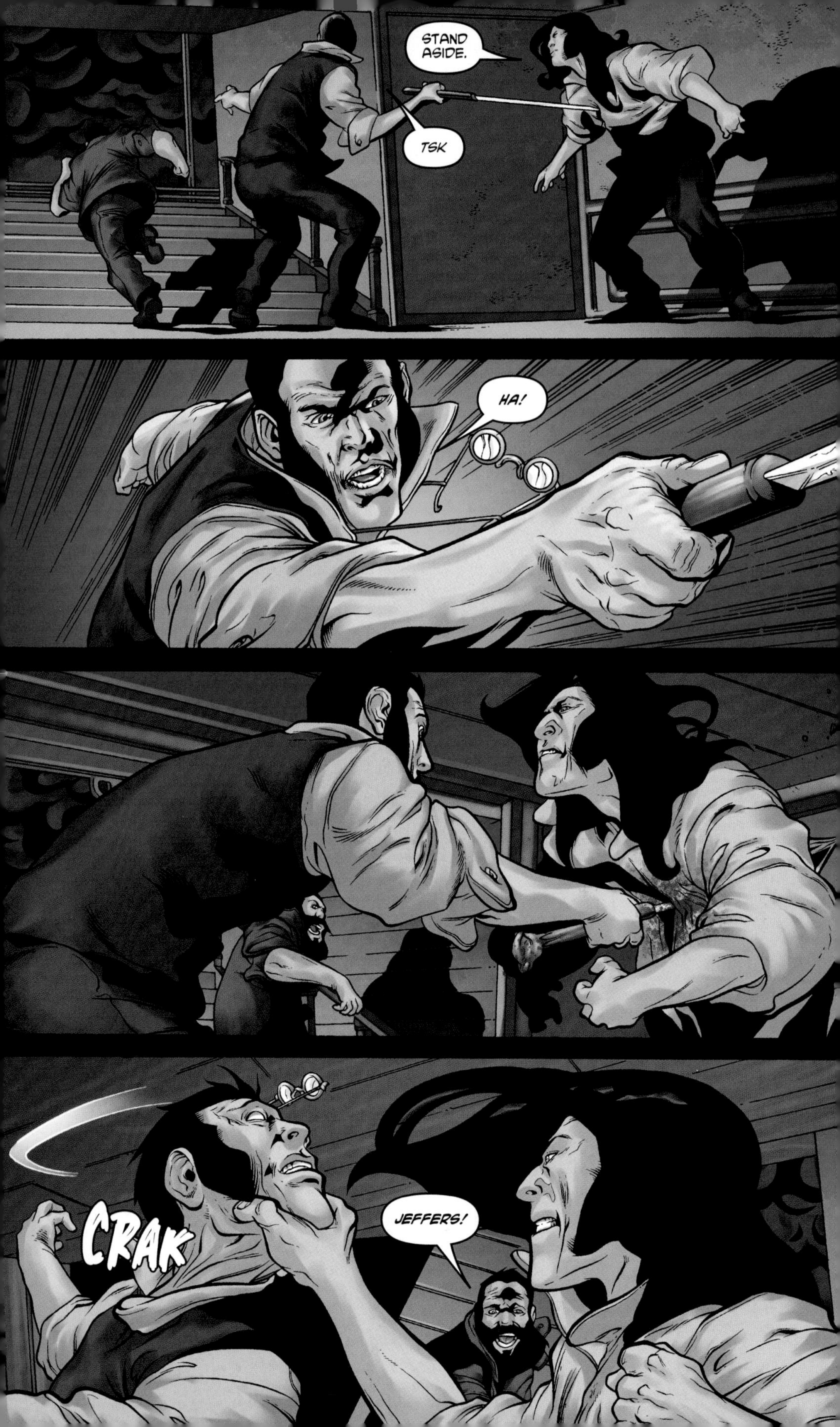
STAND ASIDE.
TSK
HA!
CRAK
JEFFERS!

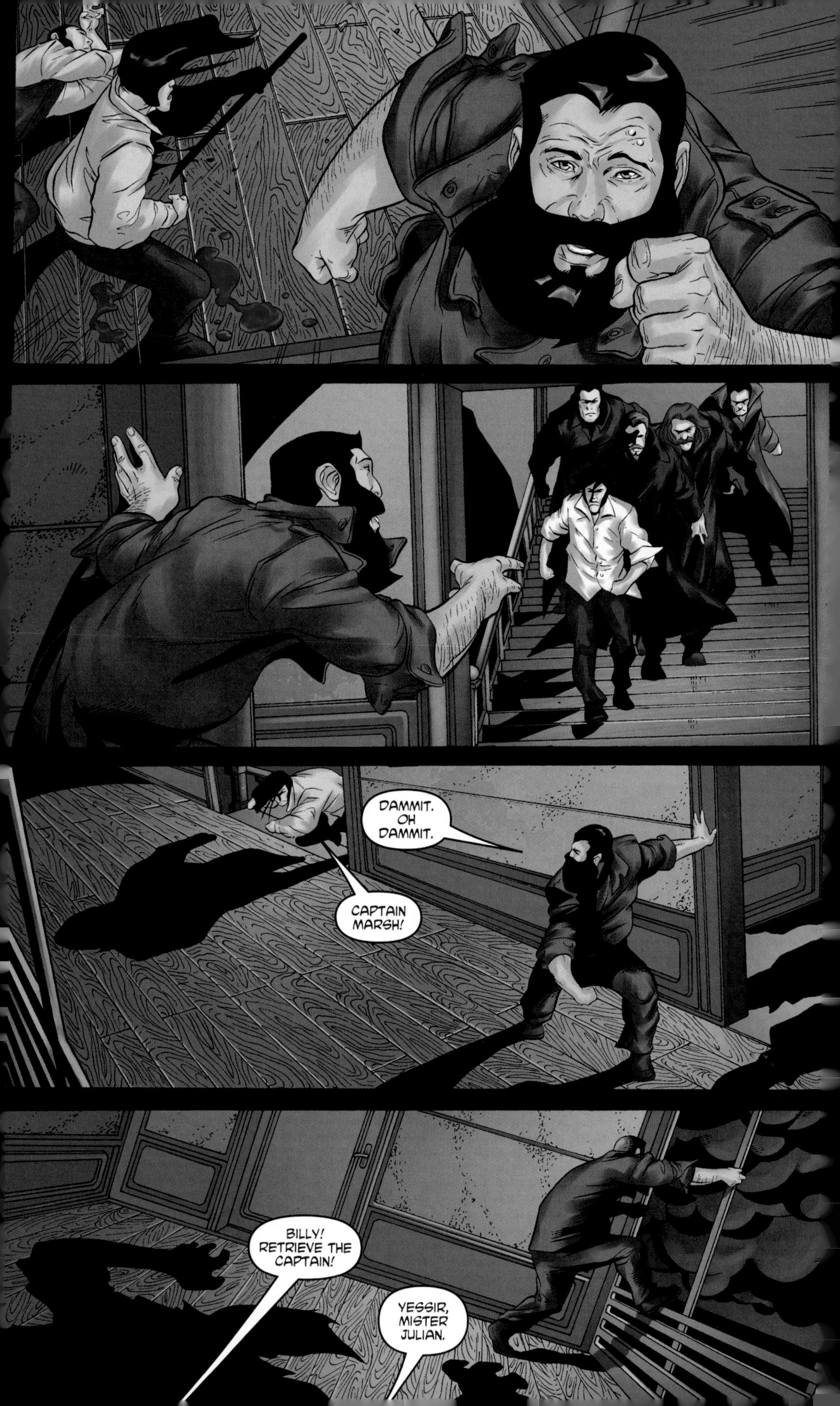

DAMMIT. OH DAMMIT.
CAPTAIN MARSH!
BILLY! RETRIEVE THE CAPTAIN!
YESSIR, MISTER JULIAN.

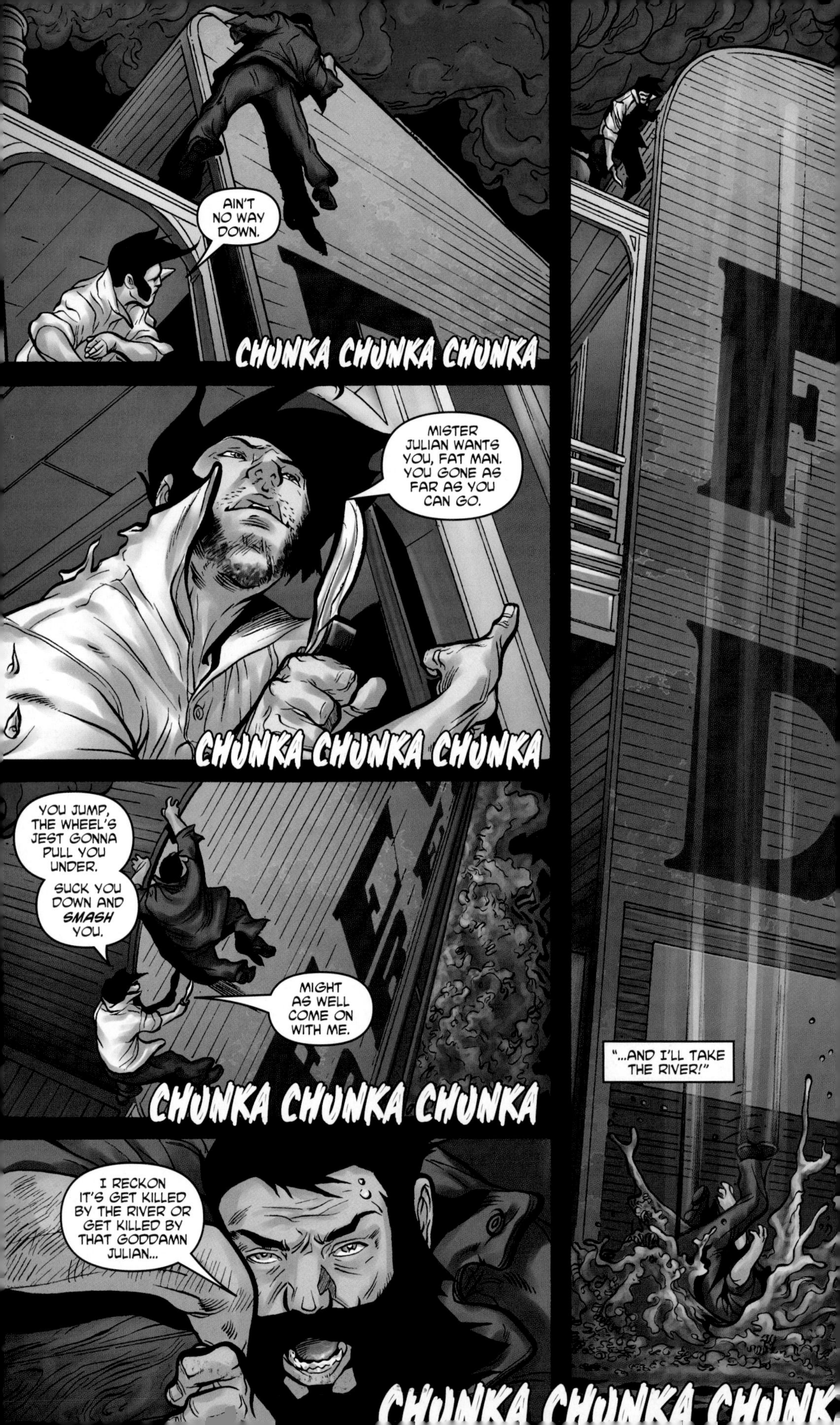
AIN'T NO WAY DOWN.
CHUNKA CHUNKA CHUNKA
MISTER JULIAN WANTS YOU, FAT MAN. YOU GONE AS FAR AS YOU CAN GO.
CHUNKA CHUNKA CHUNKA
YOU JUMP, THE WHEEL'S JEST GONNA PULL YOU UNDER.
SUCK YOU DOWN AND SMASH YOU.
MIGHT AS WELL COME ON WITH ME.
CHUNKA CHUNKA CHUNKA
I RECKON IT'S GET KILLED BY THE RIVER OR GET KILLED BY THAT GODDAMN JULIAN...
"...AND I'LL TAKE THE RIVER!"
CHUNKA CHUNKA CHUNK

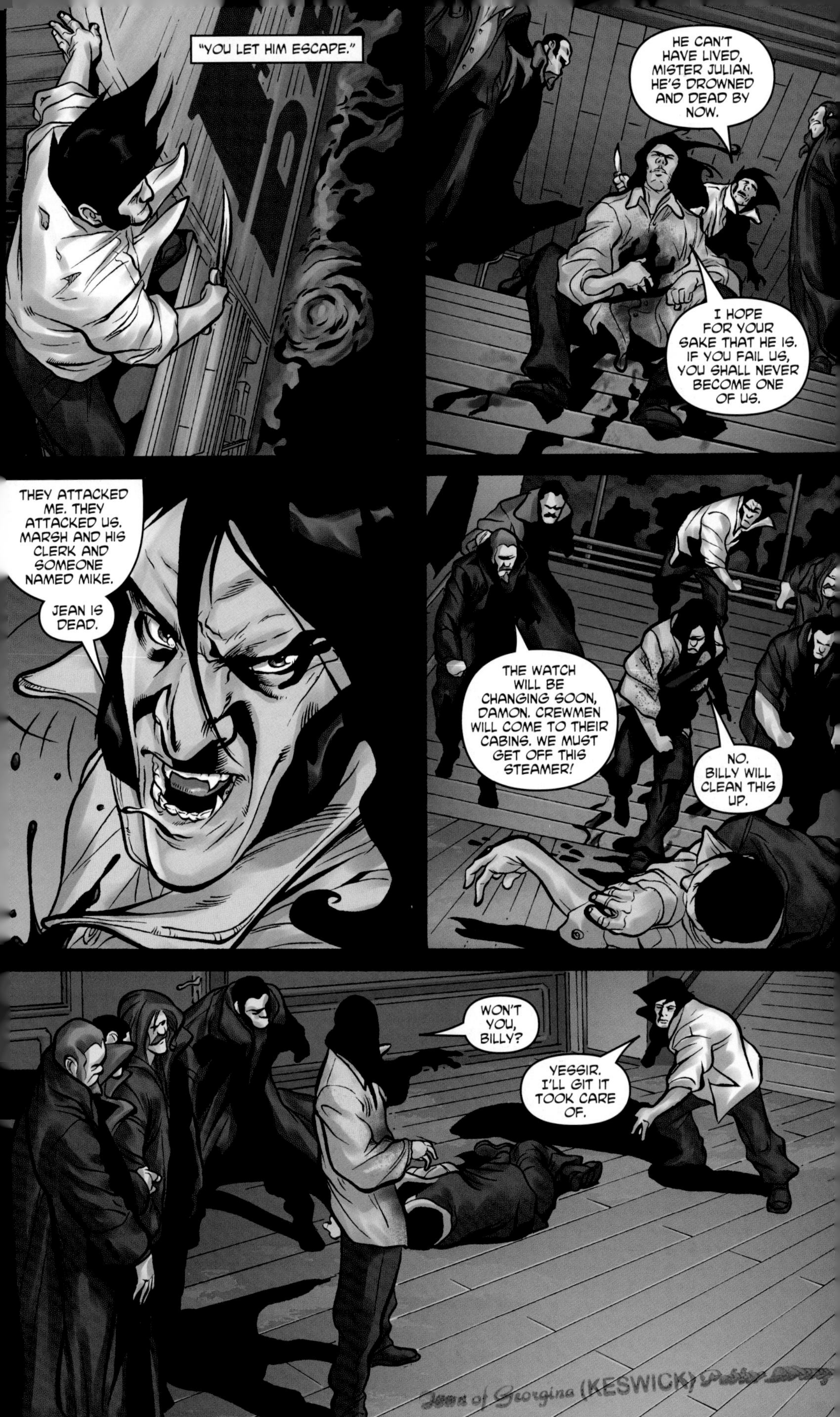
"YOU LET HIM ESCAPE."
HE CAN'T HAVE LIVED, MISTER JULIAN. HE'S DROWNED AND DEAD BY NOW.
I HOPE FOR YOUR SAKE THAT HE IS. IF YOU FAIL US, YOU SHALL NEVER BECOME ONE OF US.
THEY ATTACKED ME. THEY ATTACKED US. MARSH AND HIS CLERK AND SOMEONE NAMED MIKE.
JEAN IS DEAD.
THE WATCH WILL BE CHANGING SOON, DAMON. CREWMEN WILL COME TO THEIR CABINS. WE MUST GET OFF THIS STEAMER!
NO. BILLY WILL CLEAN THIS UP.
WON'T YOU, BILLY?
YESSIR. I'LL GIT IT TOOK CARE OF.

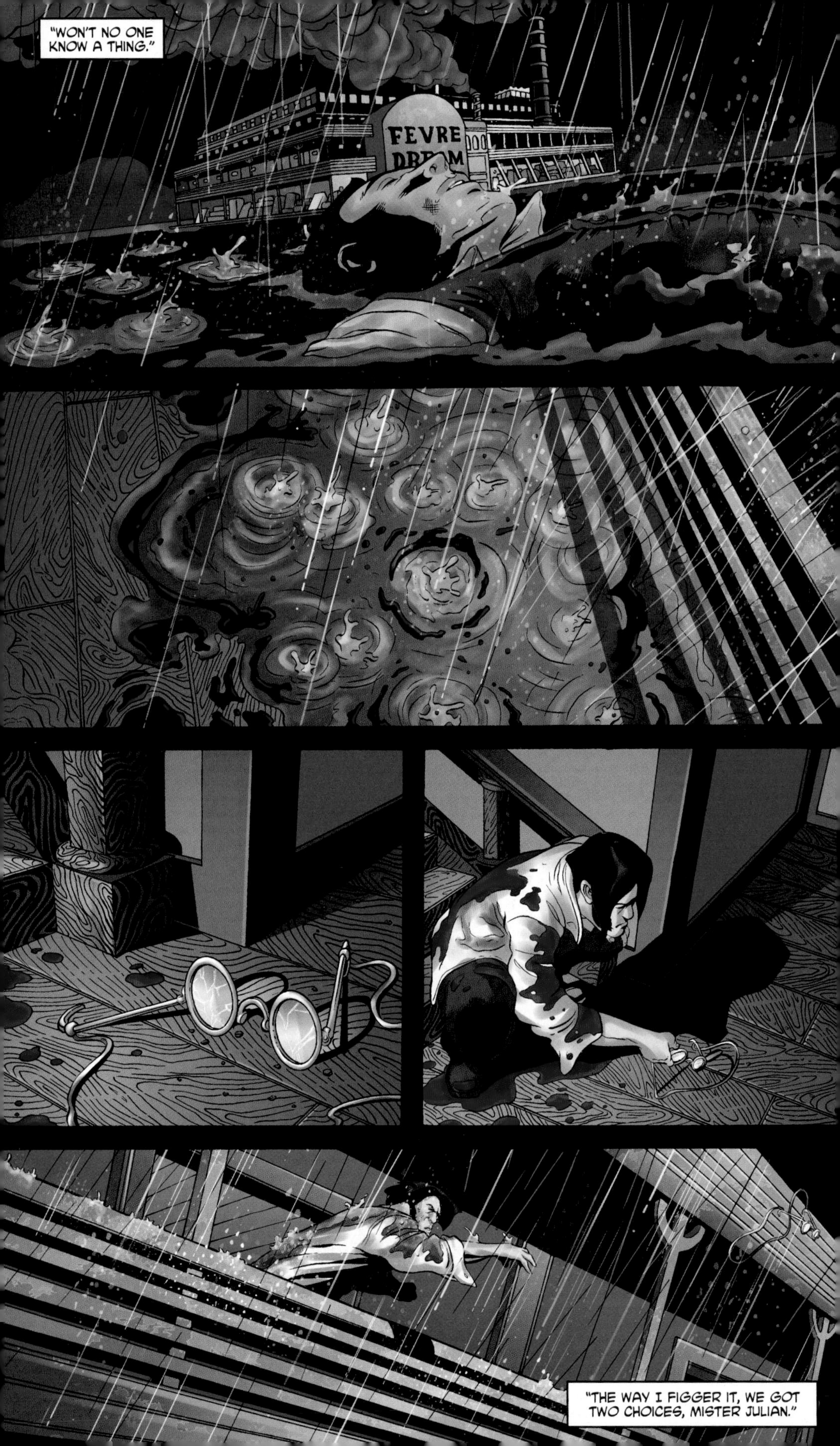
"WON'T NO ONE KNOW A THING."
FEVRE DREAM
"THE WAY I FIGGER IT, WE GOT TWO CHOICES, MISTER JULIAN."

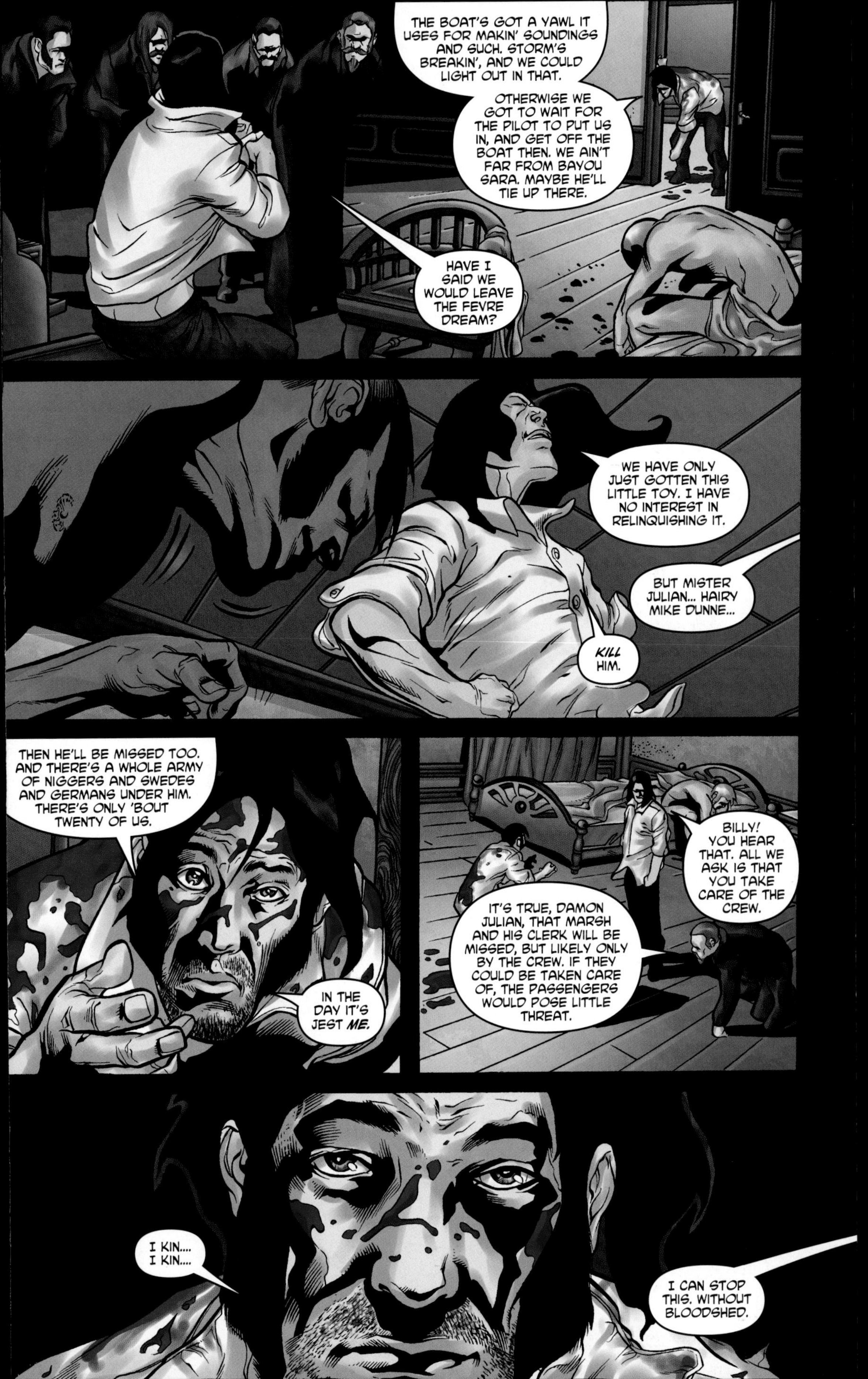
THE BOAT'S GOT A YAWL IT USES FOR MAKIN' SOUNDINGS AND SUCH. STORM'S BREAKIN', AND WE COULD LIGHT OUT IN THAT.
OTHERWISE WE GOT TO WAIT FOR THE PILOT TO PUT US IN, AND GET OFF THE BOAT THEN. WE AIN'T FAR FROM BAYOU SARA. MAYBE HE'LL TIE UP THERE.
HAVE I SAID WE WOULD LEAVE THE FEVRE DREAM?
WE HAVE ONLY JUST GOTTEN THIS LITTLE TOY. I HAVE NO INTEREST IN RELINQUISHING IT.
BUT MISTER JULIAN... HAIRY MIKE DUNNE...
KILL HIM.
THEN HE'LL BE MISSED TOO. AND THERE'S A WHOLE ARMY OF NIGGERS AND SWEDES AND GERMANS UNDER HIM. THERE'S ONLY 'BOUT TWENTY OF US.
IN THE DAY IT'S JEST ME.
IT'S TRUE, DAMON JULIAN, THAT MARSH AND HIS CLERK WILL BE MISSED, BUT LIKELY ONLY BY THE CREW. IF THEY COULD BE TAKEN CARE OF, THE PASSENGERS WOULD POSE LITTLE THREAT.
BILLY! YOU HEAR THAT. ALL WE ASK IS THAT YOU TAKE CARE OF THE CREW.
I KIN.... I KIN....
I CAN STOP THIS. WITHOUT BLOODSHED.

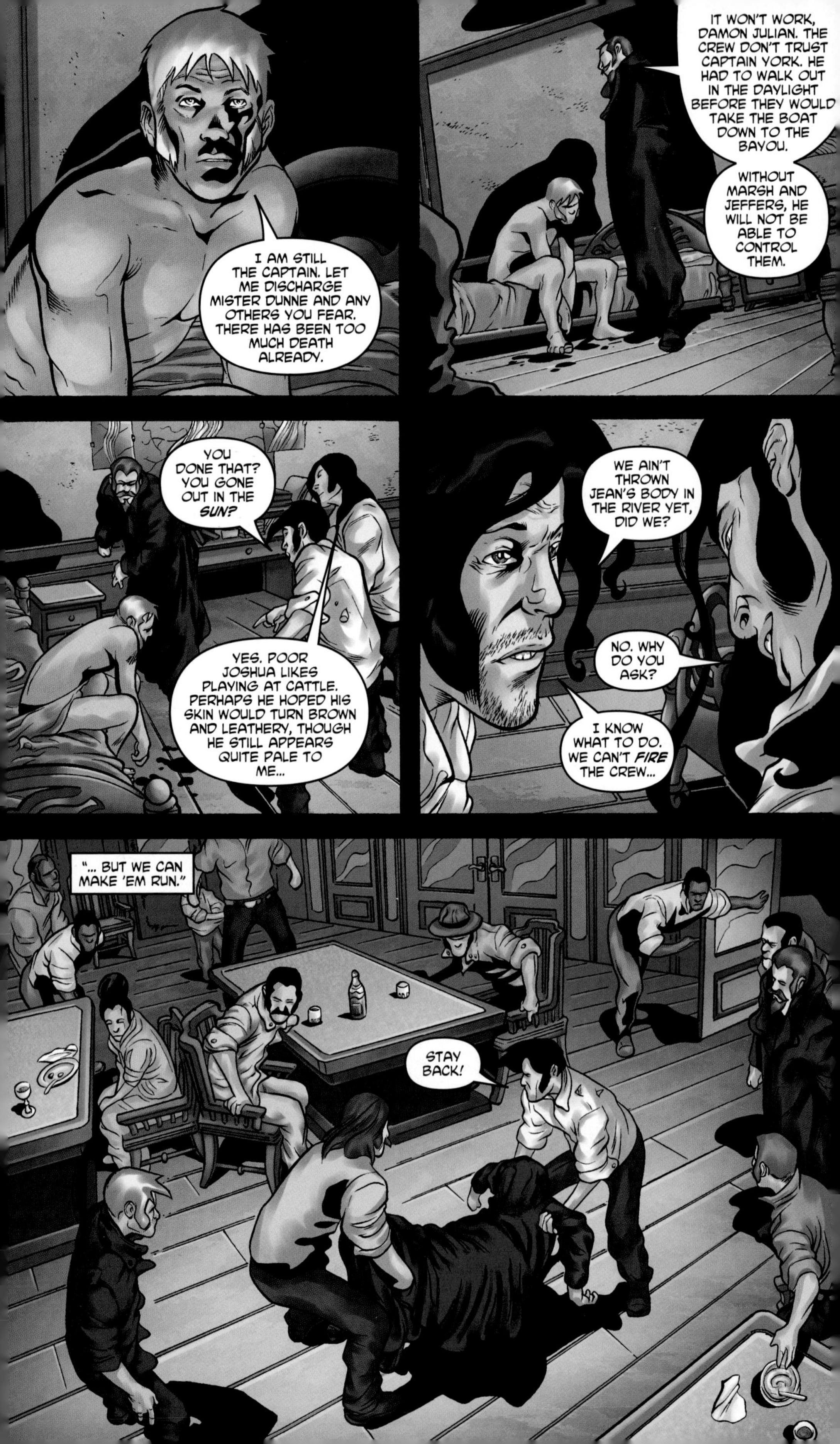
I AM STILL THE CAPTAIN. LET ME DISCHARGE MISTER DUNNE AND ANY OTHERS YOU FEAR. THERE HAS BEEN TOO MUCH DEATH ALREADY.
IT WON'T WORK, DAMON JULIAN. THE CREW DON'T TRUST CAPTAIN YORK. HE HAD TO WALK OUT IN THE DAYLIGHT BEFORE THEY WOULD TAKE THE BOAT DOWN TO THE BAYOU.
WITHOUT MARSH AND JEFFERS, HE WILL NOT BE ABLE TO CONTROL THEM.
YOU DONE THAT? YOU GONE OUT IN THE *SUN?*
YES. POOR JOSHUA LIKES PLAYING AT CATTLE. PERHAPS HE HOPED HIS SKIN WOULD TURN BROWN AND LEATHERY, THOUGH HE STILL APPEARS QUITE PALE TO ME...
WE AIN'T THROWN JEAN'S BODY IN THE RIVER YET, DID WE?
NO. WHY DO YOU ASK?
I KNOW WHAT TO DO. WE CAN'T *FIRE* THE CREW...
"... BUT WE CAN MAKE 'EM RUN."
STAY BACK!

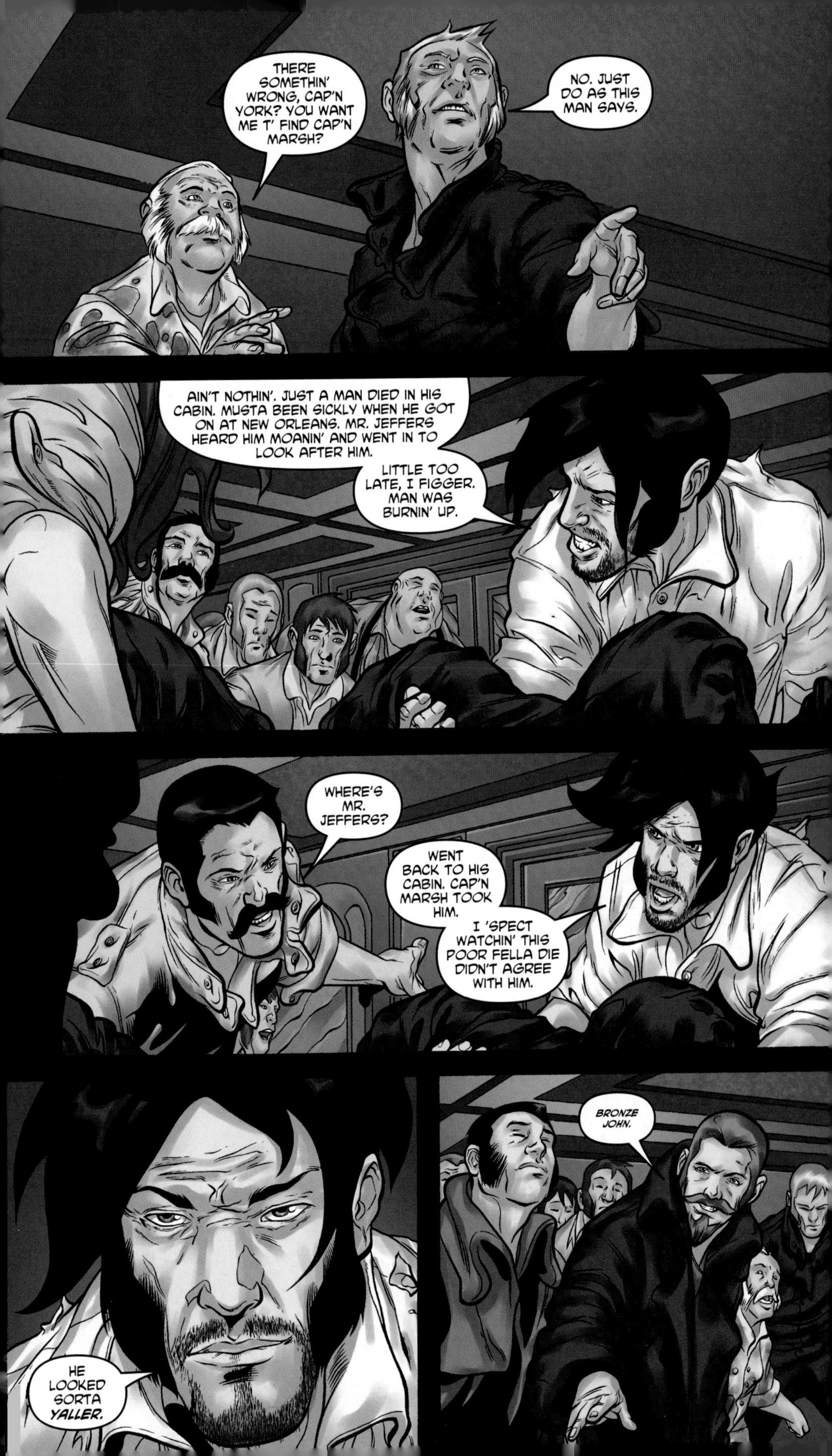
THERE SOMETHIN' WRONG, CAP'N YORK? YOU WANT ME T' FIND CAP'N MARSH?
NO. JUST DO AS THIS MAN SAYS.
AIN'T NOTHIN'. JUST A MAN DIED IN HIS CABIN. MUSTA BEEN SICKLY WHEN HE GOT ON AT NEW ORLEANS. MR. JEFFERS HEARD HIM MOANIN' AND WENT IN TO LOOK AFTER HIM.
LITTLE TOO LATE, I FIGGER. MAN WAS BURNIN' UP.
WHERE'S MR. JEFFERS?
WENT BACK TO HIS CABIN. CAP'N MARSH TOOK HIM.
I 'SPECT WATCHIN' THIS POOR FELLA DIE DIDN'T AGREE WITH HIM.
HE LOOKED SORTA *YALLER.*
BRONZE JOHN.

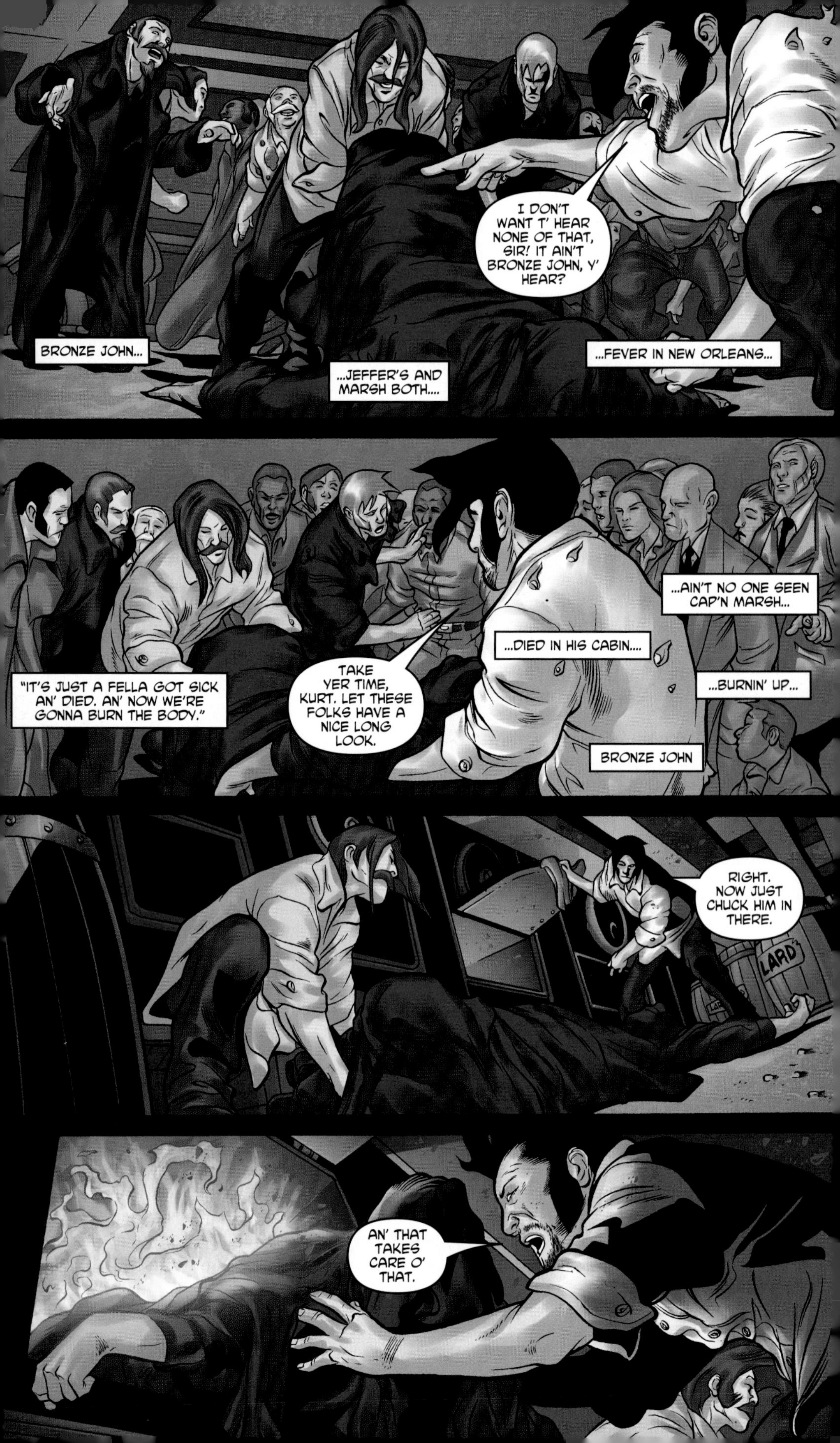
I DON'T WANT T' HEAR NONE OF THAT, SIR! IT AIN'T BRONZE JOHN, Y' HEAR?
BRONZE JOHN...
...JEFFER'S AND MARSH BOTH....
...FEVER IN NEW ORLEANS...
"IT'S JUST A FELLA GOT SICK AN' DIED. AN' NOW WE'RE GONNA BURN THE BODY."
TAKE YER TIME, KURT. LET THESE FOLKS HAVE A NICE LONG LOOK.
...DIED IN HIS CABIN....
...AIN'T NO ONE SEEN CAP'N MARSH...
...BURNIN' UP...
BRONZE JOHN
RIGHT. NOW JUST CHUCK HIM IN THERE.
LARD
AN' THAT TAKES CARE O' THAT.

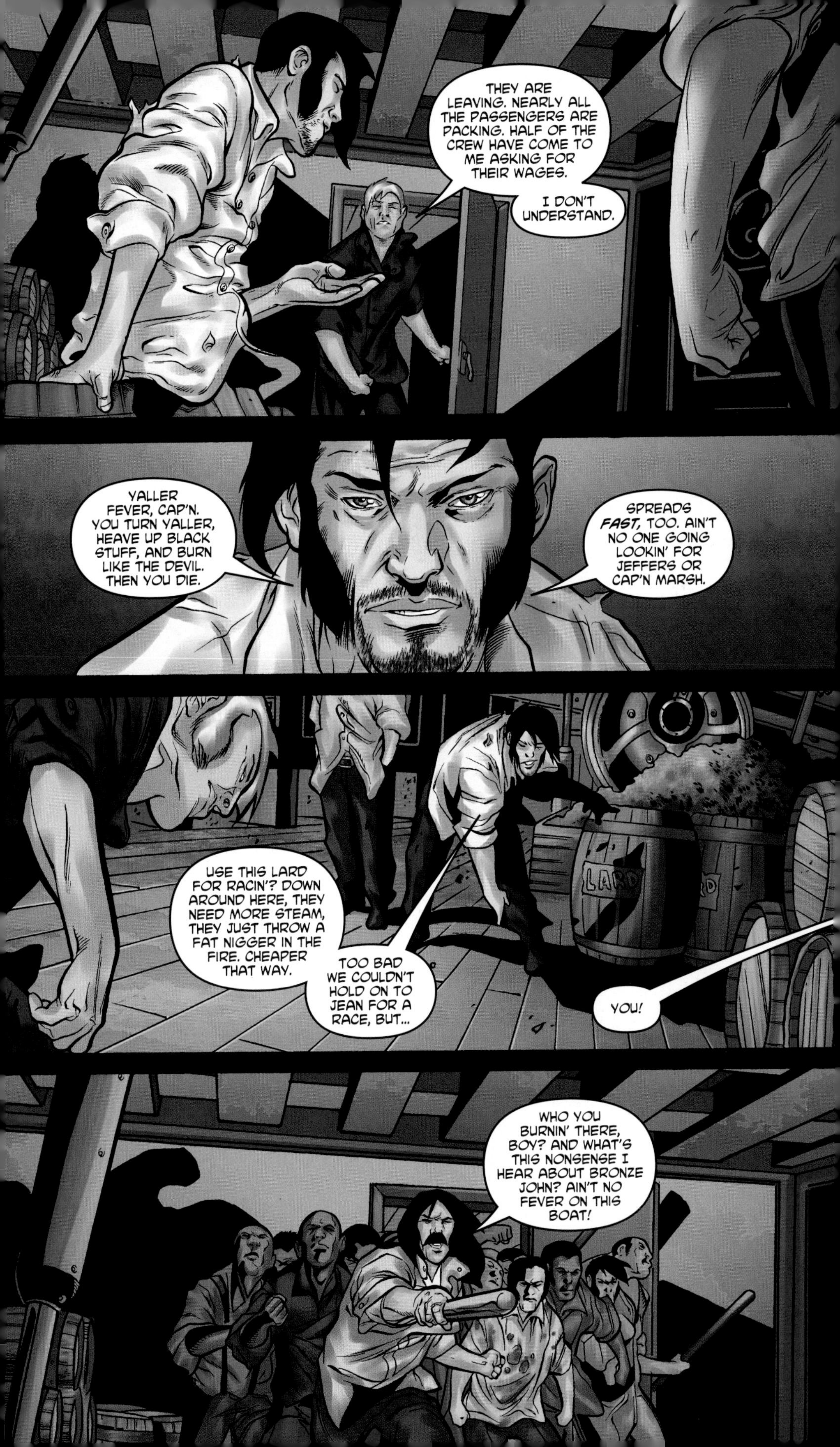
THEY ARE LEAVING. NEARLY ALL THE PASSENGERS ARE PACKING. HALF OF THE CREW HAVE COME TO ME ASKING FOR THEIR WAGES.
I DON'T UNDERSTAND.
YALLER FEVER, CAP'N. YOU TURN YALLER, HEAVE UP BLACK STUFF, AND BURN LIKE THE DEVIL. THEN YOU DIE.
SPREADS FAST, TOO. AIN'T NO ONE GOING LOOKIN' FOR JEFFERS OR CAP'N MARSH.
USE THIS LARD FOR RACIN'? DOWN AROUND HERE, THEY NEED MORE STEAM, THEY JUST THROW A FAT NIGGER IN THE FIRE. CHEAPER THAT WAY.
LARD
TOO BAD WE COULDN'T HOLD ON TO JEAN FOR A RACE, BUT...
YOU!
WHO YOU BURNIN' THERE, BOY? AND WHAT'S THIS NONSENSE I HEAR ABOUT BRONZE JOHN? AIN'T NO FEVER ON THIS BOAT!

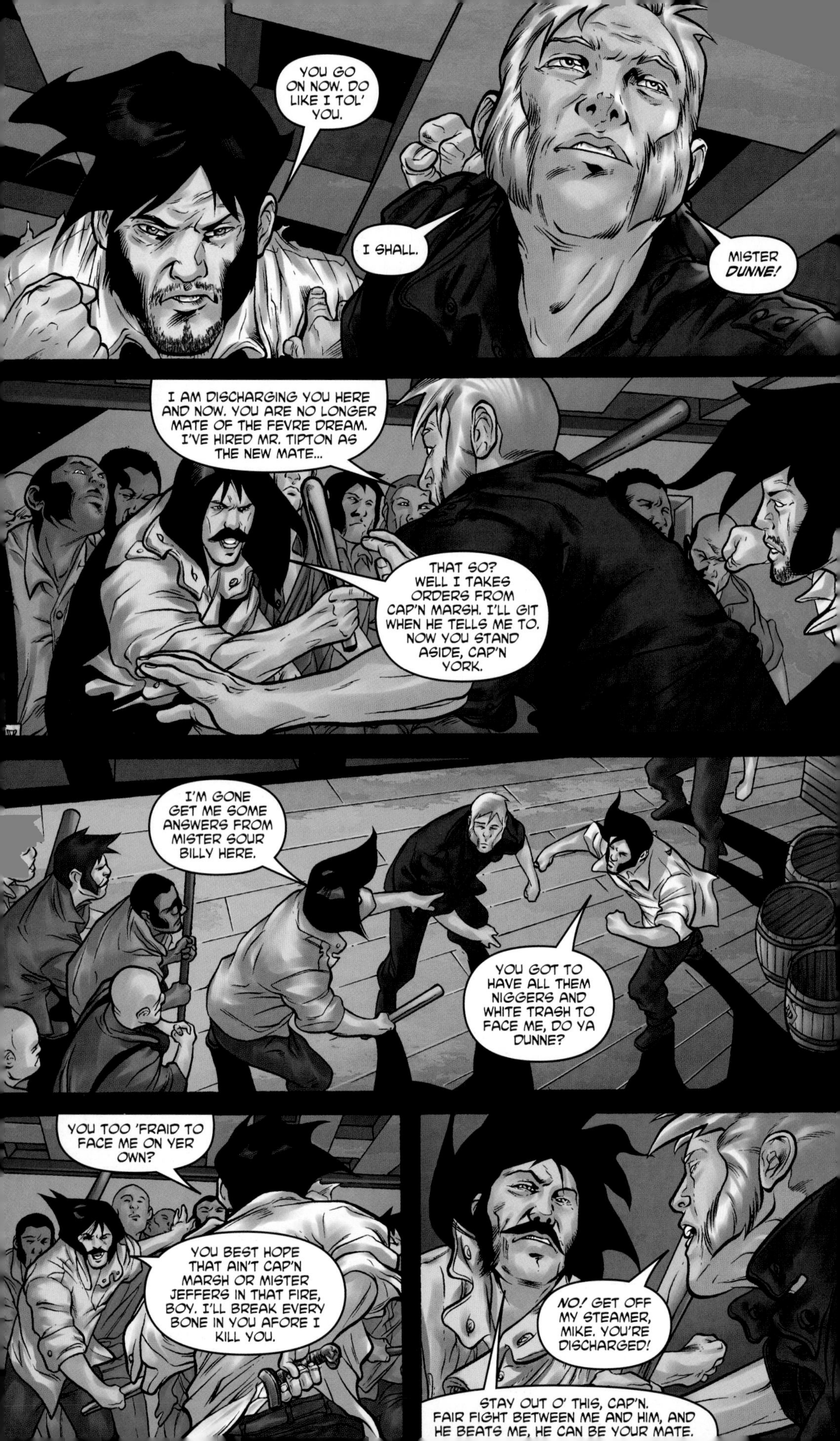
YOU GO ON NOW. DO LIKE I TOL' YOU.
I SHALL.
MISTER *DUNNE!*
I AM DISCHARGING YOU HERE AND NOW. YOU ARE NO LONGER MATE OF THE FEVRE DREAM. I'VE HIRED MR. TIPTON AS THE NEW MATE...
THAT SO? WELL I TAKES ORDERS FROM CAP'N MARSH. I'LL GIT WHEN HE TELLS ME TO. NOW YOU STAND ASIDE, CAP'N YORK.
I'M GONE GET ME SOME ANSWERS FROM MISTER SOUR BILLY HERE.
YOU GOT TO HAVE ALL THEM NIGGERS AND WHITE TRASH TO FACE ME, DO YA DUNNE?
YOU TOO 'FRAID TO FACE ME ON YER OWN?
YOU BEST HOPE THAT AIN'T CAP'N MARSH OR MISTER JEFFERS IN THAT FIRE, BOY. I'LL BREAK EVERY BONE IN YOU AFORE I KILL YOU.
NO! GET OFF MY STEAMER, MIKE. YOU'RE DISCHARGED!
STAY OUT O' THIS, CAP'N. FAIR FIGHT BETWEEN ME AND HIM, AND HE BEATS ME, HE CAN BE YOUR MATE.

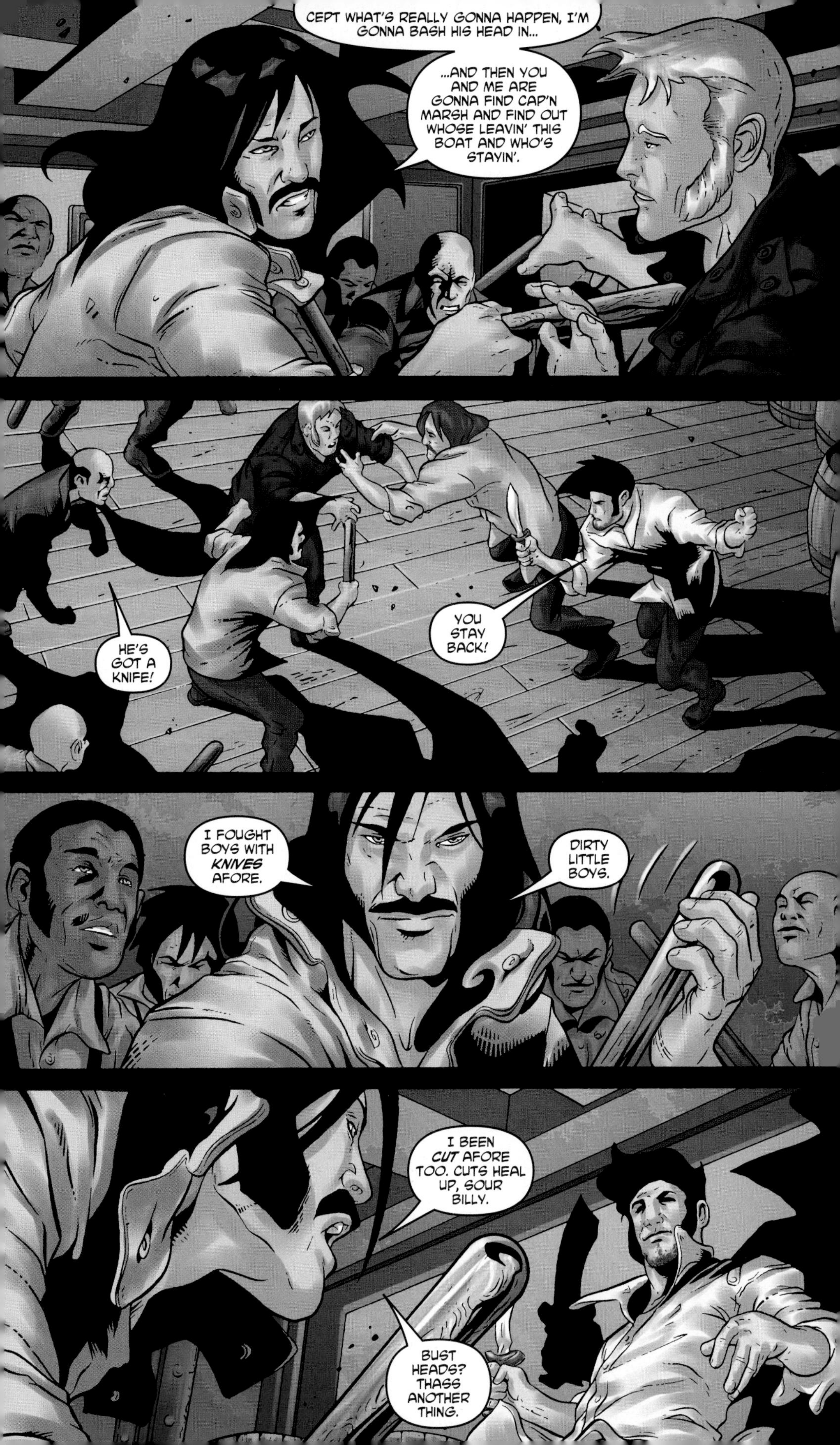
CEPT WHAT'S REALLY GONNA HAPPEN, I'M GONNA BASH HIS HEAD IN...
...AND THEN YOU AND ME ARE GONNA FIND CAP'N MARSH AND FIND OUT WHOSE LEAVIN' THIS BOAT AND WHO'S STAYIN'.
HE'S GOT A KNIFE!
YOU STAY BACK!
I FOUGHT BOYS WITH *KNIVES* AFORE.
DIRTY LITTLE BOYS.
I BEEN *CUT* AFORE TOO. CUTS HEAL UP, SOUR BILLY.
BUST HEADS? THASS ANOTHER THING.

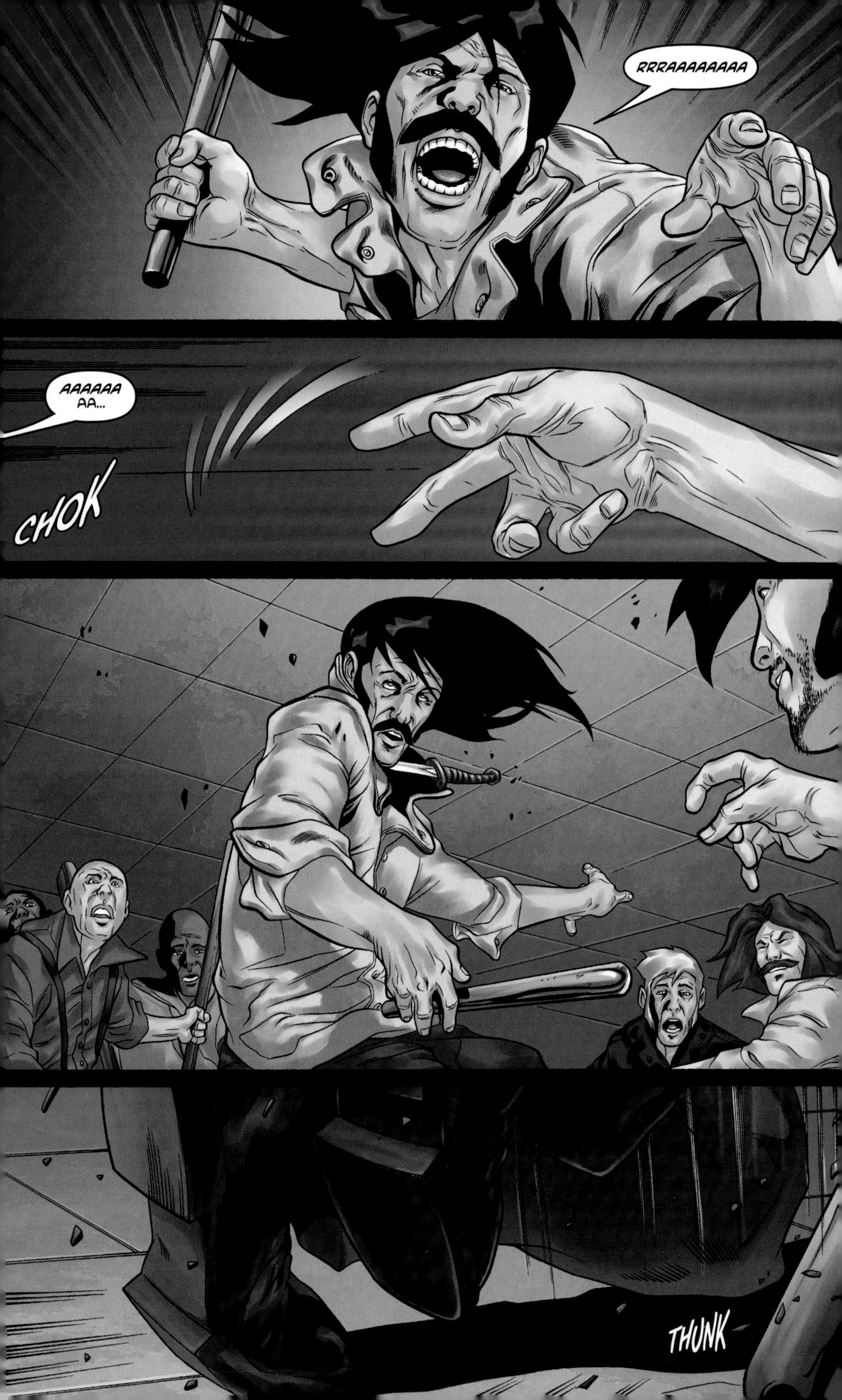
RRRAAAAAAAAA
AAAAAA AA...
CHOK
THUNK

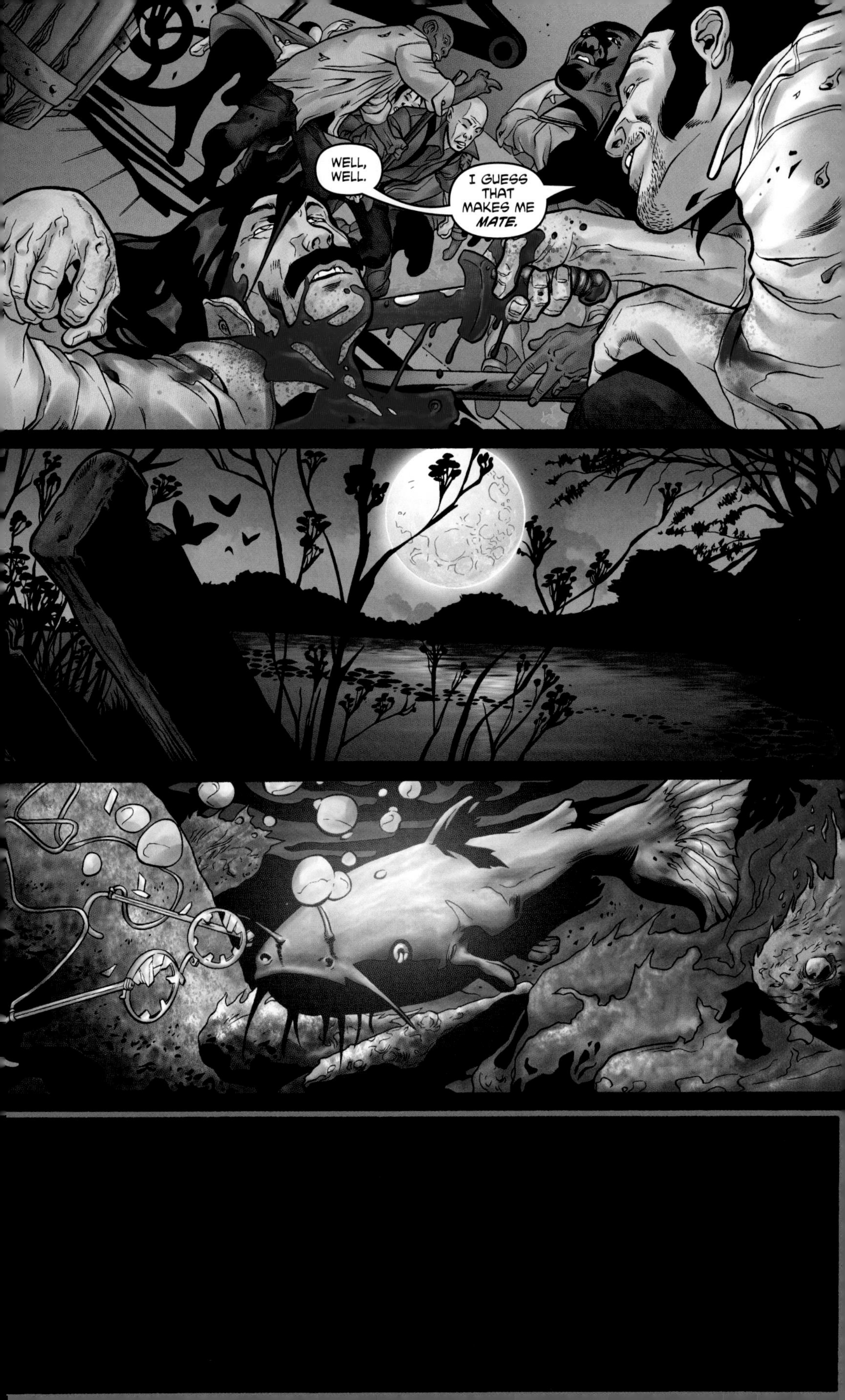
WELL, WELL.
I GUESS THAT MAKES ME *MATE.*

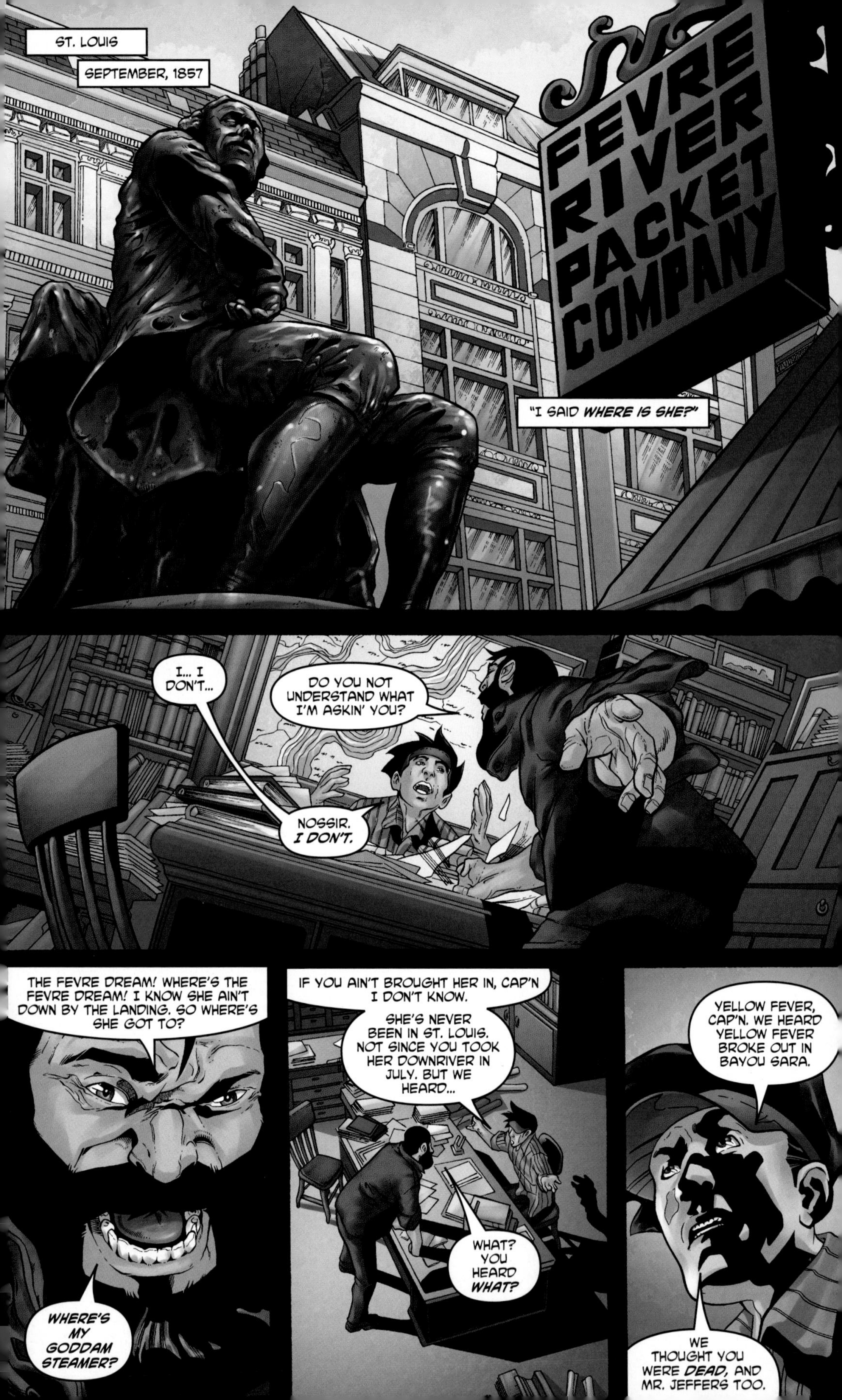
ST. LOUIS
SEPTEMBER, 1857
FEVRE RIVER PACKET COMPANY
"I SAID WHERE IS SHE?"
I... I DON'T...
DO YOU NOT UNDERSTAND WHAT I'M ASKIN' YOU?
NOSSIR. I DON'T.
THE FEVRE DREAM! WHERE'S THE FEVRE DREAM! I KNOW SHE AIN'T DOWN BY THE LANDING. SO WHERE'S SHE GOT TO?
WHERE'S MY GODDAM STEAMER?
IF YOU AIN'T BROUGHT HER IN, CAP'N I DON'T KNOW.
SHE'S NEVER BEEN IN ST. LOUIS. NOT SINCE YOU TOOK HER DOWNRIVER IN JULY. BUT WE HEARD...
WHAT? YOU HEARD WHAT?
YELLOW FEVER, CAP'N. WE HEARD YELLOW FEVER BROKE OUT IN BAYOU SARA.
WE THOUGHT YOU WERE DEAD, AND MR. JEFFERS TOO.

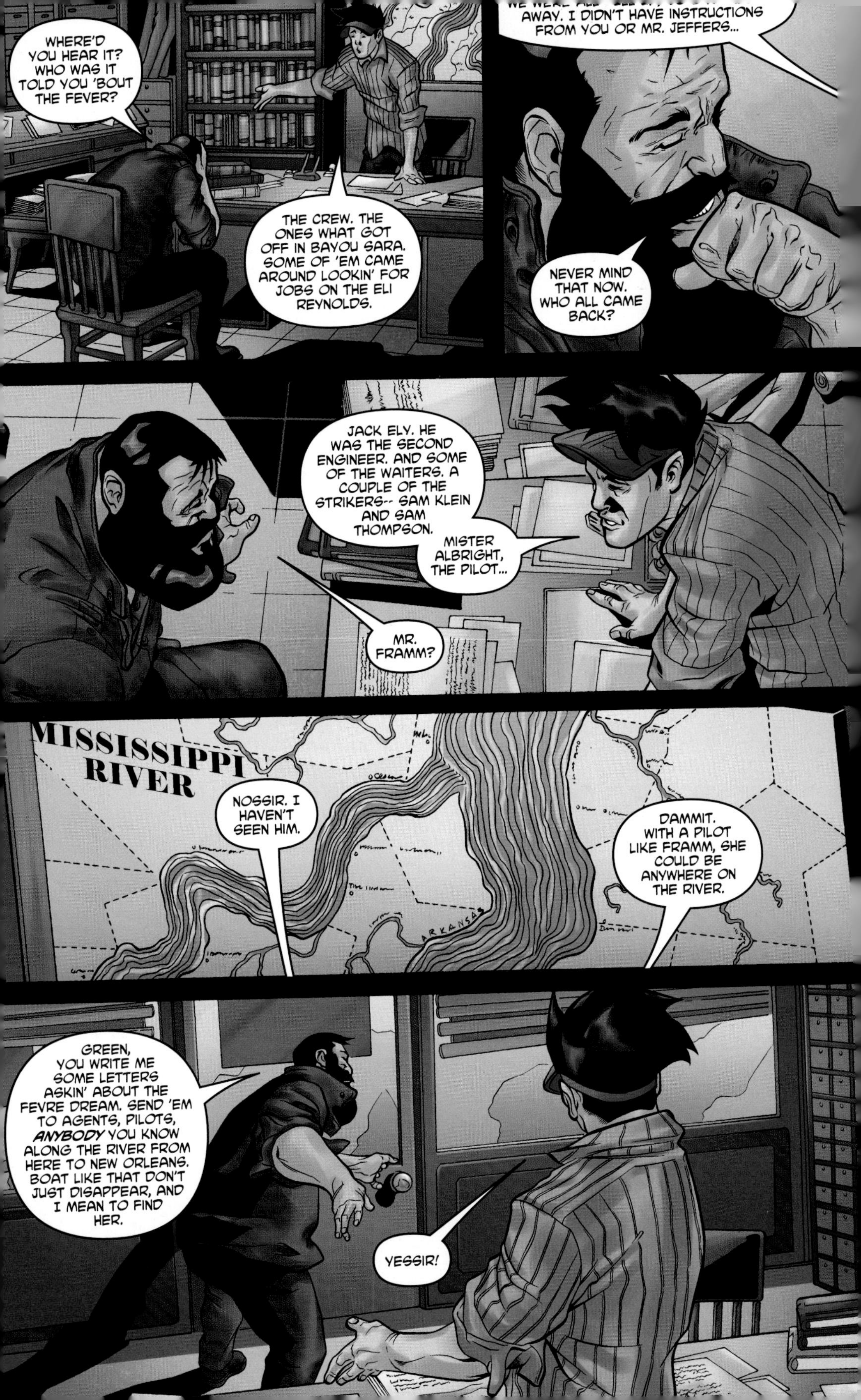
WHERE'D YOU HEAR IT? WHO WAS IT TOLD YOU 'BOUT THE FEVER?
THE CREW. THE ONES WHAT GOT OFF IN BAYOU SARA. SOME OF 'EM CAME AROUND LOOKIN' FOR JOBS ON THE ELI REYNOLDS.
AWAY. I DIDN'T HAVE INSTRUCTIONS FROM YOU OR MR. JEFFERS...
NEVER MIND THAT NOW. WHO ALL CAME BACK?
JACK ELY. HE WAS THE SECOND ENGINEER. AND SOME OF THE WAITERS. A COUPLE OF THE STRIKERS-- SAM KLEIN AND SAM THOMPSON.
MISTER ALBRIGHT, THE PILOT...
MR. FRAMM?
MISSISSIPPI RIVER
NOSSIR. I HAVEN'T SEEN HIM.
DAMMIT. WITH A PILOT LIKE FRAMM, SHE COULD BE ANYWHERE ON THE RIVER.
ARKANSAS
GREEN, YOU WRITE ME SOME LETTERS ASKIN' ABOUT THE FEVRE DREAM. SEND 'EM TO AGENTS, PILOTS, *ANYBODY* YOU KNOW ALONG THE RIVER FROM HERE TO NEW ORLEANS. BOAT LIKE THAT DON'T JUST DISAPPEAR, AND I MEAN TO FIND HER.
YESSIR!

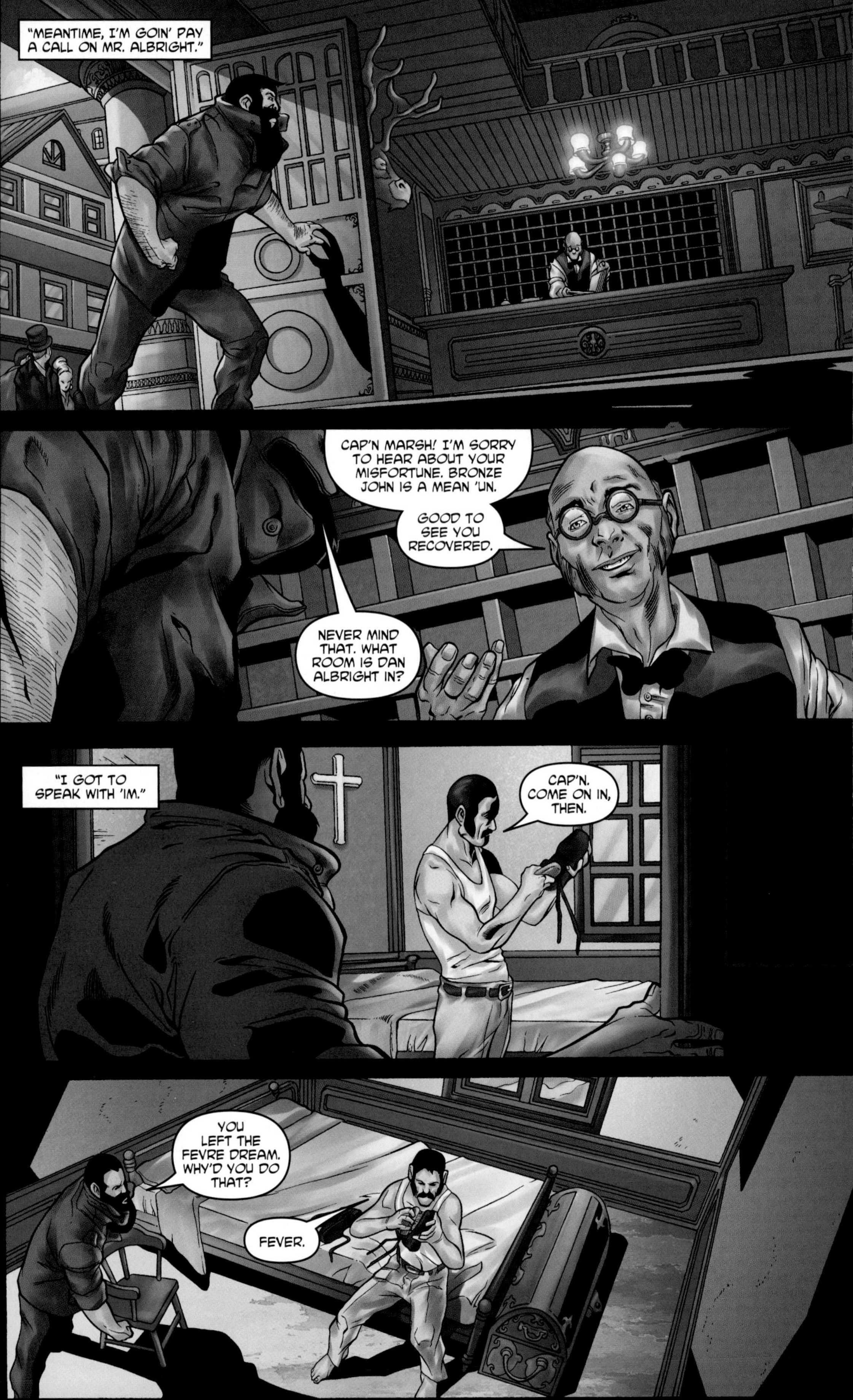
"MEANTIME, I'M GOIN' PAY A CALL ON MR. ALBRIGHT."
CAP'N MARSH! I'M SORRY TO HEAR ABOUT YOUR MISFORTUNE. BRONZE JOHN IS A MEAN 'UN.
GOOD TO SEE YOU RECOVERED.
NEVER MIND THAT. WHAT ROOM IS DAN ALBRIGHT IN?
"I GOT TO SPEAK WITH 'IM."
CAP'N. COME ON IN, THEN.
YOU LEFT THE FEVRE DREAM. WHY'D YOU DO THAT?
FEVER.

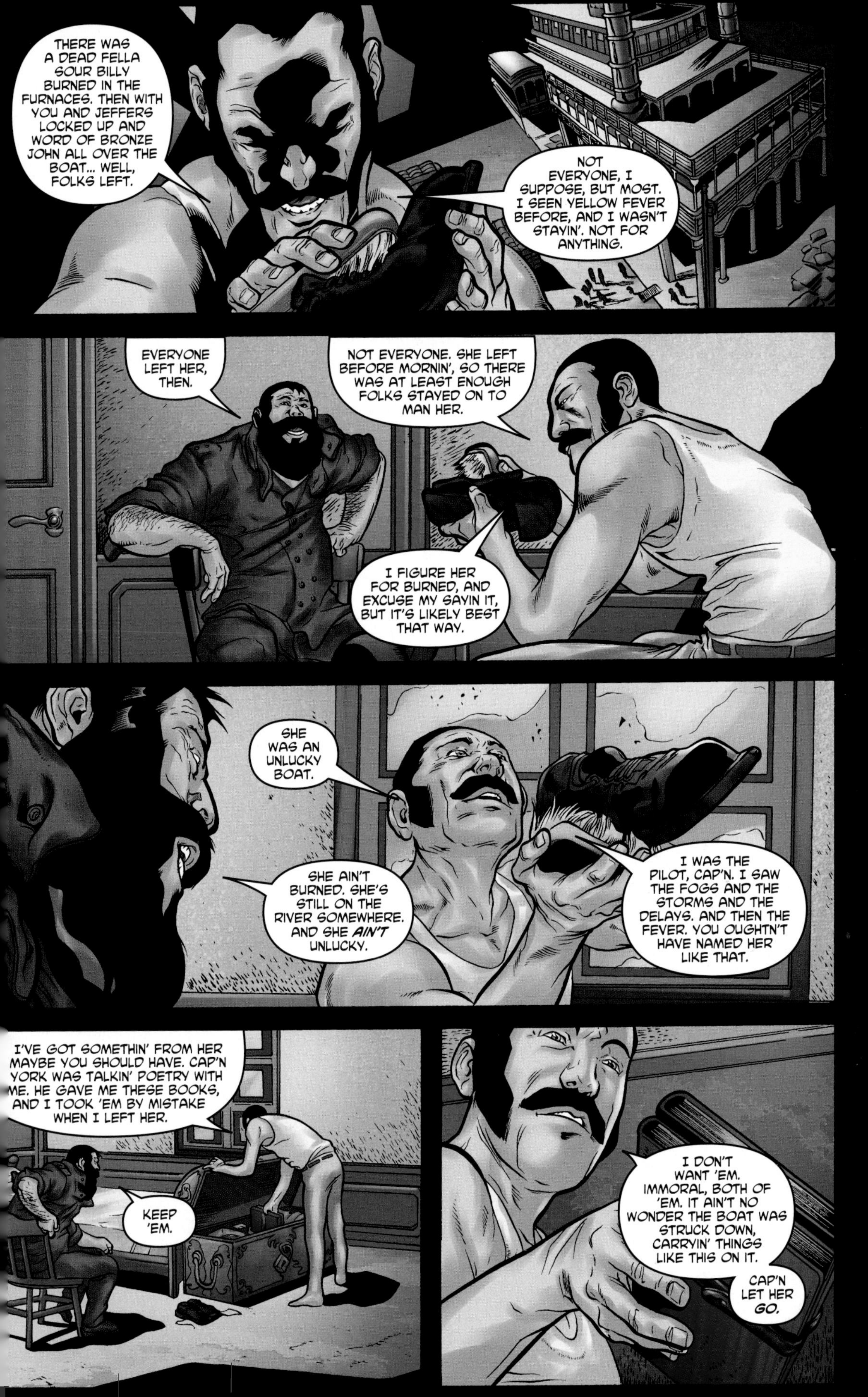
THERE WAS A DEAD FELLA SOUR BILLY BURNED IN THE FURNACES. THEN WITH YOU AND JEFFERS LOCKED UP AND WORD OF BRONZE JOHN ALL OVER THE BOAT... WELL, FOLKS LEFT.
NOT EVERYONE, I SUPPOSE, BUT MOST. I SEEN YELLOW FEVER BEFORE, AND I WASN'T STAYIN'. NOT FOR ANYTHING.
EVERYONE LEFT HER, THEN.
NOT EVERYONE. SHE LEFT BEFORE MORNIN', SO THERE WAS AT LEAST ENOUGH FOLKS STAYED ON TO MAN HER.
I FIGURE HER FOR BURNED, AND EXCUSE MY SAYIN IT, BUT IT'S LIKELY BEST THAT WAY.
SHE WAS AN UNLUCKY BOAT.
SHE AIN'T BURNED. SHE'S STILL ON THE RIVER SOMEWHERE. AND SHE *AIN'T* UNLUCKY.
I WAS THE PILOT, CAP'N. I SAW THE FOGS AND THE STORMS AND THE DELAYS. AND THEN THE FEVER. YOU OUGHTN'T HAVE NAMED HER LIKE THAT.
I'VE GOT SOMETHIN' FROM HER MAYBE YOU SHOULD HAVE. CAP'N YORK WAS TALKIN' POETRY WITH ME. HE GAVE ME THESE BOOKS, AND I TOOK 'EM BY MISTAKE WHEN I LEFT HER.
KEEP 'EM.
I DON'T WANT 'EM. IMMORAL, BOTH OF 'EM. IT AIN'T NO WONDER THE BOAT WAS STRUCK DOWN, CARRYIN' THINGS LIKE THIS ON IT.
CAP'N LET HER *GO.*

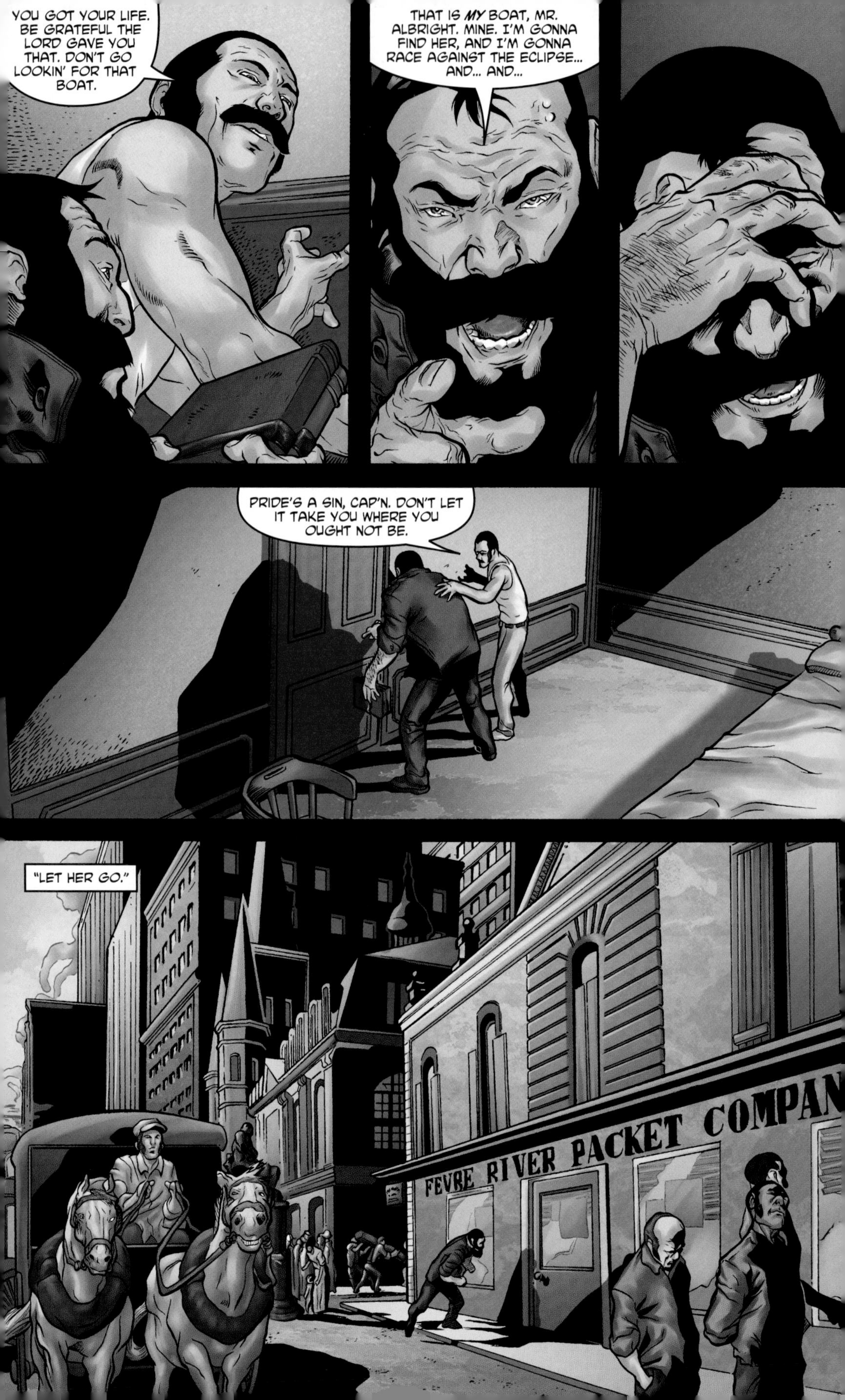
YOU GOT YOUR LIFE. BE GRATEFUL THE LORD GAVE YOU THAT. DON'T GO LOOKIN' FOR THAT BOAT.
THAT IS MY BOAT, MR. ALBRIGHT. MINE. I'M GONNA FIND HER, AND I'M GONNA RACE AGAINST THE ECLIPSE... AND... AND...
PRIDE'S A SIN, CAP'N. DON'T LET IT TAKE YOU WHERE YOU OUGHT NOT BE.
"LET HER GO."
FEVRE RIVER PACKET COMPAN

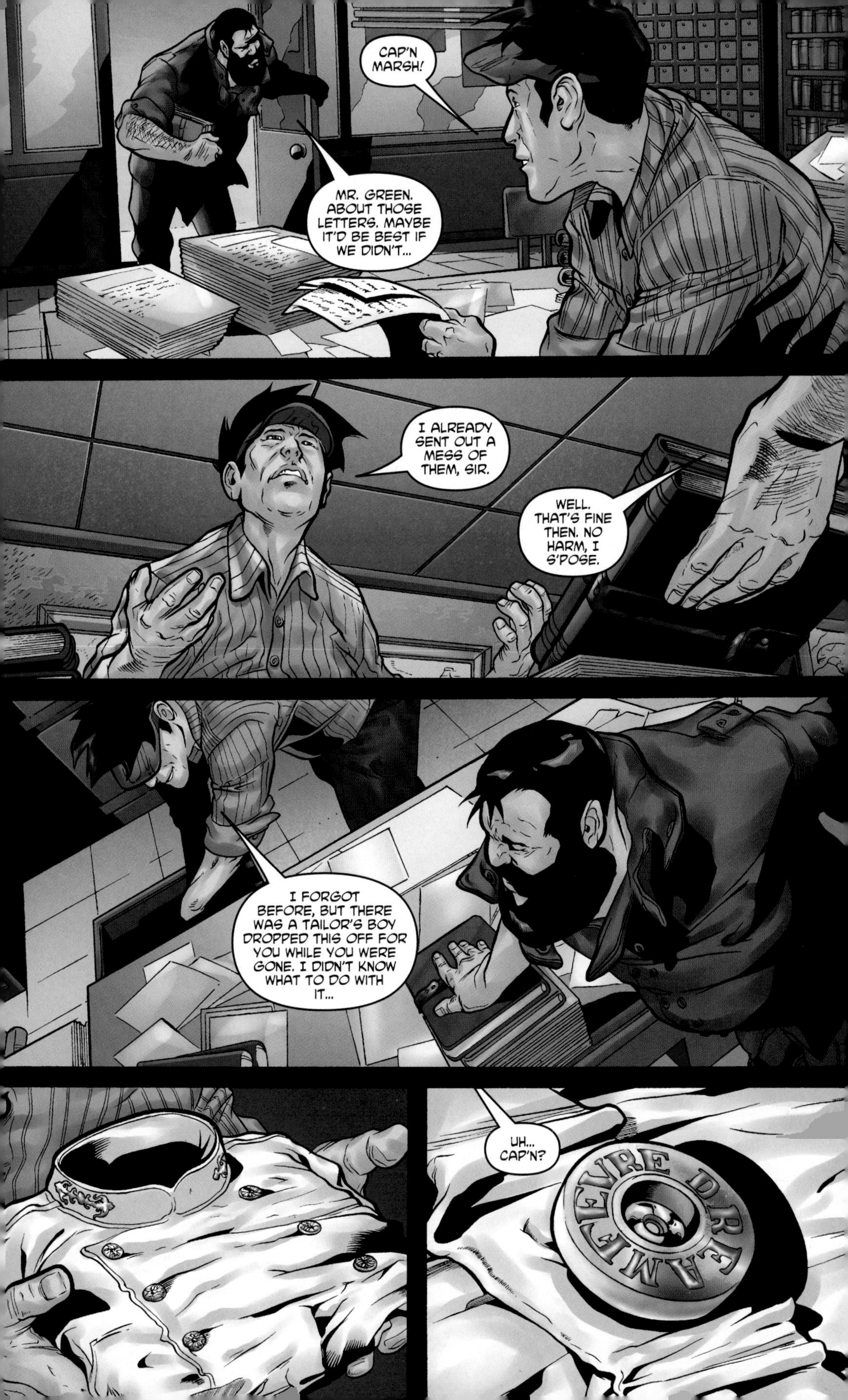
CAP'N MARSH!
MR. GREEN. ABOUT THOSE LETTERS. MAYBE IT'D BE BEST IF WE DIDN'T...
I ALREADY SENT OUT A MESS OF THEM, SIR.
WELL. THAT'S FINE THEN. NO HARM, I S'POSE.
I FORGOT BEFORE, BUT THERE WAS A TAILOR'S BOY DROPPED THIS OFF FOR YOU WHILE YOU WERE GONE. I DIDN'T KNOW WHAT TO DO WITH IT...
UH... CAP'N?

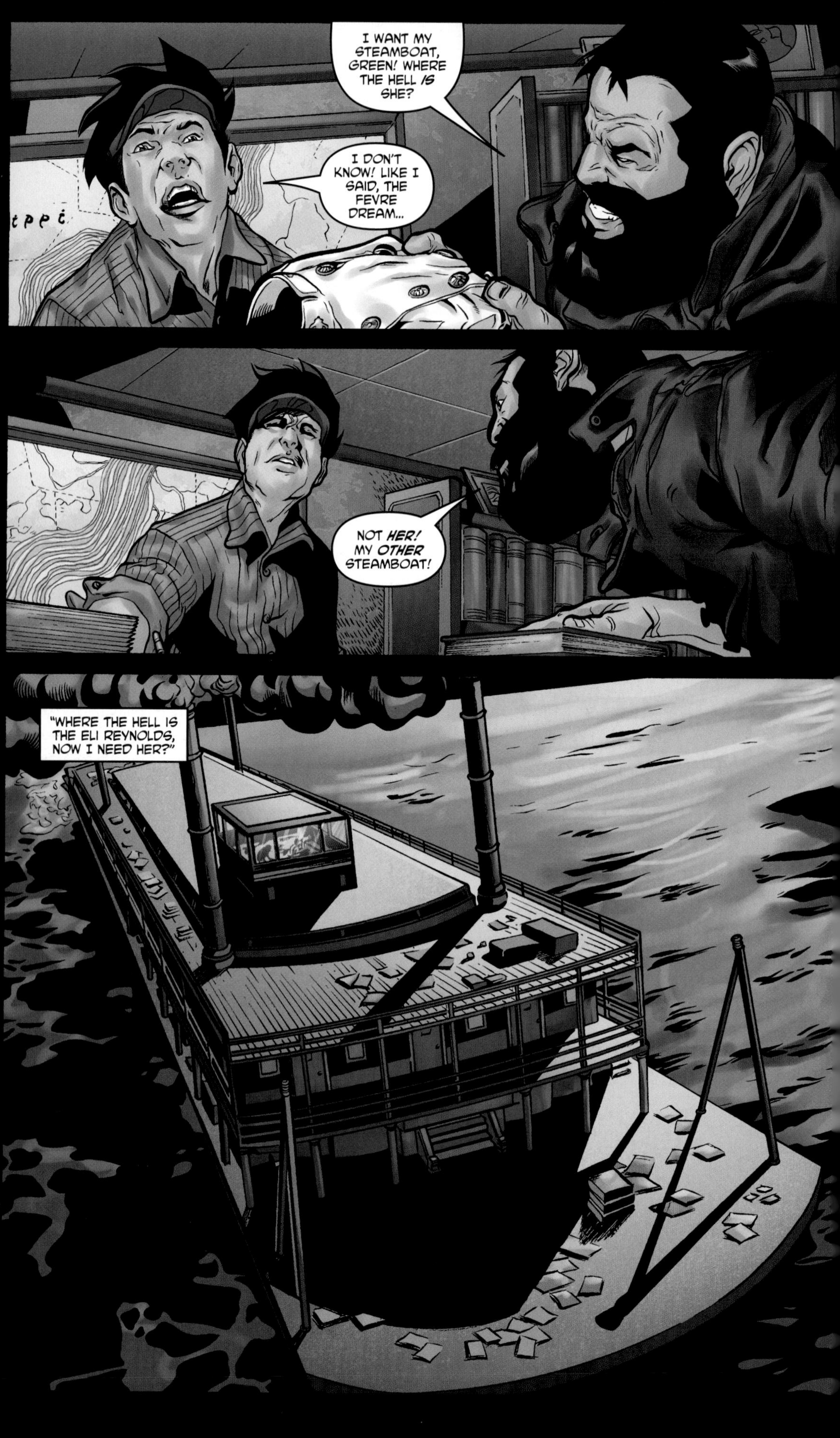
I WANT MY STEAMBOAT, GREEN! WHERE THE HELL *IS* SHE?
I DON'T KNOW! LIKE I SAID, THE FEVRE DREAM...
NOT *HER!* MY *OTHER* STEAMBOAT!
"WHERE THE HELL IS THE ELI REYNOLDS, NOW I NEED HER?"

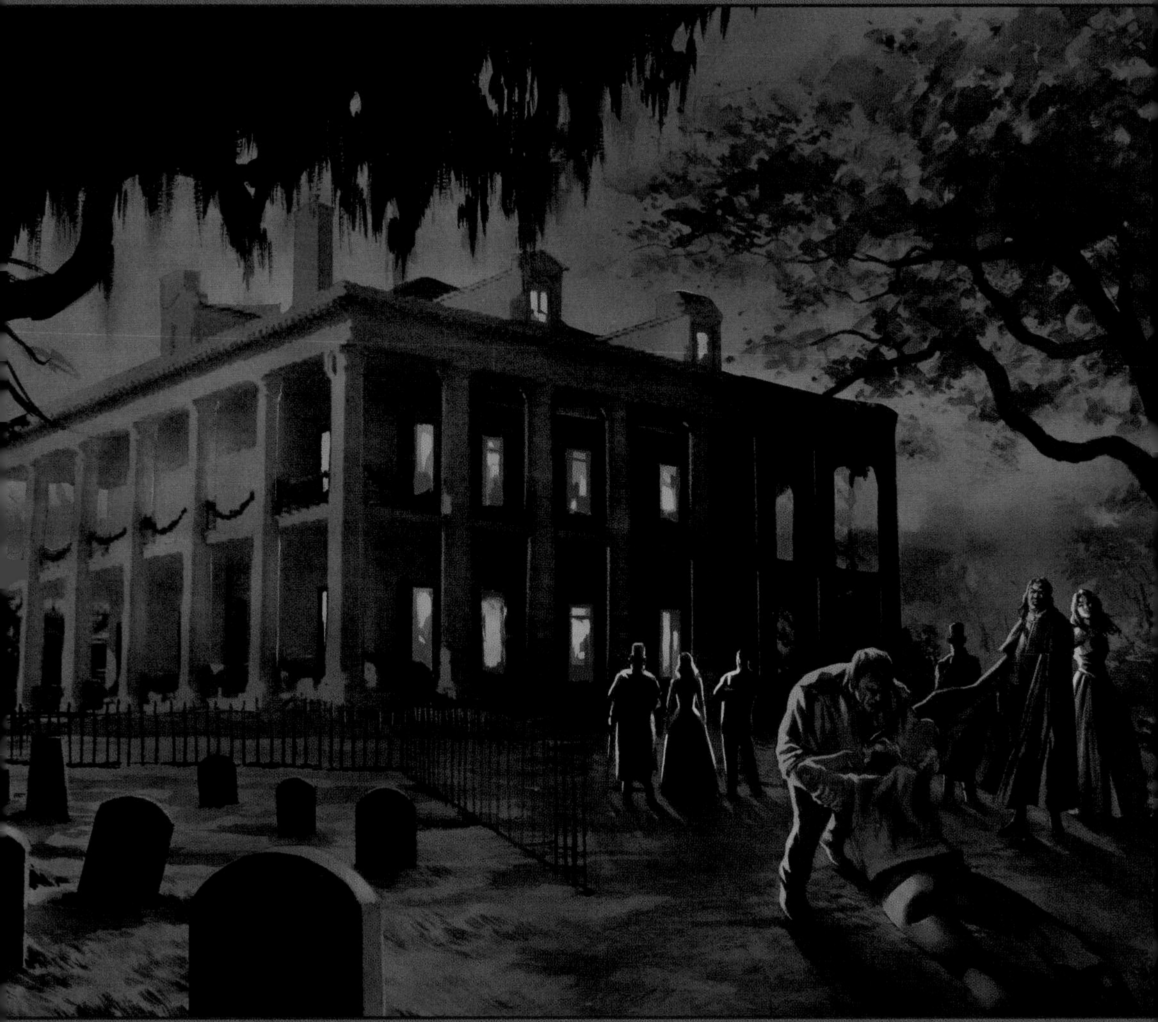

CHAPTER 8

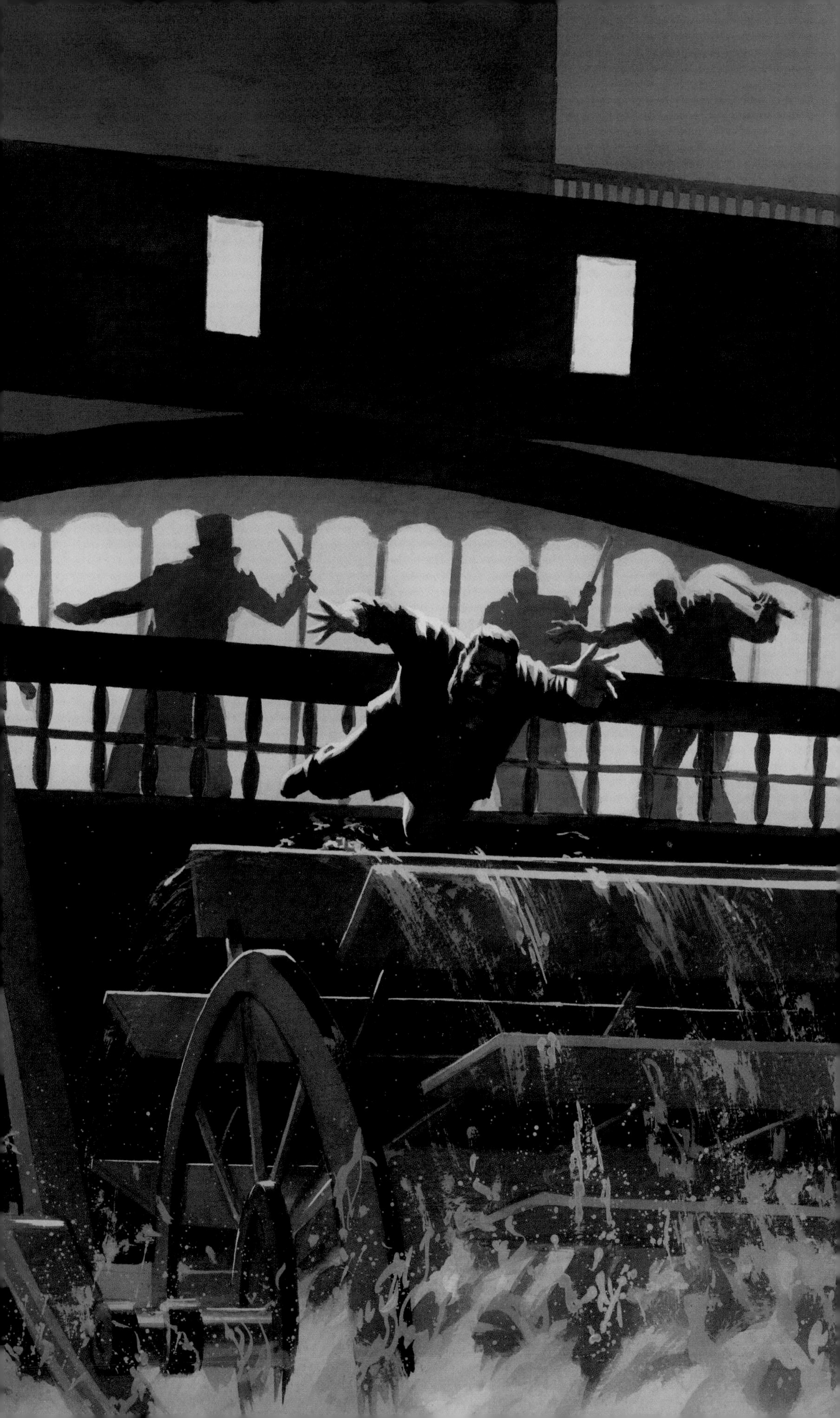

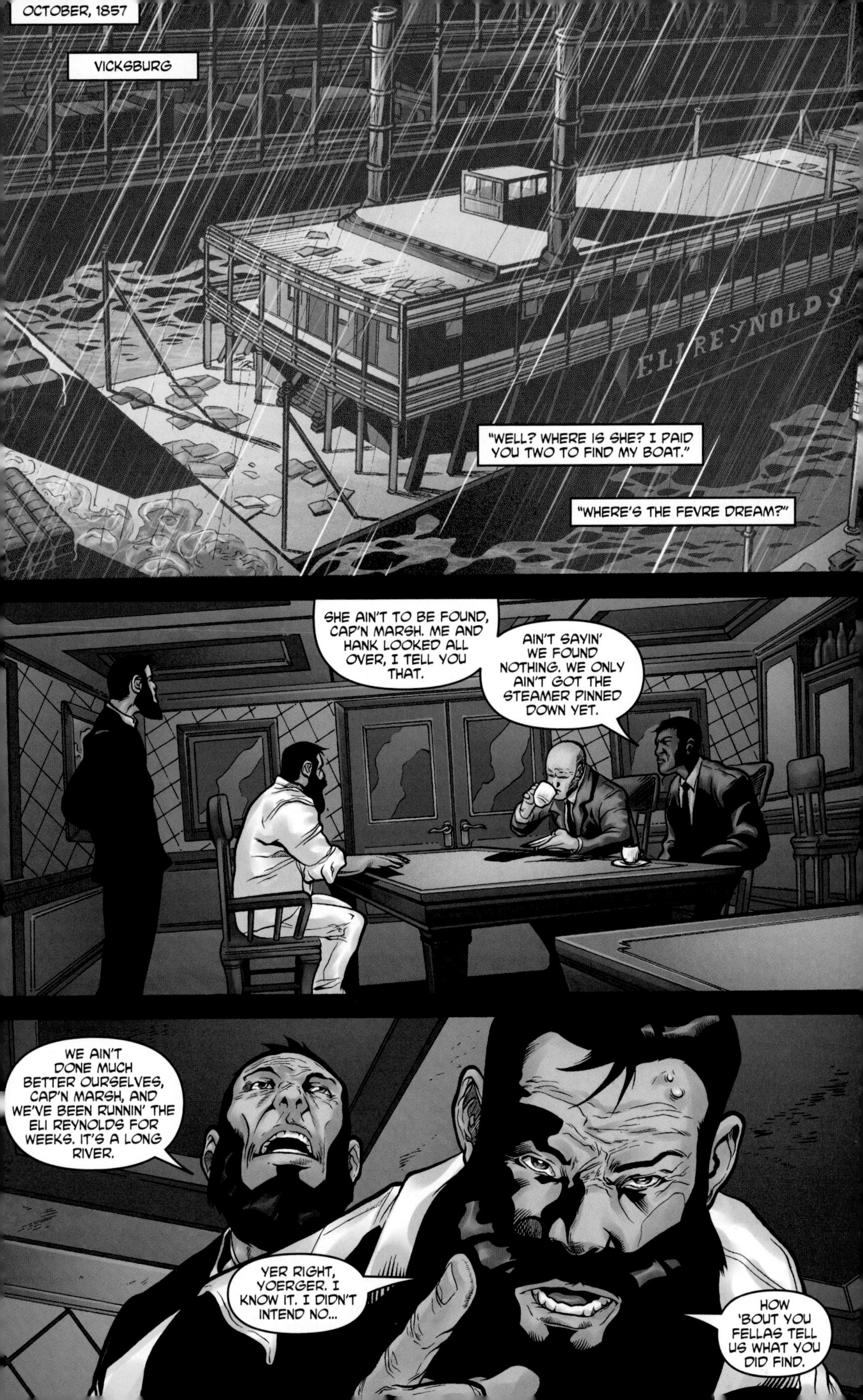

OCTOBER, 1857
VICKSBURG
ELI REYNOLDS
"WELL? WHERE IS SHE? I PAID YOU TWO TO FIND MY BOAT."
"WHERE'S THE FEVRE DREAM?"
SHE AIN'T TO BE FOUND, CAP'N MARSH. ME AND HANK LOOKED ALL OVER, I TELL YOU THAT.
AIN'T SAYIN' WE FOUND NOTHING. WE ONLY AIN'T GOT THE STEAMER PINNED DOWN YET.
WE AIN'T DONE MUCH BETTER OURSELVES, CAP'N MARSH, AND WE'VE BEEN RUNNIN' THE ELI REYNOLDS FOR WEEKS. IT'S A LONG RIVER.
YER RIGHT, YOERGER. I KNOW IT. I DIDN'T INTEND NO...
HOW 'BOUT YOU FELLAS TELL US WHAT YOU DID FIND.

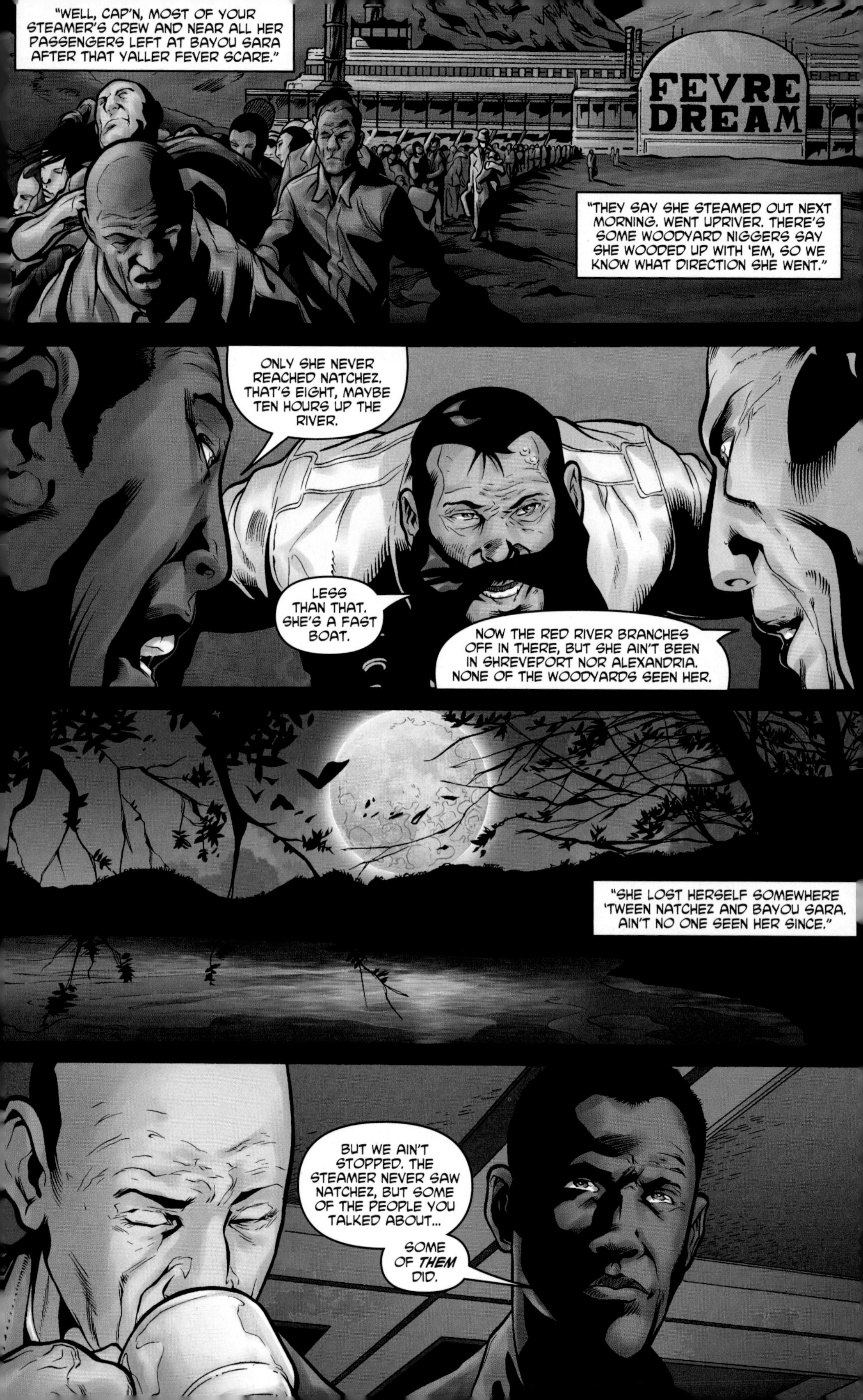
"WELL, CAP'N, MOST OF YOUR STEAMER'S CREW AND NEAR ALL HER PASSENGERS LEFT AT BAYOU SARA AFTER THAT YALLER FEVER SCARE."
FEVRE DREAM
"THEY SAY SHE STEAMED OUT NEXT MORNING. WENT UPRIVER. THERE'S SOME WOODYARD NIGGERS SAY SHE WOODED UP WITH 'EM, SO WE KNOW WHAT DIRECTION SHE WENT."
ONLY SHE NEVER REACHED NATCHEZ. THAT'S EIGHT, MAYBE TEN HOURS UP THE RIVER.
LESS THAN THAT. SHE'S A FAST BOAT.
NOW THE RED RIVER BRANCHES OFF IN THERE, BUT SHE AIN'T BEEN IN SHREVEPORT NOR ALEXANDRIA. NONE OF THE WOODYARDS SEEN HER.
"SHE LOST HERSELF SOMEWHERE 'TWEEN NATCHEZ AND BAYOU SARA. AIN'T NO ONE SEEN HER SINCE."
BUT WE AIN'T STOPPED. THE STEAMER NEVER SAW NATCHEZ, BUT SOME OF THE PEOPLE YOU TALKED ABOUT...
SOME OF *THEM* DID.

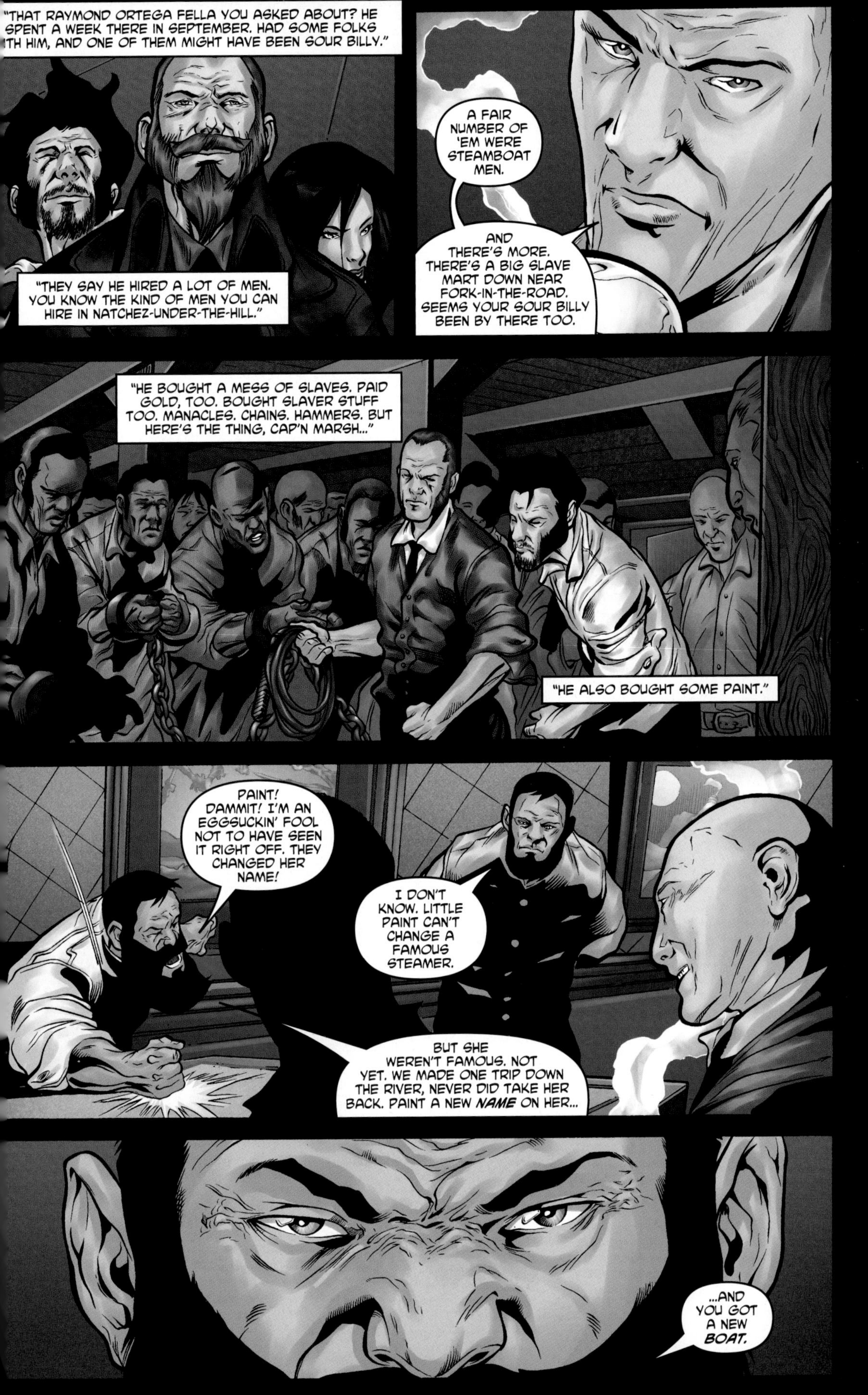
"THAT RAYMOND ORTEGA FELLA YOU ASKED ABOUT? HE SPENT A WEEK THERE IN SEPTEMBER. HAD SOME FOLKS ITH HIM, AND ONE OF THEM MIGHT HAVE BEEN SOUR BILLY."
"THEY SAY HE HIRED A LOT OF MEN. YOU KNOW THE KIND OF MEN YOU CAN HIRE IN NATCHEZ-UNDER-THE-HILL."
A FAIR NUMBER OF 'EM WERE STEAMBOAT MEN.
AND THERE'S MORE. THERE'S A BIG SLAVE MART DOWN NEAR FORK-IN-THE-ROAD. SEEMS YOUR SOUR BILLY BEEN BY THERE TOO.
"HE BOUGHT A MESS OF SLAVES. PAID GOLD, TOO. BOUGHT SLAVER STUFF TOO. MANACLES. CHAINS. HAMMERS. BUT HERE'S THE THING, CAP'N MARSH..."
"HE ALSO BOUGHT SOME PAINT."
PAINT! DAMMIT! I'M AN EGGSUCKIN' FOOL NOT TO HAVE SEEN IT RIGHT OFF. THEY CHANGED HER NAME!
I DON'T KNOW. LITTLE PAINT CAN'T CHANGE A FAMOUS STEAMER.
BUT SHE WEREN'T FAMOUS. NOT YET. WE MADE ONE TRIP DOWN THE RIVER, NEVER DID TAKE HER BACK. PAINT A NEW NAME ON HER...
...AND YOU GOT A NEW BOAT.

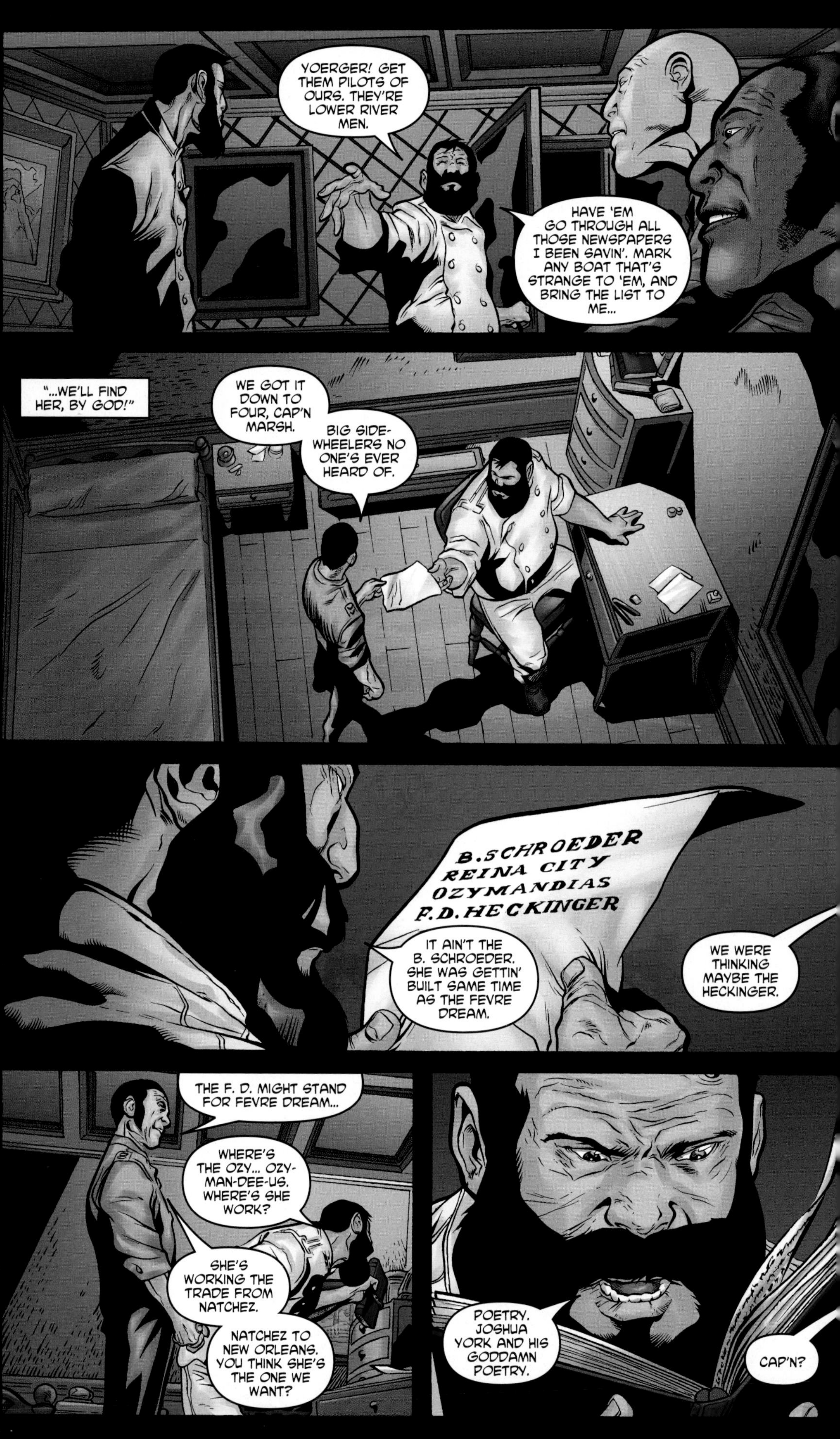
YOERGER! GET THEM PILOTS OF OURS. THEY'RE LOWER RIVER MEN.
HAVE 'EM GO THROUGH ALL THOSE NEWSPAPERS I BEEN SAVIN'. MARK ANY BOAT THAT'S STRANGE TO 'EM, AND BRING THE LIST TO ME...
"...WE'LL FIND HER, BY GOD!"
WE GOT IT DOWN TO FOUR, CAP'N MARSH.
BIG SIDE-WHEELERS NO ONE'S EVER HEARD OF.
B. SCHROEDER
REINA CITY
OZYMANDIAS
F.D. HECKINGER
IT AIN'T THE B. SCHROEDER. SHE WAS GETTIN' BUILT SAME TIME AS THE FEVRE DREAM.
WE WERE THINKING MAYBE THE HECKINGER.
THE F. D. MIGHT STAND FOR FEVRE DREAM...
WHERE'S THE OZY... OZY-MAN-DEE-US. WHERE'S SHE WORK?
SHE'S WORKING THE TRADE FROM NATCHEZ.
NATCHEZ TO NEW ORLEANS. YOU THINK SHE'S THE ONE WE WANT?
POETRY. JOSHUA YORK AND HIS GODDAMN POETRY.
CAP'N?

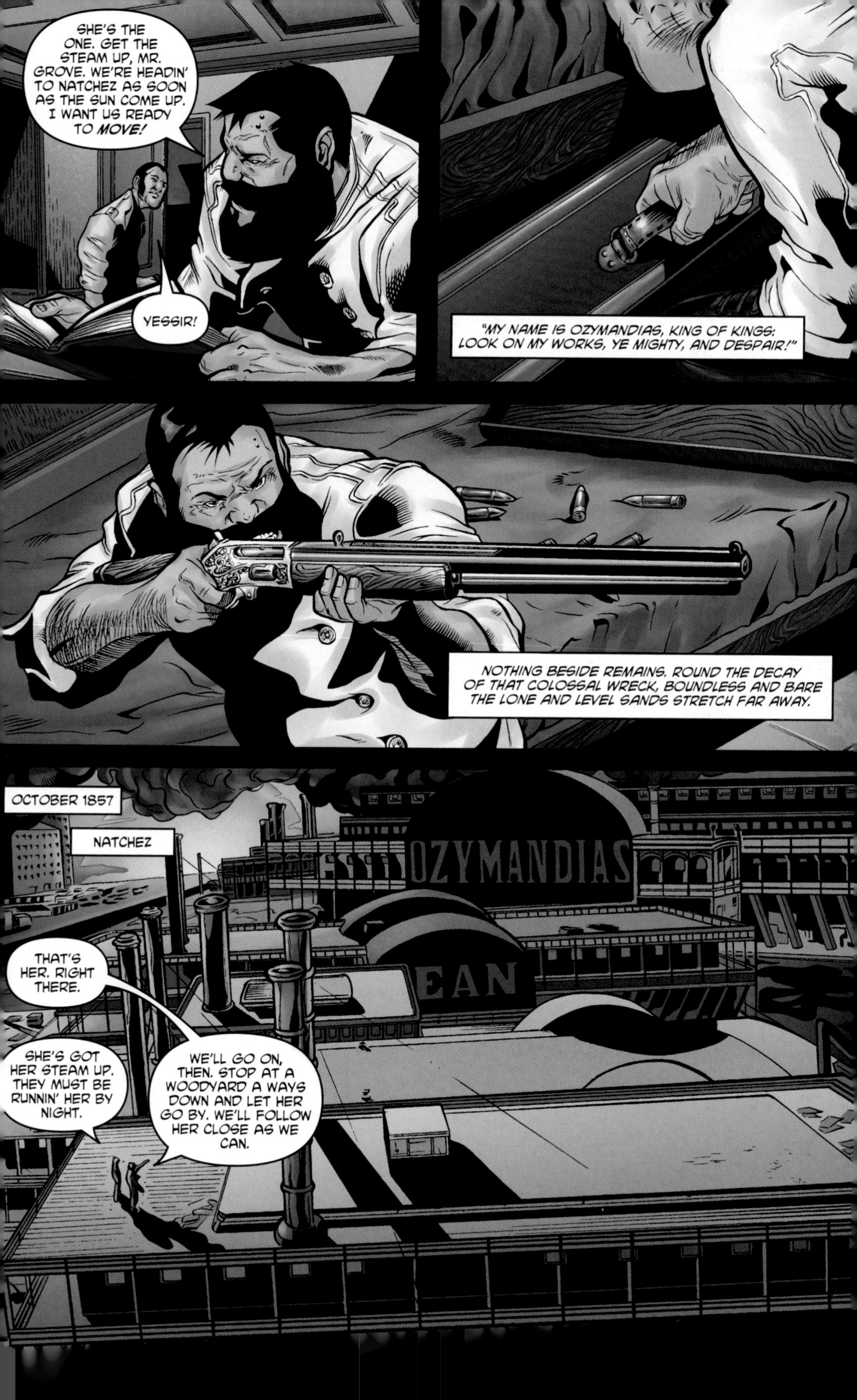
SHE'S THE ONE. GET THE STEAM UP, MR. GROVE. WE'RE HEADIN' TO NATCHEZ AS SOON AS THE SUN COME UP. I WANT US READY TO MOVE!
YESSIR!
"MY NAME IS OZYMANDIAS, KING OF KINGS: LOOK ON MY WORKS, YE MIGHTY, AND DESPAIR!"
NOTHING BESIDE REMAINS. ROUND THE DECAY OF THAT COLOSSAL WRECK, BOUNDLESS AND BARE THE LONE AND LEVEL SANDS STRETCH FAR AWAY.
OCTOBER 1857
NATCHEZ
OZYMANDIAS
EAN
THAT'S HER. RIGHT THERE.
SHE'S GOT HER STEAM UP. THEY MUST BE RUNNIN' HER BY NIGHT.
WE'LL GO ON, THEN. STOP AT A WOODYARD A WAYS DOWN AND LET HER GO BY. WE'LL FOLLOW HER CLOSE AS WE CAN.

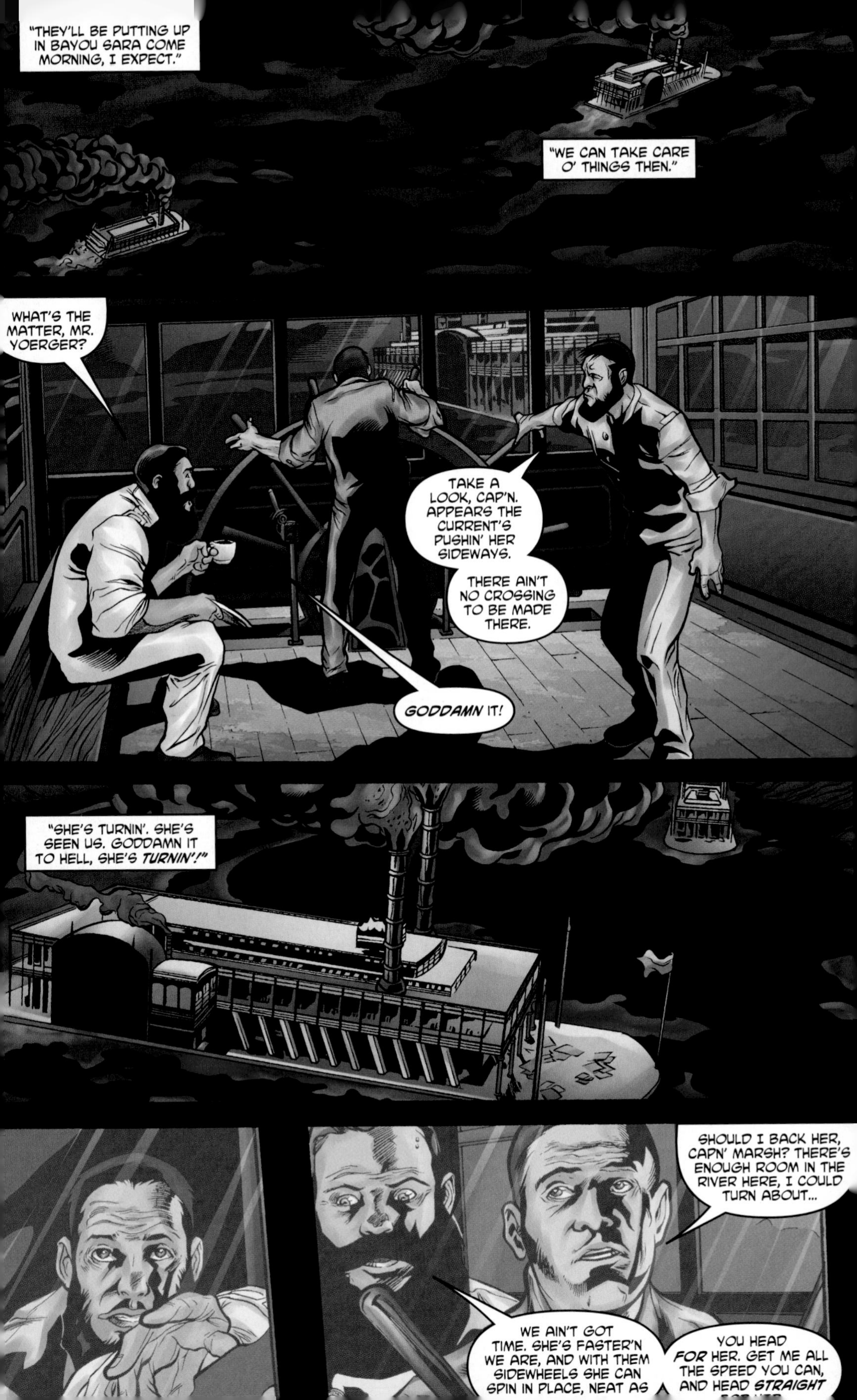
"THEY'LL BE PUTTING UP IN BAYOU SARA COME MORNING, I EXPECT."
"WE CAN TAKE CARE O' THINGS THEN."
WHAT'S THE MATTER, MR. YOERGER?
TAKE A LOOK, CAP'N. APPEARS THE CURRENT'S PUSHIN' HER SIDEWAYS.
THERE AIN'T NO CROSSING TO BE MADE THERE.
GODDAMN IT!
"SHE'S TURNIN'. SHE'S SEEN US. GODDAMN IT TO HELL, SHE'S *TURNIN'*!"
SHOULD I BACK HER, CAPN' MARSH? THERE'S ENOUGH ROOM IN THE RIVER HERE, I COULD TURN ABOUT...
WE AIN'T GOT TIME. SHE'S FASTER'N WE ARE, AND WITH THEM SIDEWHEELS SHE CAN SPIN IN PLACE, NEAT AS
YOU HEAD *FOR* HER. GET ME ALL THE SPEED YOU CAN, AND HEAD *STRAIGHT*

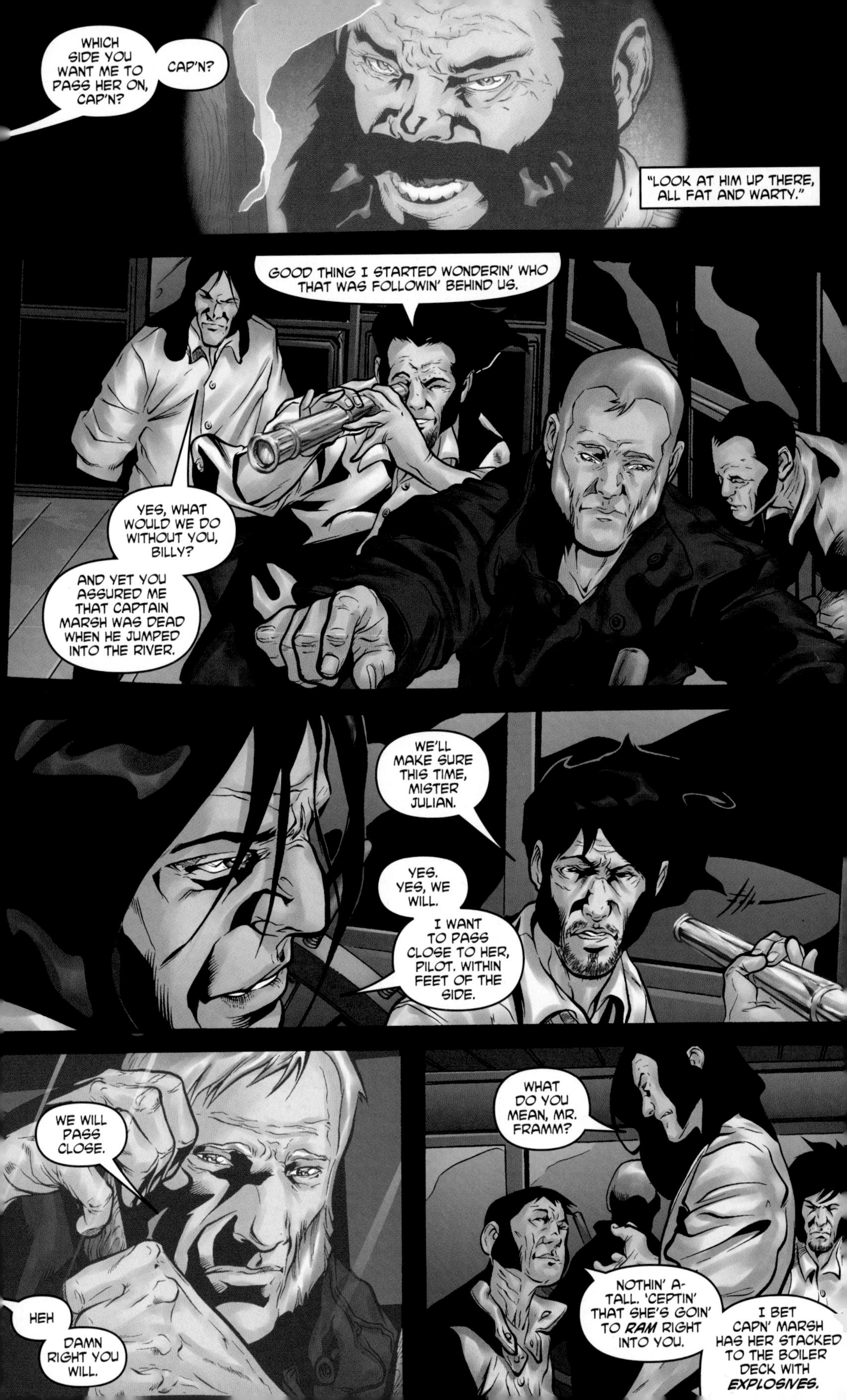
WHICH SIDE YOU WANT ME TO PASS HER ON, CAP'N?
CAP'N?
"LOOK AT HIM UP THERE, ALL FAT AND WARTY."
GOOD THING I STARTED WONDERIN' WHO THAT WAS FOLLOWIN' BEHIND US.
YES, WHAT WOULD WE DO WITHOUT YOU, BILLY?
AND YET YOU ASSURED ME THAT CAPTAIN MARSH WAS DEAD WHEN HE JUMPED INTO THE RIVER.
WE'LL MAKE SURE THIS TIME, MISTER JULIAN.
YES. YES, WE WILL.
I WANT TO PASS CLOSE TO HER, PILOT. WITHIN FEET OF THE SIDE.
WE WILL PASS CLOSE.
HEH
DAMN RIGHT YOU WILL.
WHAT DO YOU MEAN, MR. FRAMM?
NOTHIN' A-TALL. 'CEPTIN' THAT SHE'S GOIN' TO *RAM* RIGHT INTO YOU.
I BET CAPN' MARSH HAS HER STACKED TO THE BOILER DECK WITH ***EXPLOSIVES.***

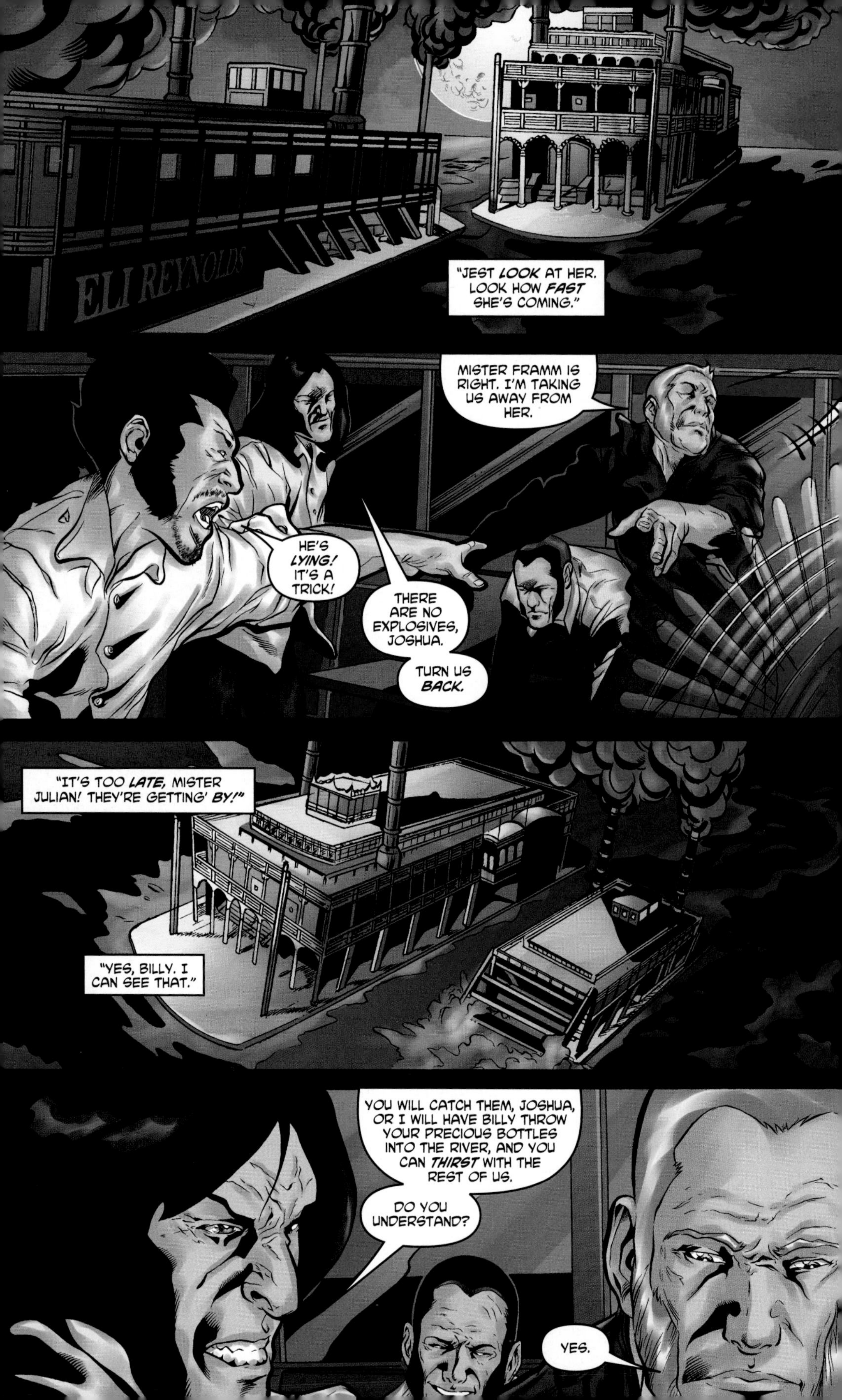
ELI REYNOLDS
"JEST *LOOK* AT HER. LOOK HOW *FAST* SHE'S COMING."
MISTER FRAMM IS RIGHT. I'M TAKING US AWAY FROM HER.
HE'S *LYING!* IT'S A TRICK!
THERE ARE NO EXPLOSIVES, JOSHUA.
TURN US *BACK.*
"IT'S TOO *LATE,* MISTER JULIAN! THEY'RE GETTING' *BY!*"
"YES, BILLY. I CAN SEE THAT."
YOU WILL CATCH THEM, JOSHUA, OR I WILL HAVE BILLY THROW YOUR PRECIOUS BOTTLES INTO THE RIVER, AND YOU CAN *THIRST* WITH THE REST OF US.
DO YOU UNDERSTAND?
YES.

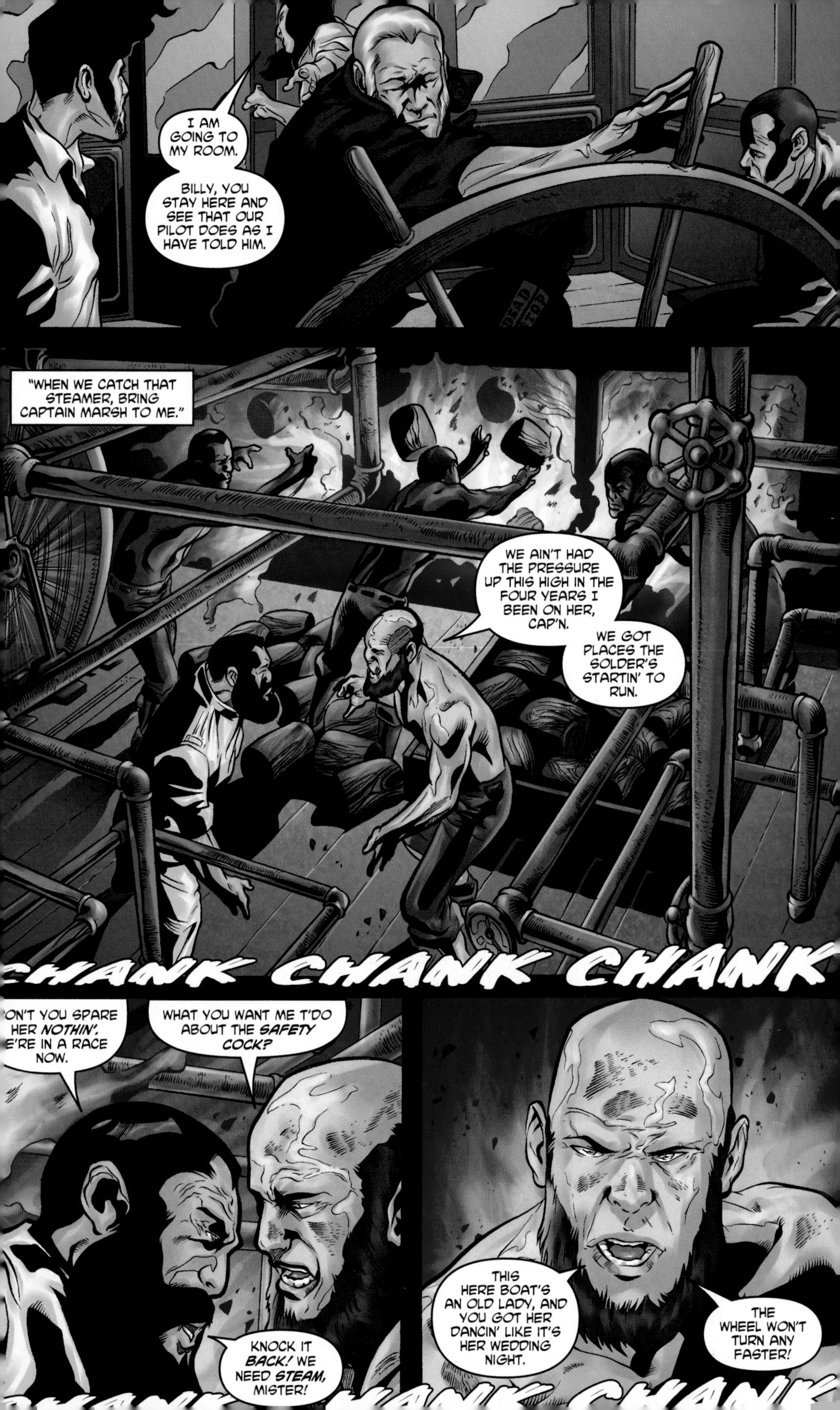
I AM GOING TO MY ROOM.
BILLY, YOU STAY HERE AND SEE THAT OUR PILOT DOES AS I HAVE TOLD HIM.
"WHEN WE CATCH THAT STEAMER, BRING CAPTAIN MARSH TO ME."
WE AIN'T HAD THE PRESSURE UP THIS HIGH IN THE FOUR YEARS I BEEN ON HER, CAP'N.
WE GOT PLACES THE SOLDER'S STARTIN' TO RUN.
CHANK CHANK CHANK
ON'T YOU SPARE HER *NOTHIN'*. E'RE IN A RACE NOW.
WHAT YOU WANT ME T'DO ABOUT THE *SAFETY COCK?*
KNOCK IT *BACK!* WE NEED *STEAM*, MISTER!
THIS HERE BOAT'S AN OLD LADY, AND YOU GOT HER DANCIN' LIKE IT'S HER WEDDING NIGHT.
THE WHEEL WON'T TURN ANY FASTER!

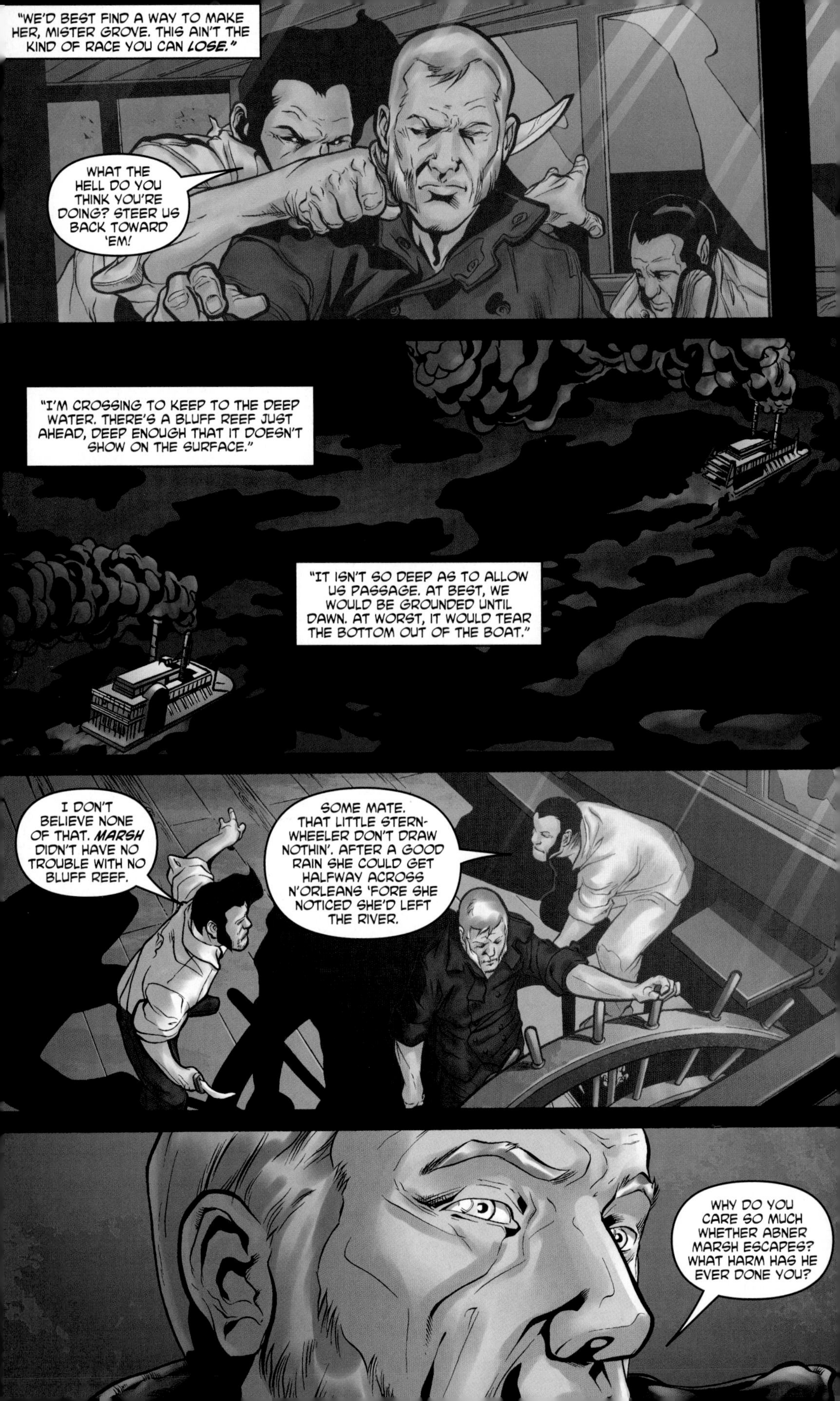
"WE'D BEST FIND A WAY TO MAKE HER, MISTER GROVE. THIS AIN'T THE KIND OF RACE YOU CAN LOSE."
WHAT THE HELL DO YOU THINK YOU'RE DOING? STEER US BACK TOWARD 'EM!
"I'M CROSSING TO KEEP TO THE DEEP WATER. THERE'S A BLUFF REEF JUST AHEAD, DEEP ENOUGH THAT IT DOESN'T SHOW ON THE SURFACE."
"IT ISN'T SO DEEP AS TO ALLOW US PASSAGE. AT BEST, WE WOULD BE GROUNDED UNTIL DAWN. AT WORST, IT WOULD TEAR THE BOTTOM OUT OF THE BOAT."
I DON'T BELIEVE NONE OF THAT. MARSH DIDN'T HAVE NO TROUBLE WITH NO BLUFF REEF.
SOME MATE. THAT LITTLE STERN-WHEELER DON'T DRAW NOTHIN'. AFTER A GOOD RAIN SHE COULD GET HALFWAY ACROSS N'ORLEANS 'FORE SHE NOTICED SHE'D LEFT THE RIVER.
WHY DO YOU CARE SO MUCH WHETHER ABNER MARSH ESCAPES? WHAT HARM HAS HE EVER DONE YOU?

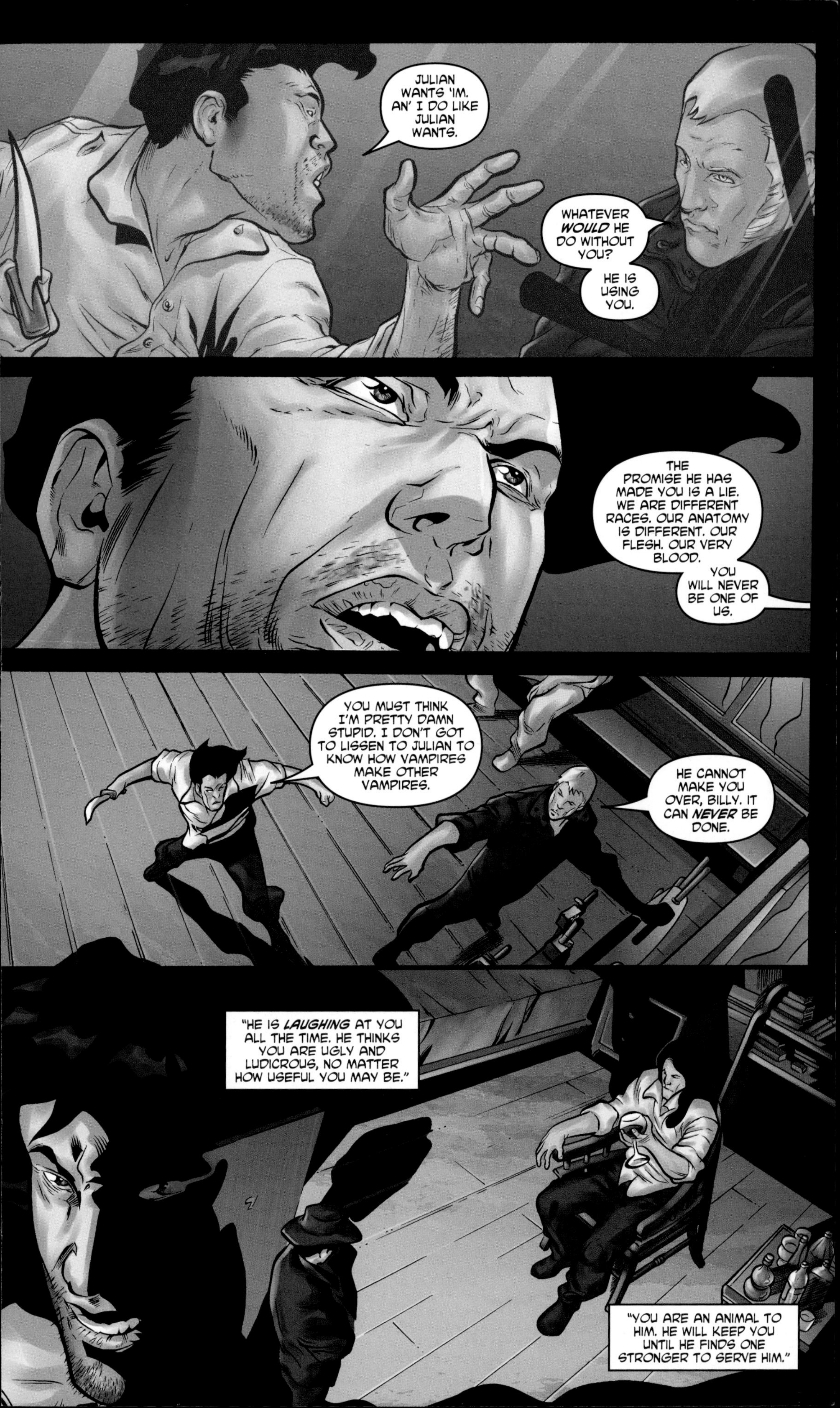
JULIAN WANTS 'IM. AN' I DO LIKE JULIAN WANTS.
WHATEVER *WOULD* HE DO WITHOUT YOU?
HE IS USING YOU.
THE PROMISE HE HAS MADE YOU IS A LIE. WE ARE DIFFERENT RACES. OUR ANATOMY IS DIFFERENT. OUR FLESH. OUR VERY BLOOD.
YOU WILL NEVER BE ONE OF US.
YOU MUST THINK I'M PRETTY DAMN STUPID. I DON'T GOT TO LISSEN TO JULIAN TO KNOW HOW VAMPIRES MAKE OTHER VAMPIRES.
HE CANNOT MAKE YOU OVER, BILLY. IT CAN *NEVER* BE DONE.
"HE IS *LAUGHING* AT YOU ALL THE TIME. HE THINKS YOU ARE UGLY AND LUDICROUS, NO MATTER HOW USEFUL YOU MAY BE."
"YOU ARE AN ANIMAL TO HIM. HE WILL KEEP YOU UNTIL HE FINDS ONE STRONGER TO SERVE HIM."

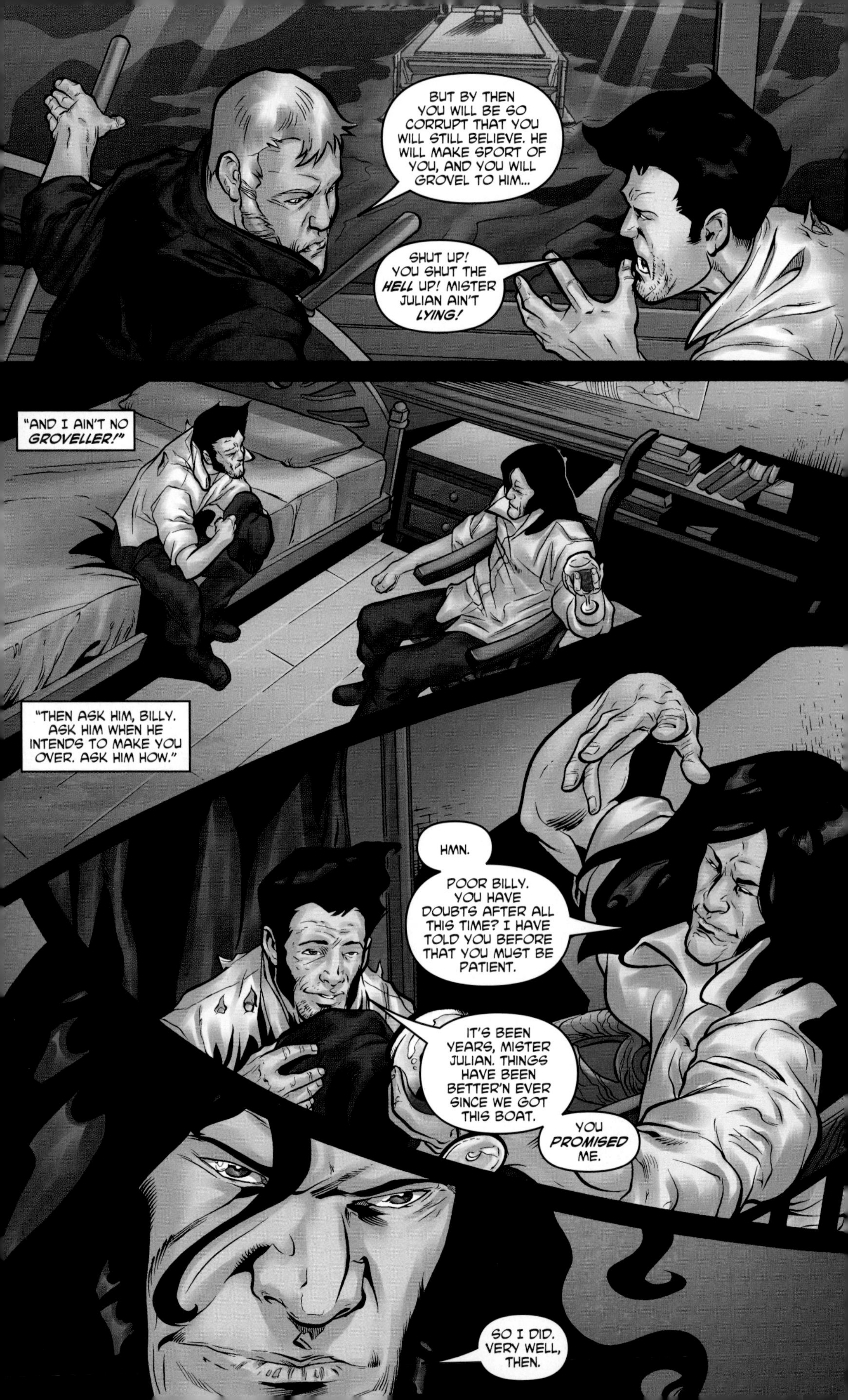
BUT BY THEN YOU WILL BE SO CORRUPT THAT YOU WILL STILL BELIEVE. HE WILL MAKE SPORT OF YOU, AND YOU WILL GROVEL TO HIM...
SHUT UP! YOU SHUT THE HELL UP! MISTER JULIAN AIN'T LYING!
"AND I AIN'T NO GROVELLER!"
"THEN ASK HIM, BILLY. ASK HIM WHEN HE INTENDS TO MAKE YOU OVER. ASK HIM HOW."
HMN.
POOR BILLY. YOU HAVE DOUBTS AFTER ALL THIS TIME? I HAVE TOLD YOU BEFORE THAT YOU MUST BE PATIENT.
IT'S BEEN YEARS, MISTER JULIAN. THINGS HAVE BEEN BETTER'N EVER SINCE WE GOT THIS BOAT.
YOU PROMISED ME.
SO I DID. VERY WELL, THEN.

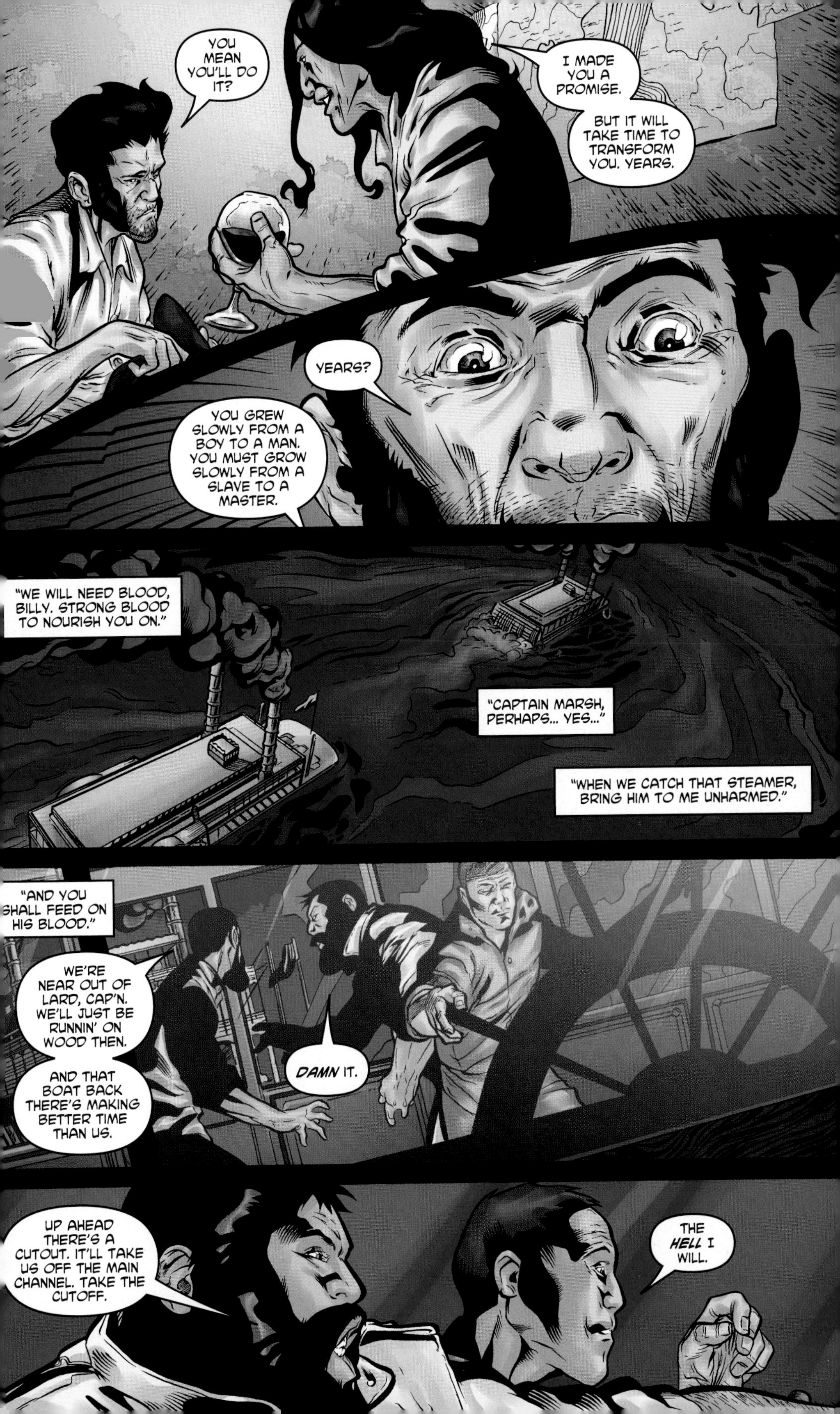
YOU MEAN YOU'LL DO IT?
I MADE YOU A PROMISE.
BUT IT WILL TAKE TIME TO TRANSFORM YOU. YEARS.
YEARS?
YOU GREW SLOWLY FROM A BOY TO A MAN. YOU MUST GROW SLOWLY FROM A SLAVE TO A MASTER.
"WE WILL NEED BLOOD, BILLY. STRONG BLOOD TO NOURISH YOU ON."
"CAPTAIN MARSH, PERHAPS... YES..."
"WHEN WE CATCH THAT STEAMER, BRING HIM TO ME UNHARMED."
"AND YOU SHALL FEED ON HIS BLOOD."
WE'RE NEAR OUT OF LARD, CAP'N. WE'LL JUST BE RUNNIN' ON WOOD THEN.
AND THAT BOAT BACK THERE'S MAKING BETTER TIME THAN US.
DAMN IT.
UP AHEAD THERE'S A CUTOUT. IT'LL TAKE US OFF THE MAIN CHANNEL. TAKE THE CUTOFF.
THE *HELL* I WILL.

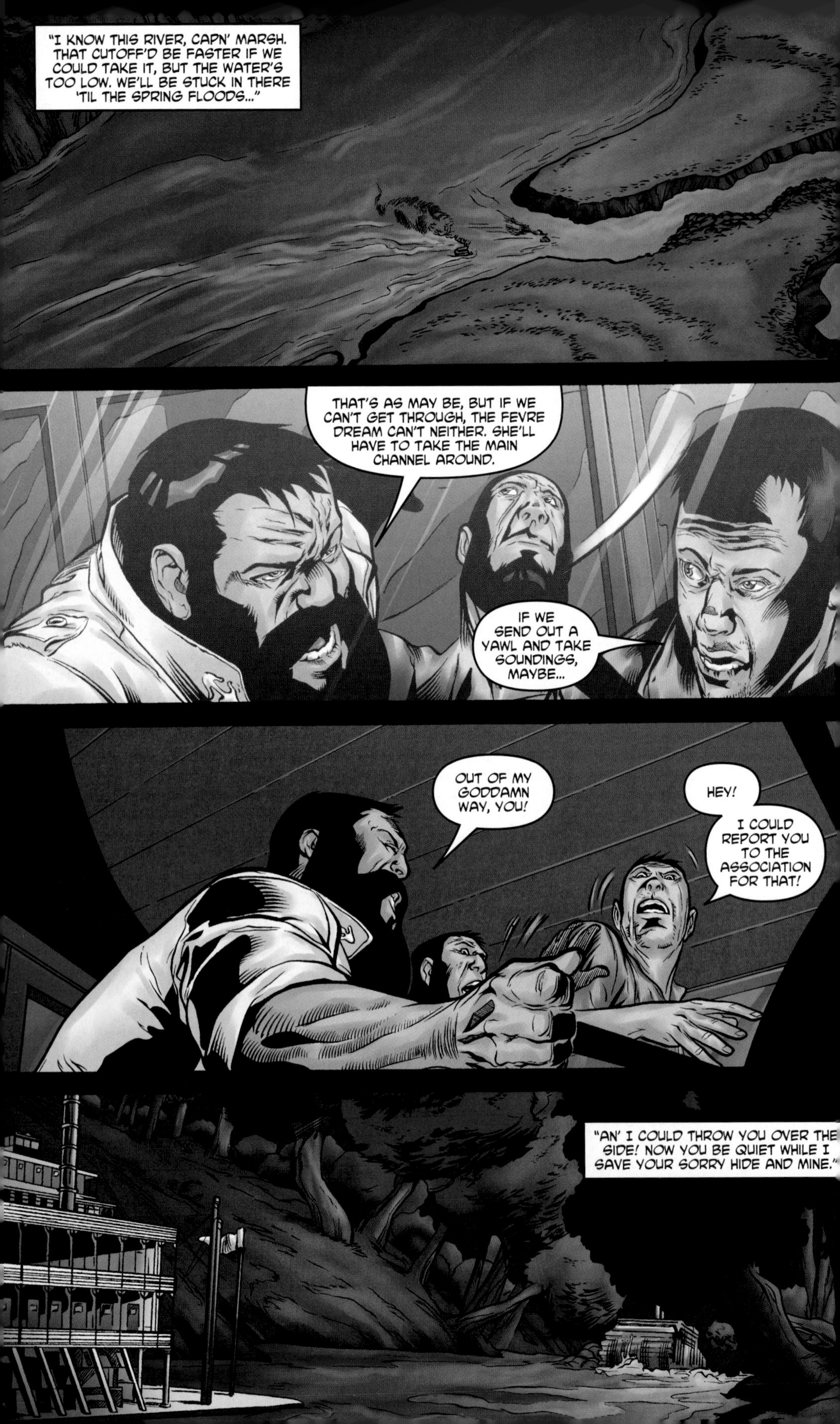
"I KNOW THIS RIVER, CAPN' MARSH. THAT CUTOFF'D BE FASTER IF WE COULD TAKE IT, BUT THE WATER'S TOO LOW. WE'LL BE STUCK IN THERE 'TIL THE SPRING FLOODS..."
THAT'S AS MAY BE, BUT IF WE CAN'T GET THROUGH, THE FEVRE DREAM CAN'T NEITHER. SHE'LL HAVE TO TAKE THE MAIN CHANNEL AROUND.
IF WE SEND OUT A YAWL AND TAKE SOUNDINGS, MAYBE...
OUT OF MY GODDAMN WAY, YOU!
HEY!
I COULD REPORT YOU TO THE ASSOCIATION FOR THAT!
"AN' I COULD THROW YOU OVER THE SIDE! NOW YOU BE QUIET WHILE I SAVE YOUR SORRY HIDE AND MINE."

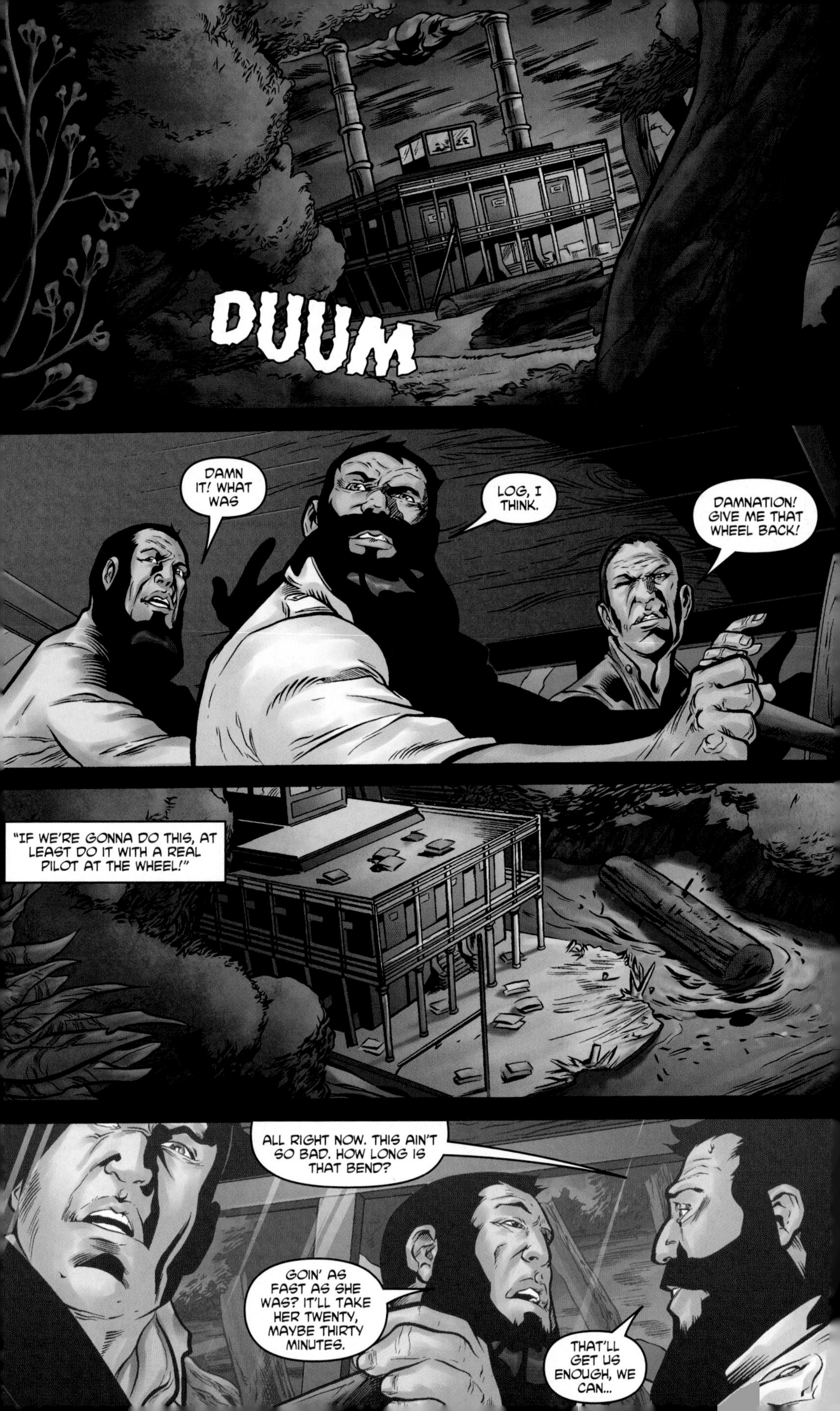
DUUM
DAMN IT! WHAT WAS
LOG, I THINK.
DAMNATION! GIVE ME THAT WHEEL BACK!
"IF WE'RE GONNA DO THIS, AT LEAST DO IT WITH A REAL PILOT AT THE WHEEL!"
ALL RIGHT NOW. THIS AIN'T SO BAD. HOW LONG IS THAT BEND?
GOIN' AS FAST AS SHE WAS? IT'LL TAKE HER TWENTY, MAYBE THIRTY MINUTES.
THAT'LL GET US ENOUGH, WE CAN...

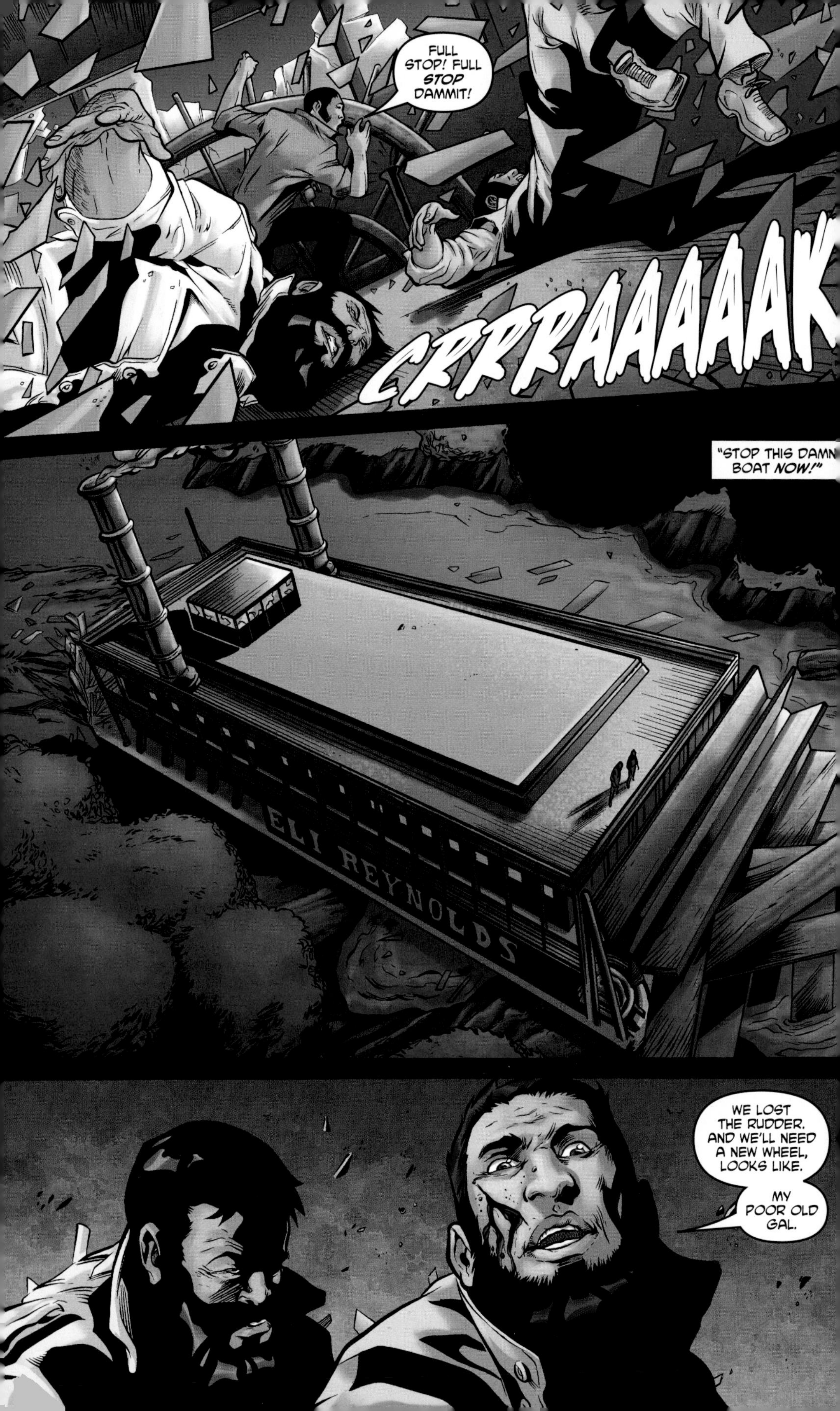

FULL STOP! FULL STOP DAMMIT!
CRRRAAAAAK
"STOP THIS DAMN BOAT NOW!"
ELI REYNOLDS
WE LOST THE RUDDER. AND WE'LL NEED A NEW WHEEL, LOOKS LIKE.
MY POOR OLD GAL.

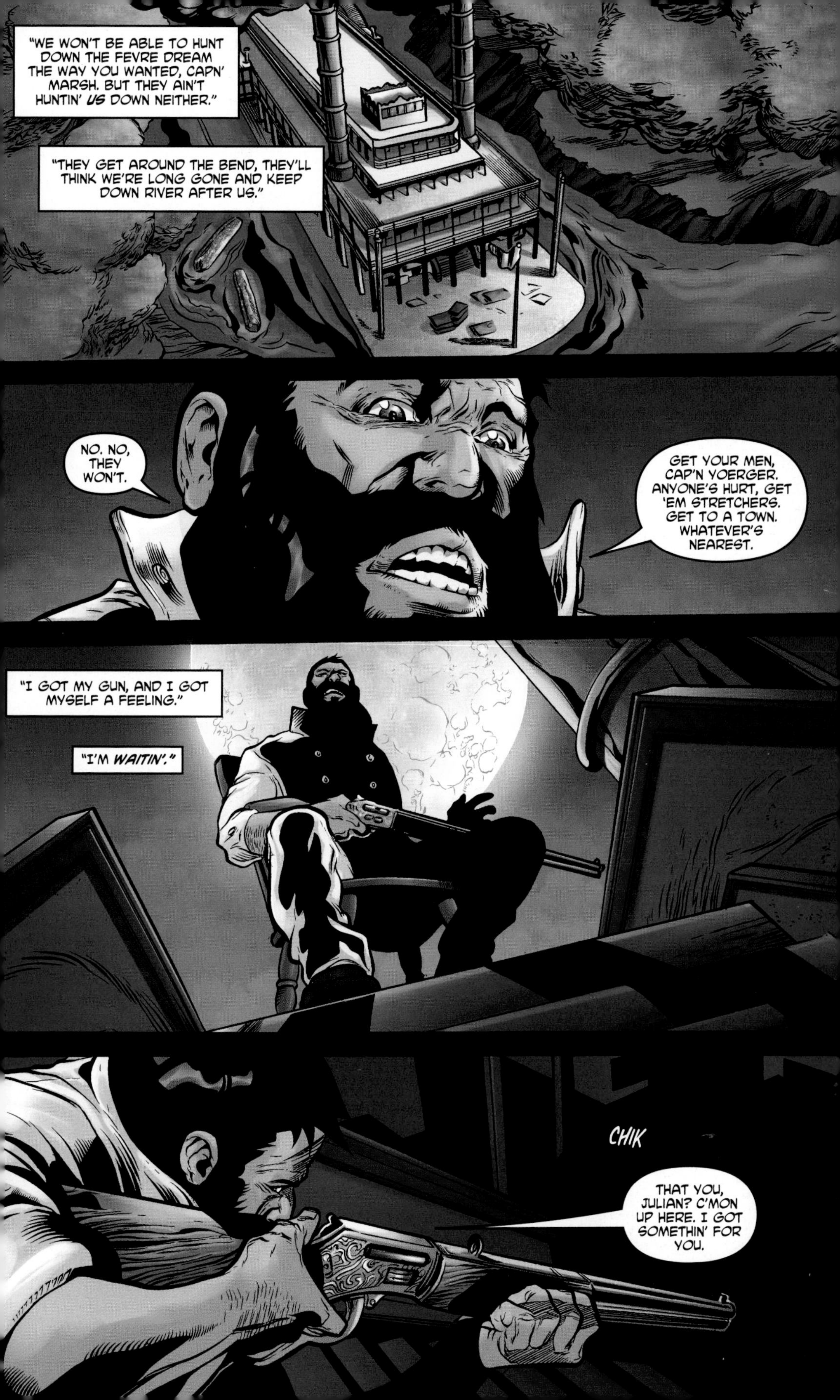
"WE WON'T BE ABLE TO HUNT DOWN THE FEVRE DREAM THE WAY YOU WANTED, CAPN' MARSH. BUT THEY AIN'T HUNTIN' *US* DOWN NEITHER."
"THEY GET AROUND THE BEND, THEY'LL THINK WE'RE LONG GONE AND KEEP DOWN RIVER AFTER US."
NO. NO, THEY WON'T.
GET YOUR MEN, CAP'N YOERGER. ANYONE'S HURT, GET 'EM STRETCHERS. GET TO A TOWN. WHATEVER'S NEAREST.
"I GOT MY GUN, AND I GOT MYSELF A FEELING."
"I'M *WAITIN'*."
CHIK
THAT YOU, JULIAN? C'MON UP HERE. I GOT SOMETHIN' FOR YOU.

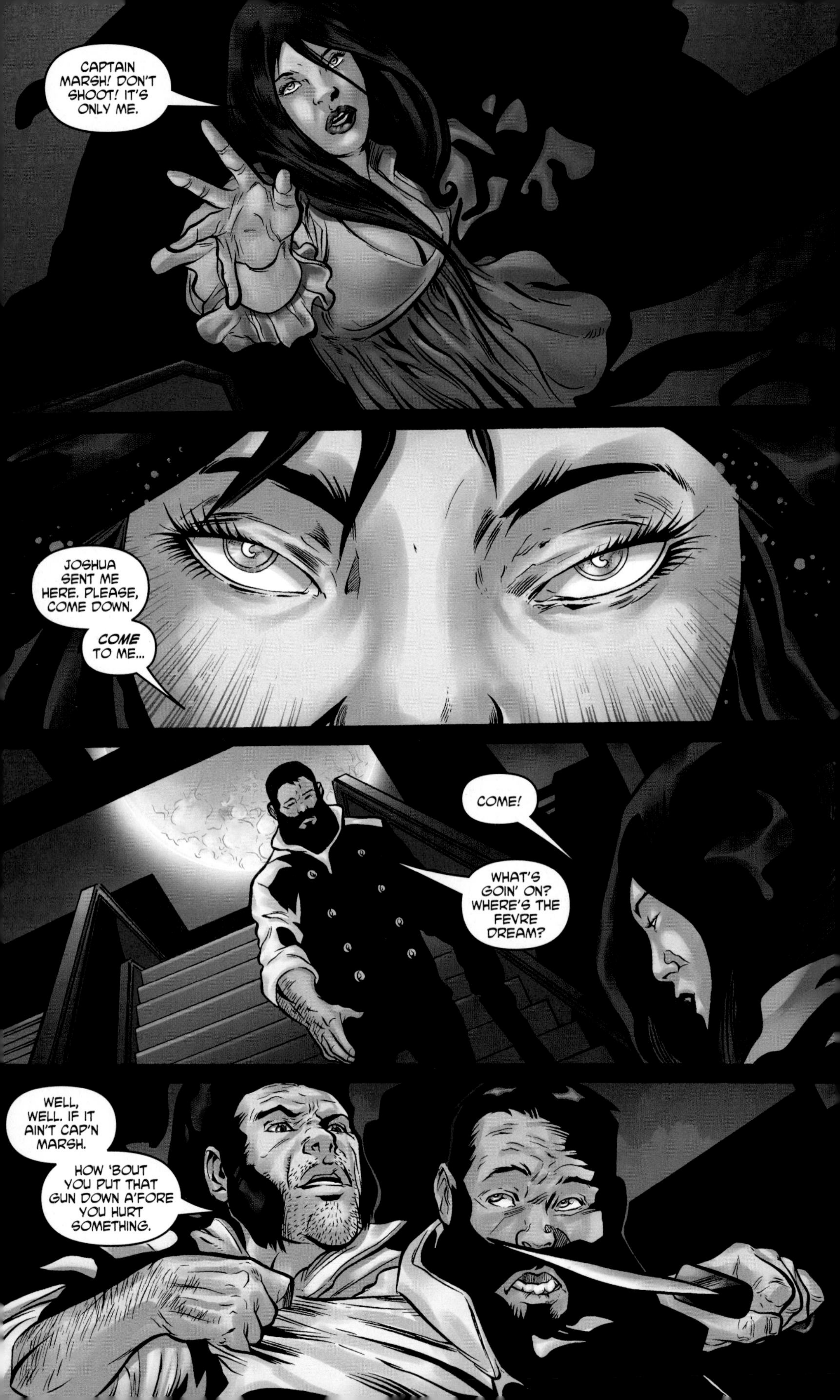
CAPTAIN MARSH! DON'T SHOOT! IT'S ONLY ME.
JOSHUA SENT ME HERE. PLEASE, COME DOWN.
COME TO ME...
COME!
WHAT'S GOIN' ON? WHERE'S THE FEVRE DREAM?
WELL, WELL. IF IT AIN'T CAP'N MARSH.
HOW 'BOUT YOU PUT THAT GUN DOWN A'FORE YOU HURT SOMETHING.

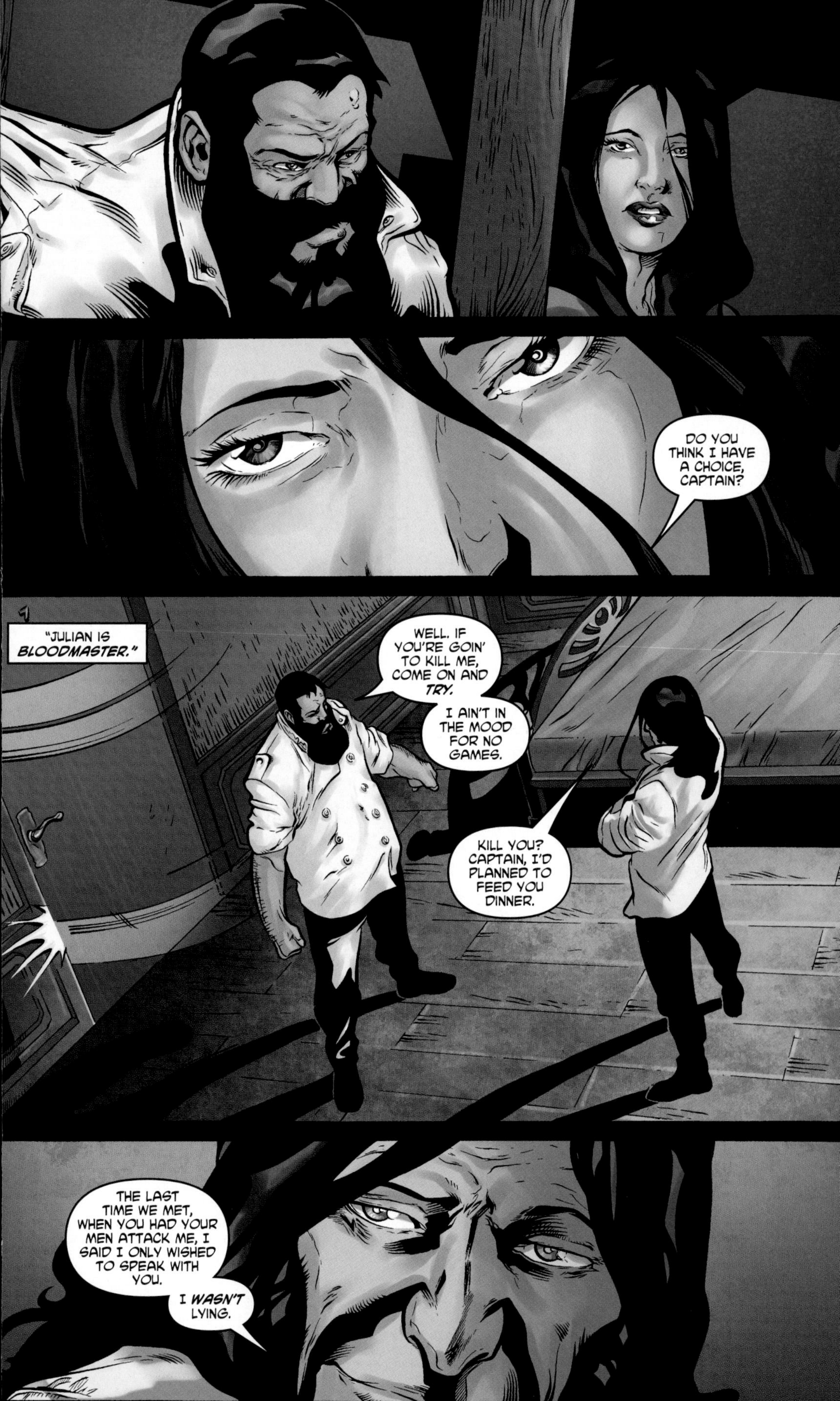
DO YOU THINK I HAVE A CHOICE, CAPTAIN?
"JULIAN IS BLOODMASTER."
WELL. IF YOU'RE GOIN' TO KILL ME, COME ON AND TRY.
I AIN'T IN THE MOOD FOR NO GAMES.
KILL YOU? CAPTAIN, I'D PLANNED TO FEED YOU DINNER.
THE LAST TIME WE MET, WHEN YOU HAD YOUR MEN ATTACK ME, I SAID I ONLY WISHED TO SPEAK WITH YOU.
I WASN'T LYING.

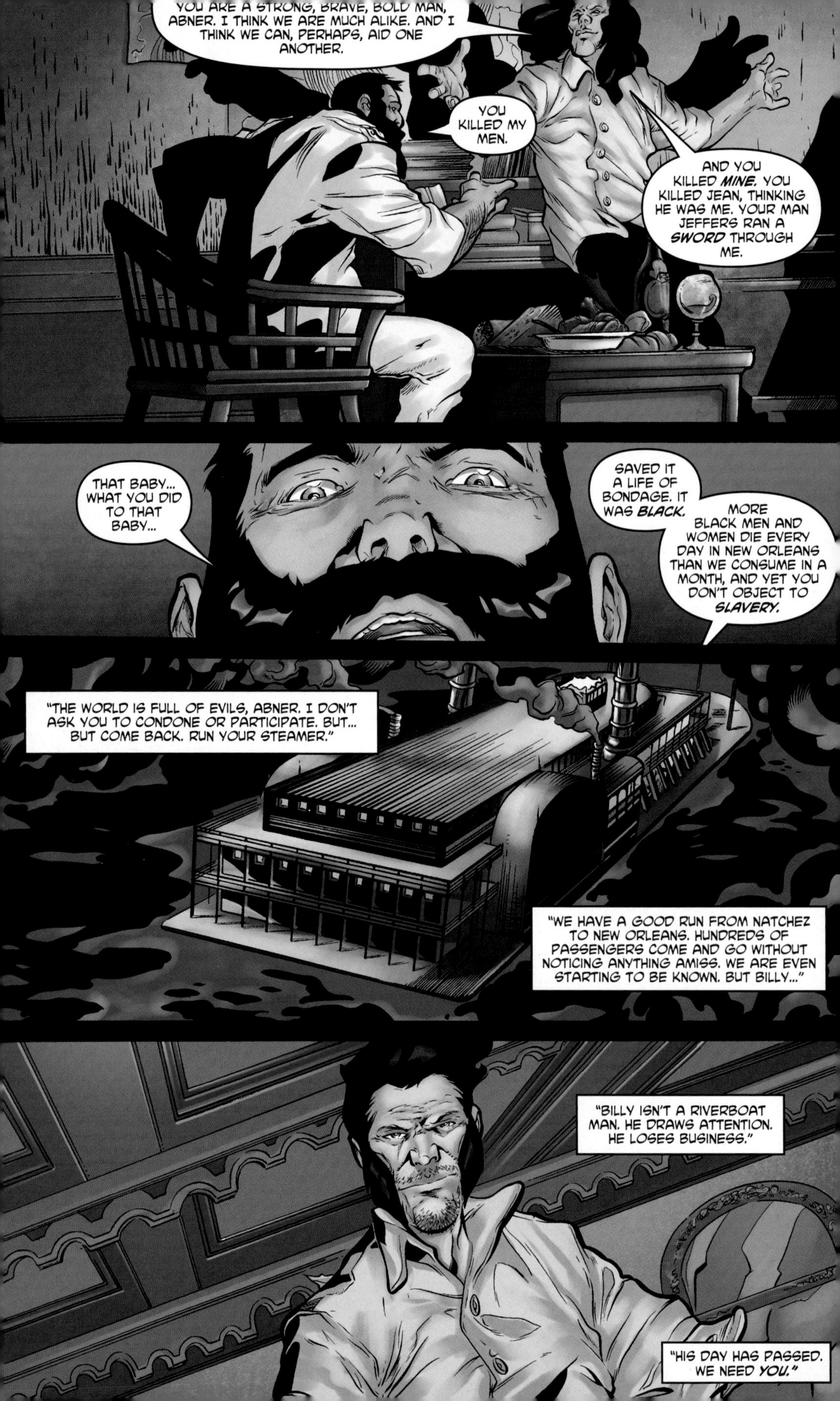
YOU ARE A STRONG, BRAVE, BOLD MAN, ABNER. I THINK WE ARE MUCH ALIKE. AND I THINK WE CAN, PERHAPS, AID ONE ANOTHER.
YOU KILLED MY MEN.
AND YOU KILLED *MINE.* YOU KILLED JEAN, THINKING HE WAS ME. YOUR MAN JEFFERS RAN A *SWORD* THROUGH ME.
THAT BABY... WHAT YOU DID TO THAT BABY...
SAVED IT A LIFE OF BONDAGE. IT WAS *BLACK.*
MORE BLACK MEN AND WOMEN DIE EVERY DAY IN NEW ORLEANS THAN WE CONSUME IN A MONTH, AND YET YOU DON'T OBJECT TO *SLAVERY.*
"THE WORLD IS FULL OF EVILS, ABNER. I DON'T ASK YOU TO CONDONE OR PARTICIPATE. BUT... BUT COME BACK. RUN YOUR STEAMER."
"WE HAVE A GOOD RUN FROM NATCHEZ TO NEW ORLEANS. HUNDREDS OF PASSENGERS COME AND GO WITHOUT NOTICING ANYTHING AMISS. WE ARE EVEN STARTING TO BE KNOWN. BUT BILLY..."
"BILLY ISN'T A RIVERBOAT MAN. HE DRAWS ATTENTION. HE LOSES BUSINESS."
"HIS DAY HAS PASSED. WE NEED *YOU.*"

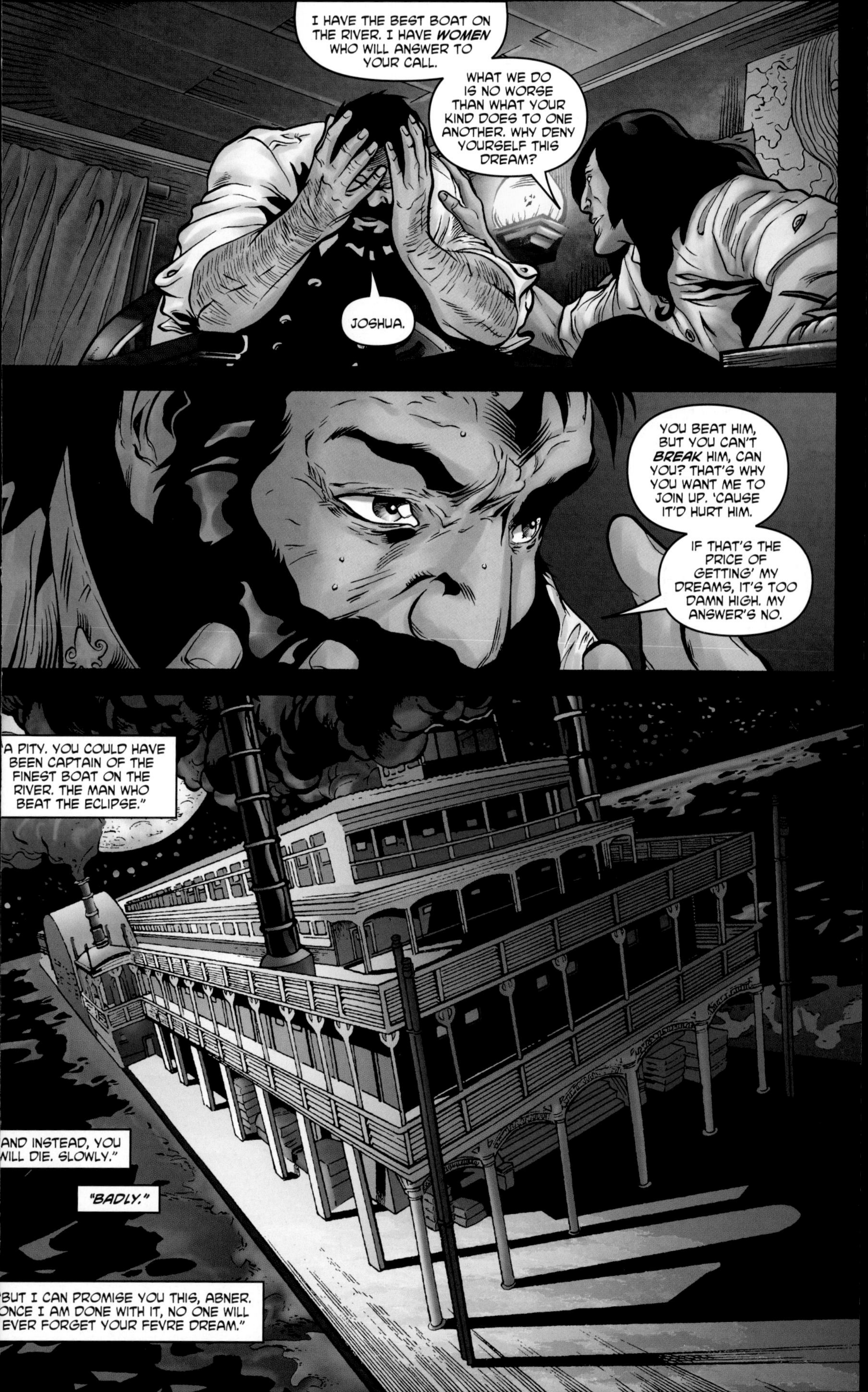
I HAVE THE BEST BOAT ON THE RIVER. I HAVE *WOMEN* WHO WILL ANSWER TO YOUR CALL.
WHAT WE DO IS NO WORSE THAN WHAT YOUR KIND DOES TO ONE ANOTHER. WHY DENY YOURSELF THIS DREAM?
JOSHUA.
YOU BEAT HIM, BUT YOU CAN'T *BREAK* HIM, CAN YOU? THAT'S WHY YOU WANT ME TO JOIN UP. 'CAUSE IT'D HURT HIM.
IF THAT'S THE PRICE OF GETTING' MY DREAMS, IT'S TOO DAMN HIGH. MY ANSWER'S NO.
"A PITY. YOU COULD HAVE BEEN CAPTAIN OF THE FINEST BOAT ON THE RIVER. THE MAN WHO BEAT THE ECLIPSE."
AND INSTEAD, YOU WILL DIE. SLOWLY."
"*BADLY.*"
"BUT I CAN PROMISE YOU THIS, ABNER. ONCE I AM DONE WITH IT, NO ONE WILL EVER FORGET YOUR FEVRE DREAM."

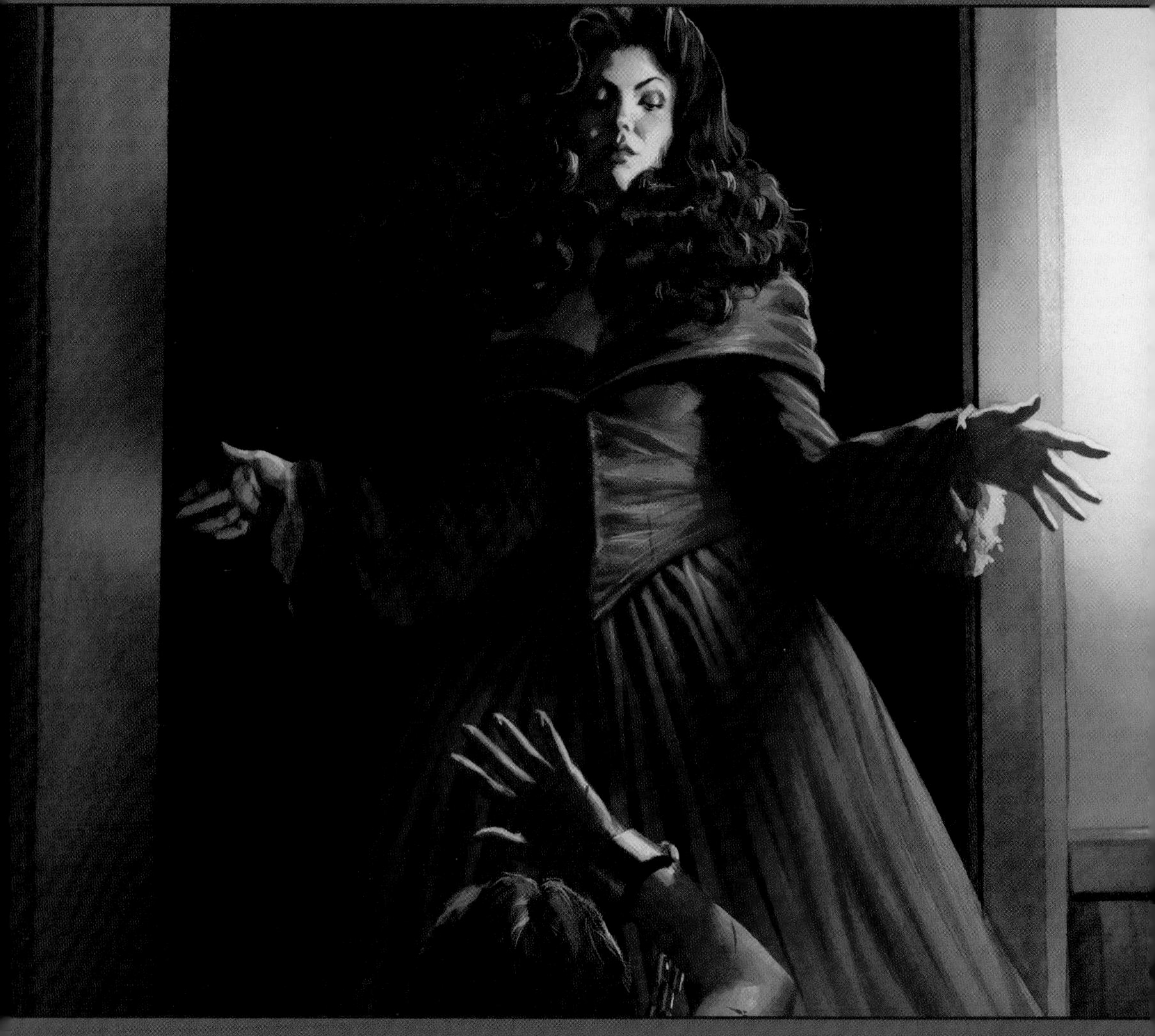

CHAPTER 9

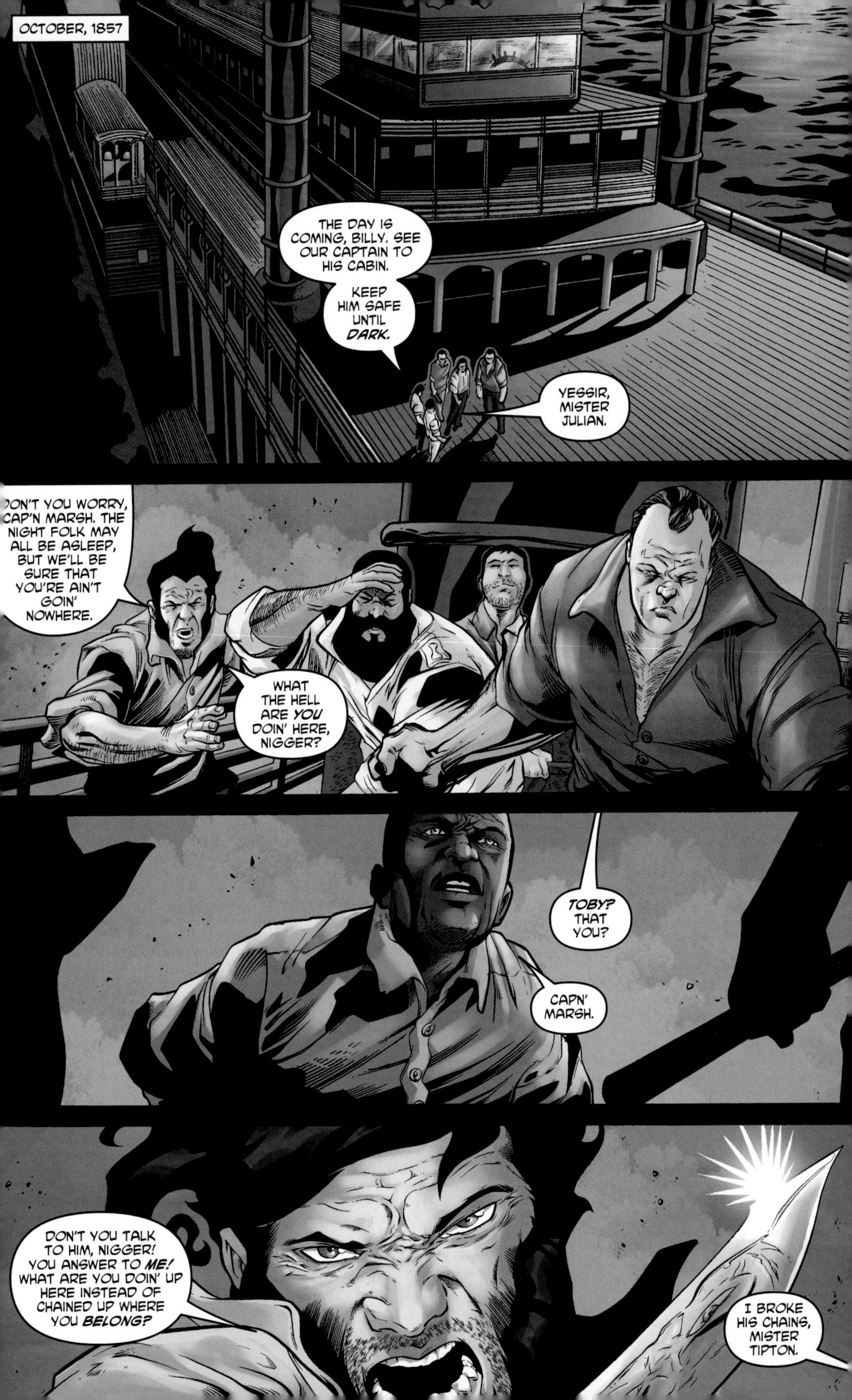
OCTOBER, 1857
THE DAY IS COMING, BILLY. SEE OUR CAPTAIN TO HIS CABIN.
KEEP HIM SAFE UNTIL *DARK.*
YESSIR, MISTER JULIAN.
DON'T YOU WORRY, CAP'N MARSH. THE NIGHT FOLK MAY ALL BE ASLEEP, BUT WE'LL BE SURE THAT YOU'RE AIN'T GOIN' NOWHERE.
WHAT THE HELL ARE *YOU* DOIN' HERE, NIGGER?
TOBY? THAT YOU?
CAPN' MARSH.
DON'T YOU TALK TO HIM, NIGGER! YOU ANSWER TO *ME!* WHAT ARE YOU DOIN' UP HERE INSTEAD OF CHAINED UP WHERE YOU *BELONG?*
I BROKE HIS CHAINS, MISTER TIPTON.

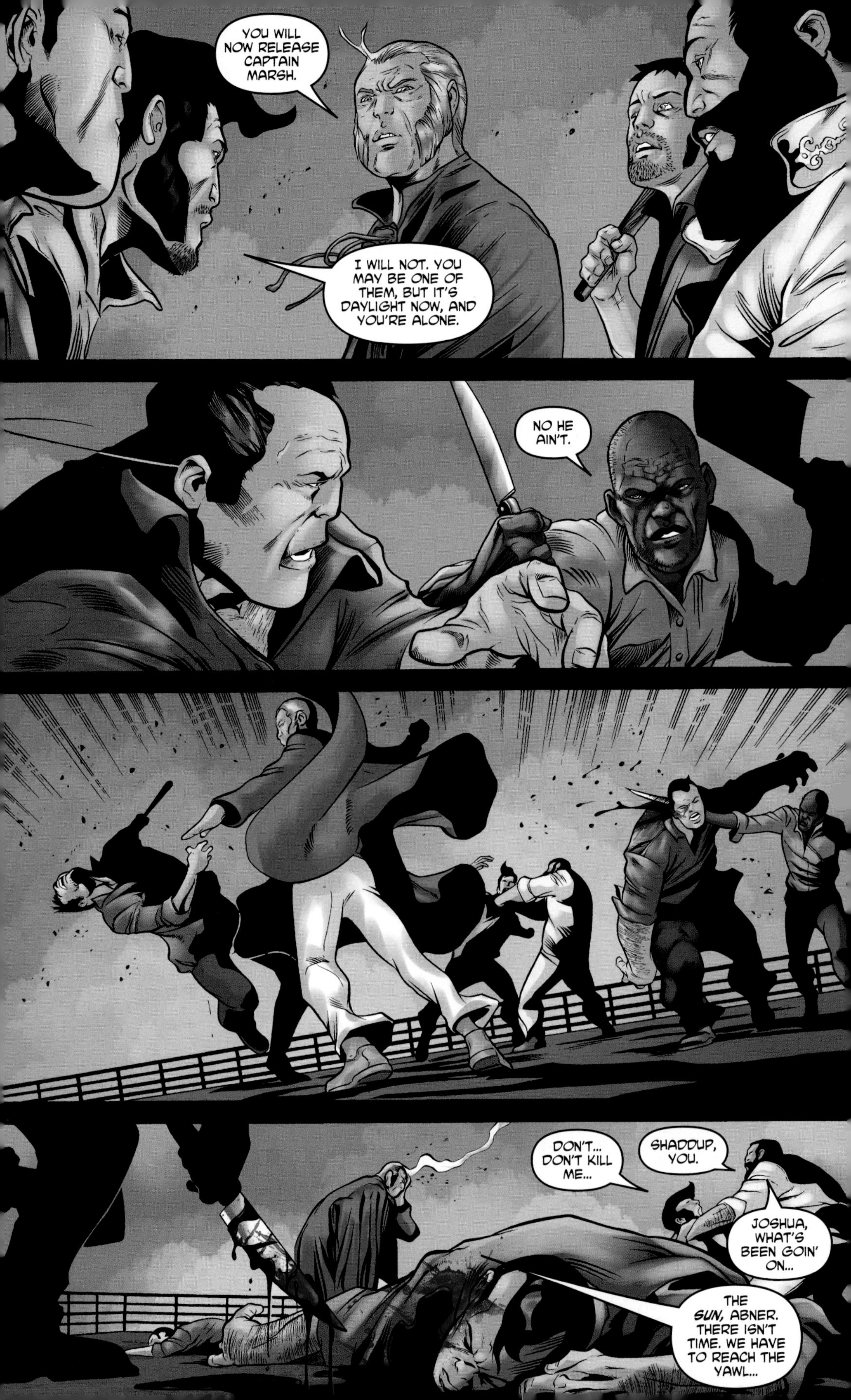
YOU WILL NOW RELEASE CAPTAIN MARSH.
I WILL NOT. YOU MAY BE ONE OF THEM, BUT IT'S DAYLIGHT NOW, AND YOU'RE ALONE.
NO HE AIN'T.
DON'T... DON'T KILL ME...
SHADDUP, YOU.
JOSHUA, WHAT'S BEEN GOIN' ON...
THE *SUN,* ABNER. THERE ISN'T TIME. WE HAVE TO REACH THE YAWL...

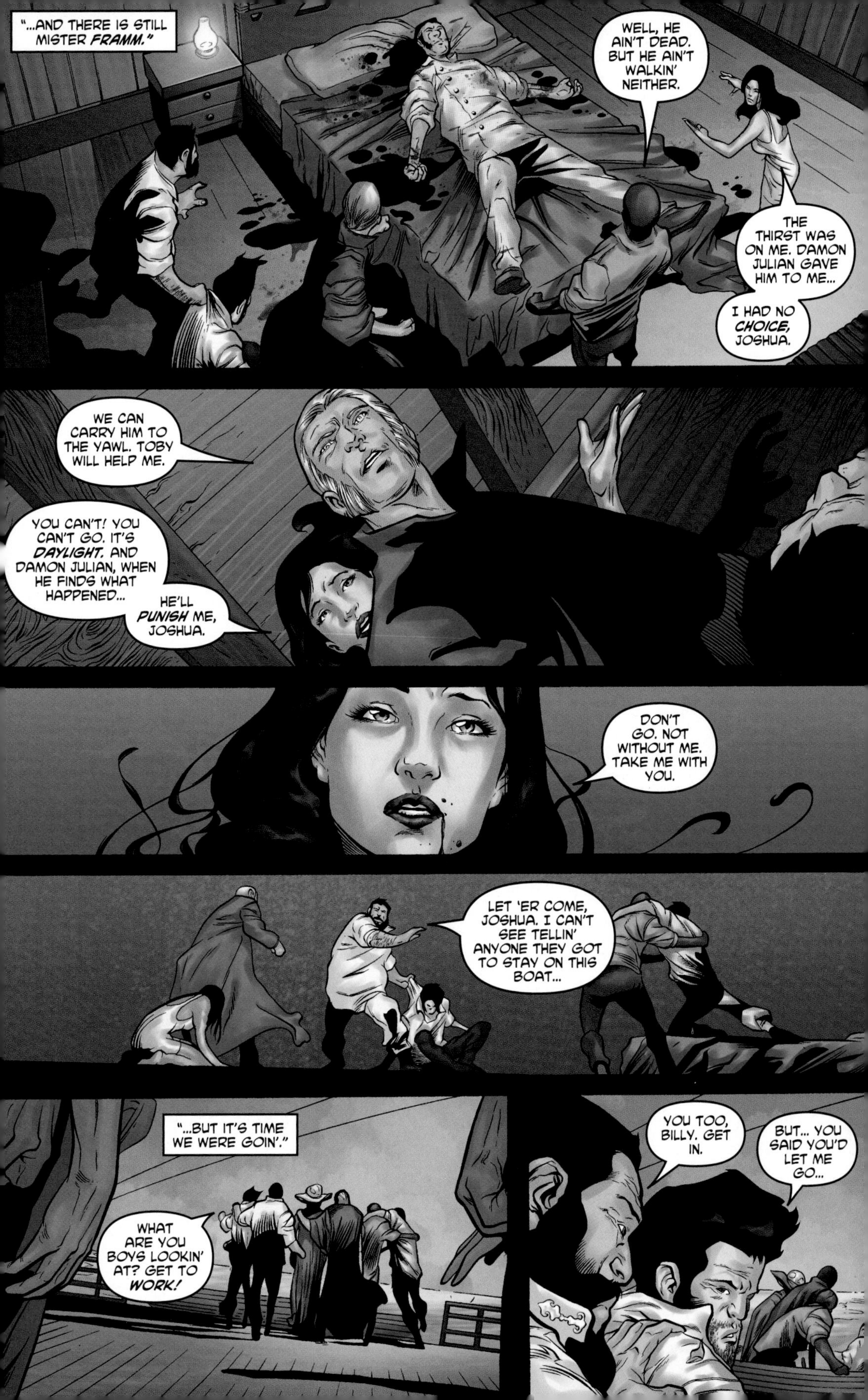

"...AND THERE IS STILL MISTER FRAMM."
WELL, HE AIN'T DEAD. BUT HE AIN'T WALKIN' NEITHER.
THE THIRST WAS ON ME. DAMON JULIAN GAVE HIM TO ME...
I HAD NO CHOICE, JOSHUA.
WE CAN CARRY HIM TO THE YAWL. TOBY WILL HELP ME.
YOU CAN'T! YOU CAN'T GO. IT'S DAYLIGHT. AND DAMON JULIAN, WHEN HE FINDS WHAT HAPPENED...
HE'LL PUNISH ME, JOSHUA.
DON'T GO. NOT WITHOUT ME. TAKE ME WITH YOU.
LET 'ER COME, JOSHUA. I CAN'T SEE TELLIN' ANYONE THEY GOT TO STAY ON THIS BOAT...
"...BUT IT'S TIME WE WERE GOIN'."
WHAT ARE YOU BOYS LOOKIN' AT? GET TO WORK!
YOU TOO, BILLY. GET IN.
BUT... YOU SAID YOU'D LET ME GO...

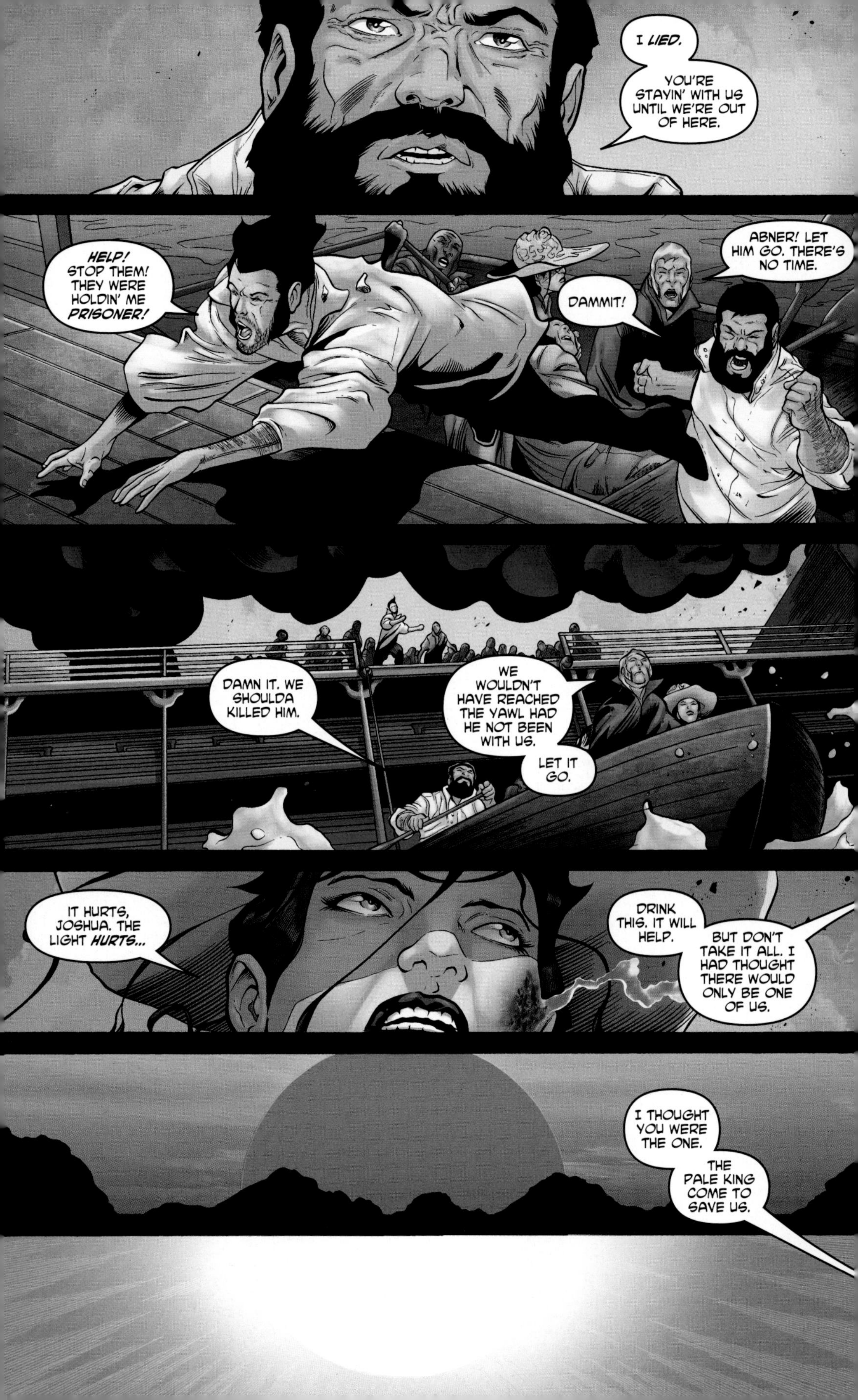
I LIED.
YOU'RE STAYIN' WITH US UNTIL WE'RE OUT OF HERE.
HELP! STOP THEM! THEY WERE HOLDIN' ME PRISONER!
ABNER! LET HIM GO. THERE'S NO TIME.
DAMMIT!
DAMN IT. WE SHOULDA KILLED HIM.
WE WOULDN'T HAVE REACHED THE YAWL HAD HE NOT BEEN WITH US.
LET IT GO.
IT HURTS, JOSHUA. THE LIGHT HURTS...
DRINK THIS. IT WILL HELP.
BUT DON'T TAKE IT ALL. I HAD THOUGHT THERE WOULD ONLY BE ONE OF US.
I THOUGHT YOU WERE THE ONE.
THE PALE KING COME TO SAVE US.

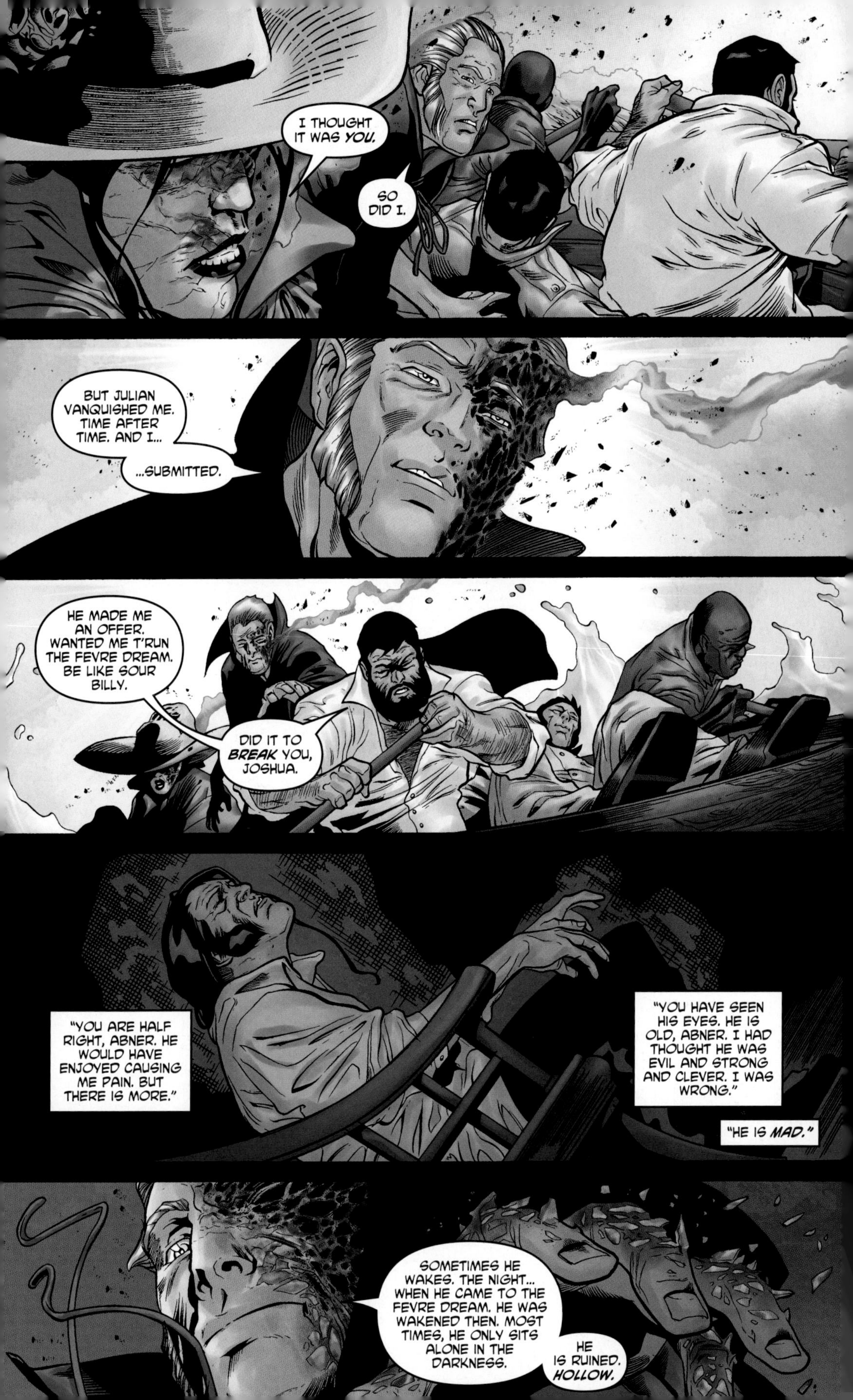
I THOUGHT IT WAS *YOU.*
SO DID I.
BUT JULIAN VANQUISHED ME. TIME AFTER TIME. AND I...
...SUBMITTED.
HE MADE ME AN OFFER. WANTED ME T'RUN THE FEVRE DREAM. BE LIKE SOUR BILLY.
DID IT TO *BREAK* YOU, JOSHUA.
"YOU ARE HALF RIGHT, ABNER. HE WOULD HAVE ENJOYED CAUSING ME PAIN. BUT THERE IS MORE."
"YOU HAVE SEEN HIS EYES. HE IS OLD, ABNER. I HAD THOUGHT HE WAS EVIL AND STRONG AND CLEVER. I WAS WRONG."
"HE IS *MAD.*"
SOMETIMES HE WAKES. THE NIGHT... WHEN HE CAME TO THE FEVRE DREAM. HE WAS WAKENED THEN. MOST TIMES, HE ONLY SITS ALONE IN THE DARKNESS.
HE IS RUINED. *HOLLOW.*

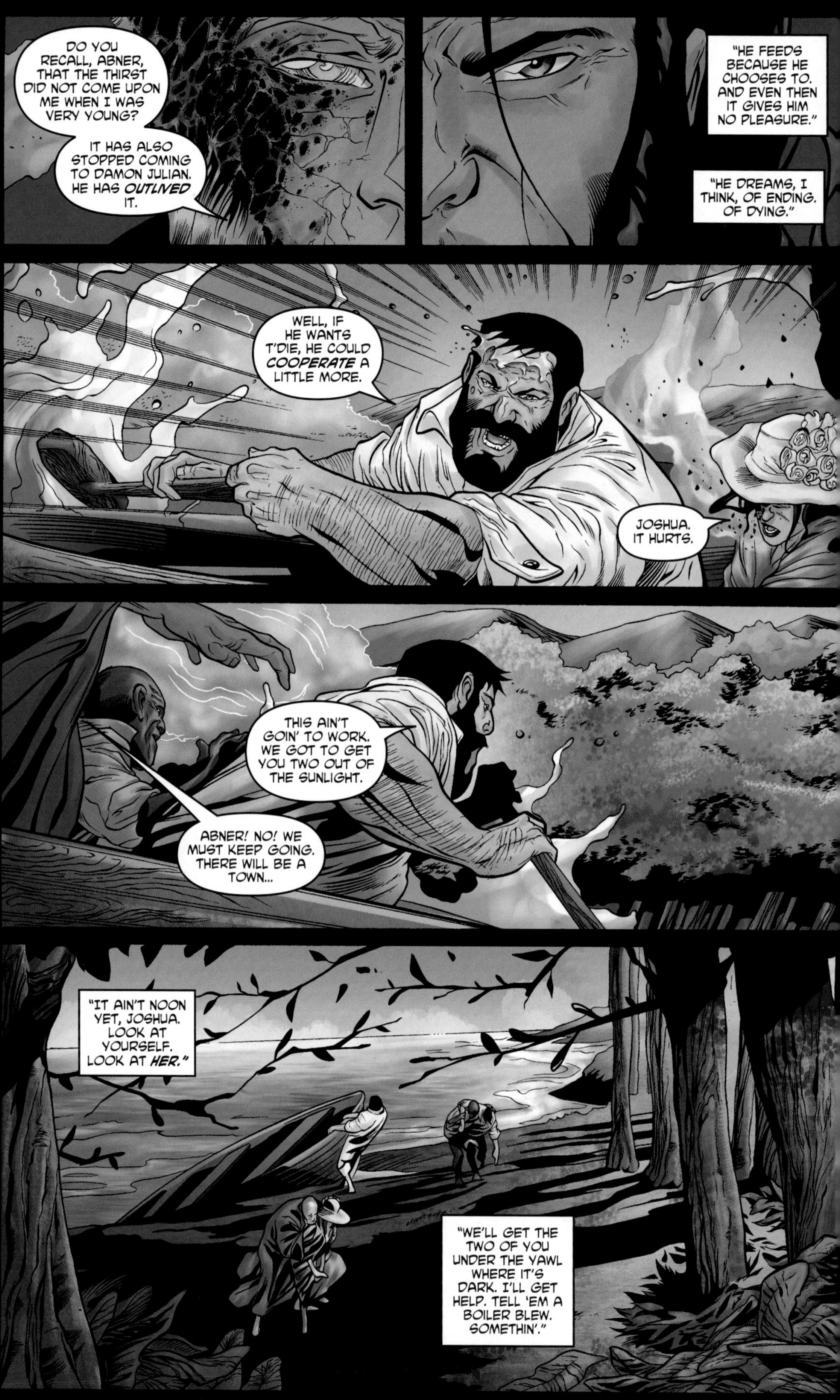
DO YOU RECALL, ABNER, THAT THE THIRST DID NOT COME UPON ME WHEN I WAS VERY YOUNG?
IT HAS ALSO STOPPED COMING TO DAMON JULIAN. HE HAS OUTLIVED IT.
"HE FEEDS BECAUSE HE CHOOSES TO. AND EVEN THEN IT GIVES HIM NO PLEASURE."
"HE DREAMS, I THINK, OF ENDING. OF DYING."
WELL, IF HE WANTS T'DIE, HE COULD COOPERATE A LITTLE MORE.
JOSHUA. IT HURTS.
THIS AIN'T GOIN' TO WORK. WE GOT TO GET YOU TWO OUT OF THE SUNLIGHT.
ABNER! NO! WE MUST KEEP GOING. THERE WILL BE A TOWN...
"IT AIN'T NOON YET, JOSHUA. LOOK AT YOURSELF. LOOK AT HER."
"WE'LL GET THE TWO OF YOU UNDER THE YAWL WHERE IT'S DARK. I'LL GET HELP. TELL 'EM A BOILER BLEW. SOMETHIN'."

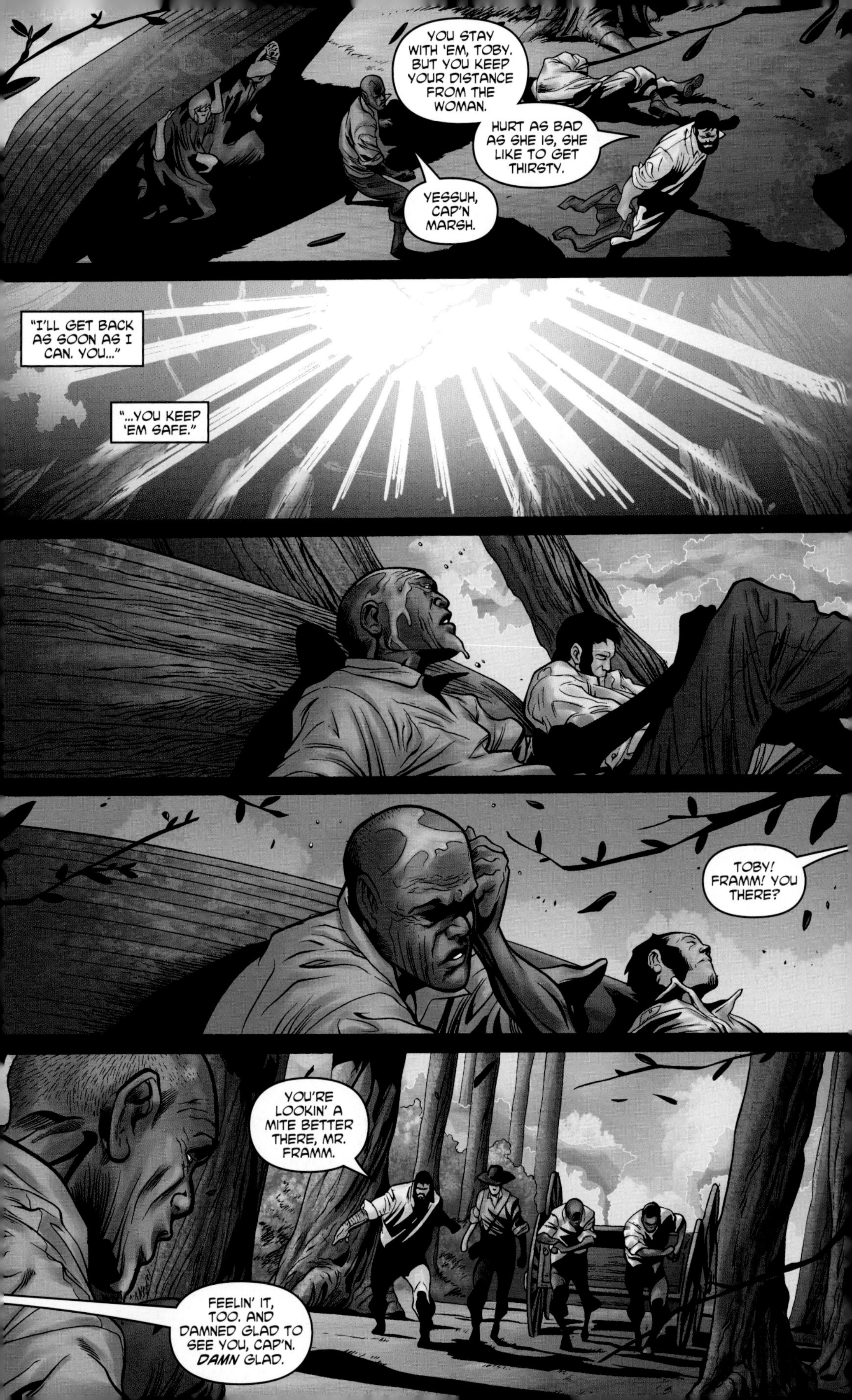

YOU STAY WITH 'EM, TOBY. BUT YOU KEEP YOUR DISTANCE FROM THE WOMAN.
HURT AS BAD AS SHE IS, SHE LIKE TO GET THIRSTY.
YESSUH, CAP'N MARSH.
"I'LL GET BACK AS SOON AS I CAN. YOU..."
"...YOU KEEP 'EM SAFE."
TOBY! FRAMM! YOU THERE?
YOU'RE LOOKIN' A MITE BETTER THERE, MR. FRAMM.
FEELIN' IT, TOO. AND DAMNED GLAD TO SEE YOU, CAP'N. *DAMN* GLAD.

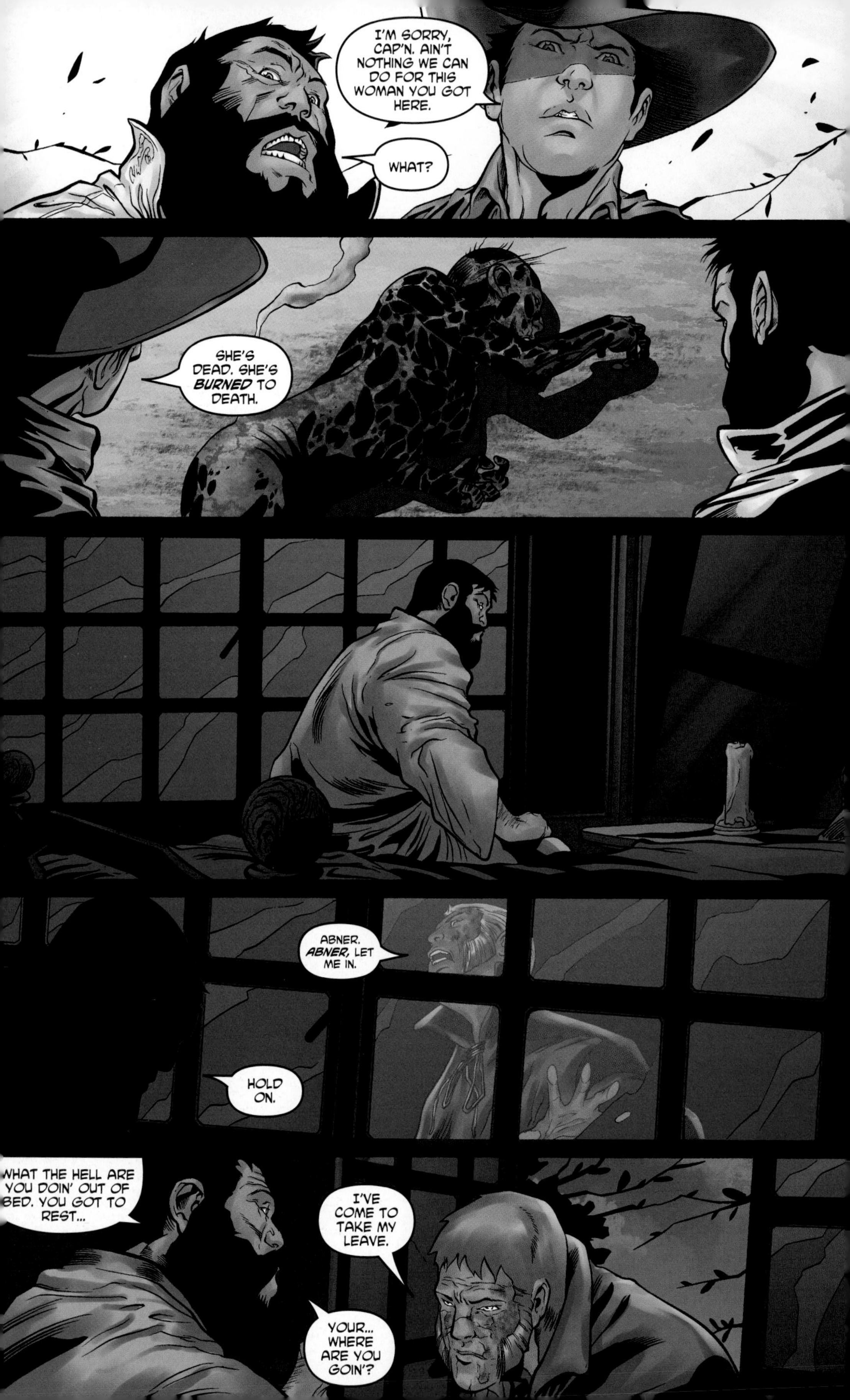
I'M SORRY, CAP'N. AIN'T NOTHING WE CAN DO FOR THIS WOMAN YOU GOT HERE.
WHAT?
SHE'S DEAD. SHE'S BURNED TO DEATH.
ABNER. ABNER, LET ME IN.
HOLD ON.
WHAT THE HELL ARE YOU DOIN' OUT OF BED. YOU GOT TO REST...
I'VE COME TO TAKE MY LEAVE.
YOUR... WHERE ARE YOU GOIN'?

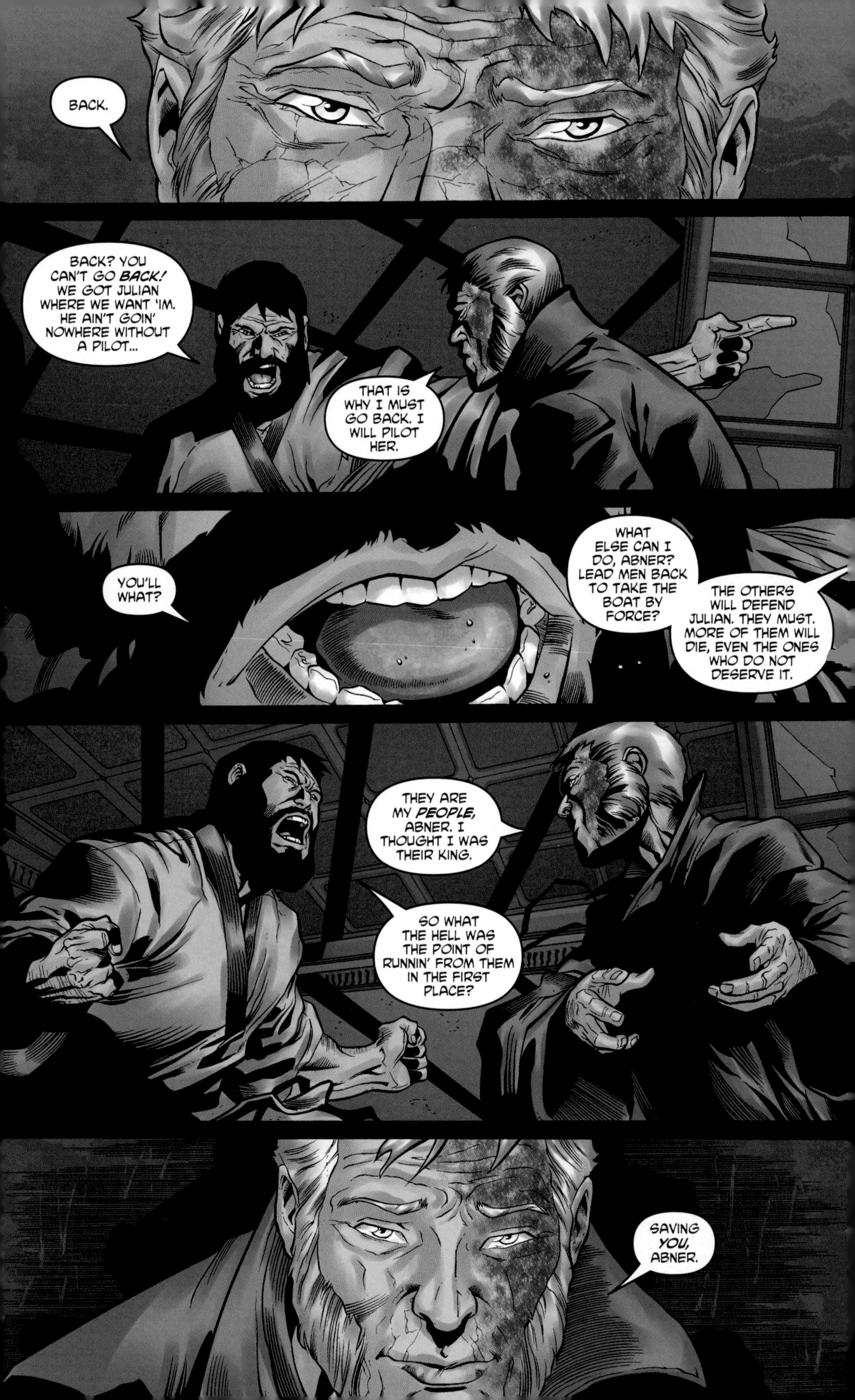
BACK.
BACK? YOU CAN'T GO *BACK!* WE GOT JULIAN WHERE WE WANT 'IM. HE AIN'T GOIN' NOWHERE WITHOUT A PILOT...
THAT IS WHY I MUST GO BACK. I WILL PILOT HER.
YOU'LL WHAT?
WHAT ELSE CAN I DO, ABNER? LEAD MEN BACK TO TAKE THE BOAT BY FORCE?
THE OTHERS WILL DEFEND JULIAN. THEY MUST. MORE OF THEM WILL DIE, EVEN THE ONES WHO DO NOT DESERVE IT.
THEY ARE MY *PEOPLE,* ABNER. I THOUGHT I WAS THEIR KING.
SO WHAT THE HELL WAS THE POINT OF RUNNIN' FROM THEM IN THE FIRST PLACE?
SAVING *YOU,* ABNER.

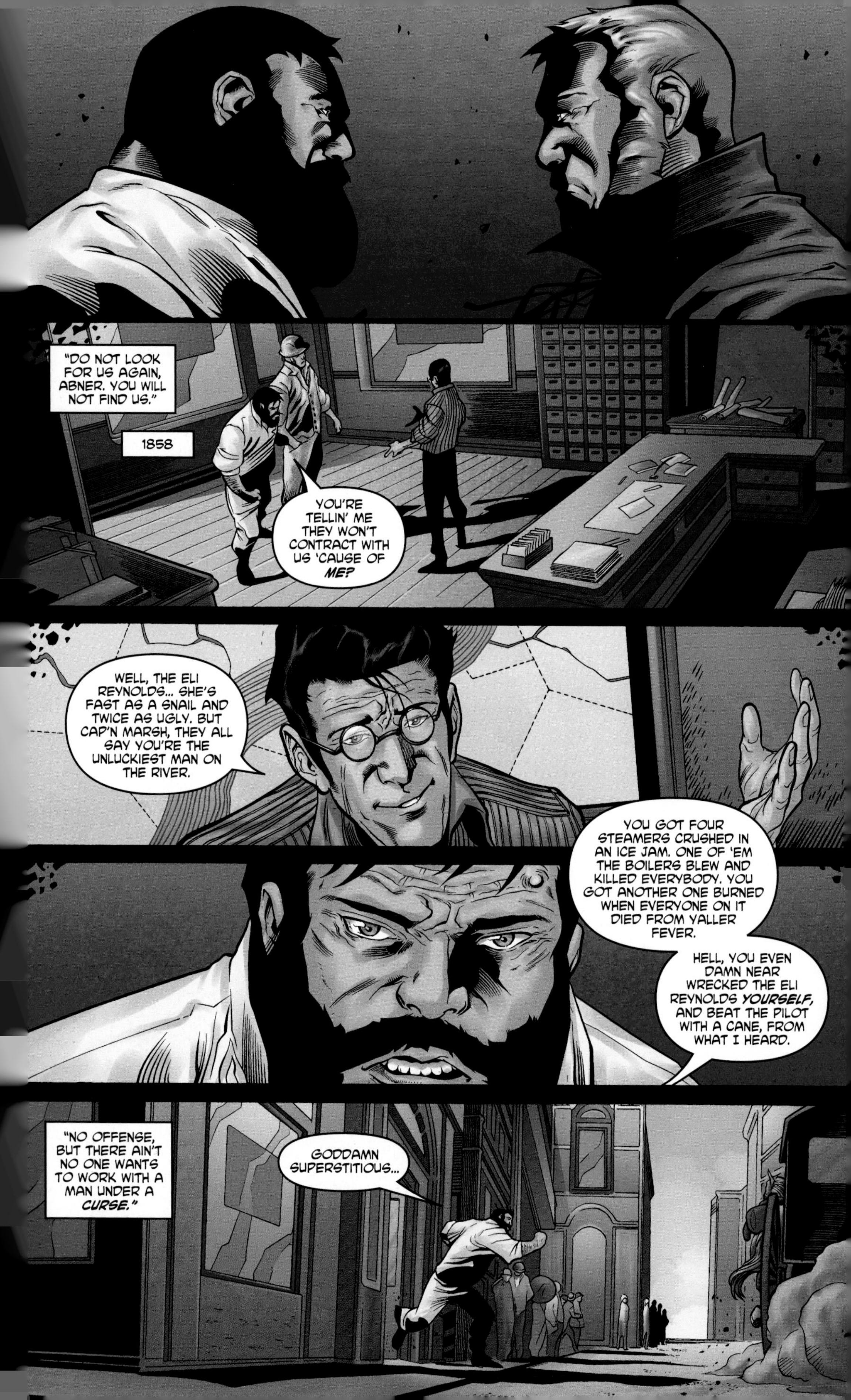
"DO NOT LOOK FOR US AGAIN, ABNER. YOU WILL NOT FIND US."
1858
YOU'RE TELLIN' ME THEY WON'T CONTRACT WITH US 'CAUSE OF *ME?*
WELL, THE ELI REYNOLDS... SHE'S FAST AS A SNAIL AND TWICE AS UGLY. BUT CAP'N MARSH, THEY ALL SAY YOU'RE THE UNLUCKIEST MAN ON THE RIVER.
YOU GOT FOUR STEAMERS CRUSHED IN AN ICE JAM. ONE OF 'EM THE BOILERS BLEW AND KILLED EVERYBODY. YOU GOT ANOTHER ONE BURNED WHEN EVERYONE ON IT DIED FROM YALLER FEVER.
HELL, YOU EVEN DAMN NEAR WRECKED THE ELI REYNOLDS *YOURSELF,* AND BEAT THE PILOT WITH A CANE, FROM WHAT I HEARD.
"NO OFFENSE, BUT THERE AIN'T NO ONE WANTS TO WORK WITH A MAN UNDER A *CURSE.*"
GODDAMN SUPERSTITIOUS...

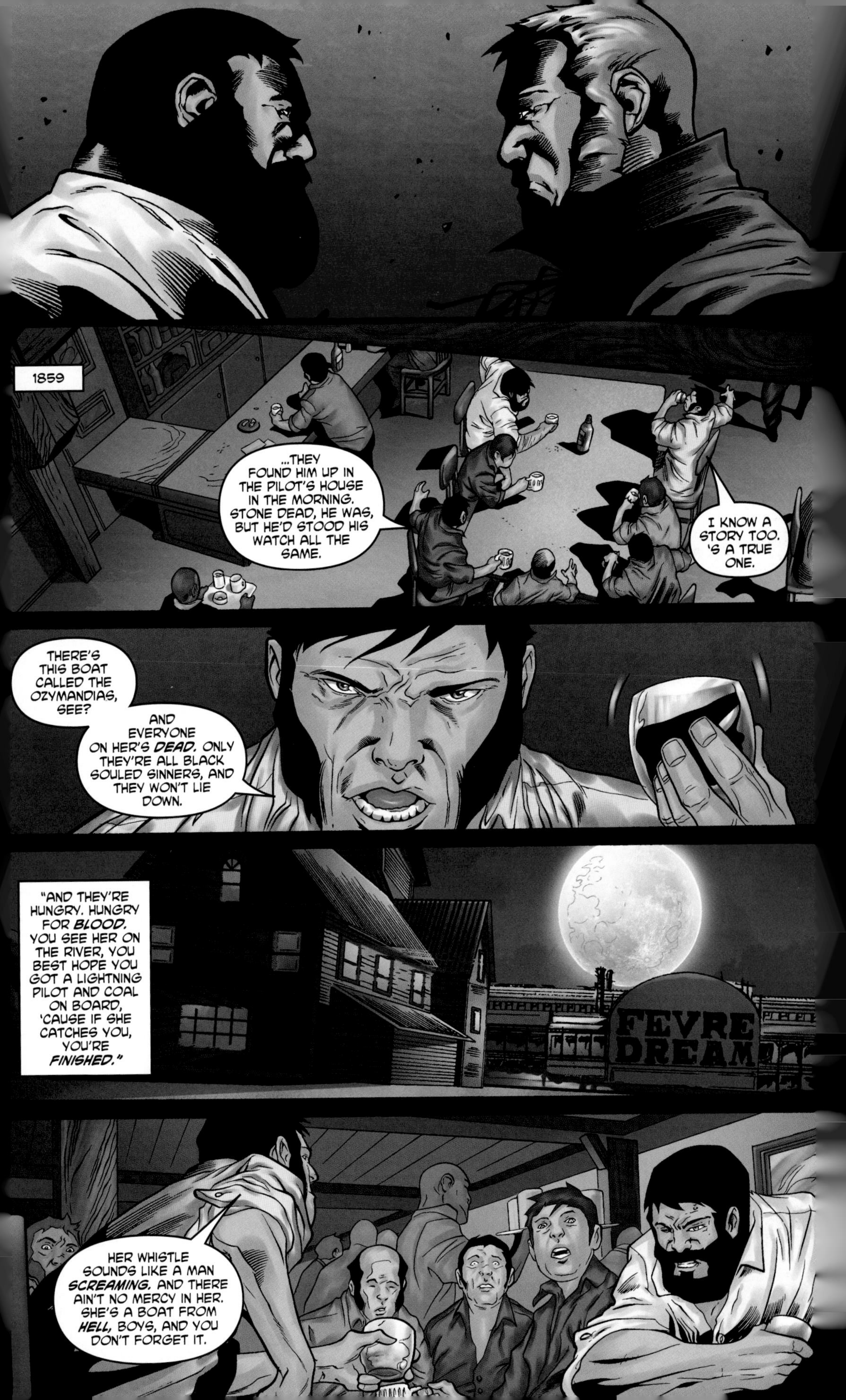
1859
...THEY FOUND HIM UP IN THE PILOT'S HOUSE IN THE MORNING. STONE DEAD, HE WAS, BUT HE'D STOOD HIS WATCH ALL THE SAME.
I KNOW A STORY TOO. 'S A TRUE ONE.
THERE'S THIS BOAT CALLED THE OZYMANDIAS, SEE?
AND EVERYONE ON HER'S DEAD. ONLY THEY'RE ALL BLACK SOULED SINNERS, AND THEY WON'T LIE DOWN.
"AND THEY'RE HUNGRY. HUNGRY FOR BLOOD. YOU SEE HER ON THE RIVER, YOU BEST HOPE YOU GOT A LIGHTNING PILOT AND COAL ON BOARD, 'CAUSE IF SHE CATCHES YOU, YOU'RE FINISHED."
FEVRE DREAM
HER WHISTLE SOUNDS LIKE A MAN SCREAMING, AND THERE AIN'T NO MERCY IN HER. SHE'S A BOAT FROM HELL, BOYS, AND YOU DON'T FORGET IT.

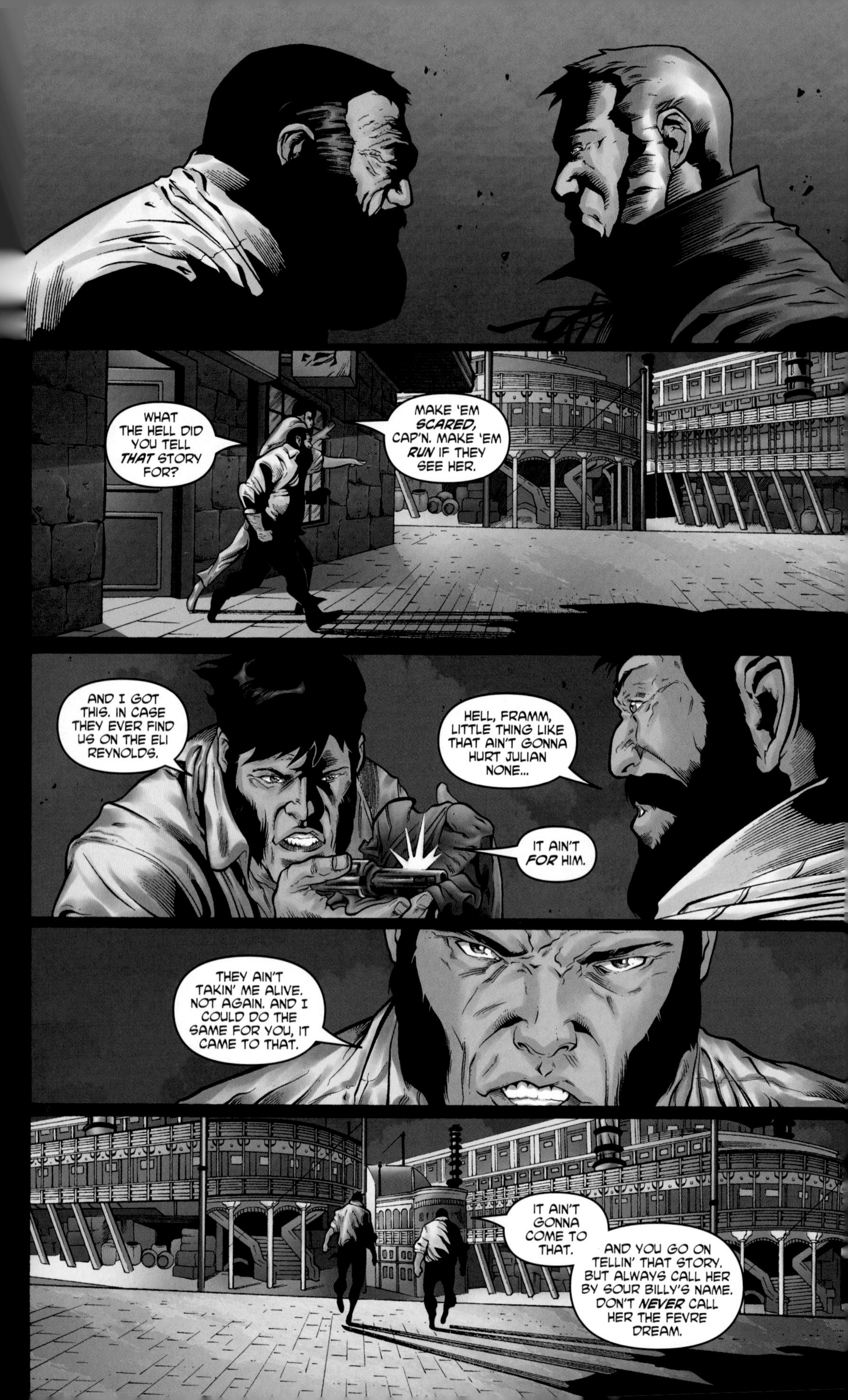

WHAT THE HELL DID YOU TELL THAT STORY FOR?
MAKE 'EM SCARED, CAP'N. MAKE 'EM RUN IF THEY SEE HER.
AND I GOT THIS. IN CASE THEY EVER FIND US ON THE ELI REYNOLDS.
HELL, FRAMM, LITTLE THING LIKE THAT AIN'T GONNA HURT JULIAN NONE...
IT AIN'T FOR HIM.
THEY AIN'T TAKIN' ME ALIVE. NOT AGAIN. AND I COULD DO THE SAME FOR YOU, IT CAME TO THAT.
IT AIN'T GONNA COME TO THAT.
AND YOU GO ON TELLIN' THAT STORY. BUT ALWAYS CALL HER BY SOUR BILLY'S NAME. DON'T NEVER CALL HER THE FEVRE DREAM.

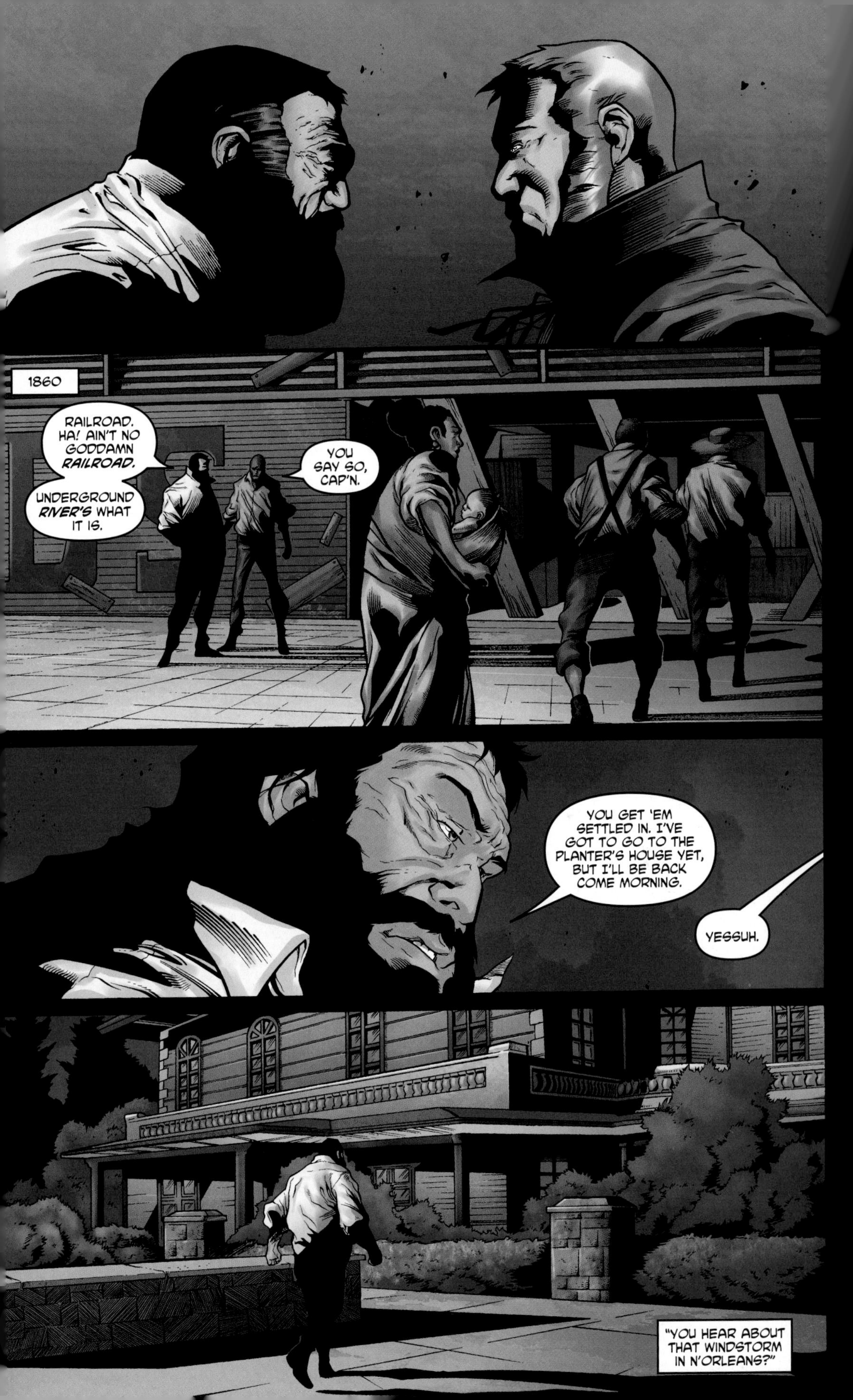
1860
RAILROAD. HA! AIN'T NO GODDAMN RAILROAD.
UNDERGROUND RIVER'S WHAT IT IS.
YOU SAY SO, CAP'N.
YOU GET 'EM SETTLED IN. I'VE GOT TO GO TO THE PLANTER'S HOUSE YET, BUT I'LL BE BACK COME MORNING.
YESSUH.
"YOU HEAR ABOUT THAT WINDSTORM IN N'ORLEANS?"

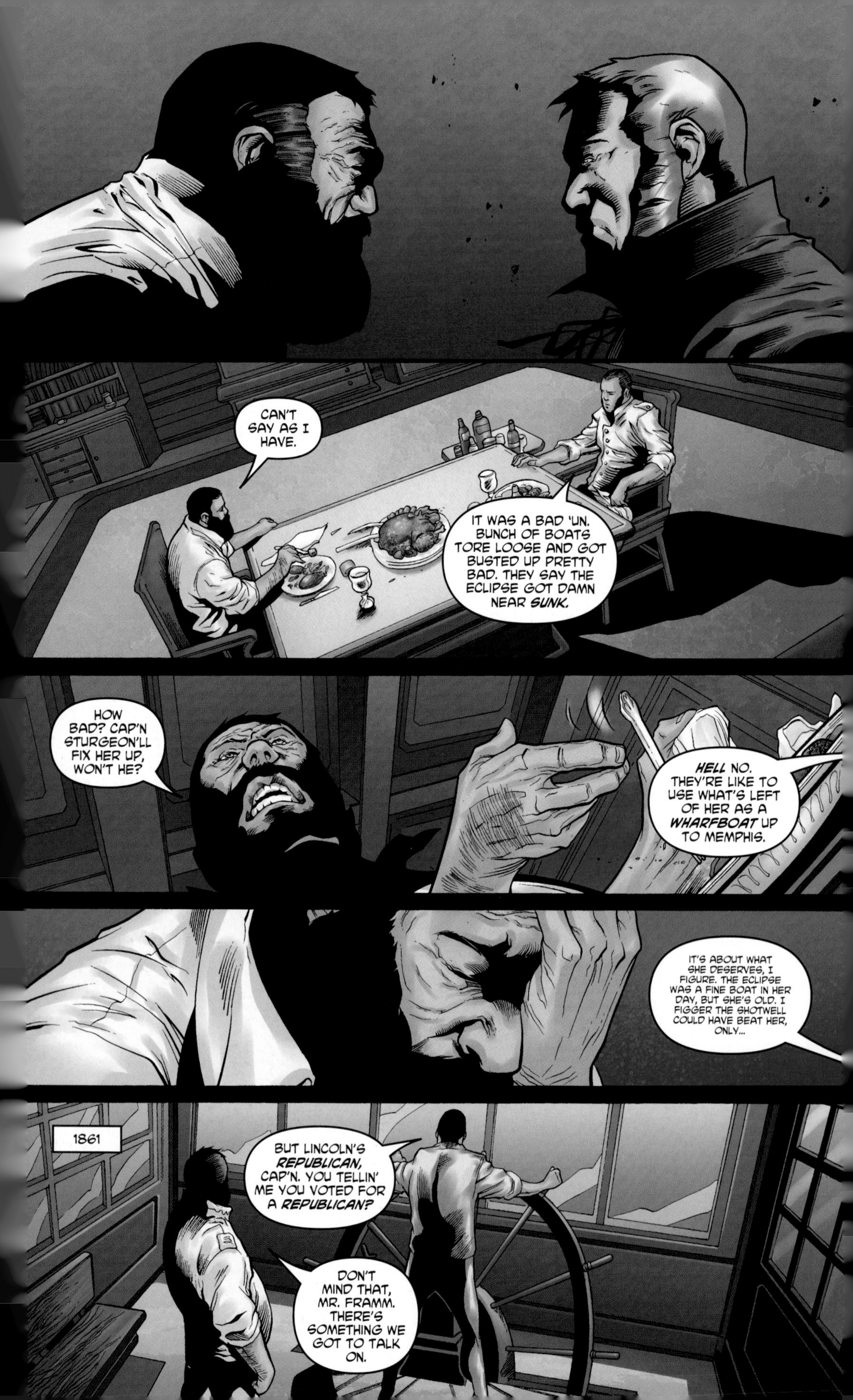
CAN'T SAY AS I HAVE.
IT WAS A BAD 'UN. BUNCH OF BOATS TORE LOOSE AND GOT BUSTED UP PRETTY BAD. THEY SAY THE ECLIPSE GOT DAMN NEAR SUNK.
HOW BAD? CAP'N STURGEON'LL FIX HER UP, WON'T HE?
HELL NO. THEY'RE LIKE TO USE WHAT'S LEFT OF HER AS A WHARFBOAT UP TO MEMPHIS.
IT'S ABOUT WHAT SHE DESERVES, I FIGURE. THE ECLIPSE WAS A FINE BOAT IN HER DAY, BUT SHE'S OLD. I FIGGER THE SHOTWELL COULD HAVE BEAT HER, ONLY...
1861
BUT LINCOLN'S REPUBLICAN, CAP'N. YOU TELLIN' ME YOU VOTED FOR A REPUBLICAN?
DON'T MIND THAT, MR. FRAMM. THERE'S SOMETHING WE GOT TO TALK ON.

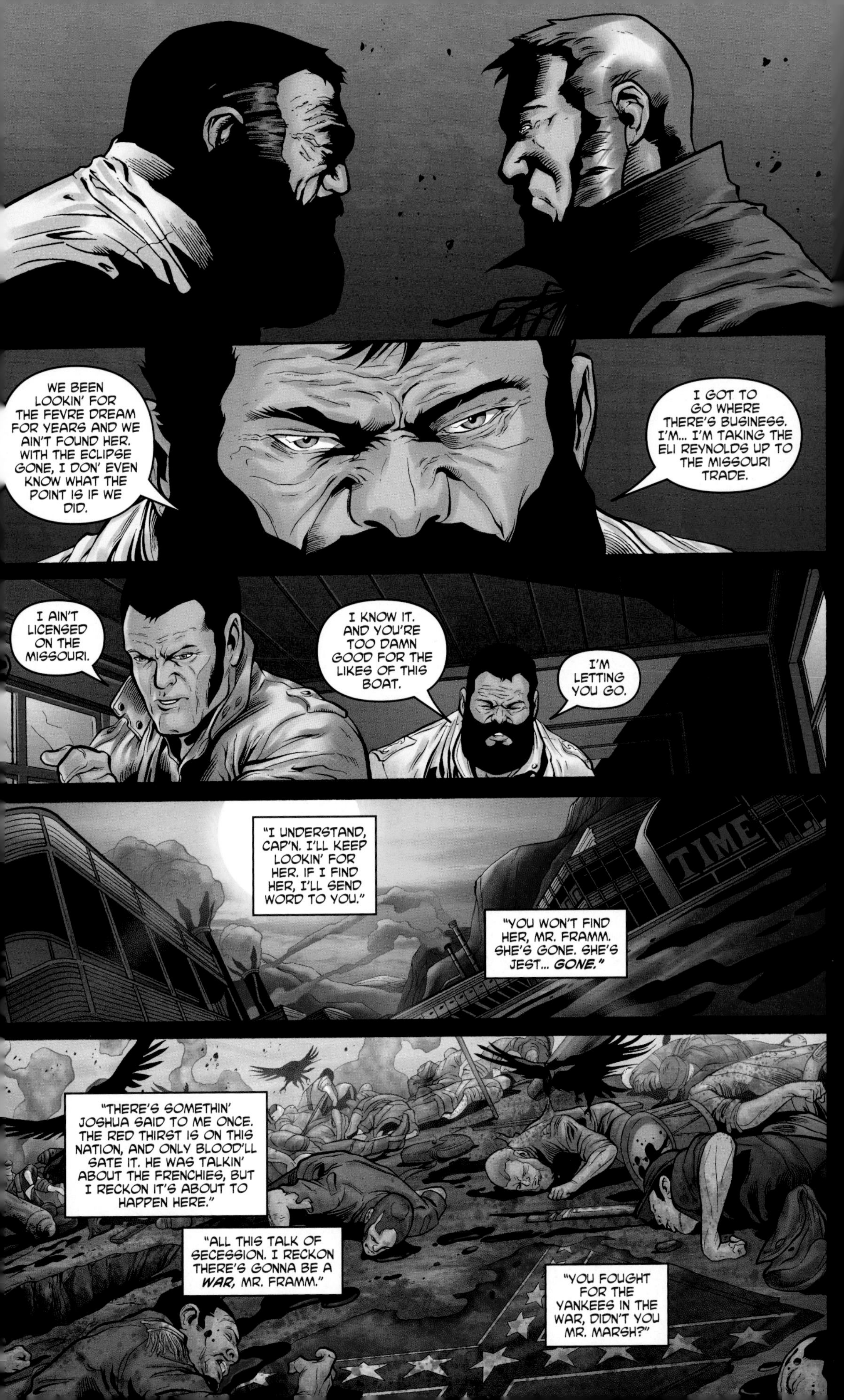
WE BEEN LOOKIN' FOR THE FEVRE DREAM FOR YEARS AND WE AIN'T FOUND HER. WITH THE ECLIPSE GONE, I DON' EVEN KNOW WHAT THE POINT IS IF WE DID.
I GOT TO GO WHERE THERE'S BUSINESS. I'M... I'M TAKING THE ELI REYNOLDS UP TO THE MISSOURI TRADE.
I AIN'T LICENSED ON THE MISSOURI.
I KNOW IT. AND YOU'RE TOO DAMN GOOD FOR THE LIKES OF THIS BOAT.
I'M LETTING YOU GO.
"I UNDERSTAND, CAP'N. I'LL KEEP LOOKIN' FOR HER. IF I FIND HER, I'LL SEND WORD TO YOU."
TIME
"YOU WON'T FIND HER, MR. FRAMM. SHE'S GONE. SHE'S JEST... *GONE.*"
"THERE'S SOMETHIN' JOSHUA SAID TO ME ONCE. THE RED THIRST IS ON THIS NATION, AND ONLY BLOOD'LL SATE IT. HE WAS TALKIN' ABOUT THE FRENCHIES, BUT I RECKON IT'S ABOUT TO HAPPEN HERE."
"ALL THIS TALK OF SECESSION. I RECKON THERE'S GONNA BE A *WAR,* MR. FRAMM."
"YOU FOUGHT FOR THE YANKEES IN THE WAR, DIDN'T YOU MR. MARSH?"

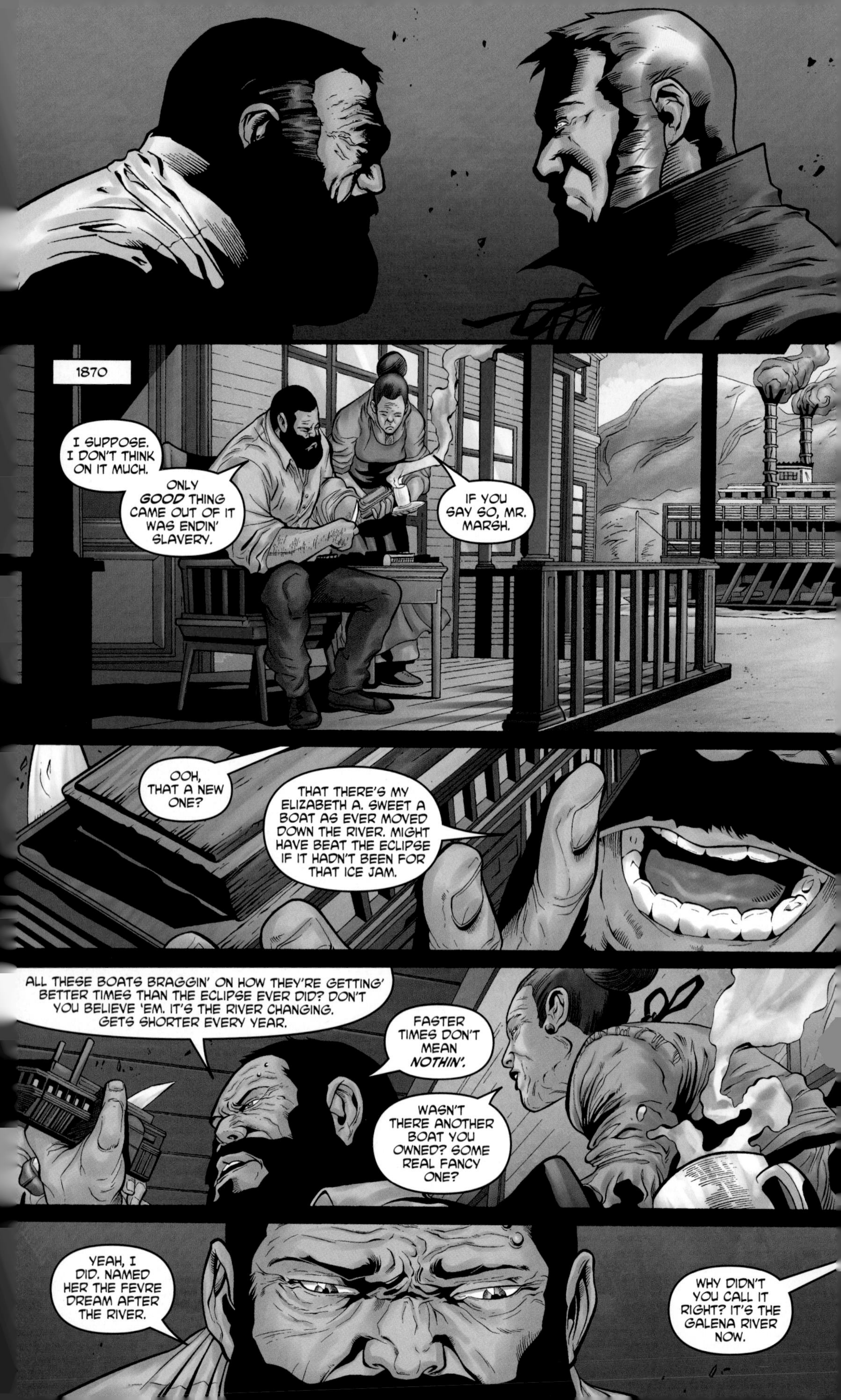
1870
I SUPPOSE. I DON'T THINK ON IT MUCH.
ONLY *GOOD* THING CAME OUT OF IT WAS ENDIN' SLAVERY.
IF YOU SAY SO, MR. MARSH.
OOH, THAT A NEW ONE?
THAT THERE'S MY ELIZABETH A. SWEET A BOAT AS EVER MOVED DOWN THE RIVER. MIGHT HAVE BEAT THE ECLIPSE IF IT HADN'T BEEN FOR THAT ICE JAM.
ALL THESE BOATS BRAGGIN' ON HOW THEY'RE GETTING' BETTER TIMES THAN THE ECLIPSE EVER DID? DON'T YOU BELIEVE 'EM. IT'S THE RIVER CHANGING. GETS SHORTER EVERY YEAR.
FASTER TIMES DON'T MEAN *NOTHIN'*.
WASN'T THERE ANOTHER BOAT YOU OWNED? SOME REAL FANCY ONE?
YEAH, I DID. NAMED HER THE FEVRE DREAM AFTER THE RIVER.
WHY DIDN'T YOU CALL IT RIGHT? IT'S THE GALENA RIVER NOW.

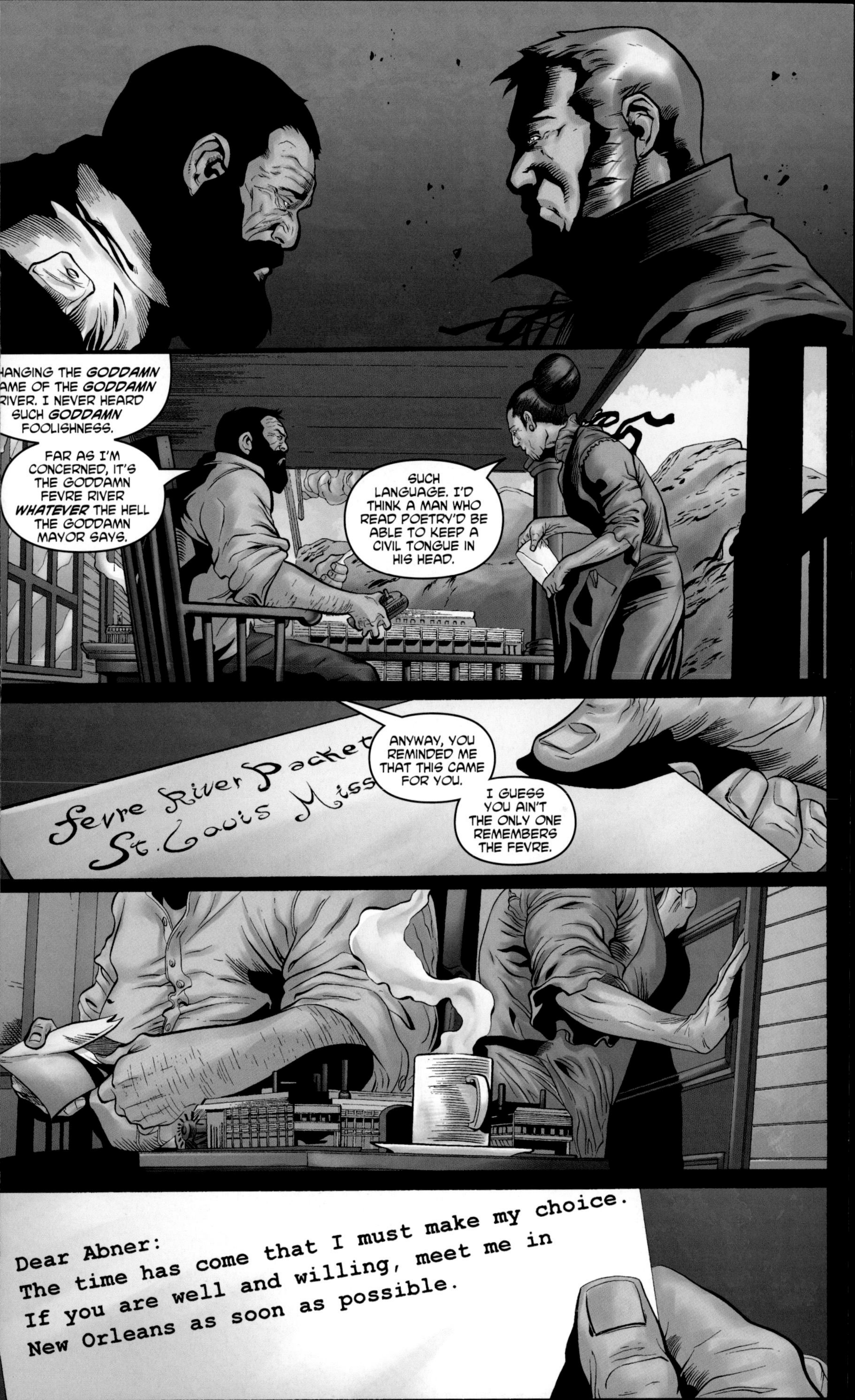

HANGING THE GODDAMN AME OF THE GODDAMN RIVER. I NEVER HEARD SUCH GODDAMN FOOLISHNESS.
FAR AS I'M CONCERNED, IT'S THE GODDAMN FEVRE RIVER WHATEVER THE HELL THE GODDAMN MAYOR SAYS.
SUCH LANGUAGE. I'D THINK A MAN WHO READ POETRY'D BE ABLE TO KEEP A CIVIL TONGUE IN HIS HEAD.
Fevre River Packet
St. Louis Miss
ANYWAY, YOU REMINDED ME THAT THIS CAME FOR YOU.
I GUESS YOU AIN'T THE ONLY ONE REMEMBERS THE FEVRE.
Dear Abner:
The time has come that I must make my choice.
If you are well and willing, meet me in
New Orleans as soon as possible.

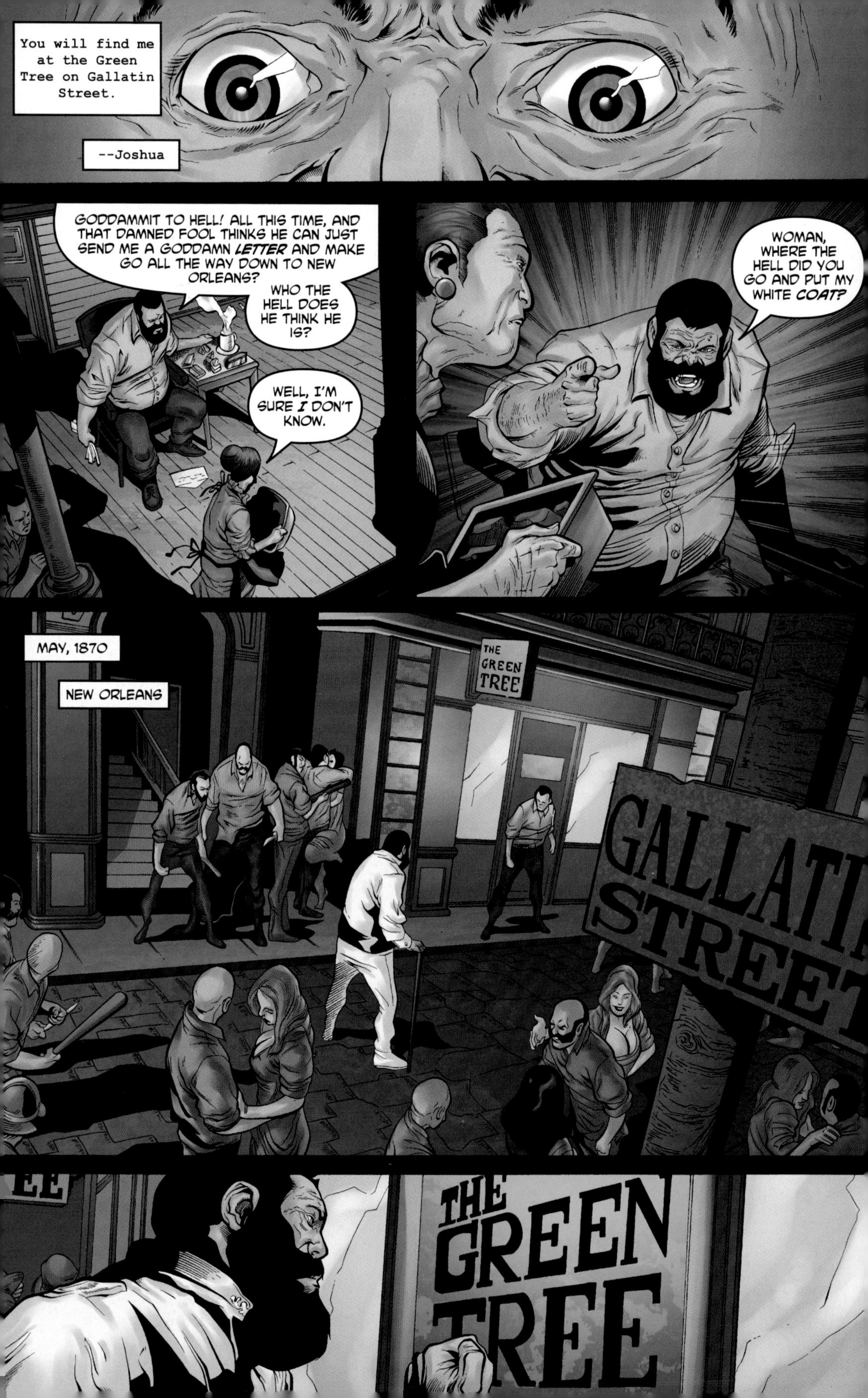
You will find me at the Green Tree on Gallatin Street.
--Joshua
GODDAMMIT TO HELL! ALL THIS TIME, AND THAT DAMNED FOOL THINKS HE CAN JUST SEND ME A GODDAMN LETTER AND MAKE GO ALL THE WAY DOWN TO NEW ORLEANS?
WHO THE HELL DOES HE THINK HE IS?
WELL, I'M SURE I DON'T KNOW.
WOMAN, WHERE THE HELL DID YOU GO AND PUT MY WHITE COAT?
MAY, 1870
NEW ORLEANS
THE GREEN TREE
GALLATI
STREET
THE GREEN TREE

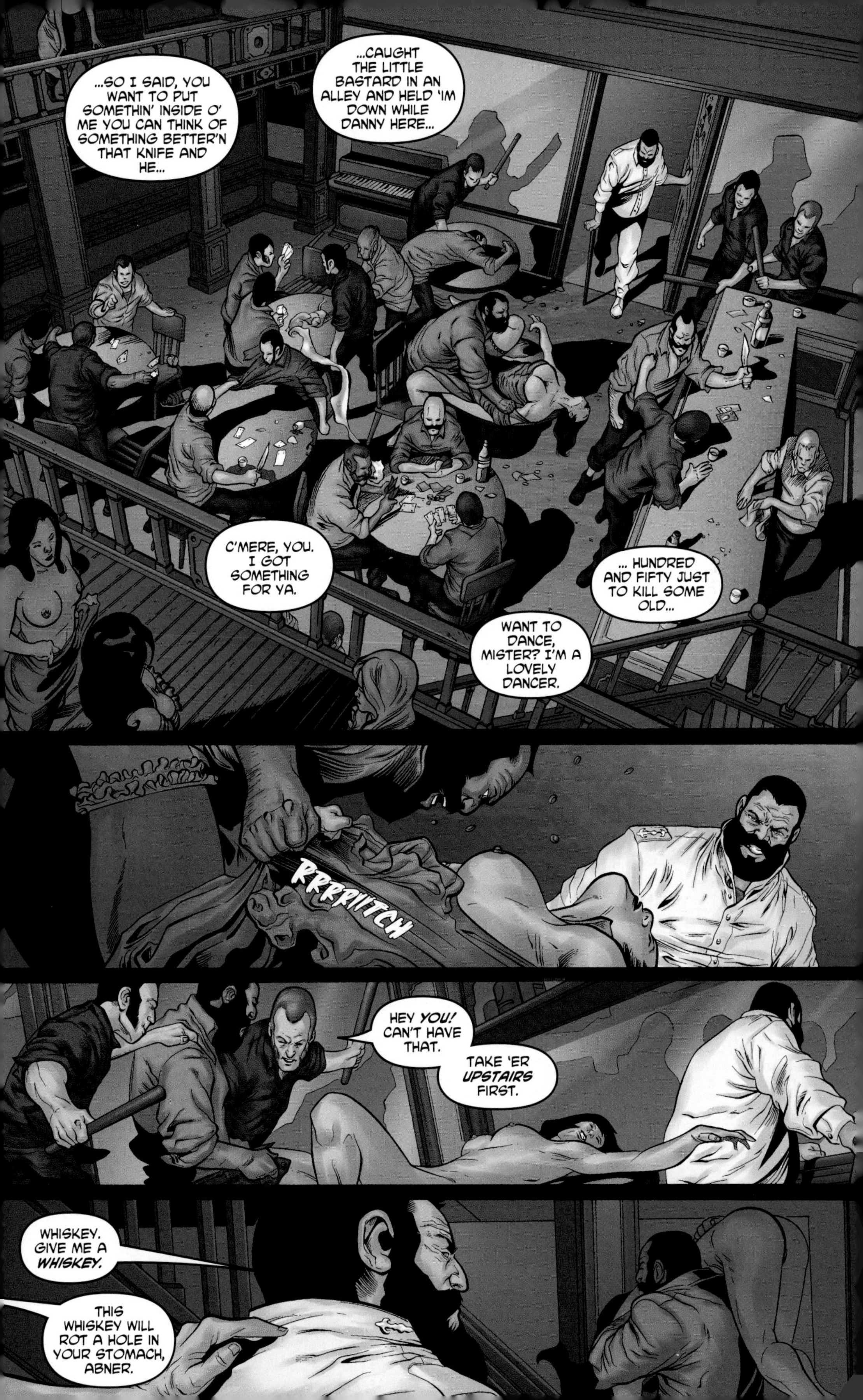
...SO I SAID, YOU WANT TO PUT SOMETHIN' INSIDE O' ME YOU CAN THINK OF SOMETHING BETTER'N THAT KNIFE AND HE...
...CAUGHT THE LITTLE BASTARD IN AN ALLEY AND HELD 'IM DOWN WHILE DANNY HERE...
C'MERE, YOU. I GOT SOMETHING FOR YA.
... HUNDRED AND FIFTY JUST TO KILL SOME OLD...
WANT TO DANCE, MISTER? I'M A LOVELY DANCER.
RRRRIITCH
HEY *YOU!* CAN'T HAVE THAT.
TAKE 'ER *UPSTAIRS* FIRST.
WHISKEY. GIVE ME A *WHISKEY.*
THIS WHISKEY WILL ROT A HOLE IN YOUR STOMACH, ABNER.

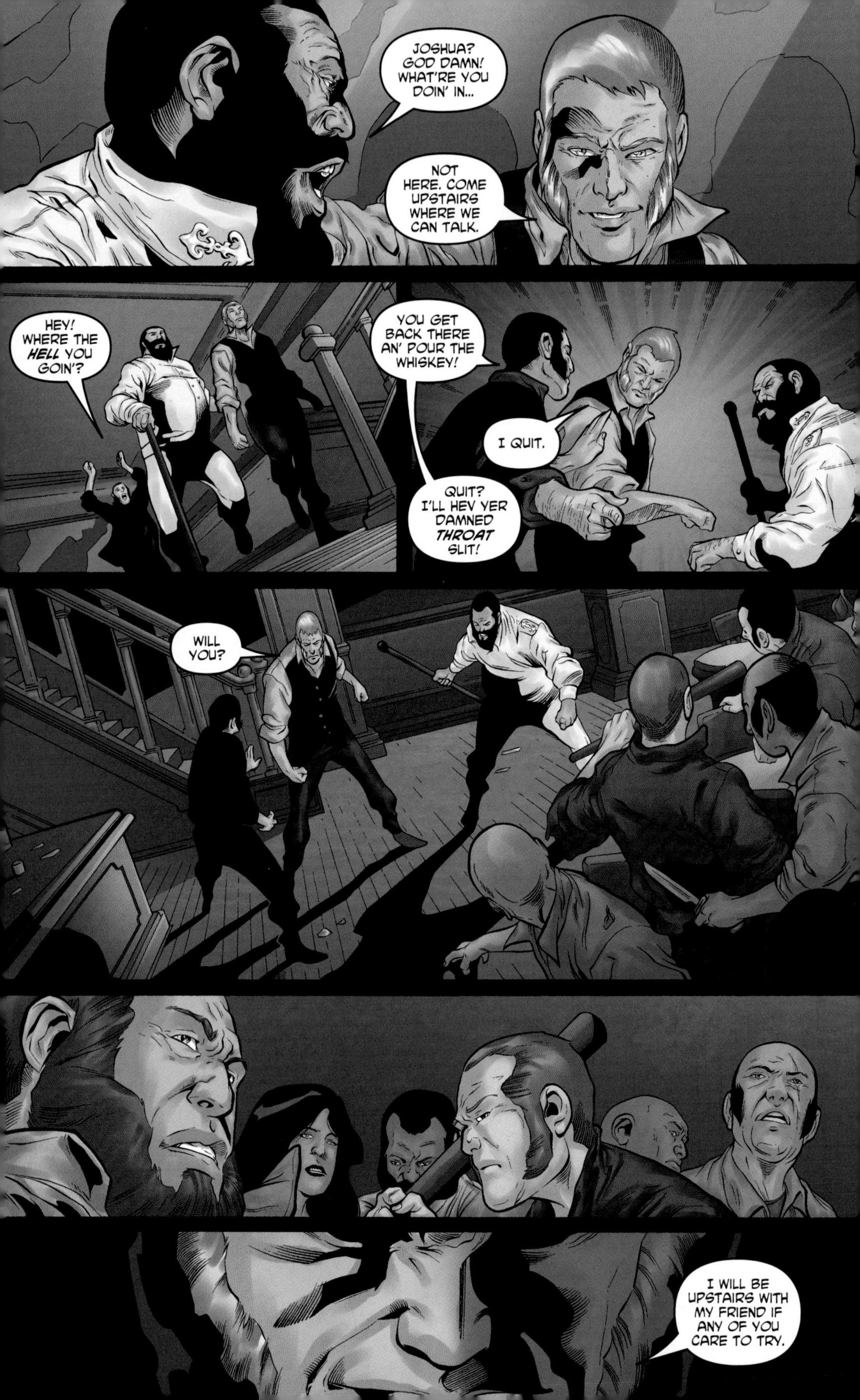
JOSHUA? GOD DAMN! WHAT'RE YOU DOIN' IN...
NOT HERE. COME UPSTAIRS WHERE WE CAN TALK.
HEY! WHERE THE *HELL* YOU GOIN'?
YOU GET BACK THERE AN' POUR THE WHISKEY!
I QUIT.
QUIT? I'LL HEV YER DAMNED *THROAT* SLIT!
WILL YOU?
I WILL BE UPSTAIRS WITH MY FRIEND IF ANY OF YOU CARE TO TRY.

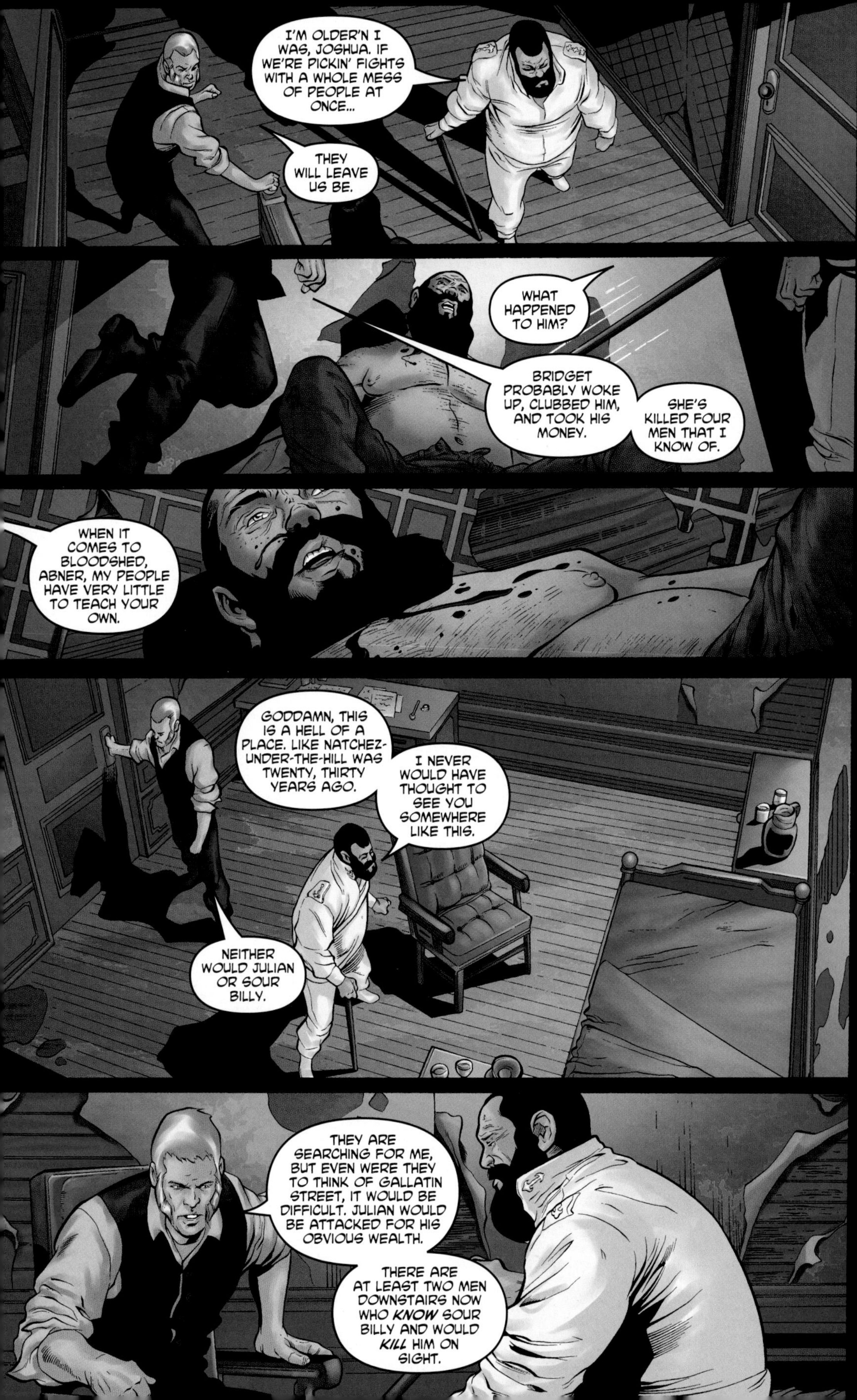
I'M OLDER'N I WAS, JOSHUA. IF WE'RE PICKIN' FIGHTS WITH A WHOLE MESS OF PEOPLE AT ONCE...
THEY WILL LEAVE US BE.
WHAT HAPPENED TO HIM?
BRIDGET PROBABLY WOKE UP, CLUBBED HIM, AND TOOK HIS MONEY.
SHE'S KILLED FOUR MEN THAT I KNOW OF.
WHEN IT COMES TO BLOODSHED, ABNER, MY PEOPLE HAVE VERY LITTLE TO TEACH YOUR OWN.
GODDAMN, THIS IS A HELL OF A PLACE. LIKE NATCHEZ-UNDER-THE-HILL WAS TWENTY, THIRTY YEARS AGO.
I NEVER WOULD HAVE THOUGHT TO SEE YOU SOMEWHERE LIKE THIS.
NEITHER WOULD JULIAN OR SOUR BILLY.
THEY ARE SEARCHING FOR ME, BUT EVEN WERE THEY TO THINK OF GALLATIN STREET, IT WOULD BE DIFFICULT. JULIAN WOULD BE ATTACKED FOR HIS OBVIOUS WEALTH.
THERE ARE AT LEAST TWO MEN DOWNSTAIRS NOW WHO *KNOW* SOUR BILLY AND WOULD *KILL* HIM ON SIGHT.

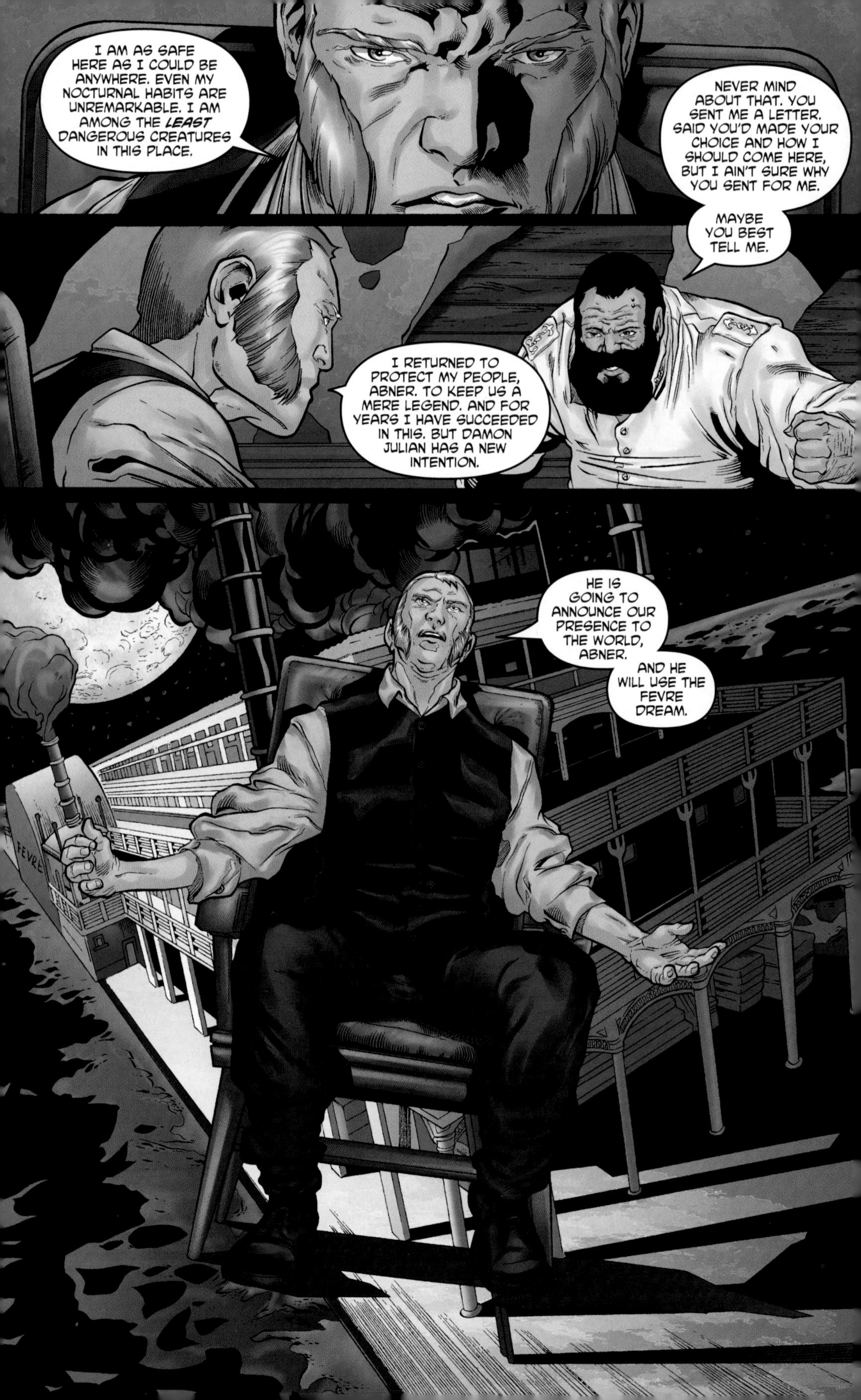
I AM AS SAFE HERE AS I COULD BE ANYWHERE. EVEN MY NOCTURNAL HABITS ARE UNREMARKABLE. I AM AMONG THE *LEAST* DANGEROUS CREATURES IN THIS PLACE.
NEVER MIND ABOUT THAT. YOU SENT ME A LETTER. SAID YOU'D MADE YOUR CHOICE AND HOW I SHOULD COME HERE, BUT I AIN'T SURE WHY YOU SENT FOR ME.
MAYBE YOU BEST TELL ME.
I RETURNED TO PROTECT MY PEOPLE, ABNER. TO KEEP US A MERE LEGEND. AND FOR YEARS I HAVE SUCCEEDED IN THIS. BUT DAMON JULIAN HAS A NEW INTENTION.
HE IS GOING TO ANNOUNCE OUR PRESENCE TO THE WORLD, ABNER.
AND HE WILL USE THE FEVRE DREAM.
FEVRE

CHAPTER 10

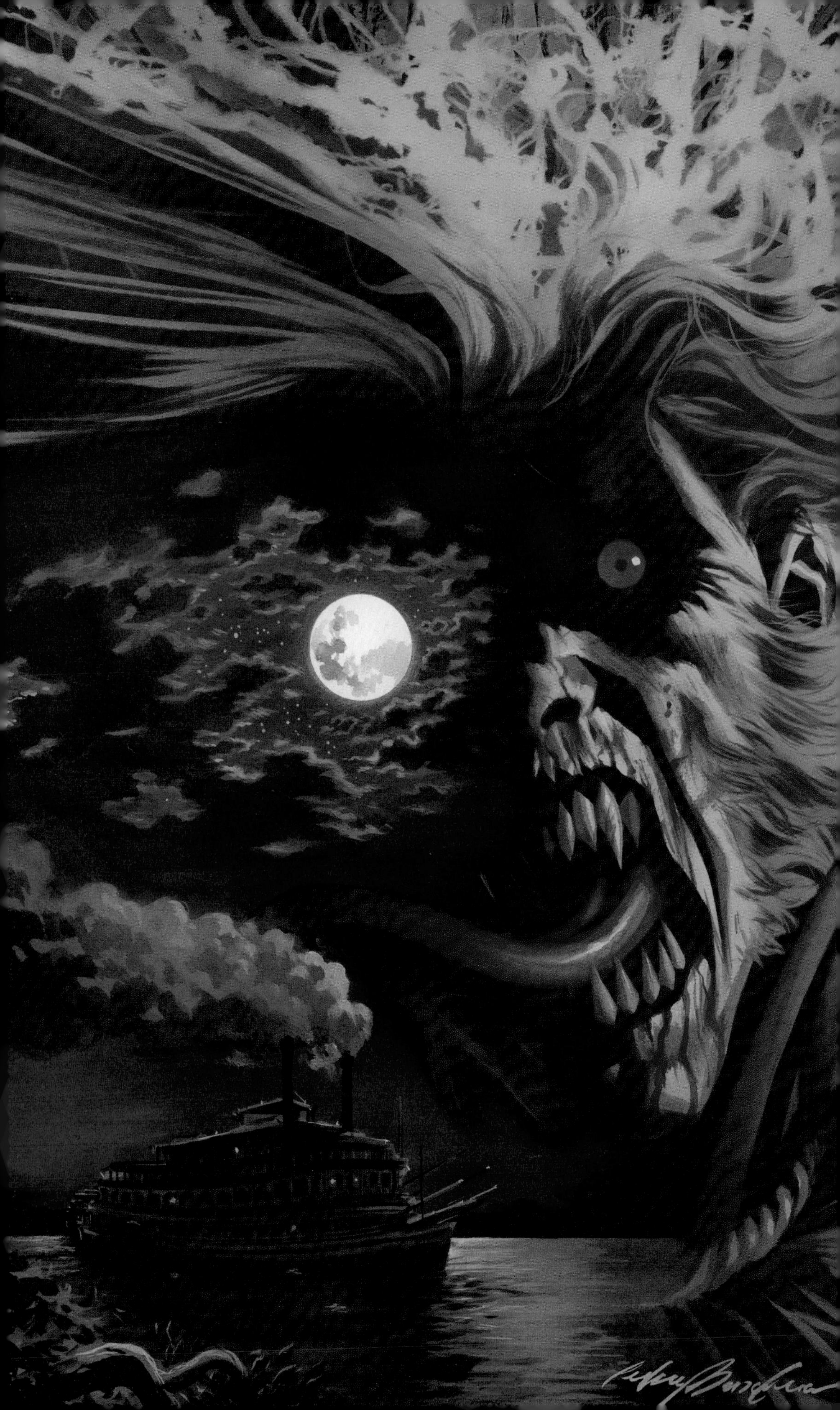

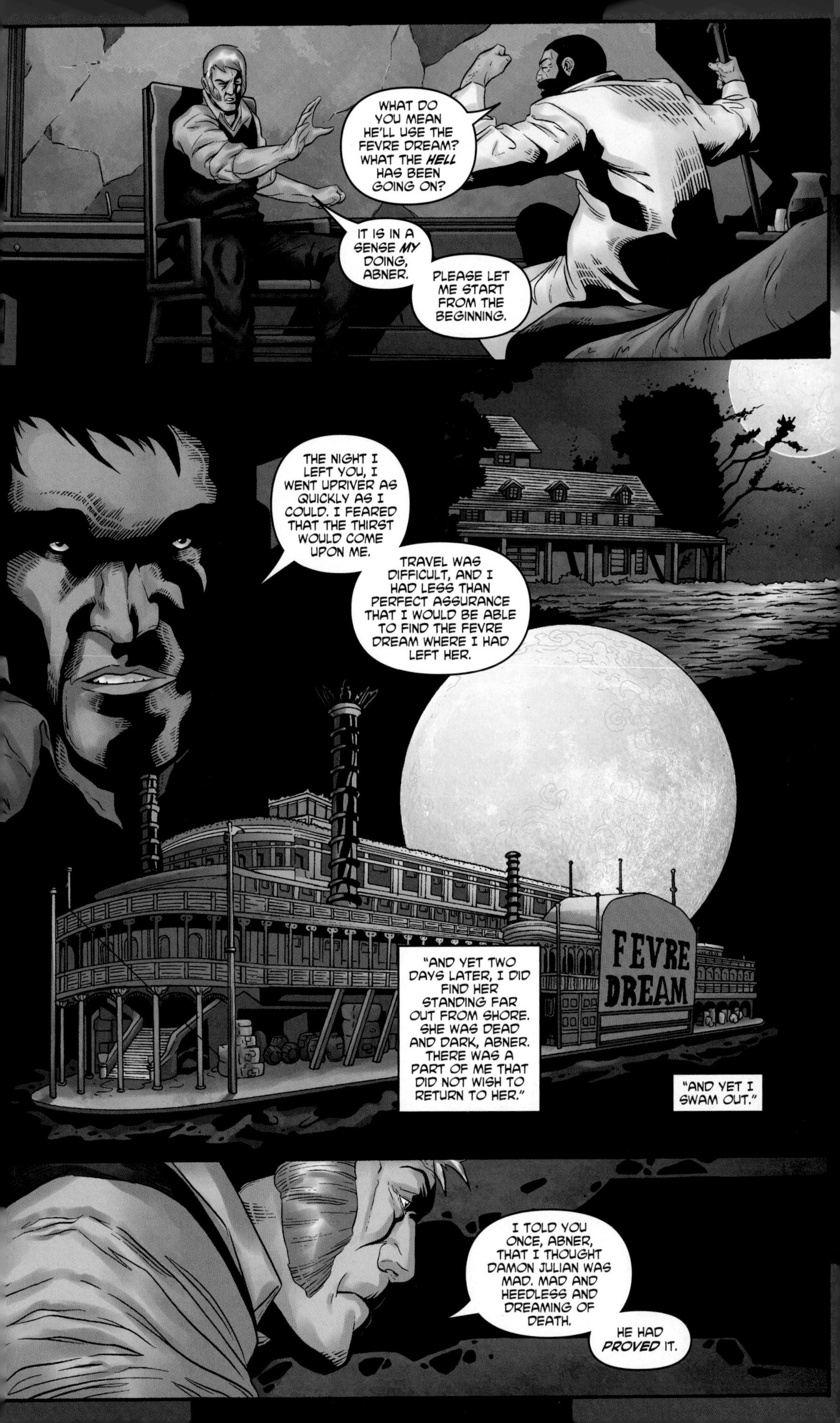
WHAT DO YOU MEAN HE'LL USE THE FEVRE DREAM? WHAT THE *HELL* HAS BEEN GOING ON?
IT IS IN A SENSE *MY* DOING, ABNER.
PLEASE LET ME START FROM THE BEGINNING.
THE NIGHT I LEFT YOU, I WENT UPRIVER AS QUICKLY AS I COULD. I FEARED THAT THE THIRST WOULD COME UPON ME.
TRAVEL WAS DIFFICULT, AND I HAD LESS THAN PERFECT ASSURANCE THAT I WOULD BE ABLE TO FIND THE FEVRE DREAM WHERE I HAD LEFT HER.
FEVRE DREAM
"AND YET TWO DAYS LATER, I DID FIND HER STANDING FAR OUT FROM SHORE. SHE WAS DEAD AND DARK, ABNER. THERE WAS A PART OF ME THAT DID NOT WISH TO RETURN TO HER."
"AND YET I SWAM OUT."
I TOLD YOU ONCE, ABNER, THAT I THOUGHT DAMON JULIAN WAS MAD. MAD AND HEEDLESS AND DREAMING OF DEATH.
HE HAD *PROVED* IT.

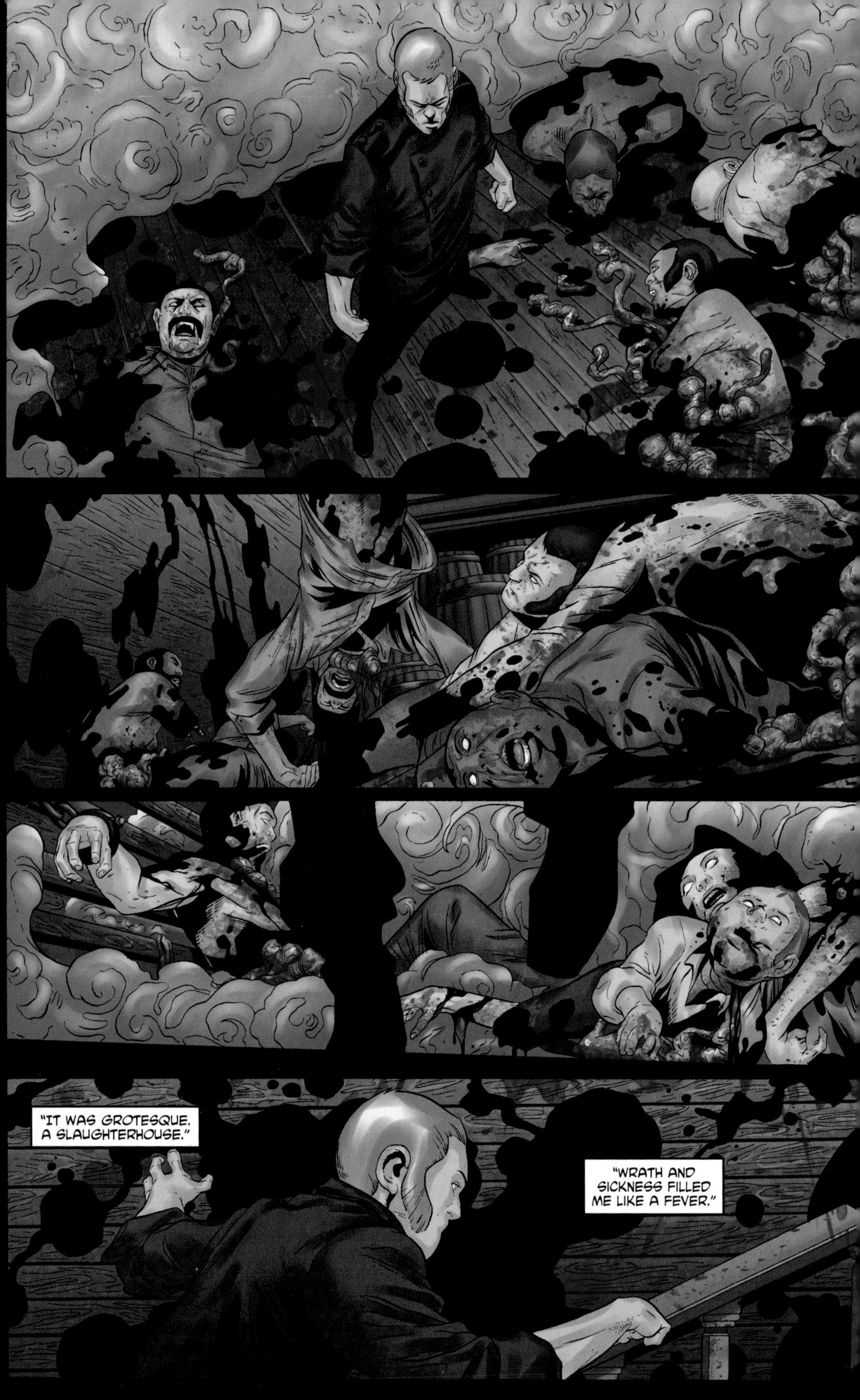
"IT WAS GROTESQUE. A SLAUGHTERHOUSE."
"WRATH AND SICKNESS FILLED ME LIKE A FEVER."

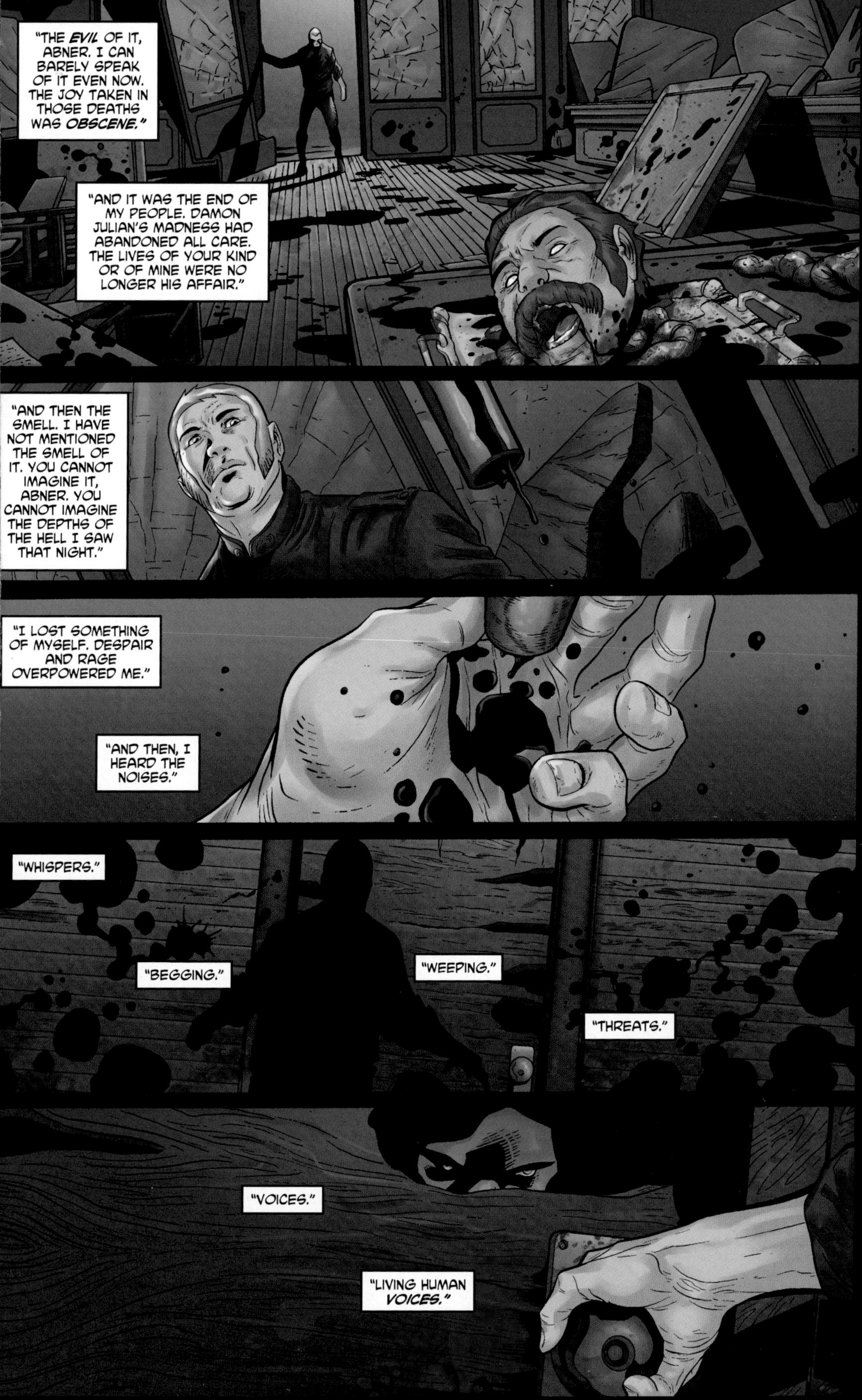
"THE EVIL OF IT, ABNER. I CAN BARELY SPEAK OF IT EVEN NOW. THE JOY TAKEN IN THOSE DEATHS WAS OBSCENE."
"AND IT WAS THE END OF MY PEOPLE. DAMON JULIAN'S MADNESS HAD ABANDONED ALL CARE. THE LIVES OF YOUR KIND OR OF MINE WERE NO LONGER HIS AFFAIR."
"AND THEN THE SMELL. I HAVE NOT MENTIONED THE SMELL OF IT. YOU CANNOT IMAGINE IT, ABNER. YOU CANNOT IMAGINE THE DEPTHS OF THE HELL I SAW THAT NIGHT."
"I LOST SOMETHING OF MYSELF. DESPAIR AND RAGE OVERPOWERED ME."
"AND THEN, I HEARD THE NOISES."
"WHISPERS."
"BEGGING."
"WEEPING."
"THREATS."
"VOICES."
"LIVING HUMAN VOICES."

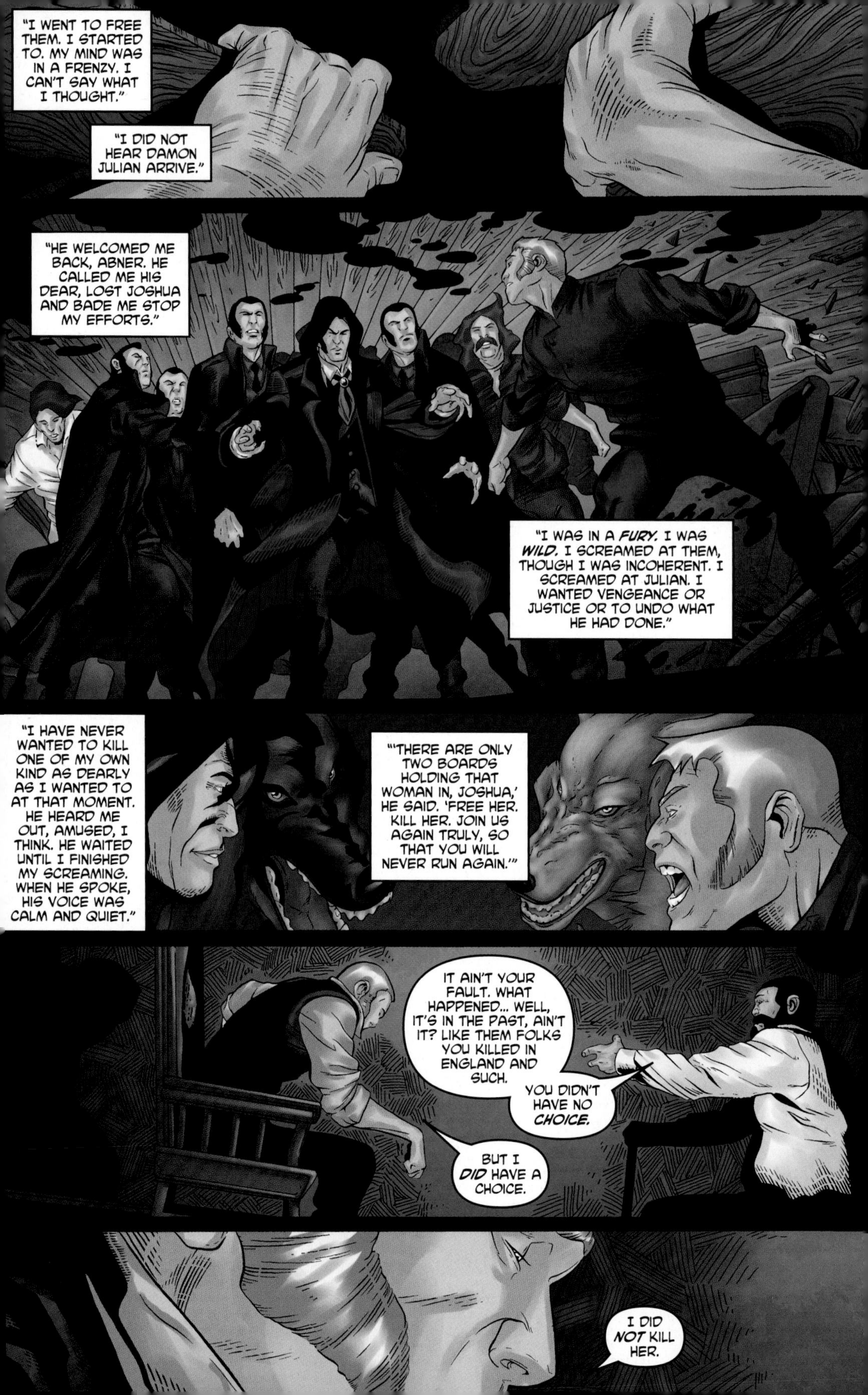
"I WENT TO FREE THEM. I STARTED TO. MY MIND WAS IN A FRENZY. I CAN'T SAY WHAT I THOUGHT."
"I DID NOT HEAR DAMON JULIAN ARRIVE."
"HE WELCOMED ME BACK, ABNER. HE CALLED ME HIS DEAR, LOST JOSHUA AND BADE ME STOP MY EFFORTS."
"I WAS IN A FURY. I WAS WILD. I SCREAMED AT THEM, THOUGH I WAS INCOHERENT. I SCREAMED AT JULIAN. I WANTED VENGEANCE OR JUSTICE OR TO UNDO WHAT HE HAD DONE."
"I HAVE NEVER WANTED TO KILL ONE OF MY OWN KIND AS DEARLY AS I WANTED TO AT THAT MOMENT. HE HEARD ME OUT, AMUSED, I THINK. HE WAITED UNTIL I FINISHED MY SCREAMING. WHEN HE SPOKE, HIS VOICE WAS CALM AND QUIET."
"'THERE ARE ONLY TWO BOARDS HOLDING THAT WOMAN IN, JOSHUA,' HE SAID. 'FREE HER. KILL HER. JOIN US AGAIN TRULY, SO THAT YOU WILL NEVER RUN AGAIN.'"
IT AIN'T YOUR FAULT. WHAT HAPPENED... WELL, IT'S IN THE PAST, AIN'T IT? LIKE THEM FOLKS YOU KILLED IN ENGLAND AND SUCH.
YOU DIDN'T HAVE NO CHOICE.
BUT I DID HAVE A CHOICE.
I DID NOT KILL HER.

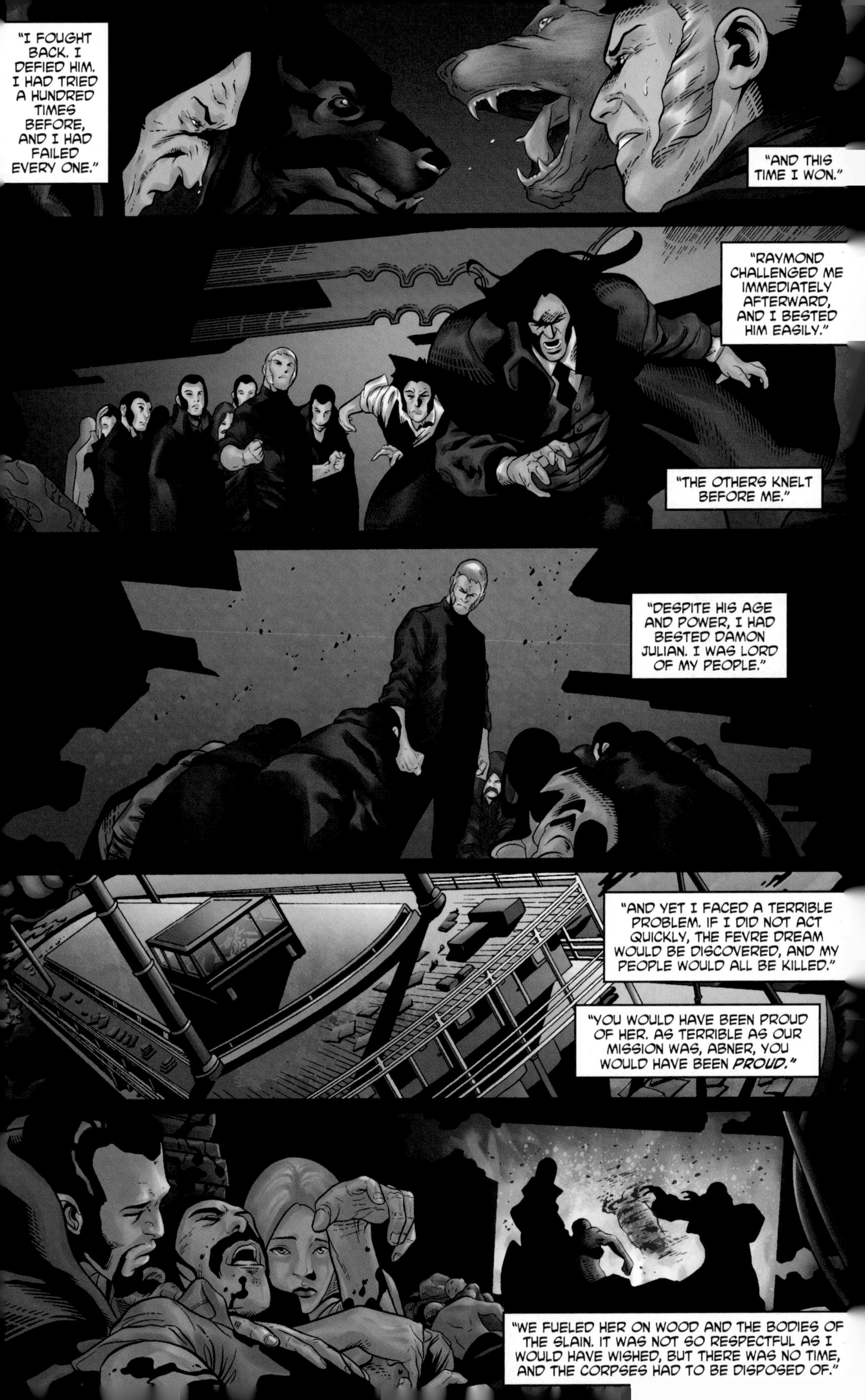
"I FOUGHT BACK. I DEFIED HIM. I HAD TRIED A HUNDRED TIMES BEFORE, AND I HAD FAILED EVERY ONE."
"AND THIS TIME I WON."
"RAYMOND CHALLENGED ME IMMEDIATELY AFTERWARD, AND I BESTED HIM EASILY."
"THE OTHERS KNELT BEFORE ME."
"DESPITE HIS AGE AND POWER, I HAD BESTED DAMON JULIAN. I WAS LORD OF MY PEOPLE."
"AND YET I FACED A TERRIBLE PROBLEM. IF I DID NOT ACT QUICKLY, THE FEVRE DREAM WOULD BE DISCOVERED, AND MY PEOPLE WOULD ALL BE KILLED."
"YOU WOULD HAVE BEEN PROUD OF HER. AS TERRIBLE AS OUR MISSION WAS, ABNER, YOU WOULD HAVE BEEN *PROUD.*"
"WE FUELED HER ON WOOD AND THE BODIES OF THE SLAIN. IT WAS NOT SO RESPECTFUL AS I WOULD HAVE WISHED, BUT THERE WAS NO TIME, AND THE CORPSES HAD TO BE DISPOSED OF."

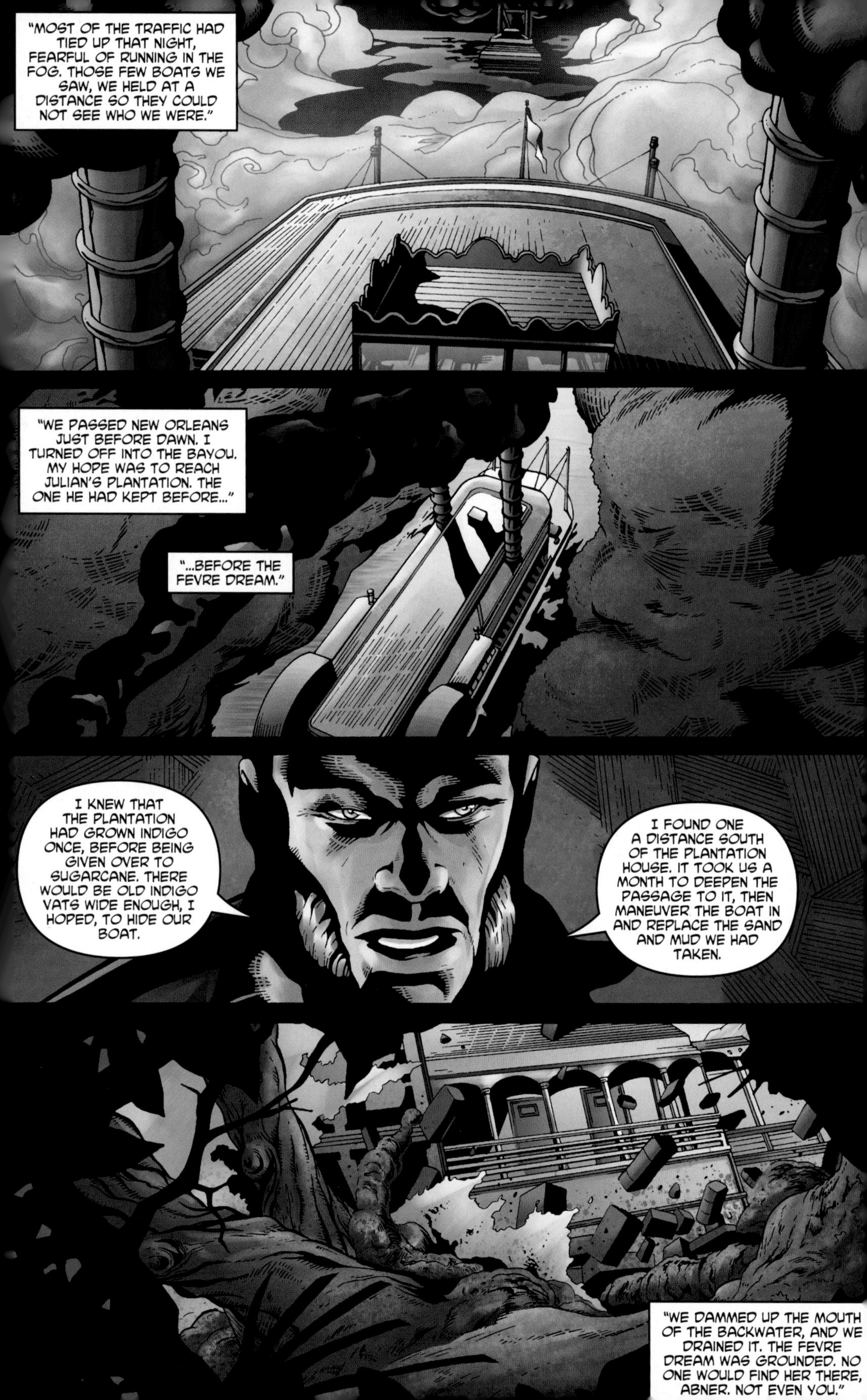
"MOST OF THE TRAFFIC HAD TIED UP THAT NIGHT, FEARFUL OF RUNNING IN THE FOG. THOSE FEW BOATS WE SAW, WE HELD AT A DISTANCE SO THEY COULD NOT SEE WHO WE WERE."
"WE PASSED NEW ORLEANS JUST BEFORE DAWN. I TURNED OFF INTO THE BAYOU. MY HOPE WAS TO REACH JULIAN'S PLANTATION. THE ONE HE HAD KEPT BEFORE..."
"...BEFORE THE FEVRE DREAM."
I KNEW THAT THE PLANTATION HAD GROWN INDIGO ONCE, BEFORE BEING GIVEN OVER TO SUGARCANE. THERE WOULD BE OLD INDIGO VATS WIDE ENOUGH, I HOPED, TO HIDE OUR BOAT.
I FOUND ONE A DISTANCE SOUTH OF THE PLANTATION HOUSE. IT TOOK US A MONTH TO DEEPEN THE PASSAGE TO IT, THEN MANEUVER THE BOAT IN AND REPLACE THE SAND AND MUD WE HAD TAKEN.
"WE DAMMED UP THE MOUTH OF THE BACKWATER, AND WE DRAINED IT. THE FEVRE DREAM WAS GROUNDED. NO ONE WOULD FIND HER THERE, ABNER. NOT EVEN YOU."

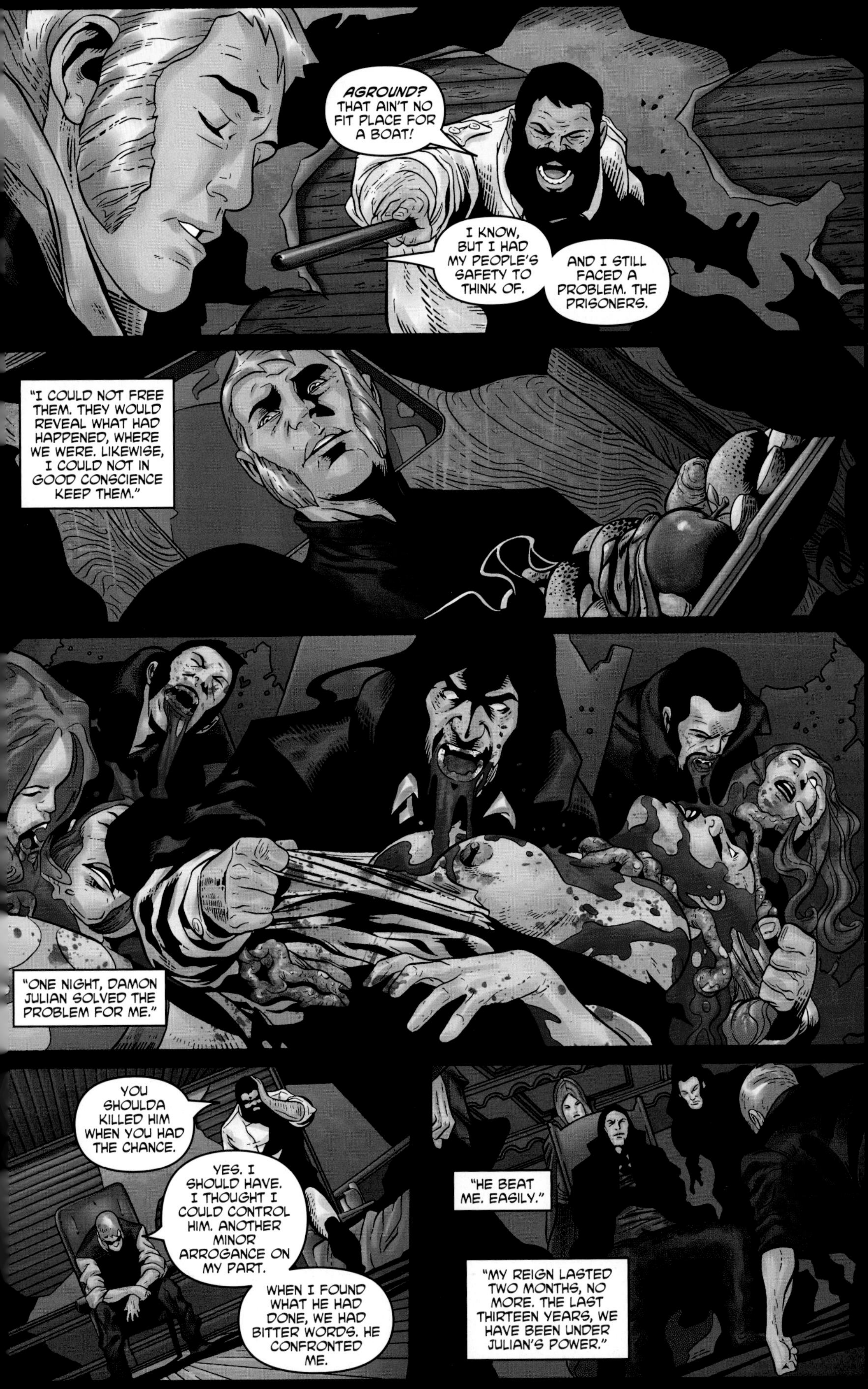

AGROUND? THAT AIN'T NO FIT PLACE FOR A BOAT!
I KNOW, BUT I HAD MY PEOPLE'S SAFETY TO THINK OF.
AND I STILL FACED A PROBLEM. THE PRISONERS.
"I COULD NOT FREE THEM. THEY WOULD REVEAL WHAT HAD HAPPENED, WHERE WE WERE. LIKEWISE, I COULD NOT IN GOOD CONSCIENCE KEEP THEM."
"ONE NIGHT, DAMON JULIAN SOLVED THE PROBLEM FOR ME."
YOU SHOULDA KILLED HIM WHEN YOU HAD THE CHANCE.
YES. I SHOULD HAVE. I THOUGHT I COULD CONTROL HIM. ANOTHER MINOR ARROGANCE ON MY PART.
WHEN I FOUND WHAT HE HAD DONE, WE HAD BITTER WORDS. HE CONFRONTED ME.
"HE BEAT ME. EASILY."
"MY REIGN LASTED TWO MONTHS, NO MORE. THE LAST THIRTEEN YEARS, WE HAVE BEEN UNDER JULIAN'S POWER."

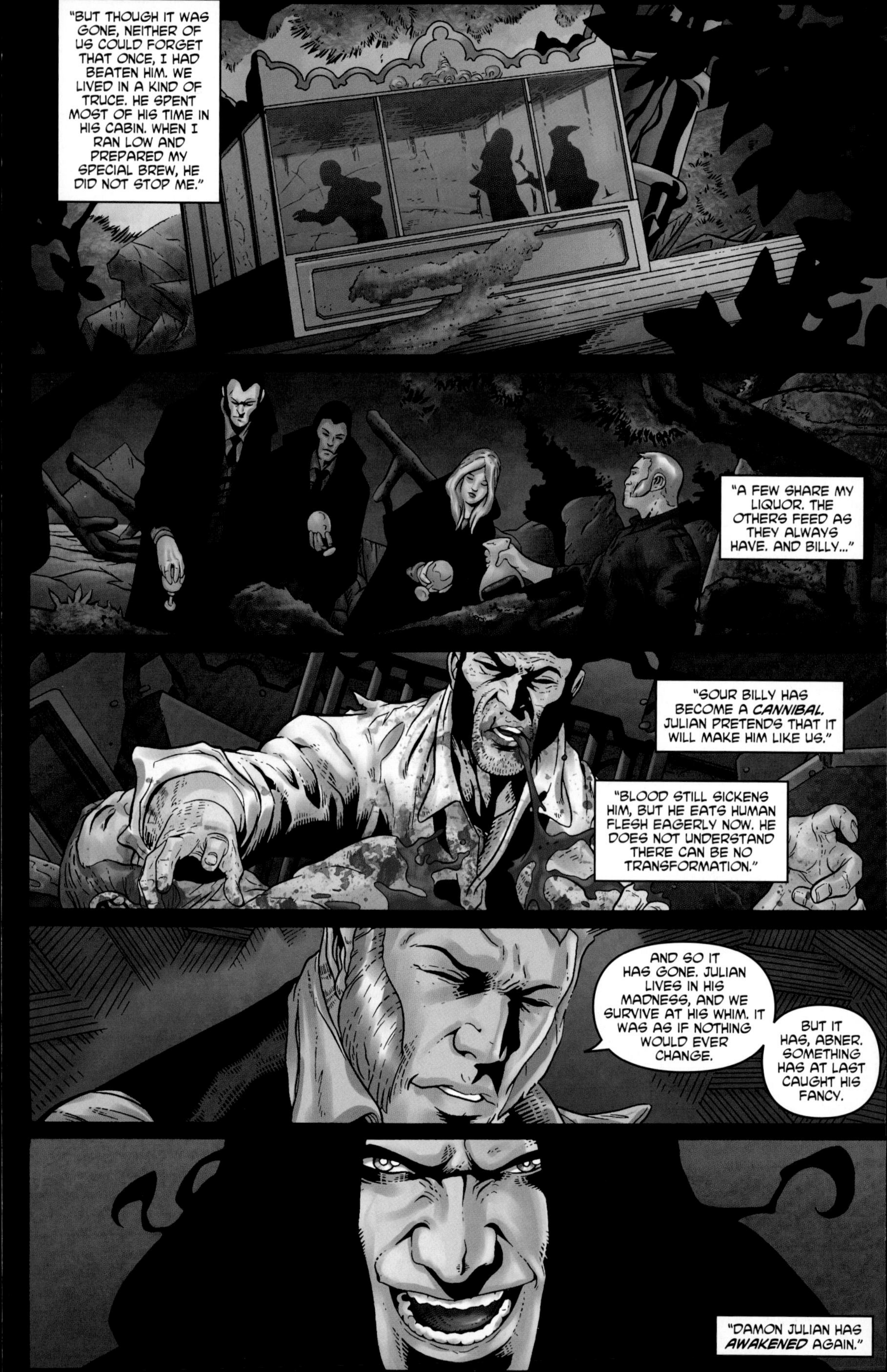
"BUT THOUGH IT WAS GONE, NEITHER OF US COULD FORGET THAT ONCE, I HAD BEATEN HIM. WE LIVED IN A KIND OF TRUCE. HE SPENT MOST OF HIS TIME IN HIS CABIN. WHEN I RAN LOW AND PREPARED MY SPECIAL BREW, HE DID NOT STOP ME."
"A FEW SHARE MY LIQUOR. THE OTHERS FEED AS THEY ALWAYS HAVE. AND BILLY..."
"SOUR BILLY HAS BECOME A *CANNIBAL.* JULIAN PRETENDS THAT IT WILL MAKE HIM LIKE US."
"BLOOD STILL SICKENS HIM, BUT HE EATS HUMAN FLESH EAGERLY NOW. HE DOES NOT UNDERSTAND THERE CAN BE NO TRANSFORMATION."
AND SO IT HAS GONE. JULIAN LIVES IN HIS MADNESS, AND WE SURVIVE AT HIS WHIM. IT WAS AS IF NOTHING WOULD EVER CHANGE.
BUT IT HAS, ABNER. SOMETHING HAS AT LAST CAUGHT HIS FANCY.
"DAMON JULIAN HAS *AWAKENED* AGAIN."

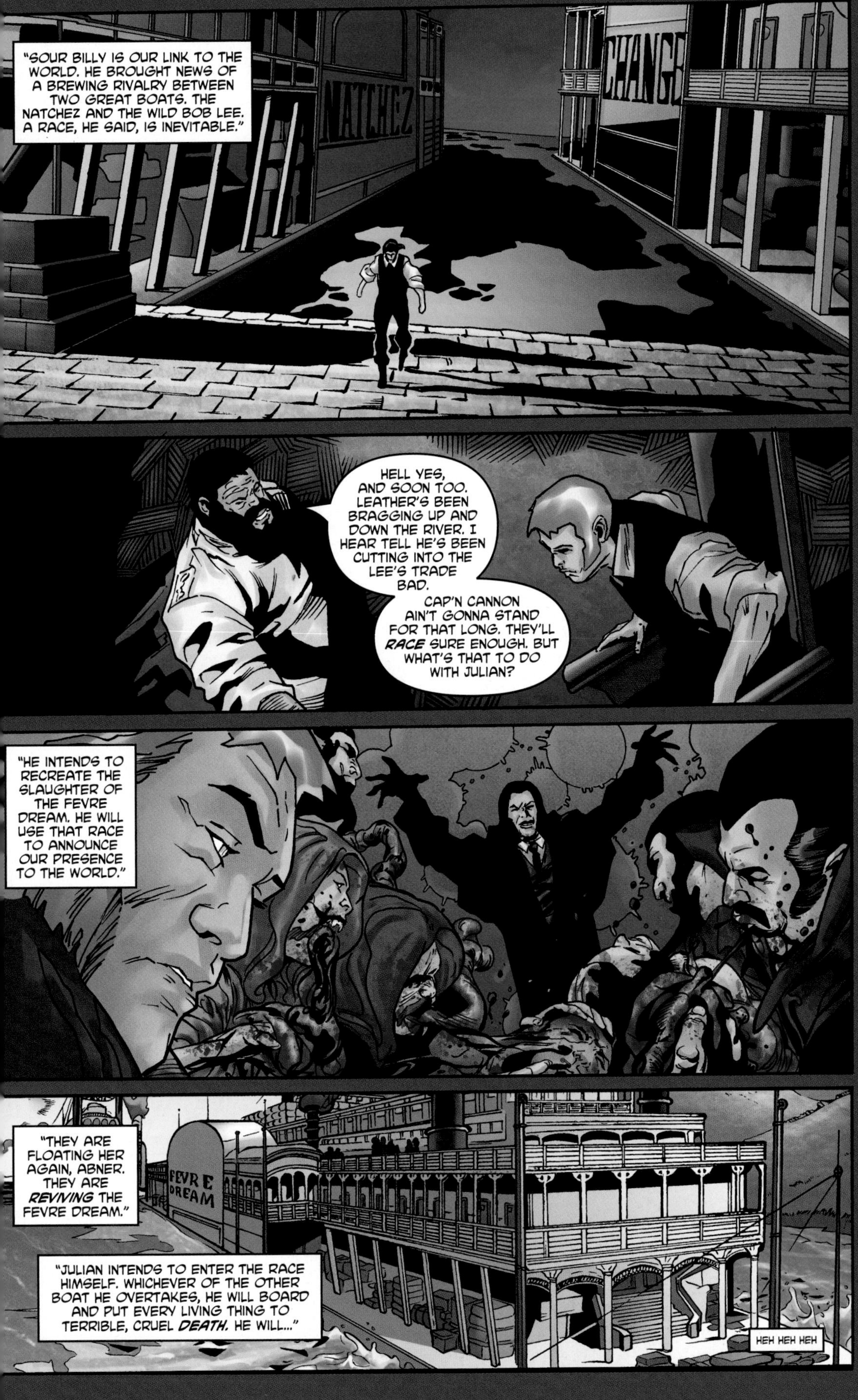
"SOUR BILLY IS OUR LINK TO THE WORLD. HE BROUGHT NEWS OF A BREWING RIVALRY BETWEEN TWO GREAT BOATS. THE NATCHEZ AND THE WILD BOB LEE. A RACE, HE SAID, IS INEVITABLE."
NATCHEZ
CHANGE
HELL YES, AND SOON TOO. LEATHER'S BEEN BRAGGING UP AND DOWN THE RIVER. I HEAR TELL HE'S BEEN CUTTING INTO THE LEE'S TRADE BAD.
CAP'N CANNON AIN'T GONNA STAND FOR THAT LONG. THEY'LL *RACE* SURE ENOUGH. BUT WHAT'S THAT TO DO WITH JULIAN?
"HE INTENDS TO RECREATE THE SLAUGHTER OF THE FEVRE DREAM. HE WILL USE THAT RACE TO ANNOUNCE OUR PRESENCE TO THE WORLD."
"THEY ARE FLOATING HER AGAIN, ABNER. THEY ARE *REVIVING* THE FEVRE DREAM."
FEVRE DREAM
"JULIAN INTENDS TO ENTER THE RACE HIMSELF. WHICHEVER OF THE OTHER BOAT HE OVERTAKES, HE WILL BOARD AND PUT EVERY LIVING THING TO TERRIBLE, CRUEL *DEATH.* HE WILL..."
HEH HEH HEH

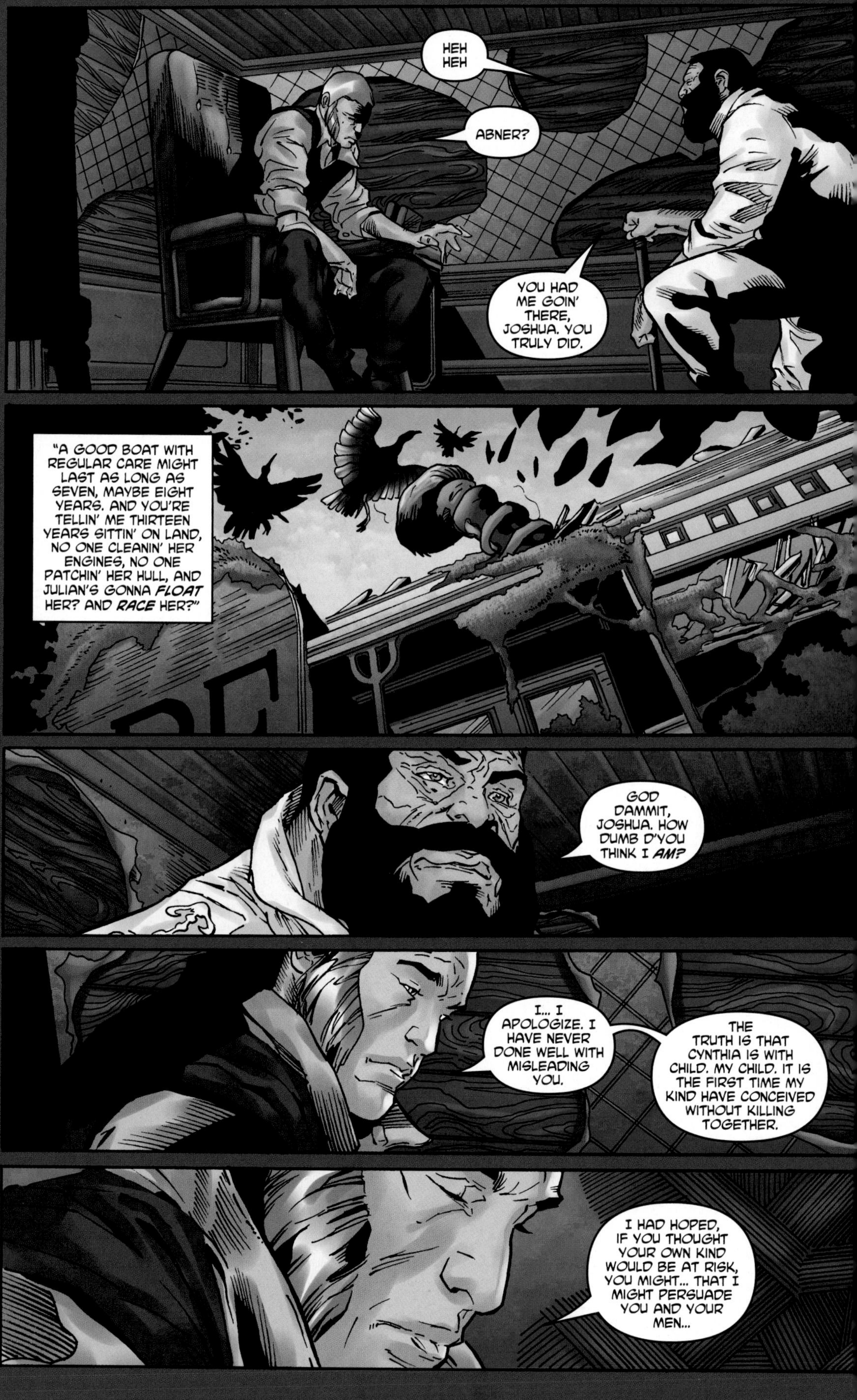
HEH HEH
ABNER?
YOU HAD ME GOIN' THERE, JOSHUA. YOU TRULY DID.
"A GOOD BOAT WITH REGULAR CARE MIGHT LAST AS LONG AS SEVEN, MAYBE EIGHT YEARS. AND YOU'RE TELLIN' ME THIRTEEN YEARS SITTIN' ON LAND, NO ONE CLEANIN' HER ENGINES, NO ONE PATCHIN' HER HULL, AND JULIAN'S GONNA *FLOAT* HER? AND *RACE* HER?"
GOD DAMMIT, JOSHUA. HOW DUMB D'YOU THINK I *AM?*
I... I APOLOGIZE. I HAVE NEVER DONE WELL WITH MISLEADING YOU.
THE TRUTH IS THAT CYNTHIA IS WITH CHILD. MY CHILD. IT IS THE FIRST TIME MY KIND HAVE CONCEIVED WITHOUT KILLING TOGETHER.
I HAD HOPED, IF YOU THOUGHT YOUR OWN KIND WOULD BE AT RISK, YOU MIGHT... THAT I MIGHT PERSUADE YOU AND YOUR MEN...

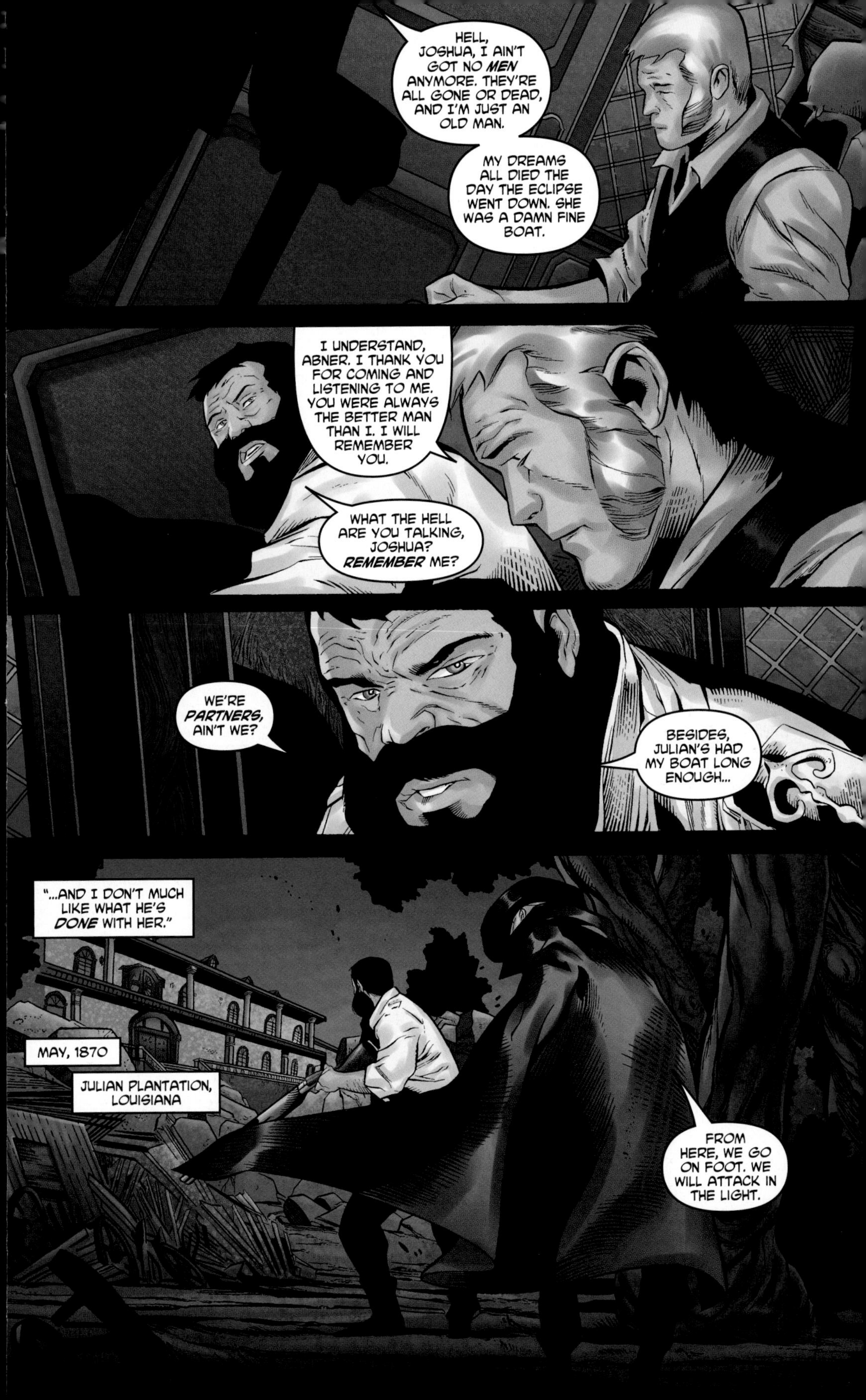
HELL, JOSHUA, I AIN'T GOT NO *MEN* ANYMORE. THEY'RE ALL GONE OR DEAD, AND I'M JUST AN OLD MAN.
MY DREAMS ALL DIED THE DAY THE ECLIPSE WENT DOWN. SHE WAS A DAMN FINE BOAT.
I UNDERSTAND, ABNER. I THANK YOU FOR COMING AND LISTENING TO ME. YOU WERE ALWAYS THE BETTER MAN THAN I. I WILL REMEMBER YOU.
WHAT THE HELL ARE YOU TALKING, JOSHUA? *REMEMBER* ME?
WE'RE *PARTNERS,* AIN'T WE?
BESIDES, JULIAN'S HAD MY BOAT LONG ENOUGH...
"...AND I DON'T MUCH LIKE WHAT HE'S *DONE* WITH HER."
MAY, 1870
JULIAN PLANTATION, LOUISIANA
FROM HERE, WE GO ON FOOT. WE WILL ATTACK IN THE LIGHT.

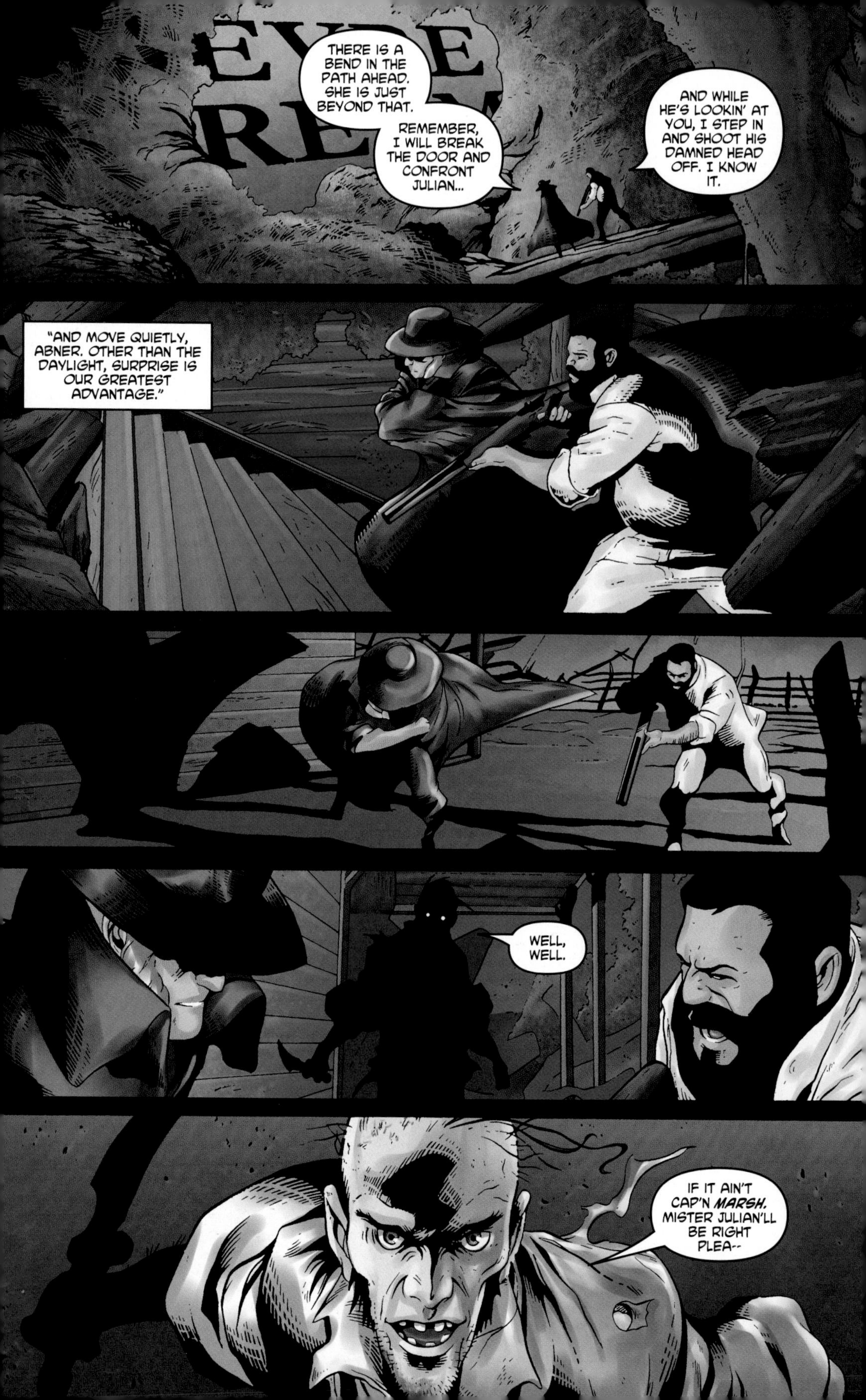
THERE IS A BEND IN THE PATH AHEAD. SHE IS JUST BEYOND THAT.
REMEMBER, I WILL BREAK THE DOOR AND CONFRONT JULIAN...
AND WHILE HE'S LOOKIN' AT YOU, I STEP IN AND SHOOT HIS DAMNED HEAD OFF. I KNOW IT.
"AND MOVE QUIETLY, ABNER. OTHER THAN THE DAYLIGHT, SURPRISE IS OUR GREATEST ADVANTAGE."
WELL, WELL.
IF IT AIN'T CAP'N *MARSH.* MISTER JULIAN'LL BE RIGHT PLEA--

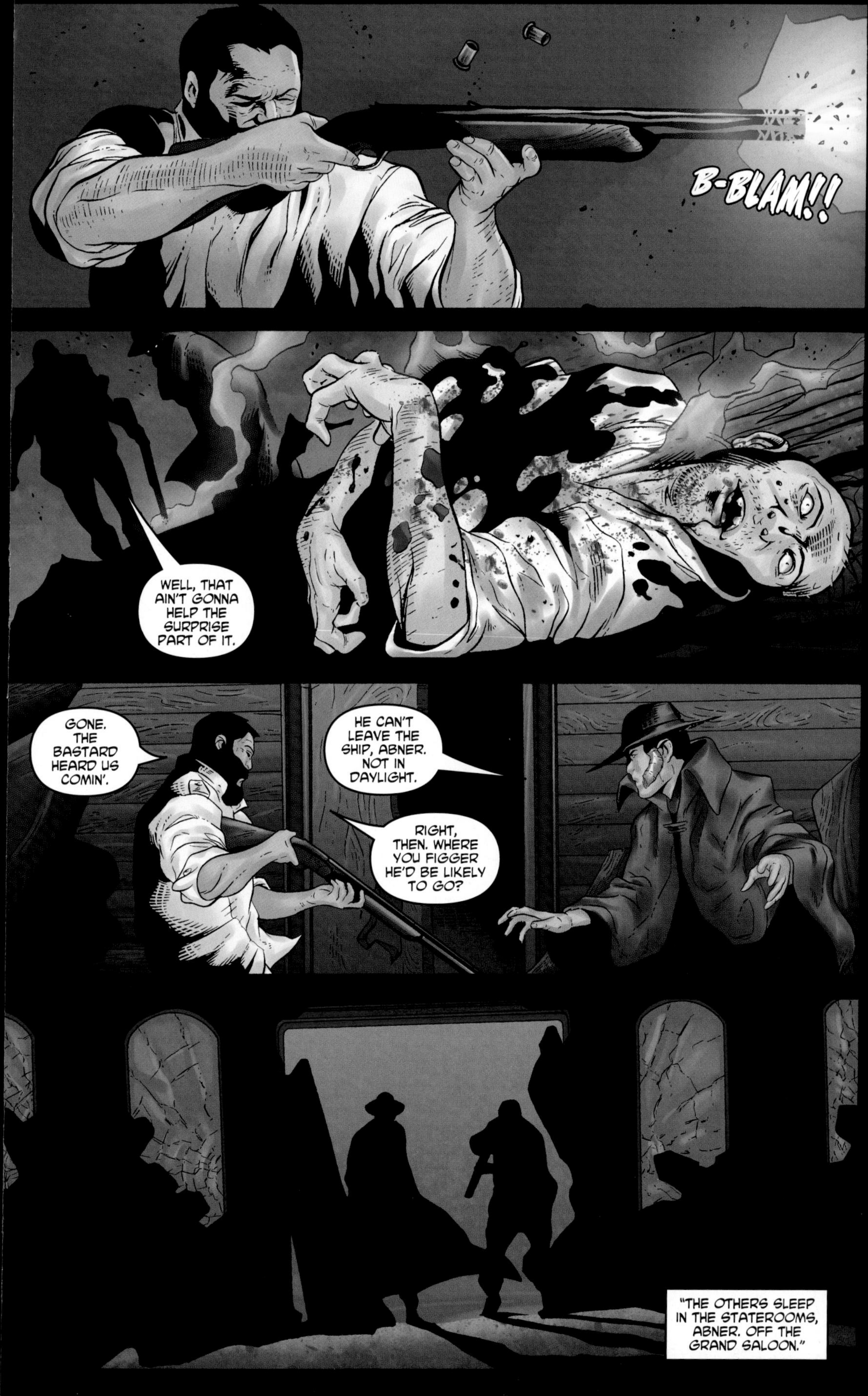
B-BLAM!!
WELL, THAT AIN'T GONNA HELP THE SURPRISE PART OF IT.
GONE. THE BASTARD HEARD US COMIN'.
HE CAN'T LEAVE THE SHIP, ABNER. NOT IN DAYLIGHT.
RIGHT, THEN. WHERE YOU FIGGER HE'D BE LIKELY TO GO?
"THE OTHERS SLEEP IN THE STATEROOMS, ABNER. OFF THE GRAND SALOON."

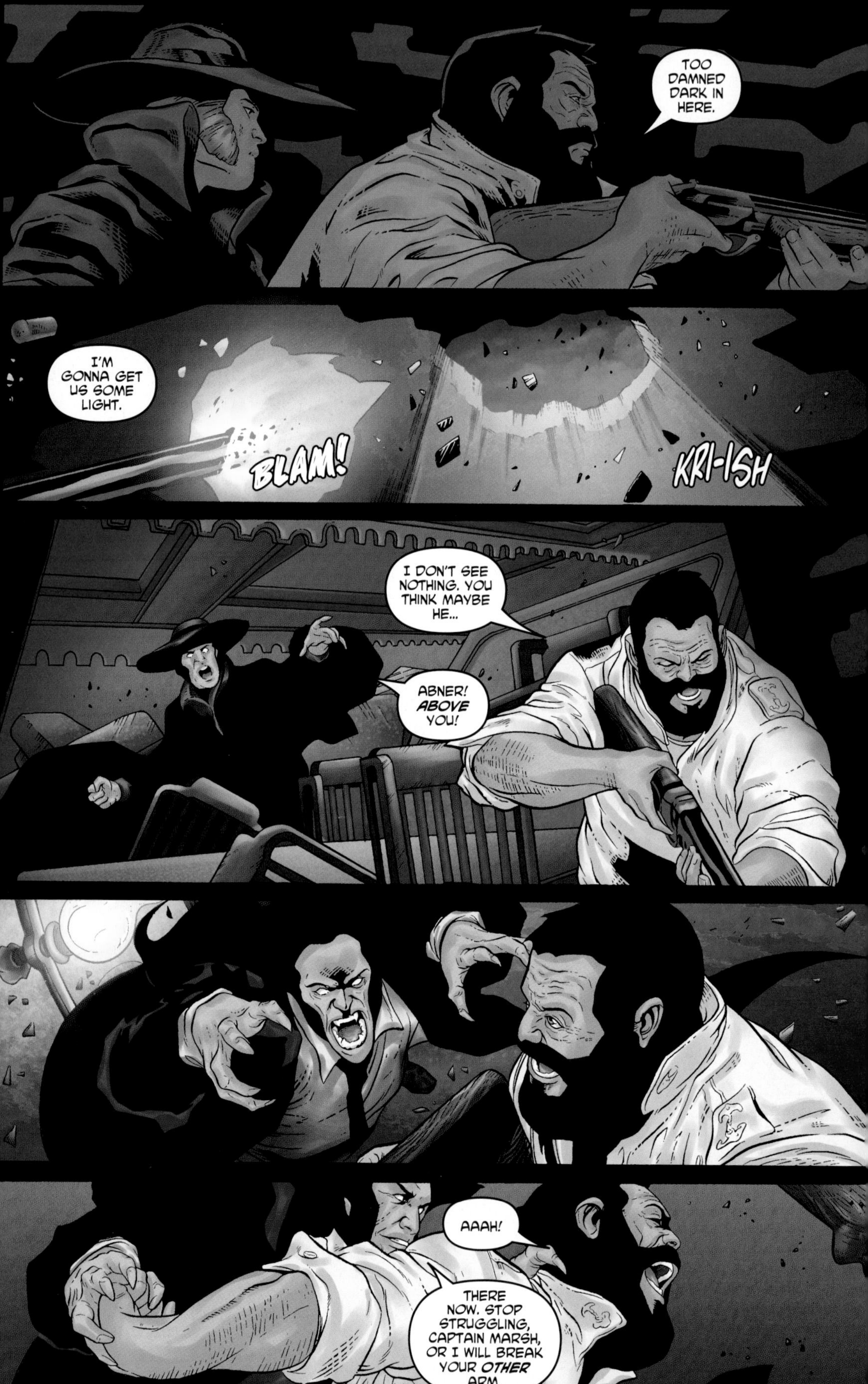
TOO DAMNED DARK IN HERE.
I'M GONNA GET US SOME LIGHT.
BLAM!
KRI-ISH
I DON'T SEE NOTHING. YOU THINK MAYBE HE...
ABNER! *ABOVE* YOU!
AAAH!
THERE NOW. STOP STRUGGLING, CAPTAIN MARSH, OR I WILL BREAK YOUR *OTHER* ARM.
CRACK!

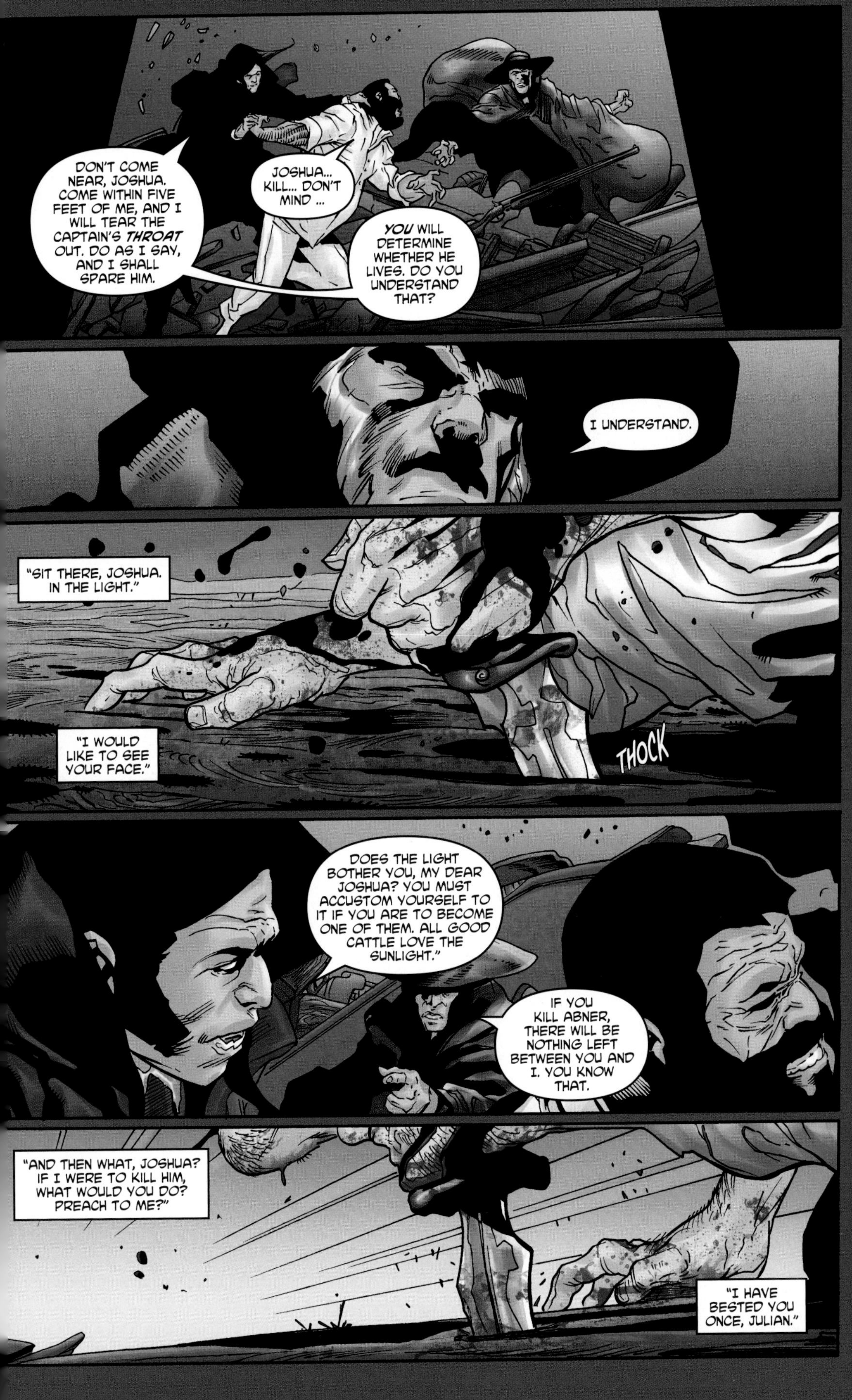
DON'T COME NEAR, JOSHUA. COME WITHIN FIVE FEET OF ME, AND I WILL TEAR THE CAPTAIN'S THROAT OUT. DO AS I SAY, AND I SHALL SPARE HIM.
JOSHUA... KILL... DON'T MIND ...
YOU WILL DETERMINE WHETHER HE LIVES. DO YOU UNDERSTAND THAT?
I UNDERSTAND.
"SIT THERE, JOSHUA. IN THE LIGHT."
"I WOULD LIKE TO SEE YOUR FACE."
THOCK
DOES THE LIGHT BOTHER YOU, MY DEAR JOSHUA? YOU MUST ACCUSTOM YOURSELF TO IT IF YOU ARE TO BECOME ONE OF THEM. ALL GOOD CATTLE LOVE THE SUNLIGHT."
IF YOU KILL ABNER, THERE WILL BE NOTHING LEFT BETWEEN YOU AND I. YOU KNOW THAT.
"AND THEN WHAT, JOSHUA? IF I WERE TO KILL HIM, WHAT WOULD YOU DO? PREACH TO ME?"
"I HAVE BESTED YOU ONCE, JULIAN."

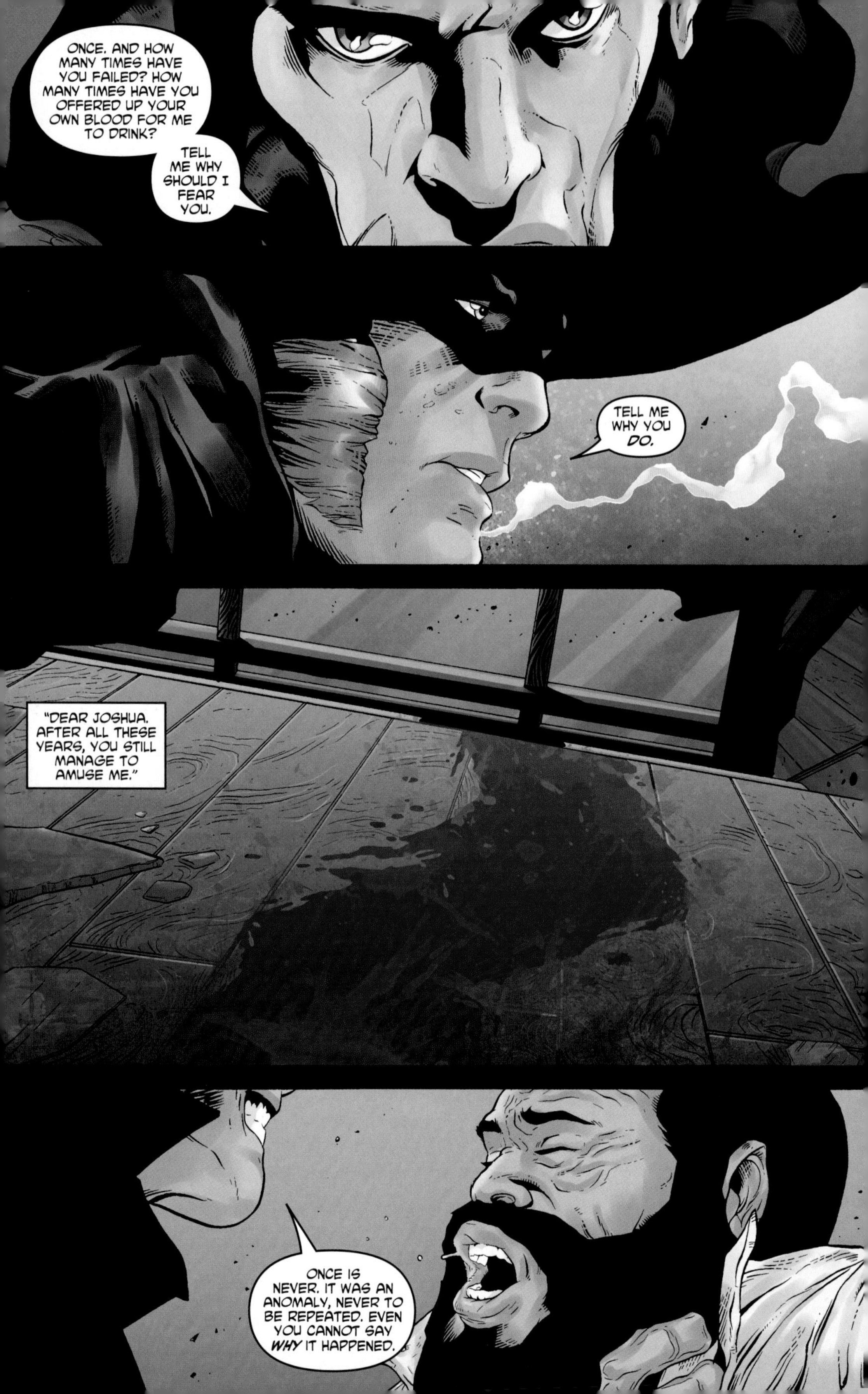
ONCE. AND HOW MANY TIMES HAVE YOU FAILED? HOW MANY TIMES HAVE YOU OFFERED UP YOUR OWN BLOOD FOR ME TO DRINK?
TELL ME WHY SHOULD I FEAR YOU.
TELL ME WHY YOU *DO.*
"DEAR JOSHUA. AFTER ALL THESE YEARS, YOU STILL MANAGE TO AMUSE ME."
ONCE IS NEVER. IT WAS AN ANOMALY, NEVER TO BE REPEATED. EVEN YOU CANNOT SAY ***WHY*** IT HAPPENED.

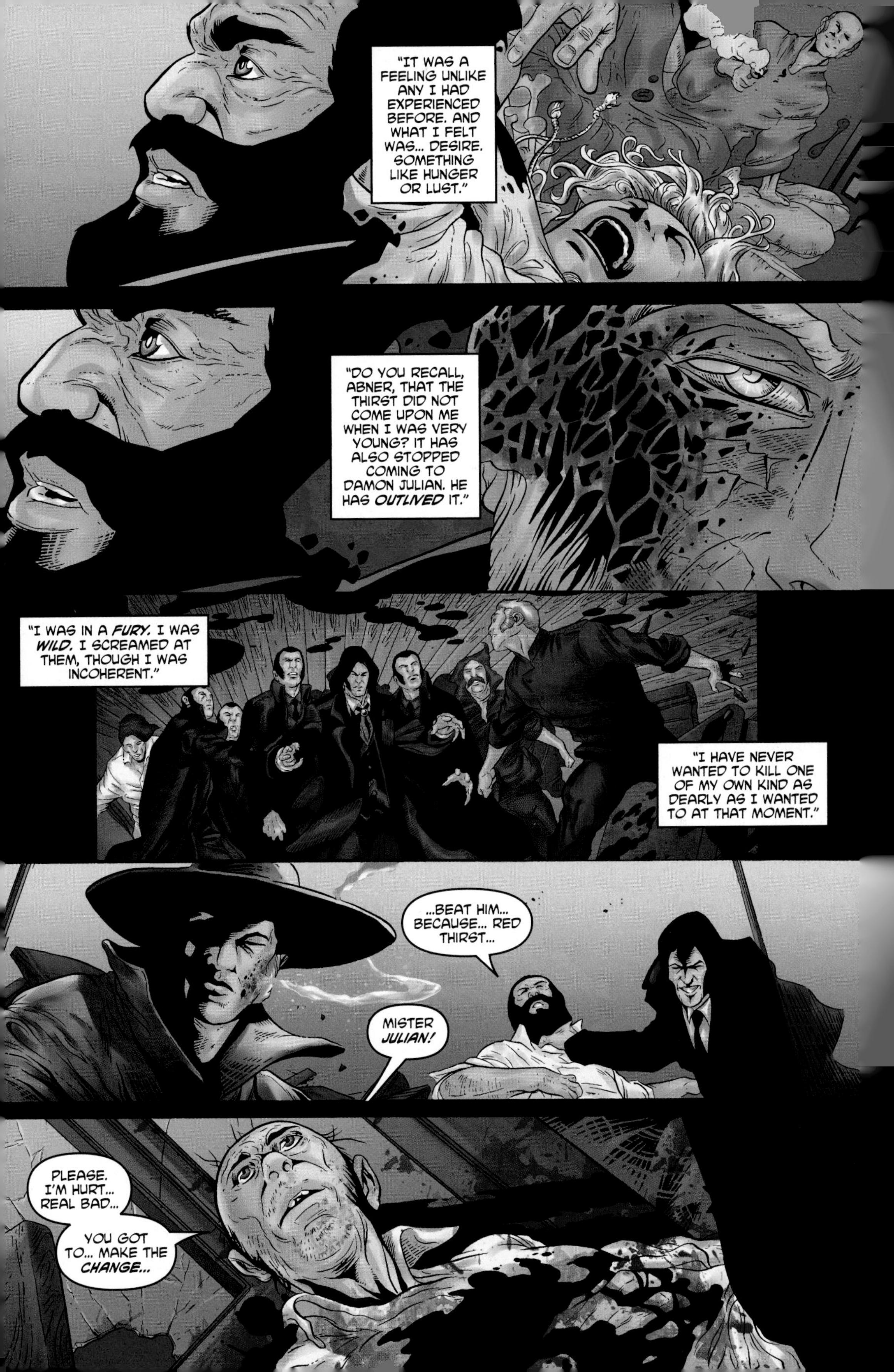
"IT WAS A FEELING UNLIKE ANY I HAD EXPERIENCED BEFORE. AND WHAT I FELT WAS... DESIRE. SOMETHING LIKE HUNGER OR LUST."
"DO YOU RECALL, ABNER, THAT THE THIRST DID NOT COME UPON ME WHEN I WAS VERY YOUNG? IT HAS ALSO STOPPED COMING TO DAMON JULIAN. HE HAS *OUTLIVED* IT."
"I WAS IN A *FURY*. I WAS *WILD*. I SCREAMED AT THEM, THOUGH I WAS INCOHERENT."
"I HAVE NEVER WANTED TO KILL ONE OF MY OWN KIND AS DEARLY AS I WANTED TO AT THAT MOMENT."
...BEAT HIM... BECAUSE... RED THIRST...
MISTER *JULIAN!*
PLEASE. I'M HURT... REAL BAD...
YOU GOT TO... MAKE THE *CHANGE*...

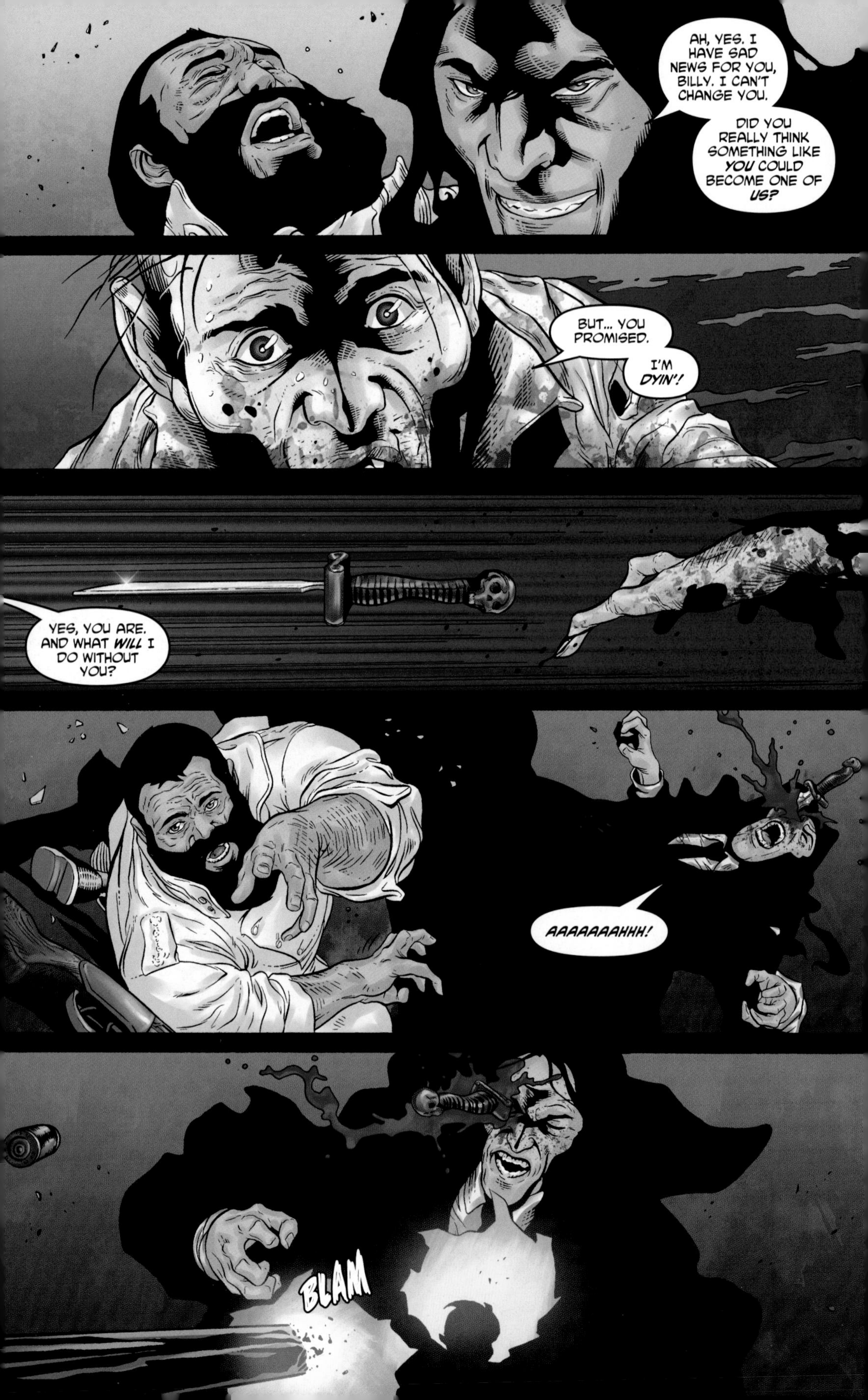
AH, YES. I HAVE SAD NEWS FOR YOU, BILLY. I CAN'T CHANGE YOU.
DID YOU REALLY THINK SOMETHING LIKE *YOU* COULD BECOME ONE OF *US?*
BUT... YOU PROMISED.
I'M *DYIN'!*
YES, YOU ARE. AND WHAT *WILL* I DO WITHOUT YOU?
AAAAAAAHHH!
BLAM

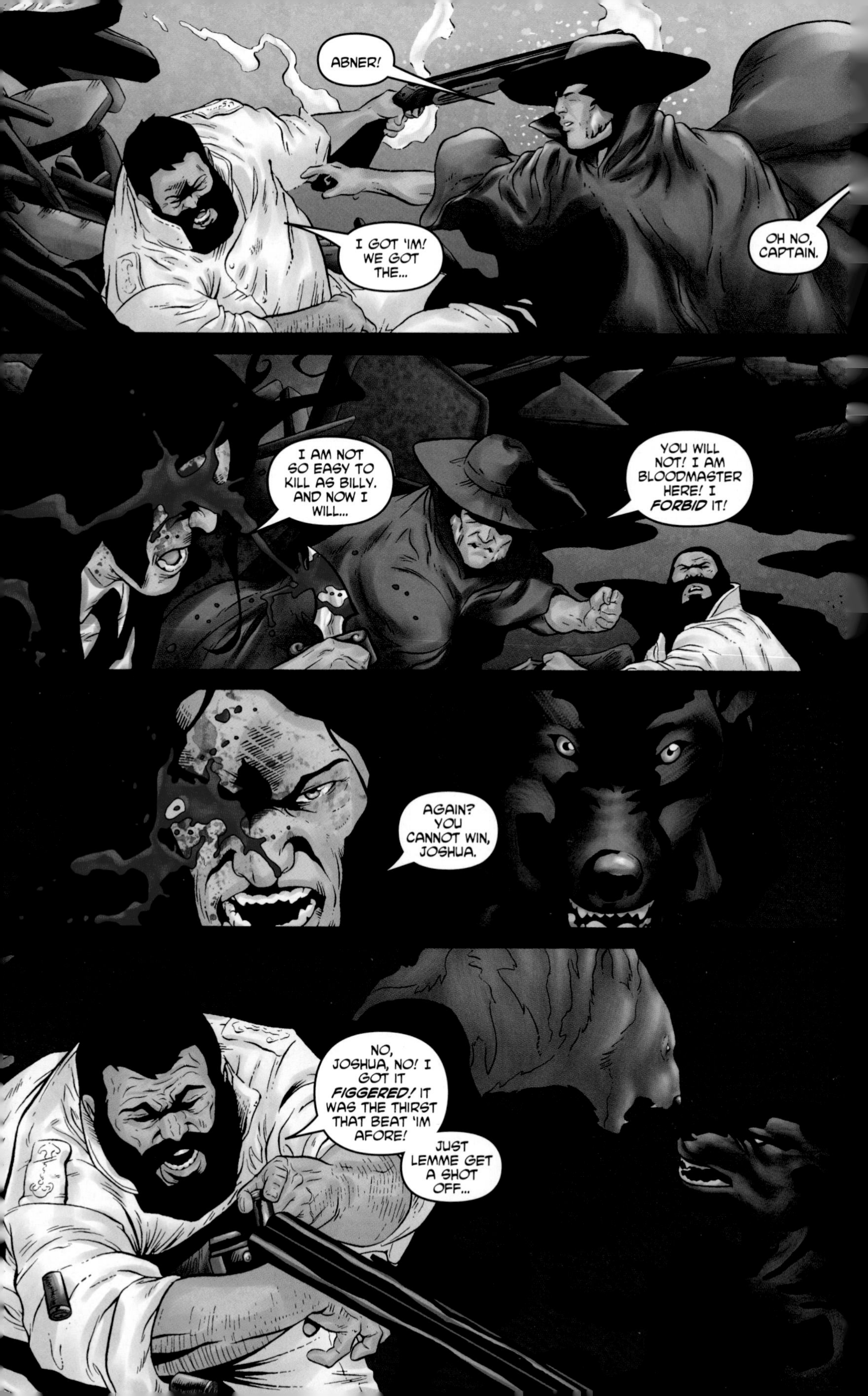
ABNER!
I GOT 'IM! WE GOT THE...
OH NO, CAPTAIN.
I AM NOT SO EASY TO KILL AS BILLY. AND NOW I WILL...
YOU WILL NOT! I AM BLOODMASTER HERE! I *FORBID* IT!
AGAIN? YOU CANNOT WIN, JOSHUA.
NO, JOSHUA, NO! I GOT IT *FIGGERED!* IT WAS THE THIRST THAT BEAT 'IM AFORE!
JUST LEMME GET A SHOT OFF...

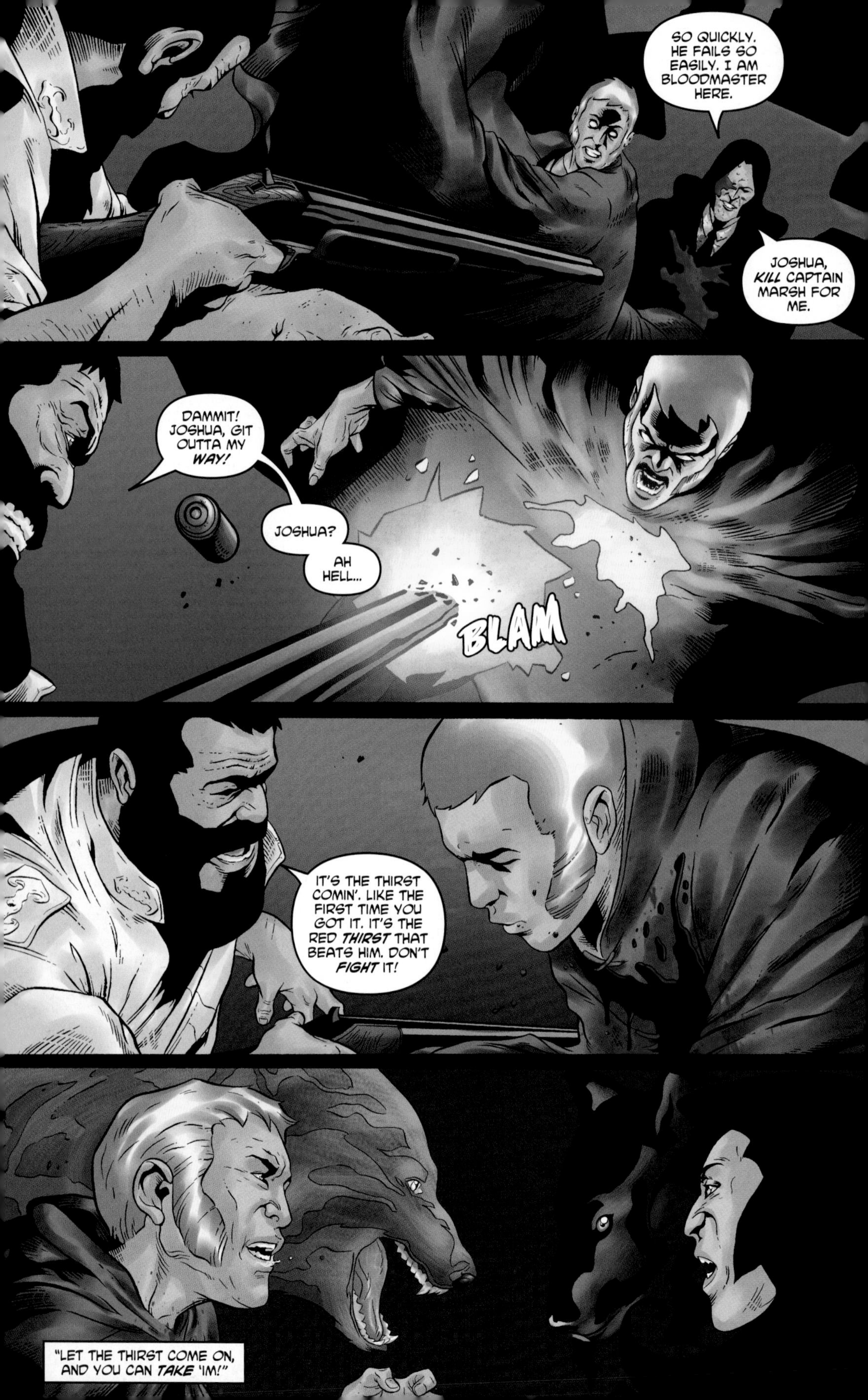
SO QUICKLY. HE FAILS SO EASILY. I AM BLOODMASTER HERE.
JOSHUA, KILL CAPTAIN MARSH FOR ME.
DAMMIT! JOSHUA, GIT OUTTA MY WAY!
JOSHUA?
AH HELL...
BLAM
IT'S THE THIRST COMIN'. LIKE THE FIRST TIME YOU GOT IT. IT'S THE RED THIRST THAT BEATS HIM. DON'T FIGHT IT!
"LET THE THIRST COME ON, AND YOU CAN TAKE 'IM!"

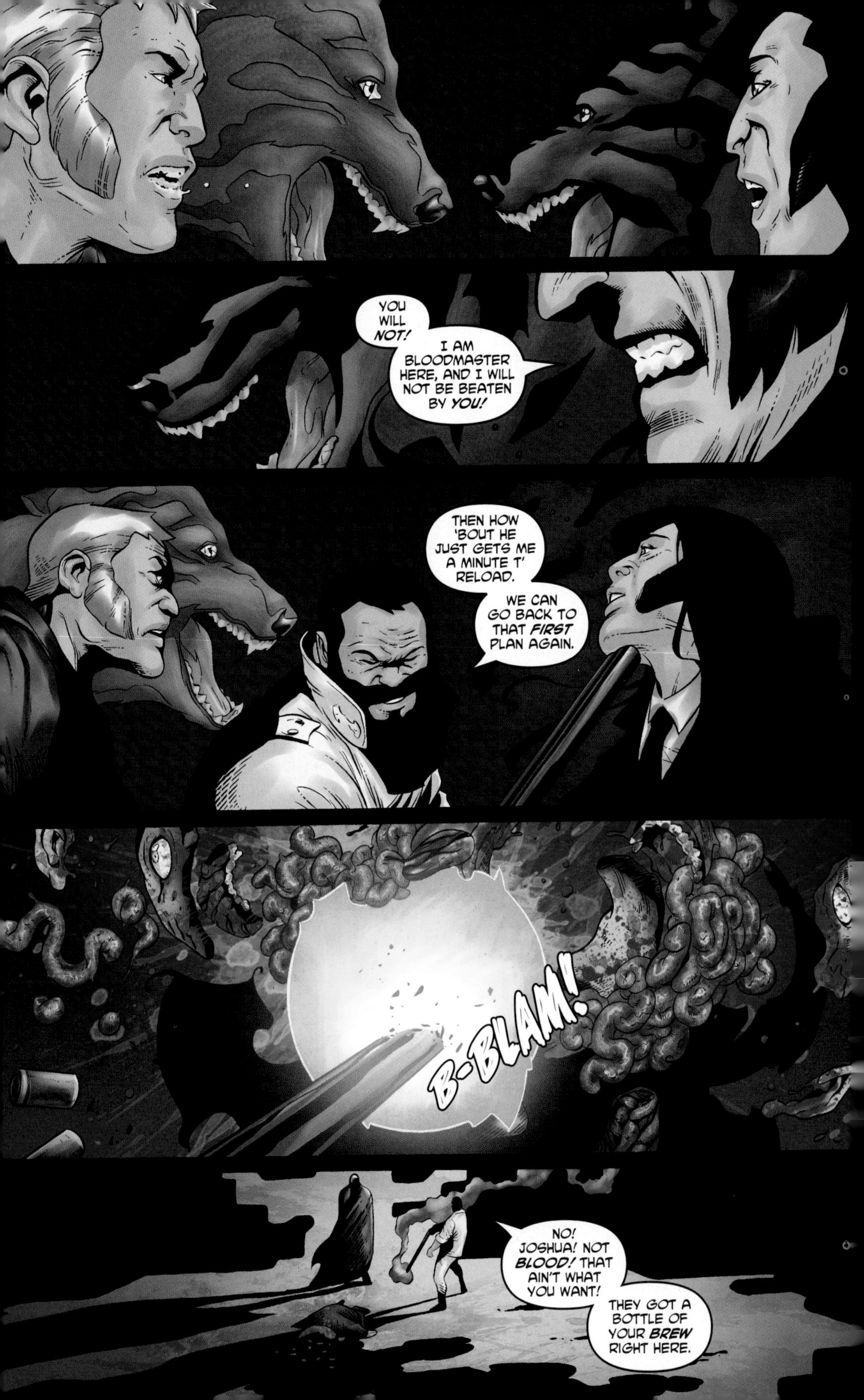

YOU WILL NOT!
I AM BLOODMASTER HERE, AND I WILL NOT BE BEATEN BY YOU!
THEN HOW 'BOUT HE JUST GETS ME A MINUTE T' RELOAD.
WE CAN GO BACK TO THAT FIRST PLAN AGAIN.
B-BLAM!
NO! JOSHUA! NOT BLOOD! THAT AIN'T WHAT YOU WANT!
THEY GOT A BOTTLE OF YOUR BREW RIGHT HERE.

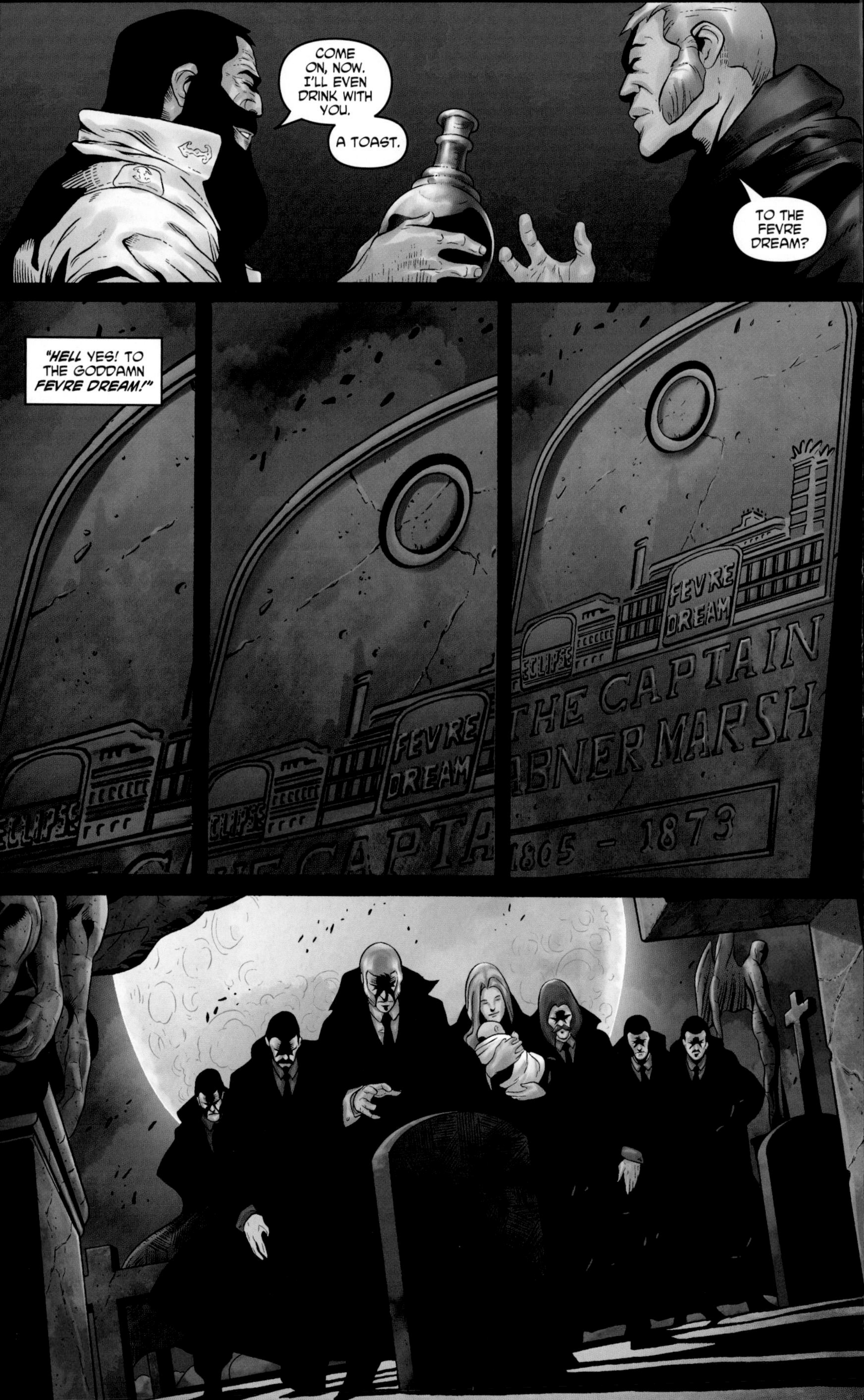
COME ON, NOW. I'LL EVEN DRINK WITH YOU.
A TOAST.
TO THE FEVRE DREAM?
"HELL YES! TO THE GODDAMN FEVRE DREAM!"
FEVRE DREAM
ECLIPSE
THE CAPTAIN
ABNER MARSH
1805 - 1873

GALLERY

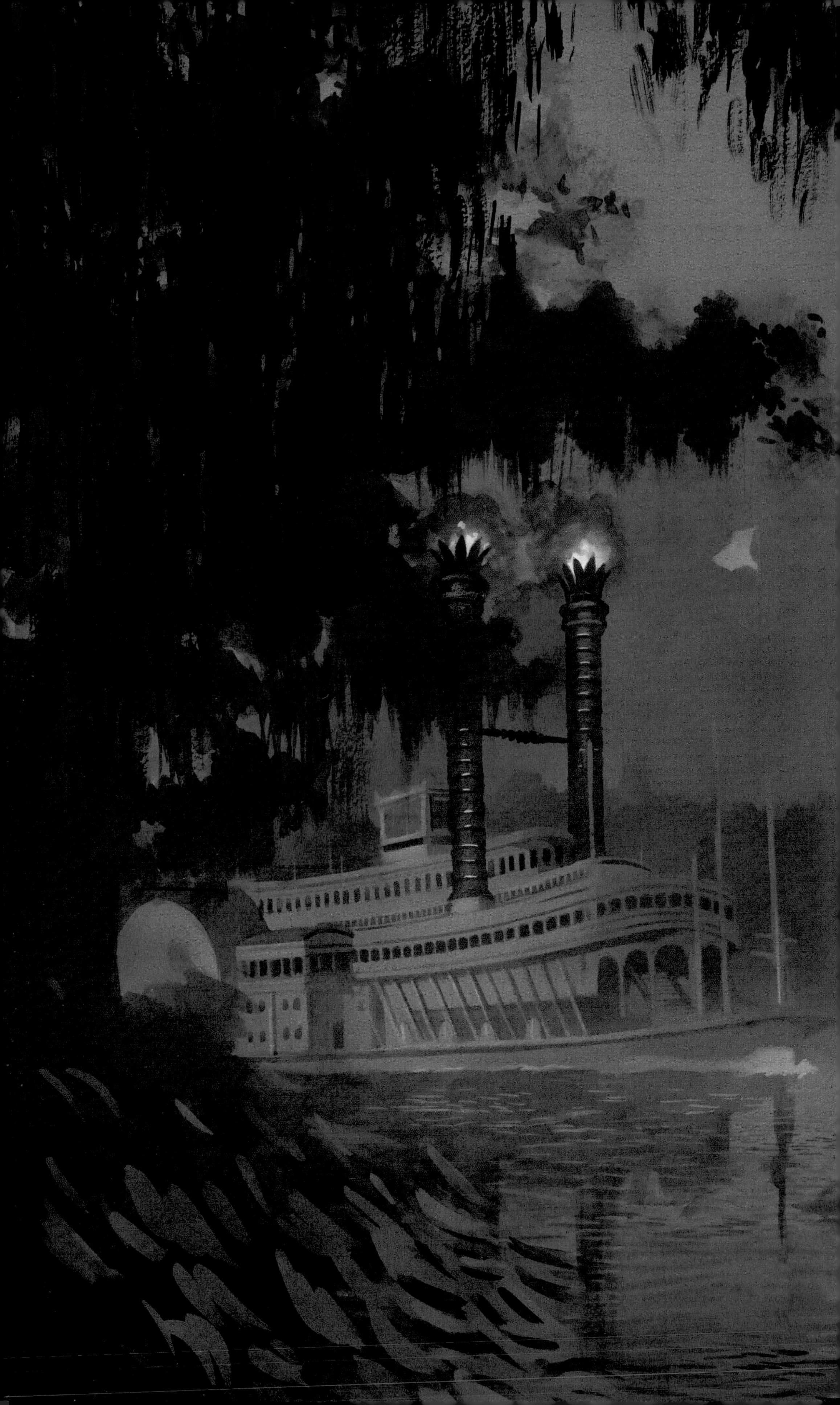

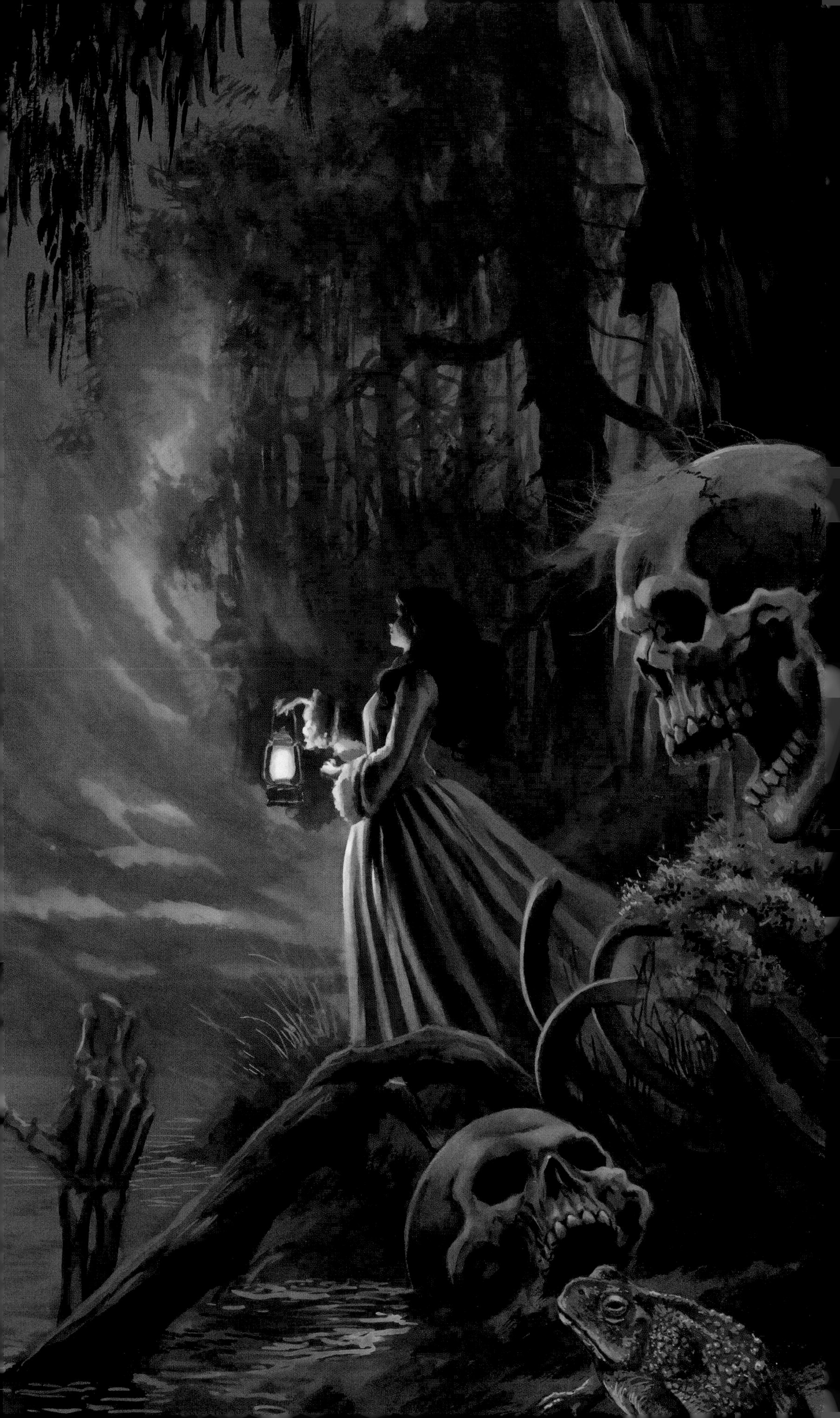

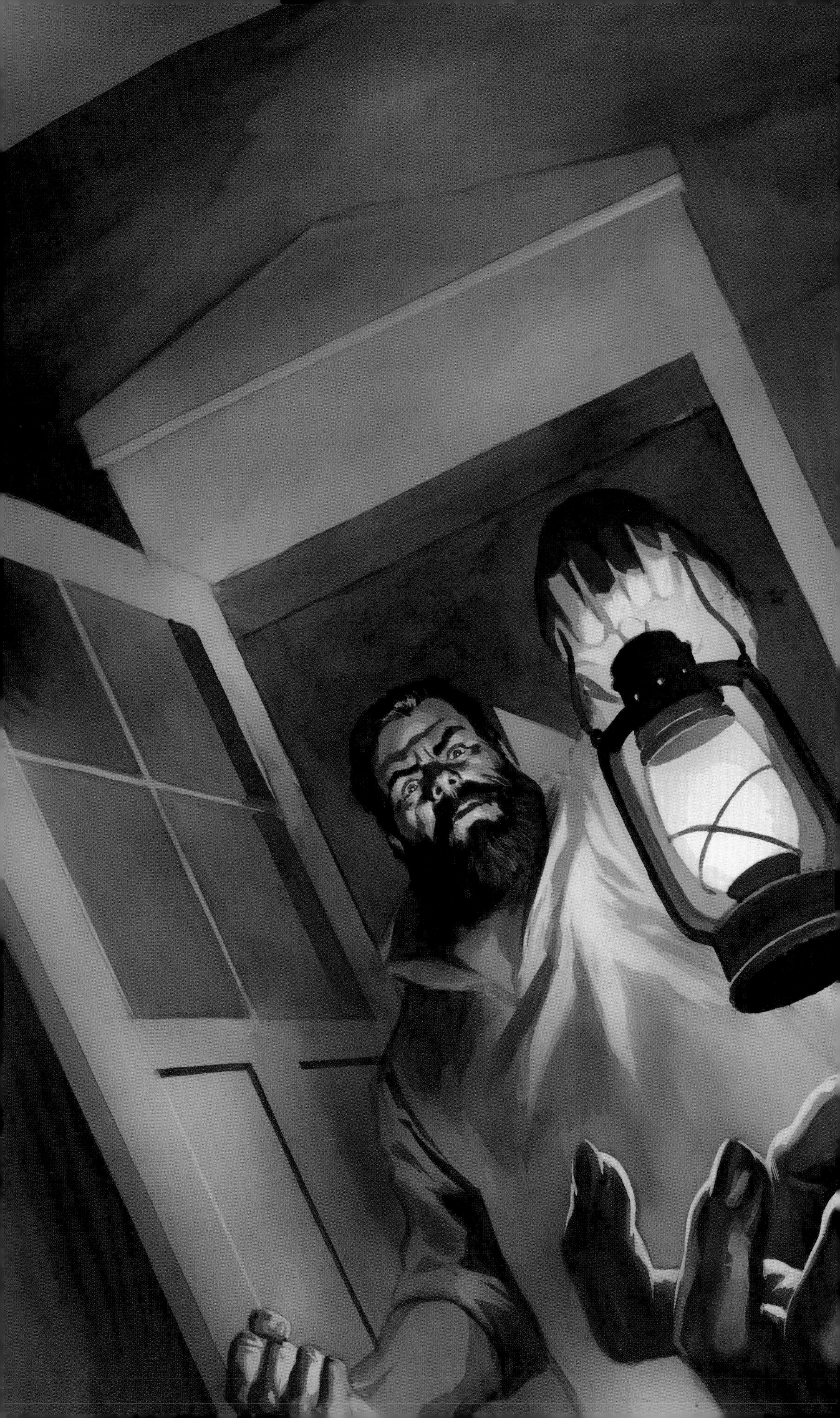

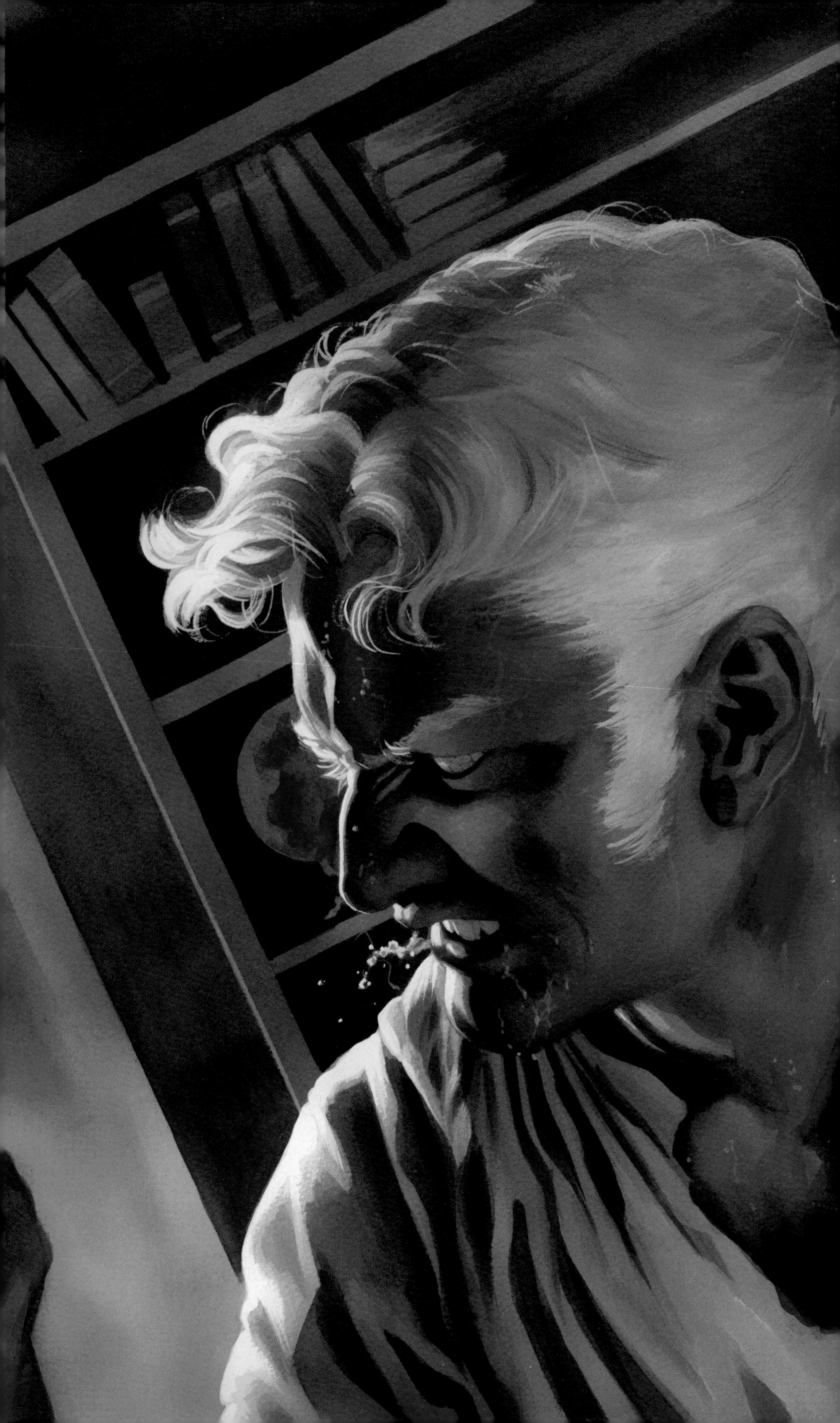

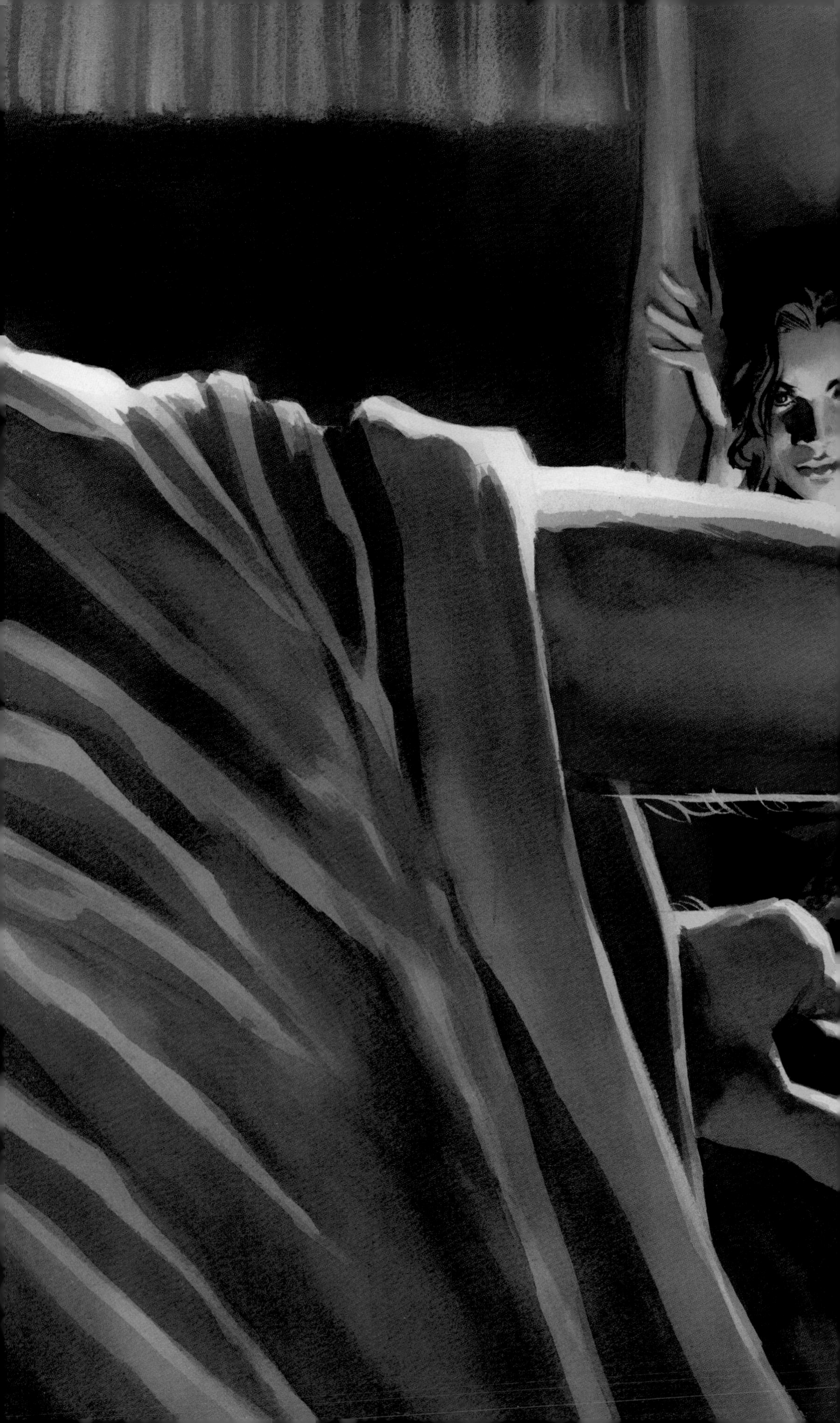

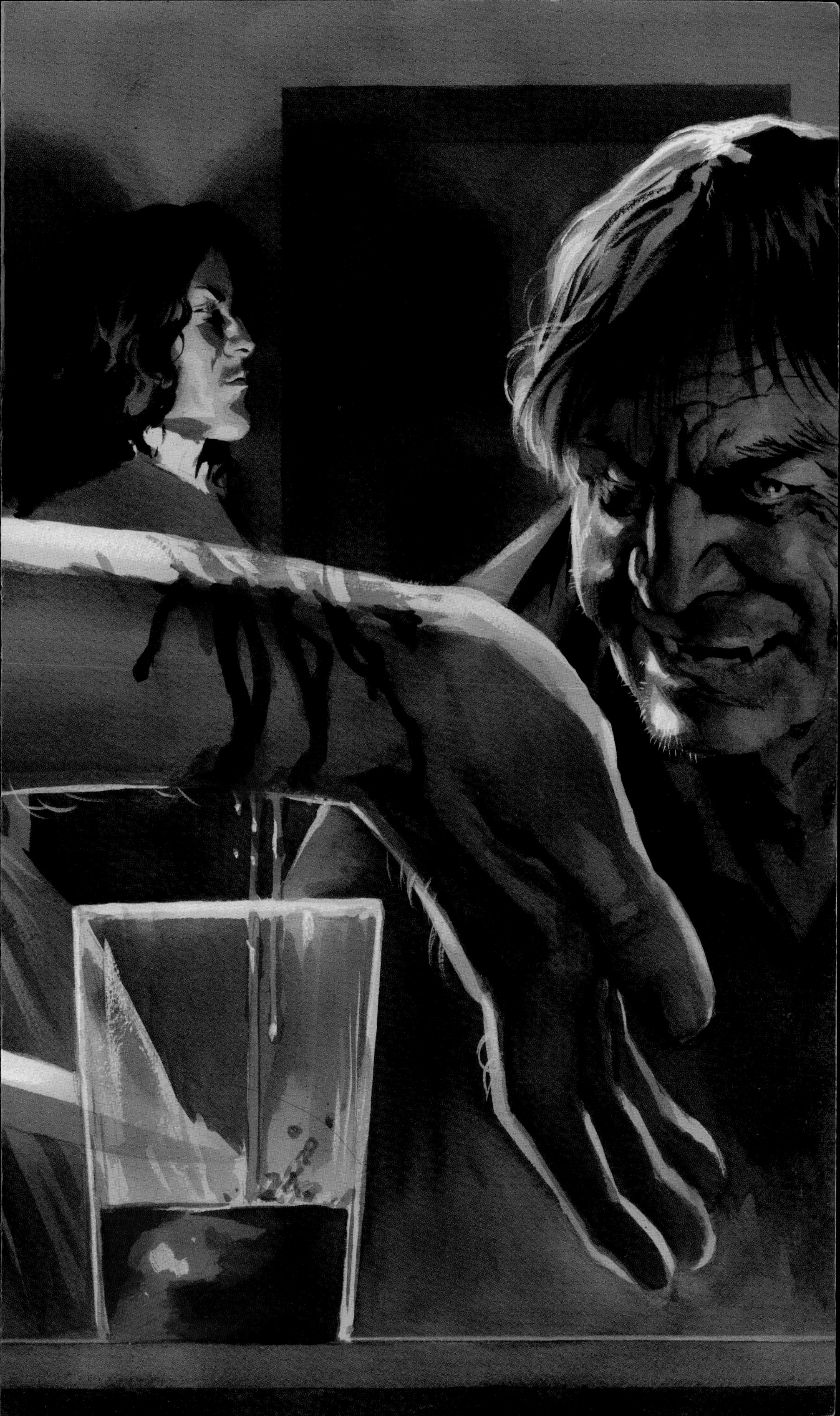

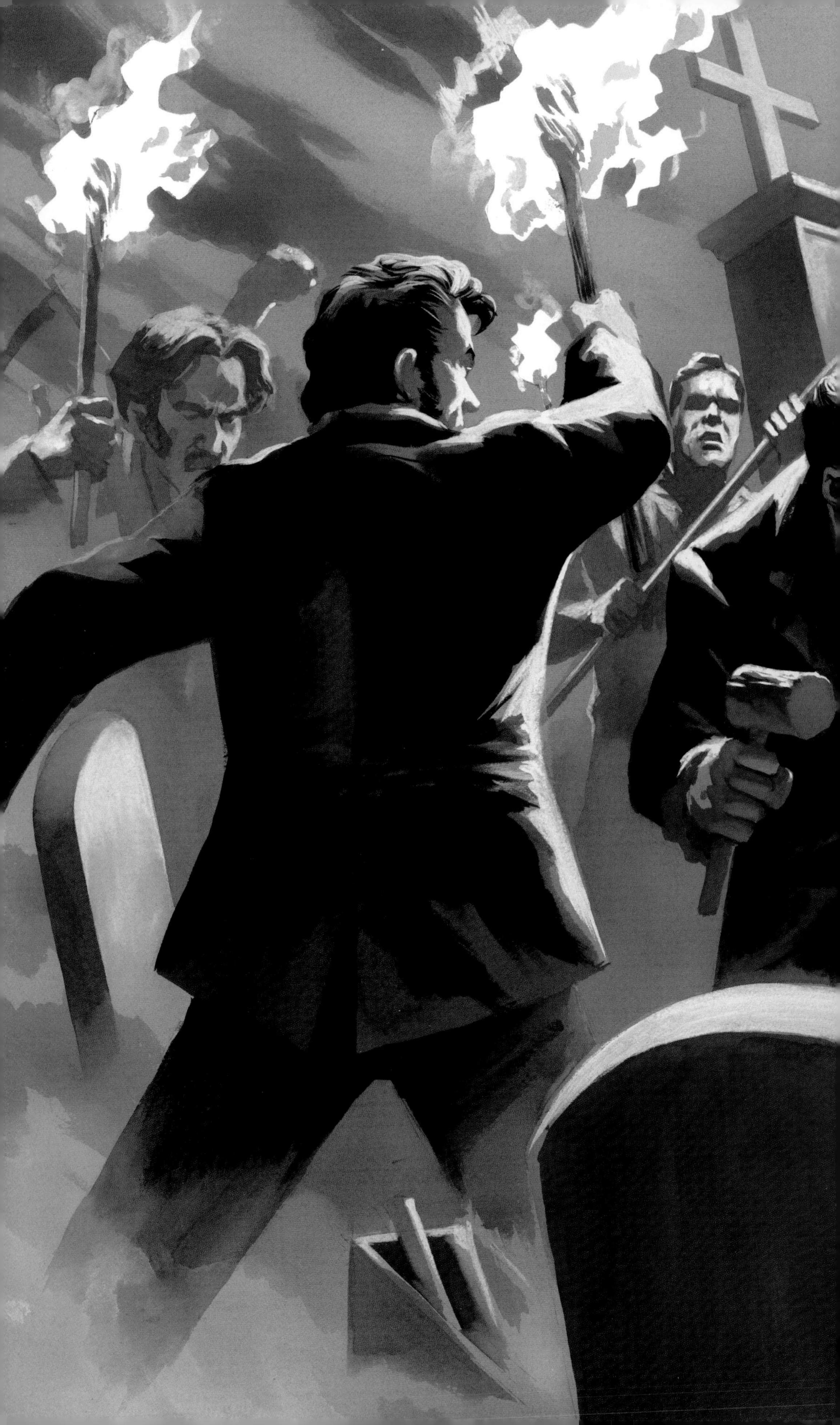

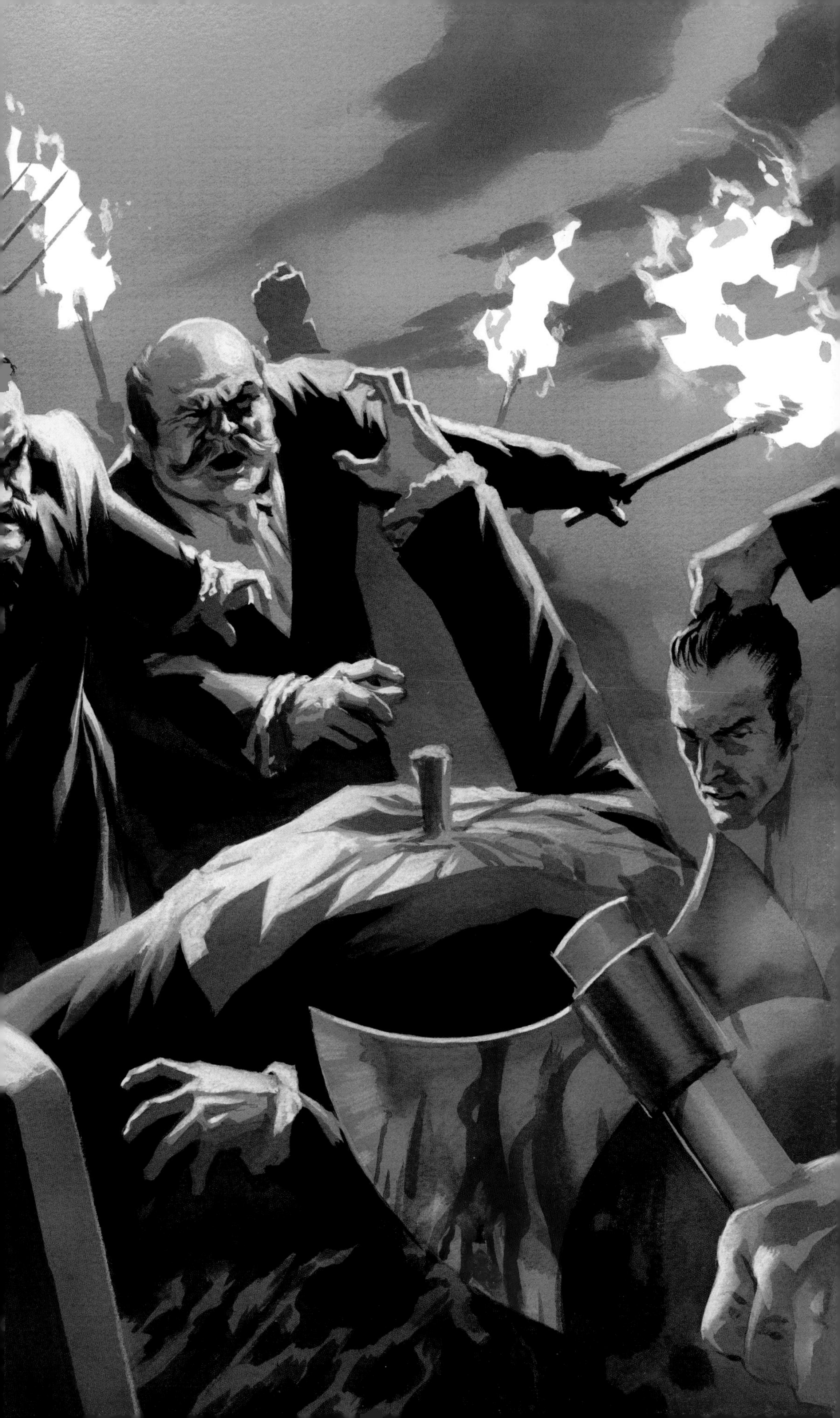

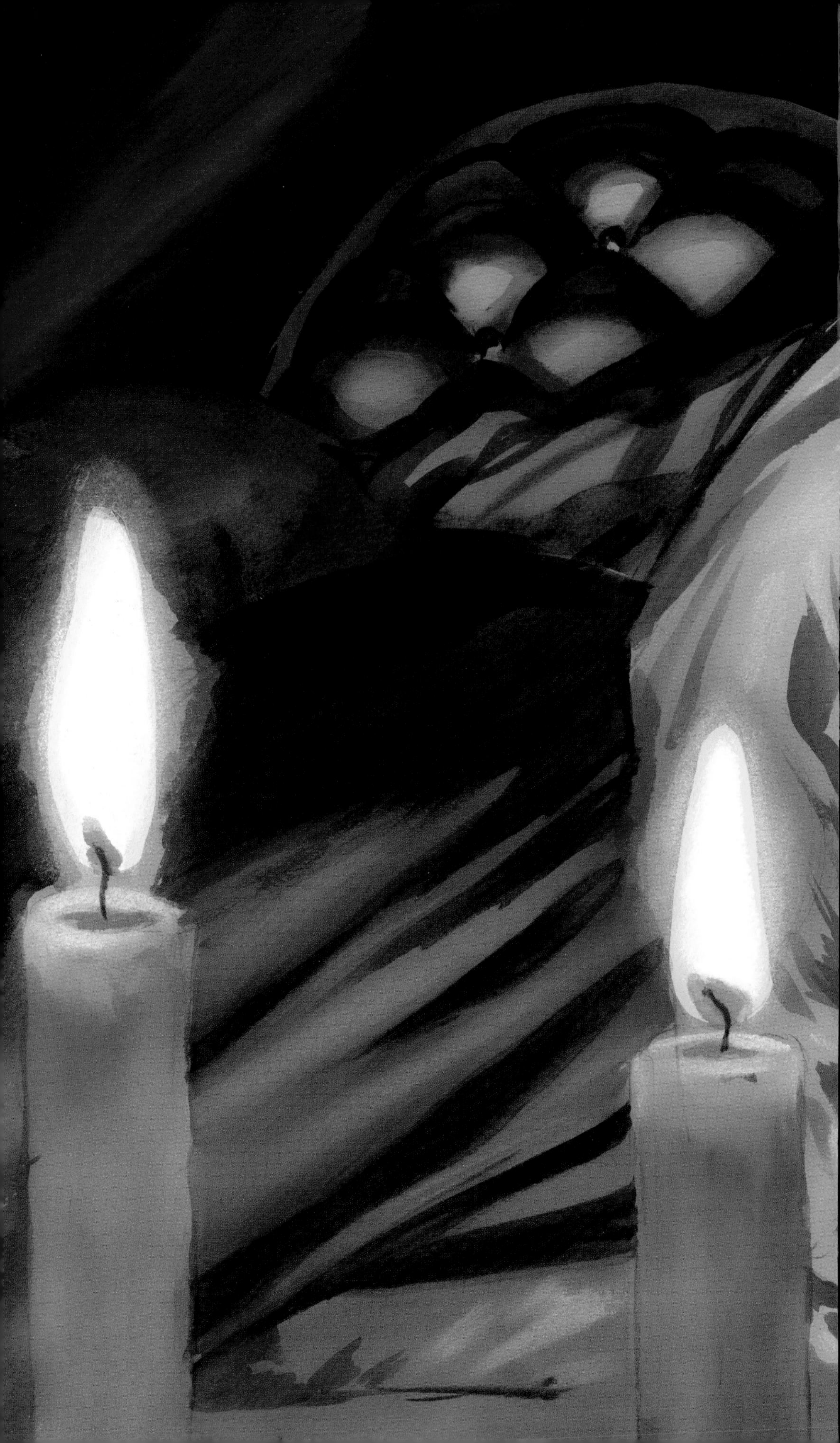

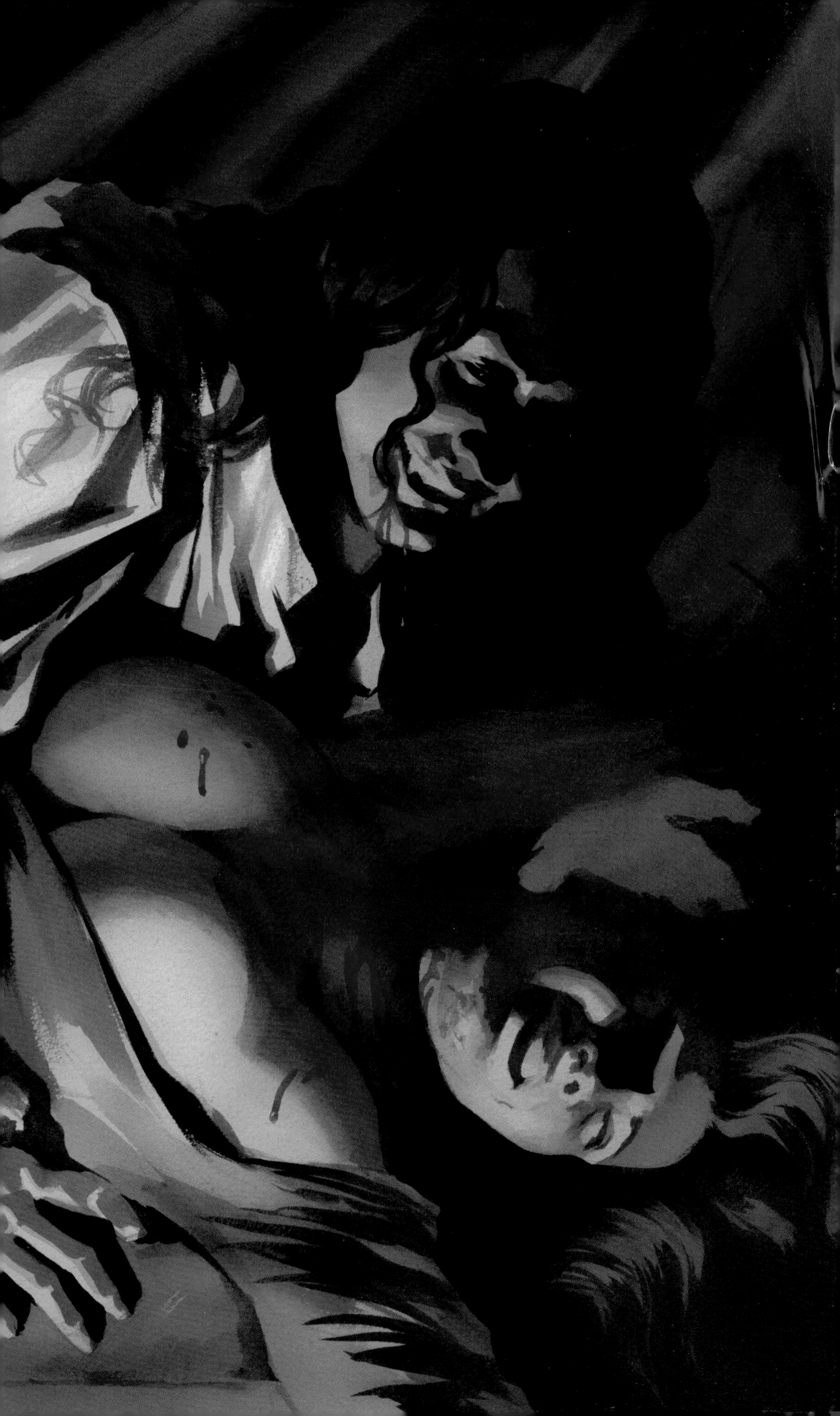

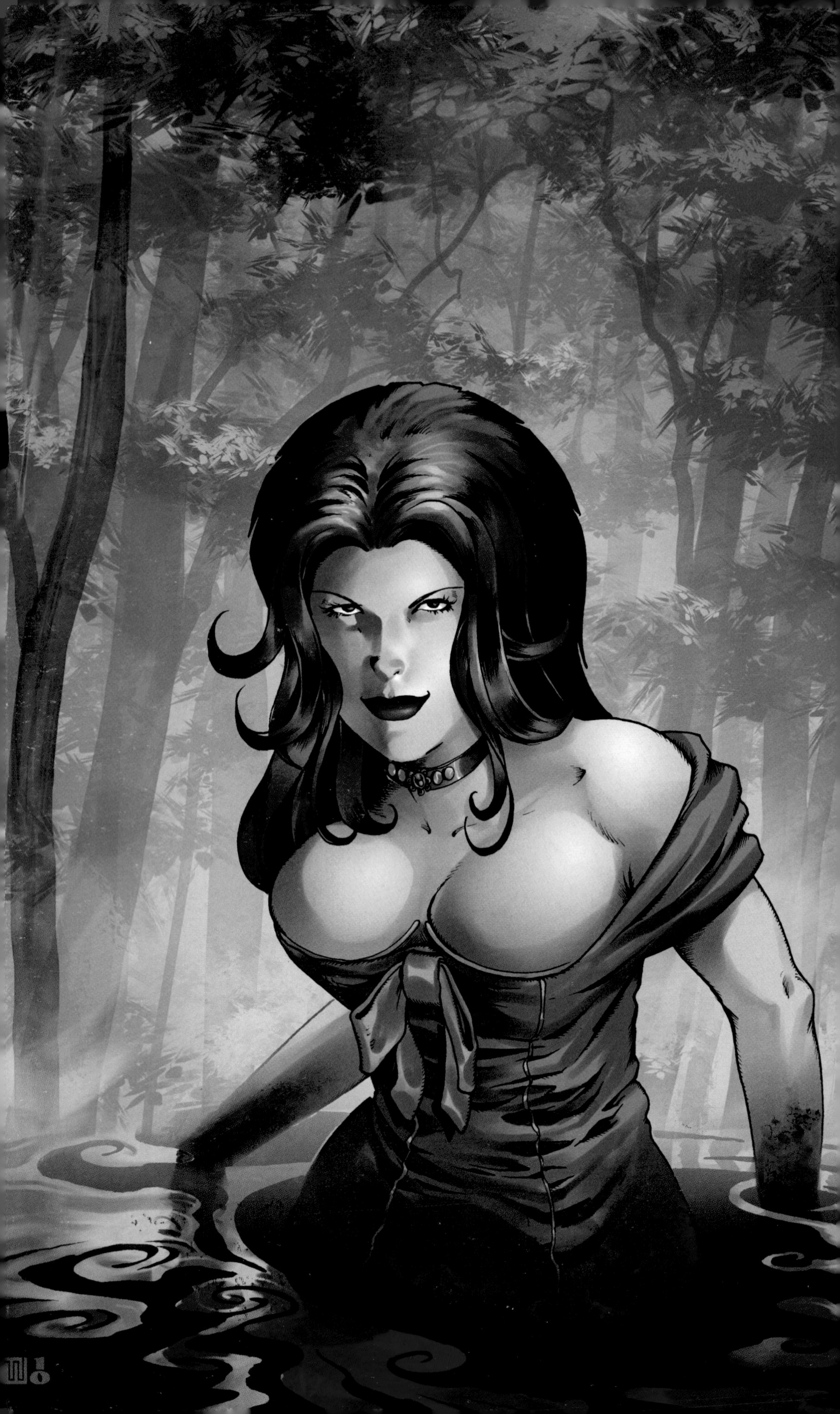